The All Colour Dictionary of
House plant Care

General editor: *David Longman*
Contributors: *Tom Gough, David Longman,*
John Pilbeam, Norman Simpson

The All Colour Dictionary of
House plant Care

259 indoor plants illustrated in colour

Foliage and Flowering Houseplants
Cacti and other Succulents
Palms and Ferns
Windowbox and Balcony plants
Indoor Bulbs and Annuals

Peter 🯅 Lowe

Contents

6 *Indexes*

12 *Introduction*

14 *Foliage and flowering houseplants*

25 *Spring and summer bulbs*

27 *Windowbox and balcony plants*

32 *Cacti and other succulents*

42 *The plants*

560 *Hints and precautions*

ISBN 0 85654 643 7

The material in this book originally appeared in the 'How to care' series on Foliage Houseplants (2 volumes), Flowering Houseplants (2 volumes), Palms and Ferns, Windowbox and Balcony Plants, Indoor Bulbs and Annuals, Cacti, Succulents.

Printed in Spain
3.88-2-2-6

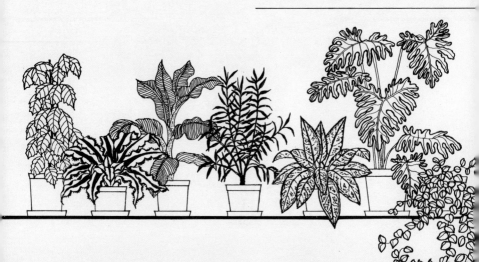

- 6 Index of common names • 9 Index of scientific names

• 12 How to use this book, Tools for indoor gardening

• 14 Watering and spraying, Feeding • 15 Cleaning the leaves, Humidity
• 16 Repotting • 17 Changing the topsoil, Bottle gardens • 18 Insect-eaters,
Hydroculture • 19 Planting a self-watering planter • 20 Lighting, Shading a
greenhouse • 21 Air plants, How to make a moss pole, Climbers and trailers
• 22 Growing from seed • 23 Propagation, Taking cuttings, Layering, Offsets
• 24 Pricking out, Dividing ferns, Pruning

• 25 Containers and compost, Planting bulbs • 26 Forcing bulbs • 27 Storing
bulbs, Dividing tubers

• 27 Containers and composts • 28 Feeding, Preparing a container
• 29 Watering and spraying, Propagation, Months and seasons • 30 Planting a
mixed container • 31 Insecticides, Taking care with insecticides

---

• 32 Light and temperature, Succulent families • 33 Watering, Feeding
• 34 Compost, Repotting • 35 Treating damaged roots, Propagation, Cactus
cuttings • 36 Growing from seed, Grafting cacti • 37 Handling spiny plants,
Root mealy bug, Vine weevils, Mealy bug • 38 Cacti: What goes wrong

---

• 42 Care instructions • What goes wrong

• 560 Buying houseplants, using Chemicals, Acknowledgements

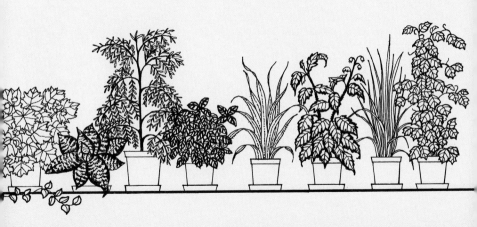

Common names

46 Acanthocalycium
56 Aeonium
478 African violet
62 Ageratum
68 Aloe
442 Aluminium plant
326 Amaryllis
74 Anemone
134 Angel wings
86 Ardisia
166 Areca palm
90 Arthrocereus
96 Asparagus fern
94 Asparagus fern
464 Australian bracken
444 Australian laurel
470 Azalea
272 Baby's toes
376 Banana, dwarf
274 Barrel cactus
116 Begonia, fibrous
110 Begonia 'fireglow'
114 Begonia, king
108 Begonia, tiger
112 Begonia, tuberous
146 Bell flower
102 Birdsnest fern
104 Bishop's cap cactus
532 Black-eyed Susan
178 Bleeding heart vine
122 Blossfeldia
534 Blue flowered torch
130 Browallia
342 Busy Lizzie

488 Butterfly flower
422 Button fern
174 Calamondin orange
438 Canary Island date palm
318 Canary ivy
352 Cape cowslip
256 Cape heath
290 Cape jasmine
452 Cape leadwort
230 Cape marigold
522 Cape primrose
334 Carrion flower
404 Carrion flower
516 Carrion flower
150 Carrion plant
390 Cartwheel plant
98 Cast iron plant
60 Century plant
44 Chenille plant
354 Chilean bell flower
142 China aster
64 Chinese evergreen
360 Chinese fan palm
324 Chinese rose
490 Christmas cactus
168 Chrysanthemum
212 Cigar plant
500 Cineraria
176 Cleistocactus
432 Climbing philodendron

382 Clog plant
182 Coconut palm
186 Coffee plant
158 Conifers, dwarf
192 Conophytum
152 Coxcomb
280 Creeping fig
204 Crocus, Dutch
184 Croton
260 Crown of thorns
214 Cyclamen
216 Cymbidium orchid
380 Daffodil
222 Dahlia
426 Desert privet
48 Desert rose
254 Devil's ivy
226 Dianthus
494 Donkey's tail
238 Dracaena
236 Dragon tree
242 Dudleya
228 Dumb cane
370 Dwarf coconut palm
244 Echeveria
248 Echinocereus
250 Echinopsis

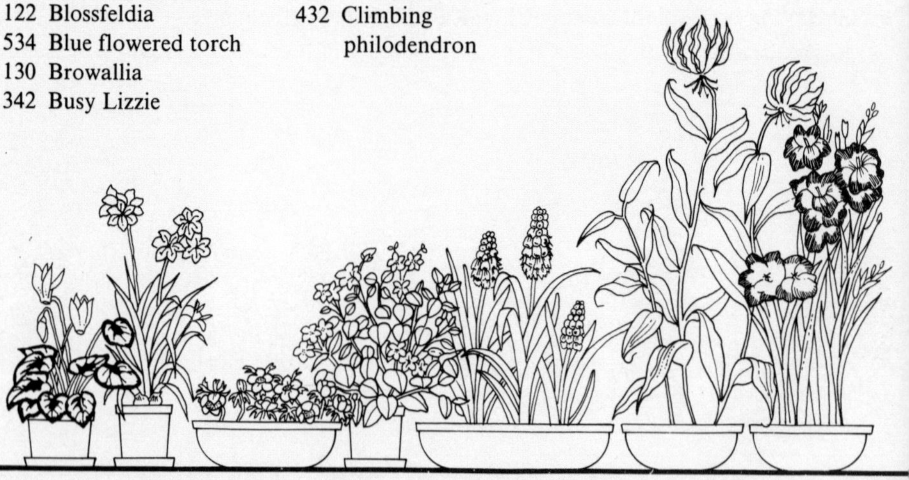

Common names

530 Elephant foot plant
106 Elephant foot tree
258 Espostoa
162 European fan palm
456 Fairy primrose
268 False castor oil plant
234 Finger plant
206 Firecracker flower
188 Flame nettle
198 Flaming dragon tree
78 Flamingo flower
552 Flaming sword
42 Flowering maple
88 Fossil cactus
340 Freckle face
284 Freesia
528 French marigold
286 Fuchsia
292 Gasteria
420 Geranium
298 Gibbaeum
504 Gloxinia
246 Golden barrel cactus
66 Golden trumpet
190 Goldfish plant
526 Goose foot plant
378 Grape hyacinth
172 Grape ivy
394 Guernsey lily
308 Gymnocalycium
124 Hairy old man of
    the Andes

436 Hare's foot fern
312 Haworthia
322 Heliotrope
220 Holly fern
336 Hyacinth, Roman
512 Indoor lime tree
344 Iris, dwarf
316 Ivy
318 Ivy, Canary
320 Ivy, indoor
266 Ivy tree
202 Jade tree
454 Jade tree, miniature
346 Jasmine
180 Kaffir lily
348 Kalanchoe
170 Kangaroo vine
114 King begonia
350 Kleinia
468 Lady palm
356 Lily
194 Lily of the valley
58 Lipstick vine
88 Living rock
450 Living rock
358 Living stone
362 Lobelia
364 Lobivia
410 Lollipop plant
70 Love lies bleeding
240 Madagascar dragon
    tree

520 Madagascar jasmine
40 Maidenhair fern
366 Mammillaria
508 Mind-your-own-
    business
330 Miniature wax plant
492 Mini bulrush
196 Morning glory, dwarf
472 Moses in the
    bullrushes
100 Mother fern
482 Mother-in-law's
    tongue
484 Mother of thousands
302 Mozambique lily
540 Nasturtium
384 Nemesia
386 Neochilenia
388 Neoporteria
210 Never-never plant
84 Norfolk Island pine
396 Oleander
402 Opuntia
252 Orchid cactus
148 Ornamental chilli
    pepper
408 Pachypodium
282 Painted net leaf
550 Pansy
126 Paper flower
328 Paradise palm
160 Parlour palm

Common names

414 Parodia
416 Passion flower
156 Peanut cactus
510 Pearl plant
264 Persian violet
428 Petunia
536 Piggy-back plant
72 Pineapple
232 Pink allamande
52 Plover's egg plant
92 Plume asparagus
262 Poinsettia
460 Polyanthus
424 Polynesia
140 Pot marigold
136 Prayer plant
368 Prayer plant
440 Pygmy date palm
498 Queen of the night
120 Queen's tears
224 Rabbit's foot fern
496 Rainbow moss
458 Rash primrose
82 Rat's tail cactus
466 Rebutia
418 Regal pelargonium
462 Ribbon fern
154 Rosary vine
474 Rose, miniature
278 Rubber plant
514 Sail plant

480 Salvia
306 Scarlet star
546 Scarborough lily
412 Screw pine
372 Sensitive plant
118 Shrimp plant
304 Silk oak
200 Silver crown
502 Silverleaf
138 Slipper flower
338 Snowball flower
288 Snowdrop
164 Spider plant
554 Spineless yucca
446 Stag's horn fern
208 Starfish
518 Stenocactus
406 Sugared almond plant
524 Sulcorebutia
448 Swedish ivy
434 Sweetheart plant
374 Swiss cheese plant
392 Sword fern
300 Sword lily
144 Tea plant
400 Teddybear cactus

108 Tiger begonia
270 Tiger's jaws
398 Tobacco plant
476 Trailing velvet plant
296 Transvaal daisy
294 Treasure flower
128 Trompetilla
542 Tulip
544 Uebelmannia
218 Umbrella grass
486 Umbrella tree
430 Upright philodendron
54 Urn plant
310 Velvet plant
548 Verbena
314 Veronica
538 Wandering Jew
556 Wandering sailor
76 Wax flower
332 Wax plant
276 Weeping fig
506 Winter cherry
132 Yesterday-today-and-tomorrow
80 Zebra plant
558 Zinnia

Scientific names

42 Abutilon hybridum
44 Acalypha hispida
46 Acanthocalycium
48 Adenium obesum
50 Adiantum capillus veneris
52 Adromischus cooperi
54 Aechmea fasciata
56 Aeonium arboreum
58 Aeschynanthus speciosus
60 Agave utahensis
62 Ageratum houstonianum
64 Aglaonema
66 Allamanda cathartica
68 Aloe variegata
70 Amaranthus caudatus
72 Ananas comosus
74 Anemone coronaria
76 Anthurium andreanum
78 Anthurium scherzerianum
80 Aphelandra squarrosa
82 Aporocactus
84 Araucaria heterophylla
86 Ardisia crenata
88 Ariocarpus
90 Arthrocereus
92 Asparagus meyerii
94 Asparagus plumosus

96 Asparagus sprengeri
98 Aspidistra elatior
100 Asplenium bulbiferum
102 Asplenium nidus
104 Astrophytum
106 Beaucarnea recurvata
108 Begonia bowerii
110 Begonia elatior
112 Begonia multiflora
114 Begonia rex
116 Begonia semperflorens
118 Beloperone guttata
120 Billbergia nutans
122 Blossfeldia
124 Borzicactus
126 Bougainvillea glabra
128 Bouvardia
130 Browallia speciosa
132 Brunfelsia calycina
134 Caladium bicolor
136 Calathea lancifolia
138 Calceolaria hybrida
140 Calendula officinalis
142 Callistephus chinensis
144 Camellia japonica
146 Campanula isophylla
148 Capsicum annuum
150 Caralluma frerei
152 Celosia plumosa
154 Ceropegia woodii
156 Chamaecereus
158 Chamaecyparis
160 Chamaedorea elegans

162 Chamaerops humilis
164 Chlorophytum comosum
166 Chrysalidocarpus lutescens
168 Chrysanthemum
170 Cissus antarctica
172 Cissus rhombifolia
174 Citrus mitis
176 Cleistocactus
178 Clerodendrum thomsonae
180 Clivia miniata
182 Cocos nucifera
184 Codiaeum variegatum
186 Coffea arabica
188 Coleus blumei
190 Columnea microphylla
192 Conophytum spectabile
194 Convallaria majulus
196 Convolvulus tricolor
198 Cordyline terminalis
200 Cotyledon undulatum
202 Crassula ovata
204 Crocus vernus
206 Crossandra infundibuliformis
208 Cryptanthus bivittatus
210 Ctenanthe oppenheimiana
212 Cuphea ignea
214 Cyclamen persicum

Scientific names

216 Cymbidium
218 Cyperus diffusus
220 Cyrtomium falcatum
222 Dahlia hybrida
224 Davallia
226 Dianthus chinensis
228 Dieffenbachia maculata
230 Dimorphotheca sinuata
232 Dipladenia sanderi
234 Dizygotheca elegantissima
236 Dracaena fragrans
238 Dracaena fragrans massangeana
240 Dracaena marginata
242 Dudleya brittonii
244 Echeveria agavoides
246 Echinocactus
248 Echinocereus
250 Echinopsis
252 Epiphyllum
254 Epipremnum aureus
256 Erica hiemalis
258 Espostoa
260 Euphorbia milii
262 Euphorbia pulcherrima
264 Exacum affine
266 Fatshedera lizei
268 Fatsia japonica
270 Faucaria tigrina
272 Fenestraria rhopalophylla
274 Ferocactus
276 Ficus benjamina
278 Ficus elastica

280 Ficus pumila
282 Fittonia verschaffeltii
284 Freesia refracta
286 Fuchsia
288 Galanthus nivalis
290 Gardenia jasminoides
292 Gasteria liliputana
294 Gazania
296 Gerbera jamesonii
298 Gibbaeum dispar
300 Gladiolus colvillei
302 Gloriosa superba
304 Grevillea robusta
306 Guzmania lingulata
308 Gymnocalycium
310 Gynura sarmentosa
312 Haworthia attenuata
314 Hebe
316 Hedera
318 Hedera canariensis
320 Hedera helix
322 Heliotropium arborescens
324 Hibiscus rosa-sinensis
326 Hippeastrum hortorum
328 Howea forsteriana
330 Hoya bella
332 Hoya carnosa
334 Huernia primulina

336 Hyacinthus orientalis
338 Hydrangea macrophylla
340 Hypoestes phyllostachya
342 Impatiens walleriana
344 Iris reticulata
346 Jasminum polyanthum
348 Kalanchoe blossfeldiana
350 Kleinia tomentosa
352 Lachenalia tricolor
354 Lapageria rosea
356 Lillium
358 Lithops
360 Livistona chinensis
362 Lobelia erinus
364 Lobivia
366 Mammillaria
368 Maranta leuconeura
370 Microcoelum weddelianum
372 Mimosa pudica
374 Monstera deliciosa
376 Musa acuminata
378 Muscari botryoides
380 Narcissus
382 Nematanthus radicans
384 Nemesia strumosa
386 Neochilenia

Scientific names

388 Neoporteria
390 Neoregelia carolinae
392 Nephrolepis exaltata
394 Nerine sarniensis
396 Nerium oleander
398 Nicotiana
400 Notocactus
402 Opuntia
404 Orbea variegata
406 Pachyphytum oviferum
408 Pachypodium succulentum
410 Pachystachys lutea
412 Pandanus veitchii
414 Parodia
416 Passiflora caerulea
418 Pelargonium regale
420 Pelargonium zonale
422 Pellaea rotundifolia
424 Pellionia
426 Peperomia magnoliaefolia
428 Petunia hybrida
430 Philodendron bipinnatifidum
432 Philodendron erubescens
434 Philodendron scandens
436 Phlebodium aureum
438 Phoenix canariensis

440 Phoenix roebelinii
442 Pilea cadierii
444 Pittosporum tenuifolium
446 Platycerium bifurcatum
448 Plectranthus australis
450 Pleiospilos
452 Plumbago capensis
454 Portulacaria afra
456 Primula malacoides
458 Primula obconica
460 Primula vulgaris
462 Pteris cretica
464 Pteris tremula
466 Rebutia
468 Rhapis excelsa
470 Rhododendron simsii
472 Rhoeo spathacea
474 Rosa
476 Ruellia mackoyana
478 Saintpaulia ionantha
480 Salvia splendens
482 Sansevieria trifasciata
484 Saxifraga stolonifera
486 Schefflera arboricola
488 Schizanthus hybridus
490 Schlumbergera
492 Scirpus cernuus
494 Sedum morganianum
496 Selaginella uncinata
498 Selenicereus

500 Senecio hybridus
502 Senecio maritima
504 Sinningia speciosa
506 Solanum capsicastrum
508 Soleirolia soleirolii
510 Sonerila margaritacea
512 Sparmannia africana
514 Spathiphyllum wallisii
516 Stapelia pulvinata
518 Stenocactus
520 Stephanotis floribunda
522 Streptocarpus
524 Sulcorebutia
526 Syngonium vellozianum
528 Tagetes patula
530 Testudinaria elephantipes
532 Thunbergia alata
534 Tillandsia cyanea
536 Tolmeia menziesii
538 Tradescantia albiflora
540 Tropaeoleum
542 Tulipa
544 Uebelmannia
546 Vallota speciosa
548 Verbena hybrida
550 Viola tricolor
552 Vriesia splendens
554 Yucca elephantipes
556 Zebrina pendula
558 Zinnia elegans

Introduction

How to use this book

Houseplants have now become so much part of everyday life that they are available at many types of shops from garden centres to motorway service stations. With the wide range of plants on sale, it is easy to make expensive mistakes. Despite the brief instruction labels provided with most purchases, a plant that has taken a nurseryman years to grow can be destroyed in a matter of weeks by either the wrong treatment or simply from being in the wrong position. This book, which features more than 250 different plants, is here to help you.

The book covers the complete range of plants grown indoors: flowering and foliage plants, palms and ferns, cacti and other succulents, and many bulbs and flowering annuals that can be grown indoors in pots and bowls. It also describes plants that are particularly suitable for windowboxes and balconies.

The plants are listed alphabetically and each one has a self-contained two-page entry. On the left is a general description of the plant with details of how to look after it. There is also a colour photograph of part or the whole of a healthy specimen. On the opposite page is a colour illustration of the plant showing all the things that can possibly go wrong with it. Since this picture shows all the troubles at once, some of the plants look very sick indeed! To find out what is wrong with your plant, read the caption next to the part of the picture that shows the same symptoms. It tells you what is wrong and how to put it right. Cacti tend to suffer from common problems which give exactly the same symptoms on most cactus species. To avoid wasteful repetition, these problems are shown in a special section on pp. 38-41, with advice on how to deal with them.

Different plants require different conditions and it is important to know each one's special requirements. Make sure you read the detailed care instructions for your plant.

Tools for indoor gardening

It is possible to look after plants with the minimum of equipm a watering can, sprayer and plastic sponge are the real esser However, for long-term houseplant care, you will need a muc more comprehensive collection, which can be acquired grad as the need arises.

Keep separate sprayers and watering cans for insecticides and fungicides and a stock of basic insecticides. Methylated spirits is useful for removing some pests. Mark all containers used for insecticides clearly and wash them out regularly.

Leafshine adds gloss but some plants react badly. These should be cleaned with a damp sponge or soft cloth, or with a fine mist spray. For delicate leaves use a feather duster or dry paintbrush. A paintbrush and cotton wool are useful for removing pests.

A small garden trowel and fork are useful when repotting or adding topsoil. A large spoon is a good substitute. A plastic bucket is essential for mixing composts, wetting peat and for giving very dry plants a thorough soaking.

Keep a selection of loam-based and peat-based composts, some pure moss or sedge peat. Some plants require lime-free mixtures. Sharp sand can be obtained from garden centres. Fertilizer, hormone rooting powder and charcoal are all useful.

Scissors, secateurs and a sharp knife are useful for taking cuttings and removing dead or damaged fronds. They are also useful for removing damaged stems from succulents and cacti, but always wear gloves when doing this.

Two watering cans to which a rose can be attached are useful, one pint (½ litre) size, the other holding about a gallon (4½l). Never use your normal watering can for insecticides or fungicides.

Keep a small stock of flower pots and saucers, both plastic and clay. Old clay flower pots can be broken up to make excellent drainage material. Outer pots, with no drainage holes, can be used to hide the standard pot.

Twine, string, raffia and plant rings are essential for climbing plants, with a selection of canes, sticks and moss poles.

Foliage and flowering houseplants

Watering and spraying

More houseplants are killed by incorrect watering (mainly of the little and often variety) than by anything else. Most prefer to be given a good soaking, then left almost to dry out before they are watered again. Some must be kept always moist — but in these cases the pot must be well drained so that the roots do not become waterlogged. Others prefer to dry out more thoroughly between waterings. Some need more water at one time of year than another. Always test the compost before watering to see how dry it is below the surface. In cold weather do not use cold water straight from the tap or the shock may damage the plant. Use tepid water for both watering and spraying.

Spraying keeps a plant's leaves clean and also provides extra humidity in hot, dry rooms. Avoid tap water if possible as the lime it contains clogs the pores of the leaves. Rainwater collected in a tank or bucket, water from melted ice in the freezer or boiled water which has been allowed to cool are all more suitable. Do not spray in bright sunlight as the water acts like a magnifying glass and may cause burn or scorch marks. A few plants dislike water on their leaves so before spraying check each plant entry.

Feeding

Most composts contain fertilizer but for healthy growth plants also need extra nourishment, usually in spring and summer. Houseplant food or fertilizer is available as a liquid, diluted before use, as a powder and in granules, pills and slow-release sticks and mats. You can also obtain a foliar feed which is sprayed onto the leaves. For most houseplants a liquid food is most suitable. It is clean, has no smell and is easy and economical to use. There are several brands available and it is a good idea to try several and to change from time to time. Normally you can simply follow the instruc-

Watering

1. Test compost for dryness with finger or knife blade before watering. If blade comes out clean or soil dry and crumbly, compost is drying out. If soil sticks, it is still moist. Check instructions for each plant: some like a dry interval, others must be always moist.

2. Add water to top of compost, filling pot to the brim. Excess water will drain into saucer. After 15 minutes, empty any water remaining in the saucer. Do not allow pot to stand in water.

3. If plant is very dried out and does not mind water on its leaves, plunge pot into bowl so that water covers pot rim. Spray leaves. Leave for 15 minutes, then take it out and allow it to drain.

4. If plant cannot tolerate water on its leaves, add water to fill the saucer and wait for 15 minutes for it to be absorbed. Empty excess so plant does not stand in water. Or, plunge pot into bowl or bucket of water to just below pot rim. Leave for 15 minutes, then take out and allow to drain.

5. Bromeliads such as the Scarlet star (Guzmania) need to have water in their central well. Use rainwater if possible and fill whenever watering compost.

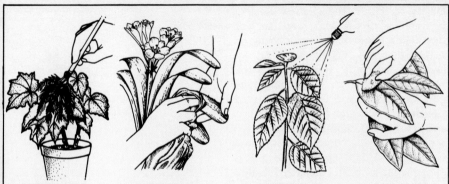

Cleaning the leaves
1. Flick very dusty plants with a feather duster before cleaning.

2. Wipe larger leaves with a damp cloth or sponge to remove dust and any insects such as red spider mite. Use soft water if possible. Remember to wipe the undersides of the leaves as well as the tops.

3. Spraying (with soft water if possible) is often enough to keep plants clean. The lime in hard tap water may mark the leaves and clog the pores. Do not spray the flowers and do not spray in sunlight.

4. Very few flowering plants tolerate leafshine on their leaves as they are easily burned or clogged by the oils it contains. Check instructions and never use more than once a month.

Humidity
Many plants require higher humidity than is found in normal rooms, especially in dry, centrally heated homes. A group of plants will create its own more humid atmosphere but you can improve the humidity around them in several ways.

1. Spray regularly with soft water, holding spray about 6in (15cm) from plant. Do not spray in strong sunlight. Spray may mark or rot flowers, so check plant's requirements when in flower.

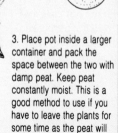

2. Put pebbles in plant's saucer and stand pot on top. Add water to saucer until it comes half way up the pebbles. Do not let bottom of pot touch water or plant will become waterlogged and roots will rot away. Water vapour will rise from the damp pebbles, providing extra humidity under the leaves. Add more water to saucer when pebbles begin to dry. A group of plants can be placed together on a tray of damp pebbles for even better local humidity.

3. Place pot inside a larger container and pack the space between the two with damp peat. Keep peat constantly moist. This is a good method to use if you have to leave the plants for some time as the peat will hold moisture well.

1. Spray plants in hanging baskets every day in spring and summer as they dry out quickly.
2. To provide constant humidity, hang a drip tray under the basket and keep it half filled with water. Humidity will rise around the plant as the water evaporates

tions on the bottle, adding a few drops to the water in the can when watering. For some plants, however, the mixture must be weaker than the manufacturer recommends on the bottle. If it is used at too concentrated a strength, it will damage the roots. Never increase the recommended strength and be careful with tablets and fertilizer sticks. If they are too close to the roots, the concentrated fertilizer may cause root damage. If in doubt, don't feed. It is always better to slightly underfeed than to overfeed - and never feed a sick plant.

Repotting

Plants need repotting either because the roots have totally filled the existing pot and can no longer develop or because the nutritional value of the compost has been used up. It is quite easy to tell if a plant needs repotting. Remove it from its pot (see right). If there is a mass of roots and no soil showing, it needs repotting - it is potbound. If any soil is visible, don't repot, but replace the plant in its old pot and gently firm it back in position. Other signs are roots growing through the pot base and weak, slow growth. Newly purchased plants should not normally need repotting. Do not repot unhealthy plants: the shock may kill them. If in doubt, don't repot.

Repotting is usually done in spring - March or April in the northern hemisphere, September or October in the southern. Most plants require good drainage so that water can run through the compost freely and air can get to the roots. Never use a container without drainage holes in its base. (In fact, bulbs can be grown in bowls which do not have drainage holes, but in that case they need to be placed in a special porous fibre - see p.26.) Broken crocks from old clay flower pots or a layer of coarse gravel at the bottom of the pot will provide drainage. Put a piece of paper or a layer of moss over the drainage crocks to stop the compost from blocking the holes and inspect the root ball for pests. Remove old stones, damaged roots and old soil and gently remove old, loose compost from the

Repotting

1. Prepare clean, dry pot not more than 2 sizes larger than old one. Place broken crocks or coarse gravel in bottom as drainage, then a piece of paper or moss and layer of new compost. Water plant well.

2. Hold pot upside down as shown. Gently tap rim of pot on edge of table and remove pot with other hand. If pot sticks, tap in several places.

3. Remove damaged or dead roots with sharp knife.

4. Gently break roots at bottom of ball and remove any bits of crock or stone. Remove all loose, old compost from top, to a depth of about ½in (1cm). Always handle with care so as not to damage leaves or buds.

5. Lower plant into new pot and add more compost round root ball, firming it with fingers or a round stick. Continue adding compost until pot is filled to within ½–¾in (1–1½cm). Leave for 3 days without water in shade.

Changing the topsoil

Large plants in tubs over 15in (40cm) are difficult to repot completely. Carefully scrape away about 2–3in (5–7cm) old topsoil.

Add new compost, leaving watering space of ½-¾in (1-1½cm) between compost and pot rim. Firm down with palm of hand. Water well, including diluted houseplant food with the first watering.

Bottle gardens

Bottle gardens provide a self-contained environment, and are ideal for most small ferns and palms as a very high level of humidity is produced. Like ships in bottles, they appear impossible to plant but with a simple homemade tool, can easily be set up. The bigger the bottle the better garden you will be able to make.

How to make a special tool

Using an old teaspoon and old kitchen fork, bend the bowl of the spoon so that it is at right angles to the handle, and bind the handles to the opposite ends of a strong cane, using insulating tape.

Planting a bottle garden

1. Make a sheet of paper into a cone shape. Place in neck of bottle. Pour in finely broken crocks or gravel, and a few grains of charcoal. Tip bottle to spread mixture evenly ½in (1cm) deep.

2. Add compost mixture to bottle, tipping so that the level is higher (5in, 13cm) one side than the other (3in, 8cm).

3. Use the fork end of your tool to move the compost about, then firm down with the back of the spoon.

4. Decide where to place plants, taller plants at the back, shorter plants at the front. Dig a hole for each, starting at the back.

5. Knock plants from pots, and loosen compost from roots. Drop plants into holes.

6. Move compost around root ball with the fork and firm it down with the spoon.

7. Water so that water runs down the inside of the bottle wall to wash off excess compost. Wipe inside with a cotton wool swab tied to the spoon. Do not use too much water, make soil just moist. Leave stopper off until condensation disappears. With stopper in place, enclosed environment will last without water for months.

top to about ½in (1cm). Then place the plant in a new pot and add fresh compost.

After repotting, leave the plant without water for 2-3 days. The roots will spread out into the new compost in search of water. If it is very hot, spray the leaves every day.

Choosing the right compost: The correct type of compost or soil is very important for indoor plants. Don't use garden soil, which is usually too heavy and stifles the roots of young plants. Compost types vary considerably as some houseplants need a very light peat-based compost and some a heavy loam. The correct combination for each plant is given in the individual entries.

The two most commonly used types of compost are loam-based and peat-based. Loam-based compost is made up of sterilized loam (soil) mixed with peat and grit or coarse, washed sand. It is usually sold with fertilizer added, following formulae developed by the John Innes Institute for Horticultural Research. The numbers 1, 2 and 3 indicate the different proportions of fertilizer added. In this book they are called 'loam-based No. 1,2 or 3'.

Peat-based composts are more open in texture, sterile, and hold moisture longer. They are normally composed of 10 parts of peat to 1 part of coarse sand with fertilizer added in the same proportions as loam-based compost. Do not firm peat composts into the pot too hard.

Ericaceous or lime-free compost is available for plants that do not tolerate lime. Sphagnum moss is useful for some plants which are grown on cork bark, or for lining a hanging basket. Sharp sand is fine, washed sand, available from garden centres. It is sometimes mixed with loam to give a specially well-drained compost. Never use coarse builders' sand. Small polystyrene balls lighten the soil and rotted leafmould and manure are useful.

Mixing compost: If mixing your own blend of compost, put the different items into a plastic bucket, using the same measure for each one. A plant pot or old cup will do. Mix the items together with a trowel or stick so that they are well blended.

Insect-eaters

Insect-eating plants such as the Venus' Flytrap (*Dionaea muscipula*) trap and digest small flies that land on them. They are usually sold as very young, newly germinated plants in pots covered with a clear plastic top which provides them with a mini-greenhouse. This is ideal, for they are bog plants and need a very moist atmosphere. Keep them in good indirect light and well watered always. They can even stand in a saucer of water. They grow in ordinary room temperatures but prefer to be under 60°F (18°C) in winter, though not below 40°F (4°C). In summer they grow spikes of white flowers.

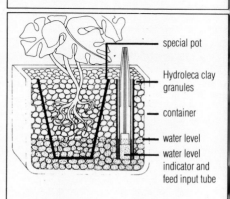

- special pot
- Hydroleca clay granules
- container
- water level
- water level indicator and feed input tube

Hydroculture

The art of growing plants in water is an easy way for the forgetful to enjoy indoor plants. The technique is relatively simple but has taken a long time to perfect. The plant is either grown as a cutting in water or converted (by a long process). The roots are held in position by granules of expanded fired clay which has no nutritional value.

The plant is fed by a special ion-exchange fertilizer which, over a long period, releases nutrients into the water. The chemicals in ordinary tap water activate the fertilizer and the plant takes it up through the roots as and when it needs nourishment. It is therefore not possible to over or underfeed a plant, provided that the fertilizer is renewed every 6 months. Making sure that the water is up to the right level as shown on the inbuilt water gauge is the only care required, except of course for an occasional dusting of the leaves. Overwatering, which kills so many plants, is impossible! Not all foliage plants are suitable but the range is wide. They are well worth buying and make ideal office plants.

Planting a self-watering planter

These are available in sizes from single pot size to large units for a mixture of plants. An 18in (45cm) square will take about five plants, including one up to 4ft (1.2m) high. A drainage layer is not necessary as the base of the soil compartment is perforated and there is a gap between this and the surface of the water below.

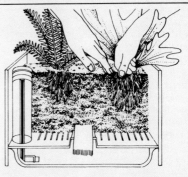

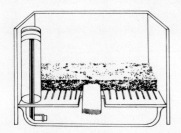

1. Place a layer of compost in the bottom of the planter.

2. Knock all plants out of their pots.

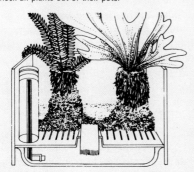

3. Place them in the planter so that the tops of their rootballs are level with each other, adjusting the level of the compost below each one.

4. Fill planter with compost, leaving ¾in (1½cm) gap between top of soil and lip of planter. Firm down well around plants.

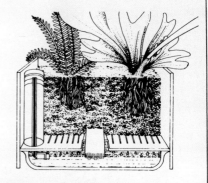

5. Pour water onto the soil. This will pass through the soil and soil compartment floor into the reservoir. Stop when the water gauge reads 'Maximum'.

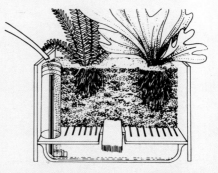

6. Water again by filling the reservoir when the indicator reads 0. Fill until it reads 'Maximum'.

19

Lighting

1. If plants are in too dark a corner they will not grow well and will turn their leaves and flower stems in the direction of the brightest light.

2. Full sunlight may damage leaves or flowers. Shade from direct midday sun with a fine gauze curtain. This will filter and diffuse the light. A plant placed opposite a white wall which faces the sun will also benefit from diffused light.

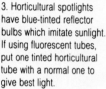

3. Horticultural spotlights have blue-tinted reflector bulbs which imitate sunlight. If using fluorescent tubes, put one tinted horticultural tube with a normal one to give best light.

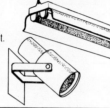

Shading a greenhouse

Midday summer sun in a greenhouse is too strong for some houseplants. Stretch horizontal wires above plants and hang fine shading netting over to protect them.

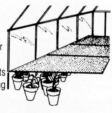

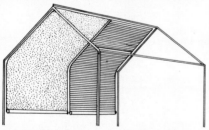

The best, but most expensive way of providing shade is to fit adjustable roller blinds made from wooden slats or thin material. These can be moved easily and do not restrict access to the plants. Your local garden centre will advise you. Finally, the easiest, cheapest way is to spray the outside with powdered shading paint mixed with water. This may wash off in the rain and must be removed in winter or the light will be too dim.

Lighting

Houseplants need different amounts of light, though most flowering houseplants prefer a high level of diffused sunlight, but not direct sunlight. Diffused light is indirect sunlight, i.e. bouncing off a wall onto the plant or filtering through a net curtain. Each plant's special requirements are described in detail in its entry.

Artificial light: To compensate for lack of daylight you can install fluorescent tubes or spotlights. However, conventional artificial light is not as intense as natural daylight and certain plants will not thrive under it.

This problem occurs particularly in offices with windows covered by a solar screen, or with no windows at all. Special horticultural spotlights and fluorescent tubes are available which imitate diffused sunlight more closely and these have a good effect on plants.

Spotlights: To imitate diffused daylight, a blue coating is added to the front of the bulb. The light seems the same as that of a conventional spotlight but in practice plants do actually grow as though they are in daylight. Unfortunately, the problem of heat has not been solved. A 150w reflector lamp mounted closer than 39in (1m) to the plant will overheat its leaves. At 39in (1m) sufficient light will be produced over an area 39in (1m) in diameter but at a distance of 78in (2m), only a quarter of that light will fall on the leaves. Although it is sometimes difficult to position the lights so as to get enough light and not too much heat, spotlights are the most adaptable types.

Fluorescent lights: These are a much more efficient method of providing light. They do not give out much heat and are available with a wide range of intensities. Special horticultural tubes fit standard fittings and are available in the same lengths as conventional tubes. They can be combined with standard tubes to give a less stark light. They are obviously not so flexible as spotlights but if a combination of the two types is used, plants in darker areas will benefit. Most specialist plant shops will be able to advise you.

Climbers and trailers

Some flowering plants grow very fast. In a greenhouse or permanent sun porch they can be trained around the walls but in ordinary rooms they need a hoop or cane. A simple frame can be made by bending a wire coathanger or using a piece of flexible cane or plastic coated wire.

Training round a hoop

1. Push ends of wire hoop or thin cane so that they are ⅔ down the pot on opposite sides. Bend stem to one side of hoop and gently twist it around the hoop. Do not damage the leaves or stem.

2. Tie a length of twine to one end of hoop and thread it along, looping it loosely around the stem. Do not tie tight knots. The growing tip will continue to follow the line of the hoop. When it reaches the other end, it can be trained round again or twisted back the other way.

Air plants

These curious-looking plants grow naturally without soil. Most are *Tillandsia* (members of the Bromeliad family) and come from Central and South America. Their tiny root systems are used only for support and they live by taking moisture and nutrients from the air. They make ideal houseplants and are usually sold mounted on coral, sea shells, minerals or driftwood. Their care is simple. They should be kept in an airy position in good indirect or diffused light and sprayed daily in summer, every other day in winter, with a mist spray. Hold the spray about 1ft (30cm) from the plant and spray it lightly so that it dries out again within an hour. In summer add liquid houseplant food to the spray water once a month, diluting it to ¼ maker's recommended strength. They will stand a wide range of temperatures, down to 45°F (7°C) in winter — and any normal room temperature in summer.

How to make a moss pole

Larger plants are best trained on a moss or foam pole. These retain moisture and any aerial roots will grow into the moss.

2. Bind moss along cane with string, tying off at top with a firm knot.

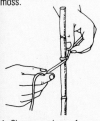

1. Choose a piece of strong cane long enough to reach top of plant from base of pot. Tie a piece of string to it, about 9in (23cm) from end. Take some sphagnum moss large enough to cover rest of cane and loosen it a little with a stick or pencil.

3. Push uncovered end of cane into compost when repotting. If at any other time, be careful not to damage roots. Tie plant loosely to moss pole in several places. Keep moss moist at all times to help humidity around plant.

Canes

1. A single cane will support a tall plant. Insert cane when repotting, after positioning plant but before adding all the compost. Cane should be a few inches from main stem, stopping about ⅔ down the pot.

A larger support can be made from two canes joined at the top by a stiff wire.

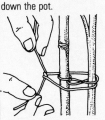

2. Loop a 9in (23cm) length of string around stem and tie in firm knot against cane. Or use a plant ring.

For three plants in one pot, place three canes around pot edge and tie at the top.

Growing from seed

1. Fill clean seed tray to rim with seedling compost, using slight pressure only at corners.

2. Press down lightly with flat board to level off surface.

3. Water through a fine rose cap, using clean tap water, until water comes through bottom of tray. Leave to drain for at least 2 hours.

4. Sow seed thinly on surface of compost. Large seeds can be spaced individually, very fine seed can be mixed with 20 times its volume of fine, dry sand.

5. Dust over with fresh, dry seedling compost, just enough to anchor seed.

6. Do not water again but insert label and place in propagator or clean plastic bag, turning open end under box so moisture is retained.

7. Keep at temperature recommended on packet and cover with sheet of brown paper. Keep away from windows.

8. When first signs of growth appear, remove paper and bag and place in full light (not hot sun).

9. When seedlings are large enough to handle, prepare small containers with potting compost. Water them and allow to drain.

10. Make small hole in compost with flat-ended stick.

11. Push plant label or ice lolly stick into seed tray and spoon up seedling.

12. Place in palm of hand, then hold by leaves to drop into hole in new pot. Do not press compost round stem.

13. Spray with fine mist spray of clean tap water and leave in shade for 2 days to recover.

14. Move into full light including morning or afternoon sun. Move to bigger pot only when roots fill small one.

Taking cuttings

This is the most common way of propagating houseplants though seeds of some species are available. First prepare a small pot with drainage and special rooting compost.

3. Dust the cut ends with hormone rooting powder.

5. Place in heated propagator or cover with polythene and keep in warm place (70°F, 21°C). Keep watered and remove cover for 5 minutes a day.

6. When cuttings begin to grow, pot singly in small pots.

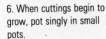

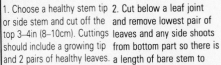

1. Choose a healthy stem tip or side stem and cut off the top 3–4in (8–10cm). Cuttings should include a growing tip and 2 pairs of healthy leaves.

2. Cut below a leaf joint and remove lowest pair of leaves and any side shoots from bottom part so there is a length of bare stem to insert into compost. Prepare other cuttings the same way.

4. Make holes around edge of new pot. Insert several cuttings and firm compost gently round them. Water well.

Propagation

Houseplants can be grown from seeds or cuttings or by dividing or layering. The best method for each is shown in the individual plant entries. Indoor flowering annuals and most plants for windowboxes and balconies are grown from seed. Few people have a heated greenhouse in which to propagate but by following the instructions in this book, excellent plants can be raised ready for planting in early summer and at little cost on a sunny window-sill indoors.

The basic preparation is common to all seed sowing (see left), while any special requirements are given under individual plant entries. Clean trays, sterile seedling compost and clean tap water are the main essentials.

Small, lightweight plastic seed trays or pots are ideal for sowing and are more sterile than wood. Plastic pots will be needed for sowing, taking cuttings and potting on. The most useful sizes are 3in (8cm), 3½in (9cm), 4¼in (11cm) and 5½in (14cm). Cut flat presser bonds from thin hardboard to fit the tray size, adding a small block of wood as a handle. Keep a small airtight jar full of dry, fine sand for mixing

Layering

1. Some climbing or trailing plants can be layered. First prepare small pot with drainage and compost of half loam, half sharp sand.

2. Choose strong stem and make slit in lower surface below a leaf.

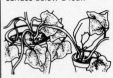

3. Bend stem so that slit stem lies on compost in new pot. Weight with pebble or peg closely to compost. Water. Roots will grow from slit and when these are firmly fixed, cut stem

Offsets

Bromeliads such as Scarlet star (*Guzmania lingulata*) produce offsets which can be separated from the parent plant when they are about half its size and have their own root system.

1. Remove offset and roots from parent plant with sharp knife.

2. Pot offset in new pot, firming compost around base. Water plant well. Keep warm (75°F, 24°C).

23

with fine seed: to get the sand really fine, pass it through an old nylon stocking.

A heated propagator is useful for both seeds and cuttings but a plastic bag wrapped around the tray makes a good substitute as long as the pots or trays can be kept in a warm, even temperature. Most seeds will germinate in half light and a brown paper cover will provide this. Once germinated, the seedlings can be kept on a windowledge with double glazing or protected from draughts by a sheet of plastic. Always label seed when sown so that progress can be checked from the date on the label.

Pricking out

As soon as the first signs of growth are seen, remove the tray from its plastic bag or propagator into a light position, though not in scorching sun. It is important to prick out (transplant) the seedlings into a tray or pot of fresh compost as soon as they are large enough to handle; the seedling will then hardly be aware that it has been moved.

Dividing ferns

It is possible to propagate some ferns from their spores, using a heated propagator but for most, root division is the most successful way of increasing your stock.

1. A plant that has become very bushy can be divided into 2, 3 or even 4 parts. First prepare as many smaller pots as you need – see Repotting (p.16).

3. Gently pull roots and stems apart with your hands.

4. For a very pot-bound plant with a mass of roots, use a sharp knife.

2. Remove plant from pot and shake away loose soil.

5. Repot the divided sections into smaller pots.

Pruning

Old flowering plants may grow straggly and produce fewer flowers. Pruning back leggy stems in spring encourages new side shoots which in turn produce more flowers. Slow-growing foliage plants rarely need pruning but quicker growing types may need cutting back.

Cut off dead flowers so that plant's energy goes to new buds and leaves.

Palms cannot be pruned to prevent further growth since most of them grow only from the top. If new growth is removed, the whole plant will eventually die.

1. Remove old dead leaves by cutting off as close to the trunk or stem as possible with a sharp knife.

2. In some palms the stump of the leaf stem will fall off, creating an attractive herringbone pattern on the trunk.

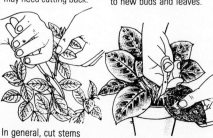

In general, cut stems down by half, just above a leaf or side shoot. But read individual instructions as some must never be pruned.

Old dead leaves should be cut off as close to the stem as possible. This encourages new young leaves to develop.

Ferns may become bushy and older leaves can be removed with a pair of sharp scissors if absolutely necessary for space reasons. Do not pinch out ferns or palms to try to make them bushy. It will stunt growth or kill them. If tips of leaves or fronds turn brown and dry, they can be removed with sharp scissors. Cut just inside brown area to avoid damaging healthy tissue.

Spring and summer bulbs

Bulbs, tubers, corms and rhizomes are all forms of underground storage organs. They are particularly valuable indoors since many flower in winter or early spring and are easy to grow well. Remember, though, that the hardy ones such as daffodils and hyacinths grow naturally in very cold conditions and will fail indoors unless they are given a long cold, dark spell in which to develop roots before the top shoots appear.

If you have a garden, the best way to achieve this is to bury the bulbs in their pots under a 3-6in (8-15cm) layer of sand. If this is impossible, then put the pots in a box with a lid or wrap them in thick black plastic and keep them in the coolest possible place, on a balcony or windowledge or in a cold cupboard. For some reason many people think the airing cupboard is the right place but this is not so. Pots buried (or 'plunged') outside should always have drainage holes but will not need watering. Others will need watering to keep the compost moist but never let them get soggy or the bulbs will rot.

When shoots begin to show above the compost it is time to bring them into the light, but check the individual care instructions to make sure they are not moved into a warm room too early. Bulbs 'plunged' outside in pots can be transferred to bowls as soon as they are brought indoors, but take care not to damage their delicate roots.

Forcing bulbs means bringing them into flower before their natural season and this is done by cooling them and giving them a dark period earlier in the year than usual. Specially prepared bulbs are sold at the correct time of the year for planting. They can only be forced once and will then revert to their normal flowering time.

Bulbs can be grown in bowls without drainage holes if in special porous fibre but they will need some crocks, pebbles or charcoal in the bottom and careful watering. Choose bowls deep enough to hold bulbs at least an inch (2½cm) above drainage layer at the correct depth below

Planting bulbs

1. When planting more than one bulb in a pot, always leave at least ¼in (6mm) between each one. This will prevent infected bulbs from contaminating others.

2. Vigorous rooting bulbs such as hyacinths may push up out of the soil if in small pot.

3. Make sure compost is loose underneath bulb and that shoulder of bulb is covered to anchor it.

4. Bulbs can be planted at different levels in a deep pot. They will all flower at same time and height.

5. Amaryllis and other tropical bulbs benefit from bottom heat after potting, to start roots developing. Radiator shelves are useful for this.

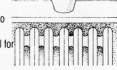

6. Stem rooting lillies need at least 6–8in (15–20cm) compost above the bulb. If no deep pots available, fit a 6in (15cm) length of plastic drainpipe (diameter about 5in, 13cm) inside rim of pot for extra height.

Forcing bulbs

1. Soak bulb fibre and squeeze out excess water. Fibre should cling together without oozing water.

2. Prepare pot or bowl with layer of charcoal lumps and sphagnum moss, then fibre or moist compost.

3. Plant bulbs in position. Most kinds should be buried with half their depth of fibre above; some should have tips of bulbs protruding. Check plant entries.

4. Cover bowl with black plastic to keep out light and keep in cool cupboard or on a windowledge or balcony. Check weekly to make sure it does not dry out.

5. Or, dig plunge hole outside in protected position and stand pot inside. Cover with 6in (15cm) sand or weathered ash to prevent frost. Pots in plunge must have drainage holes.

6. When shoots are right out of bulb uncover but shade from full light for 2–3 days.

7. When flower buds appear, move into warmer position but check temperature requirements for individual plants.

the surface (see individual plant entries).

A home-made mixture of 2 parts clean garden soil, 1 part sharp sand and 1 part grit can be used for bulbs but if only a few are needed, a bought compost is best.

Bulb fibre made of peat, crushed shell and crushed charcoal, can be used for all kinds of bulbs and is good for bowls without drainage holes since it is very porous. However, it contains hardly any nutrients and there is little chance of using bulbs planted in it again.

If bulbs are to be saved for the next year, they must be well fed while growing, continuing until the leaves die down naturally. Leaves should never be cut down after flowering for at this time the embryo

flower for next year is forming in the bulb and it depends on the leaves for its supply of nutrients.

Most summer flowering bulbs should be removed from their pots for the winter resting season or, if in the garden, lifted and stored. Keep them in a dry, frost-free place, protected from mice and other pests. Bulbs lifted from the garden should be dipped in fungicide before storing.

Most bulbs produce offsets which can be separated from the parent bulb and potted in good compost or planted out to develop in the garden. The best time to do this is just before the start of the growing season. Offsets may take several years to reach flowering size.

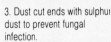

Windowbox and balcony plants

Almost any plant can be grown in a container: the selection in this book contains annuals, perennials and small shrubs, all of which can be propagated by an amateur gardener.

Many of the plants suggested are annual flowering ones, which grow from seed, flower and die in a single season. These quickly provide a colourful display and give you a chance to experiment before committing yourself to a long-term planting scheme — in which they can still feature.

Containers and composts

Any container that will hold soil and allow surplus water to drain away freely can be used but as plants are grown to improve the environment, the container should not detract from that by being ugly or unsightly. Natural hewn stone, reconstituted stone or hardwoods are ideal but the plastics industry has made great strides in producing classical designs cheaply and these are now made with more natural effect than the stark white urns of a few years ago. Even these can be improved by painting them with a natural stone finish though the surface must be well roughened with glass paper first or the paint will soon flake. Hand-thrown pottery containers, both glazed and unglazed, are also attractive.

Old sinks, halved beer barrels, old garden wheelbarrows are also much used for planting. Windowboxes may be in wood, plastic or concrete and often come with the house so that no choice is possible. Whatever is used, the judicious use of trailing plants can hide any stark outlines.

Always secure windowboxes carefully and make sure that pots or tubs on sills or balconies are stable. A container full of soil and plants can cause considerable damage if it falls down.

Containers should be filled with compost rather than soil and this may be either loam-based or loamless.

Loamless composts, based on peat, were first devised by the University of California and have largely taken the place of John

Innes for propagating purposes, being clean, light and easily handled. They are very uniform and any problems that arise in use are likely to be due to poor storage conditions. The moisture content of the peat must be exactly right at the time of mixing. If the bag is stored outside, inevitably the compost will become wetter and this will activate the slow release fertilizers and give rise to a compost that is too strong for young seedlings. So keep your compost under cover and out of the sun which will also cause slight chemical changes that may be harmful and do not waste money mixing it with unsterilized soil, putting it in dirty seed trays or watering it with contaminated water.

Feeding

Container-grown plants need more regular feeding than garden plants because each time you water the container the nutrients are washed down further and further until they have all disappeared through the drainage holes. In the garden the roots can still reach them. Liquid fertilizers are instantly available to the roots but must always be diluted to at least the maker's recommended strength. There are also a number of slow-release tabs, sticks and granules available and these can be a useful standby, especially when plants are left for some time unattended. Soil-based composts retain nutrients for longer than soil-less ones and it is for this reason that different feeding rates are given for each type.

In general, start feeding seed-grown plants 3-4 weeks after planting out. Never feed dry plants. Always water them first and allow to drain for an hour or so before feeding. Never think that a double dose will be twice as good as one: it will scorch the roots. Foliar feeds, sprayed on the leaves, are beneficial, but use them with care: dilute to the recommended strength and do not spray in bright sunshine.

When buying fertilizer, choose a balanced mixture of nitrogen, phosphate and potash, never all potash or all nitrogen or the plant's delicate balance will be upset.

Preparing a container

1. Treat wooden containers inside and out with wood preservatives before using. Follow the manufacturer's instructions carefully as many preservatives can be toxic to plants.

2. If using a light plastic urn or pot with a hollow base, pack hollow with plastic bag filled with sand to make it more stable. Choose wide-based containers where possible.

3. Make sure container has drainage holes and raise base off floor with tiles or bricks. This ensures free drainage and helps to keep pests away.

4. Place layer of stones, broken clay pots or crocks to cover base of container. Sterilize them first with solution of permanganate of potash. Crocks should be at least 1in (2½cm) deep. If no drainage holes, crocks should take up ¼ depth of container.

5. Add layer of pea gravel or very small pebbles on top of crocks.

6. Fill with compost, leaving about 2in (5cm) at top to allow for watering. Water well and leave to drain for at least 2 hours before planting. If compost settles after watering, top up with fresh.

Potash provides flowers, firmness of foliage and disease resistance. Nitrogen gives quicker growth and greenness of leaf. Phosphate promotes root growth.

Watering and spraying

Most plants will stay healthy in a moist soil, that is one that retains all the water its solid particles can hold without filling the air spaces that are so essential to the roots. In the garden, excess water can seep away over a wide area but in a container drainage holes are necessary to allow any excess to drain quickly after watering so that air can take its place. Without proper drainage, the soil soon becomes waterlogged and even moisture-loving plants will suffer and eventually die. Some plants are sensitive to even a short period without air at their roots and for these you are instructed to keep them 'on the dry side'; but don't keep them completely dry. Instead allow the soil to dry out almost to the bottom of the container between waterings.

Water from a water butt is unsuitable for seedlings. It is certain to contain disease organisms which will thrive in the warm, humid conditions of a propagator. Tap water is safe but for lime-hating species, it may contain too much calcium. For them sterilized rainwater is best.

Overwatering and contaminated water are the prime causes of failure of container-grown plants. Under individual plant entries you will find each plant's moisture preference but it is virtually impossible to recommend watering intervals outside, where rainfall and temperature radically affect the rate at which a container dries out. It is best to test the soil regularly (especially for windowboxes, which may be sheltered from the rain) and to watch for any signs of drooping leaves or flowers.

Many plants enjoy an overhead spray and this will be especially welcome to plants growing under an overhanging balcony where rain does not normally reach; plants with soft stems and leaves are likely to develop botrytis mould if they are regularly wetted and these, of course, should not be

Months and seasons

The plants in this book are suitable for a wide range of climates. To make the instructions useful for as many areas as possible, dates are given in seasons not months. The following chart gives the monthly equivalents.

Month in northern hemisphere	Season	Month in southern hemisphere
January	**Mid-Winter**	July
February	**Late Winter**	August
March	**Early Spring**	September
April	**Mid-Spring**	October
May	**Late Spring**	November
June	**Early Summer**	December
July	**Mid-Summer**	January
August	**Late Summer**	February
September	**Early Autumn**	March
October	**Mid-Autumn**	April
November	**Late Autumn**	May
December	**Early Winter**	June

sprayed. Again, individual requirements are given in the plant entries.

Propagation

To grow a windowbox or balcony plant from seed, follow the method described earlier (pp.22-24). Once the plant has grown sufficiently to be planted outside in its final container, it is ready for 'hardening off'.

This is a difficult thing to achieve and some explanation of the term is necessary first. Some plants are termed 'hardy'. These will withstand winter frosts and burst into growth again in the spring. Some are 'half hardy' and these in general comprise plants which will grow out-of-doors in the summer but will be killed by any frost. 'Tender' plants are particularly affected by cold weather and must be treated with special care. But all this has nothing to do with hardening off. Any plant introduced to the outside world from a protected indoor environment will receive a shock to its system. The art is to minimize this shock by making the introduction as gradual as possible. This process is known as hardening off. If correctly hardened off, hardy plants will still survive the winter and half hardy plants will still be killed by frost; but neither of them will be needlessly damaged by chills and shock.

Young plants are normally taken outside in mid to late spring. For the first week they should be covered with glass or plastic to allow them to adjust to cooler temperatures. If you have no cold frame, line a small crate with plastic and cover it with a sheet of glass. Air is allowed in during the day, but the cover is closed at night. At first the air should only be allowed in for 2 hours a day but after 2 to 3 days the cover can be taken off completely during fine weather. If frost is expected at night, the frame should be covered and wrapped in hessian if the plants it contains are half hardy and even for hardy ones during their first week outside. Remove the cover early in the morning or condensation will not dry off before the sun is hot and the leaves will be scorched. Late uncovering also means lost light and this is important to keep the plants growing sturdily. Half hardy plants need at least 14 days to harden off sufficiently to withstand the effects of cold spring winds, but protection must at any rate continue until all risk of frost is passed. Bought plants should be ready for planting out but if purchased early in the season, check whether they are tender or hardy before leaving them out unprotected. If in doubt, cover plants with an inverted cardboard box wrapped in newspapers, sacking and polythene on frosty nights.

One important final point. Wet protection is worse than no protection. Cover frost wraps with plastic sheet. Leaves should be dry before the frame is closed for the night. The whole spring effort of germinating and growing, the whole summer's pleasure, can be lost in one night without this care.

In cold climates, frost will completely freeze the soil in containers in winter. Wrap them in sacking and cover with a polythene sheet to keep them dry.

Planting a mixed container

1. Prepare container and assemble plants ready to be transferred. Water plants well.

2. Dig small holes with trowel where plants are to go. These should be large enough to take whole root ball. Leave plenty of space for growth.

3. Insert canes if needed for tall or climbing plants, to avoid damaging roots later on.

4. Remove plant carefully from pot or tray, disturbing root ball and soil as little as possible. For pots, knock edge and hold hand over soil while removing plant.

5. For trays, knock side and tilt whole tray forward to loosen plants, holding hand over them to prevent them falling out completely.

6. Put larger plants in position first. Do not plant too deep. They should be at same level as before. Deeper planting encourages root rot.

7. Peat pots can be planted whole. The plant's roots will grow through them.

8. Firm compost gently around plant and continue transferring in order of size until container is complete.

9. Fill any spaces with small plants to give an even look but remember to leave room for growth. Do not water for 2 days.

10. Start feeding 3–4 weeks after planting container. Feed evenly over whole soil. If feed gets on leaves, wash it off with clean water to prevent scorching.

Insecticides

Unfortunately some houseplants are vulnerable to pests and diseases. The most common are mealy bug, scale insect, red spider mite, greenfly and whitefly. These should be treated as soon as they are noticed and affected plants moved away from others to prevent the spread of infection. Plants with thin, delicate leaves, are attacked by insects such as red spider mite while greenfly and other aphids are attracted to young leaves and stems. Some pests, such as mealy bug, appear on the leaves but may be carried hidden in the soil. Plants grown outside in containers may be attacked by slugs, beetles and other garden pests.

Insecticides are available usually as concentrated liquids which are added to water and sprayed or watered onto the infected plant, and as aerosols ready for use. Less usually, some chemicals for houseplants come in powdered form. This is not suitable for all plants - check the individual instructions. Systemic insecticides are absorbed into the plant's veins (its system) and so spread the poison to any insect which feeds on them.

The least toxic insecticides are those based on pyrethrum and derris as these are both natural substances. They are most suited to whitefly and greenfly control. Derris is also suitable for whitefly and greenfly and controls red spider mite in the early stages. Methylated spirits can be used to remove scale insect and mealy bugs. Red spider can be prevented from recurring by improving humidity. Malathion is one of the most effective general insecticides and will control everything from whitefly to beetles, and especially mealy bug which is one of the most infectious and damaging insects likely to affect houseplants. It can be sprayed when diluted and also watered into the soil if the soil is infected.

Malathion may damage some sensitive plants, so read the captions carefully to make sure you choose the right treatment.

Taking care with insecticides

Insecticides and fungicides may contain deadly chemicals. Use them with care.

Never mix different types of insecticides as the chemicals may react.

Never put them into other bottles, such as soft drink or beer bottles.

Never breathe in the spray.

Never spray in windy weather.

Never pour them down the sink or drains. Do not even pour the water in which you have washed containers and sprayers down the drain.

Never make up more at one time than you will use.

Never keep diluted insecticide for more than 24 hours.

Never leave old containers lying around.

Always follow instructions carefully. Do not over or under dilute.

Always use a separate watering can and sprayer, keeping another one for normal spraying and watering.

Always keep away from food, crockery, glasses, food containers, and minerals. Derris is harmful to fish; malathion harms bees.

Always cover fish bowls when spraying.

Always store them with their sprayers and containers in a dry, frost free place, on a high shelf out of reach of children.

Always spray outside, in the evening when bees are not around.

Always wash out all sprayers and empty bottles after use, inside and out.

Always pour washing water onto ground away from food crops and water sources such as streams and rivers.

Always throw empty bottles and containers away with domestic waste.

Always wash thoroughly in hot water and detergent when you have used them.

Cacti and other succulents

These are interesting and unusual plants to grow in the home. As a group they come from dry regions where there is little rainfall and have become specially adapted to desert or near desert conditions. Stem succulents store water in thickened stems or underground tubers and produce new leaves every year, only to lose them in the dry period. Leaf succulents have thick, wax-coated leaves which shrink and shrivel but do not dry out completely. They vary in shape and size from inch-high pebble-like plants to full-sized trees, though indoors very few will grow inconveniently large. The main difference between cacti and all other succulent plants is that cactus spines grow from a felty pad or areole.

Succulents need rather different care from most other indoor plants and will not grow well in the wrong conditions. Although they are tough plants and will stand quite a lot of neglect they need correct care to develop their full potential and produce their striking flowers.

Light and temperature

The most important factor in caring for succulents is light. Their healthy growth, the development of their colouring and flowers are directly related to the amount of light you allow them. Ideally the all-round light of a sun-bathed greenhouse is what they need, but an uncurtained sunny windowsill will do very well for most. In winter months, when light levels are lower, it is more important still to ensure that they remain in the lightest position possible. If indoors, keep them on the windowsill, only removing them at night if you close the curtains; otherwise in cold climates they may be damaged in the ice-box created between the curtains and the window on frosty nights. Try not to keep them too hot in winter or their natural growing cycle will be disturbed. Around 50°F (10°C) is ideal. If in a greenhouse a minimum temperature of 40°F (4°C), or better, 45°F (7°C), should be maintained in winter.

If a greenhouse is very exposed to

Succulent families
Many of the succulent plants in this book are specially adapted members of families which also include well-known wild or garden plants.

Agavaceae: Century plant family 1
Agave

Apocynaceae: Periwinkle family 2
Adenium, Pachypodium

Asclepiadaceae: Carrion flower family 3
Caralluma, Ceropegia, Huernia, Orbea, Stapelia

Crassulaceae: Stonecrop family 5
Adromischus, Aeonium, Cotyledon, Crassula, Dudleya, Echeveria. Kalanchoe, Pachyphytum, Sedum

Compositae: Groundsel family 4
Kleinia

Dioscoreaceae: Bryony family 6
Testudinaria

Euphorbiaceae: Spurge family 7
Euphorbia

Liliaceae: Lily family 8
Aloe, Gasteria, Haworthia

Mesembryanthemaceae: Midday flower family 9
Conophytum, Faucaria, Fenestraria, Gibbaeum, Lithops, Pleiospilos

Portulacaceae: Purslane family 10
Portulacaria

summer sunshine, it may be necessary to shade the glass at times to prevent scorching. Succulent plants seem particularly vulnerable to this in the spring, when the sun suddenly shines strongly after weeks of cloudy weather and the plants are a little on the soft side, especially if they have recently been watered.

Watering

In the wild cacti and other succulent plants usually receive water at certain times of the year only, and then often in quantity, with flash floods washing over them, or even submerging them for hours at a time. However, the water drains away quickly and the plants must be able to take it up rapidly and store it for long periods of drought. This is made possible by their structure, which allows the stems or leaves to swell in times of plenty, and then store water during dry periods, releasing little by way of evaporation.

For best results indoors, try to imitate natural conditions as closely as possible. In the growing period, from spring until early autumn, water as for most other plants, but start slowly in the spring after the dry winter spell, leaving long gaps between watering so that the soil dries out almost completely each time. By early summer, when the sun is strong, the plants can be watered every week, provided still that they are almost dry from the previous watering. Never leave them in a saucer of water.

In the autumn the gaps between waterings should become longer, until by mid-autumn for plants in 5in (13cm) or larger pots, and early winter for those in smaller pots, watering should cease until the spring. Some growers believe in not allowing the soil of succulents to dry out completely, and give a little throughout the winter. This is all right if minimum temperatures of about 50°F (10°C) are maintained, but there is a danger of encouraging lanky, uncharacteristic growth, of discouraging the formation of flower-buds, or even of losing the plants. It is safer to leave them dry.

When you do water them at whatever time of year, do so generously. Quickly fill the space between the top of the compost and the rim of the pot and allow the water to drain into the soil. If any is left standing in the saucer after about half an hour, be sure to drain it off. Do not water again until the soil has nearly dried out from the previous watering. This can be tested by inserting a thin plant label or the blade of a knife into the soil: if it comes out moist leave for a few more days, and test again. If in doubt do not water.

Feeding

Provided that they are repotted each year most succulent plants do not really need feeding, but some benefit from it and instructions for feeding these plants are given with each entry. Always use a fertilizer with a high potash content, like those used for tomatoes, roses or chrysanthemums. Liquid types are probably the easiest to use. Use them at the strength

Watering Succulents

1. Test compost for dryness with knife blade or plant label before watering. If blade comes out clean, soil is dry. If soil sticks, it is still moist. Check instructions for each plant before watering.

2. Add water to top of pot, filling it to brim. Excess will drain into saucer. After ½ an hour, empty away any left in saucer. Never leave pot standing in water.

3. If plant has leaves that will be marked by water, fill saucer under pot with water. Wait for ½ an hour, then empty away what is left.

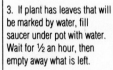

recommended for use on potted plants. Always dilute them or the plant will be damaged. If a plant which does not normally need feeding fails to grow well, the compost may be too poor. If you notice this in spring or in early to midsummer, repot in a different compost straight away. If later in the year, feed the plant until watering is reduced, then repot the following spring. Some fertilizers leave unsightly stains on plants if they are poured over the top of them so it is best to water them straight on to the top of the compost. If when watering some drops do fall on the leaves, do not brush them off but blow gently to disperse the droplets.

Compost

Cacti and other succulents need a well-drained, nutritious mixture, which will allow good root development and supply water but will not stay soggy for too long. Either loam-based or peat-based composts can be used as a basis. Do not use unsterile garden soil.

Loam-based or peat-based composts can be used neat, but to encourage more rapid drying out, they are best mixed with 1 part of coarse, gritty sand to 2 parts of compost. On no account use builders' or seashore sand which will not be sterile and may have a high lime or salt content. The amount of sand can be varied according to the needs of particular plants, and this is specified in the individual entries. Special cactus composts are available but are often worse than a good home-made mixture.

Repotting

Plastic pots have almost entirely superseded clay ones for cactus cultivation, although for some plants, such as *Ariocarpus*, which come from very arid areas, clay has advantages: it allows moisture to evaporate very quickly so that the compost is never moist for more than a few days at a time. For these more difficult cacti, increasing the grit content of the compost up to 60% or even 70% enables you to achieve similar conditions with plastic pots.

Many cacti and other succulents are shallow-rooted and will do better in half-pots or pans shallower than their width. Those with thick, tuberous roots need sufficient depth to contain the roots without cramping them.

If you have a greenhouse collection of cacti, consider using square rather than round pots. These make the maximum use of space, provide more root room, and fit together so as to hide each other from view.

The best time for repotting is in late

Repotting
1–2 weeks before repotting, water soil so that root ball will come from the pot easily.

1. Hold plant gently round base of stem, with gloves on if plant is spiny. Tap pot rim against edge of table or bench and gently ease root ball out onto a clear space. Check roots for root mealy bug and growth.

2. If root ball is compact with plenty of roots and no mealy bug, do not disturb it but prepare new pot one size larger with layer of compost deep enough to plant the root ball at the same level as before, about 1in (2½cm) below rim of pot. Place root ball on new compost.

3. If compost falls away easily but there is a good root system or if plant has reached its maximum size, carefully shake off old soil from around roots.

4. Trickle fresh compost around root ball, firming it down gently around base of plant.

5. Add a final layer of grit to top of compost. Do not water for 2 weeks after repotting.

Treating damaged roots

Examine a plant's roots when removing it from pot and check for root rot if no healthy new growth appears in spring. If the root is black and soft there is root rot. Treat the plant as follows.

 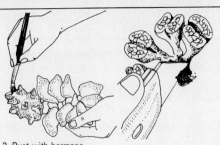

1. Pare away thinly from the base with a very sharp knife until no black specks remain. If any left, rot will return.

2. Dust with hormone rooting powder and leave to dry for 2-3 days before repotting in dry compost. Leave dry until new roots form.

3. Plants with fibrous roots are treated similarly but the stem must be cut away until only healthy tissue remains.

---

winter to early spring, before fresh roots have started to develop. Check the condition of the plant's roots when you have removed it from its pot. If the root ball is solid and there are plenty of new roots, repot it in a pot one size larger than the old one. If the compost falls away easily but there is a good root system, the plant can be repotted in the same sized pot with fresh compost. This also applies to plants that are nearly full-grown and are in pots 5in (13cm) or more. If using the same pot, wash it out well before replanting.

Always place the plant at the same level as it was before and add a final top layer of washed grit to the compost. This prevents the compost becoming compacted into a hard layer after watering, stops it splashing up around the plant and marking the lower spines and helps to prevent too rapid drying out in hot weather.

Propagation

Many succulent plants are very easily propagated from cuttings of either whole shoots or in many cases of just individual leaves. Those difficult to propagate in this way can usually be grown from seed, obtainable from specialist nurseries.

Cuttings: The best time to take cuttings of most plants is in late spring or early summer, when the plant is growing vigorously. Do not do it while the plant is actually producing flowers. The basic method of taking cuttings is illustrated on

Cactus cuttings

1. Cut stem with a sharp knife at the narrowest possible point. Cut at a slight angle.

2. Lightly dust cut stem on plant and cut end of cutting with hormone rooting powder containing fungicide and leave cutting to dry for 2 days.

4. Cover the cut end just enough to hold it upright or lean it against the side of the pot.

3. When cut surface is thoroughly dry, prepare small pot with dry compost and place cutting on surface.

5. Water after about 2-4 weeks when roots have started to grow from base. This encourages roots to penetrate compost.

p.35. Remember that, unlike any other sort of plant, cacti and other succulent cuttings must never be placed straight into fresh soil and watered — the cut surface must be allowed to dry and harden to prevent harmful fungi invading the tissue; the larger the cut surface the longer they need to be left to dry. It is a good idea to dust all cut surfaces with hormone rooting powder containing fungicide since this is the most convenient way of preventing infection. Wait for 2-3 weeks before watering.

Some succulent plants will produce a new plant from a detached, rooted leaf. Gently ease off a whole leaf from where it joins the stem. After allowing the end to dry out for a few days in an empty pot, place it on top of dry compost. Some can be laid flat, others end down. The important thing is that they are in close contact with the compost all the time. The leaf will shortly form roots, and a small plant will grow from its base.

Seeds: Succulent plant seeds need warmth and moisture to encourage germination just like those of other plants, and seedlings that survive in the wild do so usually because they have found a niche where they are protected from the drying effect of the hot sun until they are large enough to withstand it. Sowing is best carried out in a place where light and temperature can be carefully controlled. They do not need very high temperatures so a heated propagator is not essential. The seedlings in their first few

Growing from seed

1. Prepare 3½in (9cm) half pots or seed trays with soil-less or good loam based No.1 potting compost and a layer of fine grit on the surface.

2. Sow seed thinly on the surface and do not cover with compost.

3. Water from below with fungicide diluted to strength recommended for damping off of seedlings until surface looks moist.

4. Place pots or tray in polythene bag, sealing ends underneath to prevent moisture escaping. Or, seal with clingfilm.

5. Keep at 70°F (21°C) in light place, not direct sunlight, for 6 months or more, until seedlings are the size of a small garden pea. Do not water unless moisture film on polythene becomes patchy or dries out.

6. Prick out seedlings into new trays or small pots, planting about 1in (2½cm) apart.

Grafting cacti

1. Remove top inch (2½cm) of the rootstock and cut a slice from the bottom of the other cactus with a sharp, clean knife.

2. Immediately place the two cut surfaces firmly together, making sure that the rings near the centre of the stems overlap.

3. Hold firmly in place with elastic bands until new growth appears. Do not damage the outer tissue with too tight or too narrow a band.

4. To improve appearance of plant on graft, use deep pot and bury rootstock in gravel below pot rim so that only the upper cactus is visible.

Handling spiny plants
When repotting, take care not to damage spines or your hands. Wear gloves and ease plant out of pot sideways onto a padded bench, grasping the root ball not the plant body.

Root mealy bug
1. Check roots when repotting for mealy bug (white woolly patches).

2. If found, wash all soil off roots under tap and swirl in insecticide diluted to maker's instructions.

3. Leave to dry for 2-3 days, then replant in fresh compost and clean pot. Do not water for 2-3 weeks.

Vine weevils
Drastic treatment is needed to cure vine weevil attack. Vine weevils lay eggs on soil and larvae invade roots and stem. Adult flies are rarely seen by day.

1. If stem is swollen and round pieces chewed from leaves, remove from pot and inspect roots.

2. Starting at base of plant, pare away thin slices of root, then stem until soft area with larvae is reached. Cut away completely until no sign of larvae or rot remains.

3. Dust with hormone rooting powder and leave dry for 2–3 days before repotting in clean pot in new compost. Do not water for 2–3 weeks, when new roots will have formed.

weeks or even months must stay moist in a covering of polythene or cling film.

Grafting: Certain cacti are difficult to grow on their own roots and some variegated types cannot survive at all on their own roots indoors. These plants are usually grafted onto a rootstock which is easier to grow (see p.36). Unlike cuttings, the cut ends must not be allowed to dry out at all but must be pressed together immediately. The most important thing is to ensure that the rings near the centre of the stem (the vascular bundles) overlap. If the graft is successful, the upper plant should show growth after about 3 months, as it takes on the vigour of the rootstock. Remember to provide conditions that are right for the rootstock, especially if it is more demanding than the plant grafted on to it.

Mealy bug
1. Dab and remove woolly patches with small paintbrush or cotton bud dipped in methylated spirits, and spray with diluted malathion, repeating after 10 days if not clear.

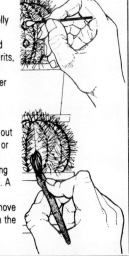

2. Brush all dead pests out from between the ribs, or moulds may set up rot. Use a typewriter cleaning brush with long bristles. A toothpick or broken matchstick helps to remove any bugs from between the spines.

If you inspect your cacti regularly and act quickly at the first sign of trouble, most conditions can be successfully treated. The pictures on the following pages show what to look out for; the captions explain what is causing the problem and how to put it right.

Brown marks appear on plant's skin, especially after winter. Brown spots and blotches appear on skin.

Skin turns light brown. Fine webs between spines and, under magnifying glass, tiny red brown mites moving about.

Patches that look like cotton wool on skin, especially near growing point or around base.

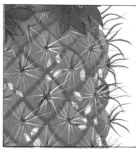

Cold marks caused by keeping plant in too low a temperature in winter.

Do not cut marks out. They are unsightly but not fatal. Check plant's temperature requirements. If on a windowsill in the home, do not leave between curtain and glass in winter.

Red spider mite.

Spray with contact insecticide to kill pests and/or systemic insecticide to protect the plant from further attack. Check that both types of insecticide specify red spider. Repeat every 2 weeks for next 3 months, then treat regularly 2 to 3 times a year as a preventive measure. Keep newly purchased plants separate until you are sure they are pest free or other plants will quickly be infected.

Mealy bug, small woodlouse-like creature about ⅛in (2–3mm) long, covered with white, flour-like coating. They surround themselves with the wool in which to lay eggs.

Remove bugs and wool with small paintbrush or cotton bud dipped in methylated spirits. This immobilizes pest but may not kill it. Use a toothpick or broken matchstick to reach between the spines. Then spray with diluted malathion or other contact insecticide or, especially for woolly plants, water systemic insecticide into soil. Repeat after 10 days.

what goes wrong

Growing point whitish or yellowish grey, plant becoming elongated with much narrower new growth than old. A plant normally free standing may need support to keep it upright.

Skin wrinkles, shrinks and looks dull.

Plant skin looks brown or black and is soft to the touch. Plant does not grow. No small flies around plant.

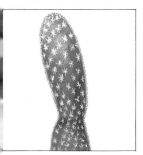

Lack of light. Plant is reaching towards best light and so growing unnaturally.

Put into better all round light position, on a sunny windowsill. For first two weeks shade with white paper to accustom plant gradually to strong sunlight. Always keep in best possible light in winter or flower buds may not form and plant will not flower the following year.

If during dry period in winter, natural contraction. If in growing season, too dry or, if watering correct, root loss or too much sudden sunshine.

In winter leave dry but spray overhead on sunny mornings. At other times of the year, check conditions. Water if dried out and if in strong sunlight, shade with white paper at hottest times of the year. If roots rotted, may be overwatering (see p. 33).

Plant is dead, usually from overwatering, watering in cold months or frosting.

Remove plant from others and dispose of plant and soil. Wash pot thoroughly before re-use and do not use soil for other plants. Be more careful to allow plants to dry out between waterings, keep dry in winter and for 2 weeks after repotting or root disturbance. Protect from low temperatures and do not trap plants between curtains and glass indoors on cold nights.

Plant does not grow but feels firm to the touch and is not surrounded by tiny black flies. On removing from pot, no roots visible. Possibly brown or orange patches on base.

Roots have rotted through, usually from overwatering or stale, compacted compost.

Brush away soil from base of plant and leave to dry for 2 days. Then with a sharp knife pare away thin layers from base of plant until no brown or orange patches remain. Dust base with hormone rooting powder containing fungicide, brush off surplus and leave plant out of its pot to dry for a week (more if the cut area is more than 1in, 3cm wide). Prepare new pot with fresh compost and place plant on top. Do not water until roots appear. Then treat normally, taking care with watering.

Small round brown patches with raised centre, like miniature limpets, on stems.

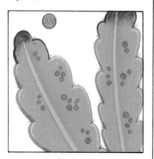

Scale insect. Tiny insect is inside waxy scale, sucking plant's sap.

Spray with contact insecticide or water soil with systemic insecticide and, after a few days, pick off scales with tweezers or thumb nail. Scale insect is unsightly but not usually fatal. As for other pests, keep infected plant isolated and examine newly bought plants carefully before putting them with others.

Small green insects cluster around buds and soft growing points, leaving sticky substance.

Greenfly.

Spray with insecticide or derris, repeating every week until clear. Keep away from other plants. Sticky substance may cause mould if not treated. Derris, a plant-based product, is safest treatment especially in the house.

what goes wrong

Plant does not grow when repotted, cotton wool-like patches found on roots, with tiny white sausage-shaped bugs about ⅛in (1-2mm) long.

Brown marks on side of plant facing the light.

Plant does not grow and tiny black flies are around base of plant.

Root mealy bug.

Wash soil off roots thoroughly to remove all traces of pest. Agitate washed roots in solution of contact insecticide. Allow to dry completely (2–3 days) before repotting in clean pot with fresh soil. Throw away old soil and scrub old pot before using again. If repotting in the growing season, do not water for at least 2 weeks or if in the winter months, not until spring. Other plants may be infected. If no obvious signs, place plants in their pots in bowl and soak them for half an hour in a solution of contact insecticide. Liquid should be deep enough to cover soil.

Plant is scorched. Soft growth made while out of direct sunlight will burn if suddenly exposed to sunshine.

Cacti are especially vulnerable in spring after the dry winter period if sun suddenly shines strongly. Accustom them to stronger light gradually by shading with white paper or moving into lighter area by degrees. Damage is irreparable, but plants will usually recover and grow on unless growing point is burned.

Plant attacked by sciara fly larvae, feeding on roots and plant tissue.

Examine roots for damage and cut back to healthy tissue. Spray plant with insecticide to kill flies and stand pot in bowl filled with solution of contact or systemic insecticide to kill larvae. Liquid should cover soil. Leave until soil thoroughly wet (½ an hour) then drain and allow to dry out. Repeat every two months or whenever flies appear.

Abutilon hybridum

Flowering maple

The delicate maple-shaped leaves of this plant set off perfectly the slightly waxy looking bell-shaped flowers. The name *Abutilon* is, in fact, the Arabic name for a species of mallow. As a plant in the home, it is rather delicate and needs copious watering in the summer. In the greenhouse, when planted out in the ground, it could reach the rafters; in the house, trained up one or two stakes, it will grow to about 39in (1m). In summer it may be put outside, provided it is sheltered from wind and the temperature is over 60°F (16°C).

The variegated Flowering maple *(Abutilon pictum)* is often grown for the beauty of its leaves alone with flowers as an extra attraction. Green-leaved Flowering maples flower more easily and if kept at 65–70°F (18–21°C) will remain in bloom from summer through to winter.

Light: Diffused. If indoors, keep out of midday summer sun. Tolerates full light if put outside in spring, but even outside protect from midday summer sun.

Temperature: 65–70°F (18–21°C) ideal. If kept at this in winter, flowering will continue. Alternatively, keep at 55°F (13°C) and water only once a week.

Water: Almost daily in summer to ensure plant does not dry out, but compost must not be waterlogged. Good drainage essential. In winter when at 55°F (13°C) water only once a week, after surface of compost has dried out.

Humidity: Spray twice weekly in summer, daily if temperature is above 70°F (21°C). Avoid flowers. If plant kept cool, do not spray in winter.

Feeding: Weekly in spring and summer, only after first flowers appear. Use liquid houseplant food diluted to normal strength.

Soil: Equal parts loam-based No. 2, peat and leaf mould, with one-eighth gritty sand.

Repotting: In spring, leaving sufficient space between soil and top of pot to allow for copious summer watering (about 1in, 2½cm).

Cleaning: Spray with soft tepid water. No leafshine. Do not spray flowers.

Webs under leaves. Red spider mite. Remove webs with damp cloth or sponge, then spray with diluted malathion, especially under leaves. Repeat every 14 days until symptoms disappear. Improve humidity by standing pot on saucer of damp pebbles.

Canes

1. Insert cane when repotting, after positioning plant but before adding all the compost. Cane should be a few inches from main stem, stopping about ⅔ down pot. Do not damage roots.

2. Loop string around stem and cane, tying firm knot against cane. Do not tie knot round plant. Or, use a plastic coated 'tie'.

Stem tips flop over. Too hot. Move to a cooler place with more ventilation. Spray daily with soft, tepid water in hot weather.

Plant grows pale and straggly with long spaces between leaves. Too much light. Move to a shadier position, out of hot summer sun.

New leaves small, no flowers appear. Needs feeding. Feed every week in spring and summer after first flowers appear. Use liquid house plant food at maker's recommended strength.

Plant flops and dies. Too cold. Keep around 55°F (13°C) in winter.

No flowers appear. Too dark and/or needs feeding. Check conditions. Move into lighter place (but not direct sunlight) and feed every week in the growing season with liquid houseplant food diluted to maker's recommended strength.

Flowers turn translucent. Damage from spraying with water. Protect flowers with paper or your hand when spraying leaves.

what goes wrong

Leaves sticky with insects where leaf joins stem. Greenfly. Spray with pyrethrum-based insecticide or diluted malathion. Repeat one week later and then every week until clear.

Leaves shrivel, flowers fall off in summer. Compost too dry. Plunge pot into bucket of water for 10–15 minutes, then drain. Keep soil constantly moist in summer, watering every day if it dries out in hot weather. Do not allow to stand in water. Spray daily with soft tepid water if temperature above 70°F (21°C).

Flies hopping around compost surface. Whitefly. Spray with pyrethrum-based insecticide or diluted malathion. Repeat weekly until clear.

Leaves fall off in winter. Compost too wet. Keep almost dry from end of autumn to spring in a temperature of 55°F (13°C). Water only when compost surface feels dry, about once a week.

Acalypha hispida

Chenille plant

The two varieties of *Acalypha* most popular as houseplants are quite different in appearance, though they need similar conditions to grow successfully. The Chenille plant has small green leaves and produces long, bright-red flower tassels without petals, which droop over the edge of the plant's pot. The other main type, 'Copper leaf' *(Acalypha wilkesiana),* has heart-shaped leaves mottled red and brown.

Light: Full daylight needed, otherwise Copper leaf's colouring will not develop and the Chenille plant will not flower well. Protect from midday sun in summer.
Temperature: Winter minimum 60°F (16°C), summer maximum 80°F (27°C).
Water: 2–3 times a week in spring and early summer to keep soil moist at all times. Plant must not stand in water. When in flower, allow compost to dry out between waterings; once a week should be sufficient. In winter, once a week.
Humidity: Spray every 2 days in spring and summer until flowers start to form, then stand pot in saucer of pebbles almost covered with water to keep humidity high. In winter spray weekly, especially if in centrally heated room. Do not spray.
Feeding: Every 14 days in spring and summer, or until it ceases flowering, with liquid houseplant food diluted according to the maker's instructions.
Soil: Equal parts of peat, fibrous loam, sand, leafmould; or loam-based No. 2 with equal parts of peat and sand added.
Repotting: After a couple of years, plants begin to look straggly and it is best to take cuttings in spring and grow new plants. Cut old plants back to 12in (30cm), just above a leaf, in early spring and repot into 5in (13cm) pots with good drainage.
Cleaning: Humidity spraying sufficient. No leafshine.

Chenille plants produce striking red tassels up to 18in (46cm) long in late summer. Healthy plants should have bright green leaves and bushy side shoots growing vigorously all the way down the main stem.

Stem-tip cuttings

1. In early spring, prepare small pot with drainage layer and compost mixed from half loam, half sand.

2. Cut off stem tip 3–4in (8–10cm) long, including growing point and at least 2 pairs of leaves. Trim off stem just below the lowest leaf.

3. Remove lowest pair of leaves. Dip cut end in hormone rooting powder.

4. Make hole in compost just deep enough to take bare stem of cutting and insert end of stem. Cut end should be at bottom of hole, lowest leaf resting on compost.

5. Water well and cover with polythene bag. Keep light and warm (about 70°F, 21°C), removing bag for 5 minutes each day to renew air. When cutting is growing well, remove bag and repot.

what goes wrong

Plant does not grow after repotting. Pot too big. 5in (13cm) pot is largest size for plant indoors.

Tassels do not form. Insufficient light, warmth and food. Move to good daylight in temperature 60–70°F (16–21°C) and feed fortnightly until tassels appear.

Flowers rot. Humidity too high. Do not spray flowers. Move plant to warm place, about 70°F (21°C), or more with good air circulation.

Leaves hang limply. Too little water in spring and summer. Keep compost moist until tassels produced, then allow to dry out between waterings.

Leaves have black patches. Leafshine damage. Do not use. Clean only by spraying with tepid water.

Healthy leaves lose colour but light is adequate. Too wet, plant standing in water. Check drainage holes in pot are clear. If soil stays damp and waterlogged even though watered infrequently, soil mixture wrong. Repot in spring using correct soil.

Leaves dry out. Air too dry. Spray with tepid water every 2 days in spring and summer. After flowering, spray once a week. Do not spray flowers.

Two-year-old plant looks straggly, long spaces between leaves. Cut back to 12in (30cm) in early spring to encourage healthy growth. Feed fortnightly in spring and summer until tassels form.

White woolly patches on leaves and stems. Mealy bug. Remove with cotton wool dipped in methylated spirits or spray every 14 days with diluted malathion until clear.

Leaves turn black. Too cold. Winter and summer minimum is 60°F (16°C). Move to warmer place. Remove black leaves.

Webs under leaves, leaves look dusty. Red spider mite. Spray every 14 days until clear with systemic insecticide particularly under leaves. Remove webs with cotton wool dipped in insecticide.

Acanthocalycium

A small genus of cacti from northern Argentina, there are 4 or 5 different species of Acanthocalycium available. They are mostly very spiny plants, with densely spiny flower-buds, too, which look like thistle buds as they emerge. They make single, unclustering, globular plants (although offsets are sometimes produced after about 5 years), up to about 5–6in (12–15cm) wide. They have black, brown or grey spines arranged on vertical ribs on a dark green stem. *Acanthocalycium violaceum* (p.47) has lilac-coloured flowers (unusual for a cactus) but other species have white, pink, orange-red or yellow flowers. They flower when about 3in (7–8cm) wide, at about 4 years, and rarely need more than a 5in (13cm) pot unless they are kept for 8–10 years when they may outgrow it.

Acanthocalycium brevispinum is less common than *A.violaceum*. Its spines are shorter and more rigid and its yellow flowers grow from the side. Like the other species, it must be allowed to dry out almost completely between watering and kept quite dry if the temperature falls to around 40°F (4°C).

Light: Maximum sunshine is needed for flower production, and to ensure good strong spines. Ideally grow outside in the summer months, bringing them gradually into full sun if they have not had much in winter. If grown in a greenhouse they will not need shading.

Temperature: Not less than 40°F (4°C); keep below 100°F (38°C) and give fresh air in summer months.

Water: Water well (overhead except when flowering), about once a fortnight in the summer months, or more frequently for smaller pots (3in, 8cm or less), making sure they have almost dried out from the previous watering before doing so. Keep dry in the 3 coldest months except for an overhead spray every 8 weeks.

Feeding: Once a month in spring and summer with a high potash fertilizer (as used for tomatoes).

Soil: Use 2 parts of either soil-less compost or loam-based No. 2 potting compost with 1 part coarse gritty sand (not builders' or seashore).

Repotting: Repot annually in the spring into next size pot, until a 5in (13cm) pot is reached, when every other year will do, unless the plant is outgrowing the pot it is in.

Cleaning and pest control: Spray overhead with a forceful spray of water if plant gets dusty and include an insecticide about 3 times a year.

Other species: Some of the rarer species are worth seeking out: *A. brevispinum* or *A. thionanthum* with deep yellow flowers and short, rigid spines like carpet tacks; *A. spiniflorum*, with pink flowers; *A. Klimpelianum*, with pure white flowers; *A. peitscheranum*, with white flowers delicately flushed pink; and the variably coloured flowers of *A. variiflorum*, which range from yellow to orange-red or carmine in colour.

46

Growing from seed

1. In spring, prepare seed tray or 2in (5cm) pots with soil-less seedling or good loam-based seed or No. 1 potting compost. Add layer of fine grit to surface, leaving ½in (1cm) space between surface and rim.

2. Sow seed thinly on surface and tap sides of pot/tray to settle seed in the grit. Then water from base with fungicide diluted to strength for 'damping off' of seedlings, until surface is damp.

3. Cover pots or tray with polythene, folding ends underneath or sealing with sticky tape to seal in moisture. Leave in light (not direct sunlight) at 70°F (21°C). Do not water again unless condensation on polythene becomes patchy or dries up.

4. After 6 months, or following spring for safety, prick out separately into 2in (5cm) pots or ½in (1cm) apart in seed trays.

These cacti need very good light all year round. If they are in too dark a position they will grow out of shape, the tip becoming elongated with the spines weaker at the top. Without full summer sun they are unlikely to flower and are best kept outside or in a greenhouse in summer.

Acanthocalycium violaceum has long, flexible, curving, yellowish-brown spines through which the pale lilac flowers push with difficulty at the top of the plant. A healthy plant will have fresh, brighter coloured spines appearing at the centre during spring and summer and should produce flowers after it is about 3in (7–8cm) wide. Each flower lasts about a week.

47

Adenium obesum

This attractive plant is popularly known as the Desert Rose as when in full bloom it looks like a rose bush covered in flowers. The thick stem, with its bulbous base, sits just above the soil and from this other more slender stems branch out. The flowers appear before the leaves, in late spring, when the plant starts to come out of its winter rest period. After flowering, the thick, waxy leaves appear and the plant grows throughout the summer. *Adenium obesum* is the species most commonly seen and is available either as seed or as seedling plants. These grow after 3–4 years to a foot (30cm) tall if repotted regularly and watered in summer. Others occasionally available are *A. swazicum* and *A. oleifolium*.

Adenium obesum, the Desert rose, has a thick swollen stem called a caudex which in the wild stores water and enables the plant to survive severe drought. The swollen part should be planted above the soil for if it is allowed to stay damp underground, it may rot.

Light: Full sunlight is essential for growth and to encourage flower production.

Temperature: Minimum 50°F (10°C) is needed. Give fresh air in summer, or stand outside when all danger of frost is past.

Water: Start watering every 2 weeks in late spring, allowing to dry out between waterings. Water weekly in hottest months, then fortnightly again in autumn. Leave dry in winter and early spring and allow plant to rest, when leaves will drop naturally. See also Introduction.

Feeding: Use high potash fertilizer in summer once a month, stop in autumn.

Soil: Use good loam-based No. 2 potting compost, or soil-less compost, with about 40% gritty sand to improve drainage.

Repotting: Every year when young and growing quickly but when over 6in (15cm) tall, better to change top inch (2½cm) soil with fresh and feed regularly as root disturbance causes the roots to rot off.

Propagation: Only possible from seeds, available from specialist nurseries.

Leaves blacken and fall, stem ends soft, tuber soft. Too cold and wet. Move to warmer place, at least 55°F (13°C) and allow to dry out before watering again. Always keep dry in winter even in normal room temperatures. Pare away rotting tissue and dust with fungicide. If conditions correct, check roots for sciara fly or vine weevil maggots (see Introduction). If rot is severe, plant will die.

Trimming dead shoots
In winter stem tips may shrivel and die if not sprayed. Wait until they are quite dry before cutting off with sharp scissors or secateurs. Cut just inside dry area to avoid damaging healthy tissue.

White woolly patches among leaves. Mealy bug. Remove with small paintbrush dipped in methylated spirits, and spray with insecticide. Repeat 2 or 3 times in growing season.

Flowers shrivel quickly. Too hot and dry. Check soil regularly in summer and water when it dries out. Do not expose to hot sun after cloudy weather: move gradually into full light.

what goes wrong

Little sign of new growth in spring. Needs feeding or repotting or root mealy bug. Check roots and if white woolly patches found, wash soil away, swirl roots in insecticide and allow to dry before repotting.

Leaves turn pale, shrivel and fall. In summer, too hot and dry or too wet. Check conditions. If dry, soak in bowl of water for ½ an hour, then drain. If soil dark and soggy, leave to dry out completely before watering again. If new leaves do not grow but stem firm, repot in fresh, dry compost. Do not water again for 2 weeks. Leaves fall naturally in autumn/winter and grow again in spring.

Tips of shoots die back, becoming brown and hard; shoots break out from well below tips in spring. Spraying tips in winter will stop this excessive drying up. Remove damaged tips when absolutely dry with sharp scissors.

Leaves turn pale green or yellow-green, no flowers. Too dark. Bring gradually into full sun over 2 weeks.

Leaves marked with brown or white patches. Brown is scorch from sudden hot sun in stuffy place. White is from insecticides or hard water spray. Remove with rainwater and small paintbrush.

When received plant has soft patches in bulbous stem or roots, and on cutting, orange patches in the tissue are revealed. Damage to roots has allowed orange rot to get a hold. Pare away narrow slices with sharp clean knife until no sign of orange is visible. Dust with hormone rooting powder containing fungicide; allow to dry thoroughly before rerooting in dry compost.

49

Maidenhair fern

This is the most popular variety of maidenhair fern. It requires a humid atmosphere, so generally does well in a steamy kitchen or bathroom with good light. Maidenhair ferns acclimatize themselves to some extent to a particular position, so should not be moved from room to room. If the fronds dry up, the plant can usually be revived if it is cut back just above soil level. If kept moist and humid, new shoots will soon appear. It dislikes cigarette smoke and gas fumes. *A. cuneatum*, a similar fern, needs similar care but tolerates drier air.

Light: Diffused daylight, not direct sunlight. If only artificial light available fit a horticultural spot light or fluorescent tube.
Temperature: Winter minimum 50°F (10°C), summer maximum 70°F (21°C).
Water: Twice a week in hot weather (over 65°F, 18°C), once a week when cooler, to keep moist at all times. Water by submerging pot until bubbles stop rising, then drain. If plant is in centrally heated room water twice weekly all year round.
Humidity: Spray daily with tepid soft water. Stand on saucer of pebbles almost covered with water or plant pot in larger container with damp peat. Keep away from radiators.
Feeding: Every 14 days in summer only, with houseplant food diluted with water. Use half the amount recommended by the maker.
Soil: Use a proprietary soil-less compost containing ready-mixed fertilizer.
Repotting: Every two years only, in plastic pot, as plant likes being pot-bound. Pack new soil loosely round root ball, leaving air gaps. Good drainage essential, so put broken clay pieces or pebbles in pot.
Cleaning: Mist with tepid soft water. No leafshine.

The Maidenhair fern's small green leaves look like miniature versions of the leaves of the Maidenhair tree. A healthy plant should have leaves of a strong green colour, growing closely on the stems. They should show no signs of brown or curling edges.

Leaves dried, brown at edges. Needs watering. Water twice a week all year round if centrally heated. Improve humidity.

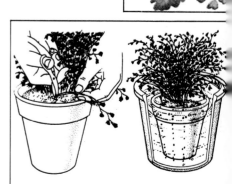

Reviving a dried-up plant
1. With scissors, cut out all dried fronds including stems, just above compost.

2. Water by plunging in bucket of water; repeat twice weekly, and spray daily with tepid soft water. Do not feed until new leaves appear.

Leaves curl while green. Too wet, may be standing in water. Allow to dry out before watering again and move to a warmer place. Do not feed until plant recovers.

Young leaves turn brown and crisp at tips. Too hot. Do not exceed 70°F (21°C) in summer. Move plant to cooler place where air circulates freely. Spray regularly.

All fronds drop. Kept much too dry for too long; air also too dry. Or gas fumes. Cut down, then water and spray regularly. Keep in fume-free room.

Whole fronds dry out. Air too dry. If not dealt with promptly, all fronds will dry. Spray daily and move away from radiators, boilers etc.

Some leaves turn black. Leafshine damage. Do not use leafshine of any kind. Clean only by spraying with soft water.

Small flies hopping around soil surface. White fly, attracted by high humidity. Spray every 14 days with pyrethrum until clear. Do not use malathion, leaves will turn black.

Leaves pale. Light too strong. Move to area of diffused light.

what goes wrong

Leaves thin, stems weedy. Needs feeding. Feed every 2 weeks throughout summer, using liquid houseplant food at half recommended strength.

Adromischus cooperi

No more than five species of this small, beautifully spotted genus are widely known in cultivation though others can be found at specialist nurseries. They come from South Africa, and make good indoor or greenhouse plants, provided they get enough sun to bring out their colouring. *Adromischus cooperi* grows to about 2in (5cm) high and spreads 4–6in (10–15cm) across. It has thick roots, like underground stems or rhizomes and these are best kept with the top just above the surface of the compost, to avoid any risk of rotting. The other species usually grown are: *Adromischus trigynus* (often named *A. maculatus*), *A. marianae*, *A. mammillaris* and *A. triebneri*. Do not use insecticides such as malathion or any labelled as unsuitable for Crassulas or Crassulaceae. Pyrethrum-based types are safe.

Adromischus cooperi, also known as the Plover's egg plant from the attractive mottling on its leaves, will not usually outgrow a 5 or 6in (15cm) pan. It needs very good light to keep the colouring of its leaves and if cared for correctly will produce its long spike of flowers in late summer. New plants are easy to propagate from single leaves.

Light: Maximum sunlight is needed for best colouring and to keep them compact.
Temperature: A minimum of 40°F (4°C). Give fresh air in summer and if in a greenhouse, keep under 100°F (37°C).
Water: Start watering fortnightly in spring. Leave to dry out between waterings. Water weekly in hot weather, then fortnightly again in the autumn. Leave dry in winter. See also Introduction.
Feeding: Not necessary but if not repotted, feed once or twice in summer with high potash fertilizer.
Soil: Use good loam-based No. 2 potting compost, or soil-less compost, with about 40% coarse gritty sand to improve drainage.
Repotting: Every spring in size larger half-pot or pan, being careful not to dislodge weakly attached leaves. Keep top of thick roots just above soil to prevent rotting.
Propagation: From leaves.

No new growth. Needs feeding. Feed twice in summer with high potash fertilizer. If fed regularly, check roots for root mealy bug. If white woolly patches on roots, swirl in pyrethrum-based insecticide and allow to dry before repotting in fresh compost and clean pot. Leave dry for 2 weeks.

Propagation
1. In late spring when new leaves appear, gently remove 3 or 4 from near top. Leave in safe place such as in empty pot to dry for 2 days.

2. Place on pot of dry compost with end touching surface; do not insert into compost but lean against pot rim or hold in place with soil. Do not water until new roots show. A new plantlet will grow from base of leaf but do not remove old leaf until quite dead and dry.

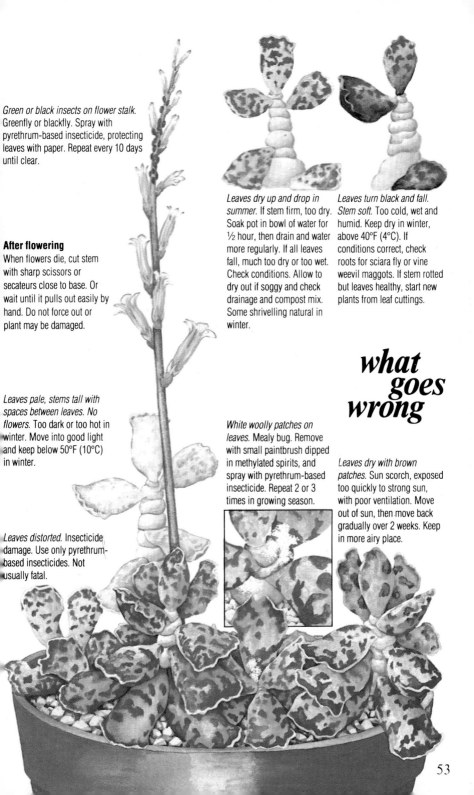

Green or black insects on flower stalk.
Greenfly or blackfly. Spray with
pyrethrum-based insecticide, protecting
leaves with paper. Repeat every 10 days
until clear.

After flowering
When flowers die, cut stem
with sharp scissors or
secateurs close to base. Or
wait until it pulls out easily by
hand. Do not force out or
plant may be damaged.

*Leaves dry up and drop in
summer.* If stem firm, too dry.
Soak pot in bowl of water for
½ hour, then drain and water
more regularly. If all leaves
fall, much too dry or too wet.
Check conditions. Allow to
dry out if soggy and check
drainage and compost mix.
Some shrivelling natural in
winter.

*Leaves turn black and fall.
Stem soft.* Too cold, wet and
humid. Keep dry in winter,
above 40°F (4°C). If
conditions correct, check
roots for sciara fly or vine
weevil maggots. If stem rotted
but leaves healthy, start new
plants from leaf cuttings.

*what
goes
wrong*

*Leaves pale, stems tall with
spaces between leaves. No
flowers.* Too dark or too hot in
winter. Move into good light
and keep below 50°F (10°C)
in winter.

*White woolly patches on
leaves.* Mealy bug. Remove
with small paintbrush dipped
in methylated spirits, and
spray with pyrethrum-based
insecticide. Repeat 2 or 3
times in growing season.

*Leaves dry with brown
patches.* Sun scorch, exposed
too quickly to strong sun,
with poor ventilation. Move
out of sun, then move back
gradually over 2 weeks. Keep
in more airy place.

Leaves distorted. Insecticide
damage. Use only pyrethrum-
based insecticides. Not
usually fatal.

53

Urn plant

This splendid Bromeliad grows naturally in trees with just enough roots to hold itself in place. Its out-stretched leaves gather rain into the central well, through which it absorbs the food it needs, and small quantities of methane gas which trigger flower formation. Shop-bought Urn plants usually have the flower bud formed; if not, the trigger for flowering may be provided by covering the plant after 18 months with a polythene bag for 4 weeks, enclosing a rotten apple core. After flowering, the parent plant begins to die, but new offsets form at its base.

The Urn plant's leaves have a soft, grey bloom which should never be rubbed off. It dies after flowering, so do not buy plants in full bloom. Choose one just coming into flower with healthy, unmarked leaves.

Light: Stands strong sunlight, survives in shade. Needs good light for flowering.
Temperature: Minimum 55°F (12°C), maximum 80°F (27°C).
Water: Fill centre well with soft water; allow excess to trickle into soil, which should be just moist. Empty well and change water every 3 weeks.
Humidity: No extra spraying necessary at normal room temperatures. Do not keep in cold, damp place.
Feeding: Not necessary but a very diluted dose of liquid houseplant food added to the water in the well every month in summer will help keep plant healthy. Use only a quarter as much food as the maker recommends.
Soil: Peat-based compost with 1 part leaf-mould or rotted pine needles to 3 parts compost. Must be lime-free.
Repotting: When plant dies, becoming dull and shrivelled, tease away offset shoots from base, carefully retaining some root. Pot up individually into 5in (13cm) pots. They will not need re-potting again.
Cleaning: Carefully with feather duster if dusty or dirty. Do not disturb grey bloom. No leafshine.

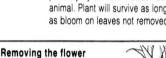

Heavy green marks on grey parts of leaves. Plant scratched, possibly by contact with domestic animal. Plant will survive as long as bloom on leaves not removed.

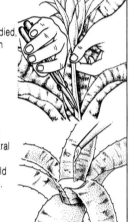

Removing the flower stem
When flower spike has died, cut its stem at base with secateurs.

Watering
Keep about 1in (2½cm) water in the plant's central well. Rainwater is best. Every 3 weeks, empty old water out and add fresh.

what goes wrong

Flower fades. Too little light. Move to better position.

Flower withers and dies. Natural after flowering.

Flower and stem rot. Soil too moist. Empty water from well and allow to dry out before watering again.

Flower and stem dry up and turn dirty pink. Too cold. Move to warmer, lighter place, at least 55°F (12°C).

Small insects in flower rosette. Blackfly. Do not spray flower. Water soil (not central well) with diluted malathion once a week for 3 weeks. Remove insects with tweezers.

Leaves shrivel. Too hot and dry. Move to cooler place, under 80°F (27°C). Water soil and ensure well in centre of plant is full of water.

Leaves distorted and sticky with small insects. Greenfly. Spray with pyrethrum or a systemic insecticide every 14 days until clear.

Leaves wither and die before flower is dead. Bloom removed from leaves, or leafshine. No cure.

White woolly patches on leaves and in leaf axils. Mealy bug. Water soil (not in well) with diluted malathion. Repeat every 3 weeks if not cured.

Leaves turn brown and droop. Lime in water or soil. Use soft water for watering. Check compost is lime-free. If not, repot in lime-free mixture.

55

Aeonium arboreum

The variety of *Aeonium arboreum* shown here, *Aeonium arboreum var atropurpureum*, has a topknot of blackish-purple leaves at the end of each spongy stem. It comes from the Canary Islands and needs very bright sunlight to bring out the purple colouring of its leaves. It will grow up to 1½–2ft (50–60cm) tall and 6–12in (20–30cm) across. It is important not to use spray insecticides labelled as unsuitable for Crassulas or Crassulacae as they will distort leaves and kill the plant. Those based on pyrethrum are safe. Other species include *A. decorum* and *A. haworthii*, like bonsai trees; *A. tabulaeforme*, with low, flat rosettes; and *A. sedifolium* with tiny rounded leaves.

Aeonium arboreum var atropurpureum is one of the darkest leaved succulent plants and may look almost black if kept in a sunny spot. Like most Aeoniums it tends to get large and straggly after a few years and it is best to start again with cuttings, which root easily. It is not easy to flower indoors.

Light: To keep the purple colouring the sunniest spot you can provide is essential, otherwise the plant becomes green and grows out of shape. Put outside in summer to increase chances of flowering.

Temperature: A minimum of 40°F (4°C) is needed; stand outside in summer and over 2 weeks gradually move into full sunlight.

Water: Start watering every 2 weeks in spring, increasing to once a week in summer but always allowing soil to dry out between waterings. Reduce gradually again in autumn and in winter water only once a month if leaves start to shrivel. See also Introduction.

Feeding: Use high potash fertilizer in summer only, once a month.

Soil: Use good loam-based No. 2 potting compost, or soil-less compost, with 30% coarse, gritty sand for improved drainage.

Propagation: Take cuttings 2–3in (8cm) long from young shoots which grow on main stem.

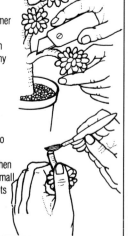

Taking cuttings

1. In spring or early summer cut 2–3in (5–8cm) long shoot from main stem with sharp knife. Choose healthy stem with good head of leaves.

2. Dust cut surfaces with hormone rooting powder to prevent infection. Allow cutting to dry for 2 days, then place on dry compost in small pot. Do not water until roots appear.

what goes wrong

Leaves small and few. Too dry or needs repotting. Check conditions. If bone dry, soak for ½ an hour in bowl of water, drain, then water more regularly except in winter. If watering correct, plant outgrowing pot. Repot in spring in next size pot.

Small green insects on and between leaves. Greenfly. Spray with pyrethrum-based insecticide and repeat every 10 days until clear.

Leaves turn black and fall, stem ends black and soft. Too cold and wet, overwatered. Move to warmer place, over 40°F (4°C) in winter. Pare away blackened stem and dust with fungicide. Keep dry in winter. At other times always allow soil to dry out before watering.

Plant thin and straggly, rosettes lose colour. Too hot and wet in winter. Keep in dry, airy place, not more than 50°F (10°C).

Leaves shrivel and fall in winter. Too dry. Add just enough water to moisten soil once a month.

Leaves scorched. Too much sun too quickly. Move out of direct sun, reintroduce gradually over 2 weeks. Keep in more airy place.

White woolly patches on leaves and stem, especially on young shoots. Mealy bug. Remove with paintbrush dipped in methylated spirits and spray with pyrethrum-based insecticide. Repeat after 10 days if not clear.

Leaves turn plain green. Too dark. Move over 2 weeks into strong sunlight.

Leaves droop. Too dry or root damage from pests or overwatering. If dry, soak in bowl of water for half an hour, drain and give more water in future. If wet, dry out, remove from pot and treat roots if rotted or infected (see Introduction).

Round pieces missing from leaf edges, stem swollen, no growth. Vine weevil. Dust around base with insecticide powder and pare away stem until larvae removed.

Little growth, white woolly patches on roots. Root mealy bug. Wash roots and swirl in insecticide. Dry for 2–3 days, then repot in fresh compost and clean soil. Leave dry for 2 weeks.

57

Aeschynanthus speciosus

Lipstick vine

The Lipstick vine is similar in general appearance to a *Columnea* (p.190). The main difference is in the flowers, which have four stamens and are more tubular in shape. The plant is best grown in a hanging pot or basket. The dark crimson flowers have an orange throat which contrasts with the dark green fleshy foliage. Pinch out flower buds during its first year, but encourage growth of stems and leaves by frequent watering. The following winter it should be kept cool and dry to rest it. Next year it will bloom profusely.

The Lipstick vine looks at its best in a hanging container and can be planted into a moss-lined basket when it it is 2 years old. For its first three years it should be kept out of direct sunlight, in a constantly humid atmosphere.

Light: Indirect daylight when plant is young. It will take full light after 3 years, avoiding midday sun.

Temperature: 75-80°F (24-27°C) in summer; winter minimum is 60°F (16°C).

Water: Every 2 days in spring and summer, especially in first year. When over 75°C, (24°C) never let compost dry out. Check it daily. Water in winter only about once a week, when compost surface feels dry.

Humidity: Spray daily all spring and summer, as very high humidity essential for good growth. In winter, spray weekly only if temperature is above 60°F (16°C).

Feeding: Once every 14 days in spring and summer after first flowers appear, using liquid houseplant food diluted to maker's instructions.

Soil: Equal parts rough sand and rich fibrous peat with one-eighth part chopped sphagnum moss added. Put charcoal and broken crocks in bottom of pot or basket.

Repotting: Annually in early years. Alternatively, plant in basket lined with sphagnum moss; or grow plant on a wooden block covered with green moss. The roots should be wrapped in sphagnum moss and fixed to the block with copper wire.

Cleaning: No leafshine.

Hanging baskets

1. Line wire basket with moss. Make 5 or 6 small holes in sheet of polythene and lay over moss. Add saucer of charcoal to absorb smells.

2. Stand basket on bucket and fill with layer of damp compost.

3. Knock plant from pot and place in centre of basket, arranging trailing stems evenly all round.

4. Fill with compost and firm round roots. Water well, allow to drain, then hang securely. Fasten drip tray below.

No flowers in second year, new leaves small. Pot too large and needs feeding. It flowers better if slightly pot bound, so do not repot again for 2 years. Feed every 2 weeks in spring and summer when flowers appear, with liquid houseplant food diluted to maker's recommended strength.

what goes wrong

Webs under leaves. Red spider mite. Remove webs with damp cloth or sponge, then spray with diluted malathion, especially under leaves. Repeat every 14 days until symptoms disappear. Improve humidity by standing pot on saucer of wet pebbles.

Plant wilts in summer. Too hot and compost too dry. Plunge pot into bucket of water for 10–15 minutes then drain. Keep compost constantly moist in summer, watering every day if it dries out in hot weather.

Leaves drop. In winter, too cold. Move to warmer place, at least 60°F (16°C). In summer if leaves drop and no flowers appear, too cold and dry. Move to warmer place, but not more than 80°F (27°C) and water by plunging pot into bucket of water for 10–15 minutes.

Flowers turn black and fall in summer. Air too dry. Spray daily with soft, tepid water and stand pot on saucer of wet pebbles.

Leaves dry out, especially in summer. Air too dry. Spray daily in spring and summer with soft tepid water and provide extra humidity by standing pot on saucer of wet pebbles.

Black spots on leaves, especially in winter. Botrytis, plant too cold and wet. Spray with fungicide then place in warmer atmosphere, at least 60°F (16°C). Allow surface of compost to dry out between waterings in winter and spray less often. Remove affected leaves.

Plant stems grow long and straggly. Too dark. Move to position in very good light including some direct sun.

59

Agave utahensis

This plant is from the desert areas of Utah and Nevada in the USA and is one of the smaller growing Agave species suitable for indoor culture, growing to between 6 and 8in (15–20cm) tall and 8–10in (20–25cm) across. Most Agaves are large plants, some up to 10ft (3m) tall and wide. The leaves are very stiff and very sharply pointed. The flowers, which will not appear for 10 or 20 years, are not welcome as the plant dies after flowering. They are known as 'Century plants' as it was believed they flowered only once in 100 years. Other species worth growing are *A. parviflora*, *A. filifera*, *A. victoria-reginae*, and *A. americana*, a larger one.

Agave utahensis var. nevadensis. This spiky plant is grown for its leaves since the flowers do not appear for at least 10 years and the plants die after flowering. All Agaves are spiky plants and should be handled with care and kept safely out of children's reach. It is possible to receive a bad eye injury from the stiff, needle-sharp points on the leaves.

Light: As much sun as possible to keep their shape and colour.

Temperature: A minimum of 40°F (4°C) is needed for safety, although most Agaves will take quite low temperatures if dry, even a little below freezing.

Water: Start to water in spring and allow to dry out between waterings. About once a fortnight is enough in spring and summer. Leave completely dry in winter. See also Introduction.

Feeding: Use high potash fertilizer in summer once a month, stop in autumn.

Soil: Use good loam-based No. 2 potting compost, or soil-less compost, with 30% gritty sand to improve drainage.

Repotting: Every spring in size larger pot, until 7 or 8in (18–20cm) pot is reached, when soil may be shaken off and plant repotted in fresh soil in the same sized pot.

Propagation: Occasionally suckering offsets are produced, which may be removed but leaves do not root to form new plants. Agaves can also be raised from seed, but buy named species; mixtures will usually be of the bigger plants.

Leaf tips brown, rest light brown. Too dry or sunscorch. Check soil. If very dry, plunge into bowl of water, for 10–15 minutes, then drain. Water regularly in summer. If sunscorched, cover with paper to filter sun for 2 weeks. Cut off damaged leaves.

Leaf end hangs down, brown crack across leaf. Plant knocked or pushed against window. Cut off cleanly at break with sharp scissors; do not pull off or base of leaf may be damaged.

Leaves dry and brown. If only lowest leaves, natural. Cut off with sharp scissors. If upper leaves also brown, overwatered, centre rotting: if leaves pull out easily, too late to save plant.

Plant does not grow. Needs repotting and feeding. Repot each year in fresh compost and feed monthly in summer with high potash fertilizer.

what goes wrong

Removing offsets

Wear gloves to remove offsets in spring or early summer, cutting with sharp knife as close to main stem as possible. Dust cut surfaces with hormone rooting powder and leave offset to dry for 2 days before potting in dry compost.

Leaves long and pale. Too dark or too wet. Check conditions. Move to lighter place; allow to dry out before watering. Keep dry in winter.

Leaves black. Atmosphere too humid. Roots rotting. Plant may die but move to more airy position, in good bright light.

White woolly patches among leaves. Mealy bug. Remove with small paintbrush dipped in methylated spirits and spray with contact or systemic insecticide. Repeat 2 or 3 times in growing season.

Plant doesn't grow; white woolly patches on roots. Root mealy bug. Wash soil off roots, swirl in contact insecticide, and allow to dry before repotting in fresh compost and clean pot. Leave dry for 2 weeks.

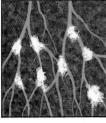

Ageratum

Ageratum is deservedly popular as a neat, continuous flowering annual. Modern hybrids rarely exceed 6in (15cm) and so are ideal for window-boxes or around the edge of a large patio or balcony tub. They are prone to fungus diseases and the best way to keep them healthy and ensure they grow bushily is to transfer them from seed tray to container as soon as they are large enough to handle.

Light: Indoors, maximum. Outdoors, no more than 2 hours shade.
Temperature: Germination, 65–70°F (18–21°C). Just before planting outdoors, 45°F (7°C). Protect from frost.
Water: Moist compost. Underwater rather than overwater. Protect from heavy rain.
Humidity: Do not syringe, spray or water overhead when in flower.
Soil: Loam-based No. 2, or soil-less potting compost. It must be completely sterile.
Feeding: Feed regularly to keep the plants growing. Feed young seedlings with half-strength liquid fertilizer. Ten days after final planting start feeding at full recommended strength. Repeat every 10 days for soil-based, every 5 days for soil-less compost.
Propagation: Prepare tray in early spring. Sow seed but do not cover with compost. Place in propagator case or plastic bag giving 70°F (21°C) bottom heat. Germination occurs within 1 week. Prick out seedlings 2in (5cm) apart as soon as they are large enough to handle. Keep at 65°C (18°C) for 1 week. Cool gradually down to 45°F (7°C) just before planting out.
Tidying: Cut off any flowers which turn brown with age. Cut at base of stem.
Varieties: Blue Mink, powder blue (6in, 15cm). Blue Danube, bright blue, dwarf, compact and early. Spindrift, white, compact and early.

Ageratums are between 4–18in (10–45cm) tall, with broad, bright green oval leaves which are slightly rough to the touch. The fluffy flowers are massed together on each stem and are usually lavender blue with more rarely white, pink and deep blue varieties.

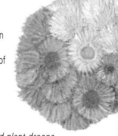

Flower heads turn brown. Insecticide or fertilizer too strong, insecticide sprayed in sunlight, or cat damage. Always use correct dilution of feed and chemicals. Do not spray in sunlight.

Leaves turn grey/green and plant droops in sun. Too dry. Water well, allow to drain until just moist before watering again.

Newly emerged seedlings collapse; stems thread-like near soil. Pythium fungus. If time, sow again in sterile compost and water only with tap water. If only some affected, plant out only those well away from affected area.

Whole plant collapses, eaten at soil level. Cutworm or woodlice. Search top inch (2½cm) of compost for cutworm (unlikely in sterilized compost). Dust with gamma BHC or destroy woodlice by hand.

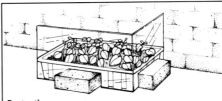

Protection

Young plants hardening off outside should be shielded from cold winds. If no cold frame available, position sheets of glass on windward side, holding in place with bricks.

Small spots on leaves. Leaf-spotting fungus. Spray with bordeaux mixture at recommended strength every 10 days until clear.

Growing point distorted and covered in tiny insects. Aphids. Spray with pirimicarb at recommended strength. Repeat after 1 week if pest returns.

what goes wrong

Plant droops, flowers lose fluffiness. Water on leaves and flowers. Do not spray or water overhead.

Holes in leaves, growing points eaten. Slug damage. Put down recommended slug bait around plant base.

Leaves of mature plant eaten. Caterpillar damage. Pick off pest or dust with gamma BHC or derris.

Plant turns black and soggy in late spring/early autumn. Frost. Protect whenever frost expected.

Leaves of young plants turn brown or bronzed. Cold winds or put outside too soon. Protect from wind.

Leaves hang down, soil dark and slimy. Waterlogged. Overwatered or badly drained. Clear drainage holes and do not water again until surface dries out.

Leaves of young plants grey and soggy. Botrytis, from wet soil and little air movement. Spray with benomyl or iprodione.

63

Chinese evergreen

A much under-rated plant for growing in the house, Chinese evergreen will live in quite difficult conditions for plants and survive away from direct light and in dry situations. It is not a large plant and, in fact, looks better when kept on the small side. The spear-shaped leaves, which droop gracefully, are about 5–6in (12–15cm) long and will deteriorate only if the plant is underfed or is too cold in winter. If grown with other plants in a bowl or jardinière, its leaf shape makes a good contrast with that of other houseplants. It is suitable for hydroculture.

The easiest way to propagate these plants is by dividing young shoots in spring. Make sure each section has a good portion of roots and keep them warm (70°F, 21°C) until they are growing well.

The variety 'Silver Queen' with its pointed green leaves overlaid with silver, is the best known. It sometimes produces a small yellow or white flower, followed by red berries. Leaves should be firm and bright, with no sign of yellowing. It is a very suitable plant for hydroculture.

Light: North-facing light best, but will tolerate most conditions.
Temperature: prefers 60°F (15°C) in winter but will survive down to 50°F (10°C) if kept dry. Summer maximum 75°F (24°C).
Water: Twice a week in summer, not more than once a week in winter, and less if very cold. Water from top, allowing surplus to drain away. Do not stand in water.
Humidity: Spray twice a week in summer, but not in direct sunshine. Do not spray in winter.
Feeding: Every 14 days in the growing season (spring and summer) with house-plant food diluted according to the maker's instructions.
Soil: Loam-based No. 2 compost.
Repotting: Annually in spring. Likes open compost, so do not firm it down too hard in the pot.
Cleaning: By hand with damp cloth or with fine mist spray in summer. No leafshine.

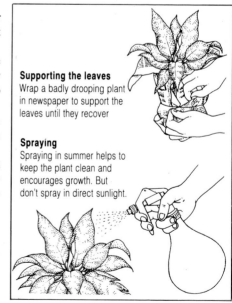

Supporting the leaves
Wrap a badly drooping plant in newspaper to support the leaves until they recover

Spraying
Spraying in summer helps to keep the plant clean and encourages growth. But don't spray in direct sunlight.

what goes wrong

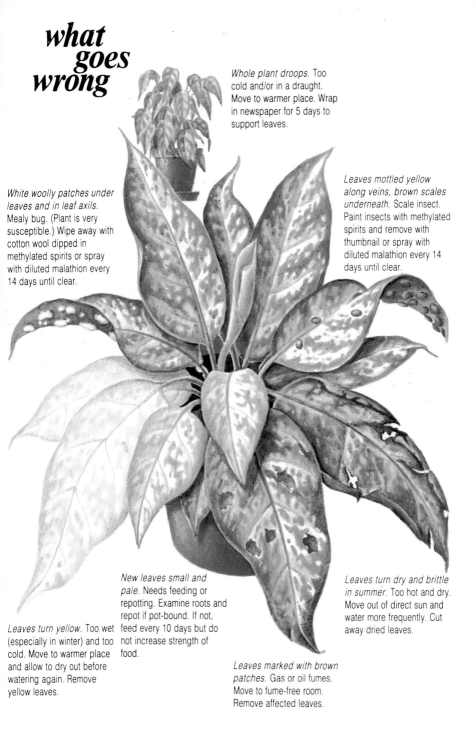

Whole plant droops. Too cold and/or in a draught. Move to warmer place. Wrap in newspaper for 5 days to support leaves.

White woolly patches under leaves and in leaf axils. Mealy bug. (Plant is very susceptible.) Wipe away with cotton wool dipped in methylated spirits or spray with diluted malathion every 14 days until clear.

Leaves mottled yellow along veins, brown scales underneath. Scale insect. Paint insects with methylated spirits and remove with thumbnail or spray with diluted malathion every 14 days until clear.

New leaves small and pale. Needs feeding or repotting. Examine roots and repot if pot-bound. If not, feed every 10 days but do not increase strength of food.

Leaves turn yellow. Too wet (especially in winter) and too cold. Move to warmer place and allow to dry out before watering again. Remove yellow leaves.

Leaves marked with brown patches. Gas or oil fumes. Move to fume-free room. Remove affected leaves.

Leaves turn dry and brittle in summer. Too hot and dry. Move out of direct sun and water more frequently. Cut away dried leaves.

Allamanda cathartica

Golden trumpet

This is an evergreen flowering plant originating in tropical America. It will climb to its maximum height of 10ft (3m) in 4 years. After flowering, it should be cut back to one joint of the old wood in midwinter, when it should be allowed to rest. It is an easily grown plant, preferring a warm greenhouse or conservatory, though it will grow well in the home if humidity is high. It should not be kept near radiators nor should it ever become waterlogged as the roots will stagnate and begin to rot.

The Golden trumpet is an evergreen climber with attractive trumpet-shaped yellow flowers. Plants are usually bought when 12–18in (30–45cm) high but will easily grow to 10ft (3m) tall, when they will need the support of canes or a trellis.

Light: Full in summer, slight shade in winter when temperature below 60°F (16°C).
Temperature: Maintain 70–80°F (21–27°C) in summer, less in winter, with minimum of 55°F (13°C).
Water: Copiously when growing to keep always moist, i.e. almost daily if temperatures high. From late summer to early spring, water only when compost surface feels quite dry, once a week or less.
Humidity: Spray every 2 days in spring and summer to maintain moist atmosphere, avoiding flowers. Place pot on saucer of pebbles almost covered with water.
Feeding: Weekly in spring and summer after first flowers appear, using liquid houseplant food diluted to maker's instructions.
Soil: Two parts loam-based No. 2 to 1 part peat and charcoal or coarse sand with one-eighth part rotten cow manure if available.
Repotting: For new plants, as soon as roots grow through bottom of pot, i.e. every month for 3 months, using pot next size up and firming compost around old root ball. After first year, repot annually as soon as new growth starts and certainly not after it has grown 6in (15cm).
Cleaning: Spray with tepid soft water, avoiding flowers. No leafshine.

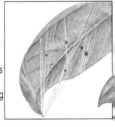

Webs under leaves. Red spider mite. Remove webs with damp cloth or sponge, then spray with diluted malathion, especially under leaves. Repeat every 14 days until symptoms disappear. Improve humidity by standing pot on saucer of wet pebbles.

Plant goes limp. In summer, compost too dry. In winter, too cold and wet. If dry, plunge pot into bucket of water for 10–15 minutes, then drain. Keep compost constantly moist in summer, watering every day if it dries out. In winter, water only when compost surface feels quite dry. Minimum winter temperature 55°F (13°C).

No flowers appear. Too dark and/or needs feeding. Check conditions. Move into lighter place (but not in direct sunlight) and feed weekly when flowering with liquid houseplant food diluted according to instructions.

New leaves small. Needs feeding. Feed with liquid houseplant food every week when flowering, diluting food to recommended strength.

Whole plant turns black. Leafshine damage. Do not use. Clean only by carefully dusting with feather duster or camel hair brush.

Pruning

1. To keep them compact and to make sure of continued flowering, plants over 2 or 3 years old should be pruned in early spring.

2. Cut stems back to about 6in (16cm) above compost, just above a leaf.

Plant grows very leggy. Not enough light and needs pruning. Move into light position (but not direct sunlight). Prune in spring.

what goes wrong

Leaves curl up in winter. Too cold. Move to warmer place above 55°F (13°C).

Leaves curl and turn brown in summer. Too cold. Move to warmer place. Do not allow temperature in summer to fall below 70°F (21°C). Try to keep at 70–80°F (21–27°C).

Leaves turn black, stems rot. Too cold and damp, especially in winter. Spray with fungicide then place in warmer atmosphere and spray and water less often.

White cotton-wool patches where leaf joins stem. Mealy bug. Spray with diluted malathion and remove bugs and 'wool' with tweezers. Repeat every 14 days until symptoms disappear. Or, paint bugs with methylated spirits and remove with tweezers.

67

Aloe variegata

This large genus of plants from South Africa and eastern parts of Africa, varies from large trees to tiny hand-sized plants. The smaller ones are very suitable for indoor or greenhouse culture, and are primarily chosen for the markings on their leaves. The red, yellow or pink flowers appear in winter or spring; they are tube shaped and many are on a long stem like bluebells. *Aloe variegata* grows well on windowsills where it can take full advantage of the sunlight and will grow to around 12in (30cm) high. Overwatering is the commonest cause of failure. Other good species are *A. albiflora*, *A. descoingsii*, *A. haworthioides*, *A. parvula*, *A. somaliensis*.

Aloe flowers are red, yellow or pink and grow on a long stem in late winter or spring. The flowers open progressively from lower down the stem to the tip and the stem should not be removed until it has dried and withered.

Light: Maximum light is needed for best colouring and flower production.

Temperature: A minimum of 45°F (7°C) is safer for these plants, as many of them like a little water in the winter months. Give fresh air or stand outside in the summer, when no danger of frost threatens.

Water: These plants want only a little water, once a month in winter. Start watering more often in spring, building up to every week in summer, tail off again in autumn. See also Introduction.

Feeding: Use a high potash fertilizer in summer once a month, stop feeding in autumn.

Soil: Use good loam-based No. 2 potting compost, or soil-less compost, with about 30% coarse, gritty sand to improve drainage.

Repotting: Every spring in size larger pot, until in 7 or 8in (18–20cm) when soil may be shaken off and plant repotted in fresh soil in same size pot.

Propagation: From offsets which appear at soil level or low on the main stem.

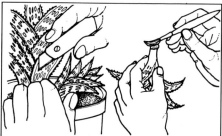

Removing offsets
1. In spring or early summer, when offsets have 3–4 pairs of leaves, remove from parent plant with sharp knife.

2. Dust cut surfaces with hormone rooting powder to prevent infection, leave to dry for 2–3 days, then plant on dry compost.

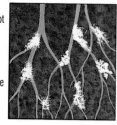

Plant does not grow, white woolly patches on roots. Root mealy bug. Wash soil off roots, swirl in contact insecticide, and allow to dry before repotting in fresh compost and clean pot. Leave dry for 2 weeks.

Green or black insects on flower stalk. Greenfly or blackfly feeding on flower's nectar. Cover leaves with paper and spray flowers with contact insecticide. Repeat weekly until clear.

what goes wrong

Leaves poor colour, no flowers. Not enough light. Keep in sunniest possible place all year round.

When flowers die, cut stalk as close to base as possible. Or, wait until it pulls out easily by hand.

Most leaves turn brown and dry. Much too dry or roots lost from overwatering earlier. If dry, soak in bowl of water for ½ an hour, then drain. If no improvement, inspect and treat roots (see Introduction).

Round, brown scales on leaves. Scale insect. Spray plant and soak soil with systemic insecticide. Remove after 1 week .

Leaves at centre of plant grow tall and thin, losing colour. Too hot and wet in winter; or too dark. Keep below 50°F (10°C) during dry resting period, with no water. But make sure light is good all year round.

White woolly patches among leaves. Mealy bug. Remove with small paintbrush dipped in methylated spirits, and spray with contact or systemic insecticide. Repeat 2 or 3 times in growing season.

Black sooty covering on leaves. Sooty mould from flower nectar. Wipe off with cloth.

Leaves badly marked. Sun scorch. Shade with paper for 2 weeks to allow to recover.

Leaves close up or wrinkle, lower leaves brown and dry. Too dry. Test compost. If very dry, soak in bowl of water for 10–15 minutes, then drain. Water more regularly in hot weather.

Stem turns black and rots. Too cold and wet in winter, overwatered in summer. Keep dry in winter and allow to dry out between waterings during rest of year.

Amaranthus caudatus

Love lies bleeding

Loves lies bleeding is a native of India but survives well in temperate climates. Its name comes from the long, rather sad-looking tassels, whose tiny flowers open progressively as the stem gets longer and are much loved by bees. From a rather weedy start, it becomes very robust as the season progresses and will, therefore, need plenty of room in a mixed container or it will hide some of its smaller companions. An annual, it will be killed by frost at the end of the summer.

Light: Maximum.
Temperature: Will survive cold but not frost, and prefers warm summers, 70°F (21°C) or more.
Water: Little and often so that the soil is always just moist. Must be well drained.
Humidity: Spraying unnecessary. It is not much affected by rain, but prefers dry weather.
Soil: Loam-based No. 2. Grows well in soil-less compost but needs a mixture of about 50% soil to support its heavy top growth.
Feeding: Liquid feed every 10 days at maker's recommended strength.
Propagation: For sowing outdoors, water compost in container 24 hours before sowing in mid to end spring. Sow 2–3 seeds in groups about 12in (30cm) apart and cover with compost until just hidden. One week after seedlings appear, thin out leaving strongest in each group. Indoors, sow very thinly on surface of well-drained compost in a 3½in (9cm) pot. When seedlings are big enough to handle, plant them singly in 3½in (9cm) pots or 2in (5cm) apart in a tray.
Tidying: Remove any yellowing leaves at the base of the plant weekly.
Varieties: Some different coloured spikes. including a dirty white are available.

Love lies bleeding grows to 2–3ft (60–90cm) if the seed has germinated indoors, less if sown outdoors. The leaves are mid-green with a red rib and have an elongated heart shape. The tiny carmine coloured flowers are clustered along a growing, willowy stem, forming long tassels which may reach the ground.

Growing point distorted and does not grow well. Aphids. Spray with liquid derris or systemic insecticide to maker's instructions. Repeat after 10 days if symptoms persist.

what goes wrong

Mature leaves have dull red markings. Caused by cold. Move to more protected position if possible.

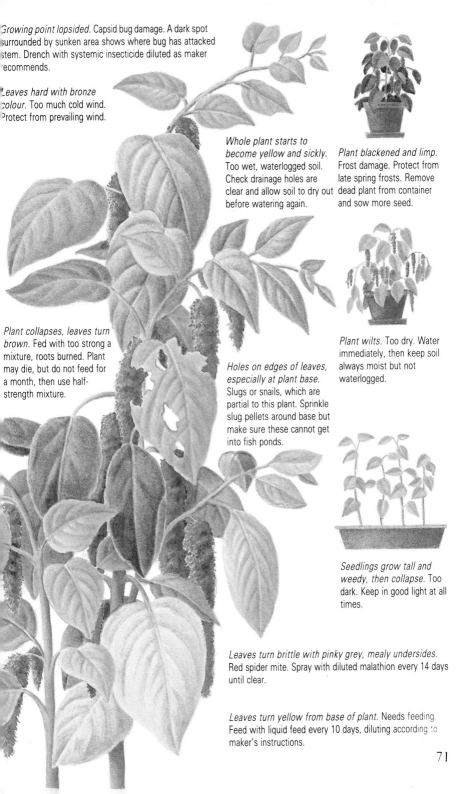

Growing point lopsided. Capsid bug damage. A dark spot surrounded by sunken area shows where bug has attacked stem. Drench with systemic insecticide diluted as maker recommends.

Leaves hard with bronze colour. Too much cold wind. Protect from prevailing wind.

Whole plant starts to become yellow and sickly. Too wet, waterlogged soil. Check drainage holes are clear and allow soil to dry out before watering again.

Plant blackened and limp. Frost damage. Protect from late spring frosts. Remove dead plant from container and sow more seed.

Plant collapses, leaves turn brown. Fed with too strong a mixture, roots burned. Plant may die, but do not feed for a month, then use half-strength mixture.

Holes on edges of leaves, especially at plant base. Slugs or snails, which are partial to this plant. Sprinkle slug pellets around base but make sure these cannot get into fish ponds.

Plant wilts. Too dry. Water immediately, then keep soil always moist but not waterlogged.

Seedlings grow tall and weedy, then collapse. Too dark. Keep in good light at all times.

Leaves turn brittle with pinky grey, mealy undersides. Red spider mite. Spray with diluted malathion every 14 days until clear.

Leaves turn yellow from base of plant. Needs feeding. Feed with liquid feed every 10 days, diluting according to maker's instructions.

71

Pineapple

This is a striking houseplant whose shape and colouring contrast well in mixed plantings. Its brightly coloured leaves are, however, sharply toothed and can easily scratch skin and tear clothing. It is a bromeliad but unlike many other plants of this type prefers to grow in normal soil not on bark or leafmould. Individual plants last only 2–3 years, but produce offsets after flowering which grow into new plants. All varieties will produce fruit though indoors there is rarely enough light (or space) for them to reach edible size.

Light: Full sunlight best but will survive in partial shade.
Temperature: Best at 65–70°F (18–21°C). If kept cooler, growth will be retarded – which can be good if in mixed plantings.
Water: Allow compost to dry out between waterings. Water once or twice a week in summer, once a week in winter.
Humidity: Benefit from high humidity. Spray overhead twice a week in summer, once a week in winter, more frequently if in hot dry room.
Feeding: Add liquid houseplant food at maker's recommended strength to water once a week in summer when growing or while fruit forming.
Soil: Likes rich compost – use loam-based No. 2.
Repotting: Repot at least twice while young rosette growing into proper plant, once 3 months after offset is separated, then again a year later when it is outgrowing its pot. But do not use too large a pot – one size larger each time. Do not firm compost down too hard – it prefers open texture. Wear gloves to protect hands from sharp leaves.
Cleaning: Wipe leaves if dusty with damp cloth. Do not use leafshine.

This small, compact Pineapple plant grows to 10–12in (25–30cm) high and the same across. Variegated ones fruit more slowly than plain green varieties and need full light all year round to keep the bright colour in their leaves. The larger *Ananas striatus* may reach 3ft (1m).

Burn marks on middle of leaves. Damage caused by spraying in sunlight. Plant needs humidity but do not spray while sun is on it. Remove unsightly leaf at base with sharp knife – wear gloves.

Rusty marks on leaves. Leafshine damage. Do not use. Clean only by wiping with damp cloth.

Propagation
Plant dies down after fruiting and a small offset grows beside it. When parent plant has shrivelled and offset is about half its size, remove both from pot and separate offset and roots with a sharp knife. Repot offset and keep moist at 70°F (21°C) for 21 days.

what goes wrong

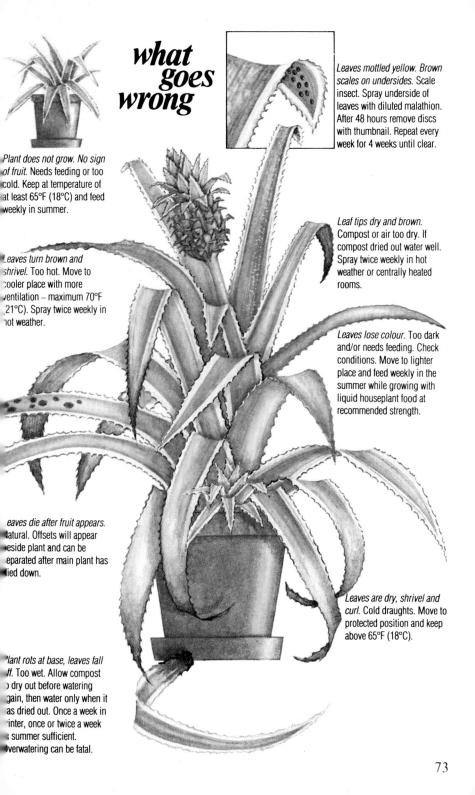

Leaves mottled yellow. Brown scales on undersides. Scale insect. Spray underside of leaves with diluted malathion. After 48 hours remove discs with thumbnail. Repeat every week for 4 weeks until clear.

Plant does not grow. No sign of fruit. Needs feeding or too cold. Keep at temperature of at least 65°F (18°C) and feed weekly in summer.

Leaves turn brown and shrivel. Too hot. Move to cooler place with more ventilation – maximum 70°F (21°C). Spray twice weekly in hot weather.

Leaf tips dry and brown. Compost or air too dry. If compost dried out water well. Spray twice weekly in hot weather or centrally heated rooms.

Leaves lose colour. Too dark and/or needs feeding. Check conditions. Move to lighter place and feed weekly in the summer while growing with liquid houseplant food at recommended strength.

Leaves die after fruit appears. Natural. Offsets will appear beside plant and can be separated after main plant has died down.

Leaves are dry, shrivel and curl. Cold draughts. Move to protected position and keep above 65°F (18°C).

Plant rots at base, leaves fall off. Too wet. Allow compost to dry out before watering again, then water only when it has dried out. Once a week in winter, once or twice a week in summer sufficient. Overwatering can be fatal.

73

Anemone

This Anemone, also called the Wind flower, can be grown outside or indoors in pots, when it will flower for up to 6 months. If growing from seed, sow in trays of seed compost in mid-spring. When seedlings are large enough to handle, prick off 5–6 plants for growing on in an 8in (20cm) pot. Plants can also be raised from corms, and some garden centres sell young plants ready for planting out or potting up in summer. If Anemones are given good indoor conditions especially good light, a pot of 5–6 plants will produce a succession of up to 150 blooms.

Light: Full light at all times for healthy blooms. Shade seedlings from full sun.

Temperature: Flower production best if constant temperature of 45°F (7°C) can be maintained, but plants will bloom at up to 60°F (16°C).

Water: Soil must be moist and well drained. Water twice a week, more in very hot weather. Newly planted corms should be left almost dry.

Humidity: Cool, dry, well ventilated position essential. Do not spray, as wet foliage becomes vulnerable to fungus diseases.

Feeding: Once plants are growing strongly in pot, feed every 10 days with liquid garden fertilizer, every 5 days in soil-less. Dilute to maker's recommended strength.

Soil: Loam-based No.2 potting compost or soil-less.

After flowering: Remove dead flowerheads to encourage new bud formation. Cut flower stem at soil level. When all flowering is finished and no new flower stems are visible, allow foliage to die back. Corms can be lifted and dried for planting in the garden, but do not grow in pots again as flowers will not be strong.

The lovely flowers of the Anemone are up to 3in (7cm) across and grow singly among 6in (15cm) high foliage. The best variety for growing in pots is DeCaen, which is small and hardy, and produces blooms in many shades of red, pink, purple and mauve.

Plant does not flower. Needs feeding. Feed with dilute liquid garden fertilizer every 10 days.

Leaves distorted and may have yellow or brown spots. No flowers. Plum rust, which is common. No cure, so destroy plant. Never spray Anemones as this makes them susceptible.

Pinholes in leaves of young plants. If standing outdoors suspect flea beetle and dust soil with gamma HCH. Plants will die if attack severe.

what goes wrong

Fluffy grey mould on any part of plant. Stems may collapse. Botrytis, common in winter. Remove affected parts and spray at 10-day intervals with benomyl or iprodione. Prevent by growing in well ventilated room, and never spray with water.

Small, wingless insects on any part of plant, leaves may be sticky or sooty. Greenfly. Spray with pyrethrum-based insecticide at 10-day intervals until plant is clear.

Leaves droop though soil moist, flowers die rapidly. Too hot. Move to cooler place, below 60°F (16°C), cooler if possible.

Flower stem splits open and looks flat. If plant has been outdoors, frost damage. Anemones are not frost-hardy, especially if grown indoors. Frosted plants may still flower.

Stems of leaves and flowers have swellings which eventually burst. Anemone smut. No cure, destroy plant.

Whole plant turns yellow. Leaves may have black streaks along veins. Waterlogging. Check drainage. Allow soil to become almost dry, then begin watering gradually to keep soil just moist. Never stand pot in saucer of water.

Buds do not open, stems pale and weak. Much too dark. Move to a well lit position.

White powder on leaves or stems. Powdery mildew, caused by hot, dry conditions affecting roots. Check and improve conditions. Spray every 10 days with dinocap.

Leaves floppy, flowers fall over. Too hot or too dry. Check conditions. Soil should be moist. Give a little water and allow plant to absorb it before giving more.

Anthurium andreanum

Wax flower

The flowers of this plant are much used by flower arrangers, especially in Japanese floristry and to produce highly stylised displays. They are often mistaken for artificial ones as they have an unreal, waxy appearance. Whether cut or growing, the flowers can last several weeks. Warmth, moisture and humidity are all important for this plant.

Light: Full diffused light but not direct sunlight.
Temperature: 70°F (21°C) all year is ideal. Tolerates maximum 85°F (29°C) for short periods provided humidity is high. Winter minimum 60°F (16°C). Try to keep around 60°F (16°C) for 6 weeks in late winter, before flowers appear.
Water: Copiously with soft water at least twice weekly in spring and summer to keep compost always moist. In winter, enough to keep roots just moist at all times, about once a week.
Humidity: Spray daily in spring and summer, once or twice a week in winter. In hot weather stand pot on saucer of pebbles almost covered with water. Keep moss around roots moist.
Feeding: Every 14 days in summer with liquid houseplant food diluted to maker's instructions.
Soil: Equal parts chopped sphagnum moss and peat-based compost. Good drainage essential.
Repotting: In winter, with above compost mixture and plenty of crocks in bottom of pot. Spread roots carefully, pack compost round them. Plant base should stand 2-3in (5-7cm) above pot level with moss around exposed roots.
Cleaning: Wipe leaves with damp cloth. Use leafshine every 8 weeks.

If kept in high humidity, Wax flowers will produce a succession of their exotic, waxy blooms from spring to late summer. Flowers are usually red but white and pink varieties are occasionally available.

Webs on leaves. Red spider mite. Remove webs with damp cloth or sponge, then spray with diluted malathion, especially under leaves. Repeat every 14 days until symptoms disappear. Improve humidity by standing pot on saucer of wet pebbles.

Leaves split and become diseased. Split caused by physical damage but leaf may then rot. Cut off damaged leaf at base of stem.

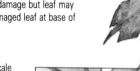

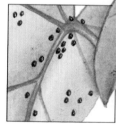

Discs on leaves. Scale insect. Spray underside of leaves with diluted malathion and, after 48 hours, remove discs with thumbnail. Repeat every week for 4 weeks until clear.

what goes wrong

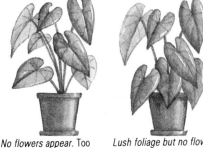

Leaves lose gloss. Air too dry. Spray daily in spring and summer with soft tepid water, once or twice a week in winter.

No flowers appear. Too dark. Move to position in good light but not direct sunlight. Or, overwatered previous winter. Water only once a week in winter.

Lush foliage but no flowers. Compost too rich. Repot in winter using correct mixture not loam-based.

New leaves small and pale, no flowers appear. Needs feeding. Feed every 14 days in summer with liquid houseplant food diluted to recommended strength.

Leaves yellow and curl under in winter. Too cold and wet. Move to warmer place, above 60°F (16°C) and allow compost surface to dry out before watering again. Try to keep temperature even. If leaves curl while green, cold draughts. Move plant to protected position.

Leaves look dry and papery, with yellowish colour. Too dry. Water immediately and keep compost always moist.

Leaves turn black. Too cold, possibly by cold glass in winter. Keep around 70°F (21°C) in summer and at least 60°F (16°C) in winter.

Brown spots on leaves. Fungus. Spray with systemic fungicide. If leaf badly affected, remove.

White cotton-wool patches under leaves and at leaf base. Mealy bug. Spray with diluted malathion and remove bugs and 'wool' with tweezers. Repeat every 14 days until clear. Or, paint bugs with methylated spirits and remove with tweezers.

Flies hopping around plant. Whitefly. Spray with pyrethrum-based insecticide or diluted malathion. Repeat one week later, then every week until clear.

Roots push up more than 3in (7cm) above soil, raising plant on stilts. Needs repotting but do not do so unless it is winter. Pack moss between and around roots.

Anthurium scherzerianum

Flamingo flower

Though not an easy plant to grow, this is most rewarding, for the exotic flowers are long-lasting and unique in their shape and texture. Normally bright scarlet, the flowers are sometimes white, pink and, rarely, white with red markings. At the flower's centre is a long tube-like spadix which sometimes has a fascinating curl. The flowers, which appear continuously, mainly in summer, are often too heavy for their stem and may need a thin stake. They may last up to 8 weeks. With care, and knowledge of its habits, this plant should flourish.

Light: Needs plenty, but must be protected from direct sunlight.
Temperature: Winter minimum 60°F (15°C), summer maximum 85°F (29°C). Flourishes best in even temperature night and day, especially in winter.
Water: At least twice a week in summer, depending on temperature, once a week in winter, with rainwater if possible. Must never dry out.
Humidity: Spray with rainwater daily in summer, twice weekly in winter to maintain humidity. Stand pot on saucer of pebbles almost covered with water.
Feeding: Every 14 days in the growing season (spring and summer) with liquid houseplant food diluted according to the maker's instructions.
Soil: 3 parts peat-based compost to 1 part chopped sphagnum moss.
Repotting: Every other year, ensuring crown, where stems emerge from roots, is above soil level, otherwise plant may rot. If roots push up above soil level, cover them with moss.
Cleaning: Wipe leaves with damp cloth. Use leafshine every 8 weeks on leaves only.

Flamingo flowers produce their long-lasting blooms mainly in summer, but in good conditions, flowers can appear at any time of the year. Healthy plants have firm, glossy leaves and, if in flower, should have new buds appearing as well.

Brown patches under leaves. Scale insect. Spray with systemic insecticide every 14 days until clear.

Leaves turn yellow at tip. Too wet, overwatering. Allow plant to dry out then cut down watering by half. Check drainage holes are clear and soil mixture is correct. Plant must not stand in water.

White woolly patches under leaves and in leaf axils. Mealy bug. Remove individually with cotton wool dipped in methylated spirits or spray with diluted malathion at 10 day intervals until clear.

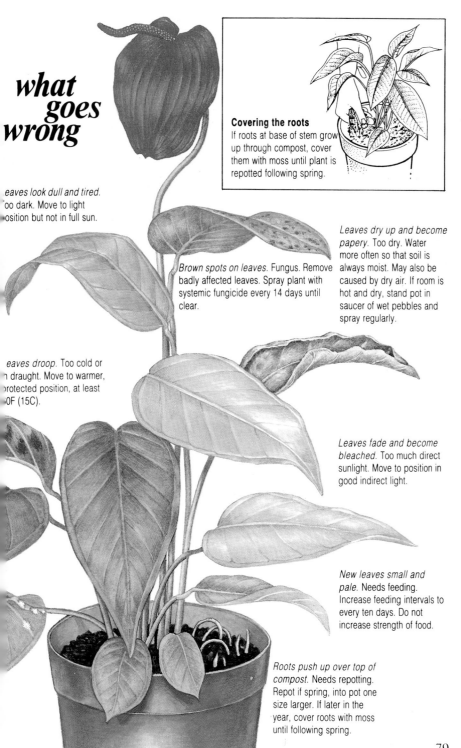

what goes wrong

Covering the roots
If roots at base of stem grow up through compost, cover them with moss until plant is repotted following spring.

eaves look dull and tired. 'oo dark. Move to light osition but not in full sun.

Brown spots on leaves. Fungus. Remove badly affected leaves. Spray plant with systemic fungicide every 14 days until clear.

Leaves dry up and become papery. Too dry. Water more often so that soil is always moist. May also be caused by dry air. If room is hot and dry, stand pot in saucer of wet pebbles and spray regularly.

eaves droop. Too cold or ı draught. Move to warmer, ırotected position, at least 0F (15C).

Leaves fade and become bleached. Too much direct sunlight. Move to position in good indirect light.

New leaves small and pale. Needs feeding. Increase feeding intervals to every ten days. Do not increase strength of food.

Roots push up over top of compost. Needs repotting. Repot if spring, into pot one size larger. If later in the year, cover roots with moss until following spring.

79

Zebra plant

Bright yellow pagoda-shaped flowers form on the tips of the leaf stems of this native of tropical and sub-tropical America. The striped foliage looks strong but *Aphelandras* can be tricky to keep. They should never dry out in the growing season; once they have flowered they should have a 6-week rest period, with water cut down to once a week.

Zebra plants are commonly available but fairly difficult to keep, the lush, striped foliage being liable to flop unless well watered when growing. A dormant period after the spring and summer flowering is the secret of keeping plants from year to year.

Light: Full diffused daylight all round plant; no direct sunlight, or plant wilts.

Temperature: Daytime maximum 80°F (27°C), night temperature 65°F (18°C) in summer. When plant resting after flowering, reduce day temperature to 65°F (18°C) and night temperature to 50–55°C (10–13°F). In winter daytime minimum 60°F (16°C).

Water: At least twice a week in spring and summer to keep moist. Once flowering has stopped, water only when compost surface feels dry, but plant must not shrivel. Once a week should be sufficient.

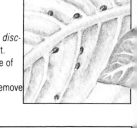

Leaves have mottled patches around small, disc-like marks. Scale insect. Paint discs on underside of leaves with methylated spirits. After 48 hours remove discs with thumbnail.

Humidity: Spray daily with soft water in growing season. Stand pot on saucer of pebbles almost covered with water. Reduce humidity when plant is resting or in low temperatures (below 55°F, 13°C).

Feeding: Every 14 days after first flower buds appear, using liquid houseplant food diluted to maker's instructions. Do not feed in winter.

Soil: Equal parts loam-based No.2 and peat with one-eighth part sand added.

Repotting: In early spring after dormant period for plants more than 2 years old. Remove as much old compost as possible and use 5in (13cm) maximum pot size. Larger pots encourage straggly plants.

Cleaning: Spray with tepid water, avoiding flowers. If leaves dusty, wipe with damp cloth. No leafshine.

Humidity

Spray every day in summer, once a week in winter. Protect flowers. For extra humidity, stand the pot on a saucer of pebbles. Add water to almost cover the pebbles but do not let the base of the pot touch the water or the roots will become waterlogged.

what goes wrong

Flies hopping around flower. Blackfly or greenfly. Spray every 14 days until clear with pyrethrum-based insecticide.

New leaves stay small. Needs feeding. Add liquid houseplant food to the water every 14 days after flower buds appear. Dilute food to maker's recommended strength.

White cotton-wool patches where leaf joins stem. Mealy bug. Spray every week until clear with diluted malathion and remove bugs and 'wool' with tweezers.

Plant grows very tall and straggly. Needs pruning, or kept too warm in winter. Keep cool (about 55°F, 13°C) for 6 weeks after flowering, allowing soil to dry out between waterings. Prune in spring.

Plant does not flower. Pot too large. Repot in early spring into smaller pot, trimming away excess roots. Prune following spring, then start feeding as soon as flower buds appear.

Flower droops and leaves look limp. Plant beginning to dry out, too wet and/or too hot. Check conditions. If dry, water well and plant should recover. Keep compost moist while growing and flowering, but never leave pot standing in water: a waterlogged plant may show same symptoms. Check temperature and keep out of direct sunlight.

Leaves turn pale. Too dark. Move into light position, but not in direct sunlight.

Base of stem rots. Too cold and wet. Move to warmer place and maintain at least 0°F (16°C). Allow compost to dry out before watering again. Then keep moist but do not allow to stand in water.

Leaves fall. Too dry or in a draught. Water first by plunging pot in bucket of water for 10 minutes. Drain and place in draught-free place. Then water twice weekly in spring and summer, weekly in winter.

Brown spots on leaves. Too much sun. Move out of direct sunlight, into position of good diffused daylight.

Brown patches on leaves. Caused by smoke or gas fire fumes. Keep in clean atmosphere and cut off marked leaves as close to main stem as possible.

Webs under leaves, leaves eventually discolour and fall. Red spider mite. Spray every week with diluted malathion for four weeks. Improve humidity around plant by standing pot on saucer of wet pebbles.

81

Aporocactus

There are some half-dozen species of this genus of hanging cactus, the commonest of which, *Aporocactus flagelliformis* (p.83), has been grown on windowsills for many years and is popularly known as the Rat's-tail cactus from the form of its limp, hanging stems. Other species have more rigidity but still make good plants for hanging baskets and are suitable for porches in the summer. They should never be left out in winter, however, for as natives of southern Mexico, they cannot stand low temperatures. *Aporocactus flagelliformis* produces flowers all along its stems in early spring. There are also some very attractive flowering hybrids, crosses between Aporocactus species and Epiphyllums (known as Aporophyllums) and other related large-flowered species. These make springy-stemmed, semi-pendant plants, also very suitable for hanging baskets, and usually flowering freely.

Aporophyllum 'Rosemary' is a hybrid produced by crossing an Aporocactus with an Epiphyllum. The inner petals are pink, the outer more salmon-coloured. Like true Aporocactus species, they are best kept in hanging baskets.

Light: Best on a sunny windowsill indoors, or hung from the upper part of the window-frame, so that their stems can hang in the light. If grown in a greenhouse, shade lightly in summer as strong sun through glass may scorch the stems.

Temperature: Not less than 40°F (4°C); keep below 100°F (38°C) and give fresh air in summer months.

Water: Water weekly in the spring and summer, so that soil just dries out between waterings and give just enough in the winter to stop them drying out completely. Once every 3–4 weeks is probably enough. Spray once a week in spring and summer and once every 6–8 weeks in winter.

Feeding: Once a month in spring and summer with a high potash fertilizer (as used for tomatoes).

Soil: Use soil-less compost with no grit.

Repotting: Repot each year in spring into next size pot until in 6in (15cm) pot or basket. After this, repot in same sized container each year with fresh compost, after shaking off as much of the old soil as possible. Leave dry after repotting for a fortnight. If becoming too large for container or available space, remove some of its stems and use as cuttings.

Cleaning and pest control: Spray with water weekly in spring and summer to keep the dust off and in winter spray about once every 6–8 weeks. Add insecticide to the spray 2 or 3 times a year.

Other species: Except *A. flagelliformis* few are seen: *A. flagriformis* and *A. conzatti* are the most likely. These are, however, less interesting than the hybrids which have flowers ranging from pale pink to deepest red.

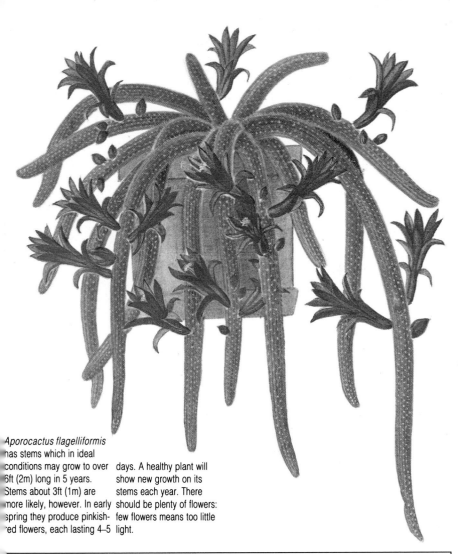

Aporocactus flagelliformis has stems which in ideal conditions may grow to over 6ft (2m) long in 5 years. Stems about 3ft (1m) are more likely, however. In early spring they produce pinkish-red flowers, each lasting 4–5 days. A healthy plant will show new growth on its stems each year. There should be plenty of flowers: few flowers means too little light.

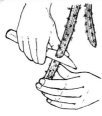

Taking cuttings
1. After flowering finished, cut lengths of stem 2–3in (5–8cm) long with sharp knife, cutting at an angle.

2. Dust end of cutting and cut end of stem with hormone rooting powder containing fungicide. Leave cutting to dry for at least 2 days.

3. Prepare 2 or 3in (5 or 8cm) pot with potting compost and place cutting on surface.

4. Cover just enough to hold it upright or rest tip against side of pot. Keep in light (not sunny) place for 2–3 weeks until roots develop. Then start watering. Repot when roots fill pot.

Araucaria heterophylla

Norfolk Island pine

This slow-growing plant is the only evergreen conifer suitable for growing in the home. Although its horizontal branches carrying soft needles seem almost oriental, it in fact comes from Norfolk Island off Australia in the south Pacific, hence its name. A very good specimen plant, it prefers to grow on its own. In its natural habitat, it grows to considerable heights, but in the home seldom reaches more than 60in (150cm). It likes plenty of air and not too high temperatures. It is related to the Monkey Puzzle tree *(A. araucana)* from Chile.

Norfolk Island pines grow very slowly, producing only one or sometimes two layers of new branches a year. The branches grow at distinct intervals on the main trunk and are covered with soft, attractive needles. These should at all times look fresh and bright: avoid plants with dried needles or stems.

Light: Keep out of direct sunlight in summer. Will tolerate shade, though prefers being near a window. Make sure that you turn the plant regularly, about once a week in spring and summer. Otherwise it will lean towards the light and lose its even shape.

Temperature: Winter minimum 40°F (5°C), summer maximum 60°F (16°C) if possible. Can be kept out-of-doors in summer.

Water: Twice weekly in summer, about every 7–10 days in winter, to keep soil just damp. Use soft water if possible.

Humidity: Spray twice weekly in summer, weekly in winter if in a centrally heated room.

Feeding: Every 14 days in the growing season (spring and summer) with houseplant food diluted with water. Use half the amount of food recommended by the maker.

Soil: A rich compost such as loam-based No. 2.

Repotting: Annually in spring when young. When over 39in (1m) tall, just replace topsoil with fresh compost.

Cleaning: Humidity spraying sufficient. No leafshine.

Branches hang down limply. Too cold. Move to warmer place, at least 40°F (5°C).

Pruning

1. Cut off bare branches cleanly close to main stem. Do not leave a jagged edge.

2. Dab cut with sulphur dust and if sap runs, use cotton wool dipped in vaseline to seal the cut ends.

what goes wrong

Plant does not grow. Needs repotting. Look at roots and if tightly packed, repot in pot one size larger.

Branches grow thin and weedy, drooping under their own weight. Needs regular feeding. Increase strength of food to three-quarters maker's recommended strength.

Needles dry up and turn yellow and brown. Too hot and dry. Move to cooler, more airy room, water and spray regularly.

White woolly patches on needles and spines. Mealy bug. If possible, remove with cotton wool dipped in methylated spirits. Or spray every 14 days with diluted malathion until clear.

Needles bleached. Too much sunlight through glass in summer. Move away from window into shadier place.

Green needles fall off. Overwatered. Allow to dry out before watering again, then water less often.

Needles sticky, with small green insects. Greenfly. Spray every 14 days with pyrethrum or a systemic insecticide until clear.

Needles drop from lower branches, leaving bare spines. In large plant, old age. Other plants may be in too dark a place. Move into lighter position and prune off dead branch close to main stem with sharp knife or secateurs.

85

Ardisia crenata

Ardisia

This unusual-looking flowering plant is well worth looking out for. Its oval, dark-green leaves about 2in (5cm) long, are carried round a central stem in layers or whorls. The small flowers, coloured white, red or purple, grow in clusters on stems that stick out horizontally beyond the leaves. The flowers gradually change to red berries, making the plant an attractive one to have at Christmas. Often, last year's berries may be on the plant with this year's flowers. Not difficult to keep, Ardisia forms a handsome plant up to 28in (70cm) tall, at which height it may lose its lower leaves.

Ardisia usually flowers in early summer. The flower clusters fade gradually, to be replaced by bright berries which often stay on the plant until new flower buds form the following spring. Healthy leaves are a good, shiny dark green.

Light: Best in a window out of midday sun.
Temperature: Winter minimum 45°F (8°C). Ordinary room temperature in summer. Does not mind heat, though berries stay on longer if kept under 60°F (15°C).
Water: 2–3 times a week in summer, weekly in winter. In autumn, when the flowers have all died away, leave it without water for 2–3 weeks as a resting period. Good drainage in pot essential.
Humidity: Spray 3 times a week in summer, once a week in winter. In dry air stand on saucer of pebbles almost covered with water. Don't allow pot base to touch the water.
Feeding: Every 14 days in the growing season (spring and summer) with liquid houseplant food diluted according to the maker's instructions.
Soil: Loam-based No. 2 compost.
Repotting: Annually in spring. Plant flowers and fruits best when slightly pot-bound.
Cleaning: Humidity spraying sufficient. Monthly spray with leafshine improves appearance.

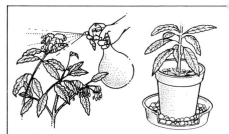

Humidity
If kept in a hot, dry room, provide extra humidity by spraying at least 3 times a week.

Stand pot on saucer of pebbles almost covered with water. Do not allow pot base to touch water or roots will become waterlogged. A combination of moist soil, good drainage and humidity will keep the plant healthy in hot, dry air.

what goes wrong

Plant does not grow well in spring and no flowers appear in summer. Too dark. Move to lighter place, but not in strong midday sunlight.

Flowers drop off before fruit has set. Too cold. Move to warmer place, but not more than 60°F (15°C) if possible.

Leaves turn yellow. Too wet, overwatered or waterlogged. Check drainage holes in pot are clear and allow to dry out before watering again. In winter, water only once a week and allow to rest without water for 2–3 weeks in autumn.

White woolly patches under leaves and on stems. Mealy bug. Remove with cotton wool dipped in methylated spirits or spray with diluted malathion every 14 days until clear.

Leaves flop and go limp in summer. Needs watering. Soak plant in bucket of water for 15 minutes, then allow to drain. Water 2–3 times a week in summer, once a week in winter.

Leaves turn pale and bleached. Too much direct sun. Move into shadier place, out of midday sun.

Leaves fall off. Air too dry. Spray regularly and if temperature over 60°F (15°C) stand pot on saucer of damp pebbles. When plant is about 28in (70cm) tall, it will lose its lower leaves naturally.

Leaves mottled with sticky webs underneath. Red spider mite. Spray every 14 days with diluted malathion or systemic insecticide until clear. Spray regularly with water to keep humidity high.

Ariocarpus

Sometimes known as Fossil cacti or 'Living rocks' these plants are the ancients of the Mexican deserts, growing so slowly and to such a great age that imported plants are often considerably older than their owners, sometimes a hundred years old or more. They were once usually seen as imported wild plants but more and more smaller, seedling plants are now being raised commercially as plants in the wild must be conserved and protected. In fact imported plants are difficult to establish and it is advisable to check that they show signs of new wool in the centre before buying them, unless you are experienced in inducing the wizened, turnip-like roots to send out fresh growth. Take care not to damage these larger roots and, if they are broken or bruised, dry them off and dust them liberally with rooting powder. Young seedling plants present fewer problems, except that they are so slow growing and may take 20 years to reach 6in (15cm) across. Grafting will help to increase the growth rate and this is best done at an early seedling stage.

Ariocarpus furfuraceus may grow as large as 7in (18cm) across and is made up of triangular tubercles like thick leaves, in a rosette three times as wide as it is tall. The large, white flower pushes up through a mass of fresh, yellow-brown wool at the centre of the plant; the appearance of new wool is a sure sign that this slow-growing plant is flourishing.

Ariocarpus kotschoubeyanus belongs to the smaller-growing group, rarely needing more than a 4in (10cm) pot. Its white or purple-pink flowers appear in late summer and autumn. Do not water until compost has dried out from previous watering — and keep dry in winter.

Light: Maximum light is essential. Keep on the sunniest windowsill or in an unshaded greenhouse.

Temperature: Not less than 40°F (4°C); keep below 100°F (38°C) and give fresh air in the summer months.

Water: Water well every 2 weeks in summer only. Keep dry in winter. Spraying is unnecessary.

Feeding: Not necessary, but will induce a little more growth; use high potash fertilizer, as for tomatoes.

Soil: A high grit content is advisable, with up to 75% coarse, gritty sand (not builders'

or seashore) to 25% soil-less or good loam-based compost.

Repotting: Avoid disturbing roots too often once plant is established, for mature plants (3–4in, 8–10cm across) repotting only every third year. Young plants may be repotted into next size pot in spring.

Cleaning and pest control: Spray lightly if dusty and gently brush up wool when dry. Add insecticide to the cleaning spray 3 or 4 times a year.

Other species: There are two main groups, the first including *A. lloydii* (below), growing up to about 7in (18cm) across. Of the other large species the best are *A. furfuraceus*, with white flowers, and *A. trigonus*, with yellow. The second group rarely outgrow a 4in (10cm) pot. Of these *A. kotschoubeyanus* (below, left) is most often seen. *A. agavoides* (still sometimes labelled *Neogomesia agavoides*) and *A. scapharostrus* are not for beginners.

Treating damaged roots

1. If a bought plant has damaged roots, they may rot, turning orange or brown at the base and becoming soft. Pare away rotting area into firm tissue with no more spots visible.

2. Dust liberally with hormone rooting powder containing a fungicide and leave for 2-3 weeks to dry thoroughly before repotting in fresh compost.

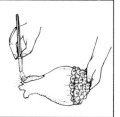

Ariocarpus lloydii has greyish-coloured, diamond-shaped tubercles which fit together like the sections of a tortoise-shell but in spirals leading to the woolly centre.

A healthy plant will produce new wool at the centre and, if given plenty of sunlight, will flower in late summer or autumn. Flowers last about 3 days.

Arthrocereus

Arthrocereus rondonianus has pinkish-lilac flowers which, unlike most in this genus, bloom in the daytime. Its finger-thick stems grow up to 12in (30cm) long.

The cacti in this genus are columnar plants from Peru, Brazil and Argentina and grow to about 6in (15cm) tall. They produce long-tubed, scented flowers, mostly white, which open in the evening. There are about a dozen species to choose from, including those more often labelled *Pygmaeocereus* or *Setiechinopsis*, but except for *Arthrocereus* (or *Setiechinopsis*) *mirabilis* (p.91), most are only available from specialist cactus nurseries. Given a little extra care and attention, however, most of them will grow and flower well, producing flowers when they are only 3–4in (8–10cm) tall. They rarely outgrow a 4in (10cm) pot.

Light: Plenty of light is needed to keep the growth spiny and compact and to induce flowering; the sunniest spot is best.

Temperature: A minimum of 40°F (4°C) will suffice if they are kept dry in winter; keep below 100°F (38°C) and give fresh air in the summer months.

Water: Water about once a week in summer months. In early autumn, reduce watering to monthly and in the 3 coldest winter months, keep plant quite dry. Begin watering again in spring, gradually increasing to summer rate. Spray overhead monthly.

Feeding: Use a high potash fertilizer once a month in spring and summer (as for tomatoes).

Soil: Use about 40% coarse gritty sand (not builders' or seashore), 60% soil-less or good loam-based compost.

Repotting: Repot every year in the spring in fresh compost, leaving dry after repotting for 2 weeks. Use same size pot unless plant is outgrowing it. Be careful not to damage roots, and dust with a rooting powder containing a fungicide if you do, to combat rot.

Cleaning and pest control: A monthly forceful overhead spray with water will keep them dust-free. Add insecticide to the spray 2 or 3 times a year.

Other species: There is one reddish-lilac flowering species, *A. rondonianus*, with yellowish-brown, short spines on stems only finger-thick but growing to about 12in (30cm) long. *A. campos portoi* is difficult to grow well or indeed at all and is better grafted, and *A. microsphaericus* is not much better; both these species have white flowers. The 2 or 3 different *Pygmaeocereus* species are not so difficult, and *Arthrocereus* (or *Pygmaeocereus) bylesianus* or *akersii* are sometimes available from specialist nurseries. They have long-tubed, white flowers, freely produced if the plants get enough sunshine.

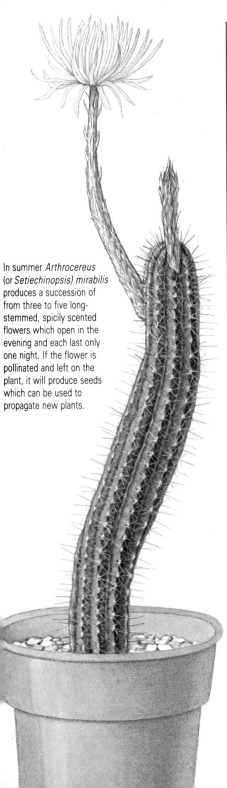

In summer *Arthrocereus* (or *Setiechinopsis*) *mirabilis* produces a succession of from three to five long-stemmed, spicily scented flowers which open in the evening and each last only one night. If the flower is pollinated and left on the plant, it will produce seeds which can be used to propagate new plants.

Collecting seeds

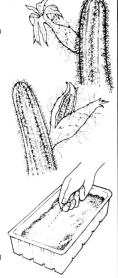

1. When flower dies and shrivels, its stem begins to swell as seeds develop.

2. After a few weeks it splits open to reveal a mass of black seeds.

3. Collect seeds carefully and prepare tray or small pot with soil-less or good loam-based No. 1 potting compost and top layer of grit. Sow seeds directly on surface.

As each flower bud develops, check each evening for the opening of the flowers. This usually starts about 8 to 10 o'clock in the evening and lasts through the night.

Arthrocereus (or *Pygmaeocereus*) *bylesianus* has long-stalked white flowers which appear two or three at a time in summer. They open in the evening when, in the wild, their colour and scent attract night-flying insects.

Plume asparagus

This is a wonderfully eye-catching plant which when mature can be 3ft (90cm) in diameter and 2ft 6in (75cm) high. Its long fronds have delicate soft leaflets growing in a bristle-like formation. The root system produces tubers which rest on the top of the pot, and a mature specimen can weigh as much as 56lb (25kg) in a 12in (30cm) pot. *A. falcatus*, the thorn fern, needs similar treatment but should be kept warmer in winter (55–60°F, 13–18°C).

Light: Shade suitable, but diffused light needed to help pale green new fronds mature to darker colour. Keep out of direct sunlight.

Temperature: Winter minimum 50°F (10°C), summer best at 55–60°F (12–15°C). If too hot, leaves will drop. Allow good air circulation.

Water: 2 or 3 times a week in summer, to keep moist. Weekly in winter.

Humidity: Mist daily with tepid water. Stand young plant on saucer of pebbles almost covered with water or pot mature plant in self-watering container.

Feeding: Every 14 days in summer only, with houseplant food diluted with water. Use half the amount of food recommended by the maker. In week between feeds, add foliar food to water for one of the daily sprays.

Soil: Loam or peat-based with low-level fertilizer content. Blend loam-based No. 1 half and half with peat.

Repotting: When roots appear through bottom of pot, repot into pot one size larger. Plant a large specimen into self-watering planter.

Cleaning: Spraying and foliage feeding will keep it clean. No leafshine.

The Plume asparagus has imposing, upright fronds which look like large bottlebrushes. They can grow to 30in (75cm) long. A healthy plant will have its main stems well covered with side branches, in turn bearing hundreds of tiny leaflets. These may dry and drop if conditions are not right.

what goes wrong

Fronds turn pale, droop and drop leaves. Overwatering. Allow to dry out before watering again.

Humidity
To provide permanent humidity around plant, put damp pebbles or gravel in saucer and stand pot on top. Keep pebbles wet but don't let base of pot actually stand in water.

or

Stand pot in outer container packed with damp peat.

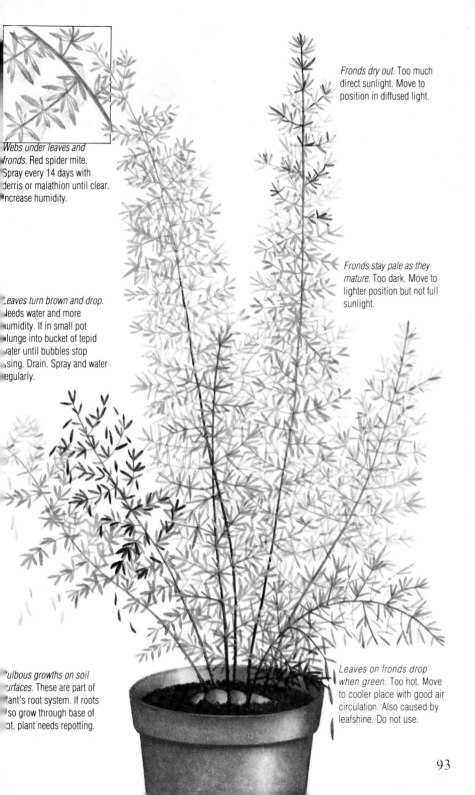

Webs under leaves and fronds. Red spider mite. Spray every 14 days with derris or malathion until clear. Increase humidity.

Leaves turn brown and drop. Needs water and more humidity. If in small pot plunge into bucket of tepid water until bubbles stop rising. Drain. Spray and water regularly.

Bulbous growths on soil surfaces. These are part of plant's root system. If roots also grow through base of pot, plant needs repotting.

Fronds dry out. Too much direct sunlight. Move to position in diffused light.

Fronds stay pale as they mature. Too dark. Move to lighter position but not full sunlight.

Leaves on fronds drop when green. Too hot. Move to cooler place with good air circulation. Also caused by leafshine. Do not use.

93

Asparagus fern

This is the fern generally used by florists with roses and for buttonholes. Like all *Asparagus* ferns, it is a member of the Lily family. Its foliage is similar to that of the asparagus vegetable and it makes a good houseplant provided it is not left in a very warm room away from windows. It requires a medium level of humidity. The thorns can scratch if care is not taken when cutting foliage or handling the plant. It prefers a clay pot but is often rather difficult to repot since its fibrous roots cling closely to the sides.

Light: Diffused daylight. Will grow in shade though foliage will remain pale. Keep out of direct sunlight.

Temperature: Winter minimum 45°F (8°C), spring and summer minimum 55°F (12°C), maximum 70°F (21°C) with good ventilation.

Water: 2 to 3 times weekly in summer, at least once a week in winter. Must not dry out.

Humidity: Spray daily with fine mist of tepid water when temperature at maximum. Otherwise, at least twice weekly. Stand on saucer of pebbles almost covered with water to help humidity.

Feeding: Every 14 days all summer, with houseplant food diluted with water. Use half the amount of food recommended by the maker.

Soil: Equal proportions of loam-based No. 1 and sterilized peat. Peat-based seed and cutting compost also suitable.

Repotting: When rootball is compact and roots show through bottom of pot. Use clay pot one size larger and gently remove old soil mixture from roots before potting up. If roots have grown into clay, twist pot around gently until they separate.

Cleaning: Spraying will keep it clean. No leafshine.

The delicate pale green leaflets of the Asparagus fern are often used in flower arrangements. With plenty of daylight, they should have lush, green foliage but direct sun can dry them out. A healthy plant should have a mass of fronds, well covered in feathery leaflets.

what goes wrong

Leaflets drop continuously. Too dark or too hot. Move to cooler, lighter place and spray daily with mist of tepid water.

Fronds remain pale. Too dark. Move to lighter place.

Fronds turn yellow in winter. Overwatered. Allow almost to dry out between waterings. Check not standing in water.

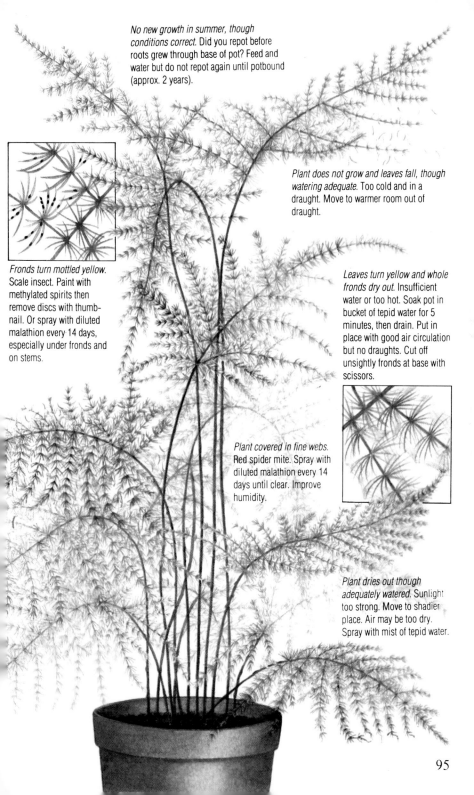

No new growth in summer, though conditions correct. Did you repot before roots grew through base of pot? Feed and water but do not repot again until potbound (approx. 2 years).

Plant does not grow and leaves fall, though watering adequate. Too cold and in a draught. Move to warmer room out of draught.

Fronds turn mottled yellow. Scale insect. Paint with methylated spirits then remove discs with thumbnail. Or spray with diluted malathion every 14 days, especially under fronds and on stems.

Leaves turn yellow and whole fronds dry out. Insufficient water or too hot. Soak pot in bucket of tepid water for 5 minutes, then drain. Put in place with good air circulation but no draughts. Cut off unsightly fronds at base with scissors.

Plant covered in fine webs. Red spider mite. Spray with diluted malathion every 14 days until clear. Improve humidity.

Plant dries out though adequately watered. Sunlight too strong. Move to shadier place. Air may be too dry. Spray with mist of tepid water.

95

Asparagus fern

This plant is called by the same common name as *Asparagus plumosus*, but looks quite different. It becomes a bushy plant with fronds both rising and trailing and is the easiest of the *Asparagus* varieties to keep. The foliage lasts well when cut and can be used as table decoration. The leaves are prickly and have sharp needles at the base. *A. sprengeri* is a good plant for the conservatory, kitchen or bathroom. When foliage becomes very overcrowded in the pot, the plant can be divided in spring. The roots are tuberous and you will need a sharp knife to separate them.

This variety of Asparagus fern has spiky, pale green foliage and must not be confused with *Asparagus plumosus*. The fronds are much less filmy, and are in fact quite prickly. They, too, are often used for flower arrangements and last well if cut.

Light: Light situation without direct sunlight. Will survive in shade.

Temperature: Winter minimum 45°F (8°C), summer minimum 50°F (10°C). Will take 70–75°F (21–24°C) in summer provided air circulation is good.

Water: 2 or 3 times a week in summer to keep very moist. Water less in winter and allow almost to dry out before watering again, probably once a week.

Humidity: Spray twice a week in summer and once a week in winter with tepid water. Spray even if out-of-doors; if very hot spray daily. Stand on a saucer of pebbles almost covered with water to keep up humidity.

Feeding: Weekly in summer with houseplant food diluted with water according to maker's instructions.

Soil: Peat-based compost blended with fertilizer ideal. If using loam-based mixture, choose one with low level of fertilizer (e.g. No. 1) and blend 50:50 with peat.

Repotting: In spring, only if plant seems pot-bound, into clay pot one size larger. Ensure good drainage in pot.

Cleaning: Spraying with water adequate. No leafshine.

Cutting off dead fronds If dead or damaged fronds are unsightly, cut them off with sharp secateurs or florists' scissors. Cut stem cleanly just above pair of leaves.

Keep fronds healthy by spraying regularly with tepid water. If very hot and dry, stand pot on saucer of damp pebbles to increase humidity.

Plant stops growing. If early summer, did you repot before roots grew through pot base? Do not repot again until pot-bound. If mid to late summer, did you feed through autumn and winter? Plant exhausted. Water but do not feed until following summer.

what goes wrong

Leaflets dry out and drop. Too hot and air too dry. Move to cooler place and increase humidity by spraying or standing pot on wet pebbles.

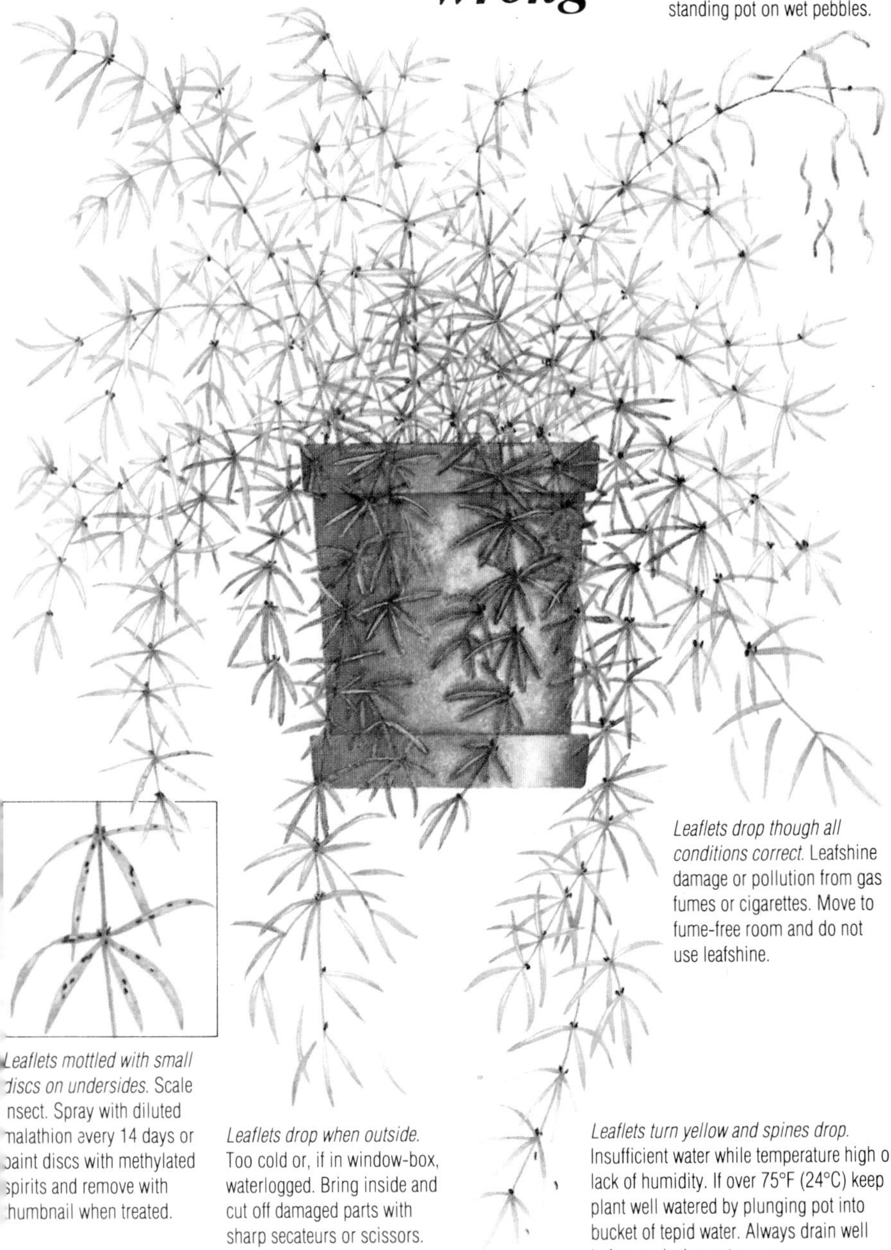

Leaflets drop though all conditions correct. Leafshine damage or pollution from gas fumes or cigarettes. Move to fume-free room and do not use leafshine.

Leaflets mottled with small discs on undersides. Scale insect. Spray with diluted malathion every 14 days or paint discs with methylated spirits and remove with thumbnail when treated.

Leaflets drop when outside. Too cold or, if in window-box, waterlogged. Bring inside and cut off damaged parts with sharp secateurs or scissors.

Leaflets turn yellow and spines drop. Insufficient water while temperature high or lack of humidity. If over 75°F (24°C) keep plant well watered by plunging pot into bucket of tepid water. Always drain well before replacing pot on saucer.

97

Cast iron plant

This is the toughest of all indoor plants. It is almost impossible to kill it without actually using poison, hence of course its common name. It was very popular in Victorian times, perhaps because it was the only plant that could stand the variable temperatures of most houses and the fumes from open coal fires and tobacco smoke. Variegated plants have handsome green and white striped leaves. A small purple flower appears occasionally out of the soil, growing quite separately from the leaves and lasting only a day or two. The plant likes to be slightly pot bound and should be kept on the dry side – though even consistent overwatering will rarely kill it.

Aspidistras or Cast iron plants, grow stems 10–12in (28–30cm) long. Although they are almost indestructible, and grow well in shaded corners, a little extra care will keep the elegant leaves bright and healthy.

Light: Will flourish in dark corners. Leaves may scorch in full sunlight.

Temperature: Normal room temperatures, 50°F–65°F (10–18°C).

Water: In winter about once a week (less if temperature below 50°F (10°C), in summer twice a week. Allow compost surface to dry out between waterings.

Humidity: Seems to like quite a dry atmosphere but an overhead mist spray once a week in summer is good.

Feeding: Do not overfeed. Once a month in summer with liquid houseplant food diluted to maker's recommended strength is enough. If leaves split, stop feeding for rest of season. Do not feed variegated plants.

Repotting: Prefers to be potbound, so repot every 3–4 years.

Soil: Loam-based No. 2 for plain green plants, seed compost or one without base fertilizer for variegated.

Cleaning: Wipe leaves with soft damp cloth when dusty. No leafshine.

Leaves pale. Compost exhausted and too dry. Repot in fresh compost and water more regularly. Do not allow to become bone dry between waterings. Once a week in summer, once a fortnight in winter correct.

Root division

1. Divide in early spring if plant so crowded with stems that pot looks almost bursting. Remove from pot and tease away stale compost with a rounded stick.

2. Grasp rootball firmly and gently pull roots and stems apart, taking care not to damage either. Repot both parts in fresh moist compost but do not water again for 2 days.

98

Leaves mottled with yellow, especially along veins. Brown scales under leaves and on stems. Scale insect. Spray under leaves with diluted malathion and after 48 hours remove discs with thumbnail. Repeat every week for 4 weeks until clear.

what goes wrong

White woolly patches under leaves. Mealy bug. Spray with diluted malathion and remove bugs and 'wool' with tweezers. Repeat every 14 days until clear. Or, paint bugs with methylated spirits and remove with tweezers. Keep plant away from others.

Brown marks or burns on leaves. Damage from sunlight. Move to position out of direct sun and remove damaged leaf at base.

Leaves covered with small spots. Leafshine damage. Do not use. Clean only by wiping leaves with soft damp cloth, using soft water if possible. Remove damaged leaf at base of stem.

Leaves turn yellow and droop. Overwatered. Compost should dry out between waterings. Water once a week in winter, less if very cold, twice a week in summer.

Leaves split. Overfeeding. Stop feeding for rest of summer and next year feed not more than once a month at only half maker's recommended strength.

Leaves discoloured, webs underneath. Red spider mite. Remove webs with damp cloth or sponge, then spray with diluted malathion, especially under leaves. Repeat every 14 days until clear. Improve humidity by weekly mist spray.

Leaves are soft and turn dark grey green. Much too cold, probably frosted. Move to warmer place and do not allow temperature to drop below 36°F (2°C).

99

Mother fern

As this attractive plant requires a very humid, though not necessarily hot, atmosphere, it grows best in an enclosed planter, greenhouse or conservatory. Young plants grow on the edge of adult leaves and can be gently removed when well developed and grown into an adult plant. This plant should be bought from a reputable seller as plants kept in normal humidity can soon blacken.

The Mother fern develops baby plantlets on its fronds. These can be removed and will grow quickly into adult plants. It can survive in a very low winter temperature (though not below freezing) but needs a high level of humidity and is therefore ideal for the enclosed environment of a bottle garden.

Light: Semi-shade best, though if too dark, plant will not grow. Keep out of strong sunlight.

Temperature: Tolerates winter temperature of 34°F (1°C), though will not grow. Best year-round temperature is 50–65°F (10–18°C). Above 65°F (18°C) plant dries out quickly.

Water: Keep moist at all times, probably watering 2–3 times a week in summer, once a week in winter. Roots rot if plant stands in water, so ensure good drainage in pot. Water less if temperature below about 50°F (10°C), allowing soil almost to dry out between waterings.

Humidity: Spray daily if not in enclosed planter. If in pot, stand on saucer of pebbles almost covered with water.

Feeding: Weekly in summer with houseplant food diluted with water. Use half the amount of food recommended by the maker. Use a foliar feed instead every week when plantlets developing, again diluted to half the maker's recommended strength.

Soil: Peat-based compost, or 1 part loambased No. 1 to 2 parts pure peat when two years. Grow plantlets in equal quantities of seed/cutting compost and sharp sand.

Repotting: In spring only when plant looks healthy, into clay pot one size larger. If compost too compressed, roots will rot.

Cleaning: Spray with soft or distilled water. No leafshine.

Fronds wither. Too much direct sunlight. Move out of sunlight.

Plant turns black in parts, some leaves turn yellow and wither. Air too dry. Spray every day or use terrarium or self-watering planter.

Fronds turn black and die. Leafshine or insecticide not sufficiently diluted. If many fronds affected, plant will die.

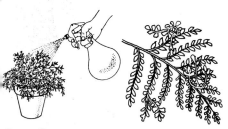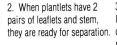

Propagation

1. When plantlets start to appear, give weekly foliar feed at half recommended strength.

2. When plantlets have 2 pairs of leaflets and stem, they are ready for separation.

3. Prepare small pot with layer of drainage and damp compost of ½ sharp sand, ½ peat. Make hole in top with stick or pencil.

4. Pull plantlet gently away from frond with your fingers and place in pot. Press compost lightly around it.

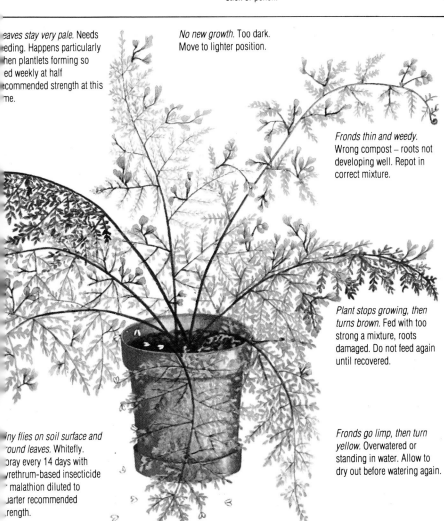

eaves stay very pale. Needs eding. Happens particularly hen plantlets forming so ed weekly at half commended strength at this me.

No new growth. Too dark. Move to lighter position.

Fronds thin and weedy. Wrong compost – roots not developing well. Repot in correct mixture.

Plant stops growing, then turns brown. Fed with too strong a mixture, roots damaged. Do not feed again until recovered.

ny flies on soil surface and round leaves. Whitefly. oray every 14 days with yrethrum-based insecticide r malathion diluted to uarter recommended .rength.

Fronds go limp, then turn yellow. Overwatered or standing in water. Allow to dry out before watering again.

Birdsnest fern

In its natural habitat, this plant grows on trees, obtaining nourishment from rainwater and decaying plant matter around it. Leaves grow from a central point, forming a well. New leaves unfurl delicately into thickish and broad adult leaves. An attractive houseplant, it is relatively easy to grow provided it is not in strong light. In imperfect conditions, older outside leaves become mottled and must be removed at their base with sharp scissors. In a shaded greenhouse or fernery, adult leaves may reach as much as 5ft (1½m) long.

The Birdsnest fern gets its common name from the way the broad leaves radiate from a central well or nest in the middle of the plant. Healthy leaves should be bright, glossy green and there should be new fronds unfurling in the cen[...]

Light: Semi-shaded position to produce healthy leaves. Strong light keeps new growth pale.

Temperature: Winter minimum 55°F (12°C), summer range 70–75°F (21–24°C).

Water: Twice a week in summer, once every 10 days in winter to keep moist at all times. If at minimum temperature in winter, plant should just dry out before being watered again.

Humidity: Plant thrives in moist atmosphere. Spray twice weekly in summer, once weekly in winter. Stand on saucer of pebbles almost covered with water to help maintain humidity.

Feeding: Weekly in summer with houseplant food diluted with water according to maker's instructions.

Soil: Peat-based compost. Not loam-based blends.

Repotting: Repot into clay pot in spring only when root-ball seems closely packed. 5in (13cm) pot adequate for 15in (38cm) high plant. It has less root than other ferns.

Cleaning: Spray with soft water, wipe leaves carefully afterwards. No leafshine.

Humidity

Provide constant humidity by standing pot on saucer of damp pebbles. Do not allow pot base to stand in water.

or

Place in outer pot packed with damp peat.

This plant has a small root system which will probably not grow through base of pot. Examine roots in spring. If they are all growing close together so that soil is obscured, repot in pot one size larger.

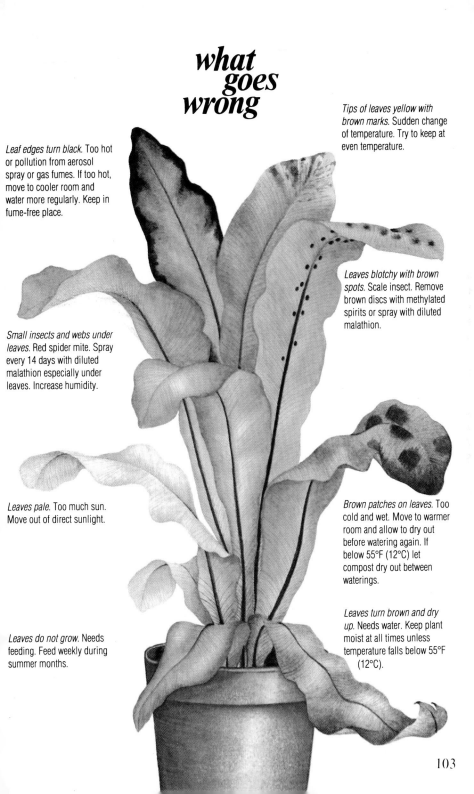

what goes wrong

Tips of leaves yellow with brown marks. Sudden change of temperature. Try to keep at even temperature.

Leaf edges turn black. Too hot or pollution from aerosol spray or gas fumes. If too hot, move to cooler room and water more regularly. Keep in fume-free place.

Leaves blotchy with brown spots. Scale insect. Remove brown discs with methylated spirits or spray with diluted malathion.

Small insects and webs under leaves. Red spider mite. Spray every 14 days with diluted malathion especially under leaves. Increase humidity.

Leaves pale. Too much sun. Move out of direct sunlight.

Brown patches on leaves. Too cold and wet. Move to warmer room and allow to dry out before watering again. If below 55°F (12°C) let compost dry out between waterings.

Leaves turn brown and dry up. Needs water. Keep plant moist at all times unless temperature falls below 55°F (12°C).

Leaves do not grow. Needs feeding. Feed weekly during summer months.

103

Astrophytum

Named for their star-like appearance, this small genus of cactus is one of the most popular with collectors. It consists of several very appealing, beautiful species, ranging in size from one growing barely above ground level and no more than 3–4in (8–10cm) wide, to another growing over 6ft (2m) tall in the wild. They come mainly from Mexico, although the smallest, *Astrophytum asterias*, also grows in Texas in the U.S.A. This one is rather difficult to keep as it is very susceptible to overwatering. *Astrophytum myriostigma* (p.105), the melon-sized 'Bishop's cap' cactus, is one of the easiest to grow.

Astrophytum asterias is very sensitive to overwatering and is therefore difficult to grow well. Reaching eventually a size of about 3–4in (8–10cm) across, it produces flowers when it is only about 1½in (3cm), after about 5 years growth. It is spineless but has rows of white woolly areoles down the centre of each section, and an attractive pattern of white spots.

Light: A sunny windowsill or greenhouse is necessary for best results, with no shading needed from the sun at all.

Temperature: Not less than 40°F (4°C); keep below 100°F (38°C) and give fresh air in the summer months.

Water: Be careful not to overwater at any time, especially *A. asterias*. Water about once every other week in the summer, or weekly for pots 3in (8cm) or less, making sure the pot has dried out from the previous watering. Keep dry in the winter months not watering in spring until the sun has gained some real strength and warmth.

Feeding: use high potash fertilizer (as used for tomatoes) once a month in summer.

Soil: Use 40% (60% for *A. asterias*) of coarse gritty sand (not builders' or seashore) in soil-less or good loam-based potting compost.

Repotting: Repot annually in the early years into large pots each year, until a 5in (13cm) pot is reached. Then every other year will do. Leave dry for a fortnight after potting.

Cleaning and pest control: Spray 2–3 times a year with an insecticide.

Other species: The small *A. asterias* has already been described as difficult to grow and

Astrophytum capricorne grows slowly to 6 or 8in (15 or 18cm) tall and produces its glorious yellow flowers with their red throat in the summer. It is covered with a tangle of long, curling, flexible spines like interlacing wire.

is not recommended for beginners. It looks like a grey-green sea urchin, has no spines and is usually covered with a pattern of white spots. If you can keep it successfully, it will produce pretty yellow flowers all through the summer. *A. capricorne* is another slow-growing species. The big fellow of the genus is *A. ornatum* which grows faster as well as larger than other species — in the wild 50 year old plants can be up to 6ft (2m). It has attractive flecking with yellow, stiff, sharp spines. It will usually produce flowers after 5–6 years, when it has grown to about 4in (10cm) tall and the same in diameter. In cultivation its usual maximum size is about 1ft (30cm).

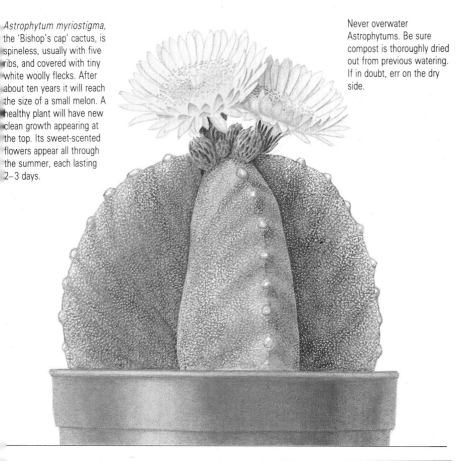

Astrophytum myriostigma, the 'Bishop's cap' cactus, is spineless, usually with five ribs, and covered with tiny white woolly flecks. After about ten years it will reach the size of a small melon. A healthy plant will have new clean growth appearing at the top. Its sweet-scented flowers appear all through the summer, each lasting 2–3 days.

Never overwater Astrophytums. Be sure compost is thoroughly dried out from previous watering. If in doubt, err on the dry side.

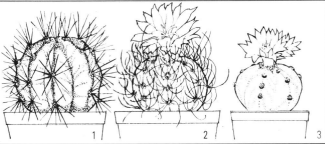

Different Astrophytums have very different types of spine. *A ornatum* (1) has long, straight, rigid ones while *A capricorne's* (2) are curling and tangled. *A myriostigma* (3) has no spines but prominent felty pads instead.

1   2   3

Beaucarnea recurvata

Elephant foot tree

This unusual plant comes from Mexico and is best known as a houseplant in the United States but it is now becoming more available elsewhere. Its large swollen stem gives it its common name and in an old plant this stem may grow into an almost sculptured shape. On top is a bunch of palm-like leaves which droop attractively over the stem. It is well worth searching for as, given plenty of light, it is an attractive and trouble-free plant. It requires rather different conditions in summer and winter, needing warmth and moisture in summer but a cooler, drier period in winter. In centrally heated homes, keep it in the coolest room in winter, but with plenty of light.

The Elephant foot tree may grow to 6 ft (2 m) or more indoors, the stem lengthening gradually from its bulb-like base. The tuft of drooping leaves give it an alternative common name of the Pony tail plant.

Light: Best in full sun though will survive in more shady positions if moved into good light from time to time.
Temperature: In winter 50–55°F (10–13°C) best. In summer 70°F (21°C).
Water: Water 2–3 times a week in summer to keep soil always moist. Water once a week in spring and autumn and only every 3 weeks in winter, to give it a drier resting period.
Humidity: Spray once a week all the year round unless temperature below 50°F (10°C).
Feeding: Use liquid houseplant food at maker's recommended strength every 14 days in summer when plant is growing.
Soil: Loam-based No. 2.
Repotting: They do not like the roots to be disturbed, so every 2 years enough for young plant. For larger plants, change top 2–3in (5–7cm) soil in spring. Make sure drainage is always good.
Cleaning: Spraying will keep leaves clean or they can be wiped with damp cloth. Use leafshine not more than once a month.

White cotton wool patches on and under leaves. Mealy bug. Spray with diluted malathion and remove bugs and 'wool' with tweezers. Repeat every 14 days until clear. Or, paint bugs with methylated spirits and remove with tweezers.

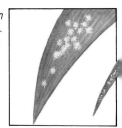

what goes wrong

Leaves droop and dry up. Too hot. Try to keep below 70°F (21°C), and spray weekly all the year round.

Brown scales under leaves. Scale insect. Spray underside of leaves with diluted malathion and, after 48 hours, remove scales with thumbnail. Repeat weekly for 4 weeks until clear. Or, paint scales with methylated spirits.

No new leaves appear and plant looks dull and tired. Needs feeding or too dark. Feed every 14 days in summer and keep in good light.

Burns on leaves. Caused by spraying in sunlight. Plant can stand direct sun but never spray when sun is on leaves. Remove unsightly leaf with sharp knife or scissors where it joins stem.

Stem shrinks and becomes gnarled. Soil too dry. Plunge pot into bucket of water for 10–15 minutes, then drain. Keep moist in summer and only allow surface to dry out in spring and autumn.

Leaves yellow and outer ones drop. Too wet, waterlogged. Drain away water in saucer and allow soil surface to dry out before watering again. Water 2–3 times a week in summer, once a week in spring and autumn. In winter allow soil to dry out completely between waterings – once every 3 weeks enough.

Leaves drop. Too cold. Keep above 50°F (10°C) and if temperature falls near minimum, keep compost dry, watering only once every 3 weeks in winter.

Tiger begonia

One of the most attractive of the small-leaved begonias, this has recently regained popularity. Grown widely in late Victorian and Edwardian times, it then virtually disappeared from commercial production until recently. It is ideal for hanging baskets, since it is compact and, though it trails naturally, rarely becomes too leggy. The flowers are small and yellow and the plant is grown mainly for its striking colouring.

Light: Good natural light but not direct sun.

Temperature: Winter minimum 55°F (13°C). Summer maximum 60–65°F (16–18°C).

Water: Twice weekly with soft water in summer, in winter about every 10 days to keep soil just moist. Water from top but do not get water on leaves.

Humidity: Spray every 3–4 days with fine mist in summer and stand pot on saucer of wet pebbles in hot weather. If temperature falls below 60°F (16°C) do not spray or stand on pebbles or leaves may become infected with mould.

Feeding: Every 14 days in growing season (spring and summer) with liquid houseplant food diluted to maker's recommended strength.

Soil: Light, open mixture of peat-based No. 2 compost or a mixture of 2 parts loam, 2 parts peat to 1 part leafmould and 1 part sharp sand.

Repotting: They do best in small pots (except when several plants are together in hanging basket) so repot only when roots look crowded. Take care not to damage delicate leaves.

Cleaning: Dust lightly with feather duster. Do not use leafshine. Do not wipe leaves or spray: leaves will mark.

The Tiger begonia's leaves are attractively marked with a pattern of lighter green and need good indirect light to look their best. They are one of the easier foliage Begonias and can be propagated by dividing roots and stems when new leaves start to appear in spring.

Propagation
This begonia can be propagated from stem cuttings or by dividing the roots and stems.

1. In spring, when new leaves start to show, prepare 2 clean pots with drainage and fresh compost. Remove plant from pot.

2. Gently pull roots and stems apart, being careful not to damage the leaves. Make sure that each section has both roots and stems.

3. Plant each section separately. Leave in shade without water for 2 days so that the roots spread out in compost to find water.

Leaves curl and go crisp at edges. Too hot. Move to cooler place with more ventilation, below 65°F (18°C). Provide extra humidity.

New leaves small in spring. Needs feeding. Feed with houseplant food diluted to maker's recommended strength every 14 days in spring and summer when growing.

New leaves dull with fine webs underneath. Red spider mite. Remove webs with damp cloth or sponge, then spray with diluted malathion, especially under leaves. Repeat every 14 days until clear. Improve humidity.

Leaves limp, plant droopy. Gas fumes. Move to fume-free room.

Leaves distorted with yellow rings and mottling. Mosaic virus. No cure. Destroy plant by burning if possible to avoid infecting others.

Grey-brown powdery patches on leaves. Too cold and damp. Spray with fungicide, then place in warmer position (above 55°F, 13°C) and spray less often. Allow compost surface to dry out between waterings. Remove damaged leaves at base of stem.

Brown patches on leaves. Caused by spraying water in sunlight. Use only fine mist spray in mornings and evenings. Small spots could be leafshine damage. Do not use.

Leaves small, lack colour, stems long and weak. Too dark. Move to lighter place but not direct sunlight.

what goes wrong

Leaves drop in winter. Too cold. Move to warmer place, above 55°F (13°C).

Begonia elatior

Begonia 'fireglow'

There are literally hundreds of different Begonias, not all, of course, suitable for growing indoors. They fall into three main groups: those with fibrous roots, those with tubers (like small potatoes) and those with rhizomes (thickened underground stems).

This is a relatively new variety of the popular flowering hybrids now available nearly all year round. It is a fibrous rooted type, and is comparatively easy to keep and gives a good show of flowers. Whilst the flower colours are mostly in shades of yellow, orange and red, new varieties are being introduced, and white and pink should soon be available. Begonias like a bright, airy position, and some care must be taken in their watering.

Begonia Fireglow's bright red flowers make it one of the most popular flowering begonias. A healthy plant will look compact, with unmarked green leaves, flowers and new buds appearing, and no signs of rot on leaves or petals.

Light: Winter minimum 60°F (15°C), summer maximum 70°F (21°C). Can collapse if becomes too hot.

Water: Twice a week in summer, about every 10 days in winter. Take care if temperature drops, as overwatering can cause stem to rot. Test compost to make sure it is dry at least half way down pot. Ensure good drainage in pot. Water on leaves can cause scorching in sun.

Humidity: Spray weekly when near summer maximum. Do not get water on the flowers. Stand pot on saucer of pebbles almost covered with water.

Feeding: Every 3 weeks when in flower with liquid houseplant food diluted according to the maker's instructions.

Soil: Loam-based No. 2 compost.

Repotting: Repot once when flowering size reached. Take care as leaves are easily damaged.

Cleaning: Not necessary. Water or leafshine will damage the leaves. If dusty, use a soft, dry paintbrush – carefully.

what goes wrong

Yellow rings and mottling on leaves. Cucumber mosaic disease or tomato spotted wilt virus. No cure, destroy plant.

Brown and black patches on leaves, followed by rot. Botrytis. Too humid and stuffy. Spray with benomyl-based fungicide and move to room with drier air and good air circulation – but not draughts. Or, gas fumes. Move to fume-free room.

Leaves droop and dry up. Too hot and dry. Water and move to cooler room, less than 70°F (21°C) if possible. Remove dried leaves.

Leaves stay small and no flowers appear in spring or summer. Needs feeding. Continue feeding every 3 weeks when flowers appear, but do not feed in winter.

Repotting
1. Take care when removing soil from root ball. Begonias have delicate stems which can easily be damaged.

2. Make sure that all roots are covered with compost in new pot, but do not press it down too hard. Leave without water in shady place for 2 days after repotting.

Leaf and petal edges scorched. Too much direct sun. Move out of bright sunlight.

'potty burn marks on ·aves and flowers. eafshine damage. Do not se.

Spots of rot on leaves, flowers and buds. Caused by spraying with water. Stop spraying.

Soft white patches on leaves. Mildew; plant probably too cold and wet. Remove affected leaves and spray with systemic fungicide. Keep in warmer, drier position.

Small blister-like spots on leaves. Leaf turns black. Bacterial wilt. Remove affected leaves and spray with systemic fungicide.

Leaves go limp and turn yellow. Too cold and wet. Allow to dry out before watering again. Move to warmer room and water only when compost feels dry below surface.

Stems rot at base. Too wet, overwatered. Allow to dry out before watering again. Move to warmer place (at least 60°F, 15°C) and water less often.

111

Tuberous begonia

Begonias are divided into three main categories, tuberous, rhizomatous, and fibrous-rooted. Tuberous begonias are descended from species introduced in 1865; even today hybrid varieties show traces of the foliage markings of *Begonia pearcei* from which they originated. The tubers are planted in early spring and by late spring have developed into young plants which will flower in summer.

Light: Full diffused light, but not direct sun.

Temperature: Summer maximum 70°F (21°C), minimum 60°F (16°C). In winter, store tubers in dry place at 50–55°F (10–13°C).

Water: Start watering dormant and divided tubers in early spring, watering whenever surface becomes dry; in summer, copiously once a week as surface begins to dry. If temperature drops below 60°F (16°C), water only when surface is dry, or tuber will rot.

Humidity: Spray weekly if temperature above 70°F (21°C). Stand pot on saucer of pebbles almost covered with water.

Feeding: Monthly after flower buds formed, with liquid food diluted to maker's instructions.

Soil: Plant new or divided tubers in equal parts peat and sand. When repotting shoots, use loam-based No.2.

Repotting: Plant or repot tubers in early spring in 3–4in (7–10cm) pots. When shoots are 3–4in (7–10cm) long, repot into 4–5in (10–14cm) pots. In winter, when leaves have died down and compost quite dry, remove tubers and store between layers of newspaper in cool, dry place. Alternatively, tubers can be left dry in their pots.

Cleaning: Not necessary, though may be dusted gently with soft brush. No leafshine.

The tuberous Begonia flowers from summer to early autumn. Many colours are available including red, orange, yellow, and shades of pink. They are usually sold as plants from early summer to the end of autumn but the tubers can be stored over winter and replanted in spring.

Leaves have black patches. Botrytis. Too cold and damp. Spray with fungicide, then place in warmer atmosphere and spray with water less often. Allow compost surface to dry out between waterings. Keep temperature above 60°F (16°C). Remove damaged leaves.

Yellow patches on leaves. Begonia mite. Remove affected leaves and burn them. Dust plant with sulphur immediately, then once a month for 3 months.

Dividing tubers
1. Prepare 2 pots with mixture of compost and sand and cut tuber in half with sharp knife. Each section must include a shoot and roots.

2. Dust cut ends with sulphur dust and pot each separately, with half tuber above compost.

what goes wrong

Leaves turn yellow. Too cold and wet. Move to warmer place, at least 60°F (16°C) and allow surface of soil to dry out before watering again. Water only when surface of soil dries out, once a week in summer should be enough.

Flowers turn transparent. Damage from water spray. When spraying plant, protect flowers by shielding with paper or your hand. Remove damaged flower.

Brown spots on flowers. Damage from water spray. Protect flowers with paper or your hand when spraying leaves. Remove damaged flower at base of its stem.

Leaves small and no flowers appear. Needs feeding. Feed once a month after flower buds form with houseplant food diluted to maker's recommended strength. If leaves grow sparsely, too dark. Plant needs good diffused light to grow well and produce flowers.

Brown scorch marks on leaves and flowers. Damage by sunlight. Move into an area of diffused daylight, out of direct sun. Remove damaged leaves and flowers.

Leaves droop and dry up. Too hot. Move to cooler place with more ventilation. Spray daily with soft, tepid water, avoiding flowers. Maximum temperature 70°F (21°C).

Stems go squashy. Too cold and damp or plant waterlogged, standing in water. Check conditions and move to position at least 60°F (16°C). Allow compost surface to dry out before watering again and drain away any water from saucer below plant. If there are signs of mould, spray stems with fungicide.

Tips of leaves curl, plant flops. Too dry. Keep soil moist in summer, watering copiously once a week, just as surface begins to feel dry.

113

King begonia

The foliage Begonias are most rewarding plants to grow for they have a wonderful variety of design and colour in each decorative leaf. They come originally from the Himalayas and are mostly used today in mixed plantings in bowls and troughs. Modern varieties owe much to nineteenth-century plant breeders, who produced the many types now available. One popular variety is *B. masoniana,* known as 'iron cross' from the brown cross pattern in the centre of its bright green leaves.

Light: Keep out of direct sunlight. Otherwise, keep as near to natural light as possible.
Temperature: Winter minimum 55°F (13°C), summer maximum 60–65°F (15–18°C).
Water: Twice weekly with soft water in summer, about every 10 days in winter to keep soil just moist. Water from the top but do not get water on leaves.
Humidity: Spray every 3–4 days with fine mist spray in summer. Stand pot on saucer on pebbles almost covered with water. If temperature drops, do not spray or stand on wet pebbles.
Feeding: Every 14 days in the growing season (spring and summer) with houseplant food diluted according to the maker's instructions.
Soil: Light, open mixture of peat-based compost or mixture of 2 parts loam, 2 parts peat, to 1 part leaf mould and 1 part sharp sand.
Repotting: Best in small pots, so repot only when roots very crowded, into next size pot. Take care not to damage leaves while handling.
Cleaning: Light feather dusting occasionally. No leafshine.

The beautifully shaped, pointed, slightly toothed leaves of foliage Begonias come in a great variety of delicate patterns in greens, reds, pinks and silvers. When buying, look for plants with crisp, unturned leaves without brown edges.

Leaves curl and go crisp at edges. Too cold and dry. Water well, avoiding crown at base of stem. Move to cooler place, below 65°F (18°C) if possible.

Leaves grow distorted and have yellow rings and mottling. Mosaic virus. Incurable. Burn plant to avoid infecting others.

Leaves drop in winter. Too cold. Move to warmer room, at least 55°F (13°C).

what goes wrong

White powdery patches spreading over leaves and stems. Powdery mildew. Spray once with benomyl-based fungicide and move plant to drier, more airy position.

Grey-brown powdery patches on leaves. Grey mould. Move to drier, more airy position and spray once with benomyl-based fungicide.

New leaves dull with fine webs underneath. Red spider mite. Spray every 14 days with derris, diluted malathion or a systemic insecticide until clear.

Leaves limp, plant droopy. Gas fumes. Move to fume-free room.

New leaves in spring stay small. Needs feeding or repotting. Examine roots and repot if they are crowded and growing through base of pot. Feed regularly.

Leaves become discoloured and then drop. Swellings on roots. Eel worm. No cure. Destroy plant.

Stem and crown rotting at base of plant. Too cold and too wet. Move to a warmer place and allow to dry out before watering again.

Roots black and rotting. Root rot, usually from overwatering. Spray roots with benomyl-based fungicide before repotting in fresh compost.

Fibrous begonia

The fibrous-rooted begonia is one of the most accommodating of all flowering plants. It can be raised from seed or from cuttings, is normally flowering by the time it is planted out and, if lifted and potted up before the frost, will continue to flower in the home until midwinter. After being cut back and given a short rest period, it will begin flowering again in early spring. At its best in dappled sunlight, it will grow in most situations from full sun to shade but, being of Brazilian origin, will not stand frosts.

Light: Seedlings, good light but not full sun. Plants, full sun if well watered. They will take quite deep shade but prefer dappled sunlight.

Temperature: Germination, 70–75°F (21–24°C). Seedlings, 60°F (16°C). Lower indoor temperature gradually to 45°F (7°C) 3 weeks before planting out. No frost.

Water: The soil must neither be dry nor waterlogged. Keep always moist, especially in first 4 weeks from seed.

Humidity: A light overhead spray during spring to early autumn.

Soil: Loam-based No. 2 but a soil-less compost is better.

Feeding: Use liquid fertilizer diluted to half maker's recommended strength, every third watering.

Propagation: From seed or cuttings. Take cuttings 2in (5cm) long from last season's plant. Insert in seedling compost round outside of a 3½ (9cm) pot. Keep moist. They root in 3–4 weeks.

Tidying: Pick off fallen flowers from foliage.

Varieties: Pink Avalanche, Organdy Mixture, Danica Rose or Scarlet, large flowered and tall and all the Ambra series of colours.

These begonias grow to 6–10in (15–25cm) high, with fleshy stems and leaves which vary in colour from bright green to deep mahogany and have a glossy surface with a slightly duller underside. The colour range is limited to white, pink and red – but there are many variations of shade.

what goes wrong

Leaves turn brown at edges. If seedlings indoors, too much sun – move to more shady place. If just moved outside, cold winds. Keep young plants cool (45°F, 7°C) for 3 weeks before planting out to acclimatize them.

Leaves lose natural gloss and are dull and grey. Too dry. Increase watering. Brightness will return but will take some days. Do not overwater if they still look dull next day.

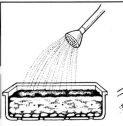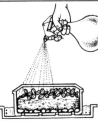

Propagation

1. Sow seed in spring, when days start to lengthen. Prepare seed tray with seedling compost and water well. Leave to drain for 2 hours.

2. Mix seed with 20 times its volume of fine sand, and sow onto surface of tray. Do not cover with compost. To sow evenly, hold seed mixture on palm of hand and tap edge of hand with index finger.

3. Place tray in plastic bag, and seal or put into propagator case. Cover with thick paper and leave at 70–75°F (21–24°C) for 10 days. When seedlings appear, remove paper but leave tray in unsealed bag in shade for 1 week.

4. If seedlings need water in first 2 weeks place tray in shallow water and mist spray daily. Later, water overhead. Prick out when large enough to handle.

New leaves pale, flowers small. Needs feeding. Feed with liquid fertilizer at half maker's recommended strength with every third watering.

Fluffy grey mould in centre of plant. Botrytis. If seedlings, give more air. Spray with benomyl and repeat in 10 days.

White powdery deposit on stems and patches on leaves. Powdery mildew. Spray with fungicide to maker's instructions and repeat every 10 days until clear.

Leaves yellow along veins. Wilt disease. Destroy plant and treat surrounding soil with cheshunt compound. Do not take cuttings from affected plant.

Plant turns yellow from base, whole plant does not thrive. Soil dark and scummy. Overwatered. Stop watering until soil nearly dry. If still wet after 2–3 days without water check drainage in container.

Leaves are blackened and droop. Frost damage. Begonias are tender. Protect from frost at all times.

Seedlings grow matted and intertwined, leaves and roots damaged when pricking out. Sown too thickly. Mix the extra-fine seed with 20 times its volume of very fine sand before sowing.

117

Shrimp plant

Also known as *Justicia brandegeana*, this plant takes its common name from its shrimp-like pink bracts; its true flowers are white and quite small. Since Shrimp plants come from tropical America, they are ideally suited to a heated greenhouse in the growing season and in the home need care, especially if in a centrally heated house which may be hot and dry at some times but cold if unoccupied during the day. If the temperature drops, watch that the atmosphere is not too humid or the bracts may rot: this is not a suitable plant for a bathroom, for example. In winter, when the plant is not growing, it should be kept cooler and drier and may lose some of its leaves.

The pink shrimp-like bracts of the Shrimp plant are its main attraction; the true flowers are small and white. Bracts and flowers appear in summer when the plant is usually available at a height of about 10–12in (25–30cm).

Light: Full light, including direct sunlight in summer. Keep in shady place in winter.

Temperature: 65°F (18°C) in spring and summer. 45°F (7°C) in winter, when plant tends to lose leaves.

Water: Profusely in summer to keep always moist, though good drainage essential. Water every day in hot weather if necessary. Water in winter only when compost surface seems dry, about once a week.

Humidity: Stand pot on saucer of pebbles almost covered with water to maintain reasonable humidity. Do not spray bracts.

Feeding: Every 3 weeks after flowering begins to end of summer, using liquid houseplant food diluted to half maker's recommended strength.

Soil: Loam-based No. 2 with good drainage.

Repotting: Prune straggly plants in early spring and repot into next size pot until in 5in (13cm). When in this size, simply remove plant from pot, knock off old compost and replace with new in same container.

Cleaning: Not necessary. If dusty spray leaves only with soft, tepid water. No leafshine. Remove dead bracts immediately.

Pruning

1. In spring, prune straggly plants before repotting and before buds appear.

2. Make cuts just above a leaf stem, using sharp scissors or secateurs.

3. Dead or discoloured bracts should be removed as they occur. Pinch them off with thumb and forefinger above first pair of leaves.

what goes wrong

Bracts turn black. Spraying damage. When flower bracts appear, do not spray. Create humidity by standing pot on saucer of damp pebbles. Remove damaged bract at its base.

Leaves turn black after cleaning. Leafshine damage. Do not use. Clean by spraying with soft, tepid water.

Leaves yellow with webs underneath. Red spider mite. Spray leaves with diluted malathion every 14 days until clear. Do not spray bracts or they will burn. Improve humidity.

Leaves pale. Needs feeding. Feed every 3 weeks from first buds to end of summer with houseplant food diluted to half maker's recommended strength.

Plant straggly and tall. Too hot and needs pruning. Move to cooler place, (65°F, 18°C) in spring and summer, 45°F (7°C) in winter. Prune in spring.

Bracts stay pale. Too dark in summer or too hot in winter. In summer, move to lighter position: plant will take full sun. Keep shaded in winter. If kept cool in winter (45°F, 7°C), bracts will have stronger colour.

Leaves distorted and sticky, with small insects. Greenfly. Spray every week for 4 weeks with pyrethrum-based insecticide.

Leaves turn yellow. Too wet, waterlogged. Check drainage in pot and allow compost to dry out before watering again. Never leave standing in water.

Leaves drop in summer. Too dry. Water compost. Keep moist throughout summer but do not allow to become waterlogged. In winter, too cold. Move to warmer place; 45°F (7°C) ideal temperature. Keep compost barely moist, allowing top layer to dry out between waterings.

Flowers drop. Natural; flowers fall about 1 week after emerging from bract but bracts remain healthy for much longer.

119

Billbergia nutans

Queen's tears

This evergreen flowering plant belongs to the large plant family known as Bromeliads. Individual plants have a limited life-span (2–3 years) and usually flower only once. However, the flowers and coloured bracts last for a long time and when the parent plant dies, it produces offsets at its base which can be carefully removed and potted up as new plants. It is almost hardy and will tolerate very low, though not freezing temperatures.

Light: Tolerates full sunlight for short periods, but prefers high levels of diffused light.

Temperature: 65–80°F (18–27°C) in summer. 60–70°F (16–21°C) in winter, though will tolerate 45°F (7°C) at night if kept dry.

Water: Twice a week with soft water in summer, allowing some water to fill central rosette of stems. In winter, if temperature is low (45°F, 7°C), water only every 14 days to keep compost dry and do not fill central well; otherwise, water weekly.

Humidity: Spraying usually unnecessary. Plant is very tolerant, though does not like very humid atmosphere if temperature below 50°F (10°C), or very dry atmosphere when in flower.

Feeding: Not necessary, provided plant is repotted annually.

Soil: Equal parts loam-based No. 2, rough peat and leafmould or silver sand.

Repotting: Annually in late spring. When offsets appear, the parent plant will eventually die. When offsets are at least 5in (13cm) long, they can be carefully separated and potted up. They will develop quickly into mature plants, but will not flower for 2 years.

Cleaning: Spray dusty plants with soft, tepid water, avoiding flowers. No leafshine.

The Queen's tears plant is a bromeliad with fairly plain, long, pointed leaves and fascinating rose-coloured bracts out of which grow clusters of long pendulous flowers. It can survive very low temperatures so is ideal for homes where the heating is off during the day.

Removing offsets

1. When flowers and leaves of parent plant have quite died down, offset will be about half the size of parent and will be ready to separate. Prepare small pot with drainage layer and mixture of damp peat and sand.

2. Knock plant from pot and cut offset and its roots from old plant with a sharp knife.

3. Place offset in new pot and firm compost around its base, covering roots. Water well and cover pot with polythene for 2–3 days to provide extra humidity. Discard parent plant.

Plant does not flower. Not enough light and/or pot too large. Move to position in good light: it will stand direct sunshine. They flower better if slightly pot bound but will only flower once in their 3-year life cycle.

what goes wrong

Leaves dry out and turn brown. Compost too dry. Plunge pot into bucket of water for 10–15 minutes, then drain. Keep compost constantly moist in summer, watering twice a week or as soon as surface begins to dry out; make sure drainage is good as must not become waterlogged. Keep water in central well.

Leaves turn black. Leafshine damage. Do not use. Clean only by spraying with soft, tepid water. Remove damaged leaf. If many are affected, plant will not recover.

Flowers dry out. Air too dry. Provide extra humidity by standing pot on saucer of wet pebbles.

Leaves curl. In summer, too cold. Move to warmer place and do not allow temperature to fall below 65°F (18°C). In winter, too hot or too wet. Best between 60-70°F (16-21°C) in winter. If in colder place (45°F, 7°C) do not water compost or well.

White cotton-wool patches round base of plant. Mealy bug. Spray with diluted malathion and remove bugs and 'wool' with tweezers. Repeat every 14 days until symptoms disappear. Or, paint bugs with methylated spirits and remove with tweezers.

Leaves turn soft and mushy with grey mouldy patches. Botrytis. Plant much too wet and cold. Allow surface of compost to dry out before watering again and keep above 65°F (18°) in summer. If 45°F (7°C) in winter, keep much drier, with no water in central well.

Stamens of flowers rot. Too wet, overwatered or standing in water. Allow surface of compost to dry out between waterings. In winter if in cool place (45°F, 7°C), water only once every 14 days with no water in well.

Flies hopping around plant. Whitefly. Spray with pyrethrum-based insecticide or diluted malathion. Repeat every week until clear.

121

Blossfeldia

A Blossfeldia grafted on to a Hylocereus as favoured by some European and Japanese nurseries and known in the trade as 'lollipops'. Hylocereus are more tender than most other cacti so plants grafted onto their rootstock must be kept above 55°F (13°C) for safety.

This is the smallest cactus, and comes from Argentina and Bolivia. In cultivation they are invariably grafted, as they are extremely difficult to grow on their own roots for any length of time. A graft on a low-growing Echinopsis rootstock gives the best effect as little of the Echinopsis shows and the Blossfeldia looks almost as if it were growing on its own. They are often, however, sold grafted onto tall green triangular Hylocereus plants — known in the trade as 'lollipops'. Not only do they look rather unnatural growing like this, but the Hylocereus rootstock will not survive in temperatures below about 50–55°F (10–13°C), though other cacti will tolerate down to about 40°F (4°C) if kept dry. Grown on a graft, a plant such as *Blossfeldia liliputana* (p.123) will form dense clusters of tiny heads, each barely half an inch (1cm) or so across, spineless and covered with tiny, flat tufts of wool, from which the flowers emerge. The flowers are creamy-white and nearly as big as the plant bodies. A cluster in full flower is almost hidden by the blooms, so prolifically are they produced in the spring and early summer. They are not really a good candidate for raising from seed, and I know of only one or two very good seed-raisers who have ever succeeded in bringing plants from seed to maturity.

Blossfeldia minima grown grafted onto an Echinopsis rootstock. If grown on their own roots, Blossfeldias are very difficult to cultivate successfully.

Light: A sunny position is needed to keep the heads tightly growing and the woolly clusters prominent, and to ensure flowering.
Temperature: If grafted on Hylocereus stock (see above) a minimum of 55°F (13°C) is needed for safety. On more usual cactus

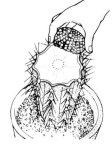

Grafting

1. Remove top inch (2½cm) of the Echinopsis plant and a slice from the bottom of the Blossfeldia with a sharp, clean knife.

2. Immediately place the Blossfeldia's bottom cut surface firmly on the Echinopsis stump, making sure the rings near the centre of the stems overlap.

3. Hold firmly in place with an elastic band until new growth appears. Do not damage outer tissue with too tight or too narrow a band.

You can disguise the rootstock of a grafted plant with gravel so the Blossfeldia appears to be growing normally.

A healthy *Blossfeldia liputana* (grown on a graft) has small heads no more than ½in (1cm) across, with prominent white tufts of wool close together. In spring and early summer, they produce masses of creamy-white flowers which almost hide the rest of the plant. Individual flowers last up to a week.

If growing a Blossfeldia on its own roots, spray weekly overhead but water the very open, gritty compost sparingly.

stock a minimum of 40°F (4°C) will suffice. Keep below 100°F (38°C) and give fresh air in summer months.

Water: Water about once a fortnight in late spring and summer, not at all in winter, and not more than once a month at other times. Spray overhead once a week all year round.

Feeding: Not necessary at all.

Soil: To keep growth in check because of the vigour of the grafting stock use gritty compost, with about half coarse, gritty sand

(not builders' or seashore) to half soil-less or good loam-based No. 1 potting compost.

Repotting: Repot every other year in the spring into next size pot, and keep dry for a fortnight after repotting.

Cleaning and pest control: The frequent spraying will keep the plants dust-free and freshened. Add insecticide to the spray 3–4 times a year to keep pests at bay.

Other species: Differences are slight. If you have one you have them all.

123

Borzicactus

This genus includes similarly flowered but very differently shaped cacti from a wide area of South America including Ecuador, Peru, Chile, Bolivia and Argentina. It includes many often sold under different genus names: those known as Oreocereus, the hairy old men of the Andes; Matucana, globular plants from Peru; Haageocereus and Seticereus, clustering, short columnar plants which grow slowly in cultivation, are densely spined in yellows and browns and flower when they are about 12in (30cm) tall; and the beautiful *Hildewintera aureispina*, a hanging, sprawling species with dense yellow spines and orange flowers. *Borzicactus trollii* (p.125) is one of the best known of the 'hairy' types.

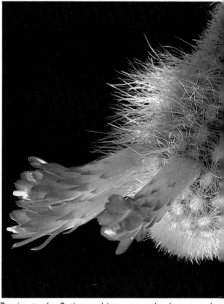

Borzicactus (or *Seticereus*) *icosagonus* develops several thick stems (about 2in, 5cm) arching away from the base of the plant. They grow to about 18–24in (45–60cm) long and eventually hang downwards. The red-orange flowers appear from extra-bristly patches at the tips of the stems.

Light: In the wild all grow in areas of strong sunlight. For good flowering and healthy spines they need the sunniest place you can find for them.

Temperature: Not less than 40°F (4°C) for safety; keep below 100°F (38°C) in summer and give fresh air when possible.

Borzicactus (or *Submatucana*) *intertextus* is a globular species with either red-orange or yellow flowers which are freely produced after it is about 2in (5cm) tall and wide. It grows to grapefruit size after about 5 or 6 years and seldom clusters though others of this type will form clumps.

Water: Water weekly in spring and summer (fortnightly if in pot 4in (10cm) or more as these hold moisture for longer). Reduce watering to monthly in autumn and keep quite dry in winter.

Feeding: Feed in spring and summer with high potash fertilizer (as used for tomatoes) once a month.

Soil: Use 1 part of coarse, gritty sand (not builders' or seashore) to 2 parts soil-less or good loam-based No. 2 potting compost.

Repotting: Repot in next size pot in spring until 5in (13cm) pots reached. Then repot every other year or shake off old soil and replace plant in fresh soil in same size pot.

Cleaning and pest control: Spray with water if dusty and add an insecticide to spray 2 or 3 times a year.

Other species: There are several other white, hairy species (often known as *Oreocereus*), all very similar to one another. The globular *Matucana* types such as *Borzicactus* (or *Matucana*) *haynei* also tend to be similar in appearance with dense white or yellowish spines and red, occasionally pink flowers. The types known as *Submatucana* are more distinct from one another and flower more easily, especially *B.* (or *Submatucana*) *pauciostata*, a clustering cactus with red flowers, *B.* (or *Submatucana*) *madisoniorum*, with red flowers and *B.* (or *Submatucana*) *intertextus* with red or yellow flowers. *Haageocereus* and *Seticereus* species are grown mainly for their densely bristled stems but do occasionally flower. The most spectacular of all the Borzicacti is *B.* (or *Hildewintera*) *aureispina*, a hanging cactus with gold-spined curving stems.

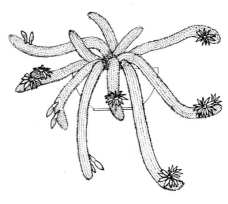

Borzicactus (Hildewintera) aureispina has thumb-thick stems up to 18in (50cm) long which are densely covered with short, stiff, bristle-like golden spines. The stems curve outwards and downwards from the centre like a golden fountain. Its salmon-pink flowers are produced in bursts along the mature stems throughout the spring and summer.

Borzicactus trollii, also known as *Oreocereus trollii*, is one of the best known of the 'hairy old men of the Andes' species. Its mahogany red spines grow through a dense covering of white, silky wool. It grows to around 12in (30cm) tall and 4–5in (10–30cm) round in about 10 years. A healthy plant will produce new, brightly coloured spines and new growth but will not usually flower. Offsets can be separated in summer or new plants grown from seed.

Paper flower

Two Bougainvillea varieties are suitable for growing indoors, doing best in a sun-room or conservatory where they can be kept light and warm. They are *Bougainvillea glabra* and *B. spectabilis,* the former being the easier of the two to grow. *B. glabra* usually pruned as a bush, has mauve bracts. *B. spectabilis* is a climbing variety which includes such hybrids as 'Mrs Butt' (orange) and 'Killie Campbell' (brick red). The bracts which provide the colour look like petals but are technically special leaves. The true flowers are very small.

A healthy Bougainvillea or Paper flower has glossy, deep green leaves and, in summer, plenty of brightly coloured bracts. The actual flowers in the centre of the bracts are hardly noticeable. *Bougainvillea spectabilis* can be trained round a hoop or up a cane; *B. glabra* is usually pruned into a bush shape.

Light: Full daylight. Stands full sunlight, loses leaves if kept in shade.

Temperature: Winter minimum 40°F (5°C), though plant loses leaves at this temperature. To maintain leaves all year, winter minimum 65°F (18°C), summer maximum 70–75°F (21–24°C).

Water: 3 times a week in summer, once a week in winter; with tap water, as Bougainvilleas like lime. Soil must not dry out and good drainage essential.

Humidity: Spray twice weekly when flower buds appear, until flowers fade. Do not spray flowers or bracts. Stand pot in saucer of pebbles almost covered in water to maintain local humidity.

Feeding: Every 14 days in spring and summer with liquid houseplant food diluted with water. Use half as much food as the maker recommends.

Soil: Loam-based No. 3 compost.

Repotting: Annually in spring into same size pot, to change spent soil. Usual size pot for adult plant is 5–7in (13–18cm).

Cleaning: Spraying adequate – but never spray flowers or bracts. No leafshine. When not spraying, dust gently with feather duster if it looks dirty.

Leaves mottled yellow along veins, small scales under leaves and on stems. Scale insect. Remove with cotton wool dipped in methylated spirits or spray every 14 days with systemic insecticide until clear.

Leaves and flowers shrivel and dry, leaving coloured bracts. Too hot and dry, probably over 75°F (24°C). Water soil and spray leaves but not flowers or bracts. Move to cooler place.

what goes wrong

Leaves turn yellow and fall, webs underneath. Red spider mite. Spray with diluted malathion and water soil with same mixture once a week until clear.

Training a climbing plant
1. Push ends of wire hoop or thin cane so they are ⅔ down pot on opposite sides.

2. Bend stem to one side of hoop and gently twist it around the hoop. Do not damage the leaves or stem.

3. Tie a length of twine to one end of hoop and thread it along, looping it loosely around the stem. Do not tie tight knots.

4. The growing tip will continue to follow the line of the hoop. When it reaches the other end, it can be trained round again or twisted back the other way.

Stains and brown marks on flowers and coloured bracts. Water damage. Do not spray these. If water gets on them, shake off gently.

Growth seems stunted. Waterlogged or, if leaves also small, needs feeding. Check drainage and make sure plant is not standing in water. Allow to dry out before watering again. In spring repot into same pot with fresh compost and feed every 14 days in spring and summer, with diluted houseplant food.

White woolly patches under leaves and at leaf joints. Mealy bug. Spray with diluted malathion and water soil with same mixture once a week until clear.

No flowers or coloured bracts appear. Too dark or overwatered. Pot may also be too large. Move plant to place where it gets full sunlight and allow almost to dry out between waterings.

Scorch marks on leaves. Leafshine damage. Do not use. Clean only by spraying or with a feather duster.

Leaves fall.
Natural in winter if temperature falls below 65°F (18°C). If leaves or flowers fall in spring or summer, too dark or too cold. Move to sunny place.

Leaves turn yellow. Too wet, overwatered. Allow to dry out until recovered, then water less often. Make sure pot is well drained.

Soft white patches on leaves. Mildew, caused by too damp an atmosphere. Move to more airy position, but not in draught.

127

Trompetilla

Named after a 17th-century horticulturalist, Dr Charles Bouvard, this plant originated in Mexico. It was once used for its medicinal properties against dysentry and hydrophobia (rabies). In Victorian times it was a popular indoor flowering plant, especially in the conservatory, and its flowers were used for buttonholes and table decorations. Some of its varieties, such as *Bouvardia humboldtii* and *jasminiflora*, are strongly scented.

The Trompetilla's clusters of flowers appear from summer to late autumn and were once popular as buttonholes and table decorations. Its growing tips must be pinched out regularly to keep it bushy and compact.

Light: Full but diffused daylight. Keep out of direct sunlight.

Temperature: Summer minimum 65°F (18°C), and maximum 85°F (29°C), but ventilation must be good. Winter minimum 55°F (13°C), keeping plant away from radiators.

Water: At least twice weekly from late spring to summer, so that compost is always moist. Reduce to once a week or less in winter, allowing surface to dry between waterings. Do not stand plant in water.

Humidity: Spray weekly in spring and summer, avoiding flowers and stopping if temperature falls below 65°F (18°C). Stand pot on saucer of pebbles almost covered with water. In winter do not spray plant, and remove from saucer of pebbles.

Feeding: Every 14 days in summer, with liquid houseplant food diluted to half maker's recommended strength. Do not feed during rest of year.

Soil: Equal parts of peat, loam-based No.3, leafmould, peat and silver sand.

Repotting: In late spring into pot 5in (13cm) maximum size. In early spring, before repotting, prune to shorten previous year's growth. Cut to 1in (2.5cm) above base of plant, cutting just above a leaf.

Cleaning: Humidity spraying adequate. No leafshine.

Insects crawling around flower buds. Greenfly. Spray with pyrethrum-based insecticide or diluted malathion. Repeat one week later, then every week until clear.

what goes wrong

White cotton-wool patches where leaf joins stem. Mealy bug. Spray with diluted malathion and remove bugs and 'wool' with tweezers. Repeat every 14 days until symptoms disappear. Or, paint bugs with methylated spirits and remove with tweezers.

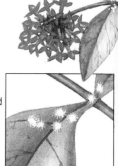

Pruning

Unless growing tips are pinched out, plant will grow straggly and not flower well. With tips of fingers, pinch out small pair of leaves at end of stems every 2 weeks. Treat one-third of stems each time.

Whole plant flops. In summer, compost too dry or too cold. Check conditions. If temperature below 65°F (18°C) move to warmer position. If soil dry, plunge pot into bucket of water for 10–15 minutes, then drain. If plant flops in winter, too wet, overwatered. Water only when compost surface has dried out.

No flowers appear. Too dark. Move into light position but not in direct sunlight.

Black marks on leaves. Too cold or leafshine damage. Move to warmer place, at least 65°F (18°C) in summer, 55°F (13°C) in winter and never use leafshine.

Webs under leaves. Red spider mite. Remove webs with damp cloth or sponge, then spray with diluted malathion, especially under leaves. Repeat every 14 days until symptoms disappear. Improve humidity.

New leaves small. Needs feeding. Feed every week while growing and flowering with houseplant food at half recommended strength.

Leaves are soft and mushy. Too cold and damp, humidity too high. Spray with fungicide then place in warmer atmosphere, at least 55°F (13°C) in winter. Spray with water less often and allow soil to dry out between waterings in winter.

Leaves dry out. Too hot and too sunny. Move to cooler place with more ventilation and out of direct sunlight. Keep under 85°F (29°C) if possible.

Plant grows straggly and out of shape with no flowers. Pinch out some growing tips every 2 weeks throughout growing season until late summer when plant should be bushy and about 18in (50cm) in diameter.

129

Browallia

This beautiful South American plant makes a magnificent display in a tub, hanging basket, trough or pot, providing it is not in a windy or draughty place. It can be raised from seed indoors in spring but should only be introduced gradually to the outside, when all danger of frost has passed. The first autumn frosts will kill it. It is sometimes grown as an indoor flowering pot plant.

Light: Indoors maximum but not direct sun. Outside, dappled sunlight: place taller plants or trellis between plant and sun. Full sun bleaches flowers and dries out plant.

Temperature: 55–70°F (13–21°C). Higher if well shaded. No frost.

Water: Good drainage and keep moist. It soon droops when dry.

Humidity: Regular syringing, 3 times a day in hottest summer days. Midday spraying safe if in shade and not already drooping.

Soil: Loam-based No. 1 or peat-based potting compost.

Feeding: Liquid feed at maker's recommended strength every 10 days in loam, every 5 in peat.

Propagation: In mid-spring, fill 3½in (9cm) pot with soil-less seedling compost pressed very lightly to make level surface. Water and drain for 2 hours. Sow seed very thinly and dust over with compost. Place in plastic bag or propagator at 55–65°F (13–18°C). Germination takes 7–10 days. Uncover and bring to light (not full sun). Prick off individually into 3in (5cm) pots as soon as big enough to handle. Water very lightly to settle soil around roots. Keep in airy room until all frost is passed. Then plant out.

Tidying: Remove yellowing leaves. Remove dead flowers which may go mouldy.

Varieties: Heavenly Bells, Blue Troll (dwarf), White Troll (dwarf).

Browallia is a tender annual which grows to 12–18in (30–45cm) depending on variety and situation. It branches freely very close to soil level, producing slender stems and light green leaves about 2in (5cm) long. White or blue flowers appear near the top of each branch throughout the season.

Leaves turn bronze, plant windswept with twisted foliage. Strong winds. Protect by moving container or screening with stronger plants.

Puckered growing points, small insects round unopened buds and stem tips. Aphid. Spray with derris following maker's instructions.

Plant and flowers wilt suddenly. Soil too dry. Water immediately, then keep always moist. Spray.

Plant turns black and soggy. Frost damage. No cure. Protect from frost at all times.

Hanging baskets
1. Line wire basket with moss. Make 5 or 6 small holes in sheet of polythene and lay over moss. Add saucer of charcoal.

2. Stand basket on bucket and fill with layer of damp compost.

3. Knock plant from pot and place in centre of basket, arranging trailing stems evenly all round.

4. Fill with compost and firm round roots. Water well, allow to drain, then hang securely.

Stem turns light brown, especially end of shoots, sometimes with fluffy grey mould. Botrytis. Spray with benomyl, repeat after 10 days, then 1 month later. Botrytis attacks when humidity high, starting on decaying flowers or damaged leaves/stems. Remove all dead flowers and leaves.

Blue flowers pale, petals have brown edges. Too strong sunlight. Protect from sun when over 70°F (21°C).

Tiny white flies, especially on underside of leaves, often with scaly deposits. Whitefly. Spray with diluted malathion every 3 days until clear. Scales will hatch daily so kill each new batch of flies as they appear until all scale gone.

Shoots become thinner, paler and lean towards light. Too dark. Move into lighter place; check plant not heavily screened by others.

what goes wrong

Leaves near base of stems turn pale yellow. Plant often dry or needs more feeding. Do not allow to dry out. If kept moist, increase feed to weekly; do not increase strength of feed.

Buds drop off or turn yellow, few flowers open. Waterlogged. Clear drainage holes and allow compost to become nearly dry before watering again.

Plant ceases to develop. Examine compost round roots for tiny, almost transparent grubs, larvae of sciarid or mushroom fly. Drench compost with diluted malathion. Grubs will come to surface and die.

131

Brunfelsia calycina

Yesterday-today-and-tomorrow

When this plant's first flush of flowers has died, a second flowering can sometimes be brought about by lowering the temperature (see below). Plants over two years old flower more profusely than young ones. Propagation is easiest by cuttings. Root them in sand and put in a warm place under a glass bell or clear polythene bag. Pot them up in the usual compost with ¼ part sand added.

Light: Keep shaded from direct sunlight when growing and in flower. Put in direct sunlight after flowering.

Temperature: Maintain 60–70°F (16–21°C) in spring and summer. After first flowering, reduce temperature to 55°F (13°C). This will encourage a second flush of flowers. After second flowering, reduce temperature to about 48°F (9°C) to harden plant, when green shoots will turn woody.

Water: Twice weekly in spring and summer to keep moist. Once every 2 weeks in autumn and winter to allow compost to dry out.

Humidity: Needs high humidity in spring and summer but do not spray once flowers appear. Stand pot on saucer of pebbles almost covered with water, or plant into another container of damp peat to maintain high humidity. In winter, reduce humidity to keep drier.

Feeding: Once in spring with nitrogen-based fertilizer to stop leaves becoming pale. Feed monthly when growing with liquid houseplant food diluted to half maker's recommended strength.

Soil: Equal parts loam-based No. 2 and peat.

Repotting: In autumn as soon as flowering is over, into pots one size larger. Prune lightly following spring.

Cleaning: Spray with soft tepid water only when not in flower, and not in winter. No leafshine.

The plant known as Yesterday-Today-and-Tomorrow flowers late spring and summer, producing an abundance of delicate, scented purple flowers which slowly change colour through to white before they are finished. To keep the plant compact, prune it lightly after the flowers have finished.

Plant grows straggly in spring. Needs pruning. Prune in spring, cutting back stems above a leaf to within 6in (15cm) of pot.

Preparing a cutting

1. Cut off tip of healthy stem including 2 pairs of leaves and growing point. Trim off stem below a leaf.

2. Remove lowest pair of leaves so there is a section of bare stem. When planted, lowest leaf should be just above compost.

3. Keep moist and warm (65–70°F, 18–21°C) for 21 days. Cover with polythene bag to keep humid, removing it for 5 minutes a day.

Foliage grows fast but no flowers appear. Too much feeding. Feed once a month only with liquid houseplant food diluted to half maker's recommended strength.

Webs under leaves. Red spider mite. Remove webs with damp cloth or sponge, then spray with diluted malathion, especially under leaves. Repeat every 14 days until symptoms disappear. Improve humidity by standing on saucer of wet pebbles.

Plant flops in summer. Too wet, waterlogged. Drain away any water from saucer and allow compost surface to dry out before watering again. Check drainage in pot.

Grey mould on leaves and stems, no growth. Too wet in winter. Keep above 45°F (7°C) and allow compost to dry out between waterings.

Leaves pale and limp. In summer, too much light. Move to shaded place, out of direct sunlight. In winter, not enough light. Move to position in very good light – will stand full sun in winter but not in summer.

Leaves pale in spring. Lack of nitrogen. Feed once only with nitrogen-based fertilizer, then monthly with half-strength houseplant food.

Leaves turn black. Leafshine damage. Do not use. Remove damaged leaf.

Flowers turn brown and fall off quickly, leaves fall later. Compost too dry. Plunge pot into bucket of water for 10–15 minutes, then drain. Keep compost constantly moist in summer, watering twice weekly or every day if it dries out in very hot weather. Do not stand in water. Spray daily with soft tepid water, avoiding flowers. If flowers are scorched, too much direct sun. Move into more shady place.

Leaves dry out in summer. Too hot and air too dry. Move to cooler place with more ventilation and stand pot on saucer of wet pebbles to improve humidity. Do not keep above 60–70°F (16–21°C) in summer if possible.

Leaves turn brown and fall off in winter. Too hot. Move to cooler place with more ventilation and spray daily with soft, tepid water. Maximum winter temperature 48°F (9°C).

what goes wrong

133

Angel wings

This is a beautiful but difficult plant belonging to the Arum family. Its leaves, almost paper-thin, are often white in background with veins marked in green, pink or red. They grow from a rhizome started into growth in heat in late winter and by spring are beginning to produce their long-stalked leaves. These continue to appear all summer, dying down again in late autumn. The rhizomes are difficult to keep through the winter and the plants are best treated as annuals. Great care must be taken not to overwater them as they soon rot if the temperature falls.

Light: Full light except midday summer sun needed to keep colour and contrast in the leaves.

Temperature: Between 60–65°F (16–18°C) in summer, maximum 75°F (24°C). Minimum in winter if you are keeping rhizomes 55°F (13°C).

Water: Keep always moist while in leaf, watering 2 or 3 times a week in hot weather. If temperature falls below 60°F (16°C) or leaves stop growing reduce watering. In winter keep dry.

Humidity: Do not spray overhead or leaves may be damaged. If possible stand with other plants as this gives more humidity.

Feeding: Feed every 21 days in growing season using liquid houseplant food at half maker's recommended strength.

Soil: Use 2 parts loam-based No. 2 to 1 part peat.

Repotting: Plant rhizomes in fresh compost after winter and do not disturb again for one year. Cover them with about their own depth of compost.

Cleaning: Light feather dusting only, no spraying, wiping or leafshine.

The Angel wing's leaves may be patterned and veined in white, green or pink. A small lily-like flower grows in summer but the spectacular leaves are the plant's main attraction. Take great care when moving these plants as stems and leaves bend and crack easily.

Overwintering

Stop watering when leaves die down and store in dry soil at 55°F (13°C). Or, remove from pots and keep in dry, dark place. Repot in spring, move to warmer place (65°F, 18°C) and start watering gradually to encourage new growth.

Leaves brown at edges, crisp. Slightly too cold. Move to warmer place, above 60°F (16°C).

Leaves and stems flop, curl up and die. Too cold. Move to warmer place, above 60°F (16°C) out of cold draughts. Leaves die down naturally in autumn.

Poor growth, leaves small. Too dark and/or needs feeding. Move to lighter place (plant takes full light except midday summer sun) and feed every 21 days in growing season with liquid houseplant food at half maker's recommended strength.

Humidity
Caladiums need humidity but spraying may damage leaves. Keep pot in outer pot filled with damp peat. Moisture from peat will rise under the leaves. But make sure drainage in plant pot is good so it does not get waterlogged.

what goes wrong

Leaves poor colour. Too dark. Move into good light, including full sun except at midday in summer.

Leaves dry up and shrivel. Too hot or compost too dry. Check conditions. Water immediately if compost feels dry, keeping always moist while in leaf. Keep below 75°F (24°C).

Leaves and stems distorted and sticky, with green insects. Greenfly. Spray with pyrethrum-based insecticide or diluted malathion. Repeat weekly until clear.

Leaves split and torn. Bad handling. Take great care when moving plant and do not wipe leaves.

Brown marks on middle of leaves. Damage by sunlight or leafshine. Move out of direct midday summer sun. Remove damaged leaf at base of stem.

Mould on stems and rhizomes. Too wet. Allow surface to dry out before watering again and never allow plant to stand in water. Keep above 60°F (16°C); if below this, allow surface to dry out between waterings.

Calathea lancifolia

Prayer plant

This is not the easiest of houseplants to grow, though it is one of the most beautiful. The long, pointed leaves appear to be hand-painted, in delicate shades of green or green and brown. Its common name derives from the fact that the leaves resemble a Moslem prayer mat, or because indoors at night its leaves tend to curl like hands in prayer. Another variety of *Calathea, C. makoyana,* has slightly rounder, beautifully marked leaves. Both originate from South America. In summer, a small white flower grows on a stem but the plant's real beauty lies in its leaves. *Calatheas* are often confused with related and very similar *Marantas*. In general, *Calatheas* are the more upright plants.

The beautifully marked leaves of the Prayer plant grow on long 6in (15cm), stems from the centre of the plant. The upper surface has a very distinctive pattern which shows less clearly on the reddish underside. When buying, make sure that the leaves are clean, undamaged and with distinct colouring.

Leaves curl and close up. Natural at night. If they stay closed in the day, too cold. Move to warmer position, out of draughts.

Light: Prefers being out of direct light. Avoid sun-facing windows in summer.

Temperature: Winter minimum 60°F (16°C). Can take summer temperatures as high as 85°F (29°C), provided humidity is also high.

Water: 2–3 times a week in summer, once a week in winter. Never allow to dry out, though withhold water if temperature drops to 60°F (16°C).

Humidity: Mist daily in summer, twice a week in winter. Stand plant on saucer of pebbles almost covered with water. High humidity essential.

Feeding: Every 14 days when growing, with liquid houseplant food diluted with water. Use half as much food as the maker recommends.

Soil: Peat-based compost. Open, porous mix best.

Repotting: Annually in spring. If plants get too big for the space available, divide them.

Cleaning: If humidity spraying does not keep leaves clean, wipe with damp cloth.

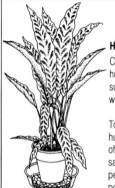

Humidity

Calatheas need high humidity. Spray every day in summer, twice a week in winter.

To provide permanent local humidity, stand pot on saucer of pebbles. Add water to saucer, almost covering pebbles but don't let base of pot touch water.

what goes wrong

Leaves fade, lose colour and look slightly transparent with webs underneath. Red spider mite. Spray with derris, diluted malathion or systemic insecticide every 14 days until clear. Improve humidity.

Leaves turn pale. Too much direct sun. Move out of sun but keep in good light position.

Leaves curl and turn brown at edges. Too cold and dry. Move to warmer position (at least 60°F, 16°C) and water regularly. Remove damaged leaves by cutting stem close to soil level.

Leaves dull with white woolly patches at bases. Mealy bug. Remove with cotton wool dipped in methylated spirits or spray with diluted malathion every 14 days until clear.

Leaves droop, look dull and lifeless with brown, curling edges. Needs watering. Soak in bucket of water for 10–15 minutes, then drain. Keep moist always unless temperature less than 60°F (16°C).

Leaves droop limply. Too hot and dry. Soak in bucket of water for 10–15 minutes, then drain. Spray every day to improve humidity. Move to cooler place if possible.

Plant produces only small leaves which do not grow. Needs feeding. Feed every 14 days in spring and summer.

137

Slipper flower

The Calceolaria is a native of the cool slopes of the Andes Mountains in South America. It needs similar conditions to survive as a houseplant and is therefore the ideal choice for a shady room or a windowsill out of the sun, where few other plants will thrive. Although it is possible to raise them from seed, they are usually sold already growing in a 6in (15cm) pot. Buy them just before they flower, in mid-spring. Flowers should last 2–3 months in cool conditions but may wither in days if kept in dry centrally heated rooms. The soft stems and leaves attract greenfly, particularly when the flower buds first appear. Treat immediately or plant may not flower.

Calceolaria, also called Lady's slipper, Slipper flower and Slipperwort, is a compact plant growing to about 10in (25cm) high. The roughly oval leaves are light sage green and crinkled. The pouch-shaped flowers are bright red, yellow or orange, often spotted with a contrasting colour.

Light: Protect from direct sunlight at all times but give good light from late autumn to early spring. Keep in shade while flowering.

Temperatures: Maximum 50–55°F (10–13°C) for best flowering. Flowers deteriorate rapidly at temperatures over 65°F (18°C).

Water: 2–3 times per week to keep compost moist but not waterlogged. Flowers will collapse if plant gets too dry. Water daily in very hot weather and make sure soil-less compost does not dry out.

Humidity: Does best in fairly dry, well ventilated rooms. Do not spray. If dusty, gently dust leaves and flowers with cotton wool.

Feeding: While flowering feed every 10 days with liquid houseplant food diluted to half recommended strength. In soil-less compost, feed every 5 days.

Soil: Loam-based No.3 potting compost or soil-less.

Sooty deposit on foliage. Excreta of whitefly, which will be seen on underside of leaves. Spray with pyrethrum-based insecticide or diluted malathion every 3 days until no more adult flies are seen.

Blotchy yellow marks on leaves in autumn. Calceolaria yellows, caused by poor light. Occurs when plant is dying back after flowering.

Small, round, yellow spots on leaves. Leaf hopper. Spray once with pyrethrum-based insecticide or diluted malathion.

Plant wilts, leaves have papery edges. Root rot, probably contracted from fungus in soil. No cure. Discard plant to avoid fungus spreading to other plants.

Fluffy grey mould on plant. Botrytis. Possible causes are watering into centre or heavy condensation settling on plant. Spray with benomyl twice in 10 days. Prevent by watering carefully into soil and keeping plant in a well ventilated room.

Support
1. When in full bloom, the plant is top heavy and may fall to one side.

2. In late winter, before flowers appear, insert 4 small sticks around edge of pot. Later growth will hide them and the plant will be held upright.

Leaves greyish, small buds and flowers. Needs feeding. Give dilute liquid houseplant food every 10 days while plant is in bloom. If in soil-less, feed every 5 days.

Leaves pale and soft, leaf stalks tall and straggly. Too dark. Move to a light situation but protect from direct sunlight.

Distorted growing points, especially at flower buds. Greenfly. Spray with pyrethrum-based insecticide. Repeat in 10 days. Weekly preventative spraying recommended as Calceolaria very susceptible to greenfly.

Brown marks on flowers. Sun scorch, likely if plant is too dry. Soak pot in water, and avoid drying out in future. Brown marks may also be caused if flowers are sprayed. Avoid spraying.

what goes wrong

Flowers turn brown and deteriorate, leaves yellowing, plant wilts. Too hot and dry. Keep in a cool, shady spot. Maximum temperature 65°F (18°C). Plant may be saved by moving to a cooler place.

White powdery film on stems or leaves. Powdery mildew. Spray with fungicide containing zineb. Spray again in 10 days if necessary.

Foliage distorted with pale streaks. Virus disease. No cure. Destroy plant as insects may transmit disease to other plants.

Leaves limp, dark and soggy. Compost dark and sour-looking. Waterlogged, due to overwatering or poor drainage. Stop watering until compost is nearly dry and ensure that drainage hole is clear.

Calendula officinalis

Pot marigold

Pot marigolds are hardy annuals which need full sun and grow quickly. The flowers have a strong scent and last well for more than a week when cut. Double at first, they become smaller and single as the season progresses. Seeds can be sown successively through the early summer, making this a useful plant for filling in any gaps caused by losses in other varieties. They self-sow very easily and may become a nuisance for this reason. To prevent unwanted plants, remove dead flower heads before the seeds form.

Light: Maximum possible.
Temperature: Germinate outdoors at 45°F (7°C), indoors 50°F (10°C). If higher, need very good light. Will stand frost.
Water: Moist, not wet. Will survive quite dry conditions once germinated.
Humidity: Keep dry. Do not spray or water mature plants overhead.
Soil: Will survive poor soil; loam-based No. 1 good.
Feeding: Begin 3 weeks after planting, then every 10 days diluting as maker recommends.
Propagation: Sow outdoors direct into prepared container from mid-spring to early summer. Place seeds ⅜ (9mm) below surface, 4in (10cm) apart and thin to 12in (30cm) apart. For early flowers, sow indoors in prepared seed tray, at 50°F (10°C). Germination takes 3 days. Prick off after 1 week and keep cool (45°F, 7°C) and light. Plant out when 3–4in (7–10cm) high, 4 to a 12in (30cm) container.
Tidying: Remove dead flowers to prevent self-seeding.
Varieties: Radar, deep orange, double with rolled petals (18in, 45cm). Fiesta Gitana, early, good for windowboxes (12in, 30cm). Orange King (12in, 30cm).

Pot marigolds grow to about 18in (45cm) high and have a woody stem with several shoots appearing from near the base. Flower buds come one at a time and may have double, or single petals in primrose, yellow or deep orange. The seeds ripen early and will produce new plants the same year.

Swellings on stem and flower stem. Crown gall caused by infected soil splashing on stems. Will not seriously affect flowering. Stand plants hardening off in clean area, not near rubbish.

Leaves have round, dark spots, turning sooty. Smut fungus. Spores will spread. Spray with bordeaux mixture every 14 days.

Leaves and stems covered with white powdery deposit. Powdery mildew. Spray with dinocap or benomyl every 10 days. Plant very susceptible.

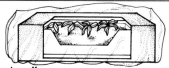

Hardening off

Young plants sown indoors need protecting when first put outside. Place trays close to wall for extra warmth and cover with cardboard box and plastic sheet for first few nights. After 1 week leave uncovered unless weather very bad. Frost will not harm them. Plant in final container after about 10 days.

Removing flowers

Remove seed head as soon as flowers die. Cut off cleanly at top of stalk. If left on, seeds will sow themselves around plant, flowering the same year.

Flower stems long and droopy, flower buds may not open. Too dark. Move into very good light – needs full sun.

Tips of leaves turn black. Overfeeding or too concentrated feed. Never exceed recommended strength.

Plant yellow and sickly, soil surface scummy. Waterlogged. Check drainage in container. Plant prefers dry soil to wet.

Leaves chewed, flower buds have holes. Caterpillar damage. Pick off pests and dust with derris. If petals have holes and ragged edges, earwigs. Dust with gamma-BHC.

Leaves droop and lie limply along stems. Too dry. Will stand all but completely dried out soil. Give container thorough soak so soil is wet right to bottom; then drain to moist before watering again.

what goes wrong

Leaves grey green, stems very woody, flowers small. Needs feeding. Feed every 10 days.

Pinpoint holes in leaves of young plants. Flea beetle. Dust very lightly with gamma-BHC. Avoid edible plants.

141

Callistephus chinensis

China aster

This beautiful flower can be grown indoors either as a pot plant or for a long-lasting cut flower, providing the right variety is selected. The dwarf 'Pinocchio' is best for pots and the medium-sized 'Milady' is good for both pots and cutting. Its main requirements are plenty of sunshine (though it will stand shade for part of the day), a fairly rich soil and a constant supply of moisture. Outdoors it will survive light frosts and indoors needs a cool, airy position: a conservatory or light porch would be ideal. It has an unfortunate susceptibility to wilt disease but if grown in sterilized loam or soil-less compost this should not be a problem indoors.

Light: Good light at all times, with full sun for most of day if possible.
Temperature: Germinate seed at 55–60°F (13–16°C). Once potted up, plants do best at a maximum of 60°F (15°C).
Water: Keep compost barely moist during germination and for seedlings. Young plants should be watered twice a week. Copious water needed during bud stage and flowering.
Humidity: Cool, airy situation is best. In hot weather (over 70°F, 21°C), spray early or late in the day.
Feeding: Begin feeding 3 weeks after potting up, using diluted liquid feed at maker's recommended strength. Feed weekly until flowering is finished.
Soil: Proprietary seed compost for germination. Pot into loam-based No.2 compost or soil-less potting compost. Always use sterile compost, not garden soil.
After flowering: Flowers can be cut for vases, but plants will not flower again. Discard after flowering is finished.

There are many varieties of China aster, all producing delicate summer or autumn flowers in shades of pink, purple, blue, red or white. For pots or containers, choose varieties marked 'dwarf', which grow 6–12in (15–30cm) high. To produce a small number of large flowers, pinch out all but one bud on each stem.

Grey mould on stems and buds. Botrytis. Plant particularly susceptible if damaged, as when flowers are cut. Spray with benomyl and keep room well ventilated.

what goes wrong

Leaves curl under and become twisted. Plum aphid. Usually affects plants grown outdoors, but can infest pot plants. Tiny insects can be seen on underside of leaves. Spray with systemic insecticide.

Plant yellows from base, dark streaks present. Leaves droopy. Aster wilt. No cure, destroy plant. Choose varieties marked WR (wilt resistant). If leaves turn yellow with dark veining, roots may be rotted due to waterlogging. Maintain good drainage.

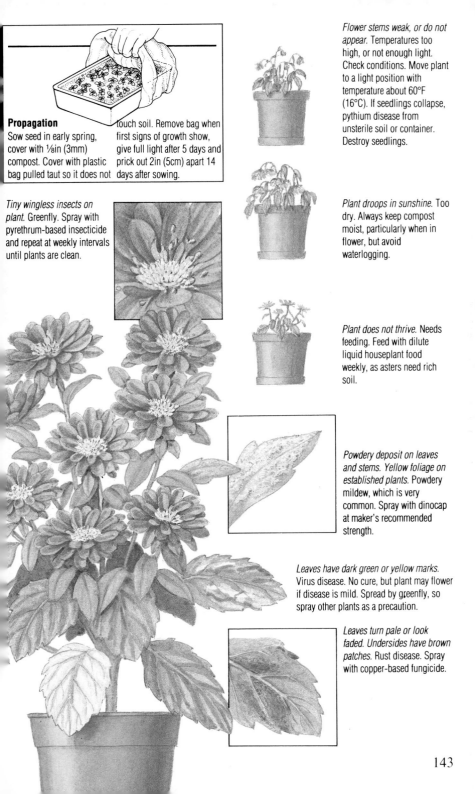

Propagation
Sow seed in early spring, cover with ⅛in (3mm) compost. Cover with plastic bag pulled taut so it does not touch soil. Remove bag when first signs of growth show, give full light after 5 days and prick out 2in (5cm) apart 14 days after sowing.

Flower stems weak, or do not appear. Temperatures too high, or not enough light. Check conditions. Move plant to a light position with temperature about 60°F (16°C). If seedlings collapse, pythium disease from unsterile soil or container. Destroy seedlings.

Tiny wingless insects on plant. Greenfly. Spray with pyrethrum-based insecticide and repeat at weekly intervals until plants are clean.

Plant droops in sunshine. Too dry. Always keep compost moist, particularly when in flower, but avoid waterlogging.

Plant does not thrive. Needs feeding. Feed with dilute liquid houseplant food weekly, as asters need rich soil.

Powdery deposit on leaves and stems. Yellow foliage on established plants. Powdery mildew, which is very common. Spray with dinocap at maker's recommended strength.

Leaves have dark green or yellow marks. Virus disease. No cure, but plant may flower if disease is mild. Spread by greenfly, so spray other plants as a precaution.

Leaves turn pale or look faded. Undersides have brown patches. Rust disease. Spray with copper-based fungicide.

143

Camellia japonica

Tea plant

These small evergreen shrubs produce strikingly uniform flowers in various strong colours, set against lush dark green leaves. They require good light to ensure flower buds form plentifully but dislike a hot, dry centrally heated atmosphere. In a cooler room, porch or conservatory where they can be kept at the right temperature and humidity, they will flourish.

Light: Full light, but plant should be kept out of bright midday sun.
Temperature: 65-70°F (18-21°C) in spring and summer to keep plant warm when growing. 55°F (13°C) in autumn and winter until flowers open, when temperature should be increased to 60°F (16°C).
Water: Twice weekly in spring to keep compost moist but plant must not stand in water. Weekly or less in summer only when compost surface dries out. Increase to twice weekly from autumn on, with good drainage in pot. Always use softened lime-free or rainwater.
Humidity: Spray weekly with soft tepid water all year except when in flower.
Feeding: Once in early spring with sequestered iron, then every 14 days all spring and summer with liquid houseplant food diluted to maker's instructions.
Soil: Ericaceous peat mixture (acid) or equal quantities brown fibrous peat, well decayed leaf soil and sand.
Repotting: Once every 2 years in early autumn, immediately after new growth has taken place, but before buds are fully formed. Put plenty of crocks in bottom of pot.
Cleaning: Spray with soft, tepid water weekly for cleaning and humidity except when in flower. Use leafshine every 4 weeks if necessary, being careful to avoid flowers and buds.

Camellias have attractive evergreen leaves and produce buds in winter for early spring flowering. The flowers are usually symmetrical and of striking colours including red, pink, and white.

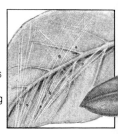

Webs under leaves. Red spider mite. Remove webs with damp cloth or sponge, then spray with diluted malathion, especially under leaves. Repeat every 14 days until symptoms disappear. Improve humidity by standing pot on saucer of pebbles almost covered in water and spray with water regularly.

what goes wrong

Leaves dusty. Needs cleaning. Use leafshine not more than once a month. Avoid flowers when spraying water or leafshine.

Leaves fall in winter. Some leaves drop naturally, part of plant's normal development.

144

Plant grows throughout winter. If this happens, no flower buds will appear. Too hot, air too dry. Keep at maximum 55°F (13°C) in winter, with humid atmosphere. Spray every week with soft tepid water and stand pot on wet pebbles.

Humidity

Spray every week all year round with soft, tepid water. Protect flowers. For extra humidity, stand pot on saucer of pebbles. Add water to almost cover pebbles but do not let base of pot touch the water or the roots will become waterlogged.

Leaves small, no flower buds appear. Needs feeding. Feed with houseplant food diluted to maker's recommended strength every 14 days in growing season, spring and summer.

Leaves turn pale green. Lime damage. Use only soft water to water and spray plant. Feed immediately with sequestered iron. Use lime-free (ericaceous) compost when repotting.

Flowers turn translucent. Leafshine damage. Protect flowers from leafshine when spraying.

Discs on leaves. Scale insect, common in camellias. Spray underside of leaves with diluted malathion and, after 48 hours, remove discs with thumbnail. Repeat every week for 4 weeks until clear.

Leaves dry out. Damage by sunlight. Move into an area of diffused daylight, out of harmful rays of sun. Remove damaged leaf.

Leaves droop and turn yellow. Too wet, waterlogged. In spring, autumn and winter keep moist but well drained. Do not stand in water. In summer allow surface of compost to dry out between waterings until buds have fully formed; once a week is probably enough to keep it correct.

Buds fall off without opening. Lime damage. Feed immediately with sequestered iron and use only soft water for watering and spraying plant. Use lime-free compost when repotting.

Compost dries out and will not absorb water. Rootball very compact. Too dry, plunge pot into bucket of water for 10-15 minutes, then drain. Keep compost constantly moist in spring, autumn and winter, watering at least twice a week. In summer allow surface to dry out between waterings, until buds are fully formed.

145

Campanula isophylla

Bell flower

The Bell flower grows well as a trailing plant in a hanging basket or in an ordinary pot provided it has plenty of light and does not become too hot in summer. White, blue or mauve flowering varieties are available, the white being known as 'Star of Bethlehem'. The plant should flower throughout summer provided it is well fed during its growing season and flowers are removed as they die. In spring, plants should be cut back almost to the compost to encourage healthy new growth. Every 2 years they can then be divided.

Light: Full indirect light essential. Can take some full sun, though will dry out quickly. Keep out of very sunny windows.

Temperature: Winter minimum 43°F (7°C); best kept below 60°F (15°C) in summer, with a cooler winter rest period. Will live outside in summer but should be brought indoors in autumn.

Water: Daily in summer if on a light windowsill, to keep damp. Keep soil just moist in winter, watering every 7–10 days depending on temperature. Likes lime in tap water.

Humidity: Spray weekly in summer unless in flower. If temperature above 60°F (15°C) provide extra humidity by standing pot on saucer of pebbles almost covered in water. Pot base must not touch water.

Feeding: Every 14 days in spring and summer with houseplant food diluted according to maker's instructions. Alkaline fertilizer sticks best if available.

Soil: Loam-based No. 1 compost.

Repotting: Keep in 5in (13cm) pots and renew top inch (2½cm) soil in spring. Every 2 years, divide by removing from pot and pulling roots gently into two equal parts. Repot in clean 5in (13cm) pots with fresh compost.

Cleaning: Humidity spraying sufficient. No leafshine.

The Bell flower will produce blooms for several weeks during the summer as long as dead flowers are removed regularly. They are available in white, blue or mauve and are usually sold in flower. Choose plants with vigorous stems and plenty of new buds among the flowers.

Leaves dry, shrivel and turn yellow. Flowers die. Too dry, needs watering. Water daily in spring and summer. In winter keep soil just damp. Spray leaves weekly.

Pruning

1. Cut back straggly, woody plants in early spring, just before they are starting to grow.

2. Cut above the first pair of leaves from compost, just above the leaf joint.

3. To make an upright, bushy plant, pinch out the tips from the main stems as they grow.

Stems grow lanky with long spaces between leaves and no flowers. Too hot and stuffy. Move to cooler room (below 60°F, 15°C) if possible, with better air circulation.

Leaves die off and no new ones appear in spring and summer. Too cold or needs feeding. Check temperature is between 50 and 60°F (10–15°C). Feed fortnightly in spring and summer.

Leaves and stems rot at base of plant. Waterlogged. Check not standing in water and that drainage holes in pot are clear. Allow to dry out before watering again.

Brown marks on leaves. Leafshine damage. Do not use. Clean with fine spray of water.

Rusty marks on flowers. Caused by spraying water on them. Spray leaves only.

Leaves turn black. If left outside on windowsill or balcony, frost damage. Bring indoors. Will not survive temperatures under 43°F 7°C).

Flowers rot while in bud. Too wet and too cold. Move to warmer place (between 50–60°F, 10–15°C) and allow to dry out completely before watering again. Do not spray buds.

Leaves turn yellow. Too dark, needs more daylight. Move to lighter place with some sun (not hot mid-day). Check feeding is regular in spring and summer, using fertilizer spikes if possible.

Leaves turn yellow and fall, webs underneath. Red spider mite. Spray with derris or pyrethrum or with a systemic insecticide every 14 days until clear. Do not spray flowers. Put pot on damp pebbles to improve humidity.

what goes wrong

147

Capsicum annuum

Ornamental chilli pepper

This plant belongs to the same family of peppers which produces, when the fruits are dried, cayenne pepper and paprika. The oval fruits are edible. They can be allowed to hang on the plant for about two weeks once they are ripe. The flowers are white, with an occasional greenish tinge, and are insignificant compared with the fruit, which starts life yellow and ripens into bright red. Ornamental chilli peppers will grow in a temperature as low as 50°F (10°C) and are therefore well suited to a house without central heating.

Light: Full light, including sunlight.
Temperature: Between 50°F (10°C) and 70°F (21°C) all year round.
Water: Daily in spring and summer, but pot should not stand in water. When flowers have set and fruit is forming reduce watering to once a week.
Humidity: Spray daily with soft, tepid water. (This also helps to control red spider.) After flowering, spray twice weekly until fruit begins to form.
Feeding: Weekly with liquid houseplant food diluted to maker's instructions from spring and summer until fruit forms, then do not feed again until following season.
Soil: Loam-based No.1.
Repotting: In early spring into pot of maximum 5in (13cm) size. Plant produces more flowers and fruit if roots are slightly crowded in pot. Put plenty of broken crocks in bottom of pot: good drainage is essential.
Cleaning: Humidity spraying sufficient. No leafshine.

Ornamental chilli peppers are grown principally for the autumn colour of their fruit which ripens from yellow to a bright red. The small white flowers appear in early summer. The fruits can be eaten but are very hot.

Spraying
Regular spraying with soft tepid water provides humidity, helps to control red spider mite and helps the fruit to set. After flowering spray twice weekly until fruit forms.

Leaves grow lush but no flowers appear. Pot too large. Plant flowers better when slightly pot bound. Do not repot for two years.

Leaves pale, no fruit or flowers. Needs feeding. Feed with liquid houseplant food every 7 days in spring and summer until fruit has formed.

148

Plant does not grow. Too cold. Move to warmer place and do not allow temperature to fall below 50°F (10°C).

what goes wrong

Stems grow long and lanky. Too hot. Move to a cooler place with more ventilation. Spray daily with soft, tepid water. Maximum temperature 70°F (21°C). Prune in spring, cutting back stems to within 2in (5cm) of pot.

New leaves distorted and sticky with green insects. Greenfly. Spray with pyrethrum-based insecticide or diluted malathion. Repeat one week later, then every week until clear.

Fruit does not turn from yellow to red. Too dark. Move to position in very good light. Plant will stand direct sunshine but make sure compost does not dry out when in full sun.

Leaves yellow with webs underneath. Red spider mite. Remove webs with damp cloth or sponge, then spray with diluted malathion, especially under leaves. Repeat every 14 days until symptoms disappear. Improve humidity by standing pot on saucer of wet pebbles, and spraying regularly with soft, tepid water.

All leaves turn yellow and drop. Too hot or plant waterlogged, standing in water. Check conditions. Move to place with good ventilation and temperature not more than 70°F (21°C). If compost heavy and damp, drain away any water from saucer and allow surface to dry out before watering again. Always throw away excess that drains through after watering.

Leaves turn black. Too cold or leafshine damage. Move to position where temperature at least 50°F (10°C). Do not use leafshine: clean by spraying with water.

Leaves turn yellow. Compost too dry. Water immediately, then water daily to keep compost moist in spring and summer. After fruit has set in winter water less often, only once a week.

Flies hopping around plant. Whitefly. Spray weekly until clear with pyrethrum-based insecticide or diluted malathion.

Leaves wilt and drop. Too dark. Move to position in good light. Plant will stand full sunlight.

149

Caralluma frerei

Carallumas come from many desert areas and have low, angular stems, often with unpleasant-smelling flowers. *Caralluma frerei* is unusual in not having flowers with this kind of smell and also in having thick leaves growing from its sprawling stem. It grows to around 2in (5cm) tall and spreads 6–8in (15–20cm) across, comes from India, and was known for a long time as *Frerea indica*. No Carallumas should be overwatered — this is the commonest cause of loss — and they need a very sunny spot for best results, particularly for flower production. Other species seen are *Caralluma hesperidum*, with almost black flowers, *C. europaea* with brown and yellow flowers, *C. dummeri* with green flowers and *C. mammillaris* with red-brown flowers.

Caralluma carnosa's thick, green succulent stems are deeply indented and, unlike those of *Caralluma frerei* (right) do not produce leaves. The flowers are pollinated by flies and are known as carrion flowers because they are said to look (and smell) like bad meat.

Light: Full sunshine all the year round.
Temperature: A minimum of at least 50°F (10°C) in winter to prevent leaves from falling, better at 55°F (13°C). Give fresh air in summer.
Water: If at 55°F (13°C) or over in winter, water monthly, to prevent leaves falling; if lower, keep dry. Water once thoroughly in spring, and after about a month start watering once a fortnight, weekly in hottest months. Tail off in autumn. See also Introduction.
Feeding: Use a high potash fertilizer once a month in summer only.
Soil: Use good loam-based No. 2 potting compost, or soil-less compost, with about 40% coarse, gritty sand.
Repotting: Every spring into larger half-pot or pan, until 7in (18cm) is reached, when plant can be repotted in same size, or broken up and started again from cuttings.
Propagation: Grows easily from cuttings.

Plant does not grow, small black flies around plant and soil surface. Sciara or mushroom fly. Roots have probably rotted. Remove from pot and pare away stem until no trace of larvae or brown rot is left in stem tissue. Dust with hormone rooting powder and leave to dry for a few days, then lay on dry soil to reroot. If stem completely rotted and tiny white larvae with dark heads are found, dispose of plant and soil.

Leaves turn brownish black and fall off, stems soft and shrivelled. Too cold and wet. Overwatering has rotted roots. Check if still rooted by lifting stems gently off soil; they will come away in your hand if roots have rotted. Treat roots (see Introduction). In future water more carefully and keep at least 55°F (13°C) in winter.

Plant shows little sign of growth. Needs feeding. If fed regularly, check roots. White woolly patches on roots are root mealy bug. Wash all soil off roots, swirl in contact insecticide, and allow to dry before repotting. Leave dry for 2 weeks.

Stems grow straggly, leaves pale at tips. No flowers in summer. Too dark. Needs full light all the year round so keep in sunniest possible place.

Scorch marks on leaves. Sunscorch. Do not allow leaves to touch glass. Keep in airy place during hot weather as scorching more likely to occur if in stuffy, badly ventilated place.

what goes wrong

Taking cuttings
1. Take cuttings in spring with sharp knife, cutting off 2–3in (5–8cm) stem tip which includes 3–4 healthy leaves. Remove lowest leaf if no bare stem below it on cutting.

2. Dust base of cutting and cut end of stem with hormone rooting powder to prevent infection and leave cutting to dry for 2 days.

3. Prepare small pot and lay stem flat on surface of dry compost. Do not water until roots appear. May take 4–6 weeks.

White woolly patches appear among leaves. Mealy bug. Remove with small paintbrush dipped in methylated spirits, and spray with insecticide. Repeat 2 or 3 times in growing season.

Leaves shrivel and fall, stem still firm. Too hot and dry in summer or too cold and dry in winter. If too dry in summer, soak in bowl, and in future give more water each time, but allow to dry out between waterings. Keep in more airy place. In winter, keep at 55°F (13°C) and water once a month.

Celosia plumosa

Coxcomb

There are two kinds of this attractive flowering pot plant. *Celosia plumosa* produces bright, feathery plume-like flowers; *C. cristata* has dense, flat, velvety heads of flowers in a variety of colours. Both are natives of tropical Asia and need the same conditions. Unfortunately they are very susceptible to red spider mite. Check that the plant is clear before buying and spray daily with clean water to help prevent attack. They can be either bought in flower or raised from seed sown in early spring. Germinate seed at 75°F (24°C) and move into full light as soon as growth starts. To avoid disease, keep them warm, in very good light in a light porch, on a sunny windowsill or in a conservatory and they will quickly reach flowering size. *Plumosa* can be put outside from early summer but cold winds quickly make it lose its sparkle.

Light: Full light at all times. Shade from midday sun in very hot weather.
Temperature: Minimum 55°F (13°C) for best flowers, although they will tolerate up to 70°F (21°C). Flowers last longer at cooler temperature.
Water: Copious water while plant is in flower, so water daily if necessary in hot weather. Make sure drainage is good.
Humidity: Spray lightly every day. Keep in a well ventilated room.
Feeding: Every 5 days with liquid houseplant food diluted to maker's recommended strength.
Soil: For taller *plumosas*, two-thirds soilless with one-third loam-based No.2 for stability. For *cristata*, soil-less.
After flowering: These are annuals and will not flower a second time. Discard when flowers die in late autumn.

Celosia plumosa grows to a height of about 24in (60cm) and produces a dramatic display of feathery yellow, red or orange flowers in summer and autumn. The smaller Celosia cristata only reaches about 12in (30cm) and has a curiously shaped flower, said to resemble the cock's comb. Both have pale green, pointed leaves, often with a rib of the same colour as the flowers.

Grey mould on leaves, flower stem soft. Botrytis. Plants in poorly ventilated room most susceptible. Increase ventilation and water soil with benomyl.

Pinpoint spots on leaves, fine webs underneath. Red spider mite. Spray with pyrethrum-based insecticide every 14 days until clear. Regular syringing with clean water will help prevent attacks.

Leaf edges turn brown. Too hot. Keep at maximum 70°F (21°C) and protect from midday sun.

what goes wrong

Flowers lose colour and look bleached. Sun too strong. Plant needs full light but must be protected from strong sunlight, especially in very hot weather.

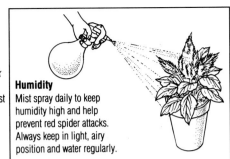

Humidity
Mist spray daily to keep humidity high and help prevent red spider attacks. Always keep in light, airy position and water regularly.

Plume pale, loose and floppy. Much too dark. Move to a spot which gets maximum light but is protected from midday sun.

Small wingless insects on any part of plant. Greenfly. Spray with pyrethrum-based insecticide every 14 days until clear. May be difficult to destroy insects established in flower plume.

Plumes lose colour, leaves yellowing. Too dry. *Plumosa* must be moist at all times while plant is in flower. However, *cristata* has a less vigorous root system and may show these symptoms if overwatered or if soil becomes waterlogged.

Tips of leaves pale yellow or brown. Trace element lacking. Feed every 5 days with a liquid plant food which contains trace elements.

Leaves greyish and small. Needs feeding. Feed every 5 days at maker's recommended strength. If leaves darker, too cold, perhaps frosted. Keep over 55°F (13°C).

Black marks at base of stem. Phytophthora, caused by waterlogging or contracted from contaminated soil or water. Avoid overwatering, check drainage. Always use sterile potting compost and clean water. Badly affected plants will not recover.

153

Ceropegia woodii

This is a tuberous rooted plant with hanging stems and heart-shaped leaves, with marks like marbling. The tiny pink and black flowers are like miniature lanterns. It makes a good plant for indoors in a hanging pot. The stems will grow to around 2ft (50–60cm) although they can grow to 8 or 9ft (2½–3m). Most other species make twining stems which need support, although a few are rigid and stick like. All bear flowers of similar structure, but differing in innumerable ways. Other species include *C. stapelii-formis*, with mottled, brown, lizard-like stems, *C. ampliata* with green and white 3in (8cm) long flowers, *C. sandersoniae*, with mottled green and white parachute-like flowers, *C. radicans* with tri-coloured flowers and many others of all shapes, colours and sizes.

Ceropegia woodii, the Rosary vine has round greyish green leaves on stems that trail prettily from a hanging basket. Other Ceropegias can be trained round a hoop or trellis and all produce similar tube-shaped flowers.

Light: The thick tuberous root of this plant prefers to be in shade, while the stems, leaves and flowers prefer to be in full light.

Temperature: Keep a minimum of 40°F (4°C) for safety. Give fresh air in summer.

Water: Water in spring and summer, once a week in hottest months, fortnightly at other times, tail off in autumn, and leave dry in winter.

Feeding: Use high potash fertilizer once a month in spring and summer.

Soil: Use good loam-based No. 2 potting compost, or soil-less compost, with 30% coarse, gritty sand.

Repotting: Every spring in size larger pot, until 6in (15cm) pot is reached, when soil can be shaken off and plant repotted in same size pot unless tuber has grown too large.

Propagation: By layering stem so that new tuber forms where stem touches soil.

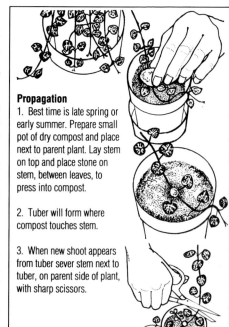

Propagation

1. Best time is late spring or early summer. Prepare small pot of dry compost and place next to parent plant. Lay stem on top and place stone on stem, between leaves, to press into compost.

2. Tuber will form where compost touches stem.

3. When new shoot appears from tuber sever stem next to tuber, on parent side of plant, with sharp scissors.

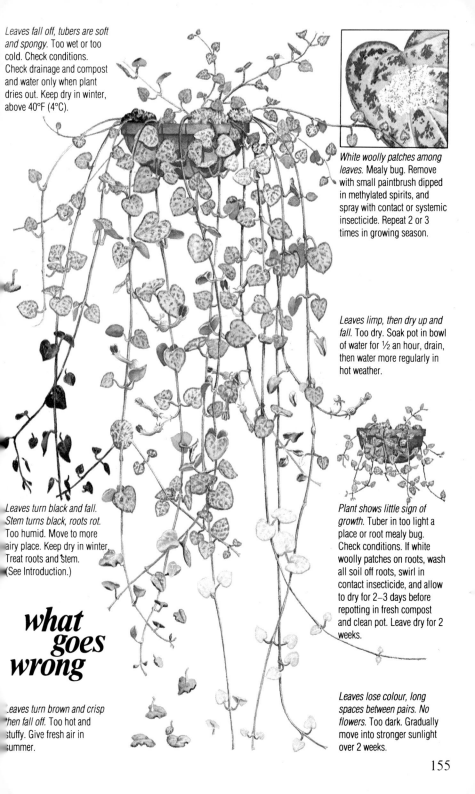

Leaves fall off, tubers are soft and spongy. Too wet or too cold. Check conditions. Check drainage and compost and water only when plant dries out. Keep dry in winter, above 40°F (4°C).

White woolly patches among leaves. Mealy bug. Remove with small paintbrush dipped in methylated spirits, and spray with contact or systemic insecticide. Repeat 2 or 3 times in growing season.

Leaves limp, then dry up and fall. Too dry. Soak pot in bowl of water for ½ an hour, drain, then water more regularly in hot weather.

Leaves turn black and fall. Stem turns black, roots rot. Too humid. Move to more airy place. Keep dry in winter. Treat roots and stem. (See Introduction.)

Plant shows little sign of growth. Tuber in too light a place or root mealy bug. Check conditions. If white woolly patches on roots, wash all soil off roots, swirl in contact insecticide, and allow to dry for 2–3 days before repotting in fresh compost and clean pot. Leave dry for 2 weeks.

what goes wrong

Leaves turn brown and crisp then fall off. Too hot and stuffy. Give fresh air in summer.

Leaves lose colour, long spaces between pairs. No flowers. Too dark. Gradually move into stronger sunlight over 2 weeks.

155

Chamaecereus

This name will survive for some time although most authorities acknowledge that the one species, *Chamaecereus sylvestrii* (p.157) is in fact an unusually shaped Lobivia (see p.364). It is often called the Peanut cactus because its stems look rather like unshelled peanuts. The stems grow to finger length, branching out as they grow. The new stems are only lightly attached and easily break off. The bright, vermilion red flowers appear all over the cactus in spring and summer. It comes from northern Argentina and is tolerant of low temperatures if dry. Of equal, perhaps more interest, are hybrids between *C. sylvestrii* and larger-flowered, more globular Lobivias. These, called 'Chamaelobivias' are like thick-stemmed versions of *C. sylvestrii* but with larger, differently coloured flowers.

Chamaelobivia 'Satsuma' has bright orange-yellow flowers opening from wool-covered buds. Chamaelobivia hybrids have thicker stems than the pure Chamaecereus cactus and are obtainable in a range of different colours.

Light: A sunny windowsill or greenhouse will ensure flowers and sturdy growth.

Temperature: For safety no lower than 40°F (4°C) though they can survive colder if quite dry; keep below 100°F (38°C) in summer and give fresh air.

Water: Keep dry in winter, water once a week in the summer, and about once a fortnight in the spring and autumn.

Feeding: Feed 2 or 3 times in the growing season (spring and summer) with high potash fertilizer (as used for tomatoes). Too much fertilizer makes them grow larger but produce fewer flowers.

Soil: Use an open, gritty soil, with 1 part coarse, gritty sand (not builders' or seashore) to 2 parts loam-based No. 2 potting compost or soil-less compost.

Repotting: This is difficult without the plant breaking up, as the stems are lightly attached to each other; the hybrids have a stronger connection. Repot every year for

Chamaelobivia 'Shot Scarlet' is one of the best hybrids, making thick, compact stems with deep crimson flowers flushed with purple. It is a hybrid between *C. sylvestrii* and *Lobivia backebergiana.*

Taking cuttings
Cuttings taken after
flowering root easily. Cut
whole stem where it grows
from plant, dust with
hormone rooting powder
containing fungicide and
leave to dry for at least 2
days before planting on
fresh compost.

the first 4 years into next size half-pot or
pan, then every other year will be enough.
Broken stems will root easily to make new
plants.

Cleaning and pest control: Spray with water
if dusty and add insecticide to the spray 2 or
3 times a year during the growing season;
these plants are especially susceptible to
damage by red spider mite.

Other species: *C. sylvestrii* is the only true
species, but some of the hybrids on the
market are well worthwhile. Many are
merely larger, red-flowering forms, but
some good colour breaks have been
produced, with yellow, purple-red, pale
orange and varying shades of crimson:
Chamaelobivia 'Kent Sunrise' has yellow
flowers with pink outer petals; *C.* 'Shot
Scarlet' has deep crimson flowers flushed
purple; *C.* 'Satsuma' is orange and
C. 'Pegler' has purple flowers.

Chamaecereus sylvestrii
produces bright red flowers
in spring and summer, each
lasting four to five days. A
healthy plant should have
short, sturdy stems with
good spines. If stems are
long and floppy or pale rather
than mid-green to brownish
red, they need more light.

Dwarf conifers

Trees in this family vary in height from 24in (60cm) after 10 years growth to 200ft (60m), so it is important to choose the right form for your container. Windowboxes need very dwarf trees. However, a very young dwarf tree will take many years to make a good display and a larger one is costly. Buy a medium-growing species and move it when it gets too big. There is a wide choice suitable for patios and balconies. Conifers should not be pruned. Best time to plant is early to mid-autumn and early to mid-spring. Young trees can be obtained either pot grown or dug from a nursery. Choose healthy, vigorous plants with no brown foliage. Always plant new trees at the same depth as at the nursery, using soil line around trunk as a guide. Deeper planting encourages root disease.

These decorative trees have layers of branches growing out almost horizontally from the stem and small, compressed leaves in various shades of green, some almost blue, others yellow. Small round cones bear the seeds. Make sure you buy the right sized plant for your container.

Light: Good, but shade tolerated.
Temperature: They stand most weathers but may get brown patches from frost.
Water: Do not leave dry or plant in dry area. Foliage will turn brown.
Humidity: Spray with hosepipe or watering can in hot dry spells or long windy periods in spring and autumn.
Soil: Loam-based No.2 best.
Feeding: Every 14 days at maker's recommended strength.
Propagation: By cuttings (see right). Seed is difficult to buy and takes a long time.
Tidying: Unnecessary. Do not prune.
Varieties: Windowboxes; Obtusa nana, Minima aurea, Pisefera nana. Patios, balconies: Lawson fletcheri, Elwoods Gold, Pisefera Boulevard, Filefera aurea. These make 3–5ft (1.6m) trees after several years. There are many others.

Cuttings

1. Cuttings can be taken at any time. Choose branch about 4in (10cm) long and cut cleanly. Trim end and dip in hormone rooting powder.

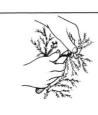

2. Prepare 3in (9cm) pot with seedling compost and insert branch about 1½in (4cm) into compost. Firm compost round base.

3. Water well and place in sealed plastic bag. Remove cover after 3 weeks.

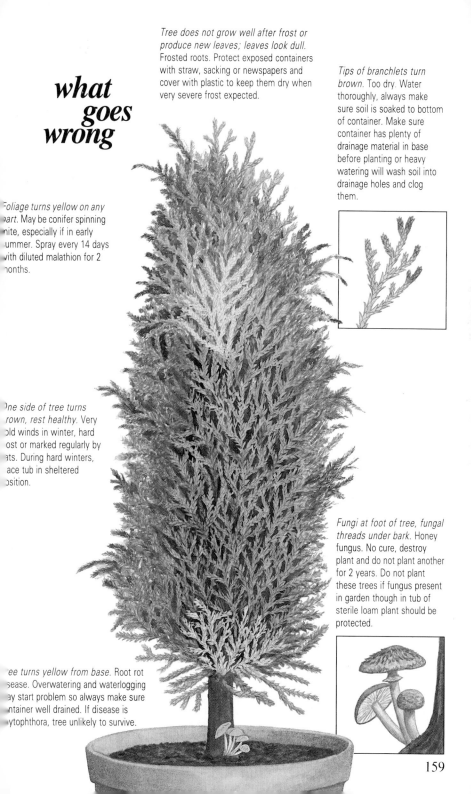

what goes wrong

Tree does not grow well after frost or produce new leaves; leaves look dull. Frosted roots. Protect exposed containers with straw, sacking or newspapers and cover with plastic to keep them dry when very severe frost expected.

Tips of branchlets turn brown. Too dry. Water thoroughly, always make sure soil is soaked to bottom of container. Make sure container has plenty of drainage material in base before planting or heavy watering will wash soil into drainage holes and clog them.

Foliage turns yellow on any part. May be conifer spinning mite, especially if in early summer. Spray every 14 days with diluted malathion for 2 months.

One side of tree turns brown, rest healthy. Very cold winds in winter, hard frost or marked regularly by cats. During hard winters, place tub in sheltered position.

Fungi at foot of tree, fungal threads under bark. Honey fungus. No cure, destroy plant and do not plant another for 2 years. Do not plant these trees if fungus present in garden though in tub of sterile loam plant should be protected.

Tree turns yellow from base. Root rot disease. Overwatering and waterlogging may start problem so always make sure container well drained. If disease is phytophthora, tree unlikely to survive.

159

Chamaedorea elegans

Parlour palm

Sometimes known as *Neanthe bella*, this plant must not be confused with rather similar Howea varieties. It is an easy plant to grow in the house, reaching a maximum height of only 3ft–3ft 6in (90–115cm) with fronds 9–24in (22–60cm) long. It can become quite bushy with age. At 3 or more years old it can produce a flower spike, not unlike mimosa. The florets will develop into small berry-like fruits. The parlour palm is particularly susceptible to red spider. Scale insect and mealy bug are less common, but they must be looked out for.

Light: High level of diffused light, but not full sun, which dries out leaves. Will survive a long time in a relatively dark place.

Temperature: Winter minimum 55°F (13°C), summer minimum 60°F (16°C), summer maximum 65°F (18°C).

Water: Keep moist at all times, watering 2–3 times a week in summer, once a week in winter.

Humidity: Spray daily with rainwater or soft water. Stand pot in saucer on pebbles almost covered with water. Steamy kitchen or bathroom are good situations.

Feeding: Every 14 days in summer only, with houseplant food diluted with water. Use half the amount recommended by the maker.

Soil: Mixture of 2 parts loam-based No. 1 and 1 part peat.

Repotting: Every year in spring, into pot one size larger. If more than 1 plant growing together, do not separate roots.

Cleaning: Once every 2 months with vegetable-oil based cleaner diluted according to maker's instructions, with milk (use 6–7 drops in a cup of water) or with liquid leafshine. No aerosol leafshine. Between cleanings, wipe with damp cloth.

The Parlour palm's soft dark green leaves grow from a stem between 9–24in (22–60cm) long. Their slightly glossy appearance can be maintained using liquid leafshines, but not aerosol types. A daily spray with soft water will keep them clean and provide the high humidity they need.

Removing dead fronds
If whole fronds are dry and discoloured, cut them off with sharp knife or secateurs close to the main stem.

Removing the flower spike
After producing berries, the spike will wither and dry. Cut it off with scissors as close to the stem as possible. If you have a heated propagator you can try to grow new plants from the seeds. They need a temperature of 80°F (27°C) to germinate.

what goes wrong

Small flat discs sticking to underside of leaves. Scale insect. Paint with methylated spirits and remove with thumbnail or spray every 14 days with diluted malathion.

Leaves turn yellow and have webs underneath. Red spider mite. Spray with diluted malathion or a systemic insecticide every 14 days until clear.

White woolly patches on leaves and stems. Mealy bug. Paint with methylated spirits and remove with thumbnail or spray with derris, diluted malathion or systemic insecticide every 14 days until clear.

Plant does not grow. Too cold and wet or needs feeding. Check and correct conditions. Move to warmer place and allow to dry out before watering again. Feed every 14 days in summer with food at half recommended strength.

Whole fronds turn brown, dry up and die. Air too dry. Stand pot on wet pebbles or put in outer pot packed with damp peat. Also caused by overfeeding. Feed every 14 days in summer only, with food at half recommended strength.

Tips of leaves turn brown. Too hot or in too sunny a position. Move to a position of indirect sunlight; water and remember to spray regularly with soft water. Can also be leafshine damage. Do not use.

Leaves rot at soil level and fall. Too cold and wet. Move to warmer room and allow to dry out before watering again.

161

Chamaerops humilis

European fan palm

This is Europe's only native palm and, although plants may vary in leaf size and shape, they all belong to a single species. It makes an ideal houseplant, especially in unheated rooms. It can reach 20ft (6m) in height but indoors is usually only 4ft (120cm) tall with leaves up to 2ft (60cm) across. It starts life with its fan-shaped leaves growing straight from the soil. As it produces new leaves, old ones die and fall off, the process producing a trunk which has stiff dark fibres near the crown. Young leaves are covered with pale woolly down which disappears as they grow.

Light: Full sunlight. Shade badly affects growth of new leaves.

Temperature: Autumn–spring, 40–50°F (4–10°C); spring–autumn, 50–60°F (10–16°C).

Water: 3 times a week in summer to keep moist, twice a week in winter. If large plant, in pot 7in (17cm) or more, may need daily watering in summer.

Humidity: Spray with soft water every week in centrally heated rooms. Planting in self-watering planter or with other plants keeps humidity adequate.

Feeding: Weekly in summer with house-plant food diluted with water according to maker's instructions.

Soil: 2 parts loam-based No. 2, 1 part decayed leafmould and sand. Good drainage essential.

Repotting: Annually in spring for young plants. When 4ft (120cm) tall, pot up into 20in (50cm) container then change top soil annually.

Cleaning: Spray with soft water. Wipe older (not young down-covered) leaves with damp sponge. No aerosol leafshine.

When young, the European fan palm's dark green fan-shaped leaves grow on stems straight from the compost. As they grow older, a trunk forms with leaf stems radiating from its top. They need full sunlight and weekly feeding in summer to grow well.

Webs under leaves. Red spider mite. Spray leaves with half-strength malathion-based insecticide every 14 days until clear. Increase humidity.

Watering

1. The plant should be kept always moist in summer. Test compost with your finger. If dry and crumbly, plant needs watering. If very dry, surface may be hard.

2. Fill space between compost and top of pot with water and allow to drain through. Leave for 15 minutes, then throw excess water away.

New fronds do not open. Too dark or too dry in summer. If in shade, move to sun-facing room or place near light window. In summer keep moist by watering at least 3 times a week – but do not stand in water.

New leaf tips turn brown. Needs water. Keep plant moist all the time in summer. Slight browning at tip is natural.

All leaves dry out. Too hot. Keep room well ventilated and do not exceed 60°F (16°C) in summer, 50°F (10°C) in winter.

what goes wrong

No new fronds appear. Needs feeding or soil replacing. If adult, change top soil. If young, repot in spring. Feed every week in summer.

New fronds grow slowly and are yellowish. Plant waterlogged. Check pot is not standing in water and has sufficient drainage in bottom.

Leaves turn black. Too cold. If outside, frosted. Move indoors if outside and if in cool greenhouse, provide heater if under 40°F (4°C). Black patches caused by spraying fronds with too concentrated malathion.

Leaves have brown patches. Leafshine damage. Do not use aerosol type. Clean leaves with damp sponge

Oldest leaves dry out. Air too dry. Down on younger leaves helps to retain moisture. Put plant in outer container packed with damp peat, especially if in centrally heated room. Spray weekly.

Brown discs on leaves and stems. Scale insect. Paint with methylated spirits and remove with thumbnail.

White woolly patches where frond joins trunk. Mealy bug. Every 14 days add liquid malathion to water. Spray stem with half-strength malathion every 14 days until clear.

163

Spider plant

This is a wonderful plant for beginners as only determined neglect will kill it. It is a very quick grower. With its long, strap-like leaves coming from the centre of the plant, it is very good in hanging baskets as it throws out long stems which produce first small flowers and then plantlets. These hang down to make an attractive decoration. Young plants, which can easily be grown from the plantlets on the end of the stems, can be used for summer bedding out-of-doors. The plant, which originates from South Africa, grows well in hydroculture. It likes to be fed well, but also likes to be pot-bound. When its stems fill the pot and the white, worm-like rhizomes bulge out over the surface, it can easily be divided.

A Spider plant's long leaves grow from the centre of the plant and are usually green at the edges with a white stripe down the middle. Some varieties have white edges and a green central stripe. Look for clean, untorn leaves, with no brown tips.

Light: Grows in most positions, though its variation is most pronounced when plant is near a window. Keep away from mid-day sun.

Temperature: Very tolerant, though must be frost-free in winter.

Water: 2–3 times a week in summer, once a week in winter. Withhold water if temperature drops below 40°F (4°C).

Humidity: Spray daily in summer, twice a week in winter if temperature is over 60°F (15°C).

Feeding: Every 14 days in the growing season (spring and summer) with house-plant food diluted according to the maker's instructions.

Soil: Loam-based No. 2, to give roots a firm hold.

Repotting: About twice a year, though plant does not mind being pot-bound. It is all right to remove some of the fat white tubers or the rhizomes if they fill surface of pot.

Cleaning: Humidity spraying sufficient. No leafshine.

Separating the plantlets

1. Prepare small pots with drainage layer and compost

2. Place new pot next to parent plant and bend stem until plantlet rests on compost. Peg stem to compost and firm soil around plantlet.

3. When plantlet grows new leaves, cut parent stem with sharp knife close to plantlet

Leaves turn dark green and lose variegation. Too dark. Move to lighter place, in window out of direct sunlight.

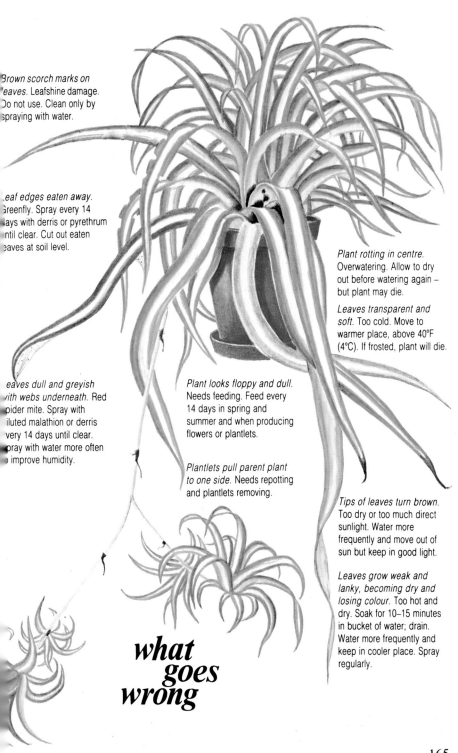

Brown scorch marks on leaves. Leafshine damage. Do not use. Clean only by spraying with water.

Leaf edges eaten away. Greenfly. Spray every 14 days with derris or pyrethrum until clear. Cut out eaten leaves at soil level.

Leaves dull and greyish with webs underneath. Red spider mite. Spray with diluted malathion or derris every 14 days until clear. Spray with water more often to improve humidity.

Plant rotting in centre. Overwatering. Allow to dry out before watering again – but plant may die.

Leaves transparent and soft. Too cold. Move to warmer place, above 40°F (4°C). If frosted, plant will die.

Plant looks floppy and dull. Needs feeding. Feed every 14 days in spring and summer and when producing flowers or plantlets.

Plantlets pull parent plant to one side. Needs repotting and plantlets removing.

Tips of leaves turn brown. Too dry or too much direct sunlight. Water more frequently and move out of sun but keep in good light.

Leaves grow weak and lanky, becoming dry and losing colour. Too hot and dry. Soak for 10–15 minutes in bucket of water; drain. Water more frequently and keep in cooler place. Spray regularly.

what goes wrong

165

Areca palm

This extremely graceful palm, sometimes known as *Areca lutescens*, has rich, soft green leaves deeply divided into long narrow segments. The plants grow in dense clusters and throw off extra trunks as suckers, which can be allowed to grow with the original provided the plants are not overcrowded. Usually, these suckers completely obscure the trunk. Up to 25ft (7½m) tall in its natural habitat, the Areca palm is sold as a houseplant between 2 and 3ft (60–90cm).

Light: Plenty needed, but should be protected from strong sun. Will tolerate shade.

Temperature: Winter minimum 50°F (10°C), though happier with 60°F (16°C). Summer maximum 80°F (27°C), though ideal is 70°F (21°C).

Water: 3 times a week in summer. In winter, once every week to 10 days, allowing soil almost to dry out between waterings.

Humidity: Spray with fine mist twice a week in summer, once in winter. When over 75°F (24°C), spray daily. Stand on a saucer of pebbles almost covered with water.

Feeding: Weekly in spring and summer with houseplant food diluted with water according to maker's instructions.

Soil: For young plant, a mixture of 1 part loam-based No. 1 and 1 part peat. For plants over 3 years old, equal parts of loam and sand, with added rotted horse or cow manure (about ⅕ of total mixture).

Repotting: Annually in spring, into plastic pot one size larger, disturbing roots as little as possible. Use broken crocks for good drainage in pot.

Cleaning: Carefully wipe with sponge or damp cloth. No leafshine.

A healthy Areca palm has rich, soft green fronds and yellow stems. Suckers grow straight from the compost and hide the stems with their fronds. Unless the pot becomes overcrowded, these can be retained to give an attractive display.

All leaves on frond go brown. Root damage caused by knocking over plant or repotting at wrong time of year. Cut off dead stem at soil surface. New suckers will soon grow.

what goes wrong

Individual leaves turn brown. Leafshine damage. Do not use any kind. Clean only with water.

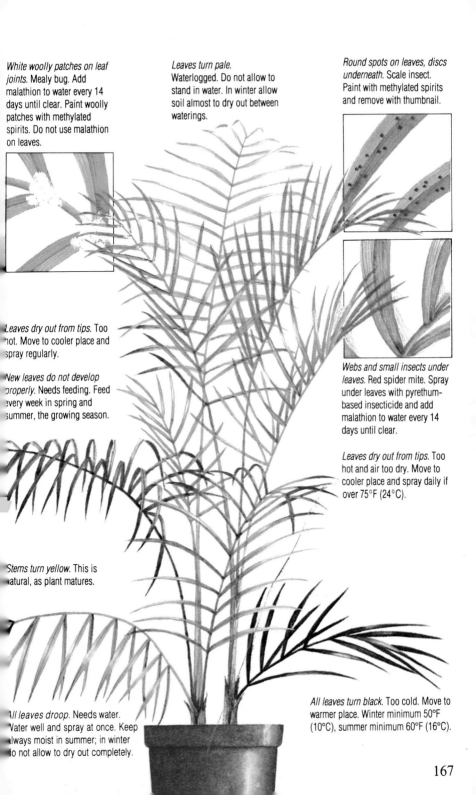

White woolly patches on leaf joints. Mealy bug. Add malathion to water every 14 days until clear. Paint woolly patches with methylated spirits. Do not use malathion on leaves.

Leaves turn pale. Waterlogged. Do not allow to stand in water. In winter allow soil almost to dry out between waterings.

Round spots on leaves, discs underneath. Scale insect. Paint with methylated spirits and remove with thumbnail.

Leaves dry out from tips. Too hot. Move to cooler place and spray regularly.

New leaves do not develop properly. Needs feeding. Feed every week in spring and summer, the growing season.

Webs and small insects under leaves. Red spider mite. Spray under leaves with pyrethum-based insecticide and add malathion to water every 14 days until clear.

Leaves dry out from tips. Too hot and air too dry. Move to cooler place and spray daily if over 75°F (24°C).

Stems turn yellow. This is natural, as plant matures.

All leaves droop. Needs water. Water well and spray at once. Keep always moist in summer; in winter do not allow to dry out completely.

All leaves turn black. Too cold. Move to warmer place. Winter minimum 50°F (10°C), summer minimum 60°F (16°C).

167

Chrysanthemum

This is the national flower of Japan, the country from which it originates. The Chrysanthemum varieties sold as pot plants are commercially grown all year round and treated with growth retardant to keep a compact shape. If planted in the garden after flowering, they will lose their compactness. Plants should always be bought with their buds showing colour, as tight-budded plants are unlikely to open in the home. They should be kept on the cool side, and their dead flowers removed as they occur. Both single and double varieties are available in a range of colours.

Chrysanthemums are among the most popular flowering houseplants and are available all the year round. Look for plants with buds that have begun to open. Keep out of very humid situations or the leaves will quickly turn yellow.

Light: Full light including sun but avoiding direct sunshine at midday.

Temperature: Best at 60°F (16°C) all year round, although will tolerate up to 70°F (21°C) for short periods if humidity is high.

Water: About twice a week all year round to keep compost evenly moist, but do not stand pot in water. Water just as surface begins to dry.

Humidity: Spray lightly once a week in centrally heated rooms, avoiding flowers. Using soft water will prevent lime spots from forming on leaves. Do not keep in very humid situations, as leaves will quickly turn yellow.

Feeding: Not necessary if bought in bud.

Soil: Equal parts loam-based No.2, peat and sand.

Repotting: Not necessary as plant is usually thrown away once flowering has finished. The roots can be planted into a cool greenhouse, but plant will revert to full size in the following season, when specialist knowledge in chrysanthemum techniques of disbudding and culture are needed for success.

Cleaning: Humidity spraying sufficient. No leafshine.

Flowers rot when leaves healthy and all conditions correct. Flower has been sprayed. When spraying with water or insecticide, shield flowers with your hand or paper. Remove damaged flower head.

Leaves turn black. Too cold. Move to warmer place, keep at 60°F (16°C) all year round. If temperature correct, leafshine damage. Do not use. Clean only by spraying with soft tepid water (avoiding flowers). Remove damaged leaf.

Leaves and stems shrivel up. Too hot. Move to a cooler place with more ventilation. Ideal temperature 60°F (16°C) all year round. Spray weekly with soft, tepid water, shielding flowers from spray.

Lower leaves turn black. Botrytis. Too cold and damp. Spray with fungicide then place in warmer position and spray with water less often. Allow compost almost to dry out on surface between waterings. Minimum temperature 60°F (16°C) all year round. Remove damaged leaves.

168

what goes wrong

*Plant grows long stems
with lanky leaves.*
Insufficient light. Move to
place in very good light. It
will stand direct sunlight
except at midday.

*Flower buds dry out and do
not open.* Compost too dry.
Plunge pot into bucket of
water for 10–15 minutes,
then drain. Keep constantly
moist in summer, watering
every day if it dries out in hot
weather. Do not allow to
stand in water.

*Many small buds do not
open.* Insufficient light. Move
to sunny position and rub off
some of the smaller buds to
encourage stronger ones to
grow. Allow up to 5 buds per
flower stem.

Leaves turn yellow.
Atmosphere too humid.
Move to drier position and do
not spray, unless in dry
centrally heated room.

*Webs on flowers and
leaves.* Red spider mite.
Remove webs with damp
cloth or sponge, then spray
with diluted malathion,
especially under leaves.
Repeat every 14 days until
symptoms disappear. Improve
humidity by spraying lightly
once a week in centrally
heated rooms.

Flies hopping around plant. Whitefly,
chrysanthemum fly or blackfly. Spray with
pyrethrum-based insecticide or diluted
malathion. Repeat one week later then every
week until clear. This is very common.

169

Cissus antarctica

Kangaroo vine

This plant was first introduced to Europe in 1790 and must have been one of the first houseplants to be exported from Australia. If allowed to climb freely it will cover a wall and it can also be trailed from a hanging basket. In northern Europe particularly it is often used as a room divider and may grow 2–3ft (60–100cm) a year, clinging to a supporting trellis with its tendrils. It is a member of the vine family but indoors will produce neither flowers nor fruit. An easy plant for a beginner but keep it out of direct sunlight which will soon dry up the leaves.

The Kangaroo vine's oval leaves are slightly rough in texture. It climbs with tendrils, which soon attach themselves to wires, canes or a trellis. If it is growing too large it can be pruned severely in spring but the miniature variety, *C. striata*, may be more suitable for smaller rooms.

Light: Needs good indirect light. Best in a window that does not get direct sun. Do not keep more than 3–4ft (1m) away from a window.

Temperature: Keep at 55–60°F (13–16°C) in winter, 65–70°F (18–21°C) in summer. If temperature over 70°F (21°C) increase humidity.

Water: Twice a week in summer, every 14 days in winter sufficient. Check compost. It should dry out on surface between waterings.

Humidity: Spray weekly in summer. If temperature over 70°F (21°C), spray daily and stand pot on saucer of wet pebbles.

Feeding: Give liquid houseplant food every 14 days in summer, diluted to maker's recommended strength.

Soil: Loam-based No. 2.

Repotting: When plant is young and growing fast, will need repotting twice a year in mid-spring and midsummer. After 3 or 4 years just replace top soil and feed weekly in summer.

Cleaning: Regular spraying keeps plant clean but leafshine can be used every 2 months.

what goes wrong

Training

1. Cissus needs a cane to climb. Insert cane when repotting; at any other time be careful not to damage roots as you push it gently into compost.

2. Loop fine twine around cane and plant stem as shown, being careful not to bruise stem: knot should be against cane not stem. Or use special plant rings or ties.

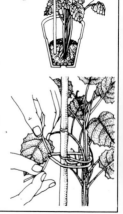

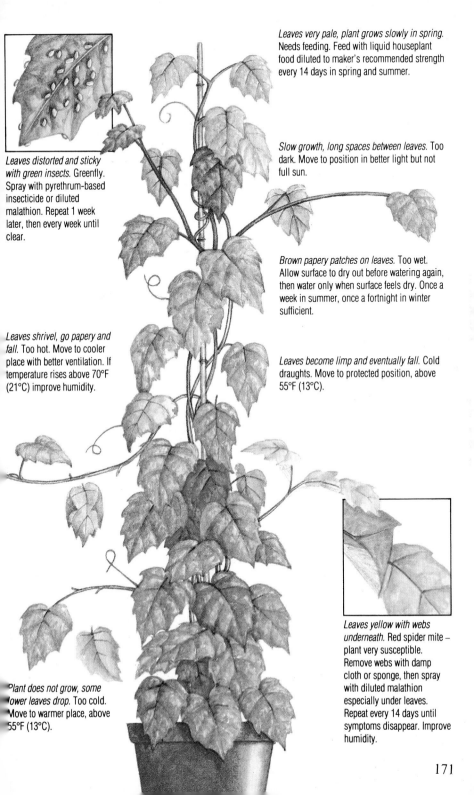

Leaves distorted and sticky with green insects. Greenfly. Spray with pyrethrum-based insecticide or diluted malathion. Repeat 1 week later, then every week until clear.

Leaves shrivel, go papery and fall. Too hot. Move to cooler place with better ventilation. If temperature rises above 70°F (21°C) improve humidity.

Plant does not grow, some lower leaves drop. Too cold. Move to warmer place, above 55°F (13°C).

Leaves very pale, plant grows slowly in spring. Needs feeding. Feed with liquid houseplant food diluted to maker's recommended strength every 14 days in spring and summer.

Slow growth, long spaces between leaves. Too dark. Move to position in better light but not full sun.

Brown papery patches on leaves. Too wet. Allow surface to dry out before watering again, then water only when surface feels dry. Once a week in summer, once a fortnight in winter sufficient.

Leaves become limp and eventually fall. Cold draughts. Move to protected position, above 55°F (13°C).

Leaves yellow with webs underneath. Red spider mite – plant very susceptible. Remove webs with damp cloth or sponge, then spray with diluted malathion especially under leaves. Repeat every 14 days until symptoms disappear. Improve humidity.

171

Grape ivy

One of the best climbing houseplants, this plant tolerates fairly shady positions and grows 2–3ft (60–100cm) a year. It makes a good room divider as it will cover a large area of trellis and also does well in a hanging basket when young. Older plants tend to develop woody stems which break easily under the weight of their hanging foliage. In mixed plantings, grape ivy should never be overwatered as plants growing together produce a humid microclimate of their own which protects them from drying out. Grape ivy is related to the true grape vine and climbs in the same way, with curling tendrils that attach themselves to a stake or trellis. It grows well in hydroculture.

Healthy Grape ivy leaves are dark, glossy green, about 2in (5cm) long with a series of small points around the edge. Young leaves may have a bronzy colour, which darkens to green as they grow. Plants should be well covered with leaves and have vigorous tendrils.

Light: Grows best by a window that does not face the sun but will survive in quite shady areas away from the window.

Temperature: Keep above 55°F (13°C) in winter and at normal room temperatures in summer.

Water: Usually twice a week in summer, every 14 days in winter. Do not overwater. Allow top layer of compost to dry out between waterings.

Humidity: Mist twice weekly in summer, same in winter if plant in hot, dry centrally-heated atmosphere. Stand pot in saucer of pebbles almost covered with water.

Feeding: Every 14 days in the growing season (spring and summer) with houseplant food diluted according to the maker's instructions.

Soil: Loam-based No. 2 compost.

Repotting: At least every spring. If growing well may require potting again in midsummer. Change the topsoil of large pots or tubs in spring.

Cleaning: Humidity spraying sufficient. Monthly spray with leafshine beneficial.

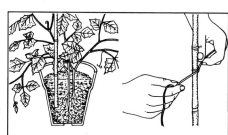

Tying to a cane

1. Push cane into compost a few inches from main stem until it is ⅔ down the pot.

2. Tie 9in (23cm) length of string to cane with knot on side next to stem.

3. Loop around stem between leaves.

4. Tie knot firmly against cane but do not crush stem with string.

172

Leaves drop and plant becomes straggly. Too dark. Move to lighter place but not in direct sunlight.

Young leaves distorted and sticky with green insects. Greenfly. Spray every 14 days with pyrethrum or derris until clear.

what goes wrong

Leaves turn yellow and have webs underneath. Red spider mite. Spray every 14 days with diluted malathion or systemic insecticide until clear.

Leaves turn pale and bleached. Too much sunlight. Move away from window that gets direct sun.

Young leaves stay small and pale. Needs feeding. Feed every 14 days while growing. If roots are showing through pot base, repot.

White woolly patches on leaves and stems. Mealy bug. Spray with diluted malathion every 14 days until clear or remove with cotton wool dipped in methylated spirits.

Leaves turn brown at tips. Scorched by sun. Move out of bright sunlight.

Leaves dry up, go thin and papery and drop. Too dry or too hot. Water more often and spray to increase humidity. Keep under 70°F (21°C) if possible.

Leaves look dull, droop and drop off. Too wet, overwatered. Allow to dry out, then water less often. Check drainage in pot is good and let top ½in (1cm) of soil dry out between waterings. Also caused by dry air. Spray to increase humidity in hot weather

173

Citrus mitis

Calamondin orange

This is a miniature orange tree which grows to a maximum height of 39in (1m). It is usually sold as a plant 2ft (60cm) high, in fruit and sometimes in flower. Its lovely, orangey scent is unmistakable. The fruits are a scaled-down version of full-size oranges, and may be candied, preserved, or used in drinks, though they are quite bitter. The plant needs a warm, light and humid position, especially at flowering time and when the fruits are ripening.

To make sure that fruits appear, spray a fine mist of tepid water on the flowers or brush each one in turn with a soft paintbrush. This transfers pollen from bloom to bloom so that fruit can form.

Light: Full light. Tolerates direct sunlight, except at midday in midsummer.
Temperature: Winter ideal 55–60°F (13–15°C); tolerates lower, but must be protected from frost. Summer maximum 65°F (18°C); good air circulation essential.
Water: Daily, with tap water, in summer. In winter allow almost to dry out between waterings. Every 7–10 days probably sufficient. Good drainage essential.
Humidity: Spray daily, early in morning. Water drops left on leaves may cause scorching in direct sun.
Feeding: Every 14 days in spring, weekly in summer, with houseplant food diluted according to the maker's instructions.
Soil: 4 parts loam-based No. 2 compost mixed with 1 part sharp sand.
Repotting: Annually in spring, taking care not to damage roots. Plants up to 2ft (60cm) happy in 5in (13cm) pots, larger plants need 7in (18cm) pots. Ensure good drainage in bottom.
Cleaning: Humidity spraying sufficient. No leafshine.

If they are to produce fruit, Calamondin oranges must be pollinated by hand. Using a camel hair paintbrush, lightly brush each flower stamen in turn so that pollen is transferred from one to another. Spray daily with tepid soft water to help fruit to set. To ripen green fruit, keep plant in a warm, sunny position.

Leaves turn quite black. Too cold. Do not allow temperature to drop below 55°F (13°C). Move to warmer place.

Leaves turn pale, then yellow. Needs feeding. Feed every 14 days in spring and summer, reducing to every 3 weeks towards end of summer. Do not feed in winter.

Plant grows leggy with long spaces between leaves. Needs pruning. Prune to neat shape in spring, cutting tops of leggy stems just above a bud, leaf or side-shoot.

Plant fails to flower. Too dark, too hot, or pot too large. Check conditions. Feed in spring to encourage new growth and do not repot again for 2 years. A 5in (13cm) pot is usually large enough.

Black dusty patches on leaves. Sooty mould. Spray with any fungicide and wipe leaves with damp cloth soaked in fungicide to prevent repeat infection.

Leaves turn brown and crispy. Too hot and stuffy. Move to cooler room (not more than 65°F, 18°C) if possible, with better air circulation.

what goes wrong

Leaves turn brown at tips and curl. Too cold and draughty. Move to warmer, sheltered place, above 55°F (13°C).

Leaves and buds or flowers drop. Needs watering and air too dry. Spray daily, best in early morning. Stand pot on saucer of damp pebbles. Water daily in summer with tap water but do not allow to stand in water.

Leaves mottled. Leaf hopper. Spray every 14 days until clear with systemic insecticide. Water soil with same mixture diluted in water once a month to prevent another attack.

White woolly patches on leaf veins. Mealy bug. Spray under leaves with diluted malathion every 14 days and water diluted malathion into soil once a week until clear.

No new growth in summer, leaves eventually turn yellow and fall. Too dark or too cold – or both. Move to warmer, lighter place (above 60°F, 15°C). Turn plant round every 3 or 4 days to make sure it grows evenly. If plant does not grow though conditions are correct, overwatering or standing in water.

Brown scales on leaves. Scale insect. Paint with cotton wool or paintbrush dipped in methylated spirits and remove with thumbnail. Spray once a month with diluted malathion until quite clear.

Scorch marks on leaves. Caused by spraying water in full sunlight. Spray in early morning or evening. Or, leafshine damage. Do not use.

Webs under leaves mottled, dusty leaf surfaces. Red spider mite. Spray under leaves with diluted systemic insecticide every 14 days until clear.

Leaves fall after turning yellow. Too wet, overwatered. Allow to dry out before watering again and make sure drainage holes in pot base are clear. In winter allow compost almost to dry out between waterings.

Small flies around plant. Whitefly. Spray with systemic insecticide every 14 days until clear.

Cleistocactus

This is a widespread genus of cactus from South America which gives the collector a chance to obtain flowers at a relatively small size on columnar plants. Most other columnar cacti are taller than their owners before flowers are likely to appear! Cleistocactus species vary from tall, column-like plants with stems as thick as your arm, to narrow, pencil-thin, sprawling stems which in the wild clamber through shrubs or over hillsides. They are noted for their dense, needle-like spines which completely clothe the stems, in colours varying from pure, glassy white to browns and yellows. Their flowers are mainly red, orange and yellow, tube-shaped with a tiny opening at the end through which, in the wild, long-tongued pollinators such as humming-birds probe in search of nectar. *Cleistocactus strausii* (p.177) is the most commonly sold species.

A group of Cleistocacti growing in a private garden (Lotus Land) in California. In good conditions these plants may grow up to 10ft (over 3m) tall, making a spectacular display.

Light: The more sunlight these plants can be given the more dense the spines will be and the greater the likelihood of flowers.

Temperature: Not less than 40°F (4°C); keep below 100°F (38°C) in summer and give fresh air whenever possible.

Water: Weekly in summer, less often for plants in 6in (15cm) pots or larger as these hold moisture for longer. Leave dry in winter. Water monthly in spring and autumn.

Feeding: Feed once a month in spring and summer with high potash fertilizer (as used for tomatoes).

Soil: Use soil-less compost or 2 parts good loam-based No. 2 potting compost (No. 3 for large plants) with 1 part coarse, gritty sand (not builders' or seashore) added.

Repotting: Repot each spring until 6in (15cm) pots are reached, when every other year will do. Get help when the plants grow too big to handle with ease. They may grow 5–6ft (up to 2m) or more. Avoid touching the spiny stems altogether for fear of damage to the brittle spines. Cut out old stems which have stopped growing.

Cleaning and pest control: Spray with water to keep dust-free; add an insecticide to the water 2 or 3 times a year to combat pests.

Other species: A good alternative to *C. strausii* is *C. ritteri*, with thinner, white-spined stems and yellow flowers. *C. santa-cruzensis* will flower at only about 8in (20cm) on pencil-thin stems with long spines; the flowers are red and yellow. An unusual, pendant species with yellow-brown, soft spines completely hiding the stems is *C. vulpis-cauda* (the name means 'fox-tail'), which has red flowers produced on and off for over 6 months; it is a good plant for a hanging pot or basket.

C.vulpis-cauda is a good candidate for a hanging basket. It is best to use a special plastic pot with saucer attached and chains for suspending it. The plant can then be potted directly into the container with the usual compost. Check regularly for moisture as hanging containers dry out more quickly than standing ones.

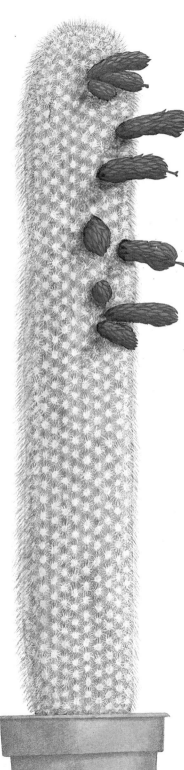

Cleistocactus strausii flowers when it is five or six years old, and about 12in (30cm) tall. The deep red flowers appear during the spring and summer months, each lasting from four to five days. A healthy plant will make several inches of fresh growth each season, producing brightly coloured spines at the growing point of the stem.

Removing old stems
1. When secondary stems begin to grow from base of plant, first stem sometimes gradually turns brown and withers.

2. Cut off old stem with a hacksaw as near to soil level as possible and dust cut surface liberally with hormone rooting powder containing fungicide.

3. When cut surface is dry, repot in centre of new pot large enough to hold all roots and the remains of the old stump. This can be disguised with a layer of gravel.

177

Clerodendrum thomsonae

Bleeding heart vine

These plants come mainly from Africa and Malaysia and are supposed to have a wide range of medicinal properties. Some varieties are hardy, but this one must be kept at a temperature of at least 55°F (13°C) if it is to survive. Plants sold in flower shops are usually sprayed with growth retardant to help keep them compact and producing abundant flowers. The unusual flowers are dark red, offset by creamy-white bracts. The foliage appears strong and glossy but is susceptible to damage by leafshine and will soon rot if too cold. Pruning the plant down to 3in (7cm) after flowering is over will encourage healthy growth in the following year.

The Bleeding heart vine is a naturally lanky plant which should be kept compact by heavy pruning after flowering. The cream-coloured bracts are strikingly shaped and have a contrasting dark red centre. They may appear at any time from spring to early autumn.

Light: Full light, including sunshine, but avoid midday summer sun.

Temperature: 65–70°F (18–21°C) from spring to late autumn; 55–60°F (13–16°C) late autumn to spring.

Water: Twice weekly from mid-spring to later summer to keep always moist, weekly from late summer to end autumn, then only when compost has almost dried out. Once a fortnight probably enough.

Humidity: Needs high humidity. Greenhouse conditions ideal. In the home, spray twice weekly from spring to end summer. Stand pot on a saucer of pebbles almost covered with water.

Feeding: Weekly with liquid houseplant food diluted to maker's instructions from spring to end summer. Do not feed in winter.

Soil: Equal parts loam-based No. 2, peat, leafmould and sand.

Repotting: In early spring. Prune the plant in autumn, after flowering has finished, down to about 3in(7cm).

Cleaning: Humidity spraying with soft tepid water sufficient. No leafshine.

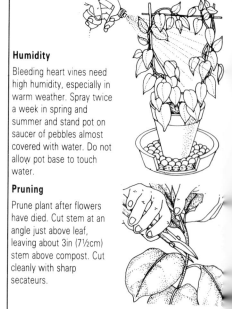

Humidity

Bleeding heart vines need high humidity, especially in warm weather. Spray twice a week in spring and summer and stand pot on saucer of pebbles almost covered with water. Do not allow pot base to touch water.

Pruning

Prune plant after flowers have died. Cut stem at an angle just above leaf, leaving about 3in (7½cm) stem above compost. Cut cleanly with sharp secateurs.

No flowers appear in spring and summer. Plant has been too hot in winter. Keep between 55–60°F (13–16°C) from late autumn to spring.

Plant grows leggy and does not flower. Too dark and/or needs feeding. Move into sunny position and feed every 7 days in growing season and when flowering, using liquid houseplant food at maker's recommended strength.

New leaves small, no flowers. Needs feeding. Feed with houseplant food every week while growing and flowering, diluting to maker's recommended strength.

Leaves turn black, flowers translucent. Leafshine damage. Do not use. Clean only by spraying with soft, tepid water. Remove damaged leaves.

Leaves rot in winter. Too wet. Overwatered. Allow surface of compost to dry out before watering again, then water only when surface dries out. Once a fortnight should be enough in winter.

Plant looks limp in spring and summer months. Compost and air too dry. Plunge pot into bucket of water for 10–15 minutes, then drain. Keep soil constantly moist in summer, watering every day if it dries out in hot weather. Spray twice weekly with soft, tepid water.

Flies hopping around compost surface. Whitefly. Spray with pyrethrum-based insecticide or diluted malathion. Repeat one week later, then every week until clear.

White cotton-wool patches where leaves join stem. Mealy bug. Spray with diluted malathion and remove bugs and 'wool' with tweezers.

Webs under leaves. Red spider mite. Remove webs with damp cloth or sponge, then spray with diluted malathion, especially under leaves. Repeat every 14 days until symptoms disappear. Improve humidity.

what goes wrong

Flower bracts fall. Too dark and/or too cold or too hot and air too dry. Check conditions. Plant should be in very good light and will stand direct sunshine. Temperature should not fall below 65°F (18°C), in summer or rise above 70°F (21°C).

179

Clivia miniata

Kaffir lily

This houseplant has very strong dark green leaves and, in early spring, a beautiful head of orange flowers borne on a single thick stem emerging from the centre of the leaves. The trumpet-shaped flowers usually come in a cluster of about ten blooms and are relatively long-lasting. Normally a brilliant orange, the flowers of some varieties have shades down to lemon. The plant flowers better if it is given a rest period in early winter. It slowly multiplies by making offsets as its base, so it is possible for an old plant to have several heads of flowers at a time. It is best to remove dead flowers before they produce seed. Otherwise they may not flower the following year.

Light: Stands shade, but flowers better if in a light window that does not get direct sun.
Temperature: Winter minimum while resting 45–50°F (8–10°C), increasing to 60°F (15°C) when flower buds appear. Summer maximum 70°F (21°C).
Water: Once or twice a week in spring and summer when flowering. Withhold for about a month when resting in winter.
Humidity: Stand pot on saucer of pebbles almost covered with water.
Feeding: Once a week from time flower stalk is half-grown to end of summer. Use liquid houseplant food diluted according to maker's instructions.
Soil: Loam-based No. 2 compost.
Repotting: Annually in spring after flowering for young plants, though they prefer small pots. With plants over about 3 years, change topsoil every 2–3 years and only repot when roots grow through soil at top.
Cleaning: By hand with damp cloth. No leafshine.

Kaffir lilies flower indoors in early spring, after their winter resting period. With modern commercial growing methods, however, they can be made to bloom at different times of the year. The cluster of flowers ranges from orange to pale lemon yellow. Healthy plants have strong, glossy leaves, growing from a bulbous stem.

Leaves shrivel. Too dry, needs watering. Soak pot in bucket of water for 10–15 minutes, then allow to drain. Water more often, especially when flowering.

Leaves brown and scorched. Direct sun on wet leaves. Move out of strong sunlight and take care when watering not to allow water on leaves.

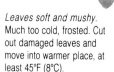

Leaves soft and mushy. Much too cold, frosted. Cut out damaged leaves and move into warmer place, at least 45°F (8°C).

Plant fails to flower in spring: Needs feeding. Feed every week when growing. If seeds were allowed to develop the year before, or plant was not given its winter rest period, it may not flower this year. If plant completely fails to grow, too cold. Move to warmer place.

New leaves pale and weak, no flowers. Too hot, air too dry. Move to cooler place, under 70°F (21°C) if possible.

Removing the flower stalk

When the flowers die, cut off stem at base before seeds begin to form.

Offsets

The small offsets that appear at plant's base can be removed to make new plants. Knock plant from pot and cut offset and its roots from parent plant with sharp knife. Repot parent and offset in separate pots.

what goes wrong

...eaves black and rotting at ...ase. Too wet, overwatered ...r badly drained. Check ...rainage holes are clear and ...low plant to dry out before ...atering again. Then water ...ss often. Soil should be ...st moist while flowering ...nd in summer. Leave without ...ater for a month in winter.

White woolly patches between leaves. Mealy bug. Remove with cotton wool dipped in methylated spirits.

Coconut palm

This palm has rather sparse foliage which grows out of a half-visible coconut. The leaves are long and grouped two to a frond, appearing to grow straight from the nut. As the plant develops, lower fronds die and new ones grow from the top of the central stem, in time producing a trunk. It is a slow grower, usually bought for its novelty. Its main problem is a rotting nut, usually caused by too frequent or over watering.

Light: Full sunlight. Care needed when spraying as water drips left on leaves can act as magnifying glasses, burning them.

Temperature: Winter minimum 65°F (18°C). Tolerates up to 80°F (27°C) in summer.

Water: Keep just moist, watering once or twice a week in summer, once a week in winter. Do not get water on nut or stand pot in water.

The Coconut palm produces dramatic, though sparse, green foliage with leaves grouped two to a frond. The nut from which the fronds grow lies half buried in the compost and should never be allowed to get wet. When spraying the fronds, be careful not to get moisture on the nut.

Humidity: Should be high. Stand pot in saucer of pebbles almost covered with water, or put pot into larger one with damp peat between the two.

Feeding: Every 3 weeks in summer with houseplant food diluted with water. Use half the amount recommended by the maker.

Soil: Mixture of 2 parts loam-based No. 2, 1 part peat, 1 part sand. Include small amount of vermiculite balls if available, e.g. 1 eggcup full in 7in (17cm) pot. Good drainage essential.

Repotting: Only when entirely pot-bound, into pot one size larger. Otherwise, leave roots undisturbed and replace 1in (2½cm) of topsoil with soil mixture above. A heavier loam required for a very large plant (6ft, 2m), 3 parts loam-based No. 2 to 1 part peat and 1 part sand.

Cleaning: Wipe with damp cloth. No leaf-shine.

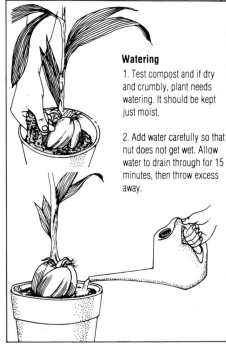

Watering

1. Test compost and if dry and crumbly, plant needs watering. It should be kept just moist.

2. Add water carefully so that nut does not get wet. Allow water to drain through for 15 minutes, then throw excess away.

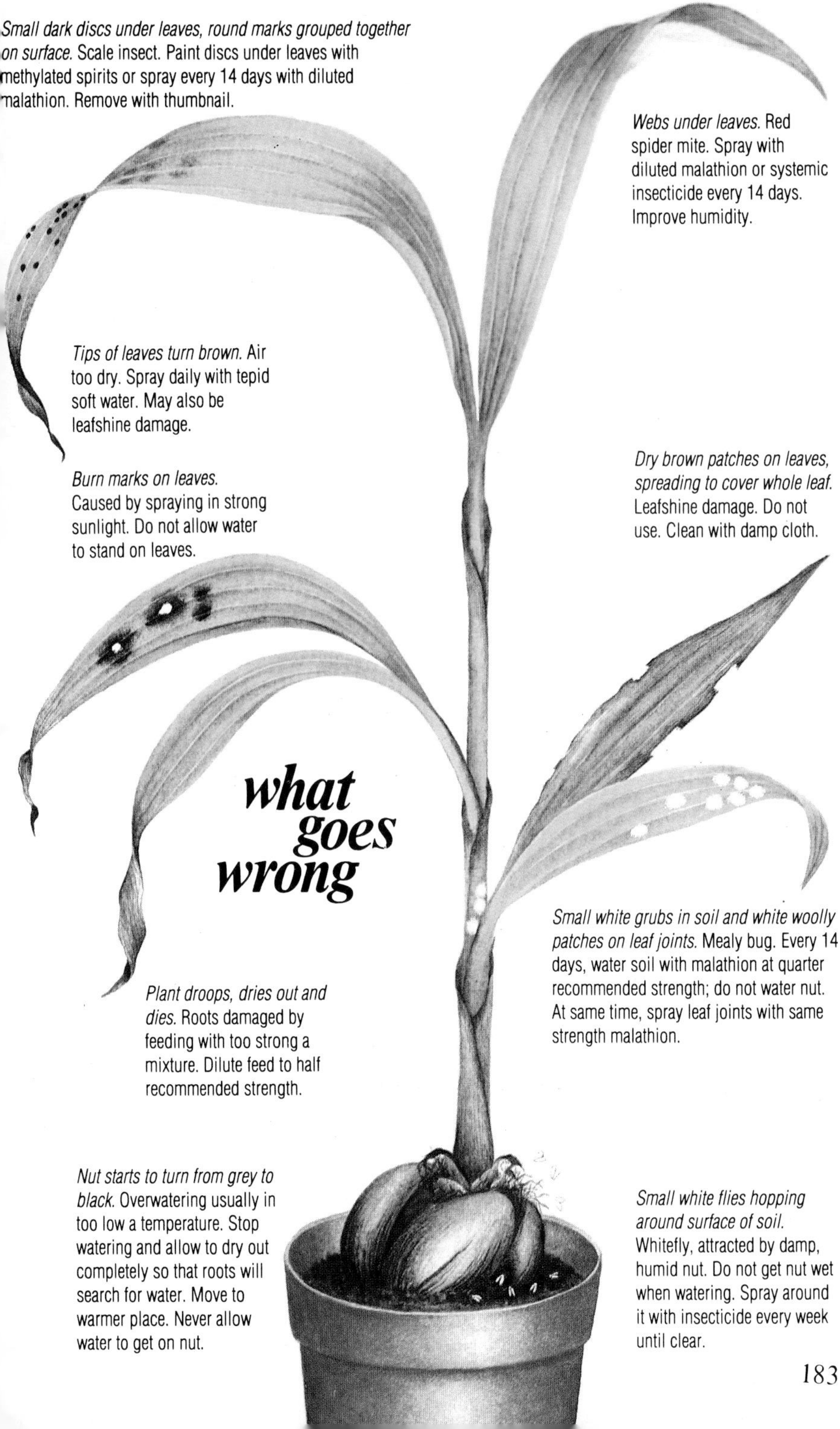

Small dark discs under leaves, round marks grouped together on surface. Scale insect. Paint discs under leaves with methylated spirits or spray every 14 days with diluted malathion. Remove with thumbnail.

Webs under leaves. Red spider mite. Spray with diluted malathion or systemic insecticide every 14 days. Improve humidity.

Tips of leaves turn brown. Air too dry. Spray daily with tepid soft water. May also be leafshine damage.

Burn marks on leaves. Caused by spraying in strong sunlight. Do not allow water to stand on leaves.

Dry brown patches on leaves, spreading to cover whole leaf. Leafshine damage. Do not use. Clean with damp cloth.

what goes wrong

Small white grubs in soil and white woolly patches on leaf joints. Mealy bug. Every 14 days, water soil with malathion at quarter recommended strength; do not water nut. At same time, spray leaf joints with same strength malathion.

Plant droops, dries out and dies. Roots damaged by feeding with too strong a mixture. Dilute feed to half recommended strength.

Nut starts to turn from grey to black. Overwatering usually in too low a temperature. Stop watering and allow to dry out completely so that roots will search for water. Move to warmer place. Never allow water to get on nut.

Small white flies hopping around surface of soil. Whitefly, attracted by damp, humid nut. Do not get nut wet when watering. Spray around it with insecticide every week until clear.

183

Codiaeum variegatum

Croton

This is one of the most colourful of all houseplants, well deserving its other common name, Joseph's Coat. It needs plenty of light if it is to flourish. It is also difficult to overwinter in the house, so it is best regarded as a plant for one season only. When large, they are beautiful grown on their own, otherwise they are best in mixed bowls, where they benefit from the humidity provided by the other plants. The leaf shapes found on Crotons vary considerably, some being oval, some like large oak leaves and others narrow and strap-like. New leaves may be mainly green, developing their colours as they mature.

Light: Needs plenty. Can be put in full sun, but if so should be sprayed in the middle of the day.

Temperature: Winter minimum 60°F (15°C), summer maximum 80°F (27°C). Prefers a steady temperature.

Water: 2–3 times a week in summer, every 4–5 days in winter, using tepid water. Never allow to dry out.

Humidity: Spray daily in summer, but not in direct sunlight. Spray weekly in winter. Stand on saucer of pebbles almost covered in water to help humidity. Don't allow pot base to touch water.

Feeding: Every 14 days in the growing season (spring and summer) with houseplant food diluted according to the maker's instructions.

Soil: Loam-based No. 2 compost.

Repotting: Annually in late spring, if plant has survived the winter. They prefer to be in a pot which is slightly too small.

Cleaning: By hand with damp cloth, or give a monthly spray of leafshine.

Though Croton leaf shapes vary, all are multicoloured, with strong yellow, red, or green markings and contrasting veins. New plants should have bright, glossy leaves growing right to the base of the stem.

what goes wrong

Leaves shrivel. Too hot and too dry; air too dry. Water and spray more often. Move to cooler place if possible.

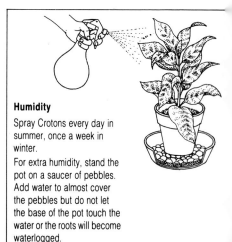

Humidity

Spray Crotons every day in summer, once a week in winter.

For extra humidity, stand the pot on a saucer of pebbles. Add water to almost cover the pebbles but do not let the base of the pot touch the water or the roots will become waterlogged.

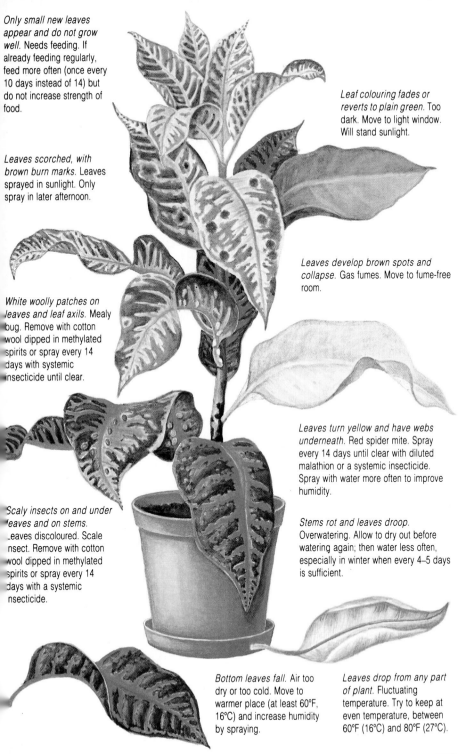

Only small new leaves appear and do not grow well. Needs feeding. If already feeding regularly, feed more often (once every 10 days instead of 14) but do not increase strength of food.

Leaf colouring fades or reverts to plain green. Too dark. Move to light window. Will stand sunlight.

Leaves scorched, with brown burn marks. Leaves sprayed in sunlight. Only spray in later afternoon.

Leaves develop brown spots and collapse. Gas fumes. Move to fume-free room.

White woolly patches on leaves and leaf axils. Mealy bug. Remove with cotton wool dipped in methylated spirits or spray every 14 days with systemic insecticide until clear.

Leaves turn yellow and have webs underneath. Red spider mite. Spray every 14 days until clear with diluted malathion or a systemic insecticide. Spray with water more often to improve humidity.

Scaly insects on and under leaves and on stems. Leaves discoloured. Scale insect. Remove with cotton wool dipped in methylated spirits or spray every 14 days with a systemic insecticide.

Stems rot and leaves droop. Overwatering. Allow to dry out before watering again; then water less often, especially in winter when every 4–5 days is sufficient.

Bottom leaves fall. Air too dry or too cold. Move to warmer place (at least 60°F, 16°C) and increase humidity by spraying.

Leaves drop from any part of plant. Fluctuating temperature. Try to keep at even temperature, between 60°F (16°C) and 80°F (27°C).

185

Coffee plant

Given the right conditions, it is almost possible to grow one's own coffee as well as drink it, for a *Coffea arabica* over three years old produces pretty little white, scented flowers which eventually produce cherry-like fruit which turn from green to red to black and so to coffee beans. The plant makes a handsome little shrub that does well in the house, for it enjoys semi-shade. Indoors it grows to about 4ft (just over 1m) tall, and there is a dwarf variety, *C. arabica* 'Nana'. It likes a good, airy position, but must not be in direct draughts.

Light: Does well in light windows that do not face the sun. Keep out of direct sunlight.

Temperature: Tolerates winter minimum of 45°F (8°C) if water withheld, but prefers 60°F (15°C). Normal room temperatures acceptable in summer.

Water: Up to 3 times a week in summer, depending on temperature. Do not let the compost dry out completely. Once a week is enough in winter. If temperature falls to 45°F (8°C) allow compost to dry out.

Humidity: Spray twice a week in summer, more often if over about 75°F (24°C). Spray every 14 days in winter with tepid water.

Feeding: Every 14 days in the growing season (spring and summer) with houseplant food diluted according to the maker's instructions.

Soil: Peat-based compost, with fertilizer at same strength as loam-based No. 2 .

Repotting: Annually in spring when plant starts to grow.

Cleaning: Humidity spraying sufficient. Use leafshine but not more than once a month.

The Coffee plant's leaves are oblong-oval, with a distinct point. When young they have a coppery tinge but soon turn a dark, glossy green, with a very shiny surface. If conditions are correct, the plant will flower – and produce a small crop of coffee beans.

Brown scorch marks on leaves. Caused by water left on leaves after spraying in sunlight. Spray in the evening.

Removing damaged leaves
Cut off single discoloured or dead leaves with scissors at point where leaf stem joins plant stem.

If dead leaf is at the end of a stem, make cut just above the next leaf down the stem, to keep plant's natural growth pattern.

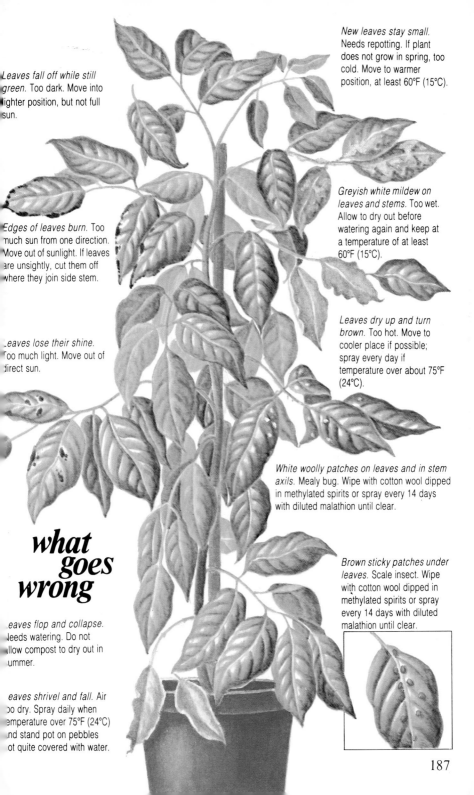

New leaves stay small. Needs repotting. If plant does not grow in spring, too cold. Move to warmer position, at least 60°F (15°C).

Leaves fall off while still green. Too dark. Move into lighter position, but not full sun.

Greyish white mildew on leaves and stems. Too wet. Allow to dry out before watering again and keep at a temperature of at least 60°F (15°C).

Edges of leaves burn. Too much sun from one direction. Move out of sunlight. If leaves are unsightly, cut them off where they join side stem.

Leaves dry up and turn brown. Too hot. Move to cooler place if possible; spray every day if temperature over about 75°F (24°C).

Leaves lose their shine. Too much light. Move out of direct sun.

White woolly patches on leaves and in stem axils. Mealy bug. Wipe with cotton wool dipped in methylated spirits or spray every 14 days with diluted malathion until clear.

what goes wrong

Brown sticky patches under leaves. Scale insect. Wipe with cotton wool dipped in methylated spirits or spray every 14 days with diluted malathion until clear.

Leaves flop and collapse. Needs watering. Do not allow compost to dry out in summer.

Leaves shrivel and fall. Air too dry. Spray daily when temperature over 75°F (24°C) and stand pot on pebbles not quite covered with water.

187

Coleus blumei

Flame nettle

The appropriately named Flame nettle is grown for its brilliant foliage. Plants can be bought in leaf and were once grown mainly from cuttings; but modern varieties are so easy to grow from seed and have such good colours and leaf forms that cuttings are unnecessary. Flowers, which appear in summer, are small. Pinch out the flower buds to keep the plant bushy. If this is done while the buds are young, the stem will not be damaged and the plants will continue to give colourful display for months.

Flame nettles are available in colours ranging from variegated grey and green to brilliant gold, orange, crimson and purple. They grow to between 6–24in (15–60cm) with leaves up to 8in (20cm) long and 4in (10cm) across. The leaves, which in some varieties are scented, are more attractive than the small blue flowers.

Light: Good indirect light but not direct sunlight which may dull the colours.

Temperature: Best around 70°F (21°C). Flame nettle will survive up to 100°F (38°C) if given plenty of water. Colour may fade if below 50°F (10°C).

Water: Vigorous root system needs copious water, especially in hot weather. Water daily if necessary; keep compost just moist when overwintering, watering about once a week.

Humidity: Spray twice a week in summer. Stand pot in saucer of damp pebbles.

Feeding: Give nitrogen-rich plant food during growing season, every 10 days in loam-based, every 5 in soil-less composts.

Soil: Loam-based No.2 or soil-less. Use broad-based pots with soil-less to prevent taller plants from getting top heavy.

After flowering: Flowers should be pinched out in bud stage. Flame Nettle is often discarded when foliage begins to die back in autumn, although it can be overwintered and brought into growth the following spring. Gradually decrease watering, keeping compost just moist. Keep plant in a light place, no colder than 50°F (10°C). Move to warmer, lighter position in spring, about 70°F (21°C).

Seedlings collapse. Pythium disease, contracted from soil or container. Discard plants. Always use clean pots and water and sterile compost.

Leaves small and pale. Needs feeding. Give dilute liquid fertilizer rich in nitrogen once a week.

what goes wrong

Small white flies on undersides of leaves. Whitefly. Spray with pyrethrum-based insecticide. Repeat weekly until clear.

Stem black and sunken. Black leg. Fungus contracted from soil or water, usually affecting plants raised outdoors. Destroy plant and treat soil with cheshunt compound.

Plant wilts, soil very wet. Waterlogging, which may cause root rot. Do not allow plant to stand permanently in water. Allow to dry out before watering again.

Leaves turn black. If plant has been placed outdoors, frost damage. Flame Nettle is not hardy and needs frost protection.

Flower stem bare and black at tip. Flower bud pinched out too late. Always pinch out buds as soon as they appear.

Propagation
Sow in spring and cover with light dust of dry compost. Place in propagator or plastic bag at 70°F (21°C) and move into full light when shoots show. Prick out 2in (5cm) apart then choose best colours to pot separately in 3½in (9cm) pots.

Edges of leaves turn brown. Too dry or too hot. Keep well watered, spray in hot weather, and stand pot on moist pebbles to maintain humidity.

Plant does not thrive. Leaves dull and uninteresting. Too cold. Move to a warmer place, over 50°F (10°C).

Wingless insects on growing points. Greenfly. Spray with pyrethrum-based insecticide. Repeat weekly until plant is clean.

Leaves turn yellow at edges, spreading towards centre. Fern eelworm, which usually only infests plants raised outdoors. No cure, destroy plant.

Leaves lose some brightness. Too much direct sunlight. Protect from sun on hot days.

Growth is weedy, stems thin. Much too dark. Move to a light position but shade from strong sunlight.

189

Columnea microphylla

Goldfish plant

This is a spectacular flowering plant which looks at its best in a hanging basket. In spring it produces a succession of bright orange flowers down the length of its hanging stems. Viewed from the side, the flowers look like leaping fish. In its natural habitat, the goldfish plant grows on trees or dead wood, but the roots merely support the plant and do not take their nourishment from the host. When grown in baskets, however, the plants do benefit from feeding.

Light: Full diffused daylight but avoid direct sunshine.
Temperature: 55–60°F (13–16°C) is best, if possible. Temperatures up to 75°F (24°C) can be tolerated if humidity is high.
Water: At least twice weekly in summer to keep compost constantly moist, though plant must not stand in water. Reduce to weekly watering in autumn; and in winter, only after surface has quite dried out – in practice, about once every 10 days.
Humidity: Spray daily with soft water in spring and summer to maintain high humidity, especially if temperature over 60°F (16°C). Avoid spraying flowers. Stand pot on saucer of pebbles almost covered with water; with a hanging basket, keep water in drip tray.
Feeding: Use liquid houseplant food every 14 days in spring and summer, diluted to maker's instructions.
Soil: 3 parts loam-based No.1 with 1 part extra peat added.
Repotting: Only every 2 or 3 years, in late spring. If replanting a hanging basket, remove chains first, being careful not to damage the long trailing stems. Put plenty of crocks in bottom of pot or basket.
Cleaning: Humidity spraying adequate. No leafshine.

Another variety of Goldfish plant is *Columnea gloriosa* which has larger leaves than *C. microphylla* but very simila blooms. Like the smaller-leaved plant, it has striking red flowers which appear among its trailing stems.

White cotton-wool patches at base of leaves. Mealy bug. Spray with diluted malathion and remove bugs and 'wool' with tweezers. Repeat every 14 days until symptoms disappear. Or, paint bugs with methylated spirits and remove with tweezers.

Humidity

1. Spray plants in hanging baskets every day in spring and summer, as they dry out quickly.
2. To provide constant humidity, hang a drip tray under the basket and keep it half filled with water. Humidity will rise around the plant as the water evaporates.

Leaves drop, stem starts to rot. Too cold and/or too wet. Move to warmer place, at least 55°F (13°C). Check compost is not waterlogged. Drain away any excess water from saucer and allow surface of compost to dry out before watering again. Never allow pot to stand in water.

Leaves turn black, flowers transparent. Leafshine damage. Do not use. Clean only by spraying with soft, tepid water but do not allow even water on the flowers.

Tips of stems shrivel, in summer then all leaves. Compost too dry. Plunge pot into bucket of water for 10–15 minutes, then drain. Keep constantly moist in summer, watering at least twice a week. Do not allow to stand in water. Spray daily with soft, tepid water.

Scorch marks on flowers. Too much direct sunlight. Keep in good diffused light, not sunlight.

Leaves healthy but no flowers appear. Not enough light. Move to position in diffused daylight but not direct sun. If new leaves small, also needs feeding. Feed every 2 weeks in spring and summer.

Leaves dry, plant looks dull. Air too dry. Spray daily with soft tepid water in spring and summer. Provide extra humidity by standing pot on saucer of wet pebbles. Do not position hanging baskets over radiators.

Leaves yellow with webs underneath. Red spider mite. Remove webs with damp cloth or sponge, then spray with diluted malathion, especially under leaves. Repeat every 14 days until symptoms disappear. Improve humidity by regular spraying with soft tepid water.

Stems straggly with long spaces between leaves. Needs feeding. Feed with houseplant food at recommended strength every 2 weeks in spring and summer.

what goes wrong

Leaves turn brown and no flowers appear. Too hot. Move to cooler place with more ventilation. Spray daily with soft, tepid water. Maximum temperature 75°F (24°C).

191

Conophytum spectabile

Conophytums are divided into two main groups: those with large heads of long leaves and those with smaller heads of round leaves. *Conophytum spectabile* is one of the smaller headed types. It has a network of dark markings on the surface and spicily scented flowers. Careful watering is needed and a long dry spell in winter and spring, after which the new heads will emerge as from a chrysalis.

Light: Take care in spring when Conophytums are liable to be scorched, especially if a month of cloudy weather is followed by bright sunshine. Shade in spring, reduce shade gradually in early summer to none in autumn.

Temperature: Minimum of 40°F (4°C) in winter; give fresh air in summer.

Water: Conophytums have unusual water requirements. Keep them dry from midwinter to early summer for long-leaved types, to mid-summer for small-leaved. Then water weekly, tailing off to fortnightly in autumn and early winter. During the dry period they will shrivel and look sick but the new body is forming and water at this time is fatal.

Feeding: Not necessary, but if not repotted for 2 or 3 years feed 2 or 3 times in summer with high potash fertilizer.

Soil: Use good loam-based No. 2 potting compost, or soil-less compost, with 50% coarse, gritty sand.

Repotting: Conophytums do not grow well if the roots are disturbed so only repot if not growing or if outgrowing pot.

Propagation: Cut off individual heads with a sharp knife in early summer when plump after first watering. Dust base with hormone rooting powder, dry off for 2 days and place in dry compost. Water after 3 weeks when roots have formed.

Conophytum spectabile grows to only about 1in (2cm) high and spreads to around 3in (7–8cm). The thick, fleshy leaves shrivel away gradually as a new pair grows between them and must not be removed until they are dry and papery and fall away naturally. The delicate flowers appear between the leaves in late summer or autumn.

Double heads form one inside the other, both still fleshy. Watering started too soon. Leave dry from mid-winter until old head has shrivelled and dried up completely.

Plant light brown and shrivelling on one side. Sun scorch. Shade from strong sunshine. When plant is growing in summer, cut out shrivelled head and dust with fungicide.

what goes wrong

Plant does not grow. Needs repotting or roots damaged by pests or overwatering. Remove from pot and check roots. If rotting, treat and dry out (see Introduction). If root mealy bug, see right. If clear, repot in fresh compost/grit in clean pot.

All plant heads become brown and papery, but feel firm. Natural in spring and early summer. New head will grow in its place.

Root mealy bug
1. When repotting, or if plant does not grow but is otherwise healthy, check roots for white woolly patches – root mealy bug.

2. Wash soil off roots if found and swirl in bowl of insecticide diluted with water, following maker's instructions.

3. Leave to dry 2–3 days before repotting in new compost and clean pot.

Heads elongate in summer, no flowers appear by late summer. Too dark or watered at wrong time. Move gradually to sunnier spot. Keep dry from midwinter to early or midsummer, watering only when old heads have shrivelled to paper thin shells.

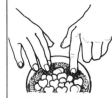

White woolly patches, especially in crevices. Mealy bug. Remove with small paintbrush dipped in methylated spirits, and spray with insecticide. Repeat 2 or 3 times in growing season.

Heads turn black, go soft and rot. Too cold and wet. Keep dry, above 40°F (4°C) in winter. To save plant, pare away blackened part of stem and roots and dust with hormone rooting powder containing fungicide, leave to dry before rerooting in dry compost. Water when new roots appear.

Convallaria majalis

Lily of the valley

Lily of the valley is a hardy woodland plant which does best in a cool, moist shady place. The scented flowers, small white bells clustered around a central stem, come into bloom in mid-spring but special varieties are available for growing indoors and these can be forced to flower from mid-winter through to late summer. It is also possible to force flowers from crowns (or rhizomes) raised outdoors, although these must be stored at a temperature of 32°F (0°C) before potting, to imitate winter conditions. Treat the crowns like bulbs and pot up to 10 in 6in (15cm) pot in autumn. Cover and keep in a cold, dark place for at least 4 weeks, then bring into a warmer place and uncover.

Lily of the valley has broad, pale green leaves which partly surround and protect the small, bell-shaped flowers. Both leaves and stems emerge from a fleshy root known as a rhizome. The most common variety is a white, single flowered one but a rose-coloured single and a white double are also available.

Light: Darkness for 4 weeks, then bring into full light. Avoid direct sun.

Temperature: If growing untreated rhizomes, store at 32°F (0°) for 4–5 days before potting. Once uncovered keep at 60° (16°C). Can be forced at up to 80°F (27°C) for rapid growth.

Water: Keep compost moist at all times. Water twice a week, more frequently if at high temperatures. Use tepid water.

Humidity: Spray weekly after leaves appear.

Feeding: Not necessary for indoor growth.

Soil: Light peat-based potting compost. Do not use bulb fibre.

After flowering: If growing specially treated crowns, discard after flowering as they will not grow again. If growing ordinary garden ones, which have been kept in cool conditions, they may flower again if planted out in the garden. Cut back foliage after flowering and plant out in mid-autumn.

Growing stems not strong. If raised in the garden, swift moth caterpillar may have eaten stem below soil level. Discard plants. Dust soil with gamma-HCH.

Leaves turn yellow and collapse, stems and roots rotting. Waterlogged. Discard badly affected plants, as they will not recover. Keep soil moist at all times and ensure that drainage is good.

Brown rot at base of stem, grey mould on stem or leaves. Botrytis. Can be caused by overwatering and waterlogging. Allow to dry out before watering again. Plant will not recover if stem is rotted.

No flowers. Too dry. Soil must be moist at all times. Or rhizomes may have been too small or have been forced before. Best to purchase specially treated ones for indoor cultivation.

Flowers fail to open at the same time. Rhizomes of different sizes planted together. Choose ones of the same size for potting together.

Forcing

1. Place crowns in plastic bag and leave in refrigerator at 32°F (0°C) for 4–5 days. Allow to thaw completely before potting, then keep cold and dark for 4 weeks. Keep moist.

2. Remove cover and bring into light when leaves sprout. Keep at 60°F (16°C) for gentle forcing, up to 80°F (27°C) for early flowering.

what goes wrong

Buds shrivel and go papery, flowers have brown edges, new stems shrivel up. Too dry while flowering. Give plenty of water, daily if necessary, while in flower.

Brown edges on flowers. Too hot, or too much direct sun. Move to a cooler, shadier spot.

Small wingless insects on flower buds. Aphids. Spray with a pyrethrum-based insecticide. Repeat in a week if still seen.

Leaves very pale and soft, no flowers. Too dark or too hot (over 80°F, 20°C). Move to a cooler, well lit position.

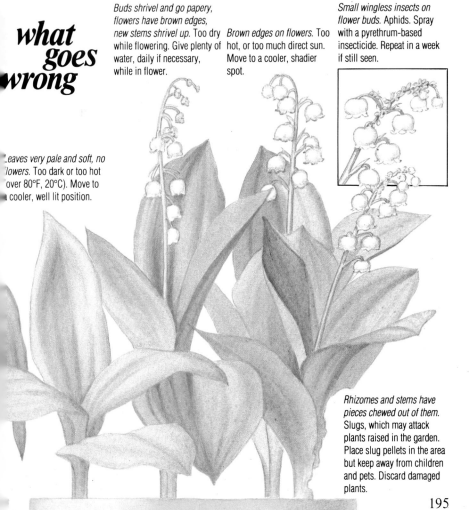

Rhizomes and stems have pieces chewed out of them. Slugs, which may attack plants raised in the garden. Place slug pellets in the area but keep away from children and pets. Discard damaged plants.

195

Dwarf morning glory

This plant has little in common with the rampant weed known as *Convolvulus,* though it, too, grows easily and it gives a mass of colour from just a few seeds. It can be sown where it is to flower, germinates easily, will survive frost and is not too troubled by pests and disease. In colder climates it should be started in a cold frame for protection. An ideal plant for filling out containers (for example where an evergreen has yet to reach a good size), one packet of seeds will fill 6 windowboxes with a blue carpet of flowers.

Light: Sun, but will take an hour or two of shade.

Temperature: Germination, 50–55°F (10–13°C). Will stand frost.

Humidity: Dry, but after a very hot day give a light spray.

Soil: Rich but light such as loam-based No.2.

Feeding: Feed when the seedlings are 4–5 weeks old, using a liquid fertilizer at maker's recommended strength. Repeat every 10 days until early autumn.

Propagation: Sow in mid-spring. If sowing in final container, fill with potting compost to 2in (5cm) from top, water and drain for 2 hours. Add 1in (2½cm) seedling compost and level off with flat board. Water again and drain for 3–4 hours. Sow seed (about 20 to a 12in, 30cm) container) and cover with ⅛in (2mm) compost. A few strands of black cotton will deter birds. Thin seedlings to 10. Or, sow in small pots, 3 to a pot, and place in cold frame. Transfer to final container when about 3in (7cm) high.

Tidying: Remove any yellow leaves.

Varieties: Blue Flash, deep rich blue with yellow centre and white surround. Petite Mixed, rose, blue and white shades with white centre.

Dwarf morning glory is a bushy, compact plant about 12in (30cm) high with medium green leaves wider at the tip than the base. The bell-shaped flowers, usually deep blue with a strong yellow centre, bloom through most of the summer.

White froth, especially where leaf joins stem. Froghopper, concealed in froth. Wash off with hose or spray with diluted malathion at half maker's recommended strength.

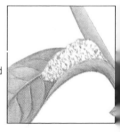

what goes wrong

Plant loose in soil, may be rocking about. Earthworms entering through drainage holes disturbing compost round roots. Worm casts on soil surface confirm. Water with solution of permanganate of potash to bring worms to surface; then remove by hand. Raise container on bricks to prevent further access.

Whole plant droops. Too dry. Give container thorough soak, then allow to become just moist before watering again.

Whole plant yellow and sickly. Waterlogged. Check drainage holes not clogged and water less. Allow to drain until almost dry before watering again.

Spraying

When temperature over 80°F (27°C) mist spray or syringe plants all over in the evening. Do not spray in bright sunlight.

Protecting

Place sticks around edge of container and stretch black cotton between them to deter birds.

Clusters of tiny insects smother growing points. Aphids. Spray with pirimicarb or other insecticide. Repeat in 10 days if not quite clear.

Leaves have white wriggly lines. Leaf miner. Spray with diluted malathion and repeat after 10 days to kill larvae. Or press finger nail into leaf at end of trail, where grub shows as darker area.

Plant loses colour and does not thrive. Needs feeding. Feed every week instead of every 10 days but do not increase strength of feed.

Some stems wilt while rest of plant fresh. If base of stem damaged, slugs. Slime trails will confirm. If eaten cleanly through, woodlice. Put down slug bait as maker recommends or spray with gamma-BHC for woodlice. Keep both cures away from fishponds; gamma-BHC will taint edible crops grown in same soil following years. Kill woodlice by hand if possible instead

197

Cordyline terminalis

Flaming dragon tree

The Flaming dragon tree's bright red colouring makes it a popular houseplant. In fact its lower leaves tend to remain green and only the upper leaves are brightly coloured. Many varieties are grown, the favourite being 'Prince Albert' which grows to about 2ft (60cm) indoors. There is a slightly larger variety called 'Lord Robertson' and a miniature called 'Red edge' which, as its name suggests has red-edged leaves, growing to only about 5in (13cm) long. Not a plant for the novice, but a good one if you have a little experience. Cordylines are closely related to Dracaenas (pp. 236–240) and there is often confusion in naming the varieties.

The Flaming dragon tree has dark green leaves, spectacularly splashed with red and purple. Buy plants with bright leaves growing right down to the bottom of the stem unless the plant is growing on a thick cane, when there should be a bunch of healthy leaves at the top.

Light: They need strong light to maintain colour but keep away from direct midday sun. Green varieties tolerate shade.

Temperature: To maintain growth and colour keep at 65–70°F (18–21°C). Will stand down to 55°F (13°C) if kept almost dry. Maximum summer temperature 75°F (24°C). If higher, increase mist spraying to improve humidity.

Water: Keep always moist, watering once or twice a week in summer, depending on temperature, once a week in winter.

Humidity: Spray twice weekly in summer and winter but never in direct sunlight. If over 75°F (24°C), spray daily.

Feeding: Add liquid houseplant food at maker's recommended strength to water every 14 days during growing season.

Soil: Either loam-based or peat-based No. 2.

Repotting: Every other year enough. Always ensure drainage hole is clear.

Cleaning: Wipe leaves with damp cloth. Leafshine may be used once a month except on 'Red edge' variety.

Pruning

1. If your plant has lost its lower leaves and stem looks bare, you can prune it to make it shoot new leaves further down stem.

2. Cut stem just above a leaf scar with secateurs or a sharp knife. Dust tip with fungicide to prevent infection and keep stem under polythene bag to give extra humidity.

3. New leaves will sprout from further down the stem to give a better balanced shape.

what goes wrong

Leaves lack colour. Not enough light. Move into position of good diffused light but not strong midday summer sun.

Leaf edges brown or spots on leaves. Damage caused by spraying in sunlight. Needs humidity but do not spray while sun is on leaves. Remove unsightly leaf at base of stem.

Leaves yellow with webs underneath. Red spider mite. Remove webs with damp cloth or sponge, then spray with diluted malathion, especially under leaves. Repeat every 14 days until symptoms disappear.

Brown scales under leaves and on stems. Scale insect. Spray with diluted malathion and, after 48 hours, remove discs with thumbnail. Repeat weekly for 4 weeks until clear.

Leaves distorted and sticky with green insects. Greenfly. Spray with pyrethrum-based insecticide or diluted malathion. Repeat 1 week later, then weekly until clear.

New leaves small and distorted. Needs feeding. Feed with liquid houseplant food at maker's recommended strength every 14 days in the growing season.

Leaves shrivel and dry up. Too hot. Keep below 75°F (24°C) if possible and if temperature near maximum provide extra humidity.

Leaf tips turn brown, lower leaves drop. Air too dry. Spray plant twice weekly with soft, tepid water and if over 75°F (24°C) stand on wet pebbles for extra humidity.

Leaves rot and drop off, no new ones appear. Too cold or too wet. Check conditions. Move to warmer place, above 60°F (16°C), and if compost waterlogged, allow surface to dry out before watering again. Always test compost before watering.

199

Cotyledon undulatum

This attractive meal-covered species with wavy-edged leaves makes a good plant either indoors or in the green-house. It can reach 16–20in (40–50cm) tall and 6–8in (15–20cm) across. After four or five years, if grown well, it will produce hanging, bell-shaped pink flowers. Other species include *Cotyledon orbiculata*, with mealy, smooth but red-edged leaves and *C. ladismithiensis*, with fat, green, hairy, wavy-edged leaves. All are fairly simple to grow, but the leaves are sometimes easily dislodged and the mealy covering is easily marked. When using insecticides it is therefore better to choose a systemic type that can be watered into the soil.

Cotyledon undulatum, or Silver crown, is unlikely to flower until it is 4 or 5 years old. Flowers can then appear in spring, summer or autumn but its wavy-edged leaves make the plant attractive all year round.

Light: A sunny spot is best, with no shade, to keep plants compact and well coloured.
Temperature: A minimum of 40°F (4°C), but fewer leaves will fall if kept at 50°F (10°C). Give fresh air in summer.
Water: Start to water once a fortnight in spring, weekly in hottest summer months, tailing off in autumn. If under 50°F (10°C) in winter keep dry, if higher, give a little water monthly.
Feeding: Use high potash fertilizer once a month in summer only.
Soil: Use good loam-based No. 2 potting compost, or soil-less compost, with 30% coarse, gritty sand.
Repotting: Every spring in size larger pot being careful not to handle leaves, and so mark the floury covering.
Propagation: The leaves will not root. Remove a shoot about 2–3in (8cm) long with a sharp knife, and dust the cut ends with hormone rooting powder. Leave to dry for 2–3 days before inserting in dry compost. Water after 3 weeks when roots have formed. Best time is early summer. Seed is sometimes available.

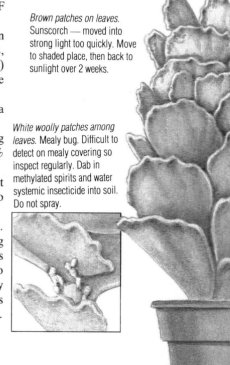

Brown patches on leaves. Sunscorch — moved into strong light too quickly. Move to shaded place, then back to sunlight over 2 weeks.

White woolly patches among leaves. Mealy bug. Difficult to detect on mealy covering so inspect regularly. Dab in methylated spirits and water systemic insecticide into soil. Do not spray.

Repotting

When repotting, take care not to damage the soft floury covering. Prepare new pot one size larger than old. Ease plant out sideways onto surface padded with newspaper, grasping root-ball not plant body. Lower gently into new pot and firm compost around roots. Do not water again for 2–3 weeks.

Leaves drop off leaving topknot on each stem. Many causes. May be too dry, need feeding or repotting or overwatering may have caused black rot. If dry in summer, soak pot for ½ hour in bowl of water, then drain and water more generously each time. In winter water monthly. If roots rotted, pare away soft area (see Introduction) and repot. If all conditions correct, check for root mealy bug .

Leaves, stems and roots black and rotting, leaves fall. Too cold and wet, too humid. Move to warmer place, over 50°F (10°C) in winter and allow soil to dry out. Give just enough water to stop leaves shrivelling — once a month enough. Pare away blackened stem and roots and dust with fungicide before rerooting (see Introduction).

what goes wrong

If stems grow tall they may become topheavy, and may lean and flop over. Insert cane beside plant to support it or repropagate from shoots.

Long gaps between leaves, leaves pale with thin mealy covering. Too dark. Move to lighter place over 2 weeks.

Marks on leaves, meal rubbed off. Damage by humans, curtains or pets. Move to protected place and plant will recover.

Round pieces missing from edges of leaves, lower stem thickened and no new growth. Vine weevil. Dust soil with insecticide powder. Slice stem from base until brown area in centre removed. Dust with fungicide and leave to dry. Inspect roots for damage and treat as stem. Reroot in dry compost.

201

Crassula ovata

This plant is among the larger and more showy species of Crassula: it can easily grow to 3ft (1m) tall. It is often labelled wrongly *Crassula portulacea* and is commonly known as the jade tree. It has shiny jade green, spoon-shaped leaves, sometimes with red edges. On mature plants that get plenty of sunlight in winter, clusters of star-shaped pink or white flowers 2–3in (6–8cm) across are produced. Another large one is *Crassula arborescens* with disc-like silvery-green leaves. *C. falcata* and *C. lactea* will make plants a foot (30cm) tall or wide. Smaller Crassulas include *C.* 'Morgan's Beauty', *C. columella*, *C. nealeana*, *C. cornuta*, *C. arta*, *C. deceptor*, *C. socialis*, *C. justi-corderoyi*, *C. cooperi*, *C. pubescens*, *C. teres*, *C. tecta* and many more.

The smaller Crassulas, including this *Crassula* 'Morgan's Beauty', flower more quickly than the large *Crassula ovata* (right). They are also useful where space is limited as many will never outgrow a 4 or 5in (10 or 12cm) pot. The striking flowers appear in winter and last a week or more.

Light: A light, sunny position is needed.
Temperature: A minimum of 40°F (4°C). Give fresh air in summer.
Water: Start watering fortnightly in spring, weekly in hottest months, tailing off in autumn. Give just a little every month to prevent leaves shrivelling in winter. See also Introduction.
Feeding: Not necessary, unless plant has not been repotted in spring. If not, use high potash fertilizer 2 or 3 times in summer.
Soil: Use good loam-based No. 2 potting compost, or soil-less compost, with 30% coarse, gritty sand.
Repotting: Every spring in size larger pot.
Propagation: In spring or summer shoots of 3–4 leaves can be removed with a sharp knife, dried for a day or two and inserted in or laid on dry compost. Water after 2–3 weeks when roots have appeared. Individual leaves may be gently prised off and treated similarly and will form new plants.

Brown marks on leaves. Sunscorch, moved into bright sun too quickly. Move out of sun, then reintroduce over period of 2 weeks. Give fresh air in summer.

Leaves distorted, as virus. Reaction to insecticide, especially malathion. Stop using insecticide and plant will recover.

White woolly patches among leaves. Mealy bug. Remove with small paintbrush dipped in methylated spirits and spray with contact or systemic insecticide. Repeat 2–3 times in growing season.

Leaves turn black and fall, stem and roots rot. Black rot — too cold and wet. Keep above 40°F (4°C) in winter, best around 50°F (10°C). Allow to dry out. Pare away blackened area and dust with fungicide. Leave to dry for 2–3 days before rerooting in dry compost.

Stems grow long with long spaces between leaves, and bend towards light. Too dark. Keep in full sunlight all year round.

Leaves dry up and drop. Some leaf-fall natural in winter. In summer, too dry or overwatered. If dry, give more water at each watering. If wet, allow to dry out thoroughly.

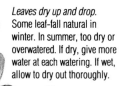

what goes wrong

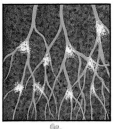

Plant does not grow. Needs feeding or repotting. If conditions correct, check roots for root mealy bug (white woolly patches). Wash all soil off roots and swirl in contact insecticide. Allow to dry before repotting in fresh compost and clean pot. Leave dry for 2 weeks.

Round pieces missing from edges of leaves, little new growth, stem swollen. Vine weevil. Dust soil with insecticide powder. Slice stem from base until brown central area with larvae reached. Dust with fungicide and reroot (see Introduction).

Crocus vernus

Dutch crocus

Although there are many species of crocus, including both autumn and winter-flowering types, the spring-flowering Dutch crocus is best for growing in pots and bowls. Some varieties can be forced to flower for Christmas but all need a cool, airy place and will not succeed in the average living-room. A light porch or landing is ideal. They grow from corms which can be planted up to 10 in a 5in (13cm) pot in autumn and just covered with compost. Place in a cool, dark place for at least 8 weeks. Under sand or ash in the garden is ideal but wrapped in black plastic and newspaper in a cold room or on a window ledge will do. Move into light when shoots show, and only bring into the living-room for flowering.

Spring-flowering Dutch crocus are easy to grow as long as they are kept cool. The flowers rise from the short, spiky green leaves, encased in a papery sheath. Although not very long-lived, they appear in succession, growing 4–6in (10–15cm) high.

Light: Total darkness for at least 8 weeks, diffused light for 2 weeks, then full light.

Temperature: Maximum 45°F (7°C) while in darkness and growing. Maximum 65°F (18°C) for flowering.

Water: Keep compost just moist while in darkness, so check every week and water into the edge of the pot if quite dry. Water twice a week while flowering.

Humidity: Dry, cool, airy situation best, so do not spray or botrytis may develop.

Feeding: Unnecessary unless keeping corms, when feed every 14 days with liquid food at maker's recommended strength until leaves die down.

Soil: Any good proprietary potting compost or bulb fibre.

After flowering: Remove dead flowerheads immediately. Corms which have been forced will not flower again, so discard after flowering. If you have a garden, corms can be planted out in autumn.

Flowers droop. Too dark or hot, or soil too dry. Check conditions. If not given enough light, supporting sheath will not be strong enough to hold up flower. If soil is allowed to dry out, flowers may not recover, so keep moist at all times. Keep below 65°F (18°C) while flowering.

Leaf tips brown and dry. Soil or air too dry, gas fumes in atmosphere. Keep compost just moist at all times. Move to a cooler position or away from fumes.

Small holes in corm or stem. Slug or snail damage if pots have been kept outdoors. Put down slug bait (keep away from pets and children), or keep pots in a cool, dark place indoors.

Corms produce leaves but no flowers. Most likely cause is pots kept in hot, dry atmosphere. Crocus will fail in too much heat. No remedy now, but keep plants in a cool, dry place under 50°F (10°C) if possible and keep compost moist next year.

Few flowers produced. Corms planted too late for maximum development. Plant as early in autumn as possible.

Corms

Crocus corms are round, flattened with a slightly hollow centre. Always inspect before planting.

1. If chewed or eaten away, mice or squirrels have found them while pots stored outside or in a shed. Protect with fine mesh wire and stand pots on solid base to prevent tunnelling.

2. Black sunken marks indicate bulb rot. Reject affected corms and dip others in solution of benomyl before planting.

Flowers open fully, then shrivel rapidly. Too hot while flowering. Keep in coolest room, under 65°F (18°C).

what goes wrong

Grey fluffy mould on leaves and buds just before flowering. Air too humid or compost too wet. Move to a cool, airy place and spray with benomyl or iprodione. Water into edge of compost.

Flowers die quickly. Too much direct sun. Move out of midday sun to a shadier position.

Leaves yellowing. Too wet. Keep compost moist but not waterlogged. Or, Vine weevil may be eating corms if grown outdoors. Search soil for small white C-shaped grubs and dust soil with gamma HCH if found.

Crossandra infundibuliformis

Firecracker flower

Although a bit tricky to keep, with correct care the Firecracker flower can be made to bloom almost continuously from spring to late summer. The plant prefers a dry atmosphere and will rot if too humid. It has orange flowers growing from green bracts not unlike ears of corn; the dark green glossy leaves are attractive but deceptively tender. The plant can be easily increased by taking cuttings at almost any time of year and rooting them in sand. Newly bought plants should have shiny leaves with no black marks anywhere.

Light: Shade from direct light in spring and summer; in winter, give full daylight including sunshine.

Temperature: Best at 65°F (18°C) all year round, with summer maximum of 70°F (21°C) if kept very dry.

Water: Only when compost surface dry, using tepid soft water. This applies all year round and probably means once a week in summer, once every 10 days in winter, depending on the temperature. Avoid getting water on the leaves; never stand plant in water. Overwatering will kill this plant.

Humidity: Atmosphere must be dry with a good circulation of air. In very hot weather (over 70°F, 21°C), stand pot on saucer of pebbles almost covered with water. Never spray plant or keep in humid greenhouse.

Feeding: Weekly during growing period only with liquid houseplant food diluted to maker's instructions.

Soil: 2 parts loam-based No. 2 and 1 part added sand.

Repotting: In early spring into pot with plenty of broken crocks in bottom for good drainage, no leafshine.

The Firecracker flower's blooms are produced from late spring onwards, and make a strongly coloured contrast to the lush foliage. The leaves look glossy and strong but wilt rapidly if they become wet. A good plant for a dry atmosphere.

Flowers and leaves rot. Botrytis. Plant too cold and damp. Spray with fungicide following maker's instructions, then place in warmer position, at least 55°F (13°C) in winter, 65°F (18°C) in summer. Always allow surface to dry out between waterings. Remove damaged leaves and flowers.

Leaves curl up and edges turn black. Compost too moist and too much humidity. Allow surface of soil to dry out before watering again, then water only after surface dries out each time. Once a week in summer, once every 10 days in winter should be enough. Do not spray.

Removing flowers

Flowers open and fall progressively, from base of flower spike. Remove dead ones as they fall. When all have died, cut off flower stem just above the topmost pair of leaves.

Lanky growth, no flowers. Too dark. Move to lighter place, will take full sun in winter.

Flowers turn translucent. Plant has been sprayed with water. Do not spray. Provide humidity by standing pot on saucer of wet pebbles if temperature over 70°F (21°C).

Plant does not grow. Too cold. Move to warmer place, at least 55°F (13°C) in winter; 65°F (18°C) in summer.

what goes wrong

Many leaves turn black all over. Too cold. Move to warmer place. Do not allow temperature to drop below 55°F (13°C) in winter; best between 65°F (18°C) and 70°F (21°C) in summer. Or, leafshine damage.

New leaves small in spring. Needs feeding. Feed weekly in spring and summer with houseplant food diluted to recommended strength.

Leaves shrivel and turn brown. Too hot and dry, air too dry. Water if surface of compost has dried out and move to cooler position, under 70° (21°C) if possible. Do not spray, but provide extra humidity by standing pot on saucer of wet pebbles.

Leaves develop brown spots, plant wilts and collapses. Gas fumes. Move to fume-free room.

Webs under leaves. Red spider mite. Remove webs with a dry cloth and add systemic insecticide such as malathion to water for compost. Do not spray with insecticide. Repeat treatment after 10 days if pest persists. Improve humidity by standing pot on wet pebbles.

Leaves go limp. Compost too moist and/or in a cold draught. Allow surface to dry out between waterings – once a week in summer, once every 10 days in winter should be enough. Move plant out of draughts.

Some flower petals fall from flower spike. Natural. Flowers appear and fade progressively from the bottom of the spike to the top.

Cryptanthus bivittatus

Starfish

One of the smallest plants in the family known as Bromeliads, the Starfish plant is a real sun lover, and the more light it gets the brighter is the colour on its flat leaves. The plant has a poor root system, which tethers it rather than giving nourishment, so it grows well in a little moss wired to a piece of log or bark. Thus it makes a good hanging decoration, though, with its striped leaves, it also looks attractive in the front of a bowl of mixed plants. Young plantlets are produced in the axils of the leaves and, unlike other Bromeliads, the mother plant does not die after producing them. Several species are available with differently patterned or coloured leaves.

The Starfish plant has leaves which grow to only about 4in (10cm) long. It grows well with other plants in bowls or bottle gardens and, because it has a small root system, can easily be grown attached to a piece of bark.

Light: The more the better. Do not allow water on the leaves in full sun, as it will scorch them.
Temperature: Winter range 60–65°F (15–18°C), summer maximum 75°F (24°C).
Water: 2–3 times a week in summer, especially if tied to moss. About every 10 days in winter. They do not need to have water in their central well, keeping the roots moist is sufficient.
Humidity: Spray every day in summer with fine mist when temperature is near maximum.
Feeding: Not essential, though a weak dose of houseplant food every 21 days in summer will help keep it in good condition. Dilute the food so that it is half the strength recommended by the makers.
Soil: Peaty compost mixed with a handful of sphagnum moss if in pots.
Repotting: Not required, as pot is really only a means of anchoring plant. Every 2 or 3 years is enough.
Cleaning: Spray or dust if dirty. No leafshine.

what goes wrong

Leaves shrivel and become thin and papery. Too hot and dry. Water more often, spray regularly and move to a cooler place if possible.

Leaves dull and droopy. Too dark. Move to lighter place. Can stand full sunlight.

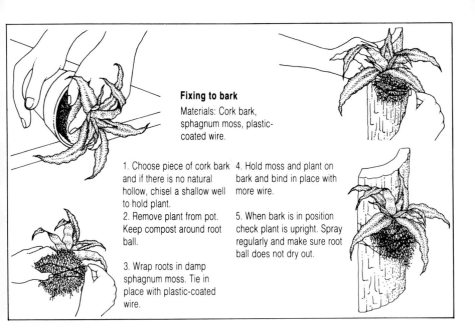

Fixing to bark

Materials: Cork bark, sphagnum moss, plastic-coated wire.

1. Choose piece of cork bark and if there is no natural hollow, chisel a shallow well to hold plant.

2. Remove plant from pot. Keep compost around root ball.

3. Wrap roots in damp sphagnum moss. Tie in place with plastic-coated wire.

4. Hold moss and plant on bark and bind in place with more wire.

5. When bark is in position check plant is upright. Spray regularly and make sure root ball does not dry out.

White woolly patches in centre of plant. Mealy bug. Wipe off with cotton wool dipped in methylated spirits.

Scorch marks on tips of leaves. Water left on leaves in direct sun. Do not allow wet leaves to stand in sunlight.

Leaf tips turn brown. Air too dry. Spray more frequently – every day if around 75°F (24°C). Trim off tips, cutting just outside healthy area.

Plant rotting at base. Too cold and too wet. Probably overwatered. Move to warmer place (at least 60°F 15°C) and allow to dry out. If left wet too long, will die.

209

Ctenanthe oppenheimiana

Never-never plant

This beautiful foliage plant is a distant relative of the Marantas (p.368) but grows in a more upright manner. It is also sometimes sold as a Calathea. A native of Brazil, its name comes from the Greek word for comb and refers to the shape of the flower which is only produced on mature plants. Another species, *Ctenanthe lubbersiana*, is also sometimes available. This has plainer leaves, mottled with light green or cream and is a rather tougher plant.

Light: They do not like strong light and should not be in a window that receives full midday or afternoon sun. Will survive well in shade but will benefit from more light in winter.

Temperature: Best above 60°F (16°C) in winter but will survive down to 50°F (10°C) if compost kept almost dry. Up to 80–85°F (27–29°C) in summer if humidity kept high.

Water: Compost must be kept very moist at all times. Water 2–3 times a week in summer, once a week in winter. If around 50°F (10°C) in winter, water only every 10–12 days.

Humidity: Need high humidity to flourish. Spray daily in summer, twice a week in winter. Place pot on saucer of wet pebbles for constant local humidity.

Feeding: Feed every 14 days in growing season (summer) using liquid houseplant food at half maker's recommended strength.

Soil: Peat-based No. 2 compost, must be open, porous mix.

Repotting: Once a year in late spring. Make sure drainage is good and do not press compost down too much.

Cleaning: Spraying will keep leaves clean; if very dusty wipe with damp cloth. No leafshine.

The Never-never plant's leaves turn at right angles, parallel to the ground. A healthy plant may reach 3ft (90 cm) with 15in (33cm) long leaves, though most plants on sale are only around 12in (30cm) tall.

Brown scales under leaves and on stems. Scale insect. Spray underside of leaves with diluted malathion and, after 48 hours, remove discs with thumbnail. Repeat every week for 4 weeks until clear. Or paint with methylated spirits.

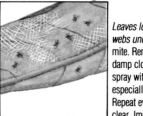

Leaves lose colour and have webs underneath. Red spider mite. Remove webs with damp cloth or sponge, then spray with diluted malathion, especially under leaves. Repeat every 14 days until clear. Improve humidity.

Leaves pale and small. Needs feeding. Feed with liquid houseplant food at half maker's recommended strength in summer growing season.

Plant collapses. Soil too dry or waterlogged. If dry, plunge pot into bucket of water for 10–15 minutes, then drain. If soil wet and dark, allow to dry out before watering again.

Leaves curl and wither. Too hot, air too dry. Spray daily in summer and stand pot on wet pebbles, especially if temperature over 80°F (27°C).

Leaves curl up and do not open. Too cold or too much light. Check conditions. Move out of strong sunlight and keep above 60°F (16°C).

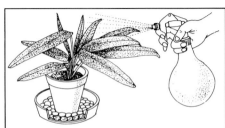

Humidity
Never-never plants need constant high humidity and moist soil. Place pot on saucer of pebbles half covered in water but do not allow pot base to stand in water or roots will rot. In hot weather spray every day and water whenever soil begins to dry out.

Leaves lose colour. Too dark. Does not need full light but must not be too shaded. In winter, move to light position.

what goes wrong

Rust marks on leaves. Leafshine damage. Do not use. Clean only by spraying with soft tepid water. Remove damaged leaf at base of stem.

Leaves droop and look limp. Too hot. Move to cooler place, below 80°F (27°C) if possible and spray daily to keep humidity high.

211

Cuphea ignea

Cigar plant

The Cigar Plant is really a perennial, but when grown indoors is best treated as an annual. It is an easy plant to raise from seed. Sow in early spring in a tray of seed compost, lightly cover with compost and place in a plastic bag. Cover with paper until germinated, then move into light. Prick off seedlings into small containers when large enough to handle and keep them just moist at all times. Choose the strongest ones for potting on to individual 4½in (11cm) pots.

Light: Full light at all times, direct sun if possible. Plant will not flower in shade.
Temperature: Minimum 70°F (21°C) for germination. Grows best at 55–65°F (13–18°C), but will continue to thrive down to 45°F (7°C) if kept in full light.
Water: Does best in soil which is just moist, so water weekly, or twice a week in very hot weather.
Humidity: Spray daily when not in flower if over 75°F (24°C).
Feeding: Feed with liquid house-plant food for 3 weeks at maker's recommended strength after potting in final pot, then weekly.
Soil: Any well-drained, sterile loam-based compost or a home mix of 3 parts loam, 2 parts peat, 1 part sand with trace elements.
After flowering: Flowers are not long-lived but are produced freely for months. Remove dead flowerheads to encourage plant to produce more. When buds stop forming in late autumn/early winter, plant is usually discarded. It is possible to take cuttings or overwinter the plant but this gives no advantage over spring sowing except slightly earlier flowers. If overwintering, keep in a well lit room at 45°F (7°C), water only about every week to 10 days to keep just moist. Bring into warmer room and sunlight in early spring.

If kept in a cool, sunny room, this attractive bushy evergreen will grow to about 12in (30cm) high and flower from midsummer to early winter. The woody stems have small dark green oval leaves and the unusual, cigar-like flowers are long crimson tubes with curious black and green tops. Overwintered plants will have a smaller crop of flowers in their second year.

Edges of leaves turn brown. Damage by leafshine or gas fumes. Do not use leafshine or keep near gas fire.

Plant becomes black and soggy. If plant has been outdoors suspect frost damage and discard. Cigar plant is not hardy and must have frost protection.

Leaves floppy. Much too dry. Water sparingly but do not allow to dry out completely.

what goes wrong

Plant does not thrive in good conditions. Check soil for C-shaped grubs of vine weevil. Dust with gamma HCH if found.

Leaves curled or distorted. Look for wingless insects. Greenfly. Spray with pyrethrum-based insecticide, repeat every 10 days until clear. If no insects, virus infection. Destroy plant.

Flowers few, growth weak. Too dark. Cigar plant must have full light to thrive, so move to well lit position.

Leaves grow strongly, few flowers. Pot too large or soil too rich. Use max. 4½in (11cm) pot; reduce feeding to every 14 days.

Pinpoint spots on leaves, webs underneath. Red spider mite. Spray with pyrethrum-based insecticide or diluted malathion. Repeat in 10 days if still present.

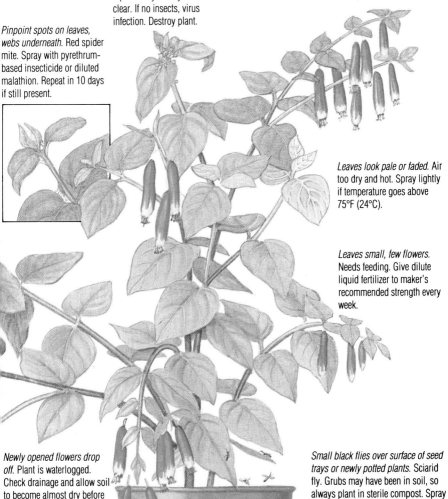

Leaves look pale or faded. Air too dry and hot. Spray lightly if temperature goes above 75°F (24°C).

Leaves small, few flowers. Needs feeding. Give dilute liquid fertilizer to maker's recommended strength every week.

Newly opened flowers drop off. Plant is waterlogged. Check drainage and allow soil to become almost dry before watering again. Keep soil just barely moist.

Small black flies over surface of seed trays or newly potted plants. Sciarid fly. Grubs may have been in soil, so always plant in sterile compost. Spray flies with pyrethrum-based insecticide.

213

Cyclamen

Though winter to spring flowering is still usual, there are now cyclamen varieties which flower all year round. It can be difficult to grow, because it is very susceptible to botrytis which causes the corm, from which leaves and flowers grow, to rot. Another problem is an insect pest, cyclamen mite. When grown successfully, however, the cyclamen produces an abundance of flowers in the depth of winter. It should be bought from a reputable seller, as if it is not well cared for it may suffer damage which will not show for 2 or 3 weeks. It should not be moved around the house, as it likes to stay in one place.

Light: Full light essential, but shade from direct sun.

Temperature: 45–60°F (8–15°C) ideal. Likes cool, airy situation. Beware central heating, sudden temperature changes. While resting without leaves, keep cool.

Water: Twice weekly when flowering, once weekly when no flowers, from below. Increase frequency when new leaves appear, so that compost is always just moist. Never cover corm with soil or water it: it will rot. Do not stand in water or allow soil to get sodden.

Humidity: Stand on saucer of pebbles almost covered in water to maintain essential humidity. Do not spray.

Feeding: Every 14 days when growing and flowering with houseplant food diluted according to the maker's instructions.

Soil: Loam-based No. 2 compost.

Repotting: Into a fresh clay pot after flowering and when old leaves have died down. Flowers better if pot-bound, so do not use too large a pot. Leave top half of corm above soil.

Cleaning: Brush leaves gently with soft brush or cotton wool. Do not moisten or use leafshine.

Cyclamen are usually sold just coming into flower. The leaves should look firm and clean and there should be new buds appearing below the leaves. Plants may have flowers at three stages all together: small tight green buds, larger buds showing their colour and fully developed flowers.

Leaves turn yellow and fall apart. Too hot and dry. Water and move to cooler place.

Grey mouldy patches on leaves. Botrytis. Remove damaged leaves and spray rest with fungicide to prevent infection.

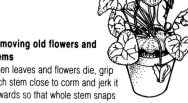

Removing old flowers and stems
When leaves and flowers die, grip each stem close to corm and jerk it upwards so that whole stem snaps off cleanly.

Plant collapses, all leaves drooping. If between waterings, needs water. If soil feels moist, caused by sudden drop in temperature, or plant too cold. Move to warmer room, but not more than 60°F (15°C).

what goes wrong

New leaves stay small, no flowers appear. Needs feeding. Feed every 14 days when new leaves start to grow.

Leaves have brown patches. Leafshine damage. Do not use.

Webs under leaves, leaves discoloured. Red spider mite. Remove affected leaves and add diluted malathion to the water when watering once a week until clear. Do not spray.

Leaves stunted and hard, dust on undersides. Cyclamen mite. No cure. Remove affected leaves and, if you have other cyclamen plants, destroy affected one.

Leaves shrivel and flop. Much too hot and dry. Wrap plant in paper so that all leaves are upright and stand pot in 2in (5cm) water for half an hour. Allow to drain and leave wrapped in paper for 24 hours in cooler room. Unwrap and continue watering normally but keep in cooler room, out of direct sun.

Stem and/or corm rots. Stem rots if corm is covered with soil. Remove surface layer to expose corm. Corm rots if it gets wet. Water always from below. Cut out rot with sharp knife and allow soil to dry right out before watering again.

Stems grow long and weak. Overfeeding or pot too large. Check conditions. Stop feeding until plant recovers and never give more than recommended dose of food. Repot in smaller pot after flowering.

215

Cymbidium orchid

There are about 50 species of the cymbidium orchid and modern propagation techniques have produced literally thousands of hybrids of the once rare and expensive plant, bringing it within reach of everyone. Cymbidiums are easy to cultivate though it is important to get both temperature and humidity right.

Light: Abundant light essential for regular flowering. Stands full sunlight except when in or about to flower. Benefits from being out-of-doors in summer.

Temperature: Winter minimum 45°F (8°C) if dry; otherwise 50°F (10°C) at night, 50–55°F (10–13°C) during day. In summer keep night temperatures as low as possible; up to 70–80°F (21–27°C) in the day.

Water: While growing and flowering, water 2–3 times a week to keep it moist. After flowering, reduce watering to once or twice a week for a resting period. Good drainage is essential.

Humidity: Spray every day with soft, tepid water to encourage moist atmosphere with good air circulation. Stand pot on saucer of pebbles almost covered with water to improve humidity but if colder than 45°F (8°C), remove this and do not spray.

Feeding: Weekly in the growing and flowering season with liquid houseplant food diluted according to the maker's instructions. Do not feed during the resting period after flowering until new growth starts.

Soil: 3 parts special fern (osmunda) fibre and 1 part sphagnum moss. Ready-mixed orchid mixtures are available though experienced orchid growers experiment.

Repotting: After flowering in spring if plant is pot-bound. Check roots. Usually necessary every second year.

Cleaning: Humidity spraying should keep leaves clean. If dusty, wipe with moist cloth. Do not touch flower spikes. No leafshine.

Cymbidium flowers, carried up to thirty to a stem, vary in colour from reddish brown to white. Each flower lasts for about six weeks and they open gradually along the spike. If buying plants in bloom, choose one with flower buds still to open and firm, leathery leaves.

what goes wrong

Leaves turn brown. Too hot. In winter, maximum temperature 55°F (13°C), in summer 80°F (27°C) with a cooler night temperature. Problem worse if air also dry, so keep spraying regularly.

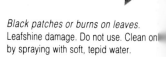

Black patches or burns on leaves. Leafshine damage. Do not use. Clean only by spraying with soft, tepid water.

Flowers have patchy, watery marks. Caused by spraying. Do not spray water or insecticide on flowers or buds.

Plant does not flower. Not enough light. Needs full light, with direct sun except when in or about to flower. When flowers appear, shade slightly to prevent scorching.

Opened flowers marked. Sun scorch. Shade from direct sun but continue to give full indirect light.

Leaves turn pale, flowers translucent. Badly drained or standing in water. Use correct compost, porous enough to allow air between the roots so that water drains rapidly away. Never stand pot in water.

Flower buds fail to open. Not enough light and needs feeding. Keep in full indirect light when flowering. Feed every week while growing and flowering.

Leaves turn black. Too cold. Minimum winter temperature 50° (10°C) unless kept dry. If dry, down to 45°F (8°C) all right for short periods.

Flower stems turn black and rot. Too humid in cold temperature. If temperature drops to 45°F (8°C) do not provide humidity.

Leaves dry out in summer. Needs watering. Soil must be always moist while growing, but plant must not stand in water. Good drainage and the correct compost are very important.

Small flies around soil surface. Whitefly, attracted by damp, humid compost. Spray with pyrethrum-based insecticide every 14 days until clear.

217

Cyperus diffusus

Umbrella grass

This is a more unusual plant for the adventurous collector. Though it is not particularly difficult to grow, it benefits from careful attention as its stems bend and crease easily. It is a graceful and elegant plant, taking its common name from the way its green, slender leaves hang down from the top of its long stems. The stems of Umbrella grass grow to 39in (1m) tall, while those of a smaller variety, *Cyperus alternifolius*, are about half this length. Small brown flowers grow out from the centre of the top of the stem. Since this is really a bog plant, it likes plenty of water.

They can be divided in early spring if they are becoming very large. New plants can also be grown from flower heads. When flowers die, cut off the tips of the leaves on one stem and bend the stem so the leaves are submerged in a bowl of tepid water. Keep warm, changing water every 3–4 days and new plantlets will grow from the old leaf.

Light: Prefers a light position, but keep away from mid-day sun.

Temperature: Winter minimum 55°F (12°C). Summer up to 68–77°F (20–25°C), if well watered.

Water: Keep compost wet at all times; better if standing in water. Water every day in summer, and if in centrally heated rooms.

Humidity: Spray daily in summer, 3 times a week in winter.

Feeding: Every 14 days in the growing season (spring and summer) with house-plant food diluted according to the maker's instructions.

Soil: Loam-based No. 2 compost.

Repotting: Annually in spring, though prefers a pot slightly too small.

Cleaning: Humidity spraying sufficient. Soft summer rain good. No leafshine.

The stems of Umbrella grasses, topped by an elegant cluster of slender leaves, grow up to 39in (1m) tall. Small brown flowers appear in the centre in summer. Handle the plant with care as the stems easily bend and crease. Make sure new plants have no yellow leaves.

Leaves turn quickly yellow or brown. Needs water urgently. Soak in bucket of water for 10–15 minutes. Place on saucer to drain, and leave standing in water that soaks through. Spray regularly.

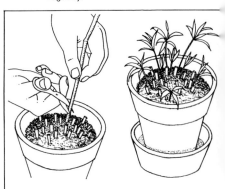

Cutting down stems

1. If plant dies down in winter, cut off stems with scissors just above soil level.

2. Keep pots standing in water and in spring, the stems will reshoot.

Plant does not grow or produce new leaves in summer. Feed every 7 days for about 3 weeks, then continue at 14 day intervals. Do not increase strength of food.

White insects on leaves which fly off when leaves touched. Whitefly. Spray every 14 days with derris or pyrethrum-based insecticide until clear.

what goes wrong

Leaves sticky and covered with small green insects. Edges of leaves nibbled. Greenfly. Spray every 14 days with pyrethrum or diluted malathion-based insecticide until clear.

Leaves bleached. Too much sun. Move out of direct sunlight.

Leaves look scorched. Leafshine damage. Do not use. Cut off damaged leaves.

Leaves look dull and limp. Too dark. Move to lighter place but not full sunlight.

Leaves die in winter. Too cold. Cut off withered foliage. It will reshoot in spring. Keep above 55°F (12°C).

Stem bent and damaged. Plant has been knocked. Stems crease easily so keep in a safe position. Cut off broken stem at soil level.

219

Cyrtomium falcatum

Holly fern

This attractive fern, sometimes also known as the Fishtail fern, is often sold in mixed batches of small ferns. With its glossy, leathery leaves it will thrive in a room where other plants will suffer from smoke or draughts, and is equally happy in the house or an unheated greenhouse. It grows quite rapidly, its fronds reaching 2ft (60cm) long and makes a well-balanced decorative plant. The furry stems grow from an underground rhizome which can be divided in spring. Each section should have roots and 3–4 stems.

Light: Diffused. Does not tolerate direct sunlight.
Temperature: Cool to moderate, 50–65°F (10–18°C) all year round. Remove to coolest part of house if central heating on. Cool greenhouse is ideal.
Water: 3 times a week in summer, once a week in winter; for young plants keep soil always moist.
Humidity: Spray with tepid water twice weekly in summer, once weekly in winter. Provided it is kept cool, requires less humidity than other ferns. Stand on saucer of pebbles almost covered with water if over 65°F (18°C).
Feeding: Weekly in summer with houseplant food diluted with water according to maker's instructions.
Soil: Compost of equal parts of loam-based No. 1 or 2, peat and silver sand.
Repotting: Annually up to 7in (18cm) pot, into next size plastic pot, only when rootball fills pot. Do not compress soil too much, or growth will be slowed. If larger, change topsoil in spring.
Cleaning: Spray with solution of 6 or 7 drops of milk in cup of water to clean and give gloss to leaves. Then wipe with soft cloth. No leafshine.

The Holly or Fishtail fern has bright, glossy, leathery leaves which look rather unlike those of a typical fern. These help it to survive in less humid situations than some ferns, and also make it less susceptible to fumes or smoke in the atmosphere. Though shiny, the leaves should never be treated with leafshine.

Leaves turn brown and crisp. Too dry. Water 3 times a week in summer, once a week in winter. Remove dead fronds.

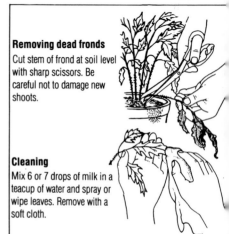

Removing dead fronds
Cut stem of frond at soil level with sharp scissors. Be careful not to damage new shoots.

Cleaning
Mix 6 or 7 drops of milk in a teacup of water and spray or wipe leaves. Remove with a soft cloth.

what goes wrong

Brown burn marks on leaves. Leafshine damage. Do not use. Clean with milk and water mixture **(see below left)**.

Leaves turn dull and soft with webs and small insects underneath. Red spider mite. Spray with diluted malathion, especially under leaves. Use weekly for 3 weeks. Increase humidity.

New leaves much smaller than old ones. Needs feeding. Feed every week in summer while growing with houseplant food at full recommended strength.

Leaves pale and no new ones appear. Too dark. Move to lighter place but not full sunlight.

Plant droops. In summer or if central heating high in winter, ʍo hot. Move to cooler place. ⸏temperature correct, check ▮lant is not standing in water. ⸏so, allow to dry out before ▮atering again.

Leaves turn pale and die in summer though conditions seem correct. Too much direct sunlight. Move to shadier place. Continue watering and spraying regularly.

221

Dahlia

Dahlias vary in height and for most containers bedding or dwarf plants are best. Natives of Mexico, they are very tender and young plants must be carefully protected from spring frosts. At the end of the season when frost has killed the leaves, dig up the tubers, dry thoroughly and dust with fungicide. Store in dry sand, peat or old newspapers in a frost-free place until late winter.

Light: Good at all times.
Temperature: Germination and cuttings, 60°–65°F (16–18°C). Outside, little growth below 45°F (7°C).
Water: keep moist but not soggy.
Humidity: Spray seedlings and cuttings, not mature plants.
Soil: Loam-based No. 3 or soil-less.
Feeding: Start 14 days after planting, at recommended strength, then every 10 days for loam-based, every 5 for soil-less composts.
Propagation: Prepare seed tray in early spring. Sow and cover with ¼in (7mm) compost; put in plastic bag at 60–65°F (16–18°C) until seedlings appear. Move to full light. Prick out when large enough to handle but do not plant out until frosts finished. From tubers, plant in trays of soil or soil-less compost in late winter, covering tuber but not crown. Water a little each day. When shoots 3in (8cm) long, cut them off right down to tuber and dip ends in rooting powder. Plant 1in (2½cm) deep in seedling compost in 3in (9cm) pots. They root in 3 weeks. Then treat as seedlings.
Tidying: Remove dead flowers. Take off buds below main flower to improve its size.
Varieties: From seed Coltness Gem, red or yellow, single dwarf, double or semi-double. Figaro, dwarf, early, many colours. Redskin, dwarf, bushy, mixed colours.

Dahlia flowers come in almost every colour and shade from red through yellow to white, in single, semi-double and double blooms. To be sure of getting the shape and colour of flower you want, buy cuttings from a dahlia specialist; but plants can also be successfully grown from seed.

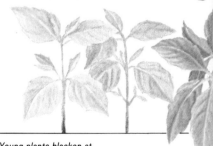

Flower only partly opens, and is lopsided. Capsid bug. Dark sunken mark under flower confirms. Spray with systemic insecticide.

Young plants blacken at base of stem, plant yellowing. Root or stem rot. Treat with soil fungicide but do not plant out affected plants.

Plant grows straggly and weak. Not enough light. Dahlias need good light at all times.

Young plant turns yellow, soil dark and sour. Waterlogged. Check drainage in container.

Young plants yellow, leaves pale but compost not too wet. Needs feeding. Feed every 10 days in loam-based soil, every 5 in soil-less compost. If feeding intervals correct, feed more often but do not use stronger food.

Seedlings or young plants outside turn black overnight. Frost. Protect from frost in spring.

Plant has holes and looks chewed. If flowers ragged with small holes in petals, earwigs. Trap in upturned pot or jar filled with dry grass or straw and destroy. Or, use gamma-BHC with care. If leaves, flowers and buds eaten with many holes and slimy trails, slugs or snails. Put down slug pellets as maker instructs. Keep away from animals and fish ponds.

Grey mould on flowers. Botrytis. Spray with benomyl. Do not spray mature plants with water.

Young growth has small spots gradually enlarging. Sooty moulds develop. Smut disease. Spray weekly with bordeaux mixture.

Holes in leaves, flower buds eaten. Caterpillar. Search for pest and remove. Or use gamma-BHC with care.

Shoots, buds and flowers have clusters of small insects. Aphid. Spray with malathion or systemic insecticide. Repeat weekly until clear.

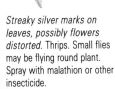

Streaky silver marks on leaves, possibly flowers distorted. Thrips. Small flies may be flying round plant. Spray with malathion or other insecticide.

Irregular blackish streaks, some yellow mottling on leaves. Virus disease. Will not badly affect flowers but do not use for cuttings. If aphids around, do not use any plants for cuttings as disease will spread.

what goes wrong

Flower droops. Too dry. Water immediately and keep soil always moist but not waterlogged.

223

Davallia

Rabbit's foot fern

This fern produces a rhizome which hangs over the top of the pot, looking uncannily like a rabbit's foot. Although in it natural habitat, its fronds grow to 18in (45cm), as a houseplant they usually reach only 6–12in (15–30cm). It differs from most ferns in that it should not be sprayed to help humidity and it is sensitive to salt, so should be watered with soft water. The rhizome should not be planted in the soil but raised above soil level and grown over the edge of the pot. They are good plants for hanging baskets as their furry 'feet' make an attractive display.

Light: Good light, near window that does not get full sun best. Keep out of direct sunlight.
Temperature: In summer 64–68°F (18–20°C), reasonably steady 60°F (15°C) in winter.
Water: 2 or 3 times a week in summer, once or twice a week in winter with soft water. Keep soil moist but not soaked.
Humidity: Does not thrive in dry air (e.g. central heating) but do not spray with water. Stand pot on pebbles almost covered with water. A kitchen which is sometimes steamy is ideal.
Feeding: Every 14 days in growing season with liquid houseplant food diluted with water. Use half the amount recommended by the maker. No 'plant sticks' or granulated food.
Soil: Compost of 3 parts fibrous peat or well-rooted leaf mould, 1 part chopped sphagnum moss, 1 part silver sand.
Repotting: In spring into clay pot one size larger. Good drainage essential: line pot with broken clay pots.
Cleaning: Dust lightly with feather duster. No leafshine.

A healthy Rabbit's foot fern has slightly glossy leaves but is often bought for its striking, furry-looking rhizomes which hang down over the top of the pot like a rabbit's foot. Unlike most ferns, it should not be sprayed and if it is necessary to treat it with insecticides, these should be added to the soil when watering. Hard water can cause the rhizomes to turn black, so always use soft or rain water.

White mould on stems and leaflets in summer. Mildew. Plant too wet or sprayed, possibly pot-bound. Repot and water once with systemic fungicide.

Leaflets pale, tips turn brown. Too much sun. Keep in light place but not direct sunlight.

Whole fronds turn black. Damage from spraying with either water or insecticide. Do not spray at all.

Leaflets fall in winter. Some leaf loss natural but if all leaflets fall, too cold. Place in warmer room (at least 60°F, 15°C) in winter.

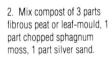

Repotting

1. Carefully remove plant from old pot. Do not damage rhizomes.

2. Mix compost of 3 parts fibrous peat or leaf-mould, 1 part chopped sphagnum moss, 1 part silver sand.

3. Add broken crocks or pebbles to provide drainage in pot 1 size larger.

4. Put layer of compost in new pot and place plant on it. Cover with rest of compost allowing rhizomes to remain above surface.

Whole fronds turn brown. Too ~~h~~ot, air too dry, probably ~~c~~entral heating. Keep between ~~6~~0°F (15°C) and 68°F (20°C). ~~D~~o not spray but place pot on ~~w~~et pebbles.

what goes wrong

Plant does not grow. Too dark. Move to area of diffused daylight. If growth stunted and no rhizomes appear, compost too heavy. Repot in spring using suggested compost mixture.

Fronds have black patches and are distorted. Leafshine damage. Clean only with feather duster.

Leaflets turn brown at tips in summer. Humidity too high. Do not spray.

Leaflets shrivel in summer. Direct sunlight. Move to area of diffused light.

Tiny black-winged insects on leaves. Growth stunted. Thrips. Do not spray plant but add systemic insecticide to water every 14 days until clear.

White insects hopping in soil. Whitefly. Add systemic insecticide to water every 14 days until clear. Do not spray plant.

Rhizomes turn black. Hard water used or salt in water. Also caused by plant fertilizer sticks or granulated plant food.

Dianthus

As Dianthus species cross easily there are many hybrids. All are suitable for containers as are the many annual and perennial species. Recent hybrids, all annuals, have the longest flowering periods, from early to late summer. If buying plants in spring, choose bushy, healthy ones as they will produce more flowers.

Light: Maximum at all times.
Temperature: Winter germination 60°F (16°C). After pricking out, 50°F (10°C).
Water: For germination, moist. Otherwise almost dry, well-drained soil.
Humidity: Dry. Do not spray.
Soil: Well-drained, sandy, or loam-based No:2. Plants grown for 1 season only may be in soil-less compost.
Feeding: Liquid fertilizer every 14 days in soil, every 7 in soil-less. Perennials in second and later years benefit from soil dressing of nitrochalk (5g per plant) but this must not touch plant.
Germination: Sow annuals as soon as days start to lengthen, on surface of well-drained seedling compost. Cover with ⅛in (2mm) dry compost and brown paper. Germination takes about 10 days. Prick out as soon as large enough to handle. Sow perennials in early summer in cold frame in shade. Plant out in early autumn for summer flowering. Perennials can be layered or propagated from cuttings.
Tidying: Pick off seed pods.
Varieties: Annuals: Magic Charms, bushy, strong, mixed colours (6in, 15cm). Snowfire, white with cherry eye (12in, 30cm). Queen of Hearts, brilliant scarlet (12in, 30cm). Telstar, long flowering, mixed colours (9in, 20cm). Perennials: Spring Beauty, early flowering, mixed colours (12in, 30cm). Deltoides Flashing Lights, ruby red, (12in, 30cm). Alpinus, very small and compact.

Dianthus has a woody base from which grow light green branching stems, each ending with a single flower. Flower colours range from white through to pink and red and blooms may be bicoloured. There is also a pale yellow variety. Most have very narrow leaves, a few are even grass-like.

Plant turns yellow from base. If stem blackening, waterlogged. Check drainage holes and allow to dry out between waterings. Use less water. If top growth also wilts in hot weather, recovering by early morning, carnation wilt disease. Cut stem and if core discoloured, remove plant and destroy. Sterilize soil with fungicide. If only 1 shoot affected, cut off and burn. Plant may survive. Do not use affected plants for cuttings.

what goes wrong

Small dark spots on leaves, erupting to form reddish powdery deposits. Rust disease. Spray with copper based fungicide to maker's instructions.

Plant grows leggy not bushy. Too hot while growing indoors. Keep at 50°F (10°C) while at seedling stage.

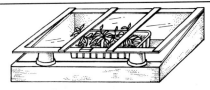

Hardening off
For good flower production keep young plants cool. When seedlings growing, cool gradually to temperature of outside cold frame and transplant. Keep covered with glass for 1 week, then raise glass during day except in snow or heavy frost. Move to final container in early to mid-spring.

Black sooty deposit in centre of open flowers. Leaves or buds distorted. Anther smut. Remove and destroy plant to prevent spread. Not common on annuals.

Small clusters of lice on new growth or flowers. Aphid. Spray in the evening with pirimicarb.

Young plant just taken outside turns very dark. Frost or cold wind. Protect during first week outside and at night. Will probably recover but not grow well.

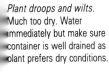

Plant droops and wilts. Much too dry. Water immediately but make sure container is well drained as plant prefers dry conditions.

Spots with reddish edges on leaves. Dianthus ring spot. Spray every 10 days with bordeaux mixture until clear.

Leaves pale, plant does not grow but no obvious pests or diseases. Examine base of plant for root aphid. If found, spray with diluted malathion to maker's instructions. If no aphid, needs feeding. Feed every 14 days in soil, every 7 in soil-less compost. If feeding regularly feed more often.

Seedlings have very thin stem near soil and later fall over. Pythium disease. Unlikely in sterile soil and cool temperatures. Prick out unaffected seedlings. Do not use diseased ones or those around them. Treat soil with fungicide.

227

Dumb cane

Now that plant breeders have introduced new, more compact and stronger varieties, this plant has rightly increased in popularity. A member of the Arum family it was first introduced from Brazil in 1830, being grown first in the Imperial Palace in Schönbrunn, Austria, by the head gardener, Herr Dieffenbach. Take care when handling it as the sap is poisonous, causing swellings if it touches the mouth or lips. Always wash your hands after touching it and wear gloves for pruning. Smaller plants do well in mixed groups but the larger ones are best standing alone.

Light: Good indirect light. Darker leaved plants tolerate semi-shade but if too dark, they will grow longer, less healthy stems.

Temperature: Prefers 60–65°F (16–18°C) but for short periods will stand down to 50°F (10°C), though this may cause loss of some lower leaves. If over 75°F (24°C) increase watering and humidity.

Water: 2 or 3 times a week in summer, with rainwater if possible, to keep compost moist. In winter not more than once a week, allowing compost to dry out if temperature falls below 60°F (16°C).

Humidity: Spray overhead in summer, daily when near 75°F (24°C); stand pot on wet pebbles or use in mixed planting for extra humidity.

Feeding: Feed monthly in spring and summer with houseplant food diluted to maker's recommended strength.

Repotting: In spring each year. Move to pot 2 sizes larger each time as plants may grow over 12in (30cm) a year.

Soil: Loam-based No. 3.

Cleaning: Sponge leaves every 14–21 days, supporting them carefully as they snap easily. Use leafshine only once a month.

The largest Dumb canes can grow up to 5ft (2m) high but the smaller plants, varieties of *Dieffenbachia picta*, are unlikely to grow more than 3ft (1m) high. The markings vary from plant to plant and new varieties have increasingly large areas of cream.

Cleaning the leaves
Dumb cane leaves snap easily so support them gently when cleaning. Wipe carefully with damp cloth or sponge every 2 or 3 weeks. The sap is dangerous so always wash your hands after touching plant and wear gloves if cutting any part of it.

what goes wrong

Leaves small and plant grows lanky. Too dark. Move into good indirect light, not strong sunlight.

Leaves go pale and bleached. Too much light or needs feeding. Check conditions. Move out of strong sunlight and feed regularly while growing.

White woolly patches on leaves and in leaf axils. Mealy bug. Spray with diluted malathion and remove bugs and 'wool' with tweezers. Repeat every 14 days until clear.

Lower leaves yellow, with brown patches on edges. Compost too wet. Allow surface to dry out before watering again. In summer keep moist, drier in winter.

Lower leaves curl inwards and die. Natural as plant grows or if in temperature around 50°F (10°C).

Leaves yellow with webs underneath. Red spider mite. Remove webs with damp cloth or sponge, then spray with diluted malathion, especially under leaves. Repeat every 14 days until clear.

Leaves dry up and collapse. Too hot and dry. Keep moist in summer; if over 75°F (24°C), increase humidity.

Burns on leaves. Caused by spraying in sunlight. Plant needs high humidity but never spray when sun is on leaves. Remove unsightly leaf where it joins plant stem.

Some leaves and stem rot and become slimy. Botrytis. Plant too cold, damp and humid. Spray with fungicide, then keep above 60°F (16°C) and spray and water less often.

Leaves turn pale and drop. Too cold. Move to warmer place, above 55°F (13°C).

229

Dimorphotheca sinuata

Cape marigold

These graceful, lightweight flowers are attractive in both tubs and window-boxes. They are generally grown as annuals and need a warm sheltered spot since they are half hardy. Seed can be sown directly in the container or, more easily, indoors in gentle heat. They can also be sown in peat pots and transferred intact to the container.

Light: The best at all times.

Temperature: Germination, 60–65°F (16–18°C). Young seedlings, 50–55°F (10–13°C). Outside, a warm sheltered sunny spot. No frost.

Water: Keep moist. Water little and often.

Humidity: Dry, no spraying overhead.

Soil: Either loam–based No.2 or soil-less potting compost. Do not press compost down too firmly, or water cannot drain away.

Feeding: Liquid fertilizer at maker's recommended strength every 14 days in soil, every 7 days in soil-less.

Propagation: Sow seed thinly on surface of prepared, drained seedling compost in early spring. Sprinkle fine dry compost to just cover seeds. Place in 60–65°F (16–18°C) under paper cover. Seedlings will transplant more easily if pricked out as soon as large enough to handle. Place in full light. Or sow in peat pots, thinning out to 2–3 seedlings per pot. Then transfer to container in pots. If using mixed hybrid seed, do not choose only the largest seedlings when thinning. They may be all the same colour.

Tidying: Remove dead flowers, cutting stems right down for neatness.

Varieties: Aurantiaca hybrids, orange, salmon, pale yellow, apricot and white; very graceful (12in, 30cm). Aurantiaca Dwarf Salmon, ideal for windowboxes. Aurantiaca Giant Orange (12in, 30cm). Glistening White and Las Vegas (mixed) both 18in (45cm).

The Cape marigold's flowers, up to 4in (10cm) across, grow singly on a rather thin stem and usually close towards late afternoon, opening again the following morning. Colours range from apricot through salmon pink to pale yellow and white.

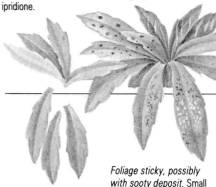

Silvery streaks on leaves, flowers may be distorted. Thrips. Spray with systemic insecticide to maker's instructions. Do not spray during day.

Small dark spots on leaves. Leaf spot fungus. Spray with bordeaux mixture or ipridione.

Foliage sticky, possibly with sooty deposit. Small insects oın buds. Aphid. Spray with pirimicarb.

Young plants in trays or peat pots eaten off at soil level. Woodlice. Trace hiding place and destroy. Use gamma-BHC with care. Common where there is undisturbed litter.

Flowers tattered, buds ragged. Earwig damage. Pests hide during day under debris, inside canes or crevices. Trap in small plant pot filled with dry grass or straw, balanced upside down on short stick. Empty trapped pests into boiling water each morning. Dust areas carefully with gamma-BHC.

Sowing in peat pots
1. Water pots and allow to drain for 2–3 hours. Sprinkle seed thinly on surface.

2. Cover with sprinkling of fine dry compost and place under paper cover in 60–65°F (16–18°C).

3. When seedlings large enough to handle, thin out weaker ones, leaving 2–3 per pot. Plant whole pot in container.

what goes wrong

Few flowers appear or flower buds do not open. Too dark. Plant must be in good bright light.

Flowers small, leaves lose freshness. Too dry. If moisture correct, needs feeding. Increase number but not strength of feeds.

Brown scorch marks on leaf and petal tips. Fertilizer too strong or sprayed in sunshine or cold winds. Check conditions. Do not use fertilizer stronger than maker recommends or spray in sun. Protect against strong cold winds.

Large holes in leaves near ground. Slugs or snails. Place slug pellets round plant as maker recommends. Remove dying slugs which may recover in warm, moist weather.

Plant does not thrive, some leaves turn yellow. Too wet. Allow container to dry out before watering again and check drainage holes clear. If watering correct, scrape away some soil from roots to see if root aphids present. If so, water with diluted malathion.

White froth on leaves. Froghopper sucking sap under froth. Pinch between finger and thumb to remove or if very many present, spray with diluted malathion.

Plant collapses and leaves turn black. Frost damage. Will not survive frosts. Protect in spring.

Dipladenia sanderi

Pink allamande

This climbing plant produces pairs of pale green leaves along the length of a fairly fast-growing stem. It can be trained round a loop of wire or up a trellis. The trumpet-shaped flowers are salmon pink with a yellow centre. The plant needs high humidity, which also helps to control red spider mite, to which it is particularly susceptible. It should be pruned hard annually after flowering to keep it compact. Propagation is by cuttings of the young shoots which appear when the plant begins to grow in spring. The shoots will soon root if kept in a warm (65°F, 18°C) humid atmosphere in a compost of equal parts of sand and peat.

Light: Full light, including sunlight except midday sun in summer.
Temperature: Average 65°F (18°C) in summer, and 60°F (16°C) in winter, not more than 70°F (21°C), not less than 55°F (13°C).
Water: 2 or 3 times a week in summer to keep moist, but plant must not stand in water or become waterlogged. In winter, water only when top layer of compost feels completely dry, about every 10 days.
Humidity: Spray daily in spring and summer. Stand pot on saucer of pebbles almost covered with water all year round, or plunge into an outer pot, with damp peat between the pots.
Feeding: Every 14 days in spring and summer with liquid houseplant food diluted to half maker's instructions.
Soil: 4 parts rough, fibrous peat and 1 part silver sand.
Repotting: In the first year, repot into next sized pot every time roots grow through bottom of pot. In subsequent years change top soil only.
Cleaning: Humidity spraying adequate. No leafshine.

The Pink allamande is a vigorous climber which flowers in summer. A trellis or cane will be required to train it and keep it under control, although it is well suited to training round a hoop. Watch for red spider mite, to which they are particularly susceptible.

Plant looks dull and lifeless, especially on warm days. Air too dry. Spray daily with soft tepid water. Provide extra humidity by standing pot on saucer of damp pebbles.

Plant flops. Too cold and wet. Allow top layer of compost to dry out before watering again and move to warmer position, at least 55°F (13°C).

232

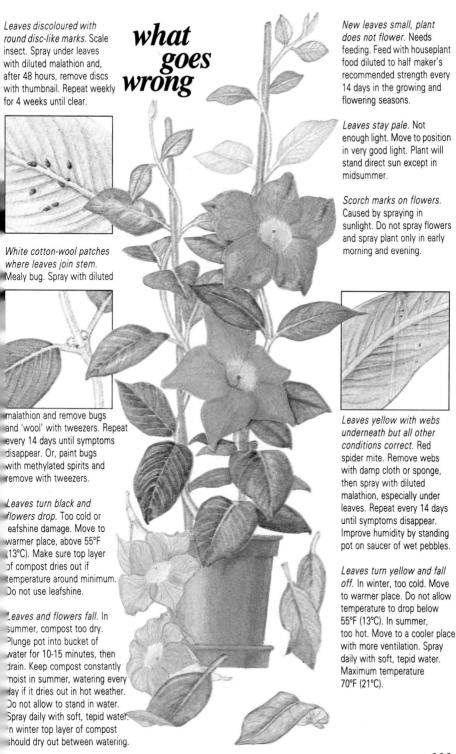

Leaves discoloured with round disc-like marks. Scale insect. Spray under leaves with diluted malathion and, after 48 hours, remove discs with thumbnail. Repeat weekly for 4 weeks until clear.

what goes wrong

New leaves small, plant does not flower. Needs feeding. Feed with houseplant food diluted to half maker's recommended strength every 14 days in the growing and flowering seasons.

Leaves stay pale. Not enough light. Move to position in very good light. Plant will stand direct sun except in midsummer.

Scorch marks on flowers. Caused by spraying in sunlight. Do not spray flowers and spray plant only in early morning and evening.

White cotton-wool patches where leaves join stem. Mealy bug. Spray with diluted malathion and remove bugs and 'wool' with tweezers. Repeat every 14 days until symptoms disappear. Or, paint bugs with methylated spirits and remove with tweezers.

Leaves turn black and flowers drop. Too cold or leafshine damage. Move to warmer place, above 55°F (13°C). Make sure top layer of compost dries out if temperature around minimum. Do not use leafshine.

Leaves and flowers fall. In summer, compost too dry. Plunge pot into bucket of water for 10-15 minutes, then drain. Keep compost constantly moist in summer, watering every day if it dries out in hot weather. Do not allow to stand in water. Spray daily with soft, tepid water. In winter top layer of compost should dry out between watering.

Leaves yellow with webs underneath but all other conditions correct. Red spider mite. Remove webs with damp cloth or sponge, then spray with diluted malathion, especially under leaves. Repeat every 14 days until symptoms disappear. Improve humidity by standing pot on saucer of wet pebbles.

Leaves turn yellow and fall off. In winter, too cold. Move to warmer place. Do not allow temperature to drop below 55°F (13°C). In summer, too hot. Move to a cooler place with more ventilation. Spray daily with soft, tepid water. Maximum temperature 70°F (21°C).

Dizygotheca elegantissima

Finger plant

As its name implies, this is a very elegant plant, with long, narrow, bronze leaves growing to 7–8in (18–20cm) long. It is also botanically interesting, as a single plant may carry three types of leaf: small baby leaves (cotyledons) at the base, juvenile leaves which are very pointed and, at the top, adult leaves which are flatter and wider. As a young plant, it is a good mixer in bowls as it makes a fine contrast in shape and colour with other plants. As it gets older, it makes a good specimen, growing into a tall tree-like plant. It flourishes in a good light, warm position, though it does not flower when grown as a houseplant. It can be grown quite easily from seed if kept around 70°F (21°C) or from stem-tip cuttings. These should also be kept warm and humid as they begin to root.

It is sometimes sold under the name of *Aralia*.

Light: Good light position away from direct sunlight.
Temperature: Winter minimum 60°F (15°C), summer maximum 70°F (21°C).
Water: Twice weekly in summer, once a week in winter, keeping moist at all times. Allow surplus to drain away. Soil must not dry out.
Humidity: Spray daily with mister, if possible, especially in summer heat.
Feeding: Every 14 days in the growing season (spring and summer) with houseplant food diluted according to the maker's instructions.
Soil: Loam-based No. 2 compost.
Repotting: Annually in spring, though plant prefers small pot.
Cleaning: Humidity misting sufficient. No leafshine.

Most Finger plants are sold while still producing only their elegantly pointed juvenile leaves. Later, their long bronze-coloured adult leaves may grow to 7–8in (18–20cm) long. Look for plants with bright leaves and branches growing all down the main stem.

Humidity
Spray daily with fine mist spray especially when temperature is near summer maximum 70°F, (21°C).

For extra local humidity, stand pot on saucer of pebbles almost covered with water. Don't let the pot base touch the water or roots will be waterlogged.

what goes wrong

Bottom leaves drop without warning. Too dark; larger top leaves may be shading lower ones. Move to lighter place, but not full sun.

Scorch marks on edges of leaves. Plant in direct sunlight. Move to light position but out of direct sun.

Plant grows slowly and new leaves are small. Needs feeding. Feed every 14 days in spring and summer.

White woolly patches on leaves and stems. Mealy bug. Wipe with cotton wool dipped in methylated spirits or spray every 14 days with diluted malathion until clear.

Upper leaves drop off when still green. Too cold. Move to warmer position, at least 60° (15°C) in winter.

Leaf surfaces sticky with brown scales underneath. Scale insect. Wipe with cotton wool dipped in methylated spirits or spray every 14 days until clear with diluted malathion-based insecticide.

Leaves sticky, twisted and distorted, with small green insects. Greenfly. Spray every 14 days until clear with pyrethrum or a systemic insecticide.

Leaves go limp and droop. Plant waterlogged from overwatering. Allow to dry out before watering again, do not stand in water and check that drainage holes in pot are clear.

Leaves go dry and brittle, then drop off. Too hot and dry. Move to cooler place, spray with water more often. Water soil regularly.

Dragon tree

This is one of many popular species of *Dracaena* and is tolerant of most room conditions. There are several varieties available, most grown with new foliage sprouting from canes from 12in (30cm) to 6ft 6in (2m) high. Adult plants produce an attractive scented flower spike with cream-coloured blossoms, but these are rarely seen indoors.

Dracaena fragrans is an all-green variety but there are others, such as *D. fragrans massangeana* (p.238) that are variegated, with a broad yellowish stripe down the centre of the leaves. Plants growing on canes of different heights can be placed together to make an unusual display.

Most Dragon trees are grown from imported sections of stem from 12in (30cm) to 6 ft 6in (2m) long and around an inch (2½cm) across. When kept under glass by the growers, these sprout an elegant rosette of new leaves. When buying this type of plant, make sure that the cane is well rooted in the pot.

Light: Prefers good light position away from direct sunlight. Plain green varieties will tolerate more shade than variegated types.

Temperature: Winter minimum 60°F (15°C), though will tolerate 55°F (12°C) if water withheld. Summer maximum 75°F (24°C).

Water: Twice a week in summer, once a week in winter. Plant must neither stand in water nor completely dry out.

Humidity: Spray with tepid water 2–3 times a week.

Feeding: Every 14 days with liquid houseplant food diluted according to the maker's instructions.

Soil: Peat-based or loam-based No. 2 compost.

Repotting: In spring, every other year, for large plants. If too awkward to handle, just change topsoil.

Cleaning: By hand with damp cloth. Use leafshine sparingly once a month. Too much leafshine will clog the pores of the leaves.

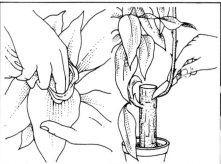

Cleaning
Clean leaves by hand with a damp cloth. Support leaf with other hand.

Cutting down an old plant
If leaves drop and plant looks bare, cut stems back close to cane with sharp knife. New shoots will appear.

236

Brown scorch marks on leaves. Too much direct sun. Move out of full sunlight. Do not spray in sunlight.

New leaves small and distorted or plant does not grow at all. Needs feeding. Feed every 14 days all the year round.

Greyish brown spots on leaves. Leaf spot fungus. Spray once with a systemic fungicide.

Stem rots from top. Too cold and draughty. Keep at temperature of at least 60°F (15°C). Move into protected position.

Leaves yellow with webs underneath. Red spider mite. Spray with derris, diluted malathion or systemic insecticide every 14 days until clear. Increase humidity by spraying daily.

Leaves discoloured with brown scales under leaves and on stems. Scale insect. Remove with cotton wool dipped in methylated spirits or spray with diluted malathion or systemic insecticide every 14 days until clear.

Plant flops, leaves turn yellow and rot; roots rot. Too wet, overwatered. Allow to dry out before watering again. Do not stand in water.

White woolly patches on leaves and stems. Mealy bug. Remove with cotton wool dipped in methylated spirits or spray with diluted malathion every 14 days.

Lower leaves droop and curl under, edges yellowing, tips brown. Needs water, may also be too hot. Water more frequently so that it never dries out. Check temperature and move to cooler place if possible. Spray daily to increase humidity. When old, the lower leaves may turn yellow and drop naturally.

Leaves fade. Too dark. Move to lighter position but not full sunlight.

what goes wrong

Bottom leaves drop. Caused by sudden changes in temperature, often on way from shop to home. New leaves will grow.

Plant sheds leaves and stops growing. Too cold. Move to warmer place, over 60°F (15°C).

237

Dracaena

Like the Ficus and Philodendron groups of plants, Dracaenas include a large number of different species, many of which are among the most popular of indoor plants. They range from species that will stand a mild frost to others that are at home in tropical jungle conditions. Members of the Lily family, their scientific name comes from the Greek word for a female dragon and many include the word dragon in their popular names. All Dracaenas have similar shaped strap-like leaves, growing as a rosette from a central stem which gradually elongates. The different types vary in colour and size. *Dracaena fragrans massangeana* grows indoors to 2–3ft (60–90cm).

The Belgian evergreen or Ribbon plant (*Dracaena sanderiana*) is another of the popular Dracaenas. It grows to about 3ft (90cm) indoors, its slender green and white leaves unfurling one above the other around the stem. In time the lower leaves fall, leaving a bare, cane-like stem.

Light: Best in good light but out of midday summer sun; will tolerate 2–3 weeks in a shady place.

Temperature: Will survive in minimum 55°F (13°C) but better at 65°F (18°C). If over 75°F (24°C) in summer, increase humidity and fresh air.

Water: Once a week in winter, at least twice a week in summer but never let plant stand in water or roots will rot.

Humidity: Spray twice weekly, more often if temperature near maximum, using rainwater if possible.

Feeding: Give liquid houseplant food at maker's recommended strength every 14 days in spring and summer.

Soil: Loam- or peat-based No.2.

Repotting: In spring annually while young. For plants over 4 years old, repot every second or third year. Make sure drainage is good.

Cleaning: By hand with damp cloth. Use leafshine not more than once a month.

Leaves go pale and fade. Too dark. Move to a lighter position.

what goes wrong

Leaves yellowed with webs underneath. Red spider mite. Remove with damp cloth or sponge, then spray with diluted malathion, especially under leaves. Repeat every 14 days until symptoms disappear. Improve humidity by standing on a saucer of pebbles almost covered in water.

Looking after the leaves
1. Clean by wiping gently with a soft, damp cloth, supporting leaf with other hand.

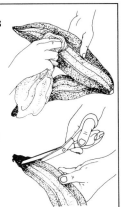

2. If tips are brown and dry, cut off just inside the dry area, to avoid scarring healthy tissue.

Plant collapses, leaves go rotten – so may stem and root. Plant waterlogged, standing in water. Drain away any water in saucer and allow surface of soil to dry out before watering again. Then keep moist but never allow pot base to stand in water. Always throw away excess that drains through after watering.

Plant drops lower leaves and stops growing. Too cold. Move to warmer place. Do not allow temperature to drop below 55°F (13°C).

New leaves small, and slow growth in spring. Needs feeding. Feed with houseplant food diluted to maker's recommended strength every 14 days in spring.

Leaves discoloured with brown scaly insects which are under leaves and on stems. Scale insect. Spray underside of leaves with diluted malathion and, after 48 hours, remove discs with thumbnail. Repeat every week for four weeks until clear.

Burn spots on leaves. Damage caused by spraying in sunlight. Plant needs high humidity but must not be sprayed when sun is shining on it or droplets will act like magnifying glasses and burn leaves. Remove unsightly leaf with sharp knife where it joins stem.

Greyish brown spots on leaves. Botrytis. Plant too cold and damp. Spray with fungicide, then keep in warmer place (above 60°F, 18°C) and spray with water less frequently. Allow soil surface to dry out between waterings. Remove damaged leaves.

Lower leaves drop. Much too dry and hot. Water more frequently and increase spraying.

Dracaena marginata

Madagascar dragon tree

This narrow-leaved Dracaena makes a splendid feature, especially when an old plant is pruned to give several heads of young leaves on top of a gnarled, almost 'bonsai' like trunk. It is an easy plant to grow and is tolerant of most conditions, though the colour of the leaves is better in good light. Dracaenas are a large family of plants, most of which make good houseplants. Some, such as the Madagascar dragon tree are commonly sold with stems ready formed. Others, such as *Dracaena deremensis* and *D. fragrans massangeana* (see p.238) may be purchased before the woody stem has developed.

The Madagascar dragon tree has narrow leaves edged with red which grow from the top of a thin, woody stem. They are usually around 18–24in (46–60cm) tall and their palm-like shape is an interesting contrast to other foliage plants. A pretty variegated type with green and white leaves is more delicate.

Light: Keep in good light but away from direct sun. If too dark, leaves lose colour.
Temperature: In winter 60°F (16°C), but will stand 55°F (13°C) if water withheld. Summer maximum 75°F (24°C).
Water: Water twice a week in summer, once a week in winter to keep moist but not waterlogged. Must never dry out completely.
Humidity: Spray with tepid water 2–3 times a week, only once a week in winter. Do not spray if below 55°F (13°C).
Feeding: Feed every 14 days in the growing season (spring and summer) with liquid houseplant food diluted to maker's recommended strength.
Soil: Peat or loam-based No. 2.
Repotting: Every other year in spring. When too large to handle easily, just replace top 2–3in (5–7cm) compost with fresh.
Cleaning: Wipe leaves with damp cloth. Use leafshine once a month but too much will clog pores and slow down new growth.

Leaves yellow with spots and underneath, webs. Red spider mite. Remove webs with damp cloth or sponge, then spray with diluted malathion, especially under leaves. Repeat every 14 days until symptoms disappear. Improve humidity by standing pot on wet pebbles.

what goes wrong

Leaves dull and droopy. Too hot and air too dry. Keep below 75°F (24°C) if possible and spray 2–ž times a week in summer. Drooping bottom leaves may be caused by sudden change in temperature. Plant should recover if kept above 60°F (16°C).

Plant flops, leaves turn yellow and rot. Roots rot. Too wet, waterlogged. Drain away any water in saucer and allow surface to dry out before watering again. Then keep moist but never allow to stand in water. Always throw away excess after watering.

Leaves discoloured with brown scales. Scale insect. Spray underside of leaves with diluted malathion and, after 48 hours, remove discs with thumbnail. Repeat every week for 4 weeks until clear. Or, paint with methylated spirits.

Brown scorch marks on leaves. Caused by spraying in sunlight. Do not spray if sun on leaves. Remove unsightly leaf where it grows from trunk.

Leaves lose colour. Too dark. Move to lighter position, but not in direct sunlight.

New leaves small, slow growth. Needs feeding. Feed every 14 days in spring and summer, with houseplant food at maker's recommended strength.

Stem rots from top, leaves drop. Too cold. Move to warmer place, above 60°F (16°C).

White woolly patches on leaves and stems. Mealy bug. Spray with diluted malathion and remove bugs and 'wool' with tweezers. Repeat every 14 days until symptoms disappear. Or, paint with methylated spirits, remove with tweezers. Keep away from other plants.

Lower leaves droop, curl under, edges yellow, tips brown. Too dry. Plunge pot into bucket of water for 10–15 minutes, then drain. Keep moist in summer, watering every day if it dries out. In winter water once a week to keep drier.

Dudleya brittonii

This species is one of the several which are covered with a mealy coating as a protection against the drying effect of the sun. This covering is easily marked by handling the leaves, or by careless watering. The plant needs to be watered either by filling a saucer in which the pot stands, or by pouring the water carefully around the edge of the plant so that it does not fall on the leaves. Sunshine is needed to bring out the best colouring. They nearly all come from Mexico where they grow on hillsides and show up as white patches on the grey-brown rock. They will reach a height of 3–4in (8–10cm) and about 8–10in (20–25cm) across. Other species include *D. albiflora*, *D. candida*, *D. densiflora*: none of these is readily available, but can be obtained from time to time.

Dudleya brittonii's intense white colouring comes from a powdery coating which protects it from drying out in bright sunlight. To avoid damaging it, always water from the base of the pot and do not spray with insecticides. Flowers are rare indoors.

Light: A sunny position is needed to keep plants in good shape and encourage dense white mealy covering.

Temperature: A minimum of 45°F (7°C) is needed for safety. Give fresh air in summer.

Water: In spring and early summer water fortnightly, weekly in hottest months. Tail off to little water in autumn and in winter water once a month to stop drying out. See also Introduction.

Feeding: Use high potash fertilizer 2 or 3 times in summer.

Soil: Use good loam-based No. 2 potting compost, or soil-less compost, with 40% coarse, gritty sand.

Repotting: Every spring in size larger half-pot or pan, being careful not to handle leaves at all, as the mealy covering is easily marked and the appearance spoiled.

Propagation: Leaves will not root and form fresh plants but whole rosettes can be separated with a sharp knife.

Leaves are marked, mealy covering removed in patches or on edges. Damaged by humans, curtains, or perhaps cats, brushing against plants. Will recover if moved to safe position.

Plant does not grow. Needs feeding or, if white woolly patches on roots, root mealy bug. Wash soil off roots, swirl in contact insecticide, and allow to dry before repotting in fresh compost and washed pot. Leave dry for 2 weeks. Feed 2–3 times in summer.

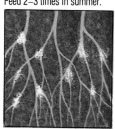

Mealy covering not very thick or white, no flowers. Not enough sunlight. Move to lighter position in sunny window.

Leaves blacken and fall, stem rots. Too cold and wet, too humid. Move to warmer, more airy position and allow to dry out before watering again. Keep dry in winter.

what goes wrong

Woolly patches on leaves. Mealy bug, difficult to see on this plant so inspect regularly. Dab with a small paintbrush just dipped in methylated spirits, and water systemic insecticide into soil. Do not spray.

Leaves long and pale in winter. Too hot, damp and humid. Move to more airy place and allow to dry out thoroughly. Keep dry in winter, even in normal room temperatures.

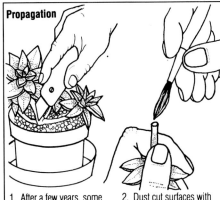

Propagation

1. After a few years, some Dudleyas will form clumps of rosettes. Individual rosettes can be separated from rest with sharp knife. Take care not to damage plant's floury covering when handling it.

2. Dust cut surfaces with hormone rooting powder to prevent infection and leave cutting to dry for 2 days before potting in small individual pot. Do not water for 2–3 weeks.

Brown scorch marks on leaves. Plant has been moved into direct sunlight too quickly. Move out of direct sun, then bring back gradually over 2 weeks. Make sure ventilation is good.

Leaves have chewed edges, lower stem swollen; plant does not grow well. Vine weevil. Dust around base of pot with insecticide powder and water soil with systemic insecticide to kill larvae in stem. Or, slice from base of stem until larvae discovered and reroot (see Introduction).

Leaves marked with small spots of green. Insecticide spray has damaged mealy covering. Water systemic insecticides into soil. Do not spray.

Lower leaves dry up. Too dry. Soak pot in bowl of water for ½ an hour, then drain. Water regularly in hot weather, whenever soil dries out.

243

Echeveria agavoides

This plant is grown for the beauty of its waxy-leaved rosette, which is grey-green with red edges to the leaves. It grows to a height of about 4in (10cm) and the rosettes reach about 6in (15cm) across. Echeverias come from Central America and vary from tiny inch-wide (2–3cm) rosettes to large shrubby plants standing 3ft (1m) tall with rosettes 2ft (60cm) across. The leaves vary from pale green, through all sorts of blues, greys and purple shades with a bloom on them that is easily damaged. Other species include *Echeveria affinis* with almost black leaves; *E. minima*, small blue, red-edged rosettes; *E. setosa* with hairy, green leaves; *E. pulvinata*, velvety green, red-edged leaves.

Light: A sunny position is needed to bring out the best colouring.

Temperature: Keep at 45°F (7°C). Give fresh air in summer.

Water: Water fortnightly in spring and summer, weekly in hottest weather, so that soil does not dry out completely. In autumn and winter give just enough once a month to stop leaves shrivelling. See also Introduction.

Feeding: Use high potash fertilizer in summer once a month.

Soil: Use a good loam-based No. 2 potting or soil-less compost, with 20% coarse, gritty sand.

Repotting: Every spring in size larger pot or larger if plant has grown well, using half pots or pans for the shallow roots, and being careful not to handle leaves and spoil the mealy or waxy covering.

Propagation: Most will make fresh plants from healthy leaves. Remove and dry for a day or two, then lay on top of dry compost. Give water after 2 weeks when leaves have roots, and plantlet formed at base.

Echeveria agavoides. These attractive flowers grow on a 6in (15cm) stem which grows from among the rosette of leaves. A collection of different Echeveria species makes a colourful display as the leaves may be powder blue, green, grey, lilac or almost pink. This species will redden, especially along the leaf edges in a sunny position.

White woolly patches between the leaves and on the stem, where young shoots are appearing. Mealy bug. Remove with small paintbrush dipped in methylated spirits, and spray with pyrethrum-based insecticide.

Round pieces missing from leaf edges, stem swollen, little new growth. Vine weevil. Sprinkle insecticide powder around base of pot and water soil with systemic insecticide to kill larvae in stem. Or slice stem from base until larvae found and reroot. (See Introduction.)

Leaves marked in patches or at edge. Coating damaged by handling. Unsightly but not fatal.

Small insects on flowers or buds. Greenfly. Spray with pyrethrum-based insecticide and repeat in 10 days if not clear.

what goes wrong

After flowering
Cut flower stem with sharp knife as close to base as possible. Remove stump by gently pulling out when absolutely dry.

To propagate new plants, remove leaf from near top of plant by hand and lay on dry compost with base touching surface. Roots will appear and new plantlet will grow at base.

Leaves and stem turn black. Leaves pull out easily. Too cold and wet. Keep no lower than 45°F (7°C) in winter in dry compost. Treat stem (see Introduction). If plant does not recover, use healthy leaves for cuttings.

Leaves distorted. Caused by excessive use of insecticides. Use only pyrethrum-based insecticides. Not fatal.

Leaves small and few. Needs repotting, or if soil dry, more water. Soak pot in bowl of water, drain, then give more water each time. but always allow to dry out between waterings.

Plant elongates in centre, leaves pale green. Too little light, move gradually over 2 weeks to a sunny spot. If too hot and wet in winter, leaves may grow like this then rot. Try to keep below 50°F (10°C) in winter with just enough water monthly to prevent leaves from shrivelling.

Plant does not grow, and on repotting white woolly patches found on roots. Root mealy bug. Wash all soil off roots, swirl in contact insecticide and allow to dry before repotting in fresh compost and clean pot. Leave dry for 2 weeks.

Leaves shrivel in winter. Too dry. Moisten soil once a month to prevent drying out completely but always make sure pot dries right out in between. Try to keep cool (under 50°F, 10°C) in winter.

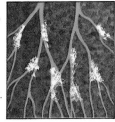

245

Echinocactus

These are the largest of the globular cacti, with some reaching about 5ft (1½m) across in the wild in Mexico and the southern United States. In cultivation they will take 5 or 6 years to get beyond a 6 or 7in (15–18cm) pot, and few will produce flowers under the size of a football. But they are handsome plants at any size, and are often seen for sale. As they get older their true beauty emerges and the spines get more and more strong and lend ferocious beauty to the plants. Kept growing vigorously they will eventually become among the most prominent in the collection.

The most popular species is *Echinocactus grusonii*, commonly known as the Golden barrel cactus. It is one of the most beautifully spined cacti there is, with stiff, bright golden yellow spines like sword-blades densely covering the globular plant.

Light: Maximum light is needed to produce strong spines.

Temperature: A minimum of 45°F (7°C) is needed, with preferably 50°F (10°C) for *E. grusonii* to prevent 'cold' marks, brown unsightly spotting. Give fresh air in summer and keep below 100°F (38°C).

Water: Weekly in summer until plants large enough for 5in (13cm) pots, then fortnightly. Keep dry from late autumn to spring.

Feeding: Feed every month in summer with high potash fertilizer (as used for tomatoes).

Soil: Use 1 part coarse, gritty sand (not builders' or seashore) to 2 parts of soil-less or good loam-based No. 2 potting compost (No. 3 for larger plants).

Repotting: Use gloves to protect your hands and avoid breaking the spines when repotting. This should be done every year into next size pot until in 6 or 7in (15 or

Echinocactus horizonthalonius is difficult to grow unless kept very well drained in a good, sunny position. It is best to water on bright, sunny days and to allow the pot to dry out thoroughly between waterings. When not in flower, a healthy plant will produce fresh wool in the centre. Flowers are produced in the summer months and last a week or more each.

A healthy *Echinocactus grusonii* is one which makes plenty of bright new spines in the summer and is not marked with brown cold marks after the winter. It is unlikely to flower in cultivation and needs to be at least the size of a football before any flowers will appear; but its beautiful yellow spines make a splendid year-round display.

Spraying occasionally overhead keeps the spines clean and bright yellow. Feeding promotes strong growth and healthy spines.

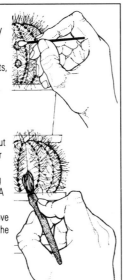
18cm) pot, then every other year will be enough.

Cleaning and pest control: Spray with water if dusty and incorporate an insecticide 2 or 3 times a year to combat pests.

Other species: A white-spined form of *E. grusonii* is available. It needs to be at least football size before the yellow flowers appear. Few others are seen except for *E. horizonthalonius*, from southern U.S.A. and Mexico. This flowers when quite small (3in, 8cm or so) with lovely pink blooms on blue-green stems with strong, curved black or brown spines. A difficult plant, it is one for the experienced grower rather than the beginner.

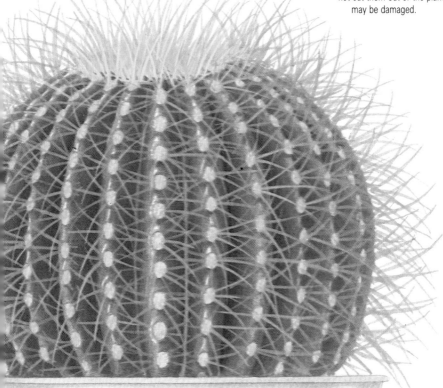

Brown cold marks are unsightly but not fatal. Do not cut them out or the plant may be damaged.

Echinocereus

Some of the largest, most sumptuous flowers of the cactus family are found in this genus. It comes from a wide area of the southern U.S.A. and Mexico, mostly forming large clumps half a metre or more across, of cylindrical stems up to 8–12in (20–30cm) tall. Many will flower at about 4in (10cm) tall and are content with shallow half-pots or pans though some have larger, tuberous roots and need deeper containers. Check which type of roots the cactus has when repotting. They fall into five main types. The larger, long-spined species such as *Echinocereus fendleri* are not easy to flower in cultivation but may grow up to 18in (50cm) across. In the wild they may reach as much as 3ft (1m). Better for flowering is the sprawling group which contains *E. blanckii* and *E. papillosus*, or the group with short spines neatly arranged like primitive combs down the ribs, such as *E. pectinatus*. These have mainly large, pink flowers, produced when the plants are only small. They rarely outgrow a 7in (18cm) pot. Another group has small, greenish-yellow or rusty-red flowers. This includes *E. davisii*, which flowers when only about 1in (2–3cm) tall. The last group consists of a few small, nearly globular species such as *E. pulchellus* which grow only about an inch (2½cm) a year but produce masses of flowers. *E. pulchellus* itself has strong, short spines in star-like clusters, often smothering itself with 20 or more blooms on one 2in (5cm) head.

Echinocereus triglochidiatus has thick, squat stems and is a very variably spined species. Although it flowers readily in the wild, it needs a sunny position to encourage flower production in cultivation. The bright red flowers, each lasting about a fortnight, are thick-textured and waxy.

Light: Give maximum light on the sunniest windowsill or in a greenhouse.

Temperature: Keep above 40°F (4°C) for

248

safety. Give fresh air in summer and keep below 100°F (38°C) if possible.

Water: Water weekly in summer, fortnightly in spring and autumn. Keep dry in winter.

Feeding: Feed with high potash fertilizer (as used for tomatoes) in spring and summer.

Soil: Use 1 part of coarse, gritty sand (not builders' or seashore) to 2 parts of soil-less or good loam-based No. 2 potting compost (No. 3 for larger plants).

Repotting: Do not put small plants in over-large pots; their roots should fill the pot. Repot every year into next size pot. If plant has very shallow root system, use a half-pot or pan. For plants that are growing strongly, repot each year into next size until 7in (18cm) reached, then every other year unless it is obviously outgrowing its container.

Cleaning and pest control: Spray with water if dusty and include an insecticide 2 or 3 times a year to combat pests.

Other species: The sprawling group is well represented by *E. blanckii* and plants are available in each of the other main groups. Larger, hard-to-flower species include *E. brandegei*, *E. maritimus* and *E. triglochidiatus*. The small 'comb' cacti include *E. purpureus*, *E. melanocentrus*, *E. reichenbachii*. The small-flowered group includes *E. chloranthus*, *E. viridiflorus*, and *E. russanthus* while the free-flowering globular species include *E. knippelianus*, with dark green stem and wispy, easily knocked off spines. It has large pink flowers with a deeper pink midstripe. *E. subinermis*, in this group, has beautiful large butter yellow flowers.

Echinocereus papillosus is a species that flowers readily in cultivation and will grow quickly to fill a 7 or 8in (18-20cm) pan with its shallow roots. Its flowers are a pale, silky yellow with red throats and appear over a 2 or 3 week period in late spring or early summer, individual flowers lasting about 7 to 10 days.

Echinocereus blanckii belongs to the sprawling group of Echinocereus. It spreads to fill a 10in (25cm) pan but has shallow, fibrous roots so does not need a deep container. Its bright purple flowers appear for about a month in spring and early summer, each lasting for a week or ten days.

Echinopsis

These are popular, night-flowering globular cacti whose flowers open in the evening to fade by the following morning. Most have white or pale pink flowers, with tubes 4–5in (10–12cm) long but some, such as *Echinopsis aurea* (p.251), have attractive yellow blooms. They grow to 2½–3in (6–8cm) tall and about 2½in (6cm) wide or larger. They offset freely and since the offsets root easily when they are removed, new young plants are widely available. Many will survive a winter outside if frost is not too severe but are better kept indoors. They come from a wide area of South America.

The name Pseudolobivia is sometimes applied to some of these plants and in addition Echinopsis species have been crossed with Lobivias to produce what are known as Echinobivias.

Echinobivia 'Ginn and Orange'. Echinobivias have shorter flower tubes (2½–3in 6–8cm) than normal Echinopsis plants but produce more blooms. Other good Echinobivias are E. 'Stars and Stripes', E. 'Mary Patricia', E. 'Peach Monach' and E. 'Sunset'.

Light: For best results, keep in the sunniest position possible. If no flowers appear, the light is probably too dull, perhaps filtered through a net curtain.

Temperature: Although these plants have been known to survive mild frost, they prefer a temperature above 40°F (4°C). Keep below 100°F (38°C) and give fresh air in summer when possible.

Water: Weekly in the summer, fortnightly in spring and autumn or if the plants are in pots of more than 5in (13cm); keep dry in winter.

Feeding: Feed every month in spring and summer with high potash fertilizer (as used for tomatoes).

Soil: Use 2 parts soil-less or good loam-based No. 2 potting compost (No. 3 for large plants) with 1 part coarse, gritty sand (not builders' or seashore).

Repotting: Repot every year into next size pot until they are in 5in (13cm) pots, when every other year will be sufficient. Then, unless plant is outgrowing its pot, repot in same size container with fresh soil.

Cleaning and pest control: Spray with water once a month to keep dust-free and incorporate an insecticide 2 or 3 times a year to combat pests.

Other species: *E. callichroma* has yellow flowers like *E. aurea* (right) but most have white or pinkish flowers. Some which have become available in recent years are worth looking out for: *E. obrepanda*, *E. kratochviliana* and *E. subdenudata* have white flowers and *E. frankii*, *E. cardenasiana* and *E. kermesina* have pink to red-violet ones. *E. kermesina* (sometimes known as Pseudolobivia) has a light green body with yellowish-brown spines. Unlike most other Echinopsis species, it produces its long-tubed flowers from the centre. The many hybrid Echinobivias come in shades of pink, red, orange and yellow.

Offsets

Offsets produced around base root easily. Remove with sharp knife when 1in (2½cm) high. Dust base with hormone rooting powder containing fungicide, dry off for 2 days and plant in fresh dry compost. Do not water for 2 weeks.

Echinopsis cardenasiana's magnificent flowers dwarf the plant's small body. The plant shown here is about 3in (7½cm) wide but they begin to produce flowers when they are only 2in (5cm) wide.

Echinopsis species come from Argentina, Bolivia, Paraguay, Uruguay and Brazil. They can stand low temperatures but are best kept above 40°F (4°C).

If your Echinopsis does not flower, move it into the sunniest possible position. Do not keep in light filtered through a net curtain.

Echinopsis aurea is usually a shining, healthy dark green, with vertical ribs and clusters of sharp spines. It grows to about 4in (10cm) indoors and flowers after 3–4 years, when it is 1½–2in (4–5cm) tall. Its yellow flowers appear in late spring, either all together or over a week or two, lasting 1 or 2 days each. The tubes from which the flowers appear are hairy and grow out from the side of the plant, just above a cluster of spines.

251

Epiphyllum

Most so-called Epiphyllums are not true Epiphyllums at all but are hybrids of hybrids whose true origins are rarely known. They are nevertheless very popular because of their large, exotically coloured blooms with their prominent swoop of stamens in the centre. The flowers give the plants their popular name of Orchid cacti and come in all shades of white, yellow, orange, red (the most common), pink or purple and combinations of these colours.

They have been bred from jungle cacti which, in nature, grow in trees as epiphytes, obtaining nourishment from the rotting vegetation accumulated among the branches, into which they root. They should therefore be treated rather differently from the desert cacti. The most commonly seen is the red-flowered *Epiphyllum ackermannii*.

Epiphyllum 'Sarabande' with its large white flowers and yellow outer sepals is one of the most attractive hybrids. Others often found are E. 'Deutsche Kaiserin', with soft pink flowers, and E. 'Reward' with yellow blooms.

Light: Like all cacti, they need a good light position for best results. A sunny windowsill is ideal. If in a greenhouse in summer, shade lightly but give full light in winter when flower buds are forming.

Temperature: Keep above 40°F (4°C) in winter and below 100°F (38°C) in summer; give fresh air when possible in summer.

Water: These plants need some water all year round. If kept below 45°F (7°C) in winter they should be almost dry, watered every 4–6 weeks, but in summer they need watering once or twice a week to keep the soil moist. Do not allow them to stand in water.

Feeding: Feed every week in spring and summer with high potash fertilizer (as used for tomatoes).

Soil: Use soil-less composts with no grit or sand added. Some growers prefer lime-free or 'ericaceous' composts which are more like the leaf debris in which the plants grow in the wild.

Repotting: Repot annually into next size pot, if plant is growing well. Pot should be large enough to take the root-ball comfortably with room for fresh soil to be added around it. Strong growers will fill 9in (23cm) or bigger pots but when they get to this size can be replaced each year in the same sized pot with fresh compost. Make sure there is good drainage in the pot.

Cleaning and pest control: Wipe the leaf-like stems clean with a damp cloth if they are dusty and spray them once a month to keep them clean. Incorporate an insecticide 2 or 3 times a year to combat pests and a fungicide to prevent brown or orange spotting.

Other species: The choice of flower colours is endless and thousands have been named in the last fifty years. There are a few cactus nurseries who specialize in these plants and it is worth a visit in spring and early summer when they are flowering to choose from the great variety available.

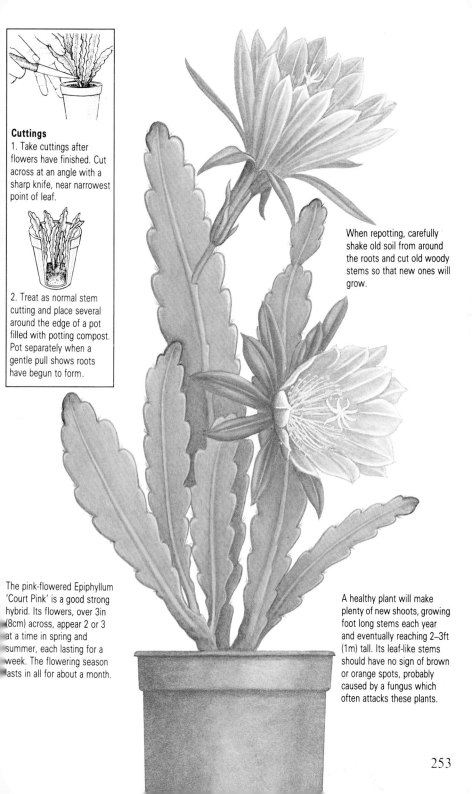

Cuttings

1. Take cuttings after flowers have finished. Cut across at an angle with a sharp knife, near narrowest point of leaf.

2. Treat as normal stem cutting and place several around the edge of a pot filled with potting compost. Pot separately when a gentle pull shows roots have begun to form.

When repotting, carefully shake old soil from around the roots and cut old woody stems so that new ones will grow.

The pink-flowered Epiphyllum 'Court Pink' is a good strong hybrid. Its flowers, over 3in (8cm) across, appear 2 or 3 at a time in spring and summer, each lasting for a week. The flowering season lasts in all for about a month.

A healthy plant will make plenty of new shoots, growing foot long stems each year and eventually reaching 2–3ft (1m) tall. Its leaf-like stems should have no sign of brown or orange spots, probably caused by a fungus which often attacks these plants.

253

Devil's ivy

This distant relation of the Philodendrons has similar habits and requirements. It is good for both climbing and hanging positions: if grown as a climber it is best with a moss pole, for it has aerial roots which will cling to the moss. The size of the pointed, heart-shaped leaves increases dramatically as the plant gets older. Take care with watering. If given too much, especially in winter, the leaves may develop brown patches. Strangely, however, it grows well in hydroculture (p.18). A vigorous climber, it will reach 15ft (over 4m) if allowed to grow unchecked. To keep it within bounds, prune back just above a leaf in spring.

Devil's ivy leaves have distinct yellow markings on a green background. If several plants are grown together in a hanging basket, preferably in a window that does not face the sun, they soon make an attractive display.

Light: Can be grown in semi-shade, though variegations fade if too dark. Keep out of direct sunlight.

Temperature: In winter best at 60°F (16°C) although it will survive down to 55°F (13°C). In summer keep below 75°F (24°C).

Water: Allow to dry out between waterings so good drainage is essential. Check compost between waterings: every 4/5 days in summer, every 7/8 days in winter enough.

Humidity: Spray with water 2–3 times a week in summer. In winter if in dry, centrally heated room, spray twice a week with tepid water.

Feeding: Feed once a month all year round with liquid houseplant food at half maker's recommended strength.

Soil: Loam-based No. 2.

Repotting: Only every other year. They do not like roots to be disturbed. Make sure drainage is good.

Cleaning: Wipe leaves weekly with damp cloth, using vegetable oil about once a month to give them a shine. No leafshine.

Inserting a moss pole

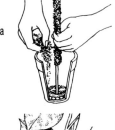

1. Epipremnum has aerial roots which will grow into a moss pole. Insert pole when repotting, before placing plant in position. Add a handful of compost to keep it upright.

2. Position plant and tie to pole with raffia or twine, making sure knot is against pole, not stem.

3. Fill pot with fresh compost and press down well. When watering allow water to trickle down pole so that moss stays damp. This helps improve humidity and gives aerial roots moisture.

254

Plant grows slowly, long spaces between leaves. Needs feeding. Feed once a month all the year round with liquid houseplant food diluted to half maker's recommended strength.

Rusty marks on leaves. Leafshine damage. Do not use. Clean by wiping leaves with damp cloth. Remove damaged leaf where it joins stem.

Brown marks and black edges on leaves. Too wet. Allow soil to dry out before watering again, and always test compost between waterings. Every 4–5 days in summer, every 7–8 days in winter enough, depending on temperature.

Leaves yellow with webs underneath. Red spider mite. Remove webs with damp cloth or sponge, then spray with diluted malathion, especially under leaves. Repeat every 14 days until symptoms disappear. Improve humidity by standing pot on saucer of wet pebbles and spray regularly.

White woolly patches on leaves. Mealy bug. Spray with diluted malathion and remove bugs and 'wool' with tweezers. Repeat every 14 days until symptoms disappear. Or, paint with methylated spirits. Remove with tweezers.

Leaves and stem look limp and dried up. Too hot and dry, air too dry. Move to cooler room, under 75°F (24°C) if possible. Water soil if it feels dry and spray plant 2–3 times a week.

Leaves turn plain green. Not enough light. Move to position in good indirect light, but not strong sun.

what goes wrong

Leaves become pale. Too much light. Move to more shaded place, out of direct sunlight.

Plant collapses. Waterlogged, probably standing in water. Or too cold. Check conditions. Allow soil to dry out before watering again, then always check surface feels dry before watering. If temperature below 60°F (16°C) move to warmer room.

255

Erica hyemalis

Cape heath

These beautiful flowering heaths are not easy to keep for long indoors as they prefer cooler winter temperatures than most people will accept. On the other hand, they will not grow outside where there is any likelihood of frost. They should be regarded as expendable, providing a little colour before winter-flowering plants such as poinsettias and azaleas become available. There are 3 varieties suitable for indoor use: pink *Erica gracilis,* white *E. nivalis* (sometimes called *E. gracilis alba),* both of which have many very small flowers, and *E. hyemalis* which has larger pink, white-tipped or yellow flowers.

Light: A window, but one that does not face direct sun ideal as plants need plenty of light.
Temperature: Winter temperature 47°F (8°C) ideal for long life. Maximum should be 60°F (15°C). Put outside in summer.
Water: 2 or 3 times a week, even in winter. Plant must never dry out, but must not stand in water.
Humidity: Spray twice weekly. Stand pot on saucer of pebbles almost covered with water or in outer pot of wet peat.
Feeding: Every 14 days when growing in spring and summer with liquid houseplant food diluted according to the maker's instructions.
Soil: 3 parts peat-based compost, with 1 part light sharp sand added. Must be lime free.
Repotting: Annually in spring after flowering. Nip out leading shoots first to keep plant bushy. Newly bought plants may be pot-bound and need immediate repotting.
Cleaning: Humidity spraying sufficient. No leafshine.

Cape heaths flower in late autumn and early winter, at a time of year when few other indoor plants are in flower. They should be kept in as cool a place as possible as they will not last long in a hot, dry atmosphere.

what goes wrong

Foliage and flowers fade and look lifeless. Too hot. Move to cooler place, under 60°F (15°C) and spray leaves with water. May also be caused by lack of light. If in dark corner, move to lighter place but not full sunlight.

Whole plant becomes brittle, leaves fall. Too dry. May be fatal but soak pot immediately in bucket of water for half an hour. Allow to drain, then water more often so that plant never dries out.

Humidity
Cape heaths need a cool but humid atmosphere. Stand pot on saucer of water filled with pebbles. Add water until it comes half way up pebbles. Do not stand pot base in water.

Another way of providing humidity is to stand the pot in an outer container, packing damp peat between the two.

Foliage and flowers darken. Too cold, probably near freezing. Move away from window at night in winter; keep above 45°F (8°C).

Irregular new growth in summer. Needs feeding. Feed every 14 days while growing. Pinch out growing tips of stems that are out of proportion.

Flowers fade. Leafshine damage. Do not use.

Brown scales on leaves and stems. Scale insect. Remove with cotton wool dipped in methylated spirits

or spray every 14 days with systemic insecticide until clear.

Leaves droop and plant smells bad. Root rot caused by bad drainage, waterlogged soil. Check plant not standing in water and that drainage holes are clear. Allow to dry out before watering again. May be fatal.

257

Espostoa

These white, woolly cacti, like small cotton-wool columns, come from the Andes in southern Ecuador and northern Peru. *Espostoa melanostele* (p.259) is an attractive example. They are slow-growing in cultivation, as in the wild, growing only about 2in (5cm) a year at most when they are young. In the wild they flower when they are about 3–4ft (1m) tall, producing an extra-thick woolly area called a cephalium at one side of the top of the stem, from which the flowers appear. Although this is very unlikely to happen in the home, they make handsome plants, the new wool produced each year swathing the top of the stem in white swirls. The wool becomes thicker as the plant ages, eventually entirely covering the stem. But beware of the spines which are half hidden by the wool and are needle sharp.

Espostoa superba produces some wool at the top of its stem but is much less woolly than other species. It grows to 2 or 3ft (1m) tall in 10 to 15 years and like other Espostoa species is unlikely to flower in the home.

Light: In the wild these cacti grow at high altitudes with high light intensity so they need maximum sunshine all the year round, on a sunny windowsill or in a greenhouse. If they do not receive enough sunshine, they will become elongated and less woolly.

Temperature: Keep above 40°F (4°C) in winter and below 100°F (38°C) in summer. Give fresh air whenever possible in summer.

Water: In spring and summer water about once a week, once a fortnight for larger plants. Always test compost. In dull weather it will not dry out so quickly and may become waterlogged. In autumn reduce watering to once every 3 weeks, then once a month. If plant is in a big pot (9in, 23cm or more) stop watering altogether in autumn to allow compost to dry out. Keep dry in winter, starting to water again in spring.

Normal stems of *Espostoa ritteri* growing from a cristate plant. Cristate plants produce multiple growing points instead of a single column, giving a ribbon-like or fan-like effect.

A healthy *Espostoa melanostele* will increase steadily if slowly in height and will make fresh, white wool at the growing point each year. As the plants get to more than 6in (15cm) the wool will get thicker and thicker, growing in a swirl around the top of the cactus. Flowers are unlikely in the home; the plant needs to be 3 or 4ft (a metre) tall and may take more than 15 years to reach this size.

Feeding will encourage quick clean growth and thicker wool.

Support the plant with a stick and a tie made of soft, loose material after repotting. Remove as soon as plant is settled, to avoid marking it.

Lightly brushing the wool will fluff it up and improve the plant's appearance. If it becomes dark and dirty do not shampoo, in spite of some advocates of this drastic measure: brush lightly with a very small amount of detergent in warm water.

For best-looking plants, repot annually to help keep plant growing quickly.

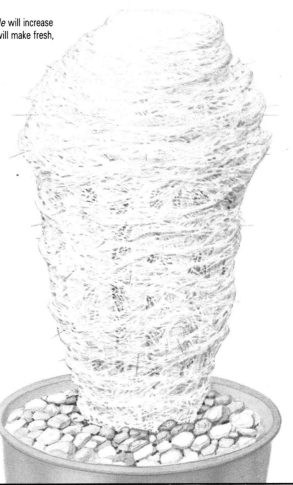

Feeding: Feed once a month in spring and summer with a high potash fertilizer (as used for tomatoes).

Soil: Use 1 part coarse gritty sand (not builders' or seashore) to 2 parts soil-less or good loam-based No. 2 potting compost (No. 3 mixture for large plants). Good drainage essential.

Repotting: Repot every year in spring into next size pot until in 5in (13cm) size. Then repot every other year. Once plant is about 2ft (60cm) tall and in a 9in (23cm) pot, keep it in the same sized container. Remove from pot each year to shake off old compost. Replace with new compost. Repotting these large plants is a two-person job.

Cleaning and pest control: Give an occasional light brushing to bring up the fluffiness of the wool. Spraying will make it look matt and unsightly. Pests are best treated with systemic insecticides, which are taken up through the roots, as the wool is difficult to penetrate with sprays and protects the pests from contact sprays. Add insecticides to the water when watering 2 or 3 times a year or if pests occur.

Other species: All the available species look very similar though some are less woolly than others. *E. ritteri* has reddish spines and sparse white wool and *E. superba* is also a less woolly one. Woolly species, apart from *E. melanostele*, are *E. lanata, E. sericata, E. nana, E. mirabilis* and some others. All are essentially similar plants.

Euphorbia milii

This popular plant grows into a small thorny shrub, which branches freely and flowers readily with red or yellow flowers. It will reach a height of 12–16in (30–40cm) with a width of 8–12in (20–30cm). Beware of the sap in all Euphorbias, which is an extreme irritant and dangerous to the eyes. This is a vast genus with well over a thousand succulent species, most of which are too large for indoor culture. Good small species include *E. obesa, E. suzannae E. decaryi, E. aeruginosa* and many others.

Light: A sunny position on a windowsill or in a greenhouse is needed for best results.
Temperature: A minimum of 45°F (7°C) is needed, but for safety some species prefer 50°F (10°C). Give fresh air in summer.
Water: Start watering in spring, fortnightly through spring and summer, weekly in hottest months, but allow to dry out between waterings. Tail off in autumn, and keep dry in winter, when leaves will fall. See also Introduction.
Feeding: Use high potash fertilizer in summer 2 or 3 times.
Soil: Use good loam-based No. 2 potting compost, or soil-less compost, with 30% coarse, gritty sand.
Repotting: Every spring in size larger pot, until 5 or 6in (15cm) pot is reached, when soil may be shaken off roots and plant repotted in same size pot with fresh soil. Do not water for 2 weeks after repotting.
Propagation: Cut off pieces of stem 2–3in (5–7cm) long in spring or summer, with a sharp knife. Dip cutting in water for a moment to stem flow of milky sap. Dust lightly with hormone rooting powder, leave to dry and after 3 days place in dry compost. Water after 3 weeks, when roots have started. Wash hands well after contact with sap.

Euphorbia milii, commonly known as the Crown of thorns, can vary in size from 1ft (30cm) tall to some with a spread of 6ft (2m). Its spiky stems have bright green, fleshy leaves which fall in winter if the temperature is below 55°F (13°C). The red 'flowers' are in fact coloured leaves called bracts. The true flower is the small yellow centre.

what goes wrong

Leaves dry up and fall. In winter, if below 55°F (13°C), natural. New leaves will grow in spring. If temperature higher, water once a month to retain leaves. In summer, overwatered or badly drained. Allow soil to dry out between waterings or roots may rot. If paring away damaged roots, take care as sap will run. Dip roots in water to stem sap flow.

Stem very thin at growing point; leaves pale greenish-yellow. Too dark or in winter too hot or too wet. Move gradually to sunny spot over 2 weeks. In winter keep dry and airy.

White marks on leaves. Caused by either insecticide spray or hard water leaving lime marks. It will not harm the plant.

Taking cuttings
When taking stem cuttings wear gloves to protect hands from poisonous sap. Cut 2–3in (5–8cm) tip in spring or early summer, just below a leaf. Remove lowest leaves if close to cut end and dip stem end in water to stop sap flowing. Drip water onto cut end on plant as well to seal.

Leaves scorched and shrivelled in summer. Too hot and dry. Move to more airy place and water when soil dries out in hot weather.

Leaves very lush but few flowers. Overfeeding. Stop feeding until next spring. Feed only 2 or 3 times in spring and summer.

Black sooty dust below where flowers have been. Sooty mould forming on the nectar. Spray weekly while flowering to dilute nectar and include a systemic fungicide in spray once a month. Dust off mould when dry.

Leaves blacken and fall, stem ends turn black and go soft, roots rot. Too humid. Move to more airy place and pare away damaged stem and roots. Dust with hormone rooting powder and leave to dry 2–3 days before rerooting. (see Introduction.)

Plants show little sign of growth, white woolly patches on roots. Root mealy bug. Wash all soil off roots, swirl in contact insecticide, and allow to dry before repotting in fresh compost and clean pot. Leave dry for 2 weeks.

261

Euphorbia pulcherrima

Poinsettia

Known almost all over the world as the flower of Christmas time, today's poinsettia is an outstanding example of scientific plant breeding. It is best treated as an annual as in a warm house in late winter it soon loses its leaves unless sprayed almost daily. In cooler conditions it can be retained to flower again the following year. Its leaves, which are slightly irregular, toothed and well veined, are thin and delicate. The top leaves, nearest the small yellow flowers, are termed bracts and turn bright red; there are also pink and white varieties. If leaves or stems are damaged, a milky sap emerges which weakens the plant; it is also said to be poisonous.

Healthy Poinsettia's have bright green leaves and red, pink or white bracts below the small flowers. They need cool conditions and often drop their leaves quickly in the hot, dr atmosphere of centrally heated rooms. Daily spraying will help to keep them alive and healthy from year to year.

Light: Stands direct sunlight in winter. When growing, protect from mid-day sun.
Temperature: When bracts are coloured, room temperature may be 55–70°F (12–21°C). Stands lower when growing but must be protected from frost.
Water: About twice a week unless very hot when it will dry out more quickly. Never let compost dry out when growing or in flower. After flowering, water only every 7 days for a 3–4 week rest period.
Humidity: Spray daily when in centrally-heated rooms or in summer.
Feeding: Every 14 days with liquid house-plant food while growing and flowering starts. Dilute food with water according to the maker's instructions.
Soil: Peat-based compost.
Repotting: Annually in midsummer after plant has rested. Prune stems before repotting. Handle roots and stems carefully and do not firm down compost too much. Use pot one size larger. If growing fast, repot again in autumn.
Cleaning: Humidity spraying sufficient. No leafshine.

Brown burn marks on leaves. Leafshine damage. Do not use.

Leaves look mouldy and dusty. Botrytis. Spray with fungicide every 7 days until clear.

Pruning
Prune when flowers die, before repotting. Wear gloves to protect from poisonous sap. Cut stems down by half, cutting just above a leaf stem. Dust cut end with sulphur dust and if sap rur seal cut with petroleum jell on cotton-wool.

what goes wrong

New leaves stay small and are pale. Needs feeding. Feed every 14 days while growing and flowering.

Leaves streaked and marbled with silver. Silver leaf virus. No cure. Burn plant.

Whole plant droops. Too cold or in a draught. Move to a protected position in a warmer room. Keep at temperature of at least 55° (12°C) when bracts are coloured. Make sure it is never exposed to frost. If too cold, plant may die.

Colour fades in patches on bracts and leaves. Too wet, overwatered, roots rotting. Allow to dry out before watering again and water less frequently in future. After flowering, allow plant to rest for 3–4 weeks, watering only once every 7 days.

Small white insects under the leaves. Whitefly. Spray every 14 days with diluted malathion until clear.

Leaves turn yellow, curl then drop. Too hot and dry.

Leaves turn pale and coloured bracts drop off. Too dark. Move to a lighter place. Plant will stand direct winter sunlight but protect from mid-day sun when growing.

Leaves shrivel and dry up. Too dry, needs watering. Put pot in bucket of water for 10–15 minutes, then drain. Water 50% more often. May also be affected by gas. Move to fume-free room.

Leaves distorted and sticky with green insects underneath. Greenfly. Spray every 14 days with pyrethrum or systemic insecticide until clear.

Move to cooler place (less than 70°F, 21°C) and spray daily to increase humidity. Check soil has not dried out and water if it feels dry below the surface during the growing period. Keep plant out of direct sunlight. Leaves drop naturally when plant is old.

Exacum affine

Persian violet

The Persian violet is a small, bushy biennial which is often treated as an annual. It is a native of the tropics and needs a light, fairly warm situation to thrive. Plants can be bought in bud in early summer or they can be raised from seed. Sow seed in a tray of seed compost in early spring. Germination takes about 3 weeks. First flowers should appear in mid-summer and plant should continue flowering through to the autumn.

Light: Full light at all times, but protect flowers from direct midday sun on hot days.

Temperature: Germination at 60°F (16°C), then keep at same temperature for best flowers. Overwinter not below 40°F (5°C), not above 60°F (16°C).

Water: Keep seedlings moist, gradually increasing water as plant begins to flower. Soil should always be moist while growing so water 2–3 times a week in summer. In winter allow to dry out thoroughly between waterings, giving a little every 10–14 days.

Humidity: In hot weather, spray lightly in the morning or evening. Do not spray in winter.

Feeding: Feed weekly with liquid houseplant food diluted to maker's recommended strength starting 4 weeks after plants are in final pots.

Soil: Soil-less potting compost.

After flowering: Can be overwintered to flower again the following summer. Allow growth to die back when flowering is finished in autumn. Cease feeding and reduce watering to keep compost just barely moist. Keep in a cool place, protected from frost, such as a light porch. In early spring, repot to a 4½in (11cm) pot and bring into a warm, light situation again.

This delicate shrub-like plant grows to a maximum height of about 6in (15cm) and produces a succession of scented lilac-blue flowers with prominent orange stamens throughout the summer. Direct midday summer sun will bleach the flowers but it needs good light all the year round.

Flowers become pale. Too much sun. Protect from direct sun on very hot days.

Young plant turns yellow, soil looks dark. Overwatering, which can be fatal. Stop watering, ensure that drainage is good. Begin watering again when soil is almost dry. Keep soil just moist.

Seedlings fail to grow. Root rot caused by too wet soil. Keep soil just moist. Rotted seedlings will not grow.

Plant wilts after a hot day. Too hot and dry. Spray with clean water to revive plant. Spray in early morning if very hot weather is predicted but do not spray in bright sunshine.

what goes wrong

Small wingless insects on leaves, buds or flowers. Greenfly. Spray with pyrethrum-based insecticide and repeat in 14 days until plant is clear.

Buds, flowers or leaves eaten. Caterpillars. Find and remove them by hand. Usually infest outdoor plants, but can be brought indoors.

Propagation

1. Seed is very fine. Mix it with fine sand for even sowing. Just cover with dry compost.

2. Place tray in plastic bag cover with paper and give full light as soon as seedlings show.

Tiny white flies on leaves or hopping around plant. Whitefly. Spray with pyrethrum-based insecticide twice in 3 days. If scale-like white eggs are found under leaves, spray every 3 days until no more scales or flies are seen.

Leaves turn yellow, plant weak. Needs feeding. Give dilute liquid houseplant food every week.

Growth thin and weak, but still green. Too dark. Move to a lighter place. Flower buds will not form in a dark place.

Leaves turn very dark in winter. Too cold. Move to a warmer place. Protect overwintered plant from frost or it will die.

Plant floppy. Much too dry. Soak pot in bowl of water for 15 minutes, then drain. Give more water at each watering but take care that soil does not become waterlogged.

265

Ivy tree

This interesting houseplant is a cross between a False castor oil plant (*Fatsia japonica)* and an ivy. Its leaves are similar to those of the False castor oil plant, but smaller, and it has tiny rather uninteresting green flowers like an ivy. It grows upright (though its thin stems need to be supported with a cane or moss pole) and will climb like an ivy. Very tolerant of different room conditions, it is also quick growing and makes a good display when several plants are grown together up a moss pole.

The most common variety has all green leaves but there is a variegated type with slightly smaller leaves.

Light: Best in good light away from direct sunlight, but quite tolerant of shady conditions. Variegated plants need more light than all green ones.

Temperature: Winter minimum 45°F (8°C), summer maximum 65°F (18°C).

Water: 2–3 times a week in summer, so that only the top ½in (1cm) of soil dries out; every 7–10 days in winter so that it is drier but does not dry out completely.

Humidity: Spray 2–3 times a week when growing in spring and summer, once a week in winter. If temperature is higher than 65°F (18°C), a daily spray will help plant to survive.

Feeding: Every 14 days in the growing season (spring and summer) with houseplant food diluted according to the maker's instructions.

Soil: Loam-based No. 2 compost.

Repotting: Annually in spring, just as plant starts to grow. Put 3 plants together in a pot for a bushier effect.

Cleaning: Humidity spraying sufficient, though leaves can be cleaned with a damp cloth if they get dusty or dirty. Use leafshine every 2–3 months.

The Ivy tree's glossy five-pointed leaves grow from a thin stem which is best trained as a climber. Variegated plants have creamy white markings, usually at the leaf edges. Healthy plants will have leaves growing all down the stems with no yellowing foliage.

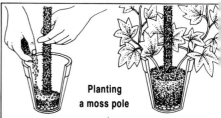

Planting a moss pole

1. Prepare pot with drainage material and position moss pole in centre. Add compost to hold it upright.

2. Place plant roots on compost. If several are planted together, space them evenly around pole.

3. Add compost to fill pot, covering roots. Firm it around both roots and moss pole. Make sure pole stands upright.

4. Fasten plant stem to pole with twine or raffia, tying loosely in space between leaves. Do not damage shoots.

what goes wrong

New shoots elongated with long spaces between leaves. Too dark. Move to lighter place.

Variegated plants turn all green. Too dark. Move to lighter place but not full sunlight.

White woolly patches on leaves and in leaf axils. Mealy bug. Remove with cotton wool dipped in methylated spirits or spray every 14 days with diluted malathion or systemic insecticide until clear.

Leaves look limp and dull. Too hot. Does not like temperatures over 65°F (18°C). Move to cool place if possible and spray regularly in hot weather.

Leaves turn soft and yellow. Too wet, overwatered. Allow to dry out before watering again, then water less often. Top ½in (1cm) of soil can dry out between waterings. In winter, water only every 7–10 days. Never stand in water.

Leaves distorted and sticky with small green insects underneath. Greenfly. Spray with derris, diluted malathion or a systemic insecticide every 14 days until clear. Increase humidity by spraying regularly.

Leaves flop. Needs water. Water immediately and then 2–3 times a week in summer, every 7–10 days in winter.

Leaves yellow with webs underneath. Red spider mite. Spray with diluted malathion or systemic insecticide every 14 days until clear. Increase humidity by spraying, especially in hot weather. Keep cooler.

Grey mouldy patches on leaves. Botrytis (grey mould). Spray with systemic fungicide and move to warmer, more airy position. Do not overwater in winter.

Plant collapses after repotting. Roots damaged. Place whole plant in polythene bag or damp newspaper for two days.

267

Fatsia japonica

False castor oil plant

This is a very easy, quick-growing and large-leaved plant and will survive in quite dark positions. Its strong, glossy finger-shaped leaves can have a spread of up to 18in (45cm) across. It is tolerant of both low and high temperatures, and will even grow outside in temperatures down to but not below freezing. It does produce flowers, a cluster of white blooms in midsummer, but it must be in a very light position for these to appear. It is also known as *Aralia* and is related to the elegant and more delicate *Dizygotheca elegantissima*, the Finger plant.

The False castor oil plant may grow 3 to 5ft (1–1½m) high and across. The handsome leaves may be plain green or variegated with cream markings outlining the leaves. The variegated ones grow more slowly than the plain green ones.

Light: For best results needs full light but it will survive in dark corners away from natural light.

Temperature: Grows in a wide range from 32°F (0°C) in winter to 70°F (21°C) in summer.

Watering: Keep moist at all times in summer, watering at least twice a week. Once a week is enough in winter but check that compost never dries out completely.

Humidity: Mist spray daily in summer if temperatures near maximum, twice weekly in winter. Likes humidity.

Feeding: Add liquid houseplant food to water every 14 days in growing season, diluting to maker's recommended strength

Soil: Loam-based No. 2.

Repotting: Repot once a year in spring as plant starts to produce new leaves. Use pot only one size larger. Plant prefers to have its roots constricted. If plant is growing straggly, stems can be cut back just above a leaf stem after repotting. Dab cut end with sulphur dust to prevent infection.

Cleaning: Regular mist spraying will keep leaves clean though they are large enough to wipe with a damp cloth. Use leafshine not more than once every 6 weeks.

Leaves distorted and sticky with green insects. Greenfly. Spray with pyrethrum-based insecticide or diluted malathion. Repeat weekly until clear.

Few new leaves grow, though feeding regular. Pot too large. Plant is growing roots, not leaves. Do not repot again for 2 years and always choose pot only one size larger than old one.

Webs under leaves with tiny red insects. Red spider mite. Remove webs with damp cloth or sponge, then spray with diluted malathion, especially under leaves. Repeat every 14 days until symptoms disappear. Improve humidity by standing pot on saucer of wet pebbles.

what goes wrong

Stems long and weak, long spaces between leaves. Too hot. Move to cooler, more airy place. Spray daily with soft, tepid water. Maximum temperature 70°F (21°C).

Whole plant droops. Waterlogged. Drain away any water in saucer and allow surface of compost to dry out before watering again. Then keep moist but never allow pot base to stand in water. Always throw away excess that drains through after watering and check plant has good drainage.

Leaves scorched and burned. Sprayed in sunlight. Spray in early morning or evening when sun not on leaves. Do not allow leaf tips to touch glass on sunny days.

Young leaves black. Frost; is plant behind curtains at night? Remove damaged leaves and move to warmer place over 34°F (1°C).

Leaves pale. Needs feeding. Feed every 14 days in growing season with liquid houseplant food diluted to maker's recommended strength.

Leaves limp. Air too dry in hot weather. Spray daily in summer, especially when near 70°F (21°C). In winter, spray twice weekly, more often if in hot, dry room.

Leaves droop. Compost too dry. Plunge pot into bucket of water for 10–15 minutes, then drain. Keep moist in summer and spray daily.

269

Faucaria tigrina

There are several species of this South African genus available, all commonly called Tiger's jaws. They make good plants for a bright windowsill display or for a greenhouse. Bright, dandelion-yellow flowers are produced in late or early autumn. They grow in clumps to fill a 5 or 6in (15cm) half-pot or pan in about 4 or 5 years and reach about 2in (5cm) tall. There is one white-flowered species not at all easy to obtain, called *Faucaria candicans*. But other good yellow-flowered species include *F. albidens* with attractive, white-edged leaves and teeth, *F. tuberculosa*, very popular for its 'fierce' teeth and swollen leaves, *F. kingiae* and *F. britteniae* somewhat similar to *F. tigrina*. All are easy to grow, provided you are careful to water at the right time of year.

Faucaria albidens. Faucarias are known as Tiger's jaws as their pairs of fleshy, spiked leaves are said to look like a tiger's open mouth. The bright yellow flowers appear in late summer and autumn but like most succulents, they will not produce them if they have been kept too hot or too wet in the previous winter months.

Light: A sunny position is needed to keep good colour and to ensure flowering.

Temperature: A minimum of 40°F (4°C) is needed. Give fresh air in summer.

Water: Start watering in spring, about once a fortnight, weekly in hottest months. Tail off in autumn, keep dry in winter. See also Introduction.

Feeding: Not necessary if repotted in spring, but if not, use high potash fertilizer 2 or 3 times in summer.

Soil: Use good loam-based No. 2 potting compost, or soil-less compost, with 30% coarse, gritty sand.

Repotting: Every year in spring, in size larger half-pot or pan. Try not to disturb roots too much. Do not water for 2 weeks.

Propagation: Take cuttings of whole shoots in spring and summer with a sharp knife. Dust them with hormone rooting powder, leave 3 days to dry before placing the base on or just in dry compost. Water after 3 weeks when roots have formed.

Flowers shrivel quickly and have brown edges. Too dry in summer or in too much strong sun. Check soil and water when soil dries out in hot weather. Protect from strong midday summer sun.

Rusty spots on leaves. Tiny webs. Red spider mite. Spray with insecticide and repeat every 2 weeks for 3 months. To prevent attack, spray regularly 2–3 times a year.

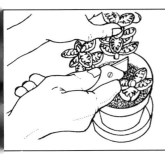

Taking cuttings

1. Cut off whole shoots with sharp knife in spring, cutting straight across stem.

2. Dust cut surfaces with hormone rooting powder to prevent infection and leave cutting to dry for 2–3 days. Place on dry compost and do not water until roots appear.

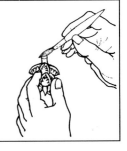

Stems long with pale leaves, no flowers by late summer. Too dark or too hot in winter. Move over 2 weeks into full sunlight and keep in airy place. Keep below 50°F (10°C) in winter.

what goes wrong

No sign of growth, though conditions correct. Check roots for root mealy bug — white woolly patches on roots. Wash all soil off roots, swirl roots in contact insecticide, and allow to dry before repotting in fresh compost and washed pot. Leave dry for 2 weeks.

Leaves shrivel, plant loses colour and does not grow in summer. Too dry or needs feeding or repotting. Check soil. If dry, soak in bowl of water for ½ hour, then drain. Repot in spring and feed 2–3 times in summer. In winter leaves shrivel naturally.

White woolly patches among leaves. Mealy bug. Remove with small paintbrush dipped in methylated spirits, and spray with contact or systemic insecticide. Repeat 2 or 3 times in growing season.

Leaves turn black and shrivel. Black rot, roots rotting. Too cold and wet or too humid. Keep over 40°F (4°C) in winter. Pare off blackened stem and dust with fungicide. Keep dry.

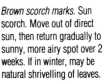

Brown scorch marks. Sun scorch. Move out of direct sun, then return gradually to sunny, more airy spot over 2 weeks. If in winter, may be natural shrivelling of leaves.

Fenestraria
rhopalophylla

There are two forms of this species, one with yellow flowers the other with white. There is also a very similar purple-pink flowered plant called *Frithia pulchra*. All have extraordinary sausage-shaped leaves with transparent ends which let in light and form tight packed bunches growing close to the soil. In the wild in South Africa, only the transparent tips of the leaves show and even then only at soil level; the rest of the plant is below ground. The yellow flowered form is sometimes labelled *Fenestraria aurantiaca*, or *F. rhopalophylla v. aurantiaca*.

Fenestraria rhopalophylla, known as Baby's toes, is wonderfully suited to survival in very dry areas. In times of drought its leaves pull themselves right down into the soil so that just the transparent leaf ends show. Light is still able to penetrate to the plant through these 'windows'.

Light: A sunny position is necessary for compact growth and to induce flowering.
Temperature: A minimum of 40°F (4°C) is needed. Give fresh air in summer.
Water: Water fortnightly in spring and summer but not overhead, weekly in hottest weather. Allow to dry between waterings. Tail off in autumn, keep dry in winter.
Feeding: If not repotted in spring, use high potash fertilizer 2 or 3 times in summer. Unnecessary if repotted that year.
Soil: Use good loam-based No. 2 potting compost, or soil-less compost, with 30% coarse, gritty sand.
Repotting: Every year in spring in size larger pot, being careful not to disturb roots too much. Leave dry for 2 weeks after repotting.
Propagation: Plant can be divided into small clumps, but individual leaves will not root to form new plants. Cut clump apart with sharp knife, dust cut surfaces with hormone rooting powder and leave dry for 3 days before repotting in fresh dry compost. Water after 3 weeks. Also fairly easily raised from seed.

Stems grow long and floppy, separating from each other and turning pale green. In winter, too hot and wet. Move to cooler position, around 50°F (10°C) in winter and allow to dry out completely, giving no water from late autumn to spring. In summer, too dark. Keep in full light to improve colour and shape.

what goes wrong

Stems shrink back into soil so only tips are exposed. Rare indoors, caused by too much light. Shade in hottest midsummer days.

Stems do not grow in spring and summer. Needs feeding or repotting. Repot in fresh compost and feed 2–3 times in growing season.

No growth though conditions correct. Stems shrink. Check roots for root mealy bug. If found, wash soil off roots and swirl in insecticide. Dry before repotting in fresh compost and clean pot. Leave dry for 2 weeks.

Individual stems dry up. Too dry or water on stems. Water from below and give more at each watering in spring and summer. Check compost regularly in hot weather.

Stems light brown and shrivelled on side nearest window. Sunscorch. Shade, then move back gradually over 2 weeks into bright sun. New stems may grow in place of damaged one. Brown marks may also be caused by cold. Keep above 40°F (4°C) in winter, away from glass.

Stems lose colour. Too dark. Move into full sunlight over 2 week period. Keep in full light all year round, only shading on hottest summer days if stems begin to shrink back into soil.

Growing from seed

1. Sow seed thinly in spring on surface of prepared tray or half-pot. Tap sides to settle seed.

2. Water from base with fungicide diluted as for 'damping off' of seedlings, until surface is damp. Place tray or pot in polythene bag with ends folded underneath to seal in moisture. Leave in light (not direct sun) at 70°F (21°C). Do not water again unless condensation on polythene becomes patchy or dries.

3. Prick out after 6 months into 2in (5cm) pots or ½in (2cm) apart in trays.

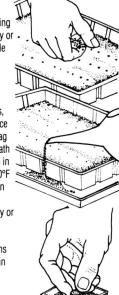

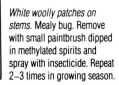

White woolly patches on stems. Mealy bug. Remove with small paintbrush dipped in methylated spirits and spray with insecticide. Repeat 2–3 times in growing season.

All stems shrivel. In summer much too dry. In winter, natural in dry resting period. In summer soak pot in bowl of water for ½ hour, drain then give more water each time.

Stems black and soft. Too cold, wet or humid. Move to warmer place, around 50°F (10°C) in winter and allow to dry out thoroughly. In summer always allow to dry out between waterings. Pare off blackened stem and dust with fungicide.

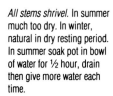

273

Ferocactus

These are the Barrel cacti of the American and Mexican deserts, said to provide the thirsty traveller with water from their succulent interior. It would be a bitter drink, but the fable persists. Many of these plants in the wild grow to massive, thick columns taller than a man, but there are a few of more modest size which will flower in cultivation. With the large species the likelihood of getting them to flowering size is remote, unless you start when you are very young for they may take 15–20 years to reach maturity. They are often worth growing for the beauty of their fierce spines. The smaller growing species such as *Ferocactus macrodiscus* (p.275) will produce flowers when they are about 4in (10cm) in diameter, after 6–8 years.

Ferocactus glaucescens has a blue-green body with bright yellow spines. Often grown for its form and colour alone, it will flower when it is about 8in (20cm) in diameter, after about 10 years growth.

Light: Maximum light is needed for good strong growth of plants and spines, as well as for the possibility of flowers in the smaller species. Keep on the sunniest windowsill or, ideally, in a greenhouse.

Temperature: For safety keep above 40°F (4°C) in winter; keep below 100°F (38°C) in summer, and give fresh air when possible.

Water: Water in spring and summer weekly (fortnightly for larger plants). Always make sure compost has dried out from previous watering before adding more. Tail off watering in the autumn to once every 3 weeks or a month and keep dry in winter.

Feeding: Use a high potash fertilizer in spring and summer about once a month (as used for tomatoes).

Soil: Use 2 parts of coarse, gritty sand (not builders' or seashore) to 3 parts of soil-less or good loam-based No. 2 potting compost (No. 3 for large plants). Good drainage essential.

Repotting: Repot annually in the early years into next size larger pot in spring. When 7in

Ferocactus gracilis has wonderfully bright red, fiercely hooked spines. The fiery red flowers are unlikely in cultivation until the plant is a foot (30cm) or more tall, which will take 12 or 15 years good growth.

(18cm) pot is reached repot every other year, or replace in same sized pot with fresh soil, after carefully shaking the old soil off the roots. Do not water for a fortnight after repotting.

Cleaning and pest control: Spray every week with water to dilute the sticky nectar which oozes from the areoles. Incorporate an insecticide 2 or 3 times a year to combat pests.

Other species: Large species (football size) worth growing for their spines are *F. gracilis* or *F. acanthodes*, noted for their colourful red or yellow dense, strong spines and *F. glaucescens*. For flowers on smaller growing species there are three that are outstanding: *F. macrodiscus* (below), *F. viridescens* and *F. fordii*. All will be 6–8 years old by the time they reach flowering size. *F. latispinus* grows more slowly but flowers at about the same size (3–4in, 8–10cm). It has pink flowers and extremely thick hooked spines.

Preventing mould

1. In spring and summer sticky nectar oozes from the areoles. Spray weekly with water to dilute it and prevent mould from forming.

2. If sooty mould forms down the ribs, spray plant with systemic fungicide every week until it can be gently brushed off.

Ferocactus macrodiscus has curving spines which are red when young, fading to yellowish buff with time. It is low-growing and flowers when it has grown to 4 or 5in (10-12cm) wide, after 6–8 years. A healthy plant will make fresh bright coloured spines each year and will slowly increase in size. It is especially important to give the plant as much sun as possible in the winter to encourage the formation of flower buds.

Ficus benjamina

Weeping fig

This is the best-known of the small-leaved varieties of *Ficus*. Its branches droop gracefully, particularly as the plant reaches adult size, making it much favoured by interior designers. Its leaves are bright mid-green, growing to about 3in (8cm) long and 1in (2½cm) wide, with many on each stem. It needs a good, light position to flourish, but is susceptible to cold draughts in winter. If it sheds leaves because of the cold, it will usually recover if moved to a warmer place, but draughts can be fatal. There are several varieties of this *Ficus,* some of which have variegated leaves. In good conditions, the Weeping fig will grow into an elegant tree up to 15ft (5m) tall. Though in time its trunk becomes strong and woody, younger plants need to be supported.

Light: Needs plenty, but must be kept out of direct sunlight.
Temperature: Winter minimum 55–60°F (13–15°C), summer maximum 75°F (24°C).
Water: Not more than twice a week in summer, once every 7–10 days in winter, with tepid water. Must not be over-watered, nor should it stand in water. Rainwater ideal, as tap water may cause lime deposits on root system, slowing growth.
Humidity: Mist spray daily, except when temperature below 60°F (15°C).
Feeding: Every 14 days in the growing season (spring and summer) with houseplant food diluted according to the maker's instructions.
Soil: Loam-based No. 2 compost.
Repotting: Annually in spring when young; just change topsoil annually when too big to handle easily.
Cleaning: Humidity spraying sufficient. Use aerosol leafshine about once a month.

The Weeping fig's leathery, waxy leaves help it to be tolerant of dry air, though it does better with a daily mist spray to provide local humidity. Do not buy plants with bare stems near the base. Protect them from cold draughts on the way home.

Leaves dry and turn brittle. Too dry, air too dry and too hot. Water more often and spray every day to increase humidity. Try to keep below 75°F (24°C).

Tying to a cane
Young and medium-sized plants need to be supported by a strong bamboo cane, especially when being carried. Tie plant to cane loosely, between side branches.

what goes wrong

Leaves drop when green. Too dark or in draught, or there has been sudden drop in temperature. In winter, water used was too cold. Check care conditions and move if necessary to warmer or lighter place. May shed some leaves naturally when new ones grow in spring.

Leaves blacken. Leaf has touched cold window. Move away from glass.

Leaves discoloured with brown scales on stems and under leaves. Scale insect. Remove with cotton wool dipped in methylated spirits or spray every 14 days with systemic insecticide until clear.

Leaves yellow and speckled with webs underneath. Red spider mite. Spray with diluted malathion or systemic insecticide every 14 days until clear. Increase humidity by spraying, especially in hot weather.

Sooty mould on leaves. Follows attack by scale insect. Wipe leaves clean with soapy water.

In spring new leaves are small, plant looks dull and lifeless. Needs repotting if small or topsoil changing. Feed after changing topsoil but not for 3–4 weeks if completely repotted.

Leaves turn yellow, then fall. Too wet, overwatered or standing in water. Drain any water from saucer and allow to dry out. Wait until soil feels dry and crumbly before watering again.

277

Rubber plant

This is still one of the most popular of all houseplants for it will grow and flourish in most homes with the minimum care. It is a native of India, where it grows to a 100ft (30m) tree but indoor varieties have been bred to grow more compactly, with smaller leaves. Take care not to break the leaves or cut the stem or they will 'bleed'. If this happens, seal the wound immediately with cotton wool or tissue dipped in petroleum jelly. Two other large-leaved *Ficus* species make good specimen plants: *F. lyrata*, the Fiddleback fig and *F. benghalensis*, the Banyan fig.

The Rubber plant's glossy leaves are about 10in (25cm) long and 6in (15cm) across when fully grown. New leaves appear at the plant's tip, covered at first by a protective sheath which falls away as the leaf unfurls. If the tip is removed, the plant should branch.

Light: Will stand some shade but will not grow so well. Keep out of direct sunlight.

Temperature: Winter minimum 60°F (16°C), summer maximum 85°F (29°C).

Water: Do not overwater – if in doubt, leave it another day or two and never leave standing in water. Water only when compost feels dry, twice a week in summer, once a week or less in winter. In winter use tepid water.

Humidity: Spray at least once a week, more often if over 70°F (21°C).

Feeding: Feed every 14 days in spring and summer when growing with liquid houseplant food diluted to maker's recommended strength.

Soil: Loam-based No. 2. Make sure it is well drained.

Repotting: Repot once a year in spring, more often if plant is growing quickly and needs larger pot to keep it stable. When too large to handle, replace top 2–3in (5–7cm) compost and feed every 10 days in summer.

Cleaning: Wipe with damp cloth, supporting leaves carefully. Use leafshine not more than once a month.

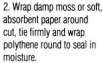

Air layering

1. If your plant has lost its lower leaves but the top is still growing, use air layering to improve its appearance. With sharp knife make shallow cut in stem below leaf or leaf scar. Insert small stone and dust cut with hormone rooting powder.

2. Wrap damp moss or soft, absorbent paper around cut, tie firmly and wrap polythene round to seal in moisture.

3. When new roots grow from cut, slice off stem below them and repot top in fresh compost. Discard lower stem or seal top with petroleum jelly and it may reshoot.

Leaves pale, new ones small and distorted. Needs feeding. Feed every 14 days in spring and summer while growing.

Leaves pale. Too much light. Move to more shaded spot, out of direct sunlight.

Yellow spots on leaves, webs underneath. Red spider mite. Remove webs with damp cloth or sponge, then spray with diluted malathion, especially under leaves. Repeat every 14 days until clear. Improve humidity.

Brown scales under leaves and on stems. Scale insect. Spray underside of leaves with diluted malathion and, after 48 hours, remove discs with thumbnail. Repeat every week for 4 weeks. Or, paint with methylated spirits.

Burns on leaves, especially after spraying. Caused by spraying in sunlight. Keep out of strong sun and never spray in sunlight. Remove leaf and stem.

Leaves hang down, curl and seem limp. Too dry. Plunge pot into bucket of water for 10–15 minutes, then drain. Allow surface to dry out between waterings but check regularly in hot weather and in centrally heated rooms.

what goes wrong

White woolly patches on leaves. Mealy bug. Spray with diluted malathion and remove bugs and 'wool' with tweezers. Repeat every 14 days until symptoms disappear. Or, paint bugs with methylated spirits, remove with tweezers.

Bottom leaves turn yellow, droop and fall. Too wet. Allow to dry thoroughly before watering again and in winter use tepid water. Very old plants lose lower leaves naturally.

Leaves from any part of plant drop suddenly. Brown patches on other leaves. Too cold. Move to warmer place, above 60°F (16°C).

279

Ficus pumila

Creeping fig

This useful and beautiful climbing plant, sometimes known as *F. repens*, flourishes in humid and damp conditions. Though it is first cousin to the rubber plant, it does not look in any way like one, having thin trailing or climbing stems and a mass of small green leaves. The plant will grow quite fast in good conditions, and will climb up the wall of a conservatory or up a moss pole, producing trails of up to 18in (46cm) in a year. It also makes a good plant for mixed bowls, in hanging baskets and in bottle gardens. The variegated variety of the plant is a slow grower. Related to the Creeping fig and similar in growth pattern is *F. radicans,* the Rooting fig, which has larger, stiffer and often variegated leaves.

The Creeping fig's small heart-shaped leaves grow close together on thin stems, forming a mass of green. Healthy plants look bushy, with no bare stems or shrivelled leaves. In spring and summer there should be signs of strong new shoots.

Light: Does well in shady situations away from a window and may become dried up in direct sunlight.

Temperature: Winter minimum 45°F (8°C). Will stand a summer temperature as high as 82°F (27°C), provided good humidity is maintained.

Water: 2–3 times a week in summer, every other day in winter to keep damp at all times.

Humidity: Spray every day in summer (twice if over 75°F, 24°C), every other day in winter.

Feeding: Every 14 days in the growing season (spring and summer) with houseplant food diluted according to the maker's instructions.

Soil: Loam-based No. 2 or peat-based compost.

Repotting: Annually in spring if necessary, though best in small pot, i.e. when plant is pot-bound.

Cleaning: Humidity spraying sufficient. No leafshine.

Stems grow straggly with leaves spaced wide apart. Much too dark. Move to lighter position, but not full sun.

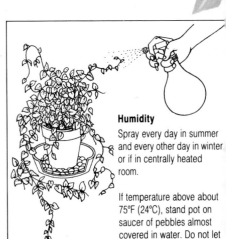

Humidity

Spray every day in summer and every other day in winter or if in centrally heated room.

If temperature above about 75°F (24°C), stand pot on saucer of pebbles almost covered in water. Do not let pot base touch water.

New leaves stay small or plant does not grow in summer. Needs repotting. Use pot one size larger.

Leaves turn yellow and drop. Too wet, pot perhaps left standing in water. Pour away any water in saucer and do not water again until compost feels barely moist.

what goes wrong

White woolly patches on leaves. Mealy bug. Remove with cotton wool dipped in methylated spirits or spray with diluted malathion or systemic insecticide every 14 days until clear.

Leaves discoloured with brown scales. Scale insect. Remove with cotton wool dipped in methylated spirits or spray every 14 days with diluted malathion or systemic insecticide until clear.

Leaves yellow with webs underneath. Red spider mite. Spray every 14 days with derris, diluted malathion or systemic insecticide until clear. Spray daily to improve humidity.

Leaves dry up and curl. Too dry or too sunny. If compost feels dry soak plant in bucket of water for 10–15 minutes, then drain. Pick off dried leaves and water regularly. Keep out of direct sun. If all leaves dry out, plant will not recover.

281

Fittonia verschaffeltii

Painted net leaf

This attractive creeping plant with its spectacular leaf markings is not, perhaps, the easiest of plants to cultivate, but is most rewarding when growing well. It is a useful plant for shady positions away from direct light, but it needs warmth and high humidity. It is also a good plant for mixed bowls and for large bottle gardens or terrariums. A Painted net leaf has attractively patterned camellia-shaped leaves about 3–4in (8–10cm) long. The small green flower which appears in the summer should be removed from the plant so that all its growing strength goes into the leaves. The miniature silvery-marked form often seen is a related species, *Fittonia argyroneura*.

Light: Tolerates shade, and will deteriorate if put in direct light, even if not in sunlight.
Temperature: Minimum all the year round 65°F (18°C) as plant likes to be warm at all times. If temperature above 80°F (27°C) humidity should also be high.
Water: At least 3 times a week in summer, more if near 80°F (27°C), and about every 5 days in winter, as plant must never dry out. Check compost regularly and use soft water if possible.
Humidity: Spray daily in summer, every other day in winter, to maintain essential high humidity.
Feeding: Every 14 days, using houseplant food diluted with water. Use half as much food as the maker recommends.
Soil: Loam-based No. 2 or peat-based compost.
Repotting: Annually in spring into shallow or half pots if possible, as plant has shallow root system. Good drainage in pot essential.
Cleaning: Humidity spraying sufficient. No leafshine.

A healthy Painted net leaf is basically green, with distinct white veins, shaded in red. A miniature form with more silvery veins is known as the silver net leaf or snakeskin plant. Plants should be compact, with no curled or dropping leaves. Though difficult to keep for long in dry, centrally heated rooms, they are well worth the extra effort.

what goes wrong

Lower leaves turn yellow. Too wet, soil waterlogged. Check drainage holes in pot are not blocked and empty any water from saucer. Allow to dry until soil is just moist.

282

Humidity
Fittonias must be kept constantly humid. Spray every day in summer, every other day in winter.

If leaves turn dull and shrivel, stand pot in saucer on pebbles almost covered with water. Make sure pot base is not touching the water.

Leaves distorted and sticky with green insects. Greenfly. Spray with pyrethrum or a systemic insecticide every 14 days until clear.

New leaves small and spaced widely on stem. Too dark. Move to lighter place but not in a window.

Leaves go dull and shrivel at the edges. Air too dry. Spray every day and stand pot on saucer of damp pebbles, making sure that pot base is not in water.

Brown burn marks on leaves. Leafshine damage. Do not use.

Leaves shrivel, turn thin and papery. Too dry and/or too much light. Soak immediately in bucket of soft water for 10–15 minutes, then drain. Move to semi-shaded position. Remove leaves that do not recover and water more often.

Leaves drop and no new ones appear. Too cold. Move to warmer room, at least 65°F (18°C) and make sure it is out of any draughts.

283

Freesia

Although they look delicate and exotic, Freesias require little heat to grow well and make excellent flowering plants for pots and bowls. They do best in a cool, airy room or porch and can be grown from either seed or corms. Plant corms in midsummer, 1in (2½cm) deep in moist compost, allowing 5–6 corms to a 5in (12cm) pot. Keep in a cool, light place without water until leaves start to grow. Sow seeds in early summer. Fill 9in (24cm) pot with potting compost with a top inch (2½cm) seedling compost. Water well and sow 15 seeds, spaced apart. Cover with ⅛in (2mm) seedling compost and shade from direct sun. Thin to 10 plants when about 1in (2½cm) high. Flowers appear in late winter.

The highly scented flowers of the Freesia grow in groups along one side of the wiry, branching stem. Single and double-flowered varieties are available, in white, yellow, pink, red, orange, or purple. Plants grow to a height of 12–18in (30–45cm), with slender, bright green leaves.

Light: Full sun except at seedling stage.
Temperature: Winter temperature 40–45°F (4–7°C). Move to temperature of maximum 55°F (13°C) for flowering.
Water: Plant corms in moist compost, then do not give any water until growth is visible. Increase watering to prevent compost from drying out. Water 2–3 times a week when in bud and flower.
Humidity: Needs a cool, dry, airy situation. If very hot, mist spray in early morning.
Feeding: Feed every week with diluted liquid garden fertilizer, beginning when buds appear, until foliage dies down.
Soil: Loam-based No.2 or soil-less.
After flowering: If fed corms can be saved and repotted to flower the following year. Cut stem when flowering is finished, but leave foliage to die back naturally. Cut back when completely dry, then lift and store corms in a cool dry place for potting up again in mid-summer.

Flowers pale, stems thin and weak. Too hot or too dark. Check conditions. Freesias need a light place with maximum temperature 55°F (13°C) for flowering.

Stems bent and untidy. Lack of support. Flower stems are straggly and need support by tying to stakes or twigs to grow straight.

Leaves turn pinky-grey, webs on underside. Red spider.

Spray with pyrethrum-based insecticide or diluted malathion. Spray again in 14 days if still visible.

Corms found to be soft after storage or purchase. Dry rot. Do not plant. If lifting corms for storage, always soak in benomyl as a precaution. Buy firm corms from a reliable source.

Support
Supporting flower stems. The flower stems will bend when flowers develop unless supported. Insert 24in (60cm) canes or twigs beside stems and tie stem loosely to cane in several places.

Small insects on buds. Greenfly. Freesias are very susceptible so spray weekly with pyrethrum-based insecticide while in bud. Do not spray flowers.

what goes wrong

Brown marks on stems, yellow blotches on leaves, which may become papery. Virus disease. No cure, so destroy corms after flowering. May be spread by greenfly, so spray with pyrethrum-based insecticide to control.

Leaf ends turn yellow, then brown. Fusarium wilt disease contracted from soil. Plant may flower, but do not save corm. Always grow in sterile compost.

Flower buds turn brown and papery or fail to open. Too dry. Increase watering when first buds appear and keep compost moist.

Plant does not grow well. In autumn, soil may be too dry or too wet. Keep just slightly moist. If corms are in second year's growth, they may not have been well fed the first year. Always feed weekly. Do not cut foliage, but allow it to die back if saving corms.

Leaves yellow. If limp or if corm is rotting, suspect overwatering. Allow plant to dry then keep compost just moist. Leaves yellow naturally after flowering. Do not cut back until fully dried out.

Fuchsia

Named after Leonard Fuchs, a six-teenth-century German botanical writer, Fuchsias originate in Central and South America. The flowers range from pale pink to dark red and purple in colour. Usually, they are given a resting period in winter, when they should be placed in a cool, light situation with a minimum temperature of 45°F (7°C). When the plant is growing, the side tips should be pinched out every 2 weeks to make it bushy.

Light: Bright light, including full sun, but not midday summer sunlight.
Temperature: Summer maximum 60°F (16°C), though tolerates 65°F (18°C) if humidity is very high. Winter 45-50°F (7-10°C), to rest until early spring.
Water: Moderately, just as surface begins to dry out – weekly in spring, twice weekly in summer. After flowering, reduce water to weekly again. In winter, allow soil surface to dry out completely between waterings. Every 14 days sufficient.
Humidity: Spray with soft water twice weekly in spring and twice daily in summer, especially in very hot weather. Spray twice weekly in late summer, and stop altogether in autumn and winter.
Feeding: As soon as flower buds appear feed weekly with liquid houseplant food diluted to maker's instructions. Stop feeding in late summer.
Soil: 1 part loam-based No. 2, 1 part peat, 1 part decayed manure, 1 part leafmould and sand.
Repotting: Early in spring, after pruning back to woody part of stem, to conserve compact shape. Use pot 2 sizes larger for first 2 years, as plants with prolific roots will flower more profusely.
Cleaning: Humidity spraying adequate. No leafshine.

New varieties of Fuchsia appear almost every year in a great number of different colours. Plants are always sold in flower, at a height of about 12–15in (30–38cm) and should be kept in a cool light place.

Leaves turn black. Leafshine damage. Do not use. Clean by spraying with water or, in winter, with feather duster if dusty.

Buds do not develop; flowers fade quickly. Too hot. Keep as cool as possible in summer, not more than 65°F (18°C) best, but not below 45°F (7°C).

what goes wrong

Buds, then open flowers and leaves drop. Air too dry or too dark. In hot weather spray twice daily with water and stand pot on saucer of wet pebbles. Move into lighter place.

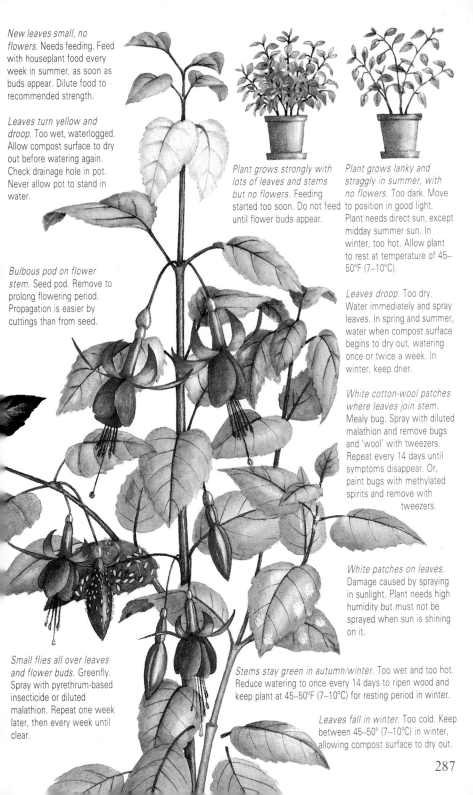

New leaves small, no flowers. Needs feeding. Feed with houseplant food every week in summer, as soon as buds appear. Dilute food to recommended strength.

Leaves turn yellow and droop. Too wet, waterlogged. Allow compost surface to dry out before watering again. Check drainage hole in pot. Never allow pot to stand in water.

Bulbous pod on flower stem. Seed pod. Remove to prolong flowering period. Propagation is easier by cuttings than from seed.

Plant grows strongly with lots of leaves and stems but no flowers. Feeding started too soon. Do not feed until flower buds appear.

Plant grows lanky and straggly in summer, with no flowers. Too dark. Move to position in good light. Plant needs direct sun, except midday summer sun. In winter, too hot. Allow plant to rest at temperature of 45–50°F (7–10°C).

Leaves droop. Too dry. Water immediately and spray leaves. In spring and summer, water when compost surface begins to dry out, watering once or twice a week. In winter, keep drier.

White cotton-wool patches where leaves join stem. Mealy bug. Spray with diluted malathion and remove bugs and 'wool' with tweezers. Repeat every 14 days until symptoms disappear. Or, paint bugs with methylated spirits and remove with tweezers.

White patches on leaves. Damage caused by spraying in sunlight. Plant needs high humidity but must not be sprayed when sun is shining on it.

Small flies all over leaves and flower buds. Greenfly. Spray with pyrethrum-based insecticide or diluted malathion. Repeat one week later, then every week until clear.

Stems stay green in autumn/winter. Too wet and too hot. Reduce watering to once every 14 days to ripen wood and keep plant at 45–50°F (7–10°C) for resting period in winter.

Leaves fall in winter. Too cold. Keep between 45–50° (7–10°C) in winter, allowing compost surface to dry out.

287

Galanthus nivalis

Snowdrop

Snowdrops are one of the first bulbs to come into flower, blooming as early as mid-winter if grown outdoors. They can also be grown in pots and bowls and brought indoors to flower. Because they are very hardy and can survive a degree of frost, snowdrops will fail completely in the heat of most living rooms. Even while flowering keep in the coldest room of the house. Plant in early autumn, allowing 10 bulbs to a 5in (12cm) pot or bowl. Cover and keep in a cold, completely dark place, preferably under ash or straw outdoors, for at least 8 weeks. When tips of shoots are just showing, bring into a cool, light room.

The Snowdrop's creamy white flowers grow on 6–8in (15–20cm) tall stems. The best variety for pots indoors is *Galanthus nivalis*, the common snowdrop, which blooms from mid-winter to mid-spring. Buy and plant bulbs as soon as they are available so that roots have the full period to develop.

Light: Total darkness for at least 8 weeks after planting, then a light position protected from direct sun.

Temperature: As cool as possible while in darkness, preferably just above 32°F (0°C). Maximum 45–50°F (7–10°C) for flowering. Plant will not thrive in warm conditions.

Water: Soak compost after planting, then do not water again until brought into light. Keep moist by watering twice a week.

Humidity: Dry, airy conditions are best. Do not spray.

Feeding: Unnecessary unless it is intended to save bulbs for planting out in the garden the following year. Give diluted garden fertilizer every 14 days if saving bulbs, from time shoots show until leaves die.

Soil: Loam-based No.2 potting compost or special bulb fibre. Or garden soil mixed with 30% sharp sand or gravel.

After flowering: Cut back flowerhead when flowering is finished and allow foliage to die back naturally. If bulbs have been fed, lift and plant out in garden. Bulbs will not flower in pots a second year.

Leaves grow but no flowers appear. Main cause is too hot conditions. Maximum temperature is 50°F (10°C) for flowering. If conditions are cool enough, bulb may have been dehydrated when planted. Always buy firm bulbs from a reliable dealer.

Small leaves, no flowers. Bulb grown indoors the previous year. Bulbs will not flower in pots a second time. Plant outdoors and buy new bulbs for growing indoors each year.

Flowers and leaves become pale, elongated and droopy. Too dark. Move to a position in full light but out of direct sun.

288

When pots taken from dark place, nose of bulbs elongated with no shoots. Possibly kept in darkness too long, or at too high a temperature. Discard as bulbs are unlikely to flower. Keep in a cold, dark place for 8 weeks when planting the next year.

what goes wrong

Leaf tips yellow and dry. Conditions too hot and dry. Keep at maximum temperature 50°F (10°C) and keep compost moist but not waterlogged.

Base of stems and tops of bulbs eaten. If grown outdoors, suspect cutworm and dust soil with gamma HCH. Rarely affects pot-grown bulbs.

Brown spots on leaves or flowers. Leaf spot disease, which usually affects plants grown in heavy soil outdoors. Rarely seen indoors.

Planting
1. In early autumn, plant bulbs 10 to a 6in (13cm) pot or bowl with good drainage. Cover with soil and water well.

2. Put outside if possible and cover to keep out light. Keep cold and dark for 8 weeks. Bring indoors to cool room when tips of shoots show. Start watering.

Growth covered in grey mould, leaves or flowers rotting. Botrytis, caused by high humidity. Cut back affected growth, move to cool, airy place and plant may recover. Do not spray.

Flowers begin to bloom, then turn brown and wither. Too wet or too dry. Soil must always be just moist, with good drainage. Bulbs may flower the next year if planted in the garden.

Leaves yellow and distorted, may have swollen areas. Stem eelworm, which usually only attacks plants outdoors. Destroy bulbs if affected as they will not flower and eelworm may spread to other bulbs.

Gardenia jasminoides

Cape jasmine

This outstanding flowering plant may be difficult to keep in the home, but its almost porcelain-like flowers with their beautiful fragrance make it rewarding. The pure white flowers are offset by glossy, thick, dark green leaves. Gardenias are lime-hating and should be watered with soft water only and planted in lime-free compost. A relatively high temperature and humidity are essential to prolong the flowering period in spring and summer.

Light: Full daylight, avoiding direct midday summer sun.
Temperature: 65-70°F (18-21°C) all spring and summer. Tolerates up to 75°F (24°C) if humidity high. Winter minimum 50°F (10°C).
Water: 2 or 3 times a week in spring and summer, once a week in autumn and winter, to allow surface to dry out a little. Use tepid, soft water only.
Humidity: Spray daily in spring and summer with soft water, avoiding flowers or buds. Stand pot on saucer of pebbles almost covered with water to maintain high humidity. Avoid centrally heated rooms unless there is a humidifier.
Feeding: Water with sequestered iron once in early spring and once again in summer. Then feed every 2 weeks with liquid houseplant food diluted to half maker's instructions until autumn.
Soil: Acid mixture using ericaceous peat blended half and half with lime-free loam.
Repotting: In early spring for first 3 years, into pot one size larger each time. Then repot only if root ball is compact, up to a maximum pot size 7in (18cm). After this, just change top soil.
Cleaning: Humidity spraying adequate. Vegetable oil-based leafshine may be used on leaves every 2 months.

The Gardinia's glossy, dark green leaves are a perfect foil for its beautiful, highly scented, pure white flowers. Buds often drop infuriatingly just as they are about to open. This is caused by a combination of lime damage, insufficient humidity and too low a temperature.

Flowers discoloured. Damage from water spray. Protect flowers when spraying.

what goes wrong

Leaves turn black in winter. Too cold. Move to warmer place and do not allow temperature to drop below 50°F (10°C).

Leaves pale. Too dark. Move to position in full daylight but not in direct midday sun.

Webs under leaves. Red spider mite. Remove webs with damp cloth or sponge, then spray with diluted malathion, especially under leaves. Repeat every 14 days until symptoms disappear. Improve humidity by standing pot on saucer of wet pebbles.

Humidity

Gardenias need high humidity, especially in spring and summer. Spray every day with soft water, protecting flowers and buds. Stand pot on saucer of pebbles almost covered in water but don't let the pot base touch the water or roots will be waterlogged.

Plant does not flower. Air too dry. Spray leaves daily with soft tepid water and provide extra humidity by standing pot on saucer of damp pebbles. When flowers appear, be careful to keep water off them, but continue spraying leaves.

Plant flops, buds drop. Too cold and wet. Allow compost surface to dry out before watering again and increase temperature to at least 60°F (16°C). As temperature rises, provide extra humidity by spraying and standing pot on damp pebbles.

New leaves small. Needs feeding. Feed every 14 days with houseplant food diluted to half maker's recommended strength. Add sequestered iron to the water once in spring and once in summer, following instructions on bottle.

Leaves discoloured with round discs. Scale insect. Spray underside of leaves with diluted malathion and, after 48 hours, remove discs with thumbnail. Repeat every week for 4 weeks until clear.

Scorch marks on leaves and flowers. Sprayed in sunlight. Spray only in early morning or evening.

Leaves turn yellow, while veins remain green. Lime damage from hard water or incorrect compost. Water with sequestered iron once in spring, following directions on bottle and once in summer. Use only soft water for watering and spraying. Repot in early spring in lime-free compost.

Flowers turn yellow. Humidity too high. Improve ventilation around plant but keep temperature at least 60–65°F (16–18°C) in summer, 50°F (10°C) in winter and do not allow humidity to fall too much or buds will drop.

White cotton-wool patches where leaves join stem. Mealy bug. Spray with diluted malathion and remove bugs and 'wool' with tweezers.

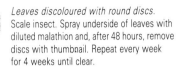

Repeat every 14 days until symptoms disappear. Or, paint bugs with methylated spirits and remove with tweezers.

Flower buds drop on healthy plant. Lime in tap water or lack of humidity. Use soft water for watering and spraying and keep humidity and temperature up in summer. Needs summer temperature of 65–70°F (18–21°C).

Leaves fall off in summer. Compost too dry. Plunge pot into bucket of water for 10–15 minutes, then drain. Keep constantly moist in summer, watering every day if it dries out in hot weather, but do not allow to stand in water.

291

Gasteria liliputana

This small, rosette-forming species belongs to a genus of larger plants, some of which grow to 2 or 3ft (1m) tall. *Gasteria liliputana* is easy to grow and puts up with a lot of neglect; but if treated well it will make a clump of stems in 3 or 4 years, and produce dainty pink and green flowers. Others worth growing include *Gasteria batesiana*, with gnarled, reptile-like leaves, *G. armstrongii*, with its blackish-green leaves and slow-growth and the heavily spotted *G. verrucosa*.

Light: A sunny position is necessary for good growth and flowering if indoors, but in a greenhouse, some shading will be necessary if over 90°F (32°C).

Temperature: A minimum of 40°F (4°C) is needed. Give fresh air in summer.

Water: Fortnightly in spring and summer, weekly in hottest months. Continue until late autumn, reducing amount and frequency until completely dry by early winter. See also Introduction.

Feeding: Use high potash fertilizer 3 or 4 times in summer months.

Soil: Use good loam-based No. 2 potting compost, or soil-less compost, with 30% coarse, gritty sand.

Repotting: Every spring in size larger pot or larger still if good growth has been made. Keep dry for 2 weeks after repotting.

Propagation: In spring cut off whole shoots (with roots) with sharp knife and replant or cut off single leaves. Do not use those around base. Dust cut end of leaf with hormone rooting powder, leave to dry for 3 days then place on dry compost. Water after 3 weeks when roots have formed. After about 8 weeks, new shoots will appear from base. Do not remove old leaf until quite dried up.

Gasteria liliputana's pink and green flowers appear in spring and early summer. Its scientific name Gasteria (from the latin word for stomach), comes from the flowers' stomach-like shape. This small species grows only a couple of inches high, though others in the genus may be up to 3ft (1m) tall.

White woolly patches among leaves. Mealy bug. Remove with small paintbrush dipped in methylated spirits and spray with insecticide. Repeat 2 or 3 times in growing season.

Leaves marked purplish-brown. Too much sunlight. Move to slightly more shaded position.

Leaves blacken and fall, roots rot. Black rot. Too cold and wet. Move to warmer place and in summer only water when dried out. In winter, keep dry.

Lower leaves turn brown, shrivel and fall. Sun scorch. Too hot and dry. Move to cooler place and in hot weather water whenever soil dries out, about once a week.

Leaves long thin and light greenish-yellow; no flowers. Too dark. Move gradually to sunnier spot over 2 weeks. Or, if kept moist in winter, too hot. Allow to dry out in winter.

Few leaves, little new growth. Needs feeding or repotting. Repot annually in fresh compost and feed monthly in summer.

Propagation

In spring cut off single leaves from centre of plant with sharp knife, cutting as close to base of leaf as possible. Rosettes growing as offsets beside main stem can be removed in the same way.

Round limpet-like patches on leaves. Scale insect. Spray and soak soil with systemic insecticide. After 2 weeks pick insects off with a sharp point e.g. a toothpick.

Flowers shrivel quickly, leaves shrivel. In summer, too dry. Give more water but allow to dry out between waterings. In winter, leaves shrivel naturally if dry, to conserve moisture.

Green insects on flower buds or flowers. Greenfly. Spray with insecticide and repeat every 2 weeks until clear.

what goes wrong

Leaf tips dry up and turn light brown, little growth. Too dry and too stuffy. Give more water with each watering but allow to dry out between. Move to more airy place.

Black spots on leaves. Cause not clear, physiological disorder. Cut out affected leaves and try putting in less sunny place and watering more often.

Plant grows slowly, white woolly patches on roots when repotting. Root mealy bug. Wash soil off roots and swirl in contact insecticide. Allow to dry before repotting in fresh compost and washed pot. Leave dry for 2 weeks.

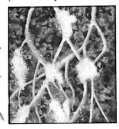

293

Treasure flower

Of South African origin, the Treasure flower is a sun worshipper and is ideally suited to a windowbox where heavy rain rarely soaks the soil as it would in a garden. The large flowers close during late afternoon, though never completely. Usually grown as an annual, they can be kept from year to year if winter temperatures are moderate but are best taken into a greenhouse or conservatory at the end of summer. Buy plants that are not too crowded in the tray, with good green colouring. Unless plants in pots or small containers, buds should not be visible.

Light: Best at all times.

Temperature: Germination 65°F (18°C), cooling gradually to outside conditions. Outside, will stand very high temperatures but not frost.

Water: Except while a seedling, prefers dry conditions. Soak container thoroughly, then leave until almost dry before watering again.

Humidity: No overhead spraying.

Soil: Loam-based No. 2 or soil-less potting compost.

Feeding: Feed every 14 days in loam-based, every 7 in soil-less, at maker's recommended strength.

Propagation: Sow seed as soon as days start to lengthen, on surface of well-drained seedling compost. Cover with ⅛in (2mm) dry compost and brown paper. Germination takes about 10 days. Prick out as soon as large enough to handle. Or, take cuttings in early midsummer.

Tidying: Cut off dead flowers at base of stem. Do not damage crown of plant.

Varieties: Mini Star, clear yellow (8in, 20cm), a European medal winner. Sunshine hybrids, large flowered mixed with stripes and dark zones (12in, 30cm). Splendens mixed (12in, 30cm).

A single Gazania flower may be as large as 4in (10cm) in diameter. Petals are usually pointed and many have a dark, round spot at the base which forms a necklace around the central zone. The leaves, crowded at the plant's base, grow to 6–9in (15–20cm) in height.

Leaves thin and pale. Much too dry. Soak soil then allow to dry out. If watering regular, needs feeding. Feed regularly for bright leaves and flowers.

Cuttings

1. Cut side shoot from outside of clump with sharp knife. Shoot should be about 4in (10cm) long. Trim off lowest leaf and dip end in rooting powder.

2. Place in 3in (9cm) pot of seedling compost. Water well and place in frame or protect from wind with glass. In full sun, protect with hessian. Rooting takes 4–6 weeks. Take indoors by mid-autumn and keep dry, cool and airy. Repot into larger pot in early spring.

what goes wrong

Leaves turn yellow, flowers distorted. Virus. No cure. Destroy plant and do not use same soil for other plantings.

Plant does not thrive, leaves turn yellow gradually and few flowers appear. Root rot, possibly from overwatering. Allow soil to dry out and plant may recover. It prefers dry conditions.

White froth on leaves. Froghopper. Pick off by hand or remove with jet of water. If badly affected, spray with diluted malathion.

Clusters of small insects, especially on buds. Aphid. Spray with pirimicarb and repeat after 10 days if not clear.

White dots or flecks on leaf surface. Underside mealy and pinkish. Red spider mite. Spray with dimethoate and repeat in 14 days.

Silvery white markings on leaves. Thrips. Spray with diluted malathion.

Soil surface erupts with fine dry mound of soil. Ants nesting or cultivating aphids on plant. Dust surface of soil with derris dust. Will not attack plant but will loosen its hold on soil.

Some leaves become limp. Probably slug attacking roots. Place slug pellets around plant, following maker's instructions but keep away from pets and fishponds. Remove dead pest.

295

Gerbera jamesonii

Transvaal daisy

The flowers of this plant are very beautiful, satiny and long-lasting, compensating for rather unattractive foliage. The leaves and strong flower stems are slightly hairy and covered with a fine down. The flowers, which may be 4–5in (10–13cm) across, are available in a wide range of colours including white, peach, red, pink, mauve and magenta. Hybrid varieties are available in all these colours with a black centre. Some varieties are best suited to a frost-proof greenhouse; some improved new hybrids may be grown out-of-doors in mild areas.

Light: Good, indirect light or sunlight most suitable. Keep in light window but not in strong midsummer sun.
Temperature: Winter minimum 45° (8°C); summer maximum 65–70°F (18–21°C), with good circulation of air.
Water: 2 or 3 times a week in summer to keep compost always moist. In winter allow compost to dry out, watering only every 10–14 days.
Humidity: Spray once a week in growing season, 2 or 3 times a week when over 70°F (21°C). Do not spray in winter or when below 60°F (15°C).
Feeding: Every 14 days with liquid houseplant food diluted to half the strength recommended by the maker. Feed in spring and summer only.
Soil: 2 parts loam-based No. 2, 1 part peat, 1 part sand. Good drainage essential.
Repotting: Annually in spring into deep pots at least 6in (15cm) in diameter. Remove sideshoots, which may be taken as cuttings, when repotting. Put plenty of drainage material in bottom of pot.
Cleaning: Humidity spraying sufficient. Do not spray flowers. Do not wipe leaves, as removing hairy surface kills plant. No leafshine.

Transvaal daisies need a good, light position and will stand sun except at midday in summer. Their striking daisy-like flowers grow on a strong, slightly hairy stem and last 2–3 weeks or 1–2 weeks as cut flowers for flower arrangements

Leaves shrivel and turn brown. Either too dry or waterlogged. Check compost to see whether it is dry or wet. In summer, water every 2 or 3 days so that soil is always moist, but do not allow to stand in water. Compost must allow water to run freely through. In winter, allow compost to dry out between waterings.

Watering
1. Always check compost before watering Transvaal daisies. In summer it should always feel moist – but not heavy and waterlogged. In winter it should feel dry and crumbly before you water it again.

2. Add water from top of pot and let it drain through into saucer. Leave for 10–15 minutes, then throw excess away. Check drainage holes in pot regularly.

Flowers do not appear, leaves elongated. Too cold and dark, needs feeding. Move to warmer place (not more than 70°F, 21°C) in good light. Will stand sunlight. Feed every two weeks with half-strength liquid houseplant food in spring and summer.

Leaves turn black. Too cold. Move to warmer room. In winter keep over 45°F (8°C) and in summer over 55°F (13°C).

what goes wrong

Plant flops. Too hot. Check temperature is not over 70°F (21°C) and move to cooler place if possible. Water and spray to increase humidity.

Black patches on leaves. Leafshine damage. Do not use. Clean only by spraying with soft, tepid water in summer. If temperature falls below 60°F (15°C) do not spray.

Small white flies hopping around. Whitefly. Spray every 14 days with pyrethrum-based insecticide until clear.

White fungus on leaves. Botrytis. Move to a warmer place (under 70°F, 21°C) and spray every week with systemic fungicide until clear.

Leaves rot in winter. Too wet, overwatered. In winter allow the soil to dry out at least half way down compost between waterings and do not spray if temperature below 60°F (15°C). Check soil mixture is correct and that drainage holes in pot are clear. Plant must be well drained.

Leaves turn brown but do not shrivel. Atmosphere too humid. May lead to botrytis. Move to warmer place, around 50°F (10°C) at least, in an airy position.

297

Gibbaeum dispar

This South African plant is awkward to grow since unlike most succulents, it grows in late autumn and winter, generally producing its purple-red flowers in spring. It therefore needs a different watering programme from most other succulents, which have their dry, dormant period in winter. It grows to about 1½in (3cm) tall and covers a base area of 4in (10cm). Other species, not easy to obtain, but worth seeking out from specialist nurseries, are *G. album*, with white or pink flowers, *G. pubescens* or *G. shandii* with violet-red flowers, and *G. velutinum* with lilac-pink flowers. All are winter growers and need the same treatment.

Gibbaeum dispar. Gibbaeums grow in winter and their special watering needs must be carefully met. They will only flower if kept in a very sunny position, especially in autumn and winter when the flower buds are forming between the pairs of fleshy green leaves.

Light: Full sun, especially in autumn and winter when buds are forming.

Temperature: Winter minimum 45°F (7°C). Give fresh air in summer.

Water: Read the general instructions for Succulents in the introduction, but remember that this plant's resting period is late spring/early summer, not winter. After flowering, leave dry for 4–6 weeks, then start watering fortnightly in late summer. In autumn and winter water monthly, increasing to fortnightly in early spring.

Feeding: Not necessary unless plant has not been repotted for 2 years. Then feed with a high potash liquid fertilizer once when watering in autumn.

Soil: Use good loam-based No. 2 potting compost, or soil-less compost, with 40% coarse, gritty sand.

Repotting: Only every 3 years to change soil, or when roots fill the pot. Use half-pots or pans. Do not water for 3 weeks after repotting.

Propagation: Separate heads with sharp knife in summer to use as cuttings. Growing from seed is difficult.

White woolly patches appear among leaves. Mealy bug. Remove with small paintbrush dipped in methylated spirits, and spray with insecticide. Repeat 2 or 3 times in growing season.

Plant turns light brown and shrivels on side nearest glass. Scorched. Move away from glass, so that air can circulate between plant and glass. Watch out in spring for sudden bright sunny spells, and shade plants for a week to accustom them to the sudden sunshine. If heads have completely dried out carefully cut them out.

Treating roots

1. Though a small plant above the surface, Gibbaeum has thick turnip-like roots. Check when repotting for root mealy bug.

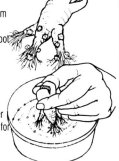

2. If found, wash soil off roots and soak in bowl of insecticide diluted as maker recommends. Leave to dry for 2 days.

3. Repot in dry compost and clean pot. Do not water again for 2–3 weeks to allow plant's roots to grow into new compost.

No flowers. Not uncommon, needs a very sunny position. Try putting outside for summer months but protect from rainfall.

Leaves lose colour and grow tall in spring/summer. Watered at wrong time of year. Keep dry for 4–6 weeks from late spring but make sure light is good.

Little growth, leaves shrivel. In summer during rest period, natural. In spring, needs repotting. In autumn, needs feeding once. In winter, too dry. Water just enough to keep leaves plump, especially when buds forming. Once a month enough.

Plant shows little sign of growth, and on repotting white woolly patches are on roots. Root mealy bug. Wash all soil off roots, swirl in contact insecticide, and allow to dry before repotting in fresh compost and clean pot. Leave dry for two weeks.

Brown limpet-like spots. Scale insect. Spray with insecticide, and pick off scales after a week or two. Spray again after a month.

what goes wrong

Irregular brown spots and patches. Too cold in winter. Keep in warmer conditions (over 45°F, 7°C). Not usually fatal.

Plant elongates, gapes, becoming yellowish-green. Too little light, move gradually over 2 weeks to sunnier spot. Needs full sun in autumn and winter when buds are forming. In poor light, plant will fail to flower.

Plant shrivels, then turns black and soft, usually in winter. Too cold or overwatered. Keep above 45°F (7°C) in winter and water monthly, allowing soil to dry out thoroughly. Keep dry in summer. A humid atmosphere will cause rot so do not spray and keep in light, airy place.

Gladiolus colvillei

Sword lily

The magnificent flower spikes of the garden Gladiolus are popular for flower arrangements but if you have a porch, greenhouse or very sunny windowsill, some varieties can be grown in pots for a longer-lasting display. Choose corms of *Gladiolus x colvillei* and plant individually 3in (7cm) deep in moist compost in 4½in (11cm) pots in early autumn. Keep in a cold, dark place for 8 weeks, then bring into a cool, light room when shoots begin to show. Plants should flower in spring.

The trumpet-shaped flowers of *Gladiolus x colvillei* are available in nearly 50 different shades. This dwarf variety of the popular garden and florists gladiolus grows to a height of 18–24in (45–60cm), making it a good choice for pots or containers.

Light: Total darkness for 8 weeks after planting, then full light as on a sunny windowsill.

Temperature: Maximum 40–45°F (5–7°C) while in darkness. Maximum 55°F (13°C) for best flowers. Flowers will last longer in cooler temperatures.

Water: Pot in moist compost, then no water until growth begins. Increase watering to 2–3 times per week while in flower. Do not let compost dry out at any time.

Humidity: Cool and dry. Do not spray.

Feeding: If corms are to be saved for growing the next year, begin feeding as soon as flower stem begins emerging from neck of corm. Give garden fertilizer weekly diluted to half maker's recommended strength. Continue feeding until leaves yellow in autumn.

Soil: Loam-based No.2 or soil-less.

After flowering: Cut back stem after all flowers die. Allow foliage to die back naturally and continue watering and weekly feeding. When foliage dies, cut back to soil level and place pot in a cool, dark place. Lift corms in autumn, separate cormlets, and repot for flowering again or store in frost-free place until following spring for planting outside.

Flower spike has few buds, or buds fail to open. Too dark. Gladiolus need full light at all times to flower.

No flower spike appears. Corms have have been too small, or was not fed in previous season. Plant corms no smaller than 3in (8cm) in diameter.

Separating offsets
When new small corms grow around original, remove from pot and wait until all have dried out completely. Then gently pull apart and repot individually. In good compost they should flower in 2 years.

what goes wrong

Flowers streaky and may be distorted. Virus disease. No cure. Plant will continue to flower, but do not save corm.

Brown spots on flowers. Botrytis. Spray with benomyl, repeat in a week if mould still visible. Do not spray with water as this encourages botrytis.

Flower buds or leaves turn yellow or brown, buds fail to develop, flowers fade. Too dry or too hot. Keep compost moist at all times. Never keep in temperature above 55°F (13°C), or plant will wilt.

Pale streaks on leaves. Buds fail to develop. Thrips. Common on Gladiolus. Spray every 10 days with pyrethrum-based insecticide, but do not spray flowers.

Leaves and buds turn yellow and die. Overwatering. Keep compost just moist and avoid waterlogging. If soil not too wet, bulb may have dry rot. Discard.

Leaves streaky, yellowing. Fusarium disease. No cure so destroy plant and corm.

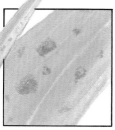

Small grey spots on leaves. Septoria disease, which usually affects outdoor-grown plants. Spray with bordeaux mixture. Do not save corms of affected plants.

Leaves and flowers eaten on outdoor-grown plants. Caterpillars or slugs. Search for pests and destroy. Dust soil with gamma HCH for caterpillars. If slime trails visible, put down slug pellets.

301

Gloriosa superba

Mozambique lily

The Mozambique Lily, sometimes called Glory Lily, needs warmth and care if it is to produce its magnificent red and yellow flowers. A native of the rain forests of tropical Africa, it is very tender and needs a warm, humid, well lit situation for best growth. Plants can be purchased, usually in late spring, or grown from tubers potted up in late winter or early spring. Pot tubers individually 2in (5cm) deep in 6in (15cm) pots of soil-less compost and keep in a light, sunny place. Tubers can be repotted each year for 3–5 years.

Light: Good at all times. Protect flowers from midday sun on very hot days.

Temperature: Start growth at 60–65°F (16–18°C). Once foliage is growing strongly increase to maximum 85°F (29°C). Rest tubers at 50–55°F (10–13°C).

Water: Keep soil just moist until growth is strong, then increase watering gradually. Daily watering may be necessary during flowering. No water during rest period.

Humidity: High, so stand pot in a saucer filled with wet pebbles. Spray around plant daily to maintain humidity.

Feeding: When growth is 12in (30cm) high, begin weekly feeds with dilute liquid houseplant food at maker's recommended strengths. Continue until foliage dies.

Soil: Soil-less potting compost.

After flowering: Remove dead flowerheads and decrease watering so that soil surface dries out each time. When foliage and stems are withered, cut back to soil level and stop watering. Place pot on its side in a dark place at temperature 50–55°F (10–13°C). Do not water. In late winter early spring, lift tubers, separate offsets and repot for another growing season. Offsets will flower after 2 years if fed regularly in the growing season.

The beautiful red and gold flowers of the Mozambique lily are up to 4in (10cm) long and appear in summer. The pale green leaves are elongated, ending with fine tendrils which cling to a wire or trellis as the plant climbs. Since they may grow up to 6ft (2m) in a season, some support is essential.

Growth weak with no flowers. Too dark, or if few flowers tuber may not have been fed in previous year, or may have been overwintered at too cold a temperature. Do not save a tuber which does not flower well. Keep in good light or provide artificial light.

Leaves dark, slow growth. Too cold or in a draught. Move to warmer place, above 65°F (18°C), out of draughts.

Holes eaten in bottom of stem and tuber. If slime trails present, suspect slugs and put down slug pellets. Keep away from pets and children.

Tubers

Inspect tuber before potting. If soft and mouldy when lifted, it was given too much water while leaves dying back or watered while resting. Discard. If chewed or eaten, attacked by mice. Store where mice cannot reach it. If tubers fail to grow well after repotting, repotted too late, after growth started. Repot in late winter/early spring to avoid damaging brittle roots.

what goes wrong

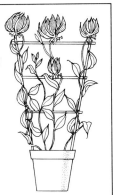

Support

Mozambique lilies grow up to 6ft (2m) in a season and cling to supports with tendrils at the ends of the leaves. Position canes or trellis when repotting, keeping at least 1in (2½cm) from tuber. If positioned at any other time, take care not to damage the stems and leaves and keep well away from bulb and roots.

Growth starts vigorously, then turns yellow from base. Too wet. Tuber needs soil which is just moist. Increase watering as growth progresses. Ensure that drainage is good.

Leaves and flowers limp. Too hot. Will stand high temperatures but shade from hot sun through glass. Or, air too dry. Stand pot on wet pebbles or, if in conservatory, damp down floor.

Leaves become hard, bronzed and crinkled. Tarsonemid mite, which is difficult to eradicate. Spray with a pyrethrum-based insecticide every 10 days, but plant may not recover. Do not spray in sunshine or leaves may be further damaged.

Leaves turn yellow green before flowering is finished. Too dry. Keep compost moist at all times, watering daily if necessary in hot weather. If compost is moist, plant may need more frequent feeding.

Plant does not grow well. If conditions are correct, suspect vine weevil. Search soil for C-shaped grubs and dust with gamma HCH if found.

Silk oak

This interesting evergreen tree makes a good house or conservatory plant when young. It has large, bronzy-green, fern-like fonds which can be as long as 12in (30cm), and which are silky on the underneath side. It will stand quite low temperatures so is hardy in temperate climates, such as the south-west of England and frost-free areas of the U.S. It is easily grown from seed and, when young, is often mistaken for a fern. It grows rapidly, however, provided it is in a good light position, even in full sun which it prefers. In its native Australia it will grow up to 100ft (30m) high and indoors may reach 6ft (almost 2m) in three years. While small it looks good in mixed plantings but when it gets bigger is best on its own.

A healthy Silk oak has bronzy-green, fern-like foliage with a smooth, silky underside. It grows best in a sunny position but does not need high temperatures. Make sure plants look fresh and vigorous, with no dry or drooping leaves.

Light: Best in full sunlight.

Temperature: Winter minimum 45–50°F (8–10°C); normal room temperature in summer, though if over 70°F (21°C), air circulation must be good.

Water: Up to 3 times a week in summer, especially if over 70°F (21°C). Once a week in winter, withholding water altogether if very cold.

Humidity: Spray twice weekly during growing season in summer. About every 14 days in winter, unless 50°F (10°C) or below.

Feeding: Every 10 days in growing season (spring and summer) with liquid houseplant food diluted according to the maker's instructions.

Soil: Likes lime-free compost if possible but loam-based No. 2 is suitable.

Repotting: Annually in spring. If it is growing fast, use a new pot 2 sizes larger than the old. When it is too awkward and heavy to handle easily, change the topsoil only and start feeding again immediately.

Cleaning: Humidity spraying sufficient. No leafshine.

Changing the topsoil
1. In spring carefully remove top inch (2½cm) soil, taking care not to damage the roots.

2. Replace with fresh compost and firm well around base of plant.

3. Water well and add dose of liquid houseplant food to the water to give immediate nourishment.

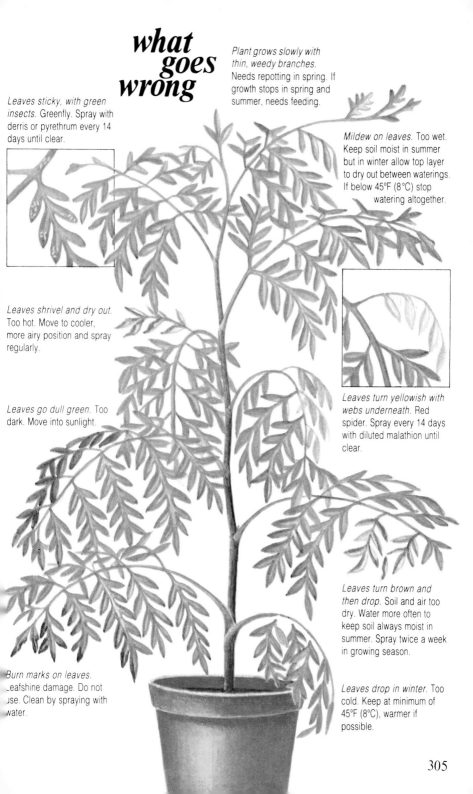

what goes wrong

Plant grows slowly with thin, weedy branches. Needs repotting in spring. If growth stops in spring and summer, needs feeding.

Leaves sticky, with green insects. Greenfly. Spray with derris or pyrethrum every 14 days until clear.

Mildew on leaves. Too wet. Keep soil moist in summer but in winter allow top layer to dry out between waterings. If below 45°F (8°C) stop watering altogether.

Leaves shrivel and dry out. Too hot. Move to cooler, more airy position and spray regularly.

Leaves go dull green. Too dark. Move into sunlight.

Leaves turn yellowish with webs underneath. Red spider. Spray every 14 days with diluted malathion until clear.

Leaves turn brown and then drop. Soil and air too dry. Water more often to keep soil always moist in summer. Spray twice a week in growing season.

Burn marks on leaves. Leafshine damage. Do not use. Clean by spraying with water.

Leaves drop in winter. Too cold. Keep at minimum of 45°F (8°C), warmer if possible.

Guzmania lingulata

Scarlet star

In its natural habitat, South America and the West Indies, this plant is usually found growing in the boughs of trees; the out-stretched leaves gather such little rain as falls into a well-shaped centre from which the flower bract grows. The strap-shaped leaves tend to lose some of their colour as the bracts develop, but the bracts themselves are wine-red and last for up to eight weeks. Small pale yellow flowers will emerge from the bract after about eight weeks. Like all Bromeliads it flowers only once in its 3-year lifespan, then produces offsets from its base.

Scarlet stars produce wine-coloured bracts from which small yellow flowers appear. This is one of many varieties of *Guzmania*, all of which require the same conditions of temperature, humidity and watering.

Light: Full diffused daylight all year round. No direct sunlight.

Temperature: Maintain 60–70°F (16–21°C) in spring and summer. Plant tolerates winter temperature as low as 55°F (13°C), provided humidity is also low.

Water: Keep moist in spring and summer by filling central well, once or twice a week, allowing water to overflow into compost. In winter, water only when surface feels dry and well is empty. Always use soft water.

Humidity: Spray daily when temperature near maximum but plant is tolerant; needs plenty of air around it. Very high humidity and low temperatures can lead to botrytis.

Feeding: Once in spring using liquid houseplant food diluted to a quarter of maker's instructions. Water into the well.

Soil: Equal parts lime-free loam and peat.

Repotting: When offsets develop. Wait until parent plant has dried up, then repot offset.

Cleaning: Every 2 months wipe leaves with vegetable oil-based leafshine. If dusty at other times wipe with damp sponge. Do not spray bracts.

Webs under leaves. Red spider mite. Remove webs with damp cloth or sponge, then spray with diluted malathion, especially under leaves. Repeat every 14 days until symptoms disappear. Improve humidity by standing pot on saucer of wet pebbles or in outer pot packed with peat.

Watering

Fill plant's central well with soft water and allow it to spill over onto compost. Keep compost moist in summer, watering twice a week in hot weather. In winter wait until well is empty and compost surface feels dry.

306

what goes wrong

Parent plant dies as side shoot develops. Natural after 3 years. Wait until parent plant has died, then carefully remove shoot and pot separately in mixture of sphagnum moss and peat.

Plant turns black in winter. Too cold. If also rotting at base, waterlogged. Move to warmer place, at least 55°F (13°C) and allow compost surface to dry out before watering again.

No flowers emerge from spike. Too cold and air too dry; or too dark; or needs feeding. Check conditions. Move to warmer place, between 60–70°F (16–21°C) and improve humidity by spraying with soft, tepid water. Move to light position: plant will stand full sunlight. Add food to central well once in spring, diluting it to ¼ maker's recommended strength.

Tips of leaves turn brown and dry, plant shrivels. Too hot and air too dry. Spray daily with soft tepid water when temperature near maximum and place pot in outer pot packed with damp peat. Keep under 70°F (21°C) if possible.

White marks on leaves. Caused by spraying with hard water. Use soft or rainwater for spraying.

Plant rots in summer. Botrytis – too cold and damp. Spray with fungicide then place in warmer place and spray less often. Allow compost surface to dry out between waterings. Best summer temperature between 60–70°F (16–21°C).

White cotton-wool patches around base of plant. Mealy bug. Spray with diluted malathion and remove bugs and 'wool' with tweezers. Repeat every 14 days until symptoms disappear. Or, paint bugs with methylated spirits and remove with tweezers.

Leaves brown and dry. Too dry. Keep central well filled and compost moist in summer. Allow surface to dry in winter. Always use soft water.

Lower leaves die. Too cold or, if after flowering, end of plant's life. Move to warmer place, between 60–70°F (16–21°C).

307

Gymnocalycium

This very popular genus of cacti comes from a wide area of South America, in Bolivia, Paraguay, Brazil, Uruguay and Argentina. It consists mainly of single-stemmed, globular, strong-spined plants, freely flowering at a few inches across, and, except for a few species, rarely needing more than a 5in (13cm) pot. *Gymnocalycium baldianum* (p.309) has red flowers but other species may have flowers coloured green, yellow, red, pink and most commonly white, often flushed with pink or red. They are readily obtainable from specialist nurseries, and are almost indestructible, putting up with a good deal of inattention.

Gymnocalycium bruchii is easy to grow and flower and will rapidly form clumps of stems, each no more than about ¾in (2cm) tall and wide. The flowers appear in early summer, 2 or 3 on each head and on a large clump there may be a hundred or more. The plant here is in a 5in (13cm) pan.

Light: As with most cacti they need a light position on a sunny windowsill. If grown in a greenhouse they need a little shading during the sunniest months.

Temperature: Keep above 40°F (4°C) for safety; keep below 100°F (38°C) and give fresh air in summer if possible.

Water: Water about once a fortnight in spring and summer, weekly in hot weather. Check compost before watering to make sure it has dried out. Tail off watering in autumn to once a month and keep dry in winter.

Feeding: Use a high potash fertilizer once a month in spring and summer (as used for tomatoes).

Soil: Use 1 part of coarse, gritty sand (not builders' or seashore) to 2 parts of soil-less or good loam-based No. 2 potting compost.

Repotting: These plants are best repotted every year into the next size pot when they are young and even when they have reached their maximum size and are in a 5in (13cm) pot they should be repotted into fresh soil each year. At this size they can be replaced in the same container. Do not water for 2 weeks after repotting.

Cleaning and pest control: Spray with water if dusty and incorporate an insecticide 2 or 3 times a year to combat pests.

Other species: For larger growing ones, *G. buenekeri* is one of the best. It makes a globular plant with few, fat ribs of matt green. The spines are well spaced out and lie close to the body, apparently more for adornment then defence. When about 10 years old it will be 6in (15cm) tall, the same across and will produce half a dozen or so robust offsets. Its flowers are a lovely shade of pink. Another large grower, but a solitary not an offsetting type, is *G. saglione*. This is magnificently spiny with curving red or yellow spines and pale pink flowers. There are many smaller growers and a good selection in addition to *G. baldianum* (right) is, *G. andreae* or *G. leeanum* (yellow flowers), *G. bicolor* (pink/white flowers), *G. bruchii* (clusters of small heads with wispy spines and pink and white flowers), *G. friedrichii* (reddish purple body and pink flowers).

Gymnocalycium bicolor, named for its two-coloured black and white spines, is a robust grower, reaching about 4in (10cm) across in 5 years or so, and wider than it is high. Its large shell-pink flowers are produced after about 3 years, when it is some 2in (5cm) wide.

Growing from seed

1. Sow seed thinly in spring on surface of prepared tray. Tap sides of tray to settle seed.

2. Water from base with fungicide diluted as for 'damping off' of seedlings until surface is damp.

3. Cover with polythene and leave in light (not sunlight) at 70°F (21°C). Do not water again unless condensation on polythene becomes patchy or dries. Prick out after 6 months into 2in (5cm) pots or ½in (2cm) apart in tray.

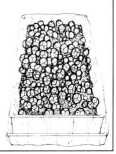

Gymnocalycium baldianum has bright red flowers which appear when it is 2–3 years old and only about 2in (5cm) across. The flowers come over a period in the summer, opening from dark green buds at the top of the plant. They each last about a week.

Gymocalyciums are best kept out of midday summer sun. If in a greenhouse, provide some shade during the hottest months.

These cacti are not usually attacked by red spider but a preventative spray with insecticide 2 or 3 times a year will keep them pest-free.

Gynura sarmentosa

Velvet plant

Looking not unlike a high-class nettle, this ornamental plant has distinctive purple, hair-covered leaves and stems. It produces small, unpleasant-smelling yellow flowers which should be removed, as they take strength away from the fast-growing leaves. The Velvet plant looks good as a young plant in mixed bowls where its colour contrasts well with green-leaved plants. It tends to become lanky when old, so it is wise to take cuttings and start new plants at least every two years. An easy plant to grow, it likes plenty of light. It can be kept bushy by pinching out the growing tips of straggly stems or can be grown as a trailer in a hanging basket, or trained round a hoop.

Light: Grows well in full sunlight, which improves the purple colour of the leaves.
Temperature: Winter minimum 60°F (15°C), though will survive 55°F (13°C) if water withheld. Summer maximum 70°F (21°C).
Water: Every other day in summer, once a week in winter. Do not water if temperature falls to 55°F (13°C) or less. Shake surplus drops from leaves to avoid scorching by sun.
Humidity: Benefits from standing in saucer of pebbles almost covered in water, but this is not essential.
Feeding: Once a month in the growing season (spring and summer) with house-plant food diluted according to the maker's instructions.
Soil: Loam-based No. 2 compost.
Repotting: Repot at start of second year, when if not grown as a trailing plant in a hanging basket it may also need staking.
Cleaning: Spray once every 3–4 weeks on a dull day. May be dusted with small hair-brush. No leafshine.

The Velvet plant's distinctive toothed leaves are covered with fine downy hairs and when healthy and kept in good light, have a rich purple colour. The flowers (which smell unpleasant) should be removed as they appear. New plants should be bushy with no sign of a flower spike.

Plant looks straggly with long spaces between leaves. Needs feeding or, if over 2 years, growing old. Take cuttings from healthy stem tips in spring.

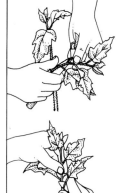

Preparing a stem-tip cutting
1. Cutt off tip of healthy stem, including 2 pairs of leaves and growing point. Trim off stem below a leaf.

2. Remove lowest pair of leaves so there is a section of bare stem. When planted lowest leaf should be just above compost. Keep moist and warm (65–70°F, 18–21°C) for 21 days. Cover with polythene bag to keep humid, removing it for 5 minutes a day.

what goes wrong

New leaves are small and a flower spike appears. Remove flowers so that growing strength goes into leaves.

Leaves distorted and sticky with green insects. Greenfly. Spray with pyrethrum or a systemic insecticide every 14 days until clear.

Leaves and stems wilt. Too dry. Soak in bucket of water for 5 minutes, then drain. If plant flops over and does not grow well but is correctly watered, may need repotting. Check roots to see if they are crowded in pot.

Burn marks on leaves though no water sprayed. Leafshine damage. Do not use.

Leaves lose purple colour and turn all green. Too dark. Move into sunny spot.

Leaves look scorched. Water left on leaves after watering or spraying. Shake surplus water off foliage. Do not spray in full sun.

Plant collapses and stems rot. Overwatered or too cold. Overwatering can kill. Allow plant to dry out before watering again and check drainage in pot. Keep above 60°F (15°C).

311

Haworthia attenuata

A very popular species of succulent which grows in a cluster. The variety shown here, often mistakenly labelled *Haworthia fasciata*, is *H. attenuata* var. *caespitosa*. It has white stripes on the outsides of the leaves and will grow to about 4in (10cm) tall and spread to between 8 and 12in (20–30cm). Most but not all are easy to grow and there are 100 or more names to choose from. A few of the best are *Haworthia reinwardtii, H. retusa, H. emelyae, H. comptoniana, H. limifolia, H. truncata, H. maughanii, H. bolusii, H. mirabilis, H. nigra, H. viscosa.*

Light: Do not need continuous sun but best if in sunlight 3 or 4 hours a day; or place on a brightly lit windowsill not in direct sun. In greenhouses, shade in the hottest summer months.

Temperature: Minimum 40°F (4°C). Give fresh air in summer.

Water: Water fortnightly in spring and summer, weekly in hottest months, but allow plant to dry out between waterings. Tail off in autumn, keep dry in winter. See also Introduction.

Feeding: Use high potash fertilizer 2 or 3 times in summer months.

Soil: Use good loam-based No. 2 potting compost, or soil-less compost, with 30% coarse gritty sand.

Repotting: Every spring in size larger pot. Shallow rooted species grow better in half-pots or pans. Do not water for 2 weeks.

Propagation: Whole shoots which have appeared around main plant, or individual leaves, may be removed with sharp knife (leaves can be gently eased off with fingers). Dust them with hormone rooting powder, dry for 3 days, then pot in fresh compost. Water after 3 weeks when roots have formed. Some leaves take longer. Small plants will appear later around the base of the rooted leaves.

Haworthia attenuata. Haworthias come from desert and mountain areas in South Africa and in the wild often grow under bushes, seeking a little shade from the fierce sun. This makes them ideal plants for windowsills and less sunny spots in the greenhouse, where they will receive just a few hours of direct sun each day.

White woolly patches especially at base and tips of leaves. Mealy bug. Remove with small paintbrush dipped in methylated spirits and spray with insecticide. Repeat 2–3 times in growing season.

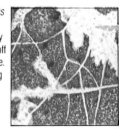

No growth though conditions correct in spring/summer. Examine roots for root mealy bug. If found, wash all soil off roots and swirl in insecticide. Leave to dry before repotting in fresh compost and clean pot. Leave dry for 2 weeks.

Green insects on flower and stem. Greenfly. Spray with pyrethrum-based insecticide and repeat every 10 days until clear.

Plant grows slowly in spring and summer. Roots lost from overwatering or soil too heavy and compacted. Remove from pot and check roots. If rotted, pare back base to fresh tissue and dust with hormone rooting powder. Reroot in fresh, compost including at least 30% coarse gritty sand.

Leaves grow long with green parts pale, white parts less bright. Too dark or, in winter, too hot and wet. Needs full light in winter and good bright light in summer with 3–4 hours full sun. Move gradually into strong light in summer to avoid scorching. In winter try to keep cooler, around 50°F (10°C), in dry soil.

what goes wrong

Leaves close up, ends shrivel. Too hot and dry. Give fresh air in summer if over 75°F (24°C) and water whenever compost dries out.

Leaves blacken and rot. Too cold and wet, too humid. In summer always allow soil to dry out between waterings. Small black spots may be signs of disease. Move out of strong sunlight and water regularly in summer. Cut out affected leaves at base with sharp knife. Do not use for propagation.

Hebe

Veronica

Hebes make attractive, long-lasting shrubs which can tolerate high winds if not subjected to heavy frosts. There are hardy dwarf varieties for windowboxes and a wide range of taller ones for patios and balconies. They may need protection from winter weather depending on where you live. Build a shelter round them or move them to a sheltered spot. Summer quarters should be sunny.

Light: Plenty, though they can take about 3 hours shade. Indoors, best light possible.
Temperature: Most survive mild frosts and, if well watered, stand high temperatures.
Water: Keep moist but well drained in summer. In winter water only enough to stop soil drying out completely.
Humidity: Spray overhead when 70°F (21°C).
Soil: Loam-based No. 2.
Feeding: Regular summer feeding with liquid or dry organic fertilizers, according to maker's instructions.
Propagation: Take cuttings about 4in (10cm) long, at any time between early and late summer. Trim to a point below a leaf joint and remove bottom leaves. Dip into rooting powder and insert in 3½in (9cm) pot, 4 round each pot. Rooting takes about 6 weeks. Then pot each cutting separately.
Tidying: After flowering, cut off flowering stems.
Varieties: For windowboxes: Carl Teschner, violet/blue, in early summer (9in, 22cm). Carnosula, white in mid-summer (6in, 15cm). Pagei, blue grey foliage, white flowers in late spring (9in, 22cm). For patios: Midsummer Beauty, lavender in early-late summer (3ft, 1m). Autumn Glory, purple in early summer – early autumn (2ft, 60cm). Speciosa hybrids, shiny leaves, purple crimson, lavender/rose flowers.

These evergreen flowering shrubs come mainly from New Zealand and vary in height from 6in to 6ft (15cm to 2m). The flowering season is equally varied, being from late spring to early autumn, in colours ranging from white to blue, purple and even crimson.

Leaves pale grey/green, flowers dull. Too dry. Water thoroughly so that bottom of container is well wetted. Then allow to dry out until surface feels just moist before watering again. If watering correct, needs feeding. Give topdressing of potash organic fertilizer and feed regularly.

Round brown spots with purple outer ring on leaves, some shoots or stems light brown and dying. Hebe leaf spot. Cut out any dying stems and spray with benomyl every 14 days until clear.

Edges of leaves turn brown. Root scorch from too strong fertilizers. Always use maker's recommended strength. Dry fertilizers must be applied only to well watered soil, then well watered in.

Foliage darkens, then turns pale, leaves fall. Frost damage. May recover in spring. Prune off damaged growth in early spring. Protect in winter or move to sheltered position.

314

Stem soft and brown with some whitish strands; whole shrub turning yellow. Honey fungus. No cure. Burn plant and do not plant trees or shrubs in garden for 2 years. Should not affect shrubs in containers unless in contaminated soil. Watch for toadstools round base of dead tree stumps.

what goes wrong

Leaves pale and thin, stem growing lanky. Too dark. Move to lighter place.

Pruning

To keep plants compact, prune when flowers have died. For small-leaved plants, trim all round bush with shears.

For large-leaved plants, trim with pruning shears, making cuts just above a leaf. Do not cut through leaves.

Yellowish specks, sometimes pale blisters on leaf surface, whitish mould under. Downy mildew. Spray with bordeaux mixture every 14 days until clear.

Pinpoint white spots on upper surface of leaf, scurfy grey below, with fine webs. Red spider mite. Spray with dimethoate and repeat until new growth clean, at maker's recommended strength and intervals.

Leaves yellow from base of plant, no growth. Waterlogged or root rot, from serious overwatering. Allow soil to drain, check drainage holes and water less often in future.

Ivy

The Ivy is a native of northern Europe and so almost completely hardy. It grows in all conditions, from deep shade to full sun, though its leaf colour is best between these extremes. Almost pest and disease free and tolerant of all kinds of weather, it is an ideal plant for container growing. Smaller-leaved dwarf varieties are best for window-boxes and last for many years while there are many vigorous ones to cover large areas. Pruning may be needed to control their growth.

Light: Variegated forms need good light.
Temperature: Survives frost. Cuttings will take quicker at 60°F (16°C), but will take anyway.
Water: Keep moist but not waterlogged.
Humidity: In hot, dry weather (over 70°F, 21°C) give an overhead spray.
Soil: Almost any except solid clay. Loam-based No. 2 is ideal.
Feeding: Liquid or dry fertilizer at maker's recommended strengths and intervals. If using dry fertilizer, water soil first and allow to drain before feeding.
Propagation: In spring or summer, cut off a shoot with aerial roots (most of them have), about 4in (10cm) long. Plant it outdoors or indoors and it will root rapidly. No rooting powder is necessary. Cuttings without ae-rial roots will also take easily, but after a longer period.
Varieties: Buttercup, small leaved, golden. Glacier, small pale green and white. Chicago, small, green and purple. Tricolour, small silver for windowboxes. *Colchia dentata aurea,* large and fast grow-ing, green splashed gold. *Canariensis,* large thick leaves, green and cream. *Sagitaefolia,* tall, lime green.

The Ivy's evergreen trailing or climbing stems carry aerial roots which cling to walls, trellises or the soil surface and enable its attractive leaves to cover a wide area. The leaves vary in size and colour, some being strongly variegated. The flowers are small but the berries are attractive.

Scales on underside of leaves, close to veins. Scale insect. Wipe off with cotton-wool dipped in methylated spirits.

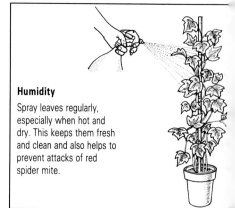

Humidity
Spray leaves regularly, especially when hot and dry. This keeps them fresh and clean and also helps to prevent attacks of red spider mite.

what goes wrong

Leaves eaten near top of plant. Caterpillar. Remove visible pests and dust plant carefully with gamma-BHC.

Pale pin-point spots on leaves, leaves fading. Underside mealy, pinkish colour. May be fine webs round leaves. Red spider mite. Spray every 14 days with diluted malathion or dimethoate until clear. Spray regularly with water to prevent attack.

Variegation of leaves not pronounced. Too dark. Plain green varieties best for dark areas. Move into better light if possible.

Wingless insects with white covering on underside of leaves. Mealy bug. Wipe off with cotton-wool dipped in methylated spirits and spray with dimethoate.

Small insects on stem tips, leaves sticky and sooty. Aphid. Spray with pirimicarb. Repeat after 10 days.

Edges of leaves brown and dry. Wind damage if plant buffeted about. Plant will grow on but leaves may fall.

White powdery deposit on stems. Powdery mildew. Sometimes occurs if plant left dry for long period. Spray with benomyl every 14 days.

Lower leaves turn yellow, stem and leaves dark; some mould on stem. Soil waterlogged. Check and clear drainage holes. Allow soil to dry out before watering again.

Small black flies running over soil surface. Sciarid fly grubs in soil. Drench soil with diluted malathion.

Leaves grey/green and thin. Too dry or needs feeding. Check conditions. Keep soil moist but not waterlogged and feed regularly.

Edges of leaves dry out and leaves fall. Much too dry. Water immediately. Do not leave for long periods without water. Spray regularly in hot weather.

Small brown or dark spots on leaves. Leaf spot fungus. Spray with fungicide and repeat after 14 days.

Silvery streaks on leaves. Thrips. Spray with diluted malathion or any systemic insecticide. Do not spray in bright sunlight.

Edges of leaves near soil eaten. If slime on soil, slugs or snails. Put down slug pellets as maker recommends. If no slime, woodlice. Dust area carefully with gamma-BHC.

Canary ivy

These large-leaved ivies are very popular as houseplants. They are not quite as hardy as the smaller-leaved *Hedera helix* (see p.320) and will not survive outside in frost. They need plenty of light, and high humidity especially in winter but must never be overwatered. Unless they are well staked, they tend to look untidy and if not pruned grow straggly. Pinch out the growing point once or twice a year for a more bushy plant. They are very susceptible to red spider.

Hedera canariensis 'Gloire de Marengo' is the most common of the large-leaved ivies. Another attractive plant is 'Golden leaf' which has two shades of green on its leaves and often reflects a gold tint in bright light. Like all variegated plants, the colour of the leaves improves if kept in good light.

Light: Best in strong light but not midday summer sun or leaves may be bleached.

Temperature: Winter minimum 45°F (7°C), summer best at 60–65°F (16–18°C). If above this, increase humidity.

Water: Water twice a week in summer, once a week in winter. Allow surface to dry out between waterings.

Humidity: Spray every day in summer or in centrally heated rooms; once a week enough if near winter minimum. For constant humidity, stand pot on saucer of wet pebbles.

Feeding: Every 14 days while growing in spring and summer, using liquid houseplant food diluted to maker's recommended strength.

Soil: Loam- or peat-based No. 2.

Repotting: Young plants grow quickly and need repotting twice a year. When over 2 years old, repot once a year in spring. When too large to handle, replace top 2–3in (5–7cm) soil annually.

Cleaning: Regular spraying will keep them clean but if very dusty, wipe leaves with damp cloth. Use leafshine not more than once a month.

Canary ivy is very susceptible to red spider mite attacks, especially in hot, dry rooms. Keep humidity high by regular spraying and stand pots on wet pebbles for extra local humidity.

what goes wrong

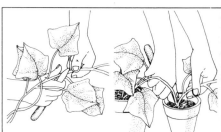

Propagation

1. Prepare small pot and place next to plant. Choose vigorous stem and cut a slit on lower surface just below a leaf. Place cut stem against compost in new pot and peg closely down.

2. Keep moist. Roots grow from cut and when these are visible and tip has signs of new growth, cut stem with sharp knife to separate plants.

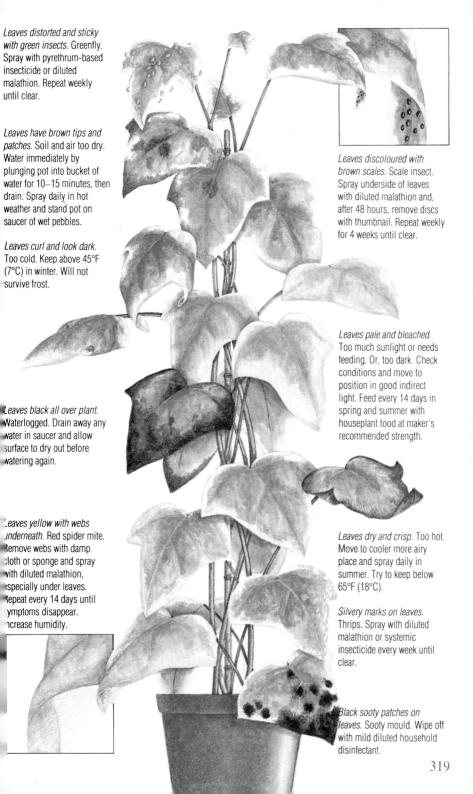

Leaves distorted and sticky with green insects. Greenfly. Spray with pyrethrum-based insecticide or diluted malathion. Repeat weekly until clear.

Leaves have brown tips and patches. Soil and air too dry. Water immediately by plunging pot into bucket of water for 10–15 minutes, then drain. Spray daily in hot weather and stand pot on saucer of wet pebbles.

Leaves curl and look dark. Too cold. Keep above 45°F (7°C) in winter. Will not survive frost.

Leaves black all over plant. Waterlogged. Drain away any water in saucer and allow surface to dry out before watering again.

Leaves yellow with webs underneath. Red spider mite. Remove webs with damp cloth or sponge and spray with diluted malathion, especially under leaves. Repeat every 14 days until symptoms disappear. Increase humidity.

Leaves discoloured with brown scales. Scale insect. Spray underside of leaves with diluted malathion and, after 48 hours, remove discs with thumbnail. Repeat weekly for 4 weeks until clear.

Leaves pale and bleached. Too much sunlight or needs feeding. Or, too dark. Check conditions and move to position in good indirect light. Feed every 14 days in spring and summer with houseplant food at maker's recommended strength.

Leaves dry and crisp. Too hot. Move to cooler more airy place and spray daily in summer. Try to keep below 65°F (18°C).

Silvery marks on leaves. Thrips. Spray with diluted malathion or systemic insecticide every week until clear.

Black sooty patches on leaves. Sooty mould. Wipe off with mild diluted household disinfectant.

319

Hedera helix

Indoor ivy

Ivy was one of the first plants to be grown in the home and is one of the few houseplants that are native to Europe. Indoor ivy is grown in many varieties with leaf sizes ranging from finger-nail size up to 2½in (6cm) across. Some are all green, others highly variegated. Ivies are very easy plants to keep and because of this are sometimes neglected. They do not like too hot or too dry an atmosphere and do best in the company of other plants. They make beautiful hanging basket plants and look good trained up to a trellis. If lower stems become bare and straggly nip out the leading shoots a couple of times a year to keep the plant bushy.

Light: Best in good light, though direct sun can bleach the leaves. The greater the leaf variation, the more light needed.

Temperature: Winter minimum indoors 45°F (7°C). Best summer temperature 60–65°F (16–18°C); if temperature higher, increase humidity.

Water: Twice a week in summer, once a week in winter sufficient.

Humidity: Spray every day in summer or centrally heated rooms, once a week in cooler positions. To increase humidity, stand plant in saucer of damp pebbles.

Feeding: Every 14 days in the growing season (spring and summer) with houseplant food diluted according to the maker's instructions.

Soil: Loam-based No. 2 or peat-based compost.

Repotting: Annually in spring for mature (2 years and over) plants. Young, quick-growing ones may need repotting twice a year if they look too large for their pot. If very large, change the topsoil every year.

Cleaning: Humidity spraying sufficient, though if very dusty wipe with damp cloth. Use leafshine once a month.

There are very many varieties of ivy with leaves of different sizes, patterned in different shades of green and white or green and cream. Healthy plants should have bright, firm leaves and be compact with strong shoots growing from the centre.

Stems grow lanky with long spaces between leaves; leaves drop. Too cold and too dark. Move to lighter, warmer place, over 45°F (7°C).

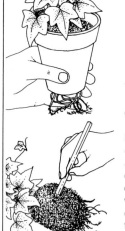

Repotting
When roots grow out of pot base and plant stops growing, it needs repotting.

Remove from old pot and carefully tease soil from around root ball. Do not damage roots. Repot in pot one size larger, and leave without water for 2 days to encourage roots to spread through soil.

what goes wrong

Leaves discoloured with brown scales. Scale insect. Remove with cotton wool dipped in methylated spirits or spray every 14 days with pyrethrum or a systemic insecticide until clear.

Variegated plants turn plain green. Overfeeding or too dark. Check conditions and move to lighter place if necessary. Stop feeding until following spring.

Leaves turn pale in summer. Too much direct sun. Move to slightly shaded place.

Leaves turn yellow with webs underneath. Red spider mite. Spray with diluted malathion every 14 days until clear.

Silvery marks on leaves. Thrips. Spray with pyrethrum or a systemic insecticide every 14 days until clear.

Leaves turn black all over. Too wet, overwatered. Allow to dry out before watering again, then water less often. In winter let top half inch (1 cm) of soil dry out between waterings.

Leaves go quite dry and crisp. Too hot and dry. Move to cooler room (under 65°F, 18°C) if possible. Spray daily to improve humidity.

Black sooty patches on leaves. Sooty mould. Wipe off with 6 or 7 drops of disinfectant mixed with a cup of water.

Leaves distorted and sticky with green insects. Greenfly. Spray every 14 days with pyrethrum or a systemic insecticide until clear.

321

Heliotropium arborescens

Heliotrope

Heliotropes are natives of Peru and can be grown in a number of ways: as a dwarf bushy plant, as a pyramid 24–30in (60–75cm) tall or as a 4ft (120cm) standard. Dwarf varieties are easy to grow in a windowbox and well worth a place for their scent. They will not stand frost and should be planted out in mild weather when all frost has finished. Overwinter them in a greenhouse or conservatory.

Light: Maximum but will stand some hours of shade. Indoors in winter, maximum possible.

Temperature: Germination, 65–70°F (18–21°C). Spring cuttings need bottom heat and surrounding temperature of 60°F (16°C). No frost.

Water: Keep moist, not waterlogged.

Humidity: Syringe after hot days.

Soil: Loam-based No. 2. Soil-less potting compost is suitable for dwarf plants but will not support standards.

Feeding: Every 10 days in loam, every 5 in soil-less, diluted to maker's recommended strength.

Propagation: From seed in early spring. Treat as Browallia (p.130), pricking off into 3½in (9cm) pots when second pair of leaves formed. Take cuttings in spring or late summer. Summer cuttings should be rooted in seedling compost around the edge of a 3½in (9cm) pot and overwintered at 45°F (7°C). In early spring, cut off the top 3in (8cm) and root each one in 3½in (9cm) pot.

Tidying: Remove dead heads with sharp knife.

Varieties: For general planting, Marine, very dwarf with a strong scent and very deep purple flowers. For training as a standard, Peruvianum, var. Gigantia, lavender, well scented.

Heliotropes are rather sombre looking plants with dark green leaves often overlaid with purple. The purple or white flowers are tiny but grow in large plate-like clusters in the centre of the plant. Their beauty lies mostly in the superb vanilla scent given off especially in the evening.

Flowers tattered or missing. Earwigs. If plants are staked, these may be hiding in the hollow of the bamboo cane. They can be killed by inserting wire into hollow.

Foliage turns very deep colour, almost black. Very cold wind. Move container to more sheltered position.

Fluffy mould on plant during winter indoors. Botrytis. This may develop on butt of removed side shoot or other damaged area. Spray once a month through winter with iprodione.

Edges of leaves turn brown and shrivelled when plant is indoors. Damage from fumes of gas or other heater. Or, damage from insecticide spray in sunshine.

Pinhead whitish spots on leaves, possibly some holes torn. The effect of a heavy hailstorm on broad, tender leaves. Protect plant in bad weather.

what goes wrong

Whole plant droops, leaves wilt. Too dry or overwatered, root rot. Check compost. If dry, water container thoroughly. If soil wet and heavy, check drainage and allow to dry out before watering again. Then keep moist but not soggy. Severe waterlogging will cause root rot and plant will die.

Small white flies on underside of leaves when plant indoors. Small clear scales present. Whitefly. Spray every 3 days with permethrin until all trace of scales and flies has gone.

Training a standard

1. Remove all side shoots from young plant or cutting in spring. Keep moist and feed regularly. Remove flower buds.

2. As stem grows, tie it every 6in (15cm) to a 48in (130cm) cane. Continue to remove side shoots. In early autumn, repot and keep almost dry in cool, light airy place over winter. Do not feed. Repot and start feeding again in early spring.

Leaves and flowers sticky with small flies. Aphid. Spray with pirimicarb. Especially important to prevent aphid on trained plants.

Small scales on underside of leaves, especially while plants growing indoors. Scale insect. Spray with diluted malathion and dab scales with paintbrush dipped in methylated spirits to loosen hold. Then lightly scrape off leaf.

Leaves lose rich colour. Possibly thrips if flecking present. Spray with diluted malathion. If no markings on foliage, plant needs feeding. Feed regularly.

Foliage is black and soggy. Plant has been killed by frost. Heliotrope will not take frost. Protect in late spring when young plants hardening off or just planted.

Holes in leaves. Slugs. Place slug pellets around area as directed by maker. Keep away from pets and fishponds.

323

Hibiscus rosa – sinensis

Chinese rose

This shrubby, sub-tropical flowering plant has exotic red, yellow or orange flowers which only last one or two days before shrivelling and falling off. If the humidity is too low, the buds may fall off before opening, although a number of hybrids have been developed recently to prevent this. When buying, check that the lower buds on the plant have not dropped.

Light: Plenty of diffused light but never direct sun.
Temperature: 65–70°F (18–21°C), in spring and summer, with summer maximum of 80°F (27°C). Reduce to 55°F (13°C) in winter.
Water: 2 or 3 times a week in summer to maintain a moist compost, though plant must not stand in water. In winter, water only when top of compost feels dry: when temperature around 55°F (13°C), this should only be once every 14 days.
Humidity: Spray daily with soft tepid water in spring and summer. Stand pot on saucer of pebbles almost covered with water. Ensure good ventilation. In winter, spray weekly.
Feeding: Every 14 days in spring and summer, especially after flower buds appear, using liquid houseplant food diluted to maker's instructions.
Soil: Equal parts loam-based No. 3 and peat, with one-third less peat for adult plants.
Repotting: Annually in spring into pot one size larger, up to a maximum 7in (18cm). Plant is more prolific if reasonably pot-bound. When in largest pot size, change top soil annually.
Cleaning: Humidity spraying adequate. Leaves may be wiped with a damp cloth. No leafshine.

The Hibiscus has exotic flowers which are available in red, yellow or orange; each bloom lasts only one or two days before drying out and shrivelling. Buds will fall if the humidity is too low, so spray daily with soft tepid water in spring and summer.

Flower buds fall off before opening. Air too dry. Spray daily in summer with soft, tepid water. In winter spray weekly. While growing in spring and summer, keep temperature between 65–70°F (18–21°C), to encourage buds to open.

Black marks on leaf. Leafshine damage. Do not use. Clean by spraying with soft, tepid water.

Leaves pale. Too dark. Move to lighter place, but not in direct sunlight.

Leaves drop while still green. In summer, too wet, waterlogged; roots are rotting. Check drainage holes in pot and allow soil to dry out on surface before watering again. Then water twice a week in summer to keep soil moist. In winter, too cold. Maintain 55°F (13°C) all winter. Remember to keep soil drier in winter, allowing surface layer to dry out between waterings.

what goes wrong

Pruning

Cut stems down by half in spring with secateurs or sharp scissors. Cut at an angle just above a leaf or side shoot. Dust cut ends with sulphur and if sap runs, smear ends with ash or petroleum jelly to seal the wound.

New leaves stay small, no flowers appear. Needs feeding. Feed every 2 weeks in spring and summer, using houseplant food at maker's recommended strength.

Plant wilts, leaves limp and dull. Too hot and dry. Water and move to cooler place, under 70°F (21°C) in summer, around 55°F (13°C) in winter.

Plant grows tall and straggly. Needs pruning but prune only in spring or summer. Dust pruning cuts with sulphur to prevent disease.

Leaves misshapen and sticky, with small insects. Greenfly. Spray with pyrethrum-based insecticide, or diluted malathion. Repeat 1 week later, then every week until clear.

White cotton-wool patches where leaf joins stem. Mealy bug. Spray with diluted malathion and remove bugs and 'wool' with tweezers. Repeat every 14 days until symptoms disappear. Or, paint bugs with methylated spirits and remove with tweezers.

Leaves lose shine, webs underneath. Red spider mite. Remove webs with damp cloth or sponge, then spray with diluted malathion, especially under leaves. Protect flowers. Repeat every 14 days until clear. Improve humidity. Do not restore gloss with leafshine.

Flowers fall after one day in bloom. Natural. Flowers last only a day once fully open.

Amaryllis

The enormous flowers of the Amaryllis lily make a wonderful display in winter and spring. Bulbs can be bought already potted and these need only heat and water to grow, but have usually been treated to flower only once. Fortunately, it is easy to pot up untreated bulbs yourself and then grow them on to flower for 3–5 years in succession. Pot them one to a 5in (12cm) pot in late winter, one-third above the soil. They will flower one year without feeding but must be fed if they are to flower the following year, since the next embryo bud starts to form as the first dies away.

Light: Good light at all times. Protect flowers from direct sun. Full light after flowering for foliage to develop and ripen.
Temperature: 60–75°F (16–24°C) during growing period, although flowers will last longer in cooler temperatures. Rest bulbs at 50°F (10°C).
Water: Soil should always be moist, so water 2–3 times a week, more during hot weather and during flowering. No water while resting.
Humidity: If room is dry, spray lightly over buds. Never spray flowers or leaves. Do not spray while resting.
Feeding: Feed weekly with liquid house-plant food at maker's recommended strengths from the time flower starts to open until foliage starts to die back.
Soil: Loam-based No.2. If planning to use next year, do not use bulb fibre.
After flowering: Do not cut stems until they have completely dried out. Gradually decrease watering, and stop completely for 6–8 weeks. Then lift bulb, separate offsets and repot parent bulb. Pot up offsets in rich potting compost. They will be ready for flowering in 2–3 years.

Amaryllis or Barbados lily produces trumpet-shaped scented flowers up to 12in (30cm) across in shades of red, orange, white and pink. Between 3 and 6 flowers grow on the 24in (60cm) tall stem and the leaves do not appear until flowering is nearly finished. If kept in the right conditions, the flowers will open in succession, each lasting several weeks.

what goes wrong

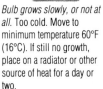

Bulb grows slowly, or not at all. Too cold. Move to minimum temperature 60°F (16°C). If still no growth, place on a radiator or other source of heat for a day or two.

Flowers look bleached. Too much direct sun. Protect flowers from direct sun. Blooms will last longer if protected from hot sun.

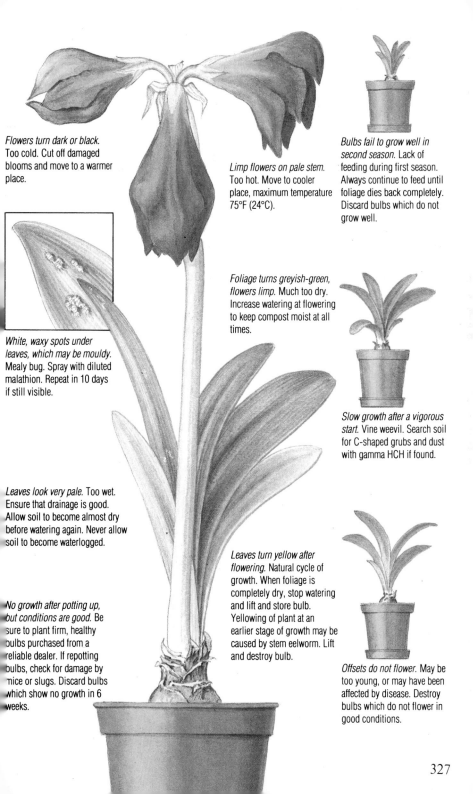

Flowers turn dark or black.
Too cold. Cut off damaged
blooms and move to a warmer
place.

Limp flowers on pale stem.
Too hot. Move to cooler
place, maximum temperature
75°F (24°C).

Bulbs fail to grow well in
second season. Lack of
feeding during first season.
Always continue to feed until
foliage dies back completely.
Discard bulbs which do not
grow well.

Foliage turns greyish-green,
flowers limp. Much too dry.
Increase watering at flowering
to keep compost moist at all
times.

White, waxy spots under
leaves, which may be mouldy.
Mealy bug. Spray with diluted
malathion. Repeat in 10 days
if still visible.

Slow growth after a vigorous
start. Vine weevil. Search soil
for C-shaped grubs and dust
with gamma HCH if found.

Leaves look very pale. Too wet.
Ensure that drainage is good.
Allow soil to become almost dry
before watering again. Never allow
soil to become waterlogged.

Leaves turn yellow after
flowering. Natural cycle of
growth. When foliage is
completely dry, stop watering
and lift and store bulb.
Yellowing of plant at an
earlier stage of growth may be
caused by stem eelworm. Lift
and destroy bulb.

No growth after potting up,
but conditions are good. Be
sure to plant firm, healthy
bulbs purchased from a
reliable dealer. If repotting
bulbs, check for damage by
mice or slugs. Discard bulbs
which show no growth in 6
weeks.

Offsets do not flower. May be
too young, or may have been
affected by disease. Destroy
bulbs which do not flower in
good conditions.

327

Paradise palm

Originating in the Lord Howe Islands of the Pacific, this is the 'Victorian' palm associated with palm courts. Mature specimens can grow to 12ft (over 3m) in the home. As *H. forsteriana* is very slow-growing, producing one leaf per plant per year, it is usually planted three or four to a pot. It is extremely tolerant of various light conditions and will survive in a dark situation for a long time. It is very susceptible to root damage if knocked over, so treat it with care.

Light: Indirect daylight preferred, but survives quite well in artificial light

Temperature: Winter minimum 50°F (10°C), summer maximum 75°F (24°C).

Water: In summer, keep just moist at all times, watering once or twice a week. In winter, once every week or ten days, allowing almost to dry out in between.

Humidity: Spray daily with fine mist of tepid soft water in summer, especially if 75°F (24°C) or over.

Feeding: Every 14 days in summer with houseplant food diluted with water according to maker's instructions.

Soil: Fibrous mixture of 4 parts loam-based No. 2, 1 part sedge or moss peat, 1 part rotted pine needles.

Repotting: In spring, only if plant is potbound, into pot one size larger. With younger plant, knock from its pot very carefully, ensuring root-ball does not crumble or the individual plants separate. With large, mature plants, do not repot, just change topsoil.

Cleaning: Wipe every week with damp cloth. Use vegetable-oil based cleaner, 6–7 drops of milk in a cup of soft water, or liquid leafshine diluted in water (make it 4 times weaker than the maker's recommended strength). No aerosol leafshine.

The Paradise palm's long, graceful fronds develop from a leaf spike which unfurls slowly. It grows at the rate of only one new frond a year. It needs good, indirect light but will grow well in artificial light, too. As with other slow-growing palms, several plants are often placed together in one pot.

Leaf tips turn brown. Natural but if brown spreads down leaf, increase humidity. Trim leaves with scissors.

Trimming the fronds and leaves
Cut out dead lower fronds. Cut as close to main stem as possible.
If the tips of the leaves are brown and dry, trim them off with sharp scissors, cutting just outside healthy leaf tissue.

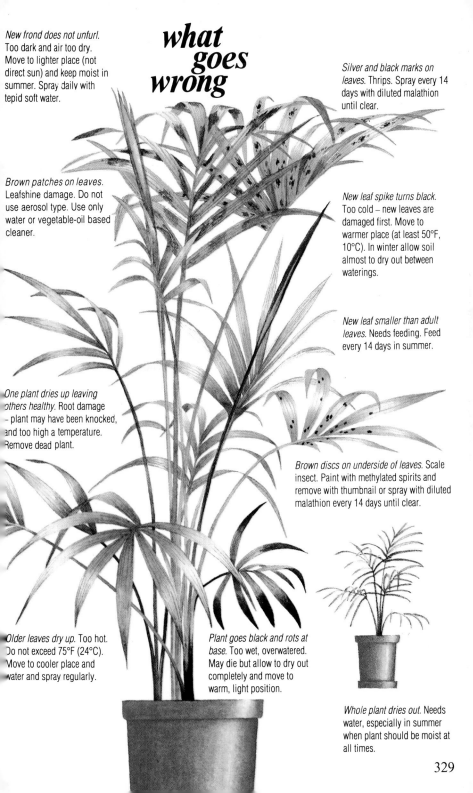

what goes wrong

New frond does not unfurl. Too dark and air too dry. Move to lighter place (not direct sun) and keep moist in summer. Spray daily with tepid soft water.

Silver and black marks on leaves. Thrips. Spray every 14 days with diluted malathion until clear.

Brown patches on leaves. Leafshine damage. Do not use aerosol type. Use only water or vegetable-oil based cleaner.

New leaf spike turns black. Too cold – new leaves are damaged first. Move to warmer place (at least 50°F, 10°C). In winter allow soil almost to dry out between waterings.

New leaf smaller than adult leaves. Needs feeding. Feed every 14 days in summer.

One plant dries up leaving others healthy. Root damage – plant may have been knocked, and too high a temperature. Remove dead plant.

Brown discs on underside of leaves. Scale insect. Paint with methylated spirits and remove with thumbnail or spray with diluted malathion every 14 days until clear.

Older leaves dry up. Too hot. Do not exceed 75°F (24°C). Move to cooler place and water and spray regularly.

Plant goes black and rots at base. Too wet, overwatered. May die but allow to dry out completely and move to warm, light position.

Whole plant dries out. Needs water, especially in summer when plant should be moist at all times.

329

Hoya bella

Miniature wax plant

This is a slender-stemmed plant, whose small, plain green, waxy leaves distinguish it from the larger-leaved *Hoya carnosa*. Requiring more heat than *H. carnosa*, a Miniature wax plant is ideally suited to growing in indoor hanging baskets. The flowers are a waxy white with a rose-crimson or violet centre, and they hang down in groups or clusters. The plant should not be placed on polished furniture, as the flowers produce a sticky nectar which can fall in droplets, causing damage. More popular in Victorian times, it can be difficult to obtain today, and is not easy to bring to flower, but efforts are well rewarded by the exquisite, scented blooms.

The Miniature wax plant's star-shaped, waxy, white flowers with a rose-crimson centre are produced at the height of summer. The flowers only measure ⅜in (1cm) but grow in clusters. Keep in temperatures of 65–70° (18–21°C) in summer, spraying twice per week in a well ventilated room.

Light: Full diffused daylight but avoid midday sun in summer. Full sun in winter.
Temperature: 65–70°F (18–21°C) in spring and summer, though peaks of up to 85°F (30°C) will do no harm for short periods. Maintain 60°F (16°C) in winter.
Water: Weekly in spring and summer; reduce to every 14 days in autumn and winter, watering only when soil surface feels dry.
Humidity: Spray at least twice weekly with soft water in spring and summer, avoiding flowers. Planting into a hanging basket is beneficial; good ventilation important.
Feeding: Every 14 days in spring and summer only, with liquid food diluted to maker's instructions.
Soil: Equal parts of loam-based No.2 and rough peat.
Repotting: In spring, and only when plant completely pot-bound: in practice, every 2 or 3 years.
Cleaning: Humidity spraying adequate. Wipe leaves occasionally – not more often than once every 6 weeks – with vegetable oil-based leafshine.

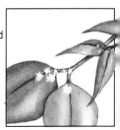

White cotton-wool patches where leaves join stem. Mealy bug. Spray with diluted malathion and remove bugs and 'wool' with tweezers. Repeat every 14 days until symptoms disappear. Or, paint bugs with methylated spirits and remove with tweezers.

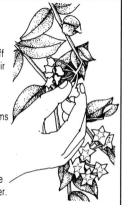

Removing flowers

When flowers die, pick off individual blooms and their flower stems. Do not remove the short side stem which carries the flower cluster. New blooms will grow from this the following year.

Flowers produce sticky nectar so protect furniture under plant while in flower.

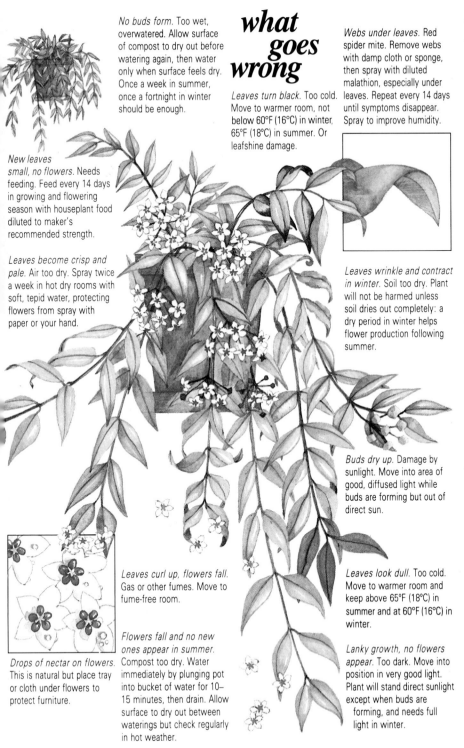

what goes wrong

No buds form. Too wet, overwatered. Allow surface of compost to dry out before watering again, then water only when surface feels dry. Once a week in summer, once a fortnight in winter should be enough.

New leaves small, no flowers. Needs feeding. Feed every 14 days in growing and flowering season with houseplant food diluted to maker's recommended strength.

Leaves become crisp and pale. Air too dry. Spray twice a week in hot dry rooms with soft, tepid water, protecting flowers from spray with paper or your hand.

Leaves turn black. Too cold. Move to warmer room, not below 60°F (16°C) in winter, 65°F (18°C) in summer. Or leafshine damage.

Webs under leaves. Red spider mite. Remove webs with damp cloth or sponge, then spray with diluted malathion, especially under leaves. Repeat every 14 days until symptoms disappear. Spray to improve humidity.

Leaves wrinkle and contract in winter. Soil too dry. Plant will not be harmed unless soil dries out completely: a dry period in winter helps flower production following summer.

Buds dry up. Damage by sunlight. Move into area of good, diffused light while buds are forming but out of direct sun.

Drops of nectar on flowers. This is natural but place tray or cloth under flowers to protect furniture.

Leaves curl up, flowers fall. Gas or other fumes. Move to fume-free room.

Flowers fall and no new ones appear in summer. Compost too dry. Water immediately by plunging pot into bucket of water for 10–15 minutes, then drain. Allow surface to dry out between waterings but check regularly in hot weather.

Leaves look dull. Too cold. Move to warmer room and keep above 65°F (18°C) in summer and at 60°F (16°C) in winter.

Lanky growth, no flowers appear. Too dark. Move into position in very good light. Plant will stand direct sunlight except when buds are forming, and needs full light in winter.

331

Hoya carnosa

Wax plant

This attractive plant would justify its place in the home just by its foliage, which is dark green, fleshy and climbs to cover a large area quite quickly. In summer, it provides the additional pleasure of waxy, star-like, flesh-coloured flowers. An established plant will be covered in blooms, have a faintly exotic aroma and produce a honey-like nectar. Moving the plant after the flower buds have set can cause them to drop off. Faded flowers should not be removed as new buds often form on them. The variegated species *H. carnosa* has attractive foliage, but is a reluctant flowerer.

Light: Good light position, but not in mid-day sun which may scorch leaves.
Temperature: Winter minimum 50°F (10°C), summer maximum 75°F (24°C).
Water: Weekly in summer, every 14 days in winter, with rainwater if possible. Good drainage essential.
Humidity: Spray at least once a week in summer, avoiding open flowers. Stand pot on damp pebbles in outer container of damp peat.
Feeding: Every 14 days with liquid houseplant food diluted to half the strength recommended by the maker.
Soil: Loam-based No. 2 compost. Crushed brick dust in pot aids flowering.
Repotting: Plant prefers to be pot-bound, so repot only every 2–3 years into clay pots. Alternatively, simply change topsoil and feed.
Cleaning: Humidity spraying sufficient. Leaves may be wiped with damp cloth. Use leafshine not more than once a month and not on open flowers.

Wax plants have all green or variegated green and white leaves and, once well established, produce blooms of up to 30 small flower heads throughout the summer months. Healthy leaves are firm and slightly fleshy and should grow all the way down the stem.

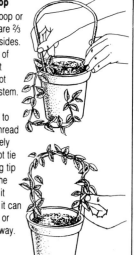

Training round a hoop
1. Push ends of wire hoop or thin cane so that they are 2/3 down pot on opposite sides. Bend stem to one side of hoop and gently twist it around the hoop. Do not damage the leaves or stem.

2. Tie a length of twine to one end of hoop and thread it along, looping it loosely around the stem. Do not tie tight knots. The growing tip will continue to follow the line of the hoop. When it reaches the other end, it can be trained round again or twisted back the other way.

No flowers appear, leaves fade and drop. Too dark. Move to lighter place, but not in direct midday sun. May also fail to flower if pot-bound. Check roots and if they look crowded, repot in spring into pot one size larger.

Brown scorch marks on leaves. Too much direct midday sun. Or water from spraying left on leaves in bright sunlight. Keep out of midday sun and spray only in early morning.

what goes wrong

White woolly patches on leaves. Mealy bug. Remove with cotton wool dipped in methylated spirits or spray with systemic insecticide every 14 days until clear. Plant is very susceptible.

Buds drop off before opening. Too cold, too near a window or plant has been moved too often. Keep above at least 50°F (10°C) in winter and do not move from place to place when flower buds have started to appear.

New leaves appear but no flowers. Needs feeding more often. Feed every 14 days all the year round with half strength liquid houseplant food. Do not increaase strength of dose.

Leaves dry up and curl. Too hot and dry. Air too dry. Keep below 75°F (24°C) and spray at least once a week in hot weather. Provide extra humidity with damp pebbles or peat. Water more often.

Brown scales on undersides of leaves, with sticky substance. Scale insect. Remove with cotton wool dipped in methylated spirits or spray every 14 days with systemic insecticide until clear.

Leaves turn yellow, wilt and rot. Too wet, over-watered. Allow to dry out before watering again and cut watering frequency by half. Good drainage is essential.

333

Huernia primulina

Though this plant belongs to a genus of 'Carrion flower' plants, it is suitable for growing indoors as its flowers do not have the group's characteristic smell of rotting meat. The stems make clumps to fill a 4 or 5in (10cm) pot and reach about 2in (5cm) tall in 3 or 4 years if grown well. Other good species are *Huernia zebrina*, with shining red and yellow flowers; *H. oculata*, chocolate brown and white; *H. hystrix*, greenish-yellow and brown; *H. hallii* creamy-yellow, and many others which are all easy to grow.

Light: Keep in sunny position on a windowsill or in a greenhouse. Shade from full midsummer sun in greenhouse. A bright but not very sunny windowsill will be tolerated, but flowering will not be so good.

Temperature: Minimum 40°F (4°C) but 50°F (10°C) is better. Give fresh air in summer months.

Water: In spring soak in a bowl until soil wet through, then leave dry for a month. Water fortnightly in summer, weekly in hottest weather; tail off in autumn and keep dry in winter if under 55°F (13°C); if warmer, give a little water once a month. See also Introduction.

Feeding: Use high potash fertilizer 2 or 3 times during summer months.

Soil: Use good loam-based No. 2 potting compost, or soil-less compost, with 40% coarse, gritty sand.

Repotting: Every spring in size larger half-pot or pan. When old stems look unsightly, discard them when repotting, as flowers are produced on young stems from current or former year.

Propagation: Take cutting with sharp knife at natural junction of stems. Divide large clumps into clusters of 3 or 4 stems.

Huernia primulina. This is the only Huernia species with really yellow flowers, most others being mixtures of red, brown or cream. It is fly pollinated, but has little noticeable smell so it is hard to see why the flies are attracted to it.

what goes wrong

Stems turn yellow, then black in winter. Too cold. Is plant shut behind curtains at night? Move to warmer place, above 40°F (4°C).

Stems black and shrivelled, some fall over. Too cold, wet and humid. Allow to dry out thoroughly and keep above 40°F (4°C) in winter. Pare away rot from stem. If roots black and rotted, treat and repot (see Introduction). Or, take cuttings from healthy stems.

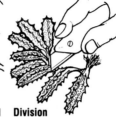

Taking cuttings
1. Take cuttings after flowering. Cut off new, outer stem where it joins old, using a sharp knife.

2. Dust base of cutting and cut end of old stem with hormone rooting powder to prevent infection and leave cutting to dry for 2 days before placing on surface of dry compost.

Division
1. Divide clumps of 6–8 stems in spring or early summer. Remove from pot and clean away any soil from lower stem. Cut through stem with sharp knife.

2. Repot half with roots as usual. Treat other half as cutting, leaving to dry for 2–3 days before rerooting.

Stems shrivel and dry. Many possible reasons. Too hot and dry in winter; too dry in spring and summer, needs feeding or root mealy bug. If soil dry in spring and summer, increase amount of water each time but allow to dry out between. In winter moisten soil monthly. If feeding and soil correct, check roots for white woolly patches. Swirl roots in insecticide, allow to dry before repotting.

Stems grow tall and pale, especially at tips. Few flowers. Too dark. Move into full light over 2 weeks. May also happen if too hot and wet in winter. Keep around 50°F (10°C) in rest period.

Brown scorch marks on stems. Sunscorch, plant moved into direct sun too quickly in stuffy place. Move out of direct light, then return gradually over 2 weeks. Keep in more airy place.

Stems shrivel, white woolly patches especially round base. Mealy bug. Remove with small paintbrush dipped in methylated spirits, and spray with contact or systemic insecticide. Repeat 2 or 3 times in growing season.

Plant collapsing or not growing, black flies around plant and soil. Sciara fly. Inspect roots and if rotted, pare back until all trace of root or larvae removed. Then treat and repot (see Introduction).

Hyacinthus orientalis

Roman hyacinth

Colourful and fragrant Dutch hya-cinths are one of the easiest bulbs to grow in pots or bowls provided three essential requirements are met. First, they need at least 8 weeks in very cool dark conditions to form their root system. Next, no heat must be given until the flower bud is quite clear of the neck of the bulb. Third, give them plenty of water when reaching full bloom. Plant bulbs one to a 3½in (9cm) pot in autumn and leave outside under sand or ashes or in a cool cupboard indoors. Bring into partial light when the green leaf tips are just showing above the soil and repot in bowl or 3–4 to a 6in (15cm) pot. Move into full light for flowering. Bulbs which have been grown in pots will not flower indoors again.

Hyacinths grow to a height of about 10in (25cm). Each bulb produces a single flower stem which carries 20–30 small, hanging bell-shaped flowers in shades of red, pink, blue, yellow or white. The flowers last for 4–6 weeks in the right conditions. For best results, choose varieties specially grown for indoor flowering.

Light: Total darkness for at least 8 weeks after planting, then partial light until foliage is bright green. Full light while flowering but protected from direct sun.
Temperature: Maximum 45°F (7°C) while in darkness, 60–65°F (16–18°C) for flower-ing. Keep cool until flower bud is com-pletely clear of bulb.
Water: Plant in moist compost, then check weekly while in dark and keep just moist. Water 2–3 times a week when in flower.
Humidity: Dry, airy place. Do not spray.
Feeding: If bulbs are to be saved for the garden, feed with houseplant food at maker's recommended strength weekly after flower buds are formed. Do not feed when in full flower.
Soil: If grown in pots with drainage holes use any good fibrous potting compost. Special bulb fibre best for bowls.
After flowering: Cut back stem to bulb after flowering. When foliage dies down, bulbs can be planted out in the garden.

Stem bends over when in full flower. Too dark. Give plenty of light but protect from full sun. Prevent before flower is fully developed by inserting thin stake in soil and tying stem to it.

New leaves become stunted or fail to grow. Hyacinth yellows disease. No cure, lift and destroy bulb, which was probably infected when purchased. Always buy firm, clean bulbs from a reputable dealer.

Bulbs planted in a large bowl do not flower at the same time. Always plant bulbs of the same variety in a group, as flowering times differ for different varieties. Do not mix colours in the same bowl.

Growing in water
Hyacinths can be grown in water, using special containers. Put a few pieces of charcoal in base and fill with soft water. Place bulb in neck of glass, base just clear of water. Roots will grow into the water.

Nose of bulb turns dark or bronzed after being brought into light. Usually affects bulbs kept in garden. Too strong light too quickly. Keep bulbs in a cool, shady place until leaves are bright green.

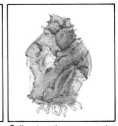

Bulb eaten when uncovered. Mice will eat bulbs planted in the garden or stored. Either store in a place where mice can not get to them, or put down traps.

Flowers, buds and leaves suddenly turn yellow and shrivelled. Soft rot. Probable causes are too rich soil or too hot. Prevent by growing in potting compost or bulb fibre. Keep in cool temperature. No cure, destroy infected plant.

what goes wrong

Leaves grow well but flower hidden. Bulb brought into warmth and light to soon. Wait until entire bud is visible above the bulb before bringing into full light.

Buds turn yellow or fail to open. Soil allowed to become either too wet or too dry. Always keep just moist.

Small, floppy leaves and no flower buds. Bulb was either too small or was forced the previous year. Always choose new, healthy bulbs for planting indoors.

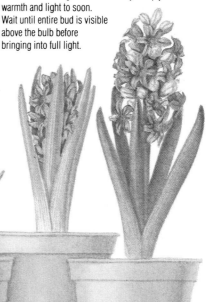

Hydrangea macrophylla

Snowball flower

Sometimes known as Hortensia, the common *Hydrangea* is well suited to growing in pots in the home and will grow happily in the garden when its flowering period is over. It needs copious watering in the flowering season or its leaves droop. It is available with pink, blue and white flowers, the latter on the beautiful 'Lace cap' variety. Pink plants may be changed to blue by adding alum (aluminium sulphate) to the soil, while blue ones may be changed to pink by adding of iron.

Light: Full light; not direct sun which dries plant out. Leaves turn yellow, growth is stunted in shade.
Temperature: Winter minimum 45°F (8°C), when dormant. Raising temperature to around 55°F (13°C) in early spring encourages growth. Summer maximum 65°F (18°C).
Water: Daily in late spring, summer, putting pot in water to cover compost for about 5 minutes or until bubbles stop rising from root-ball. Water every 2 days in early spring; only when compost appears dry in autumn, winter. Use lime-free water.
Humidity: Spray daily with soft water in spring and summer. Keep away from radiator or boiler.
Feeding: Weekly in spring and summer. Add liquid houseplant food to water in bucket, using dose recommended by maker. To avoid wasting fertilizer, drain excess back into bucket when plant fully watered and keep water/food mixture for next feed. Change mixture every 6 weeks.
Soil: Equal parts loam-based No. 2 and decayed manure, plus colourants if changing colour of flowers. Must be lime-free.
Repotting: Every year before flowering. Put plenty of drainage material in pots.
Cleaning: Humidity spraying sufficient. No leafshine.

The Hydrangea's natural flower colour is pink but can be changed to blue by adding special colourant containing alum to the water. Some soil types may produce blue flower and these can be returned to pink by adding iron filings or a colourant. A healthy plant of whatever colour should have fresh green leaves, with no sign of drooping or discolouring.

Flowers change colour. If blue flowers turn pink, add aluminium sulphate to the water and blue colour will return. It is unlikely that pink flowers will turn blue as pink is the natural colour and is changed to blue by adding special hydrangea colouring.

Leaves turn brown and crisp. Too hot and air too dry. Move to cooler place (under 65°F, 18°C) and spray daily with soft water. Keep plant away from radiators or heaters.

what goes wrong

Young leaves distorted and sticky with green insects. Greenfly. Spray every 14 days with pyrethrum-based insecticide or diluted malathion until clear. Cut off damage leaves and keep plant away from others as greenfly sprea

Watering

Hydrangeas need plenty of water in summer and their leaves droop dramatically if the compost becomes too dry.

1. Fill bucket with water and place pot inside, with water just covering compost. Leave for 5 minutes, until bubbles stop rising from soil.

2. Remove pot and allow to drain into saucer or drip tray. Pour excess away.

3. Once a week you can add liquid houseplant food to the water. In this case, keep the water from the bucket and the excess which drains out to use another time.

Young leaves yellow, veins show up in older leaves. Lime damage. Use only soft water for watering and spraying and lime-free compost. To help rapid recovery, water with sequestered iron once only.

No new growth in spring. Too cold. in early spring, move to room at least 55°F (13°C) to encourage new growth. Begin watering more frequently, every 2 days, and begin feeding every week.

Leaves turn slowly yellow and flower growth is stunted. Too dark. Move to place in good indirect light, not full sunlight.

Brown spots on leaves. Fungal infection, botrytis. Dust leaves with flowers of sulphur or spray with systemic insecticide diluted in water every 14 days until clear.

Leaves turn yellow with webs underneath. Red spider mite. Spray with diluted malathion and wipe away webs with cotton wool soaked in diluted malathion.

Whole plant is limp with drooping leaves. Eventually leaves turn brown and curl. Too dry. Plunge pot immediately into bucket of water, leave for 30 minutes then allow to drain.

Black scorch marks on leaves. Leafshine damage. Do not use. Clean by spraying with soft water.

339

Hypoestes phyllostachya

Freckle face

This plant, grown essentially for its pretty coloured oblong leaves, which grow to 1½–2in (3–5cm), has recently been improved by careful breeding. Once a rather untidy, sprawling plant, it is now much more compact and makes a good ground cover plant for mixed planted bowls. Its distinct colouring also makes a good contrast to green or variegated plants. Though it can be overwintered, it is best propagated afresh each spring to keep it neat and compact. Older plants produce delicate purple and white flowers.

It can be propagated from either stem-tip cuttings or from seed. Both need a warm place (70°F, 21°C) and cuttings should be covered with polythene to provide extra humidity.

Light: Needs good light. A window that does not face into the sun is good. Leaves lose pink markings in too dark a position, but direct sunlight will burn them.

Temperature: Winter minimum 65°F (18°C), if possible. Ordinary room temperature adequate in summer. If very hot – over 75°F (24°C) – ensure plant is in an airy position.

Water: 3 times a week in summer, once a week in winter with tepid water, when not growing.

Humidity: Unless planted in mixed bowl, stand in saucer of pebbles almost covered with water. Do not spray.

Feeding: Every 14 days with liquid houseplant food diluted in water. Use half as much food as the maker recommends.

Soil: Loam-based No. 2 compost.

Repotting: Annually in spring if plants are being kept from year to year. It is better to repropagate each spring, to keep stock young, vigorous and compact.

Cleaning: Dust carefully with soft cloth. No leafshine.

If they are not kept in good light, the leaves of a Freckle face plant will lose their attractive pink markings. Bright sunlight, however, will burn them so if they are in a sunny window, make sure the light is filtered through a fine net curtain. Leaf markings vary from tiny pink dots to larger, more widely spaced patches, all on a green background.

Humidity

Humidity is important all the year round. Spraying may damage the leaves so stand pot on saucer of pebbles almost covered in water. Don't let pot base touch the water or roots will become waterlogged.

Or pot can be placed in outer container with damp peat packed between.

Leaves lose their markings. Too dark. Move to lighter position in window but out of direct sun.

Burn marks on leaves. Direct sun. Move away from sunny window. Or leafshine damage. Do not use.

*.eaves droop and look *dull*. Too cold or water used *oo cold*. Move to warmer *·lace*, over 65°F (18°C) and *vater in winter with tepid *vater*.

Leaves turn yellow and drop off. Too wet, overwatered. Allow to dry out before watering again, then water less often. In winter once a week is sufficient, so that top half of soil dries out.

Leaves pale with brown scales. Scale insect. Remove with cotton wool dipped in methylated spirits or spray with systemic insecticide every 14 days until clear.

what goes wrong

Leaves curl inwards and go dry and papery. Too hot and dry. Place in cooler, more airy position (under 75°F, 24°C) and stand on saucer of damp pebbles to improve humidity. If soil dry, add water.

Impatiens walleriana

Busy Lizzie

This is one of the easiest plants to grow indoors. It roots in water, grows very vigorously, and has brilliant coloured flowers. It can be kept from year to year, but as it tends to become leggy, sprawly and untidy, it is better either to take new cuttings each spring or to grow new plants from seed. *Impatiens walleriana* is the usual Busy Lizzie and produces plenty of pink or red flowers. New hybrids with multi-coloured foliage have been introduced. These may be treated in the same way but require slightly higher winter temperatures.

Light: Likes direct sunshine. A sunny windowsill ideal position.

Temperature: Winter minimum 55°F (13°C), though prefers 65°F (18°C). Summer maximum 72°F (22°C).

Water: 2–3 times a week in summer. Every 10 days in winter to keep on dry side, giving less if temperature drops below minimum.

Humidity: No spraying, as may cause fungus disease and mark flowers. Stand pot on saucer of wet pebbles when temperature near or over summer maximum.

Feeding: Once a week when growing in summer with houseplant food diluted in water. Use half as much food as maker recommends.

Soil: Loam-based No. 3 compost.

Repotting: Annually after first year; it flowers better when pot-bound so do not put in too large a pot. Is best to repropagate each spring.

Cleaning: Use feather duster, or put out in rain in summer, shaking surplus water off before bringing plant back inside. No leafshine.

Busy Lizzies come in all shades of pink and red, some now with reddish or variegated leaves. Healthy plants should be compact, with well-coloured leaves and, in summer, a mass of bright flowers. Old plants tend to become untidy, with straggly, fleshy stems but they are easy to propagate from either seeds or cuttings.

Spotty burn marks on leaves and flowers. Leafshine damage. Do not use. Clean with feather duster.

Leaves turn pale, stems grow long and straggly. Needs feeding or repotting. Repot in spring with fresh soil and feed once a week when growing with half-strength food.

White insects fly away when plant is touched. Whitefly. Spray with derris or pyrethrum every 14 days until clear.

Plant collapses and leaves curl. Leaves and stems start to rot. Too cold and too humid. May be fatal but allow to dry out before watering again and move to warmer place, around 65°F (18°C). Do not spray.

Cuttings

Busy Lizzie cuttings root easily in water.

1. Prepare shallow jar filled ⅔ with water, with 3–4 pieces of charcoal in bottom. Cover with foil held by rubber band and pierced with holes to take stems.

2. Remove 3in (8cm) side shoot from plant, cutting where shoot joins main stem. Push stem through foil into water. When new roots form, repot in small pot and cover with polythene for 3 or 4 days to give extra humidity.

No flowers appear. Too dark. Move into light window, in direct sun.

Plant grows straggly with no leaves on bottom stems. Too old. Take cuttings to grow new plants.

Sooty deposits on leaves. Mould from greenfly infection. Wipe off mould with cotton-wool soaked in fungicide and spray every 14 days with diluted malathion until clear.

Leaves distorted and sticky with green insects. Greenfly. Spray every 14 days with derris or pyrethrum until clear.

what goes wrong

Leaves turn pale and have webs underneath. Red spider mite. Spray with diluted malathion every 14 days until clear.

Leaves dry out, curl and die. Too hot and dry, air too dry. Move to cooler place, not more than 72°F (22°C). Water 2 or 3 times a week in summer to keep compost moist and provide humidity.

Leaves turn pale and fall off. Too cold. Move to warmer place, preferably 65°F (18°C).

White powdery mould on leaves and stems. Fungal infection. Allow to dry out and move plant to warmer place, above 55°F (13°C) at least. Spray once with systemic fungicide.

343

Iris reticulata

Dwarf iris

Most members of the Iris family grow too tall for pot cultivation, but there are several Dwarf irises which are excellent for growing indoors. All grow from bulbs, which should be planted in early autumn for flowering in late winter to mid-spring. Plant 6–8 bulbs in a 5in (12cm) pot or bowl, covering bulbs in soil. Unlike many other bulbs, Irises do not need to be kept in a dark place after potting up. Keep in a cool, light position, such as a shady windowsill, until ready for flowering, then move into a well lit situation. Take care not to overfeed Dwarf irises, or they will produce new offsets but no flowers.

Light: Moderate light during growing period, then full light for flowering. Protect from direct sunlight while in flower.
Temperature: Keep cool, 40–45°F (4–7°C) while growing, then maximum 55–60°F (13–16°C) for flowering.
Water: Soak compost after planting, then water weekly to keep compost moist. Water 2–3 times a week during flowering.
Humidity: Cool, dry conditions essential. Do not spray.
Feeding: If planning to save bulbs for growing again, feed every 10 days with liquid houseplant food diluted to maker's recommended strength. Start when flower bud forms, stop when leaves die down.
Soil: Loam-based No. 2 potting compost or special bulb fibre.
After flowering: Cut back flowering stems after all flowering is over, but allow foliage to die back. Gradually decrease watering. Cut back yellowed foliage, lift bulb, separate any offsets, and store parent bulb for potting up or planting out in early autumn. Offsets can be planted in the garden and will flower in 2–3 years.

Dwarf irises are one of the easiest bulbs to grow in pots or bowls. *Iris reticulata, Iris danfordiae, Iris bakeriana* and *Iris histriodes* are all suitable. All grow to 4–8in (10–20cm) high and produce exotic-looking flowers in late winter or spring. Flowers are usually purple or blue, often with white markings.

Patchy surface on leaves, fine webs underneath. Red spider mite. Dip cotton bud in diluted malathion and wipe over all the leaves. Repeat in 14 days to kill any hatched eggs.

Long strips missing from edges of leaves. Iris sawfly grub, which usually only attacks plants grown outdoors. Spray with derris.

No flowers appear. Bulb may have been diseased, of poor quality, or not fed in previous season. Always choose firm, healthy bulbs from a reliable grower. Feed regularly if intending to grow on bulbs for another year.

344

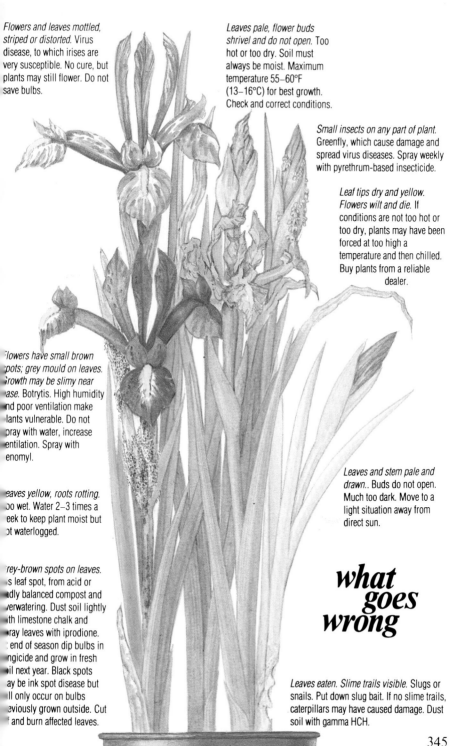

Flowers and leaves mottled, striped or distorted. Virus disease, to which irises are very susceptible. No cure, but plants may still flower. Do not save bulbs.

Leaves pale, flower buds shrivel and do not open. Too hot or too dry. Soil must always be moist. Maximum temperature 55–60°F (13–16°C) for best growth. Check and correct conditions.

Small insects on any part of plant. Greenfly, which cause damage and spread virus diseases. Spray weekly with pyrethrum-based insecticide.

Leaf tips dry and yellow. Flowers wilt and die. If conditions are not too hot or too dry, plants may have been forced at too high a temperature and then chilled. Buy plants from a reliable dealer.

Flowers have small brown spots; grey mould on leaves. Growth may be slimy near base. Botrytis. High humidity and poor ventilation make plants vulnerable. Do not spray with water, increase ventilation. Spray with benomyl.

Leaves yellow, roots rotting. Too wet. Water 2–3 times a week to keep plant moist but not waterlogged.

Grey-brown spots on leaves. Is leaf spot, from acid or badly balanced compost and overwatering. Dust soil lightly with limestone chalk and spray leaves with iprodione. At end of season dip bulbs in fungicide and grow in fresh soil next year. Black spots may be ink spot disease but will only occur on bulbs previously grown outside. Cut and burn affected leaves.

Leaves and stem pale and drawn.. Buds do not open. Much too dark. Move to a light situation away from direct sun.

what goes wrong

Leaves eaten. Slime trails visible. Slugs or snails. Put down slug bait. If no slime trails, caterpillars may have caused damage. Dust soil with gamma HCH.

345

Jasmine

This is a winter flowering plant producing hundreds of tiny white star-like flowers with an attractive scent. Often confused with *Stephanotis floribunda*, this variety of Jasmine requires quite cool conditions. It is best grown in a greenhouse or conservatory and brought into the house when in flower. When flowering is over, it should be pruned back by half to encourage it to form a compact shape the following year. In the summer, the leading shoots should be progressively pinched out every month to encourage side shoots to grow.

The Jasmine is a winter-flowering plant which produces a mass of tiny, star-shaped white or pink flowers. Dry atmospheres quickly cause both flowers and foliage to shrivel, so spray daily in centrally heated rooms.

Light: Full diffused daylight. Direct summer sun should be avoided as the plant will quickly dry out.

Temperature: Best at 60°F (16°C), and not more than 65°F (18°C) with good ventilation in summer, and 55°F (13°C) when flowering in winter: any hotter and the plant will turn brown. Minimum temperature at any time is 45-50°F (7-10°C).

Water: Every 4 or 5 days when in flower; 2 or 3 times a week in summer, keeping compost always moist, but not standing in water. In winter, water only when compost surface dried out, except while flowering.

Humidity: Spray daily if atmosphere dry, avoiding open flowers. Plant pot in another pot with moist peat between.

Feeding: Every 14 days in spring and summer with liquid houseplant food diluted to maker's instructions.

Soil: 3 parts loam-based No.2 with 1 part peat added.

Repotting: In early spring when flowering finished, after pruning. Main growing tips of the foliage, which grows in spring and summer, should be pinched out monthly until end of summer.

Cleaning: Humidity spraying adequate. No leafshine.

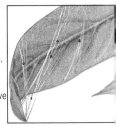

Leaves pale with webs underneath. Red spider mite. Remove webs with damp cloth or sponge, then spray with diluted malathion, especially under leaves. Repeat every 14 days until symptoms disappear. Improve humidity by standing pot on saucer of wet pebbles.

Training round a hoop

1. Push ends of wire hoop or thin cane so that they are ⅔ down pot on opposite sides. Bend plant stem to one side of hoop and gently twist around.

2. To secure plant to hoop, tie twine to one end of hoop and thread it along, looping it loosely around stem. Do not tie knots or stem may be damaged.

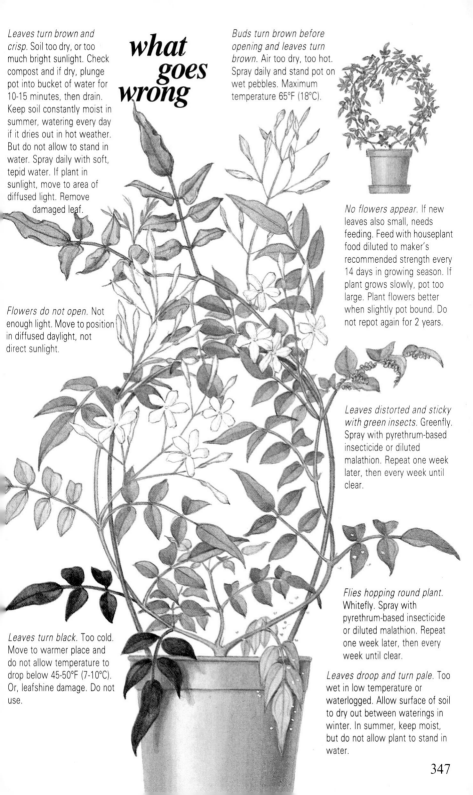

Leaves turn brown and crisp. Soil too dry, or too much bright sunlight. Check compost and if dry, plunge pot into bucket of water for 10-15 minutes, then drain. Keep soil constantly moist in summer, watering every day if it dries out in hot weather. But do not allow to stand in water. Spray daily with soft, tepid water. If plant in sunlight, move to area of diffused light. Remove damaged leaf.

what goes wrong

Buds turn brown before opening and leaves turn brown. Air too dry, too hot. Spray daily and stand pot on wet pebbles. Maximum temperature 65°F (18°C).

No flowers appear. If new leaves also small, needs feeding. Feed with houseplant food diluted to maker's recommended strength every 14 days in growing season. If plant grows slowly, pot too large. Plant flowers better when slightly pot bound. Do not repot again for 2 years.

Flowers do not open. Not enough light. Move to position in diffused daylight, not direct sunlight.

Leaves distorted and sticky with green insects. Greenfly. Spray with pyrethrum-based insecticide or diluted malathion. Repeat one week later, then every week until clear.

Flies hopping round plant. Whitefly. Spray with pyrethrum-based insecticide or diluted malathion. Repeat one week later, then every week until clear.

Leaves turn black. Too cold. Move to warmer place and do not allow temperature to drop below 45-50°F (7-10°C). Or, leafshine damage. Do not use.

Leaves droop and turn pale. Too wet in low temperature or waterlogged. Allow surface of soil to dry out between waterings in winter. In summer, keep moist, but do not allow plant to stand in water.

347

Kalanchoe blossfeldiana

This popular species, often found in florists, grows up to 12in (30cm) high with wide, fleshy green leaves. Its small red, yellow or pink flowers grow in brilliant clusters from autumn through to the spring although some can now be bought in flower at almost any time. Another good species is *Kalanchoe tomentosa* also known as the Panda plant, with velvety, silvery-green leaves with brown edges. Also available are *K. rhombopilosa* and *K. fedschtenkoi*, with lilac-purple leaves and *K. tubiflorum*, which has tiny leaf-plantlets.

Light: Sunny conditions for best leaf colour and good flowers.

Temperature: A minimum of 45°F (7°C) but most will grow better at 50°F (10°C). Give fresh air in summer months.

Water: Fortnightly in spring and summer, weekly in hottest weather if soil dries out rapidly. Tail off in autumn and if under 45°F (7°C), keep dry in winter. If at 50°F (10°C) or over, water once a month, just enough to stop leaves from shrivelling.

Feeding: Use high potash fertilizer 2 or 3 times in the summer.

Soil: Use good loam-based No. 2 potting compost, or soil-less compost, with 20% coarse, gritty sand.

Repotting: Every spring in size larger pot.

Propagation: Take whole shoots or leaf cuttings in spring or summer. Cut shoots with a sharp knife; ease leaves off gently with as much of base as possible. Dust with hormone rooting powder, leave to dry for 3 days, then lay on fresh, dry compost. Water after 3 weeks when roots should have formed. Some Kalanchoes, (also called Bryophyllums), make little plantlets on the leaves. These may be taken off at any time and treated in the same way.

Kalanchoe tomentosa, the Panda plant, has slightly furry leaves. It can be propagated easily from leaves which if gently pulled off will root on dry soil and produce several small new plants. *Kalanchoe blossfeldiana,* right, is better propagated from cuttings.

Leaves distorted as though virus infected. Usually caused by excessive use of insecticides. Use pyrethrum-based insecticides. Not fatal.

Round pieces missing from edges of leaves. Vine weevil. Sprinkle insecticide powder around base of pot and water soil with systemic insecticide to kill larvae in stem. Or slice stem from base until larvae found and reroot.
(See Introduction).

348

Little new growth after flowering. Needs repotting or feeding. Repot each spring and feed 2–3 times in summer.

Root mealy bug
1. Check roots when repotting for root mealy bug (white woolly patches).

2. If found, wash all soil off roots under tap and swirl in insecticide diluted to maker's instructions.

3. Leave to dry for 2–3 days, then replant in fresh compost and clean pot. Do not water for 2–3 weeks.

what goes wrong

Mildewed and blackened patches on leaves. Too humid. Dust with flowers of sulphur and move to more airy place. Do not get water on leaves. If too cold and wet, stems turn black and leaves fall. Keep dry in winter unless over 50°F (10°C), when give just enough water monthly to stop leaves from shrivelling.

Stems straggly, young leaves pale or yellowish-green. Too dark. Move gradually over 2 weeks to sunny spot. If too hot and wet in winter, stems may grow tall and leaves droop. Keep around 50°F (10°C) in rest period.

White woolly patches among leaves. Mealy bug. Remove with small paintbrush dipped in methylated spirits, and spray with pyrethrum-based insecticide. Repeat 2 or 3 times in growing season.

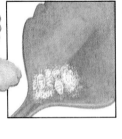

Leaves dry up and fall. Too dry or too cold. Check conditions. Best about 50°F (10°C) in winter. In summer, water when soil dries out. In winter if over 50°F (10°C) water monthly. If all conditions correct, check roots for root mealy bug (see above).

349

Kleinia tomentosa

Several members of this genus are classed as succulents, and *Kleinia tomentosa*, sometimes labelled *Senecio haworthii*, is one of the most attractive. It has stark white leaves made from a dense covering of clinging, spiderweb-like wool. A very sunny spot is needed to produce the yellow flowers in cultivation, as this plant comes from South Africa and is well adapted to withstand the strong sunlight it receives there. It will grow to between 10 and 12in (25–30cm) tall and 4–6in (10–15cm) across. Other species worth looking out for are: *Kleinia* (*Senecio*) *medley-woodii*, with flat woolly leaves and *rowleyanus*, with hanging stems and pea-like leaves.

Kleinia tomentosa. A well grown plant will have leaves all the way up the stem. It needs careful watering: if it is too dry, the lower leaves will fall, if too wet the roots will rot. Make sure it is planted in a compost containing plenty of grit so that excess water can drain off quickly.

Light: Full sunshine is needed to bring out the best colouring.

Temperature: A minimum of 45°F (7°C) is needed. Give fresh air in summer.

Water: Water fortnightly in spring and summer, but allow to dry out between waterings. Water weekly in the hottest weather. Tail off in autumn and in winter give just enough to keep soil from becoming dust dry – about once a month. See also Introduction.

Feeding: Use high potash fertilizer 3 or 4 times in the summer.

Soil: Use good loam-based No. 2 compost, or soil-less compost, with 30% coarse, gritty sand.

Repotting: Every spring in size larger pot until 5 or 6in (15cm) is reached. Then gently shake soil off roots and repot in same size clean pot with fresh soil. Do not water for 2 weeks after repotting.

Propagation: Cuttings may be taken in spring and summer, dried off for 2 or 3 days after dusting lightly with hormone rooting powder and placed in fresh, dry compost.

Leaves wrinkle and fall, leaving topknot on each stem. Stems shrivel. Too dry or too hot in winter. In winter water once a month if leaves start to wrinkle and fall and keep around 50°F (10°C). In spring and summer give more water each time, but allow to dry out between waterings. Give fresh air in hot weather.

what goes wrong

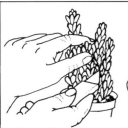

Taking cuttings
1. In spring or early summer, cut off stem about 2in (5cm) from tip, between leaves.

2. If no bare stem shows, remove lowest leaf. Dust cut ends with hormone rooting powder to prevent infection. Leave to dry for 2 days.

3. Place on surface of dry compost and do not water until roots appear in 2–3 weeks time.

Long spaces between leaves, little white covering on new ones. Too dark. Move into full sun over 2 weeks.

Leaves turn black and fall, stem black and soft. Too cold and wet or too humid. Keep warmer, above 45°F (7°C) in winter. Pare off blackened part of stem and dust with fungicide. In winter give just enough water once a month to prevent leaf fall and in summer always allow to dry out between waterings.

Little new growth, white woolly patches on roots. Root mealy bug. Wash all soil off roots, swirl roots in contact insecticide and allow to dry before repotting in fresh compost and clean pot. Leave dry for 2 weeks.

Leaves shrivel and have brown scorch marks. Too hot and stuffy, sunscorched. Give fresh air in summer and move out of bright sunlight. Reintroduce gradually over 2 weeks.

White woolly patches among leaves. Mealy bug. Remove with small paintbrush dipped in methylated spirits and spray with contact or systemic insecticides. Repeat 2 or 3 times in growing season.

Leaves on lower stem fall, little new growth. Needs repotting urgently. Repot with fresh compost each spring.

351

Cape cowslip

Providing they are kept cool, Cape cowslips will last in flower for many weeks and when massed in a large pot or bowl will make a very impressive display. The hanging variety, *Lachenalia pendula* has small red flowers on drooping stems and makes a good plant for an indoor basket. Plant bulbs as early in autumn as possible, 5–6 to a 4½in (11cm) pot, covered with ½in (1cm) compost. Place pots outside or in a cool room where there is plenty of light and in early winter bring them into a room where the temperature is no higher than 55°F (13°C) to flower.

Cape cowslips come from South Africa and flower in late winter or early spring. There are two types: *Lachenalia tricolor* has clusters of red, yellow or orange flowers on 12in (30cm) upright stems while *Lachenalia pendula* has small red flowers on drooping stems, making it ideal for a hanging basket.

Light: Full sun essential at all times, except when in flower. Shade blooms from midday sun.

Temperature: Minimum temperature 48°F (7°C), then 55°F (13°C) maximum for flowering. Cape Cowslip will not survive any degree of frost.

Water: Keep compost just barely moist after planting. Increase watering when shoots are visible. Bulbs rot quickly if soil is too wet, so avoid overwatering.

Humidity: Dry, cool airy atmosphere is best. Do not spray.

Feeding: Feed with dilute liquid garden fertilizer at maker's recommended strength, beginning when about 4in (10cm) tall, then weekly intervals until flowering is over.

Soil: Soil-less potting compost or a mixture of 2 parts loam-based No.3 potting compost with 1 part peat.

After flowering: Remove dead flowerheads, but do not cut foliage. Gradually reduce watering. When leaves are dry and withered cut back to soil level. Leave bulbs in pots in a cool, dry place in full sun. Repot in fresh compost the following autumn. Bulbs will bloom 2–3 years, and increase by offsets.

Stems floppy with few flowers. Much too hot. Move to a place with maximum temperature 55°F (13°C).

Plant is healthy but growth is very slow. Too cold. Move to a warmer place, around 50°F (10°C) best. If no flower stem appears, too dark. Move plant into full sunlight until flowers open, then shade from bright midday sun.

Leaves have dark spots or marks like warts. Natural appearance of foliage, so no action needed.

Bulbs have not produced offsets or offsets very small when bulbs are lifted. Lack of nutrients in compost. Feed weekly with dilute liquid garden fertilizer. Bulbs will probably flower another year.

Bulbs soft or mouldy when lifted for repotting. Bulbs not dried off and ripened. Stop watering after leaves are cut back. Discard unhealthy bulbs.

Small wingless insects on buds. Greenfly. Spray with pyrethrum-based insecticide. Repeat at 10-day intervals until clear.

Mould on flowers. Humidity too high. Keep in a cool, airy place and do not spray.

Brown edges on flowers. Sun too hot. Protect from midday sun while in flower.

what goes wrong

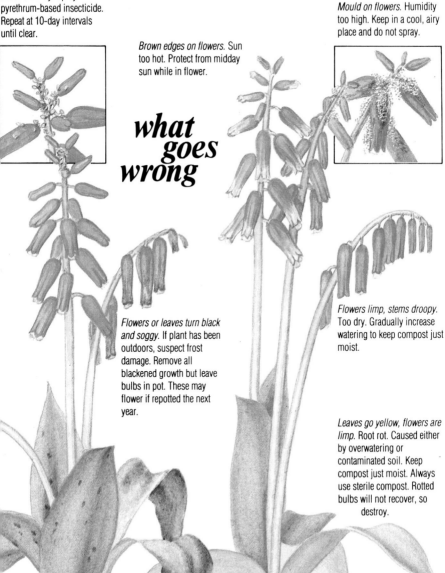

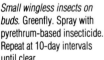

Flowers or leaves turn black and soggy. If plant has been outdoors, suspect frost damage. Remove all blackened growth but leave bulbs in pot. These may flower if repotted the next year.

Flowers limp, stems droopy. Too dry. Gradually increase watering to keep compost just moist.

Leaves go yellow, flowers are limp. Root rot. Caused either by overwatering or contaminated soil. Keep compost just moist. Always use sterile compost. Rotted bulbs will not recover, so destroy.

Lapageria rosea

Chilean bell flower

This beautiful evergreen climber produces spectacular waxy, translucent, rosy-crimson flowers which appear from late summer until late autumn. It will grow to 20ft (6m) if unpruned and can be used in the greenhouse to climb over an archway, as the flowers hang downwards. In the home, it is best trained on a trellis and kept in relatively small pots to keep the roots compact and pruned by one third after flowering. This plant is like a magnet to many of the common houseplant pests, including greenfly, which will attack young shoots in spring, thrips, mealy bug and scale insect.

The Chilean bell flower is an evergreen climber whose spectacular rosy crimson flowers hang down gracefully. If allowed to grow unchecked, it will easily reach 20ft (6m) so should be trained on a trellis and regularly pruned.

Light: Diffused daylight in summer, avoiding direct sun. Increase light in winter, including full sun.

Temperature: Maintain 65–70°F (18–21°C) in summer, with maximum 75°F (24°C). Winter minimum 55°F (13°C).

Water: At least twice a week in summer, to keep always moist. Never allow pot to stand in water. Reduce to weekly in winter, allowing compost surface to dry out between waterings.

Humidity: Spray daily in spring and summer until flowers appear. Maintain humidity when flowering by standing pot on a saucer of pebbles almost covered with water. Do not spray in autumn or winter.

Feeding: Every 14 days in spring and summer with liquid houseplant food diluted to half maker's instructions.

Soil: 3 parts fibrous peat, 1 part loam-based No.2 and 1 part equal quantities of charcoal and peat.

Repotting: In early spring for young plants, into pots one size larger to a maximum 7in (18cm). Then repot into same sized pot.

Cleaning: Spray with soft water. No leafshine.

Leaves sticky with green insects. Greenfly. Spray every week with diluted malathion to prevent attack; greenfly can quickly damage this plant.

Whole plant turns black. Leafshine damage. Do not use. Clean only by carefully dusting with feather duster or camel hair brush.

Plant fails to flower. Too dark. Move into good light position. Will stand full sunlight except in summer, when it will be too hot.

Webs on flowers and leaves. Red spider mite. Remove webs with damp cloth or sponge, then spray with diluted malathion, especially under leaves. Repeat every 14 days until symptoms disappear. Improve humidity by standing pot on saucer of wet pebbles.

Discs on leaves. Scale insect. Spray underside of leaves with diluted malathion and after 48 hours remove discs with thumbnail. Repeat every week for 4 weeks until clear.

what goes wrong

New leaves small, no flowers appear. Needs feeding. Feed every week in growing and flowering season with houseplant food diluted to maker's recommended strength.

Leaves scorched. Caused by spraying in bright sunlight. Spray only in early morning or evening if plant is in full light.

Leaves eaten away. Thrips. Spray thoroughly with diluted malathion and repeat after 1 week. If in greenhouse, fumigate.

Leaves turn black and stems rot, especially in winter. Botrytis, plant too cold and damp. Spray with fungicide, then place in warmer position, at least 55°F (13°C) and spray less often. Allow compost surface to dry out between waterings in winter.

Flies hopping around plant. Whitefly. Spray with pyrethrum-based insecticide or diluted malathion. Repeat one week later, then weekly until clear.

Plant goes limp, especially in summer. Soil too dry or too much hot sunlight. Plunge pot into bucket of water for 10-15 minutes, then drain. Keep soil constantly moist in summer. Keep out of hot summer sun.

Leaves flop and dry out. Air too dry or too hot. Spray daily with soft tepid water and provide extra humidity by standing pot on saucer of damp pebbles. Best kept at 65-70°F (18-21°C) and not more than 75°F (24°C).

White cotton-wool patches where leaves join stem. Mealy bug. Spray with diluted malathion and remove bugs and 'wool' with tweezers. Repeat every 14 days until symptoms disappear. Or, paint bugs with methylated spirits and remove with tweezers.

Flower buds fall off. Too cold. Move to warmer place, at least 55°F (13°C).

355

Lily

Lilies are among the most beautiful and elegant of all flowering bulbs. Although most are hardy and suitable only for growing outdoors, there are now several species of Asiatic and Oriental Hybrids suitable for growing in pots or containers. Lilies can be bought in pots in bud stage and need only full light and plenty of water to bloom. They can also be grown from bulbs planted up in winter, in individual 4in (10cm) pots. Keep in a cool, light position, and gradually give more water as growth increases. Pot-grown lilies will rarely flower again, so discard when all blooms have finished. Hardy lilies such as the Mid-Century hybrid 'Enchantment' can also be grown in pots without heat for early summer flowering. They need full sun at all times, otherwise treat as below.

Lilies are easy to grow in pots providing the right varieties are chosen. Recently developed Asiatic and Oriental Hybrid lilies grow to a height of 18–24in (45–60cm) and produce magnificent bell-shaped flowers in a cluster of 4–8 blooms on a single stem. Flowers are usually white or cream with red, pink or purple markings.

Light: Full light at all times, but shade flowers from hot sun.

Temperature: Does best at 55–65°F (13–18°C) but can tolerate higher or lower temperatures. Will not survive frost or extreme heat.

Water: Compost must be moist at all times. Water twice a week after potting, increasing as growth increases. Copious water needed while in bloom, daily if necessary.

Humidity: Cool, well ventilated position preferred. If weather is very hot, spray around flowers in evening.

Feeding: Use liquid houseplant food at maker's recommended strength every 10 days if in loam-based compost, every 5 days in soil-less.

Soil: Either loam-based No.2 or soil-less.

After flowering: Flowers bloom in succession. Remove dead flowerheads to encourage stronger blooms. Pot-grown plants will not flower again.

Leaves pale and small, few buds. Needs feeding. Increase number but not strength of feeds. If growth generally weak, may be too dark or too hot. Move to cool, light position. If leaves also limp, thrips. Dust soil with gamma HCH.

what goes wrong

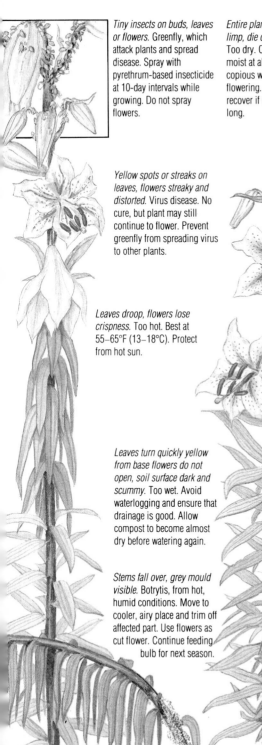

Tiny insects on buds, leaves or flowers. Greenfly, which attack plants and spread disease. Spray with pyrethrum-based insecticide at 10-day intervals while growing. Do not spray flowers.

Entire plant is limp, flowers limp, die quickly or fall off. Too dry. Compost must be moist at all times, and copious water needed during flowering. Flowers will recover if not too dry for too long.

Yellow spots or streaks on leaves, flowers streaky and distorted. Virus disease. No cure, but plant may still continue to flower. Prevent greenfly from spreading virus to other plants.

Holes in leaves, buds or flowers. Small red beetles present. Lily beetle, which usually attack plants grown outdoors but may attack pot plants. Spray with malathion. Repeat in 10 days.

Leaves droop, flowers lose crispness. Too hot. Best at 55–65°F (13–18°C). Protect from hot sun.

Flowers pale and may be brown around edges. Too much sun. Shade flowers from direct sun, especially if weather is hot.

Leaves turn quickly yellow from base flowers do not open, soil surface dark and scummy. Too wet. Avoid waterlogging and ensure that drainage is good. Allow compost to become almost dry before watering again.

Early leaves black at tips. Frosted. Do not leave pots outside in frosty weather. Leaves will recover, but tips will be bleached.

Stems fall over, grey mould visible. Botrytis, from hot, humid conditions. Move to cooler, airy place and trim off affected part. Use flowers as cut flower. Continue feeding bulb for next season.

Holes in young growth. Slime trails present. Slugs. Put down slug baits and remove any slugs seen. Keep pellets away from pets and children.

357

Lithops

This is a wonderful genus of South African plants, adapted to survive long, extreme droughts. They are good indoor or greenhouse plants but the watering instructions must be carefully followed. In their winter rest period new leaves grow and push through the old ones which shrivel and dry up completely. It is most important that the plants receive no water at this time. There are many species and forms with differing colours and patterning. The flowers are either yellow or white, appearing in late summer or early autumn. Good species include *L. optica* fa. *rubra*, with purple-pink stems, *L. dorotheae*, *L. otzeniana*, *L. werneri* and *L. lesliei*.

Light: Maximum sunshine is needed for these plants to ensure compact growth, good colouring and flower production.

Temperature: Low temperatures can be tolerated in the winter, but a minimum of 40°F (4°C) is safer. In summer give fresh air whenever possible.

Water: Start when the shrivelling pair of leaves are absolutely dry and crisp to the touch, usually in early summer, giving water about once a fortnight, or weekly in the really hot months after this. Stop altogether in the early winter, and do not start again until leaves have dried once more, in early summer. See also Introduction.

Feeding: Feed twice during the summer, if not repotted in spring, using high potash fertilizer. Feeding is not needed if plant has been repotted.

Soil: Use good loam-based No. 2 potting compost, or soil-less compost, with about 40% coarse, gritty sand.

Repotting: Every spring in size larger half-pot, being careful not to disturb roots.

Propagation: Usually from seed, although whole stems may be rooted in springtime.

Lithops dorotheae. This is one of the most popular 'Living stone' plants, chosen for its intricate markings. Individual heads grow to around 1in (2½cm) and are often planted with a group of differently coloured species in a shallow pan with pebbles between them to mimic their natural state. If grown in this way, make sure that the pan has drainage holes.

Leaves become elongated and lose colour. Too dark. Move into full sunlight gradually over 2 weeks. May also occur if kept too hot and wet in winter. Try to keep below 50°F (10°C) in dry soil.

Plants in greenhouse found out of pots, with triangular marks on leaf-ends. Bird damage. They often mistake them for berries. Repot and keep birds out of greenhouse.

1. If plant has formed clump, remove single heads in spring.

2. Dust base with hormone rooting powder and leave to dry for 2–3 days.

3. Place on surface of dry compost and do not water until roots appear.

Removing dead flowers
Do not pull away dead flower heads but leave them to shrivel away, only picking out by hand when they pull away easily. Pulling them out earlier may damage leaves.

what goes wrong

Two pairs of leaves actively growing at the same time on each head. Caused by watering before old leaves have shrivelled. When old leaves die, stop watering until they have dried up completely.

White woolly patches in crevices. Mealy bug. Remove with small paintbrush dipped in methylated spirits, and spray with contact or systemic insecticide. Repeat every 2–3 weeks until clear.

No flowers. Not enough light or watered at wrong time. Check conditions. If in shade, move over 2 weeks into full sunlight. Keep dry from early winter to early summer.

Plant turns black and soft. Too wet in summer or in winter too cold and humid; roots rotting. Keep above 40°F (4°C) in winter in dry atmosphere. Plant may be dead but remove from pot and inspect roots. If base rotting, pare away soft parts (see Introduction).

Leaves wither, turn brown and die. Natural. Each pair of leaves lasts only 1 year, then dies down. Do not remove old leaves until they pull away easily.

Leaves have burn marks. Moved into sun too quickly. Shade from midday sun in early summer.

Plant shows little sign of growth, and on repotting white woolly patches are found on roots. Root mealy bug. Wash all soil off roots, swirl roots in contact insecticide, and allow to dry before repotting in fresh compost and washed pot. Leave dry for two weeks before watering again.

Livistona chinensis

Chinese fan palm

This house palm, popular in many countries, is very decorative when young, with fan-like leaves divided half-way to the centre into long pointed segments growing on a stiff stem which rises from the centre of the plant. A mature plant can grow as high as 30ft (8m) with leaves 6ft (over 1½m) across. In their natural habitat, the leaves of some varieties are used for roofing and hats, and the leaf bases for rope. Although almost hardy, it will not tolerate frost. As a houseplant it is usually about 3ft (90cm) tall when bought. It grows very slowly to about 6ft (1½m), its trunk forming from the dead leaf sheaths.

Light: Full light, though keep out of summer sun. Shade slows growth.
Temperature: Winter minimum 50°F (10°C), summer minimum 60°F (15°C). Best all-round temperature is 65–70°F (18–22°C), with 75°F (24°C) summer maximum.
Water: Every day in summer, including trunk, to keep soil moist at all times. In winter once or twice a week.
Humidity: Spray once a week. Stand young plant on saucer of pebbles almost covered with water to increase humidity.
Feeding: Weekly in spring and summer with houseplant food diluted with water according to maker's instructions.
Soil: Equal parts loam-based No. 3, decayed stable manure. Good drainage essential.
Repotting: Annually in spring into well-drained pots for young plants. Change topsoil for larger, adult plants. Feed after changing topsoil but after complete repotting, do not feed for 2 weeks.
Cleaning: Wipe with damp cloth or sponge. No leafshine.

The Chinese fan palm has leathery, slightly glossy leaves which grow like large green fans. The pointed segments are joined together from the leaf base to about half way up and have wispy threads hanging between the points.

Brown discs on leaves and stems. Scale insect. Paint with methylated spirits and remove with thumbnail. Stems but not leaves can be sprayed with malathion every 14 days until clear.

what goes wrong

White woolly patches where frond joins trunk. Mealy bug. Water soil with liquid malathion diluted as recommended. Spray stems with same solution but do not spray leaves or they will 'burn'.

Webs under leaves. Red spider mite. Wipe with cloth dipped in pyrethrum-based insecticide diluted to half normal strength every week until clear. Do not use nicotine or malathion or leaves will burn.

No new fronds grow. Soil nutrients used up. If young plant, repot in spring. If adult, change topsoil. Feed regularly.

New fronds do not open. Too dark or needs water. Move to lighter room or place near light window. Keep moist in summer, watering every day if soil dries quickly. Do not stand in water.

Leaves grow slowly and turn yellow. Too wet, badly drained. Allow to dry out before watering again and check drainage in pot.

New leaf tips turn brown. Some browning natural but if all tips brown, needs watering. Keep moist in summer.

Brown patches on leaves. Leafshine damage. Do not use.

..eaves turn black. Too cold. If ..utside for summer, bring in .. temperature falls below ..0°F (10°C).

Leaves dry out. Too hot. Do not exceed 75°F (24°C) and in summer keep room well ventilated. 65–70°F (18–21°C) best. Oldest fronds will dry out eventually and if rest are healthy this is natural. Remove dead ones by cutting off with secateurs as close to trunk as possible.

361

Lobelia erinus

Lobelia

Lobelias are half hardy perennials but are invariably grown as annuals from seed sown as soon as the days start to lengthen. Trailing varieties are valuable for containers as they will clothe the side of a tub or trough and hang attractively from a basket or windowbox.

Light: Maximum at all stages. Outside up to 30% shade if light good for rest of the day.
Temperature: 60–65°F (16–18°C) for first month after sowing, reducing gradually to 45°F (7°C) before planting out. Protect from frost.
Water: Moist, not waterlogged.
Humidity: Spray in the evening if hot.
Soil: Well drained loam-based No. 2 or soil-less potting compost.
Feeding: Regular feeding every 10 days in soil or every 5 in soil-less. A liquid fertilizer containing more potash than nitrogen is desirable to keep the intensity of colour and prevent the plant succumbing to disease.
Propagation: Seed is very fine. Prepare tray and mix seed with half its volume of very fine sand. Sow thinly over whole surface of compost. Don't cover seed with compost, but place tray in plastic bag, seal, cover with several layers of newspaper and keep at 60–65°F (16–18°C). Uncover when germinated and prick out when large enough to handle. Plant out when frosts have finished and flowers nearly open.
Tidying: Remove stems which have turned brown from disease.
Varieties: Trailing: Sapphire, dark blue, white eye. Blue Cascade, light blue. Red Cascade, carmine. Compact varieties: Crystal Palace, rich deep blue with bronze foliage. Mrs Clibran, deep blue and white eye. Blue Gown, mid-blue. String of Pearls. mixed.

Lobelias are either dwarf, compact plants only 4–6in (10–15cm) high or trailers with stems up to 24in (60cm) long. The tiny flowers bloom over a very long season and may be white, crimson, violet and from light to very deep blue.

Leaves yellow with dark veining. Soil dark and sour. Waterlogged. Check drainage in container and allow soil to dry out before watering again,

Leaves small and grey-green. Needs feeding. Feed more often but do not increase strength of feed.

362

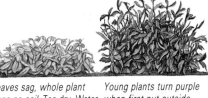

Leaves spotted with pale buff-coloured markings, which gradually join up until whole leaf is affected. Stems have streaky marks. Alternaria disease. Spray with iprodione and following week with benomyl. Alternate treatments every fortnight to prevent infection. Contaminated plants will continue to flower but will cease flowering earlier in the season than usual. Alternaria can be seed-borne so make sure purchased seed has been treated against it. But spores can also infect growing plants, especially if wet.

Leaves sag, whole plant flops on soil. Too dry. Water immediately then water more frequently so soil does not dry out.

Young plants turn purple when first put outside. Sudden cold. Plant growth will be checked, but will recover. Introduce plants to outdoors gradually. Protect from frost if out at night.

Seedlings or young plants suddenly wilt and stems are thin, cotton-like strands. Pythium disease or damping off. Remove affected plants and drench compost with soil fungicide.

what goes wrong

Puckered or distorted buds and growing points. Greenfly. Spray with general insecticide and repeat after 10 days. Do not spray in hot sunshine; wait until evening.

Leaves have papery markings on edges. Liquid fertilizer too strong. Always dilute to maker's recommended strength.

Leaves have white, dead edges. Caused by spraying insecticides in sunlight. Spray in the evening, when bees have finished visiting flowers.

Leaves have grey, dry patches. Frost damage. Protect young plants at night and harden off gradually. Lobelias will stand some frost if carefully hardened.

Flowers pale, stems soft. Feed does not contain right balance of potash and nitrogen. More potash than nitrogen is desirable. Check contents of fertilizer.

Fluffy grey mould on leaves or stems or whole crown. Botrytis. Carefully pick off affected areas and spray with benomyl or iprodione. While indoors keep plants in well ventilated position.

Lobivia

This genus of cacti comes from Bolivia (its name is an anagram of the country) but is also found in Argentina and Peru. It is outstanding for its large, freely produced flowers which come in a variety of colours from white through every shade of yellow, orange, pink, red and purple. *Lobivia maximiliana* (p.365) has bicoloured red and yellow flowers. They vary in appearance but are mostly globular plants, offsetting after 3–4 years to form clumps 6–8in (15–20cm) or more, with spines usually coloured brown or blackish. They are not at all difficult to grow and will usually flower if kept in a sunny place. Generally the more sun they receive the more flowers they will produce, although each bloom lasts only a day or two.

Lobivia jajoiana is one of the few species commonly seen which tends to stay solitary for some time and the only one with hooked spines. The flowers are brightly coloured and the black ring in the centre contrasts strikingly with the petals and with the creamy anthers which fill the cup of the flower.

Light: For maximum flower production keep on a sunny windowsill or in a greenhouse, where shading is unnecessary unless temperatures rise above 100°F (38°C). In poor light they soon grow out of shape and do not produce healthy new spines — or flowers.

Temperature: Keep above 40°F (4°C) in winter and below 100°F (38°C) in summer, giving them fresh air when possible.

Water: Water weekly in spring and summer, or fortnightly for plants in pots of 5in (13cm) or more. Always check soil has dried out from previous watering. Tail off watering in autumn to once every 3 weeks to a month, and keep dry in winter.

Feeding: Use a high potash fertilizer (as used for tomatoes) monthly in spring and summer.

Soil: Use 1 part coarse, gritty sand (not builders' or seashore) to 2 parts soil-less or good loam-based potting compost, No. 2 for small plants, No. 3 for large.

Repotting: In the early years these plants

Lobivia rebutioides var *chlorogana* is one of a complex group which are liable to nearly smother themselves with flowers. The blooms last barely a day or two but will come each year if the plant is potted on regularly into the next size of container and kept growing well.

should be repotted every year into slightly larger pots in spring, until they reach 5in (13cm) pots, when every other year will do. At this size they can be repotted into the same size pot. Shake off the old compost carefully and replace with new. Do not water for a fortnight after repotting.

Cleaning and pest control: Spray if dusty and incorporate an insecticide 2 or 3 times a year to combat pests.

Other species: The selection is considerable and the variation of types as wide as can be, from those with very few strong spines to those which are completely obscured by a dense spiny covering. Some have single heads which never grow more than 4in (10cm) tall, yet others grow in clumps up to 12in (30cm) or more across. Most flower easily and a good selection is as follows: *L. maximiliana* (below); *L. jajoiana*, with flowers varying from yellow, through orange to red, with a black throat; *L. rebutioides*, with yellow flowers; *L. backebergiana*, with carmine flowers which have a blue sheen to the petals; *L. winterana*, with long-tubed deep pink flowers; and *L. hastifera*, with pale pink flowers, white in the throat.

Removing dead flowers
It is advisable to remove dead flowers before autumn and winter. If left on the plant they may encourage rotting from the point of attachment or harbour mealy bugs.

If mealy bugs attack, remove wool with small paintbrush dipped in methylated spirits and spray plant with diluted malathion. Repeat in 10 days if not clear.

Lobivia maximiliana produces its striking red and yellow flowers in summer when it is 2in (5cm) across and 3–4 years old. They grow from the sides of the plant, beginning as small, furry buds. Once open they last for only a day or two.

L. maximiliana grows eventually to about 2½–3½in (6–8cm) tall and ½–2in (4–5cm) wide.

365

Mammillaria

Mammillarias come mainly from Mexico, where they grow in habitats which range from steep rock faces and ledges in the high mountains to sandy, flat areas within salt-spray distance of the sea. Over 200 species are known, varying from single acorn-sized plants to massive clumps that would fill a wheelbarrow. The flowers are every shade between white, yellow, pink, red and purple, produced freely by most species, growing in rings around the crown of the stems. Spines are arranged in geometric whorls and may be strong and sharp, like tentmakers' needles, or as thin and flexible as hairs; straight, curved, twisting or hooked like fish-hooks; sparse or so dense as to hide the plant's body completely; coloured from black through reds, browns and yellows to pure white, often supplemented by thick wool which gives a complete covering.

If repotted and fed regularly, *Mammillaria compressa* will form a clump 12in (30cm) or more across in about 10 years growing. The plant here is in a 15in (38cm) pan and is at least 15 years old.

Light: A sunny position, particularly in winter and spring when buds are formed.
Temperature: All but one or two species will be happy with a minimum winter temperature of 40°F (4°C), but 45°F (7°C) is safer; keep below 100°F (38°C) in summer and give fresh air whenever possible.
Water: Weekly in spring and summer, fortnightly for pots of 5in (13cm) or more. Monthly in autumn and keep dry in winter.
Feeding: Feed monthly in spring and summer with high potash fertilizer (as used for tomatoes).
Soil: Use 1 part coarse gritty sand (not builders' or seashore) to 2 parts soil-less or good loam-based No. 2 compost.
Repotting: Repot every year until plant fills 5in (13cm) pot, then every other year is sufficient unless plants outgrow their container. Use half-pots or pans except for species with thick tuberous roots.

Mammillaria candida is named for its dense covering of white spines. The shell-pink flowers appear after the plant has grown to about 3in (8cm) wide and tall, perhaps sooner if plenty of sunlight is available.

Cleaning and pest control: Spray once a month to keep dust-free and incorporate an insecticide 2 or 3 times a year to combat pests.

Other species: *Mammillaria zeilmanniana* (below), with its purple flowers is one of the most popular. It is impossible to list all the species available here and the following is only a selection of some of the most attractive and rewarding plants: *M. blossfeldiana*, hooked spines, carmine striped flowers; *M. bocasana*, white, hairy spines, cream or pink flowers; *M. candida*, white or pinkish spines, pale pink flowers; *M. carmenae*, dense yellow spines, white flowers; *M. compressa*, long white spines, deep pink flowers; *M. erythrosperma*, hooked spines, dusky pink flowers; *M. hahniana*, long white hairs, purplish-red flowers; *M. longiflora*, hooked spines, large pink flowers; *M. guelzowiana*, long hairs, hooked spines, large pink flowers, over 2in (5–6cm) across; *M. microhelia*, star-like spines, greenish or pink flowers; *M. prolifera*, clustering, yellow or brown spines, yellow flowers; *M. saboae*, tiny heads and spines, large pink flowers; *M. schiedeana*, soft golden spines, white flowers; *M. schwarzii*, dense white spines, cream flowers.

Mammillaria zeilmanniana flowers in spring and summer when it has reached about 1–1½in (3–4cm) tall. Flowers appear over a period of a month or so, each lasting for around a week. Offsets, producing their own flowers, cluster around its base when it is 2–3 years old and can be used for propagation. The plant grows to 2–2½in (5–6cm) tall, 1–1½in (3–4cm) wide in a pot.

Offsets
1. Remove offsets from around the base with a clean, sharp knife, cutting at narrowest point. Do not do this while plant is flowering. Offsets should be at least ½in (1cm) across.

2. Dust base with hormone rooting powder containing fungicide and leave to dry for at least 2 days. Then plant in fresh compost. Keep in a light place but do not water for 2–3 weeks, when roots will have developed.

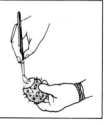

Maranta leuconeura

Prayer plant

This plant belongs to one of the most decorative families of houseplants. All have beautifully marked leaves, some looking almost as if they have been hand painted. Originating from the tropics, they need high humidity and often do best in bowls of mixed plants where a more humid atmosphere is created. The common name comes from the way that at night the young leaves curl up and seem like fingers clasped together in prayer. Some varieties are also known as 'Rabbit's tracks'.

Maranta leuconeura tricolor is the most decorative of all the Marantas or Prayer plants. Its beautifully coloured leaves have a soft, velvety bloom and need high humidity to keep them fresh and bright. Never try to make them more glossy with leafshine.

Light: Best in indirect light, away from a sunny window. In summer they do well in shade but in winter need more light.

Temperature: Will survive down to 50°F (10°C) if soil allowed to dry out between waterings but do better above 60°F (16°C). In summer up to 80–85°F (27–29°C) provided humidity is kept high.

Water: Keep moist at all times unless temperature down to 50°F (10°C). Water 2–3 times a week in summer, once a week in winter, every 10 days if around 50°F (10°C).

Humidity: High. Spray daily in summer, twice weekly in winter. If not in mixed planting, keep pot on wet pebbles.

Feeding: Add liquid houseplant food to the water every 14 days in spring and summer while growing, diluting food to half maker's recommended strength.

Soil: Need an open, porous mix. Peat-based No. 2 is good.

Repotting: Repot once a year in spring but do not firm compost down too hard. In mixed plantings, just change top 1in (2½cm) soil annually.

Cleaning: Spraying will keep it clean but if dusty, wipe leaves carefully with damp cloth. No leafshine.

Leaves limp, brown and patchy with curled edges. Too wet. Drain away any water in saucer and allow compost surface to dry out before watering again. Keep soil moist but not waterlogged. If temperature falls to 50°F (10°C), water only every 10 days.

what goes wrong

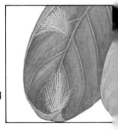

Leaves fade, webs underneath. Red spider mite. Remove webs with damp cloth or sponge, then spray with diluted malathion, especially under leaves. Repeat every 14 days until symptoms disappear. Improve humidity by standing pot on saucer of wet pebbles and spray regularly.

368

Root division

1. Large plants with many stems and a large rootball can be divided in early spring, just as new leaves start to grow.

2. First prepare 2 clean pots with drainage and compost.

Remove plant from pot and tease old compost from roots with rounded stick.

3. Grasp the rootball firmly and gradually pull it apart, making sure each section has both roots and stems.

4. Repot both sections separately, do not firm soil down too hard around roots. Leave without water for 2 days in a shady place. This allows roots to spread out in search of water. Move back into good indirect light and start watering again as usual.

Burns on leaves. Damage caused by spraying in sunlight. Needs high humidity but never spray if sun on leaves. Remove unsightly leaf where stalk joins plant.

Leaves curl and wither. Too cold. Move to warmer place, above 60°F (16°C). Or, soil too dry. Check conditions and if dry, water by plunging pot into bucket of water for 10–15 minutes. Drain. Keep always moist.

White woolly patches and grubs in leaf joints. Mealy bug. Spray with diluted malathion and remove bugs and 'wool' with tweezers. Repeat every 14 days until clear. Or, paint with methylated spirits, remove with tweezers.

Leaves pale. Too much light. Move out of direct sun, into shady place.

Leaves droop and look limp. Too hot. Move to cooler place, below 80°F (27°C) if possible and spray daily to keep humidity high.

Leaves lose colour and look lifeless. Too dark and/or needs feeding. Check conditions. Move to lighter place (but not direct sunlight) and feed every 14 days in growing season with houseplant food diluted to half maker's recommended strength.

Microcoelum weddelianum

Dwarf coconut palm

This is an attractive, deceptively delicate-looking house palm, grown for its foliage as it will not produce coconut fruits. In fact, it is tough and relatively easy to care for. Requiring a humid atmosphere, it is usually grown several to a pot and, since it grows slowly, is an ideal bottle garden plant. It dislikes having its roots disturbed. It is sometimes known as *Cocos* or *Syagrus weddeliana*.

Light: Tolerates high level of light, including direct sunlight. If daylight insufficient, use an artificial light to improve growth.

Temperature: Winter minimum 60°F (16°C), summer maximum 70°F (21°C).

Water: In summer keep moist, but not saturated, watering 2 or 3 times a week. In winter allow almost to dry out between waterings, every week to 10 days.

Humidity: Spray twice a week with fine mist of tepid soft water. Stand in saucer of pebbles almost covered with water. The humid microclimate of a bottle-garden (See p. 17) is ideal.

Feeding: Once every 2 to 3 weeks in summer with houseplant food diluted with water. Use half the amount recommended by the maker.

Soil: Mixture of 3 parts loam-based No. 1 and 1 part sedge or moss peat.

Repotting: Annually in early spring into clay pot one size larger. Knock root-ball out whole. If several are planted together, do not separate root-balls.

Cleaning: Wipe both sides of leaves every week with damp cloth and tepid, soft water. No leafshine.

Removing fronds: Cut off brown and shrivelled lower leaves with scissors or secateurs as close as possible to main stem.

The Dwarf coconut palm has delicate-looking green fronds. It grows slowly, and several plants are usually placed together in one pot to give a more bushy appearance. It is a relatively easy plant, but does require a humid atmosphere.

Leaf tips turn brown. Air too dry. Spray daily with tepid soft water in a fine mist. Avoid large droplets which may mark leaves.

New leaves dry up. Too hot. Do not exceed 70°F (21°C) unless there is good circulation of air. Spray weekly with tepid soft water to improve humidity. If plant also not growing in summer, check not standing in water. Allow to dry out before watering again.

Whole plant dries up. Roots disturbed. Has it been knocked over? Carefully firm soil back into pot and continue watering as usual. Repot carefully following spring if plant survives.

Plant does not grow. Too dark. Needs bright light all year round. If already in good position, may need repotting. Repot in following spring and feed regularly meanwhile.

what goes wrong

New leaves turn brown. Too cold. Move to warmer place, at least 60°F (16°C).

Repotting

Repot in spring when roots growing through pot and lack of new fronds show soil nutrients are used up. Prepare pot 1 size larger with drainage material and compost. Palms prefer tall, narrow pots.

1. Remove plant from pot.

2. Carefully remove stale soil from roots, using stick or pencil.

3. Place plant in centre of new pot, root-ball on compost.

4. Add new compost to fill pot. Make sure that all roots are covered. Leave in the shade without water for 2 days to encourage roots to grow into compost.

Some leaves have brown patches. Leafshine damage. Do not use. Clean both sides of leaves with tepid water only.

Lower leaves dry and crisp. Needs water. Plunge pot into bucket of water until bubbles stop rising. Drain thoroughly before replacing in position.

371

Mimosa pudica

Sensitive plant

The chief attraction of the Sensitive plant is the fascinating way it folds its leaves when touched, even by a drop of water. Because of this it has been grown for many years solely for its novelty value and although it has been the subject of numerous scientific studies, no one has yet been able to explain its response. A native of tropical South America, it needs high humidity and shade from full sunshine. In the wild it is a shrubby perennial plant and indoors needs regular feeding to keep it healthy. It is rarely worth overwintering as it grows easily from seed – but avoid the temptation to continually touch the leaves as this may lead to the plant's early demise.

The Sensitive plant's green, feathery leaves, close together along the stem when touched, the stem itself drooping at the same time. It grows to about 18in (45cm) tall with a woody, slightly barbed stem and produces small pale mauve fluffy flowers in mid-summer.

Light: A good light position protected from direct sunlight.
Temperature: Prefers 65–75°F (18–24°C) for best growth. Cannot tolerate cold.
Water: Keep compost moist at all times. Daily watering may be necessary in hot weather. Water carefully into side of pot or into saucer, to avoid disturbing leaves.
Humidity: Maintain humidity by standing pot in a saucer of pebbles half covered with water. Do not spray as water on leaves will evoke sensitive response.
Feeding: Start 3 weeks after plant in final pot, then feed weekly with liquid houseplant food at maker's recommended strength until flowering finished. In soil-less composts feed every 4 or 5 days.
Soil: Loam-based No.2 potting compost or soil-less potting compost.
After flowering: Discard in autumn after flowering is finished and foliage begins to die back.

what goes wrong

Propagation
1. Sow on prepared surface and dust over lightly with dry compost. Prick out seedlings as soon as they are large enough to handle. Transplant to 4½in (11cm) pot when growing well.

2. Water pots from below to avoid wetting the foliage and do not move them about too much as even this may cause leaves to fold.

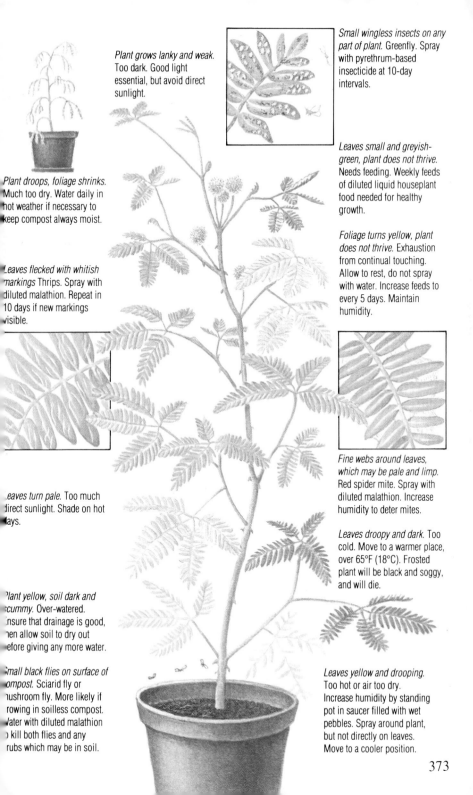

Plant grows lanky and weak. Too dark. Good light essential, but avoid direct sunlight.

Small wingless insects on any part of plant. Greenfly. Spray with pyrethrum-based insecticide at 10-day intervals.

Plant droops, foliage shrinks. Much too dry. Water daily in hot weather if necessary to keep compost always moist.

Leaves small and greyish-green, plant does not thrive. Needs feeding. Weekly feeds of diluted liquid houseplant food needed for healthy growth.

Foliage turns yellow, plant does not thrive. Exhaustion from continual touching. Allow to rest, do not spray with water. Increase feeds to every 5 days. Maintain humidity.

Leaves flecked with whitish markings Thrips. Spray with diluted malathion. Repeat in 10 days if new markings visible.

Fine webs around leaves, which may be pale and limp. Red spider mite. Spray with diluted malathion. Increase humidity to deter mites.

Leaves turn pale. Too much direct sunlight. Shade on hot days.

Leaves droopy and dark. Too cold. Move to a warmer place, over 65°F (18°C). Frosted plant will be black and soggy, and will die.

Plant yellow, soil dark and scummy. Over-watered. Ensure that drainage is good, then allow soil to dry out before giving any more water.

Small black flies on surface of compost. Sciarid fly or mushroom fly. More likely if growing in soilless compost. Water with diluted malathion to kill both flies and any grubs which may be in soil.

Leaves yellow and drooping. Too hot or air too dry. Increase humidity by standing pot in saucer filled with wet pebbles. Spray around plant, but not directly on leaves. Move to a cooler position.

Monstera deliciosa

Swiss cheese plant

One of the most handsome of the larger houseplants, this is easy to grow and very tolerant of varying temperatures. It does, however, need a lot of space if it is to show the full beauty of its deeply cut leaves. It eventually produces an edible, but to western tastes not very appetising fruit. It should always be grown up a moss pole or sturdy stake, otherwise it will spread out horizontally. An easy plant for a beginner who wants something large and showy. It grows slowly but will reach a height of 8ft (230cm) after many years.

Light: Avoid direct sunlight; does well away from windows, in shade.
Temperature: Will survive down to 50°F (10°C) in winter but prefers no lower than 55°F (13°C). In summer easily up to 75°F (24°C), higher if humidity increased.
Water: Do not overwater – allow to dry out between waterings. Once a week sufficient in summer unless temperature over 70°F (21°C); every 14 days in winter. Always check soil before watering to see that surface is dry.
Humidity: Spray 2–3 times a week in summer, once a week in winter. Use soft water if possible. Stand pot on wet pebbles.
Feeding: Do not overfeed. Add liquid houseplant food at maker's recommended strength to the water every 3 weeks in summer.
Soil: Porous, peat-based No. 3.
Repotting: Once a year in spring. When too large to handle easily, replace top 2–3in (5–7cm) of soil with fresh. Always support plant with stake or moss pole.
Cleaning: Wipe leaves with damp cloth, supporting carefully from underneath. Use leafshine once a month.

In the wild, the Swiss cheese plant grows in very windy regions and the dramatic holes and splits in its leaves may help to prevent wind damage. The aerial roots which grow from the stem are essential to the plant's health and should never be cut off.

Leaves have brown tips. Too dry. Water immediately, then check compost weekly. Surface should dry out in summer but will do this more quickly when temperatures are high.

Leaves pale with webs underneath. Red spider mite. Remove webs with damp cloth or sponge, then spray with diluted malathion, especially under leaves. Repeat every 14 days until symptoms disappear. Improve humidity.

Lower leaves yellow, then brown especially in winter. Too wet. Allow soil surface to dry out thoroughly before watering again, then water only about once every 14 days so that compost dries out between waterings.

Plant does not grow. Too dark. Needs some indirect light to flourish. If in very dark corner, provide artificial lighting.

Some leaves do not split. You have a plant called 'Philodendron pertusum' which shares the same common name. It will not grow so large.

what goes wrong

Leaves badly torn and split. Human damage. Move plant to position where it will not be knocked.

Brown marks on centre and edges of leaves in summer. Damage caused by spraying in sunlight. Never spray when sun is on leaves. Remove leaf if badly marked, cutting stalk where it joins main stem. Use sharp knife.

Black patches on leaves. Too cold. Move to warmer place, above 55°F (13°C).

Leaves turn pale. Needs feeding. Feed every 3 weeks in summer while new leaves growing.

White woolly patches where leaves join stem. Mealy bug. Spray with diluted malathion and remove bugs and 'wool' with tweezers. Repeat every 14 days until symptoms disappear.

Leaves dry up and shrivel. Soil and air too dry. Water well and spray 2–3 times a week in summer. Check compost regularly when temperatures are high.

Musa acuminata

Dwarf banana

While the Dwarf banana is easy to grow and is tolerant of most conditions, as long as it has plenty of moisture and good air circulation, it is not suitable for a small room as its long, graceful leaves can reach 39in (1m) when matured and are very delicate. They split easily along the veins if knocked or if the atmosphere is dry. When kept in good light and warm conditions, the plant will grow very quickly, making up to 39in (1m) in a year, and it will even give fruit if grown in a conservatory. Some varieties can be grown quite easily from seed.

Light: Best in light, sunny position.
Temperature: Winter minimum 60°F (16°C), normal room temperature in summer. Do not leave in closed up room in hot weather.
Water: 2 or 3 times a week in summer when growing, never allowing plant to dry out. Every 10 days sufficient in winter, when plant can be much drier. Never leave water on leaves, as this can cause scorch marks in sun.
Humidity: Spray every other day in summer, weekly in winter. Stand on saucer of wet pebbles to increase humidity.
Feeding: Every 14 days in the growing season (spring and summer) with house-plant food diluted according to the maker's instructions.
Soil: Rich loam-based No. 3 with a little manure added.
Repotting: Annually in spring. For plants that are too large to handle easily, replace topsoil.
Cleansing: Humidity spraying sufficient. If very dirty, wipe leaves carefully with soft cloth, supporting underneath to avoid damage. No leafshine.

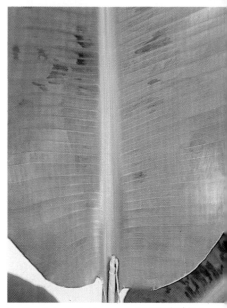

The Dwarf's banana's leaves are up to 39in (1m) long when it is fully grown but are very delicate. They unfurl one by one from the plant's centre, gradually forming a trunk-like stem. Healthy plants have no brown edges to the leaves and should show no sign of splits or tears.

Leaves torn and damaged. The delicate leaves tear easily if knocked. Move to safe position. Dry air may cause leaves to split. Spray every other day in summer or in centrally heated room, and stand pot on saucer of damp pebbles.

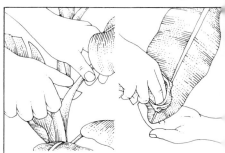

Removing a damaged leaf
Cut leaf stem with sharp knife as close to the main stem as possible. Dust cut edge with sulphur dust to protect from infection. If sap runs, seal cut with vaseline.

Cleaning
If leaves are dusty, wipe them carefully with a soft cloth and sponge with tepic water. Support the delicate leaves while cleaning.

No sign of new leaves in spring. Needs repotting (or topsoil changing) and feeding. If replacing topsoil, feed immediately. If repotting, do not feed for 14 days.

Leaves shrivel and go thin and papery. Leaf edges may also turn black and leaf gradually die. Too cold. Move to warmer place, at least 65°F (18°C) and remove dead leaves.

Burn marks on leaves. Leafshine damage or direct sun on leaves, especially after spraying. Do not use leafshine and do not spray plant in sunlight.

Leaves turn pale. Too dark. Move to lighter place. If in sunny window, do not spray while sun is on leaves.

White woolly patches in leaf axils, especially older leaves. Mealy bug. Remove carefully with cotton wool dipped in methylated spirits or spray with diluted malathion every 14 days until clear.

Slimy rot on stems and base. Too wet or sprayed too often in low temperature. Dust rot with sulphur dust and move to warmer room, at least 65F (18C).

Webs under leaves, leaves discoloured. Red spider mite. Spray every 14 days with diluted malathion until clear.

Lower leaves turn yellow. This is natural in older leaves, which gradually die and fall.

Leaf edges turn brown and leaves dry up. Too dry. Water more often and improve humidity by spraying every other day in summer or in central heating and standing pot on saucer of damp pebbles.

what goes wrong

Grape hyacinth

The Grape hyacinth is a native of Persia which has now become naturalized in most temperate climates. It is a good choice for growing in pots or bowls indoors, to flower from late winter through to mid-spring. Choose firm, clean, healthy bulbs and plant just covered, 6–8 in a 5in (12cm) half pot. Keep in a completely dark, cold place, either under ash or straw outdoors or in a cool, dark cupboard, for at least 8 weeks. When tips of shoots are beginning to show, move into a cool light airy room, taking care not to break the tender young shoots. Pots can also be kept outdoors in the garden, taking care to protect them from mice and slugs, and then brought in just as the buds are about to open.

The Grape hyacinth's small flowers are grouped in a pyramid-like cluster around the main stem, which grows to 8–10in (20–25cm) tall. The most common variety is a rich sky blue though mauve and white ones are also available.

Light: Total darkness for 8 weeks after planting, then full indirect light.

Temperature: Maximum 40–45°F (4–7°C) while in darkness. Move into light place at maximum 60°F (16°C) for flowering. Flowers will last longer if cooler.

Water: Soak compost after planting, then no water until pots brought into light. Water 2–3 times a week to keep compost moist but not waterlogged.

Humidity: Dry, airy conditions. Do not spray.

Feeding: Feed with diluted liquid houseplant food at maker's recommended strength every 14 days while growing and flowering.

Soil: Loam-based No.2 potting compost or special bulb fibre. Bulbs grown in fibre will not flower again.

After flowering: Cut back flower stem. Allow foliage to die back naturally. Cut back foliage when withered and place pot in a cool place. Lift bulbs the following autumn, separate offsets and plant both offsets and parent bulb in the garden.

Leaves pale, flower stems floppy. Too dark. Move to a lighter situation.

Grey or white mould on leaves. Fungus disease. Do not spray as this makes plants susceptible. Keep in a well ventilated room. Bulb may still produce flowers, but do not save.

Growth of bulb is slow and weak. If grown outdoors, small C-shaped grubs of vine weevil may be present. Dust soil with gamma HCH. Do not pot in garden soil.

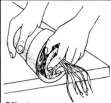   

Offsets

1. Parent bulb will produce offsets. When foliage has died down after flowering, remove bulb from pot and leave to dry out.

2. Gently separate offsets from parent bulb.

3. Plant offsets outdoors at a depth of 2–3in (5–7cm). They will be ready to flower in 2 years.

4. Parent bulb should also be planted out as it will not flower again in a pot for 2 years. Topdress before shoots appear with general garden fertilizer.

what goes wrong

Leaves but no flowers emerge. If bulb has been repotted from previous year, it may not have been well fed. Feed every 14 days with dilute liquid houseplant food if bulbs are to be saved. Do not pot up offsets, which take 2 years to come into flower.

Leaves yellow, flowers droop, scummy surface on soil. Waterlogging, which can occur easily if bulbs are grown in bowls without drainage holes. Prevent by putting a layer of gravel in bottom of bowl before planting. If soil becomes waterlogged, allow to dry out before watering again.

Flowers die quickly. Too hot and stuffy, or too much direct sun. Keep in a well ventilated room at maximum temperature 60°F (16°C). Protect from direct sunlight.

Leaves droop. Too dry. Water 2–3 times a week to keep compost just moist but not waterlogged.

Flower stems very short. Bulb planted too late in season. Plant in early autumn. Do not save these bulbs for repotting although they will bloom again if planted in the garden.

Flower stems eaten off at ground level. Seen on plants grown outdoors. Either cutworms or slugs. Put down slug pellets if slime trails present but keep away from pets and children. Dust cutworm with gamma HCH.

Daffodil

The Narcissus family is a vast one, with many hundreds of varieties. All grow from bulbs, which produce narrow, strap-like leaves and flowers which have petals grouped around a central cup, or trumpet. They are classed according to trumpet and petal lengths, generally being called daffodils when the trumpet is at least as long as the petal. For growing in pots or bowls choose one of the smaller varieties or buy bulbs specially prepared for indoor flowering. Bulbs, which may be single or double nosed should be potted in early autumn with the nose just above the soil. They need at least 8 weeks in a dark, cold place before being brought into a cool, light room when the shoots appear.

The colours of Daffodil varieties range from yellow to white with red, orange or pink trumpets. Dwarf varieties, about 12in (30cm) tall are best for indoors and may flower at any time from early winter to late spring. Touching the bulb or sap may cause slight skin irritation but this is shortlived.

Light: Complete darkness for 8 weeks. Diffused light until shoots are green and growing well, then full light for flowering.
Temperature: Maximum 40–45°F (4–7°C) while in darkness, as cool as possible until bud has cleared the bulb, maximum 60°F (16°C) for flowering.
Water: Soak compost after planting, then no water until brought in light. Increase watering to 2–3 times per week to keep compost moist at all times.
Humidity: Good ventilation.
Feeding: If bulbs are to be saved, feed weekly with dilute liquid houseplant food at maker's recommended strength, beginning when growth is 3in (7cm) high.
Soil: Loam-based No.2 with a handful of fine grit, special bulb fibre.
After flowering: If bulbs are to be saved, cut back dead flower stems. Allow leaves to die (at least 8 weeks) then cut back to soil level. Lift bulb, separate offsets, and store bulb in a cool dry place or plant out in the garden. Repot in autumn.

Flower bud becomes pale brown and stops growing. Too dry while developing. Keep moist at all times. Plant will not flower. Continue feeding until foliage dies as bulb can be saved for repotting.

Lush leaves but no flowers. Overfeeding. Begin feeding with dilute liquid houseplant food at weekly intervals when growth is 3in (7cm) high. Do not feed if growing in fibre.

Bud remains near neck of bulb. Pot brought into full light and heat too early. Shoots should be growing strongly and bud clear of neck before pot is brought into full light.

what goes wrong

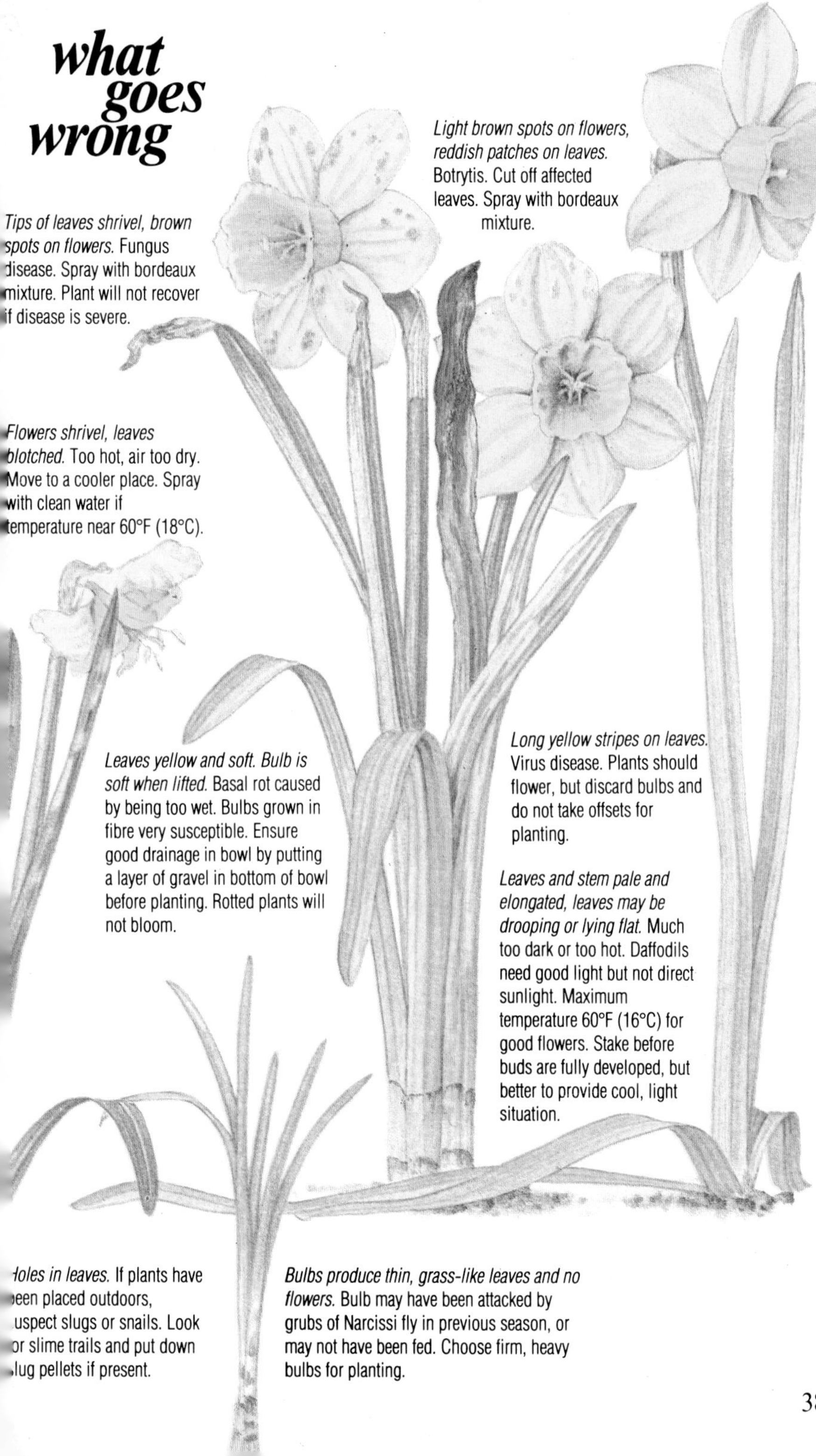

Tips of leaves shrivel, brown spots on flowers. Fungus disease. Spray with bordeaux mixture. Plant will not recover if disease is severe.

Light brown spots on flowers, reddish patches on leaves. Botrytis. Cut off affected leaves. Spray with bordeaux mixture.

Flowers shrivel, leaves blotched. Too hot, air too dry. Move to a cooler place. Spray with clean water if temperature near 60°F (18°C).

Leaves yellow and soft. Bulb is soft when lifted. Basal rot caused by being too wet. Bulbs grown in fibre very susceptible. Ensure good drainage in bowl by putting a layer of gravel in bottom of bowl before planting. Rotted plants will not bloom.

Long yellow stripes on leaves. Virus disease. Plants should flower, but discard bulbs and do not take offsets for planting.

Leaves and stem pale and elongated, leaves may be drooping or lying flat. Much too dark or too hot. Daffodils need good light but not direct sunlight. Maximum temperature 60°F (16°C) for good flowers. Stake before buds are fully developed, but better to provide cool, light situation.

Holes in leaves. If plants have been placed outdoors, suspect slugs or snails. Look for slime trails and put down slug pellets if present.

Bulbs produce thin, grass-like leaves and no flowers. Bulb may have been attacked by grubs of Narcissi fly in previous season, or may not have been fed. Choose firm, heavy bulbs for planting.

381

Clog plant

The Clog plant, originally from Brazil, has curiously shaped bright orange flowers with red tips which are produced all along the plant's stems. The fleshy, bright green succulent leaves help it to conserve moisture and it can survive without water for longer than many other flowering plants. Its common name comes from the flower shape which is thought to resemble an old-fashioned clog.

Light: Good, indirect daylight, not full sunlight. Position by light window that does not face full sun is ideal.

Temperature: Never below 55°F (13°C). Tolerates summer maximum of 75°F (24°C), but good ventilation needed.

Water: Only when soil surface feels dry as too much water causes flowers to drop off. On the other hand, insufficient water also makes flowers fall. Always test compost before watering as amount needed will vary with temperature. If near summer maximum, may need water 3–4 times a week; in winter once every 7–10 days is enough.

Humidity: Likes a dry atmosphere, so no need to spray for humidity or stand pot on damp pebbles. Spraying plant when in flower rots flowers.

Feeding: Every 14 days in spring and summer with liquid houseplant food diluted according to the maker's instructions.

Soil: 4 parts peat and leaf-mould mixed with 1 part loam and 1 part sand. Or, equal parts loam-based No. 2 and peat, with a handful of sand for drainage.

Repotting: Every 2 years in spring with new compost but into same sized pot (5in, 13cm). Good drainage layer in pot essential.

Cleaning: Spray if dirty with soft water, but only when temperatures are over about 70°F (21°C). No leafshine.

The Clog plant has glossy, almost succulent leaves and pouched, orange flowers which appear all along its stems. Because its fleshy leaves help it to conserve moisture, it needs less water than other flowering plants – but do not neglect it too much or the flowers will fall.

what goes wrong

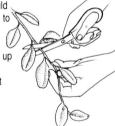

Leaf stems grow leggy with long spaces between leaves and plant fails to flower. Too dark. Move to light position but not direct sunlight. Prune plant in early spring to encourage flowering on new growth.

Pruning
Straggly Clog plants should be cut back in late spring to encourage side shoots.

Make cuts about half way up long, straggly stems, just above a leaf. Keep a neat shape.

Plant does not grow in spring and no flowers form. Needs repotting in fresh soil or feeding. May be in too large a pot. Repot every 2 years in spring into 5in (13cm) pot. Feed every 14 days in spring and summer. To encourage flowering, prune plant in early spring.

Some leaves have black patches. Leafshine damage. Do not use. Clean only by spraying with soft water.

Stem tips turn brown. Too hot. Move to cooler place, under 75°F (24°C), out of direct sunlight.

White lime marks on leaves. Plant sprayed with hard water. Use only soft or rainwater for spraying and do not spray when in flower.

Leaves and flowers turn pale and some dry out though all conditions seem correct. Sunlight too strong. Move to a good light area out of direct sun. A window that does not get sun is ideal.

Leaves turn black. Too cold. Move to warmer place, at least 55°F (13°C).

Flies hopping around plant. Whitefly. Spray and water soil once a week with systemic insecticide until clear.

Webs under leaves. Red spider mite. Spray under leaves with diluted systemic insecticide every 14 days until clear. Remove webs with cotton wool soaked in same mixture.

Leaves goes soft and spongy. Too wet or atmosphere too humid. Water only about once a week in winter if temperature falls to 60°F (16°C) to allow compost in pot to dry out. In summer water when soil surface feels dry. Move to less humid place with good air circulation. May develop grey mould if in very humid, steamy atmosphere.

Flowers fall before they are finished. Either too dry or too wet. Check compost and water only when soil surface feels dry. If temperature near summer maximum (75°F, 24°C) this may be 3–4 times a week. Never allow compost to become waterlogged.

White woolly patches on leaves and at joints of stems. Mealy bug. Wipe off with cotton wool dipped in methylated spirits. Water diluted malathion into the soil every 14 days until clear.

383

Nemesia

Nemesia comes from South Africa and is an easily grown annual suitable for all kinds of containers. It goes well, for example, with a newly planted evergreen which needs space around it to grow but looks rather bare at first. Its only drawback when used in a planting scheme is that it finishes flowering by midsummer, so needs replacing with other plants later on. Or, if cut down to 3in (8cm) after flowering, it will produce a second crop of blooms.

Light: Seedlings indoors, full light. Plants outside, full sun.
Temperature: Germination, 50–65°F (10–18°C). Down to 40°F (4°C) outside but protect from frost.
Water: Water seedlings sparingly but do not allow to dry out. For mature plants, keep compost just moist.
Humidity: Dry. Do not spray or water overhead when in flower.
Soil: Good texture, free draining. Use loam-based No.1 or soil-less potting compost.
Feeding: Start 3 weeks after planting out, diluting liquid fertilizer to half maker's recommended strength. Feed every 10 days in soil, every 5 in soil-less. Increase to maker's recommended strength only if plants stop growing well.
Propagation: Sow from early spring to early summer on well drained seedling compost, covering with dust of fine dry compost. Keep between 50–65°F (10–18°C) and when seedlings appear after 4 days, move to full light. They soon grow too long and collapse in poor light. Prick out when large enough to handle. Plant out when frosts finished.
Tidying: Remove yellow leaves and flowers dropped onto leaves.
Varieties: Carnival has the largest flowers, Triumph a wider colour range.

Nemesia flowers come in a wide range of colours in warm tones of white, yellow, orange, red and brown. The plants grow about 12in (30cm) high and give a splash of colour from early summer.

Pale spots on leaves when in seed trays. Leaf spot fungus. Treat with bordeaux mixture to manufacturer's directions. Keep foliage dry especially at night.

Seedlings collapse, stems thread-like at base. Pythium disease. Nemesia is very susceptible if not in good light and sterile conditions. This includes water supply to seedlings. Remove affected plants and water soil with soil fungicide.

Seedlings die. Possibly alternaria on seed responsible. Always purchase good quality seed from a reliable source.

what goes wrong

Plant tall and weak. Too dark or was crowded in seed tray earlier. Give plenty of room for lateral development when pricking out into seed trays. Plants need full light and sun.

Cutting down.

Cut stems down to 3in (8cm) above soil level after flowering, using sharp scissors. Add a light top dressing of dry fertilizer to container to help plant produce new leaves and flowers.

Grey fluffy mould on leaves. Botrytis. On young plants, water left on leaves overnight or planted too close together. Water in the morning. On older plants, mould, encouraged if dead fallen flowers not removed from leaves. Pick off dead flowers and leaves.

Flowers rot. Sprayed with water or heavy rain. Do not spray or water overhead when in flower.

Frothy white deposit especially where leaf joins stem. Frog hopper, a sap sucking insect hiding in the froth. Wash off with diluted insecticide or jet of water or pick off by hand.

Clusters of small insects on foliage of young plants. Aphid. Spray with insecticide and repeat in 14 days if not clean. Older plants are less susceptible.

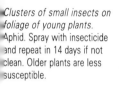

Bottom of stem turns black, foliage yellows. Phytophthora root and stem rot from contaminated water or soil. Plant unlikely to survive, so remove and treat soil with a fungicide.

Young or mature plants eaten at edges of leaves. Slugs or snails. Slugs likely to be hiding under seed tray. Snails under stones etc. Remove visible pests and put down slug pellets following maker's instructions. Keep away from pets and fishponds.

Plant wilts. Too dry. Keep soil just moist. Check daily in hot weather.

Plant collapses though still green. May be eaten off at ground level by cutworm. This will only occur if compost in container was not sterilized. Search through top 1in (2½cm) of soil surface. If not found, suspect slug and put down pellets as maker recommends.

385

Neochilenia

These cacti, from Chile, produce flowers of delicate pastel shades, unlike the bright colours of most cacti. They are usually low-growing, small, globular plants, with darkly pigmented bodies and black, brown or yellow spines. They rarely grow more than 3in (7cm) tall and do not produce offsets. *Neochilenia nigriscoparia* (p.387) is a good example of the genus.

The funnel-shaped flowers, about 1½ to 2in (3–5cm) wide, grow from the centre of the plant and come in shades of white, cream, yellow or pink. They are sometimes spicily scented.

Some botanists maintain that the name Neochilenia is incorrect and that they should either be called Nichelia or be merged into the genus Neoporteria (p.388). Few collectors and no nurseries follow their guidance and most collectors cling to the name Neochilenia for these clearly differentiated plants.

Light: Keep on a sunny windowsill, or in a greenhouse, where they should be kept shaded in the hottest months.

Temperature: Keep above 40°F (4°C) in winter, and below 100°F (38°C) in summer, giving fresh air whenever possible.

Water: Water once a month in spring, increasing in summer to once a fortnight. In hot weather, if soil dries out quickly, water once a week. Keep dry in winter. Overwatering will rot roots and may kill the plant.

Feeding: Feed once a month in spring and summer with high potash fertilizer (as used for tomatoes).

Soil: Use 2 parts soil-less or good loam-based No. 2 potting compost with 1 part coarse, gritty sand (not builders' or seashore).

Neochilenia imitans is one of the few Neochilenias which eventually grow into columns and has tiny, close-pressed spines in neat rows. The buds are almost black and the pale yellow interior of the flower when it opens comes as a surprise. It is a slow growing species, taking 5 years to reach 2in (5cm) tall.

Neochilenia kesselringianus with its flat-globular growth and dark spines is typical of the genus. The flowers, their dark throats contrasting well with pale pink petals, are spicily scented. It rarely grows to more than about 3in (8cm) wide but will flower when 3 years old and only half this size.

Repotting: Repot every year until plants fill a 4in (10cm) pot, then repot every other year or replace in same sized container with fresh soil. Be careful not to damage the thick roots when repotting and choose a pot large enough to accommodate them comfortably, with room for fresh soil around them.

Cleaning and pest control: Spray monthly to keep dust-free and incorporate an insecticide 2 or 3 times a year.

Other species: Seed is produced commercially for many of the 50 or 60 species and different species consequently appear from time to time. A good selection in addition to *N. nigriscoparia* (below) is: *N. napina*, with short black spines and cream flowers, and its variety *spinosior*, with long black spines and pink flowers; *N. imitans*, with tiny spines and pale yellow flowers; *N. jussieui*, with strong brownish spines and pink flowers with darker midstripe; *N. chilensis*, one of the most densely spined, has yellow or white spines and pink-red flowers; *N. kesselringianus* with white flowers and a neat arrangement of areoles. *N. atra*, a low-growing cactus with a very dark body and pale yellow flowers with blackish outer petals, is attractive but seldom available.

Sciara fly
If plant not growing and black flies are around soil, examine roots for sciara fly larvae. If roots are damaged, pare away soft tissue until firm healthy root remains. Dust with rooting powder.

Neochilenia nigriscoparia has a naturally dark body with long black spines. It produces fresh spines in spring and summer and after it is about 2in (5cm) wide, at 4–5 years old, funnel-shaped flowers appear from its centre in early summer. The flush of blooms lasts for about a week and it will not normally flower again until the following year.

Neoporteria

The genus of Neoporteria is sometimes considered to include Neochilenias (p.386) but as the two groups of cacti look very different, most collectors prefer to give them separate names.

Neoporteria multicolor (p.389) is typical of the group usually known as Neoporterias. These are densely spiny plants with little of the plant visible through the basketwork of interlacing, curving spines. They grow quite large, to 8in (20cm) or more tall and 4–5in (10–12cm) wide after 10 or 12 years and usually remain single headed. The spines vary in colour from creamy white through yellows and browns to black, and are mostly long, curving inwards to make an almost impenetrable, porcupine-like covering where they meet at the top of the plant. Almost but not quite impenetrable, for this is where the flowers push their way through.

Neoporteria flowers are unlike almost any other cactus flowers in shape, the outer petals curving out, the inner staying close around the centre parts of the flower. They are usually bicoloured in varying shades of pink and yellow.

Neoporteria wagenknechtii has strong, needle-sharp spines which make repotting difficult. It flowers at about 2in (5cm) wide and tall, when it is about 4 or 5 years old. This plant has buds, open flowers and the yellow remains of dead flowers.

Light: Give maximum sunshine on a sunny windowsill or in a greenhouse all year round.
Temperature: Keep above 40°F (4°C) in winter and below 100°F (38°C) in summer, giving fresh air whenever possible.
Water: Water fortnightly in summer, weekly if in pots smaller than 4in (10cm) as long as compost has dried out between waterings. In spring and autumn water monthly and keep dry in winter.
Feeding: Use a high potash fertilizer (as used for tomatoes) once a month during spring and summer.

Soil: Use 2 parts coarse gritty sand (not builders' or seashore) to 3 parts soil-less or good loam-based No. 2 potting compost.
Repotting: Repot every year until plant fills a 5in (13cm) pot, then every other year. If plant has not outgrown its container, remove it from pot, shake off the old soil and repot in same pot with fresh soil. Do not rewater for 2 weeks. Take care when repotting as the spines are very sharp.
Cleaning and pest control: Spray monthly to keep dust-free and incorporate an insecticide 2 or 3 times a year to combat pests.
Other species: Several different species are often available as seed is produced commercially and the cacti are not difficult to grow. Three good ones in addition to *N. multicolor* (right) are: *N. laniceps*, with fine, almost hair-like khaki-brown to dark brown spines; *N. litoralis*, usually with yellow spines; and *N. wagenknechtii* with strong spines and pink flowers.

Repotting

Wear gloves to protect your hands and handle plant with care to avoid damaging the sharp spines.

1. Remove plant from old pot and examine root ball. If there are plenty of hair-like white roots on surface, it needs repotting. Check for signs of pests. For treatment see pp. 38–41.

2. Gently crumble root ball with fingers to remove old compost but be careful not to break roots. If compost falls away easily and there are plenty of new roots, plant may be repotted in same pot with fresh compost.

3. If root ball is solid, prepare pot 1 size larger with drainage material and 1in (2½cm) layer of fresh compost. Place root ball on compost.

4. Trickle fresh compost around root ball, firm down gently and add final top layer of grit. Compost level should be the same as before, about 1in (2½cm) below pot rim. Do not water for 2 weeks, to allow roots to grow into new compost.

Neoporteria multicolor has spines which range in colour from almost white to nearly black, with every shade of yellow and brown between. If given enough sunlight, it will flower in late summer when it is about 3in (7cm) wide, at 5–6 years old. Between 12 and 15 flowers appear over a period of about 2 weeks and have the characteristic Neoporteria shape with outer petals curving outwards and inner ones remaining almost closed around the flower's centre.

Neoregelia carolinae

Cartwheel plant

This striking plant has long, strap-like green and cream leaves with, in the centre, a group of special leaves or bracts which turn a rich red. The actual flowers are small, usually mauve in colour, and hardly project out above the central leaves. It is a Bromeliad, one of a large family of plants which includes the Pineapple. Many of them grow in trees in their natural habitats and absorb nourishment from water that collects in their central well rather than from soil. The Cartwheel plant's leaves spread out almost horizontally and span up to 18in (46cm). A recently introduced more compact variety, 'Perfecta', has an intense red colour. There is also a widely grown plain green variety, 'Marechalli'. All make useful plants for mixed groups in large tubs or troughs.

Light: Good light position with some sun. Avoid midday sun.

Temperature: Constant all-year 60°F (15°C) ideal. Acceptable winter minimum is 55°F (13°C), summer maximum 70°F (21°C).

Water: Keep rosette centre half full with water at all times, changing the water weekly. Water compost weekly in summer, keep drier in winter, watering every 10–14 days.

Humidity: Spray overhead weekly.

Feeding: In summer, add liquid houseplant food when changing water in central well every second week. Use half as much food as the maker recommends.

Soil: Equal parts peat-based and loam-based No. 2 compost.

Repotting: Annually in early summer. Roots are small but plant may need bigger pot for support since leaves tend to spread out.

Cleaning: Wipe leaves with damp cloth. No leafshine.

The Cartwheel plant's tiny flowers grow inside its central well and it is the brightly coloured bracts that are its most striking feature. The plant flowers only once so when buying make sure that there are no signs of old flowers and that the striped outer leaves are clean and undamaged.

Leaves droop, dry out and look pale though watering correct. Too hot. Keep below 70°F (21°C), constant 60°F (15°C) ideal.

Leaves look bleached. Too much strong midday sun. Move out of direct summer sun but keep in good light.

what goes wrong

Plant dries up and shrivels. Too dry. Make sure that there is always water in the plant's well and that the soil in pot is watered regularly.

Removing offsets

When flowers and leaves of parent plant have quite died down, offset will be about half the size of parent and will be ready to separate.

1. Prepare small pot with drainage layer and mixture of damp peat and sand.

2. Knock plant from pot and cut offset and its roots from old plant with a sharp knife.

3. Place offset in new pot and firm compost around its base, covering roots. Water well and cover pot with polythene for 2–3 days to provide extra humidity. Discard parent plant.

Leaves turn pale. Too dark. Move into lighter place, with some direct sun, but not at midday in summer.

Leaves fade and have webs underneath. Red spider mite. Spray every 14 days with diluted malathion or derris.

Centre of rosette starts to die but young side shoots appear. Natural after 2–3 years. Do not separate new shoots until centre of parent plant has died.

Flowers shrivel and turn black. Leafshine damage. Do not use on flowers.

Base of plant rots. Too cold and wet. May be fatal, but allow to dry out and empty water from central well until plant recovers.

Brown scales under leaves. Scale insect. Remove with cotton-wool dipped in methylated spirits or spray with systemic insecticide every 14 days until clear.

391

Nephrolepis exaltata

Sword fern

Also known as the ladder fern or Boston fern, this is one of the more common varieties of the large *Nephrolepis* family. It is a good hanging plant and does well planted in a basket. New fronds grow from the centre and uncurl as they develop, and buyers should always look for healthy central foliage. Provided it has sufficient humidity, it is easy to keep, though the ends of the leaves can become ragged if damaged by people brushing past them. In spring it produces plantlets on runners, which root at the edge of the pot. These can be separated to make new plants.

Light: Diffused daylight, though will survive in a quite shady position. Keep out of direct sunlight.

Temperature: Summer minimum 65°F (18°C) and maximum 75°F (24°C). Winter temperatures 55–60°F (13–15°C).

Water: 2 or 3 times a week with soft water in summer to keep moist at all times. Allow almost to dry out in winter before watering, usually once a week.

Humidity: Daily spraying with tepid soft water essential for healthy growth. Stand plant on saucer of pebbles almost covered with water. Bathroom or kitchen good situations for this plant.

Feeding: Every 14 days when growing (spring and summer) with liquid house-plant food diluted with water according to the maker's instructions.

Soil: Peat-based compost or 1 part loam-based No. 1 blended with 2 parts sterilized peat.

Repotting: Annually in spring, into plastic pot one size larger. Put broken crocks in pot to provide good drainage.

Cleaning: Spray with soft water. No leaf-shine.

When buying a Sword fern, look for healthy bright green central foliage as new leaves grow from the middle of the plant. Pale green, lush fronds uncurl upwards, developing into a graceful sword shape.

Leaves turn bleached, dry and crisp. Too much direct sun. Move to shadier place.

White deposits on leaves. Lime from spraying with hard water. Use rainwater if possible.

Plant droops in winter. Too wet or standing in water. When temperature below 60°F (15°C) allow to dry out between waterings.

what goes wrong

Leaves turn black. Too cold. Move to warmer room, at least 60°F (15°C) in winter and 65°F (18°C) in summer.

New leaves pale and stunted. Needs feeding. Feed every 14 days in summer when growing. Dilute liquid houseplant food to recommended strength.

Cutting off fronds

1. Cut off brown, shrivelled fronds at base with sharp scissors.

2. If ends of fronds become ragged and dried, cut them off with scissors just inside damaged area. Do not cut into healthy leaf.

Leaves blacken and shrivel. Leafshine damage, fumes or insecticide damage. Do not use leafshine or insecticides. Keep in fume-free place.

Leaves dry out, shrivel and fall. New fronds in centre brown. Needs water. Cut shrivelled fronds off at base and water well, plunging pot into bucket of water for 1 hour. Drain.

Leaves turn brown at tips, wilt and become crisp. Too hot, air too dry. Move to cooler place and spray daily with tepid soft water.

Nerine sarniensis

Guernsey lily

Guernsey lilies are natives of South Africa and unlike many other bulbs, can be left in the same pot to flower for 4–5 years. Purchase bulbs which are firm and free of dark or sunken areas and plant in late summer or early autumn, either individually in 4in (10cm) pots or 3 to a 7in (18cm) pot. Half the bulb should be showing above the compost. Keep in a cool, airy, well lit position. Bulbs need a resting period after flowering.

Light: Bright light for as long as possible each day. Shade flowers from midday sun.
Temperature: Constant 55–60°F (13–16°C) for best growth. Resting plants can be kept at colder temperatures, but will not survive frost.
Water: Water weekly after new growth appears, increasing to 2–3 times a week while flowering and in full leaf. Soil must always be moist. Reduce watering when leaves turn yellow. Do not water at all during resting period.
Humidity: Dry, well ventilated position. Do not spray.
Feeding: Feed weekly with dilute liquid houseplant food at maker's recommended strength from the time growth appears until foliage is cut back after flowering.
Soil: Loam-based potting compost No.2. Do not grow in special bulb fibre.
After flowering: Cut back flower stem, then allow leaves to yellow and die back. Cut back to soil level, cease feeding and allow pot to dry out. Place pot in a sunny place, preferably outdoors. In late summer, topdress soil with a 1in (2½cm) layer of fresh, moist compost and place in growing position again.

Guernsey lilies produce a single flower stem 15–18in (38–45cm) tall with clusters of salmon pink or bright red flowers. The leaves may not appear until the bud is already well formed. The slightly hardier *Nerine bowdenii* has thick, glossy leaves which do not die down completely in winter, so needs a little water even while resting.

Bulbs
If bulb was healthy when planted but does not flower, cause may be pest attack, or conditions too wet or too dry. Check and remedy. If bulb fails to flower in second or following year, cause may be not enough feeding in previous year. Feed now to build new embryo bud for next year. Bulbs will flower 4–5 years, so discard if too old. If bulbs grow slimy and mouldy while resting, too wet. Do not water at all after cutting back foliage.
Bulb soft at planting time or after resting. Fusarium bulb rot, possibly caused by watering during rest period. Always buy firm, healthy bulbs from a reliable dealer. Do not water while resting. Discard soft bulbs as they will not grow.

Base of stem severed, plant topples over. Cutworm grubs, which may live in the top 1in (2½cm) layer of soil. Dust with gamma HCH if found. Always grow in sterile compost.

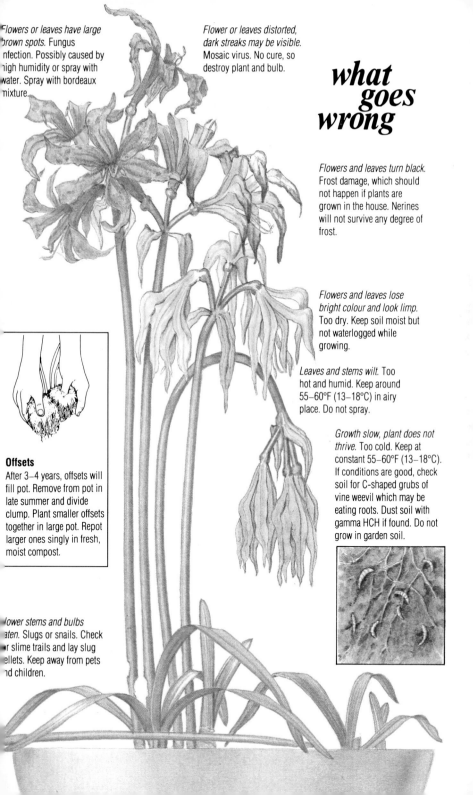

Flowers or leaves have large brown spots. Fungus infection. Possibly caused by high humidity or spray with water. Spray with bordeaux mixture.

Flower or leaves distorted, dark streaks may be visible. Mosaic virus. No cure, so destroy plant and bulb.

what goes wrong

Flowers and leaves turn black. Frost damage, which should not happen if plants are grown in the house. Nerines will not survive any degree of frost.

Flowers and leaves lose bright colour and look limp. Too dry. Keep soil moist but not waterlogged while growing.

Leaves and stems wilt. Too hot and humid. Keep around 55–60°F (13–18°C) in airy place. Do not spray.

Growth slow, plant does not thrive. Too cold. Keep at constant 55–60°F (13–18°C). If conditions are good, check soil for C-shaped grubs of vine weevil which may be eating roots. Dust soil with gamma HCH if found. Do not grow in garden soil.

Offsets
After 3–4 years, offsets will fill pot. Remove from pot in late summer and divide clump. Plant smaller offsets together in large pot. Repot larger ones singly in fresh, moist compost.

Flower stems and bulbs eaten. Slugs or snails. Check for slime trails and lay slug pellets. Keep away from pets and children.

Oleander

The oleander is a pretty plant with soft-coloured trumpet-shaped flowers in both double and single form. The leaves are long and narrow and paired down the stem. Its foliage and, in some circumstances, flowers are poisonous and should never be eaten by humans or animals. Oleanders grow up to about 18in (46cm) in a pot though in a large tub in a conservatory or sun-room they may reach over 7ft (2m). The variegated types, *Nerium oleander* 'Variegata', tend to be more compact and slower growers. Flower colours range from white through delicate pink to orange and even purple. Some are scented. After flowering, the stems which have carried flowers can be cut back to half their length. Use secateurs and cut at an angle just above a side shoot or leaf.

Light: Very light position, does not mind full sun. Too much shade prevents flowers from appearing.

Temperature: Winter minimum 40°F (5°C). Prefers to be cool in summer; if over 60°F (15°C) must be outside or in a very airy room.

Water: Daily in summer if over about 65°F (18°C) every 10 days in winter, using tepid rainwater if possible. If water is cold, flowers may not form.

Humidity: Spray with soft water once a week in summer, especially if over 65°F (18°C), but never in middle of day.

Feeding: Every seven days in summer when growing, using liquid houseplant food diluted according to maker's instructions.

Soil: Loam-based No. 3 compost.

Repotting: Usually every 2–3 years in spring. Plant flourishes in big pot. When not repotting, change topsoil in spring and feed.

Cleaning: Spray with tepid water or wipe with damp cloth if dirty. No leafshine.

Oleander flowers come out in succession all through the summer, although each one lasts only a short time. Health leaves are naturally slightly matt and leathery. When buyir choose a plant with buds as well as flowers and check leaves for signs of pests.

Side shoots

1. To encourage buds to open, cut off side shoot immediately below flowering head so that plant's energy all goes to buds.

2. Put stems into shallow jar filled ⅔ with tepid water anc covered with foil. 3 or 4 pieces of charcoal will keep water fresh. If kept warm (61–64°F, 16–18°C), new roots will form and cuttings can then be potted in small pots. Cover them with polythene for 2–3 days to give them extra humidity.

Leaves pale with no new growth. Needs feeding or repotting. Repot every 2 to 3 years in spring and change topsoil in other years. Feed weekly in summer.

Buds rot before opening. Too cold, or water too cold. Move to warmer position (not over 60°F, 15°C if possible unless in very airy room) and water with tepid water in winter.

Leaves pale, dry and shrivelled with no new growth. Too dry. Soak pot in bucket of water for 15 minutes, then drain. Water daily in summer to keep moist.

Stems grow straggly with no flower buds in summer. Too hot and dry. Water daily in summer and spray with soft water. Move to cooler place (under 60°F, 15°C if possible) or very airy room.

what goes wrong

Brown marks on leaves. Too cold, if plant outside may be frost 'burns'. Winter minimum temperature 40°F (5°C). Brown marks on flowers may be caused by leafshine. Do not use.

Scorch marks on leaves. Caused by water staying on leaves in strong sunlight. Spray only in early morning and make sure water does not stay on leaves.

White woolly patches on leaves and in leaf axils. Mealy bug. Remove with cotton-wool dipped in methylated spirits or spray every 7 days with systemic insecticide until clear.

Brown scales under leaves and on stems. Scale insect. Remove with cotton-wool dipped in methylated spirits or spray every 7 days with systemic insecticide until clear.

No flower buds appear but leaves and stems otherwise healthy. Too dark. Move to lighter position, in full sun.

397

Nicotiana

Tobacco plant

The sweet-scented Tobacco plant comes from South America and is of the same family as smoking tobacco. The scent of some varieties can be quite heady on a humid evening but the search for new colours has resulted in less perfume for others. They need a sunny spot and must always be protected from frost, however carefully they have been weaned to outside conditions.

Light: Maximum indoors and out.
Temperature: Germination, 65°F (18°C). No frost.
Water: Keep moist but not saturated.
Humidity: Dry when in flower. Spray after hot day (70°F, 21°C), especially when first planted out.
Soil: Loam-based No.3 or soil-less potting compost.
Feeding: Start when plants are outside but not planted into final containers. Feed every 2 weeks diluting to half maker's recommended strength. Two weeks after final planting start feeding every 10 days in soil, every 5 in soil-less, at maker's full recommended strength.
Propagation: Sow in mid-spring on prepared seedling compost. Do not cover seed with compost but place tray in plastic bag and cover with thick paper. Germination takes 4–5 days. Then give full light but not direct sun. Prick out when large enough to handle, leaving 3in (8cm) between plants. Will take full sun when growing.
Tidying: Remove whole flowering stem near base when flowers have died. This prevents seed pods forming so more flowers are produced.
Varieties: For patio and balcony, Affinis, white, highly scented. Crimson bedder, crimson 20in (50cm). For window boxes, Nikki series, many colours, 10in (25cm).

The varieties of sweet-scented Tobacco plant suitable for containers are usually 10–15 (25–38cm) high with colours including lime, pink, red and white. The taller white variety (affinis) is highly scented but its flowers close partially by day, opening towards evening.

Plant stops growing, soil surface dark and sickly. Waterlogged. Stop watering and check container drainage. Do not water again till almost dry.

Edges of leaves brown and shrivelled. Insecticide spray in bright sunshine or at too strong a concentration has scorched roots. Never use more than maker's recommended strength. Spray only in evening.

Early leaves have lacy holes where touching compost. Sciarid fly larvae. Drench compost with diluted malathion to maker's instructions. Rinse leaves in clear water to remove concentrated insecticide. This could cause scorch.

what goes wrong

Pale green/yellow mottling on leaves, twisted or knobbly stem. Virus disease. If severe, remove plant from container and destroy. If attack not too severe, flowering may continue to end of season. The presence of aphid on plants probably means that all will show symptoms.

Young plants in trays start to produce flower stems while still quite small, leaves are grey/green. Needs feeding. Feed at once. It is better that flower stems do not develop until planting out when roots have a full 'run'. This will not apply if plants are in large pots before going outside.

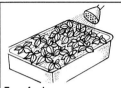

Transferring

1. Water tray well and drain. Tap end of tray on ground, hold open hand in front of plants and tilt box forward. Plants will lean away from box so whole contents can be lifted out.

2. Gently pull roots apart, leaving as much soil as possible around them, and plant singly in container.

Green/brown winged flies inside flowers and under leaves. Aphid. Spray with diluted malathion to maker's instructions.

Top of flowering stems thin and very light in colour. Few flowers. Too dark. Move to lighter place if possible.

Flower stems hard and woody to the touch. Needs feeding. Feed once a week for 2 weeks with a high nitrogen feed then feed regularly.

Holes in leaves and leaf edges eaten away. Slugs or snails. Place slug pellets around to maker's recommendations. Keep away from pets and fishponds.

lant turns black. Frost amage. Always protect from rost in early summer.

Leaves are grey green and small. Too dry. Water container and keep always moist but not soggy.

Plant leans over. Root rot from unsterile soil or overwatering. Stop watering, plant may recover. If plant turns yellow, remove.

Notocactus

The name Notocactus means 'southerly cactus' and refers to the plant's origins in South America where it grows in Argentina, Uruguay, Paraguay and Brazil. These are among the largest flowered of the cacti, usually with yellow, silky-textured blooms up to 5in (12cm) across. The flowers are freely produced once the plants are about 3in (7–8cm) wide after 4–5 years and steadily increase in size and number as the plant gets larger. Most are easy to grow and many have decorative spines as well as flowers. *Notocactus leninghausii* (p.401) is sometimes called the Teddybear cactus, and is probably the best known.

Notocactus crassigibbus produces large flowers which, in full sun, will flatten out and cover the plant body completely. It starts to flower when 2 or 3in (5–8cm) wide, at 4 or 5 years old. This plant is in a 5in (14cm) pot.

Light: Keep on a sunny windowsill for best flowering. If in a greenhouse, shade lightly in summer.

Temperature: Keep above 45°F (8°C) in winter and below 100°F (38°C) in summer. Give fresh air whenever possible.

Water: Unlike most cacti, these should not be allowed to dry out completely in winter, provided the temperature is at least 45°F (8°C). Water monthly from base of pot. In spring, increase watering to once a fortnight and in summer weekly watering may be necessary if soil is drying out quickly. Reduce watering again in autumn.

Notocactus purpureus is one of a group which tends to produce its flowers in later summer, when most cacti, including other Notocacti, have finished. Generally staying solitary, this species will flower at about 2 or 3in (5–8cm) wide, when it is about 4 or 5 years old.

Feeding: Feed monthly in spring and summer with high potash fertilizer (as used for tomatoes).

Soil: 3 parts soil-less or good loam-based No. 2 potting compost, with 1 part coarse, gritty sand (not builders' or seashore).

Repotting: Repot every year in next size pot until plants fill a 5in (13cm) pot. Then every other year will be sufficient. Some Notocactus species grow more quickly than others, so check whether plant is outgrowing its pot. There should be room for fresh soil to be added around the plant when the old has been shaken off the roots.

Cleaning and pest control: Spray monthly to keep dust-free and use an insecticide 2 or 3 times a year to combat pests.

Other species: Among those with a dense covering of spines are *N. scopa*, with red and white spines and smallish yellow flowers, *N. haselbergii*, with white spines and red flowers, *N. graessneri*, with yellow spines and small green flowers, and the superb, blue-bodied, soft yellow spined *N. magnificus*. This is much larger than most others and has large yellow flowers.

Individual heads grow to the size of a large melon, forming clusters which fill a 10in (25cm) pan. These densely spined species are sometimes known as Eriocactus or Brasilicactus. Others worth looking out for are *N. crassigibbus*, with 5in (12cm) yellow flowers, *N. buiningii*, with milky-green bodies and yellow flowers, *N. horstii*, orange flowers, *N. uebelmannianus*, purple flowers, *N. rutilans*, pink flowers, *N. ottonis*, with yellow flowers and *N. purpureus* with purplish-pink flowers.

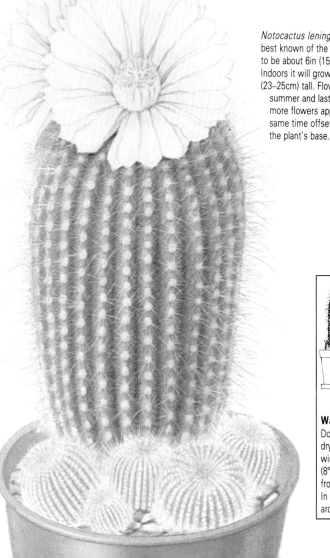

Notocactus leninghausii is probably the best known of the Notocacti though it needs to be about 6in (15cm) tall before it flowers. Indoors it will grow eventually to 9–10in (23–25cm) tall. Flowering season is early summer and lasts about a week, with 4 or more flowers appearing at a time. At the same time offsets begin to cluster around the plant's base.

Watering
Do not allow Notocacti to dry out completely in winter. Keep above 45°F (8°C) and water monthly from base of pot in winter. In summer water normally around plant or overhead.

401

Opuntia

This is the largest genus of cacti, spreading from as far south as Argentina through the Americas to Canada. It has been introduced and naturalized in many other parts of the world, particularly in the Mediterranean — and grows so freely in Australia that it has become a problem. Most Opuntias have flat, disc-shaped segments but there are small, round-jointed species and others with cylindrical segments. They range in size from a few inches to several feet. Most are easy to grow indoors though some of the larger types need more room than most people can provide. However, only a few produce flowers unless they are in a very sunny position all the year round. *Opuntia albata* (p.403) with its attractive yellow flowers is one of the easier ones and blooms when it is 3–4 years old.

Opuntia oligotricha is one of a group of papery-spined cylindrical-jointed species with segments that are easily knocked off. In the right position they will flower when they are about 6in (15cm) tall, at about 3 or 4 years old but will not do so unless they have plenty of sunshine all the year round.

Light: Maximum sunlight on a sunny windowsill is needed for strong growth. If the light is not ideal, they will soon grow out of shape and need to be supported. Full sun at all times of the year is needed for flowers.

Temperature: Keep above 40°F (4°C) in winter and below 100°F (38°C) in summer. Give fresh air whenever possible.

Water: Water once a week in summer, providing soil dries out between waterings, fortnightly in spring and autumn. Keep dry in winter.

Feeding: Use high potash fertilizer (as used for tomatoes) once a month in spring and summer.

Soil: Use 2 parts soil-less or good loam-based No. 2 potting compost, with 1 part coarse gritty sand (not builders' or seashore).

Repotting: Repot every year until plant fills a 5in (13cm) pot. Then every other year will do. To avoid touching the sharp spines, ease

Opuntia albata grows to 5–6in (13–15cm) tall but flowers after 3 or 4 years, when it is only 2½–3in (6–8cm). Flowering season is early summer and lasts for about a week. Each flowering pad produces 3–4 pale yellow flowers from its tip. A healthy *Opuntia* will produce new segments each year and, if in good light, should not need support.

A layer of grit on top of the compost helps to prevent the soil becoming hard and compacted after watering, stops the lower stem being splashed with mud and retains moisture in the pot in hot weather.

the plant out of the pot until you can grasp the root-ball. For large plants, you will need help.

Cleaning and pest control: Spray monthly to keep dust-free and incorporate an insecticide 2 or 3 times a year to combat pests. Make sure both sides of the stems are sprayed.

Other species: Few of the cylindrical jointed species are grown indoors since they rarely produce the wonderful spines they have in the wild but *O. tunicata* is sometimes available. This has glistening, creamy-white spines and loosely attached joints. Another which sometimes flowers is *O. oligotricha*. Of the low-growing small-jointed species there are many. *O. invicta* has marvellously blood-red new spines but is slow-growing, taking 5 years or more to fill a 7in (18cm) pot or pan. *O. molinensis* has dense ginger tufts of spines and *O. nigrispina* is purplish-black.

Taking cuttings

1. After flowering has finished, cut whole segment from plant at narrowest point with a sharp knife.

2. Dust end of cutting and cut end of stem with hormone rooting powder containing fungicide. Leave cutting to dry for at least 2 days.

3. Prepare 2 or 3in (5 or 8cm) pot with potting compost and place cutting on surface, bottom end against compost.

4. Cover just enough to hold it upright or rest against side of pot. Keep in good light place (not sunny) for 2–3 weeks until roots develop. Then start watering. Repot when roots fill pot.

Opuntias kept in poor light soon lose their round, disc shape and grow elongated and pale greenish-yellow. Cut off elongated stems and reposition plant in better light, moving gradually over a few weeks into a sunny position.

Opuntia albata has spines with no barbs and others of this type (but with barbs) worth growing are *O.microdasys* with yellow, red-brown or white spines; *O. basilaris,* with purplish-violet pads and *O. violacea* var. *santa-rita,* with long spines and violet pads. All these can be grown until they fill a 7in (18cm) pot but when larger than this, it is best to root one of the pads and start a new plant.

Orbea variegata

This plant, also known as *Stapelia variegata*, is probably the best known of the 'Carrion flower plants', so called because its flowers smell like rotting meat. It makes large clumps which spread to fill a 5 or 6in (15cm) half-pot or pan and reach about 2½in (6cm) high in 4 or 5 years. It produces wonderful brown and creamy-yellow flowers which form 5 pointed stars 2–3in (5–7cm) across but must have a sunny position. It is easy to propagate from stems. Other good species are *Orbea ciliata*, (formerly *Diplocyatha ciliata*), with creamy-white flowers fringed with white hairs, *O. woodii* with red flowers; *O. lutea*, with a bright yellow flower. All are obtainable from specialist nurseries.

Orbea variegata. Like most other carrion flower plants, this species is best kept in a sunny place outside while it is in flower as the smell from the blooms is intended to attract flies for pollination. To humans, it smells quite foul.

Light: A sunny position is needed to keep leaves compact and induce flowering.

Temperature: A minimum of 40°F (4°C) is needed for safety. Give fresh air in summer.

Water: Water fortnightly in spring and summer, weekly in hottest months, allow to dry out between waterings; tail off in autumn and keep dry in winter unless stems droop. Then give just enough to revive them.

Feeding: Use high potash fertilizer 2 or 3 times in summer; not necessary if repotted in spring.

Soil: Use good loam-based No. 2 potting compost, or soil-less compost, with 30% coarse, gritty sand.

Repotting: Every spring in fresh soil and size larger half-pot or pan. After 4–5 years discard older unsightly stems when repotting, retaining younger growth as this is where they flower from.

Propagation: Take cuttings of whole stems at natural junction, with sharp knife. Possible from seed, but this is difficult to obtain.

Stems shrivel, white woolly patches especially round base. Mealy bug. Remove with small paintbrush dipped in methylated spirits, and spray with contact or systemic insecticide. Repeat 2 or 3 times in growing seasons.

Stems grow long and pale, especially at tips. Few flowers. Too dark. Move into full light over 2 weeks. May also occur if too hot and wet in winter. Keep below 50°F (10°C) while resting.

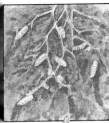

Stems shrivel and do not grow in spring, conditions correct. Check roots for root mealy bug. Swirl roots in insecticide, allow to dry before repotting in fresh compost and clean pot. Leave dry for 2 weeks.

Taking cuttings
1. Cut whole new stem in late spring or early summer where it joins older ones. Outer stems are the youngest.

2. Dust cut ends with hormone rooting powder to prevent infection, leave dry for 2–3 days.

3. Then place on dry compost in small pot. Water when roots appear.

Stems turn yellow, then black in winter. Too cold. Is plant shut behind curtains at night? Move to warmer place, above 40°F (4°C).

Brown scorch marks on stems. Sunscorch, plant moved into direct sun too quickly in stuffy place. Move out of direct light, then return gradually over 2 weeks. Keep in more airy place.

Stems shrivel and dry. Many possible reasons. Too hot and dry in winter; too dry in summer, or needs feeding. If soil dry, increase amount of water each time but allow to dry out between. In winter moisten soil monthly and keep below 50°F (10°C). Feed 2–3 times in summer.

what goes wrong

Stems not growing, some black and shrivelled, some fall over. Too cold, wet and humid. Allow to dry out thoroughly and keep above 40°F (4°C) in winter. Pare away rot from stem. If roots black and rotted, treat and repot (see Introduction). Or, take cuttings from healthy stems.

Plant collapsing or not growing, black flies around plant and soil. Sciara fly. Inspect roots and if rotted, pare back until all trace of rot or larvae removed. Then treat and repot. (see Introduction.)

405

Pachyphytum oviferum

This popular plant is sometimes known as the 'sugared-almond plant'. The plump grey almond-shaped leaves have a delicate dusty white coating and grow in rosettes. At first it grows upright, but as the stems multiply they spread sideways to cover quite a large area: it will reach a height of 3–4in (8–10cm) and spread to between 8 and 12in (20–30cm). There are not many species in cultivation, but occasionally from specialist nurseries you can get *P. viride*, with sausage-shaped olive-green leaves, and *P. bracteosum*, with thick flattish, leaves. All are easy to grow.

Pachyphytum oviferum, the Sugared almond plant. The dusty coating on this plant's plump, oval leaves gives them their special colouring and it is important not to touch and spoil them. It flowers in spring after a winter resting period. Be careful not to get water on its leaves.

Light: A sunny position will keep the leaves of this plant blue and powdery.

Temperature: A minimum of 40°F (4°C) is needed but at 50°F (10°C) fewer leaves will fall.

Water: Start fortnightly in spring and summer, weekly in hottest weather. Tail off in autumn and if below 50°F (10°C) keep dry in winter. If above this, water monthly throughout winter. See also Introduction.

Feeding: Use high potash fertilizer 2 or 3 times in summer.

Soil: Use good loam-based No. 2 potting compost, or soil-less compost, with 30% coarse, gritty sand.

Repotting: Every spring in size larger half-pot or pan, being careful not to handle leaves, as this will damage the coating.

Propagation: Whole stems or leaves can be removed, gently with the fingers for leaves, with a sharp knife for stem cuttings. Dust cut surface with hormone rooting powder, leave dry for 3 days, then lay on dry, fresh compost. Water after 3 weeks when roots have formed.

what goes wrong

Leaves marked on edges or in patches. Damaged by contact — humans, curtains, cats? Unsightly but not fatal.

Leaves distorted as though virus infected. Caused by excessive use of insecticides, especially those based on malathion. Not usually fatal.

Round pieces missing from edges of leaves, little growth, stem swollen. Vine weevil. Sprinkle soil with insecticidal powder. Pare away stem from base until brown area in centre of stem reached, dust with hormone rooting powder and reroot (see Introduction).

Taking cuttings
Leaves will root in late spring or early summer. Choose stem well covered in leaves and remove one gently by hand. Do not use leaf from base of stem. Lay leaf flat in pot of dry compost, with base touching surface.

2. Or cut 2–3in (5–8cm) stem with good head of leaves using sharp knife; dry for 2 days, dust base of cutting and cut end of plant with hormone rooting powder to prevent infection and place cutting on dry compost. Do not water until new roots appear.

Leaves stay small and few. Needs repotting, or if soil is bone dry, more water. Soak in a bowl before watering more thoroughly each time, but always allowing to dry out between waterings.

Leaves look scorched. Too much sun too suddenly or lack of ventilation. Acclimatise gradually to full sun after winter and give fresh air on hot days.

Small green insects on flowers or flower-buds. Greenfly. Spray with pyrethrum-based insecticide. Repeat every 10 days until clear.

Grows elongated in centre, leaves pale green. Too little light, move gradually over 2 weeks to a sunny spot.

No flowers. Too dark. Keep in full light all year round.

White woolly patches between leaves, and on stem. Mealy bug. Remove with paintbrush dipped in methylated spirits, taking care to avoid damaging waxy or mealy covering to leaves, and spray with pyrethrum-based insecticide.

Leaves fall, stem becomes bare. Too cold, too dry or leaves knocked off. Check conditions. Keep around 50°F (10°C) in winter. In summer water when pot dries out. Take care when handling or watering plants as leaves are lightly attached.

Stem black and rotting, plant falls apart. Too wet. Always allow to dry out between waterings. Moisten soil monthly in winter to stop leaves falling but dry out thoroughly in between.

Little sign of growth, white woolly patches on roots. Root mealy bug. Wash all soil off roots, swirl roots in contact insecticide, and allow to dry before repotting in fresh compost and clean pot. Leave dry for 2 weeks.

Lower leaves shrivel in winter. Too hot. If keeping without water in winter, try to keep below 55°F (13°C). If hotter, water about once a month.

Pachypodium succulentum

This South African species is easy to grow. It has a large tuber, generally grown half out of the compost, as its soft tissues rot easily. From the tuber thorny branches grow up, which produce flowers in spring, followed by leaves and further flowers during the summer. The flowers vary from white, to white with a red stripe or pink with a red stripe. The plant will reach between 8 and 12in (20–30cm) tall and the same across. Other good species are *Pachypodium saundersiae* with white flowers, *P. lamerei* which is tall, *P. rosulatum*, *P. baronii*, *P. lealii*, *P. geayii* and *P. namaquanum*

Light: All Pachypodiums need full sun.
Temperature: Minimum 55°F (13°C) although South African species will tolerate down to 40°F (4°C) in winter if dry.
Water: Start watering fortnightly when signs of growth appear, usually in late spring. Allow soil to dry out between waterings. Water weekly in hottest weather, tail off to fortnightly in autumn and withhold from early winter, when the leaves will go brown and fall. Do not water again until leaves begin to reappear. Spray tips of shoots monthly in winter to prevent them from drying.
Feeding: Use high potash fertilizer 2 or 3 times in summer months.
Soil: Loam-based No. 2 or soil-less compost, with 40% coarse, gritty sand.
Repotting: Avoid damage to roots when repotting each spring into a size larger pot. After 6in (15cm) pot is reached do not repot for 2 or 3 years, but feed regularly.
Propagation: Best from seed, from specialist seed nurseries. Seedlings grow quickly and the taller-growing types will reach about 8in (20cm) in 3 or 4 years.

Pachypodium succulentum. It is best to buy Pachypodiums as young seedlings rather than as larger plants which have already formed tubers and are more difficult to grow indoors. Remember to spray the stems occasionally during the winter rest period, to prevent the ends from shrivelling.

Tips of shoots die back, becoming brown and hardened; shoots break out from well below tips in spring. Spraying tips in winter will stop this excessive drying up. Remove damaged tips when absolutely dry with sharp scissors or secateurs. Do not cut into healthy stems.

White woolly patches among leaves. Mealy bug. Remove with small paintbrush dipped in methylated spirits, and spray with insecticide. Repeat 2 or 3 times in growing season.

what goes wrong

Leaves marked with brown or white patches. Brown is scorch from sudden hot sun in stuffy place. White is from insecticides or hard water spray. Remove with rainwater and small paintbrush.

Little sign of new growth in spring. Needs feeding or repotting or root mealy bug. Check roots and if white woolly patches found, wash soil away, swirl roots in insecticide and allow to dry before repotting in fresh compost and clean pot. Leave dry for 2 weeks.

Leaves blacken and fall, stem ends soft, tuber soft. Too cold and wet. Move to warmer place, at least 55°F (13°C) and allow to dry out before watering again. Always keep dry in winter even in normal room temperatures. Pare away rotting tissue and dust with fungicide. If conditions correct, check roots for sciara fly or vine weevil maggots (see Introduction).
If rot is severe, plant will die.

Flowers shrivel quickly. Too hot and dry. Check soil regularly and water when it dries out in summer. Do not expose to hot sun after cloudy weather: move gradually into full light.

Leaves turn paler, shrivel and fall. In summer, too hot and dry or too wet. Check conditions. If dry, soak in bowl of water for ½ an hour, then drain. If soil dark and soggy, leave to dry out completely before watering again. If new leaves do not grow but stem firm, repot in fresh, dry compost. Do not water again for 2 weeks. Leaves fall in autumn/winter, and grow again
in spring.

Leaves turn pale green or yellow-green, no flowers. Too dark. Bring gradually into full sun over 2 weeks.

When received plant has soft patches in bulbous stem or roots, and on cutting, has orange patches in the tissue. Damage to roots has allowed orange rot to get a hold. Pare away narrow slices with sharp clean knife until no sign of orange is visible. Dust with hormone rooting powder containing fungicide; allow to dry thoroughly before rerooting in dry compost.

409

Pachystachys lutea

Lollipop plant

A relatively recent introduction to the realm of flowering houseplants, the Lollipop plant is not unlike the more common 'Shrimp plant', *Beloperone guttata*. Both belong to the same family of Acanthaceae. The bright yellow bracts of the Lollipop plant stand upright at the top of the leaf-stems. Between the bracts are small white, snap-dragon-like flowers. The plant may be grown for its foliage when flowering is over, though it should be pruned back by half after flowering to keep it compact.

The Lollipop plant's yellow spikes are formed of special leaves or bracts; the true flowers are the small white petals which grow from the sides. A healthy plant will have firm, bright leaves all the way down the stems. If they are pale, dull or droopy, the plant needs care and attention.

Light: Full light, including summer sun. Prefers shadier position in winter when dormant.

Temperature: Summer average 60°F (16°C) preferred, with maximum 70°F (21°C). Lower in winter, though if as cool as 45°F (7°C) plant will temporarily lose leaves.

Water: In summer keep compost always moist, watering 2–3 times a week, more often if it dries out more quickly in hot weather. In winter water about once a week. Compost should never dry out completely, but do not allow to become waterlogged. Do not stand in water.

Humidity: Spray 2 or 3 times a week and stand pot on saucer of damp pebbles to give extra humidity. Do not spray when bracts are forming as they will rot.

Feeding: Weekly in growing season with liquid houseplant food diluted according to the maker's instructions.

Soil: Loam-based No. 2 compost. Good drainage essential.

Repotting: Annually in early spring. A 5in (13cm) pot adequate for plants up to 5 years old. Put plenty of broken crocks or pebbles in pot to improve drainage.

Cleaning: Gently dust with soft brush or feather duster if dirty. No leafshine.

Plant grows straggly, with long spaces between leaves. Needs pruning. Prune in early spring to encourage a bushy plant with many flowers.

Pruning
When flowers and bracts have died, cut the stems back severely to within 3–6in (7–15cm) of compost. Cut just above a leaf stem.

Humidity
Stand pot on saucer of pebbles almost covered in water to provide extra humidity but do not let base of pot stand in water, as compost must be well drained. Do not spray when bracts are forming or they will rot.

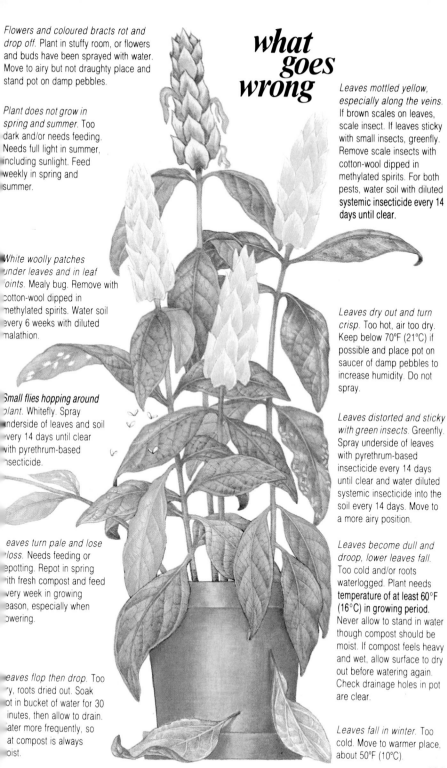

Flowers and coloured bracts rot and drop off. Plant in stuffy room, or flowers and buds have been sprayed with water. Move to airy but not draughty place and stand pot on damp pebbles.

Plant does not grow in spring and summer. Too dark and/or needs feeding. Needs full light in summer, including sunlight. Feed weekly in spring and summer.

White woolly patches under leaves and in leaf joints. Mealy bug. Remove with cotton-wool dipped in methylated spirits. Water soil every 6 weeks with diluted malathion.

Small flies hopping around plant. Whitefly. Spray underside of leaves and soil every 14 days until clear with pyrethrum-based insecticide.

eaves turn pale and lose loss. Needs feeding or epotting. Repot in spring ith fresh compost and feed very week in growing eason, especially when owering.

eaves flop then drop. Too ry, roots dried out. Soak ot in bucket of water for 30 inutes, then allow to drain. ater more frequently, so at compost is always oist.

what goes wrong

Leaves mottled yellow, especially along the veins. If brown scales on leaves, scale insect. If leaves sticky with small insects, greenfly. Remove scale insects with cotton-wool dipped in methylated spirits. For both pests, water soil with diluted **systemic insecticide every 14 days until clear.**

Leaves dry out and turn crisp. Too hot, air too dry. Keep below 70°F (21°C) if possible and place pot on saucer of damp pebbles to increase humidity. Do not spray.

Leaves distorted and sticky with green insects. Greenfly. Spray underside of leaves with pyrethrum-based insecticide every 14 days until clear and water diluted systemic insecticide into the soil every 14 days. Move to a more airy position.

Leaves become dull and droop, lower leaves fall. Too cold and/or roots waterlogged. Plant needs **temperature of at least 60°F (16°C) in growing period.** Never allow to stand in water though compost should be moist. If compost feels heavy and wet, allow surface to dry out before watering again. Check drainage holes in pot are clear.

Leaves fall in winter. Too cold. Move to warmer place, about 50°F (10°C).

411

Pandanus veitchii

Screw pine

Described by an eminent Victorian botanist as a 'stately, fine-looking plant,' the screw pine needs plenty of room to be seen at its best, as it leaves may grow over 3ft (1m) long and spread out gracefully. They grow in a circle from the central stem which appears to twist as it ages, giving the plant the first part of its common name. The 'pine' comes from the leaves' resemblance to pineapple leaves. When the plant is 2–3 years old it develops aerial roots which grow down to the soil, raising the plant as if on stilts.

The Screw pine's sharp-edged leaves are green with creamy white or yellowish stripes near the edges. Growing in a spiral pattern from the centre, they arch down gracefully, making a striking display. They need good light and because of their spiked leaves should be kept in a place where they will not be accidentally touched.

Light: Likes plenty, except mid-day sun. Needs some sunlight every day and will deteriorate if in too dark a position.

Temperature: Winter minimum 50°F (10°C), though water must be withheld at this temperature and plant better kept at 60°F (15°C). Can be in normal room temperature in summer, though if very hot (75°F, 24°C or above), needs increased humidity and plenty of air.

Water: 2–3 times a week in summer, every 10 days with tepid water in winter, withholding altogether if temperature drops to winter minimum. At all times, ensure no water left in leaf axils as this can cause rotting. Best watered from below.

Humidity: Spray with tepid water once a week in summer, every 10–14 days at other times. Keep on saucer of damp pebbles.

Feeding: Every 20 days in the growing season (spring and summer) with houseplant food diluted according to the maker's instructions.

Soil: Loam-based No. 2 compost with peat added in proportion of 4:1.

Repotting: Usually every 12–15 months in spring, though plant best in small pot.

Cleaning: Wipe leaves with damp cloth, or use leafshine every 3 weeks.

Repotting

Repot in spring when roots are very crowded and new leaves are small. Water plant well first. Prepare pot one size larger with drainage layer and layer of damp, loam-based No. 2 compost mixed with peat.

1. Hold old pot with one hand over compost, around base of plant. Tap edge of pot and plant and old compost will come out.

2. Carefully tease away stale soil but do not damage the roots or aerial roots. Place plant in centre of new pot, resting root ball on compost. Cover roots with compost but leave about 1–2in (2½–5cm) space between top of compost and pot rim.

3. If aerial roots grow later in the year, cover them with fresh compost in autumn.

Leaves turn all green, plant does not grow. Too dark. Move to lighter place. Make sure plant is in morning or afternoon sun.

Leaves pale and bleached. Too much midday sun. Plant needs morning or afternoon sun every day but not fierce noonday light.

New leaves small. Needs feeding or repotting. Check roots to see if they are very crowded in pot and if so, repot in next size of pot.

Leaves shrivel and turn brown. Too hot and dry. Water more often and move to cooler place (under 75°F, 24°C if possible).

Leaves rotting. Drops of water left on leaves after spraying or watering. Water from below and if temperature 50°F (10°C) allow soil to dry out.

Brown scales and sticky coating under leaves. Scale insect. Remove with cotton wool dipped in methylated spirits and spray with diluted malathion every 14 days until clear.

what goes wrong

Brown marks on edges of leaves. Air too dry. Stand pot on saucer of damp pebbles to improve humidity.

Webs under leaves and yellow marks on surface. Red spider mite. Spray with diluted malathion or systemic insecticide every 14 days until clear.

Base of leaf rotting. Too wet, overwatered. Allow soil to dry out before watering again. In winter allow top half of soil to dry out between waterings, and if temperatures below 50°F (10°C) do not water at all. Stem rot may be fatal.

Leaves soft, brown and mushy. Much too cold, frost damage. Cut out dead leaves at base and move to warmer room, preferably at least 60°F (15°C).

413

Parodia

Since they were introduced to cultivation some forty years ago, these cacti have become very popular with collectors because of their attractive spines and freely produced flowers. They are small plants, the largest not more than 8 or 12in (20 or 30cm) tall, and take ten years or more to reach this size. Since they have shallow roots, they do not usually outgrow a 4in (10cm) pot. Flower colours vary from deep red as in *Parodia penicillata* (p.415) through orange and yellow and spines range from pure white through yellows and browns to almost black. They come from a wide area of South America including Bolivia, Paraguay and Argentina.

Parodia comosa has neat rows of fluffy white pads called areoles, from which the contrasting dark brown spines arise. An abundance of smallish yellow flowers may be expected when the plant is 4 or 5 years old and 2in (5cm) or so tall. As with all cacti that have white wool, overhead watering or spraying should be avoided.

Light: A sunny windowsill is essential for good spine and flower production. In a greenhouse, shade lightly in the sunniest months, giving full light for the rest of the year.

Temperature: They do best about 45°F (8°C) in winter but will survive at 40°F (4°C). In summer keep below 100°F (38°C), giving fresh air whenever possible.

Parodia hausteiniana is notable for its dense, warm amber spines, many of which are hooked and may easily catch on curtains or clothing. If accidentally unpotted in this way, replace in dry compost and do not water for 2 weeks. This species flowers when it is barely an inch (2½cm) tall.

Water: Water every week in summer, every fortnight if in pots larger than 4in (10cm). Reduce to once a month in spring and autumn, keeping dry in winter in the coldest months.

Feeding: Use high potash fertilizer (as used for tomatoes) 2 or 3 times during spring and summer.

Soil: Use 3 parts soil-less or good loam-based No. 2 potting compost to 1 part coarse gritty sand (not builders' or seashore).

Repotting: Repot every year in spring into next size pot until plants are in 4in (10cm) pot. Then every other year will do. If plant has not outgrown its container, remove from pot, carefully shake old soil from around roots and replace with fresh soil.

Parodia penicillata grows 4–6in (10–15cm) tall and produces its clusters of red flowers in early summer. Flowering season may last from a week to a month with new blooms replacing those that fade. Though Parodias grow slowly, most reach flowering size when they are only about 1in (2½cm) across.

If growing from seed, leave the tray or pots covered with polythene for about a year. After 6 months the seedlings will still be only about the size of pinheads, often with a tiny root. If the covering is removed too soon, they will quickly dry up.

Most have shallow roots so half-pots or pans are suitable.

Cleaning and pest control: Spray monthly to keep dust-free except for the very woolly species such as *P. nivosa* and *schwebsiana*. Incorporate an insecticide 2 or 3 times a year.

Other species: *P. chrysacanthion* is similar to *P. penicillata* (above) but has yellow flowers produced at the centre in clusters of 10 or more. It is one of the most beautifully spined of all cacti, with dense, long, thin spines like fragile splinters of yellow glass.

Many smaller growing types are available in various spines and flower colours. These include *P. comosa* with yellow flowers and *P. hausteiniana* with hooked yellow spines and yellow flowers. *P. nivosa* is a more woolly species with snow-white spines and red flowers; *P. prolifera* makes clusters of small heads with white and yellow spines and deep yellow flowers. *P. maassii* is one of the largest with spines ranging from white to yellow or brown and yellow or orange flowers.

Passiflora caerulea

Passion flower

When grown in the home, this plant is usually trained around a hoop or on a small trellis, which is how it is generally sold as a houseplant. *Passiflora* is best suited to a conservatory or porch as it requires a very cool winter temperature; it can even be grown out of doors if protected from frost. With full light it will flower freely in summer through to winter and may even produce fruit. Choose plants with many buds still unopened, not with the remains of old flowers.

Light: Full light, including sun. If in too dark conditions it will not flower.

Temperature: Maintain 65–75°F (18–24°C) from spring to autumn, never exceeding 75°F (24°C) in summer. Maintain 55–65°F (13–18°C) from autumn to spring.

Water: Copiously every 2 days from spring to late summer to keep moist – daily if temperature goes up to 75°F (24°C). In winter water only when soil surface seems dry, i.e. every 7–10 days.

Humidity: Spray with soft water 2 or 3 times a week in summer. Do not spray in winter or when plant is in sunshine.

Feeding: Weekly in spring and summer with liquid houseplant food diluted to half maker's instructions. Do not feed in winter.

Soil: 2 parts peat, 2 parts loam and 1 part coarse sand.

Repotting: Annually in spring after plant has been pruned by about one-third to encourage strong new growth. Pot up into one size larger pot only, or plant will produce abundant foliage and few flowers that year. (If larger plant wanted, pot up into pot 2 sizes larger. Plant may not flower that year.) Remove weak shoots altogether.

Cleaning: Humidity spraying adequate. No leafshine.

Passion flowers were named by early Spanish missionaries to South America, who saw the symbols of Christ's passion in the strange form of the flowers. Different parts of the flower represent the wounds, nails, cross, crown of thorns and the apostles.

White cotton-wool patches where leaf joins stem. Mealy bug. Spray with diluted malathion and remove bugs and 'wool' with tweezers. Repeat every 14 days until symptoms disappear. Or, paint bugs with methylated spirits and remove with tweezers.

New leaves small. Needs feeding. Feed with houseplant food diluted to half maker's recommended strength every week in growing season.

Leaves distorted and sticky. Greenfly. Spray with pyrethrum-based insecticide or diluted malathion. Repeat one week later, then once a week until symptoms disappear.

Plant looks limp and leaves turn yellow. Soil too dry. Plunge pot into bucket of water for 10–15 minutes, then drain.

Whole leaves turn furry with white powder. Botrytis mould. Too cold and damp. Spray with fungicide then place in warmer place, at least 55°F (13°C). Spray with water less often. Allow compost to dry out between waterings in winter.

Pruning

Prune in spring, before buds appear. Cut back main stem by one-third, cutting at an angle just above a leaf, using sharp secateurs. Shorten side shoots by half and cut out any weedy shoots at the base.

Fruit remains yellow, with a few black spots. Too cold. Move to warmer, lighter position, at least 65°F (18°C).

what goes wrong

Flowers have scorch marks. Caused by spraying in sunlight. Do not spray flowers and spray leaves only in early morning and evening.

Plant wilts though soil is moist. Plant waterlogged, standing in water. Drain away any water in saucer and allow surface to dry out before watering again. Then keep moist in summer but never allow pot base to stand in water. Always throw away excess that drains through after watering.

Growing tips droop and flop. Too hot and air too dry. Move to position with better ventilation and improve humidity by spraying regularly and standing pot on saucer of damp pebbles. Maximum temperature 75°F (24°C).

Leaves pale with webs underneath. Red spider mite. Remove webs with damp cloth or sponge, then spray with diluted malathion, especially under leaves. Repeat every 14 days until symptoms disappear. Improve humidity around plant.

No flowers appear. Pot too large or, if new leaves also small, needs feeding. Flowers best when slightly pot bound. Do not repot for 2 years. Feed with houseplant food diluted to half maker's recommended strength every week in the growing season. If leaves are growing rapidly, too much food. Withhold for 2–3 weeks, and always use half strength food. Do not feed in winter. If other conditions seem correct, not enough light. Move to position in very good light. Plant will stand direct sunshine.

Regal pelargonium

Pelargoniums are often confused with geraniums, outdoor garden plants to which they are closely related. The varieties grown indoors as houseplants are real sun-worshippers and require the protection of a sun-facing window. They are most satisfying, colourful plants to grow in summer, and are not difficult providing they are in good light, airy positions and are well watered.

Pelargoniums have large heads of flowers, delicately coloured from the softest of pinks to the darkest of reds, often with a contrasting deeper shaded area in the middle of petals. When the flower-heads have died, break them off at the point where they join the main stem. In spring a straggly plant can be pruned back to about half its size.

Light: Sun-facing window essential to provide sufficient light all year round.

Temperature: Winter, 55–60°F (13–15°C); summer, ordinary room temperature to maximum 75°F (24°C).

Water: 2–3 times a week in summer, with good drainage in pot. About once every 10 days in winter to keep on dry side. If below 60°F (16°C), withhold water.

Humidity: Fairly dry atmosphere preferred. No overhead spraying, as this can produce stem rot. Do not stand pot on damp pebbles.

Feeding: Every 14 days in spring and summer when growing with liquid houseplant food diluted according to maker's instructions.

Soil: Peat-based or loam-based No. 1 compost.

Repotting: Twice during first year. After this, since plant flowers better if pot-bound, change topsoil each spring and feed.

Cleaning: Use feather duster if very dusty. Do not spray. No leafshine.

Healthy Pelargoniums have clean-looking green leaves, with no sign of yellowing or damaged edges. In a sunny window they produce a succession of buds from late spring to the end of summer, opening into bright clusters of flowers ranging in colour from pale pink to deep red.

Plant grows straggly, with long spaces between leaves. Bottom leaves turn/yellow. Too dark. Move into light window, facing the sun.

what goes wrong

White insects fly away from plant when touched. Whitefly. Spray with derris or pyrethrum-based insecticide every 14 days until clear.

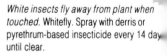

Mass of distorted shoots at soil level. Leafy gall, a bacterial disease. Destroy plant and do not use as cuttings. No cure

Lots of healthy leaves grow but no flowers. Overfeeding. Feed only every 3 weeks instead of every 14 days and never exceed recommended strength of dose. Try changing the brand of houseplant food.

Watering
1. Pelargoniums need careful watering to keep them moist but not waterlogged in summer, drier in winter. Always test compost surface before adding water.

2. Water from top of pot and allow excess to drain through. After 10 minutes empty away any that remains in the saucer. If temperature falls below 60°F (16°C) do not water.

Leaves turn yellow and have brown blotches. Too dry and stuffy. Water more often, 2 to 3 times a week in summer and move to more airy position.

Leaves darken and develop a red tinge. Too cold at night. Move to warmer place and do not allow temperature to fall below 55°F (13°C).

Pale yellow rings on distorted leaves. Virus disease. No cure. Destroy plant.

Bottom of stem turns black and rots. Fungal disease called black leg. Caused by cold and overwatering. Usually fatal but move plant to warmer room (around 60°F, 15°C) in winter and allow plant to dry out before watering again.

Pelargonium zonale

Geranium

Both Zonal and Ivy-leaved Pelargoniums are suitable for outdoor planting, though they can also be grown successfully indoors on a sunny windowsill. All should be taken inside over winter and kept cool, dry and in good light until the following spring.

Light: Seedlings, good light indoors; cuttings shade while rooting. Mature plants, good light. Dappled shade suitable.

Temperature: Germination, 70°F (21°C) or more. Cuttings indoors need bottom heat of 65°F (18°C). Harden off gradually. No frost.

Water: Use tap, not stored water. Allow container to dry out between waterings.

Humidity: Dry, no overhead spraying.

Soil: Soil-less for germination and cuttings. Then loam-based No.2 or soil-less potting compost.

Feeding: Use liquid fertilizer at half maker's recommended strength every week in soil, every 3 days in soil-less. Increase strength to full recommended rate when plants are growing well outside.

Propagation: Take cuttings outdoors in midsummer or early autumn, indoors in early autumn and early spring. Root 3-4 to a 4in (10cm) pot, giving bottom heat of 65°F (18°C) for indoor cuttings. Sow seeds in early autumn or early spring. Clip pointed ends before sowing and sow in moist compost at 70°F (21°C) or more.

Tidying: Remove dead flower stems where they join main stem. Do not leave end of stem protruding.

Varieties: From seed, Caprice, coral pink. Sprinter, scarlet. Ringo, red. Playboy, mixed, bronze leaf, small flowers. From cuttings, Paul Crampel, single scarlet. Irene, semi-double cerise. Gustav Emich, red, double. Springtime, salmon, double. Treasure chest, orange red, double.

Geraniums have few equals for brilliance of colour and long-lasting blooms and are probably the most familiar of all windowbox and balcony plants. Flowers range from white through pink to brilliant scarlet and plants can be from 6 to 30in (15 to 75cm) tall.

what goes wrong

Holes appear in buds and leaves. Caterpillar. Search for and destroy pest. Dust carefully with gamma-BHC. A whole month's flowers may be eaten in a single night.

Plant suddenly goes yellow and sick. Black leg (pythium) from unsterile, overwatered soil. No cure. Take plant carefully from container and soak area with cheshunt compound or Jeyes fluid diluted to manufacturer's instructions.

Plant has yellow edge to bottom leaves. Leaves and flowers becoming smaller. Needs feeding. Increase number of liquid feeds per week. Do not increase strength.

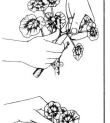

Preparing a cutting
1. Choose shoot with at least 2 pairs of leaves and growing point and cut below second pair of leaves (about 4in, 10cm long).

2. Trim end to just below leaf and remove lowest pair of leaves. Dip cut end in rooting powder and insert round edge of pot, in seedling compost.

Many lush leaves but no flowers or only small ones. Overfeeding. Feed with half-strength fertilizer when plants young, increasing to full recommended strength as plant matures.

Plant does not grow well: no flowers. Too dark. Move to lighter place, full sun if possible. Or, sciarid fly larvae on roots. Drench soil with diluted malathion to maker's instructions.

Pinpoint white/pale yellow spots on surface of leaf, leaves look mealy underneath. Red spider mite. Spray plant with dimethoate or liquid derris and repeat until growth is a fresh green.

Grey mould on spent flower heads. Botrytis. This will occur after rain followed by humid conditions or spraying whole plant regularly. Remove heads very carefully to prevent spores from spreading and spray with benomyl.

Distorted flower buds or tender young growth. Aphid damage. Spray with pirimicarb or derris to maker's instructions.

Light yellow spots on top of foliage, increasing in size, and brown snuff-like powder on the underside. Pelargonium rust. Spray with dinocap fungicide.

Leaves redden when first planted outside in spring. Due to sudden chill after being protected. Transfer from inside to outside conditions must be gradual.

Leaves begin to yellow from base. Too dry. Increase water slightly but do not allow to become waterlogged.

Plant does not look fresh, soil is dark and sickly Poor drainage or overwatering. Make sure drainage is clear. Stop watering until dry.

421

Button fern

Most ferns in the *Pellaea* family are small and best grown in hanging baskets or indoor rockeries, but *P. rotundifolia* is available in pots. It makes a good houseplant provided it is in a cool to moderate temperature in slight shade with constantly moist soil. Also grows well in a greenhouse or conservatory. Its common name derives from its round, slightly leathery leaves which grow directly from the frond alternately on each side down the length. New leaves grow from the tip of the frond.

The Button fern's slightly glossy, leathery round leaves grow from a thin brown leaf stem. The leaf edges are slightly crinkled but should not look brown or dried.

Light: Diffused daylight. No direct sunlight. Tolerates semi-shade.

Temperature: Tolerates winter minimum of 45°F (7°C). Ideal all-year-round temperature is 55°F (13°C). Summer maximum should be 65°F (18°C).

Water: At least 3 times a week in summer, once or twice a week in winter, as soil must remain moist. Do not water leaves or plant will die. Do not stand in water.

Humidity: Dry atmosphere and airy situation best. High humidity will kill the plant. Do not spray with water.

Feeding: Every 14 days from early spring to mid/late summer with houseplant food diluted with water according to maker's instructions.

Soil: Equal parts of loam-based No. 2, leafmould or peat, and crushed limestone. Good drainage is essential as plant must not be waterlogged.

Repotting: Plant has very little root and will grow in 4in (10cm) pot all its life. Change soil every two years and divide if plant becomes top heavy.

Cleaning: Remove dust with feather duster. No spraying, damp cloth or leafshine.

Whole fronds dry up. Too dry. Keep soil always moist, watering 3 times a week summer, twice a week in winter.

Watering and cleaning
Add water from base of pot. Allow to stand for 15 minutes, then empty excess from saucer. Add food to water when feeding.

Clean leaves gently with a feather duster. Do not spray or use leafshine.

Plant does not grow. Needs feeding or, if all conditions are correct, is in too large a pot. Repot in spring into smaller pot. 4in (10cm) is large enough.

what goes wrong

Whole plant turns brown. Too hot. Move to cooler place and keep soil always moist. Cut off brown foliage with scissors as near to soil as possible.

Whole plant goes limp. Bad drainage. Always throw away excess water in saucer after watering.

Individual leaves turn brown and dry up. Atmosphere too humid or leaves wet from spray or watering. Do not spray and water from below.

Leaves turn black and die. Leafshine damage, do not use. Only sprayed leaves will be affected. Cut off leaves close to stem or cut frond close to soil.

Some leaves turn brownish yellow, webs under leaves. Red spider mite. Do not spray but add systemic insecticide to water once a week until pest disappears. Remove webs with feather duster.

Leaves turn black. Too cold. Keep at 55°F (13°C) all the year round.

Fronds dry up from tips, leaves blacken. Direct sunlight. Move to area of diffused light.

Plant looks dull and lifeless, but leaves still green. Too dark. Move to lighter place but not in direct sunlight.

Polynesia

An attractive creeping plant that is moderately easy to grow and does well in hanging baskets. Two species are normally grown, *Pellionia pulchra*, also known as the Rainbow vine, and *P. daveauana*. The first has rounded, silvery green leaves with dark markings along the veins. The second has more pointed leaves with a lighter central area. Slow growers, they need careful watering in winter or they may rot. If a plant becomes leggy and loses its leaves near the centre, it is best to repropagate and start again. Cuttings taken in summer root easily.

The Polynesia plant's leaves change as they age from dull red to silvery green, marked with darker green along the veins. The young leaves are delicate and may be easily bruised if handled carelessly.

Light: Does well in shady position, but prefers indirect light away from direct sunlight.

Temperature: Minimum 60°F (16°C) in winter. Up to 80°F (27°C) in summer. Increase humidity if temperature rises too high.

Water: Keep moist at all times, unless temperature drops to minimum. Do not overwater or allow pot to stand in water; twice a week in summer, once a week in winter enough.

Humidity: Likes a humid atmosphere. Spray daily when over 70°F (21°C) in summer, once a week in winter when under 65°F (18°C).

Feeding: Every 21 days in spring and summer with liquid houseplant food at maker's recommended strength.

Soil: Likes an open compost, so use peat-based No. 2.

Repotting: Once a year in spring. Young leaves are tender, take care not to bruise them.

Cleaning: Spraying should keep it clean. Do not use leafshine.

Little green flies and sticky substance on leaves. Greenfly. Spray with pyrethrum-based insecticide or diluted malathion. Repeat one week later and every week until clear.

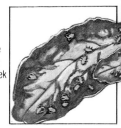

Cuttings

1. Take cuttings in summer if plant has grown leggy. Cut off stem tip 2–3in (5–8cm) long, including growing point and at least 2 pairs of leaves.

2. Trim off stem below leaf, remove lower leaves and dust end with hormone rooting powder. Insert in mixture of sand and peat, cover with polythene and keep warm until rooted.

Leaves limp, plant collapses. Compost too dry. Water immediately. Allow compost surface to just dry out before watering again. In winter water sparingly only once a week.

what goes wrong

Leaves pale, perhaps with scorch marks. Too much direct sun. Move to position in good indirect light.

Leaves go crisp and spotted. Leafshine damage. Do not use. Clean only by spraying with soft tepid water. Remove damaged leaf.

Grey mould in winter on stems near base. Botrytis. Plant too cold and damp. Spray with fungicide, then move to warmer place, over 60°F (16°C) and spray with water less frequently. Allow surface to dry out between waterings. Remove damaged leaves.

Stems rot, leaves collapse. Compost too moist. Allow surface of soil to dry out before watering again, then water only after surface has dried out. Twice a week in summer, once a week in winter should be enough but test compost before watering.

Leaves and stems go crisp and leaves drop off. Too hot. Move to a cooler place with more ventilation. Spray daily with soft, tepid water. Maximum temperature 80°F (27°C).

Plant grows leggy and drops leaves. Too dark. Move to lighter place (but not direct sunlight).

425

Peperomia magnoliaefolia

Desert privet

Desert privet plants have thick, fleshy leaves, rather like succulents. Unlike true succulents, however, they need a shady position since in the wild they grow at the foot of or in large trees. There are many varieties available. *Peperomia magnoliaefolia* is the most popular but others include *P. caperata*, with indented, dark green leaves, *P. hederifolia* with pale grey leaves and, most striking of all, *P. sandersii* or *argyreia* which has smooth green, silvery striped leaves on bright red stems. *P. magnoliaefolia's* first leaves are plain green, the variegated green and cream markings appearing as the plant grows.

Light: Keep away from direct sun, but not in half darkness: indirect light best.
Temperature: Between 60–65°F (16–18°C) in winter, though will survive down to 50°F (10°C) for short periods if kept dry. Summer maximum 75°F (24°C).
Water: Allow to dry out between waterings: every 10 days in summer, every 14–18 days in winter enough. Overwatering, especially in winter, can cause rotting and botrytis.
Humidity: They like a humid atmosphere so spray twice a week in summer and winter unless temperature below 60°F (16°C). Stand pot on wet pebbles for extra humidity.
Feeding: Give liquid houseplant food every 14 days in spring and summer, diluting to half maker's recommended strength.
Soil: Loam-based No. 1.
Repotting: In spring only if outgrowing pot. They have small root system and do better in small pots.
Cleaning: Spraying sufficient. If wiping with a damp cloth, take care as leaves are brittle. No leafshine.

The Desert privet's green and cream leaves make it attractive all the year round. A small, compact plant, it rarely grows to more than 8in (20cm) high. Some varieties produce flowers which grow in upright spikes rather like mouse tails and are usually off white in colour.

Leaves shrivel, dry up and die. Too hot. Move to cooler room, below 75°F (24°C).

Parts of leaves and base of stem go black and rot. Too wet. Allow soil to dry out before watering again, then water less often. Once every 10 days in summer, once every 14–18 days enough in winter.

what goes wrong

Leaves drop. Too cold. Move to warmer place, above 60°F (16°C).

Plant does not grow and looks dull. Needs feeding. Feed with liquid houseplant food diluted to half maker's recommended strength every 14 days in spring and summer.

Leaves dull and pale. Too much light. Move out of strong sunlight, into more shady place.

Rust spots on leaves. Leafshine damage. Do not use. Clean only by spraying or wiping leaves with damp cloth. Remove damaged leaf where it joins stem.

Cuttings
1. Take stem tip cuttings in spring. Cut off stem with 2 pairs of leaves and growing tip. Trim below bottom leaves.

2. Remove lowest pair of leaves and dip stem in hormone rooting powder. Plant in sand/leafmould and keep covered at 65°F (18°C) for 21 days.

Leaves yellow with webs underneath. Red spider mite. Remove webs with damp cloth or sponge, then spray with diluted malathion, especially under leaves. Repeat every 14 days until symptoms disappear. Improve humidity.

Leaves look blistered. Waterlogged, may be standing in water. Drain away any water in saucer and allow surface to dry out before watering again. Always throw away excess from saucer after watering.

Grey mould on stems. Botrytis. Too cold and damp. Spray with fungicide, then move to warmer room and spray with water less often. Winter minimum best above 60°F (16°C). Allow soil surface to dry out between waterings. Remove damaged leaves where they join stem.

Leaves limp. Compost and air too dry. Water immediately by plunging pot into bucket of water for 10–15 minutes, then drain. Spray twice a week all the year round unless temperature falls below 60°F (16°C).

Petunia

Petunias come from Argentina and are really half-hardy perennials though usually now grown as annuals. Few other plants flower so prolifically and they are ideal for the sheltered conditions usually given in containers. Flowers may be spoilt by rain but the actual plants recover quickly. As they will survive light frost they can be planted out early and will bloom from late spring through to late autumn. If buying plants, do not choose any with more than one flower showing.

Modern Petunias are compact, bushy plants from 12 to 18in (30–45cm) high. The bell-shaped flowers come in almost every colour of the spectrum including a recent yellow variety and some with two-coloured stripes.

Light: Seedlings need good light. Outdoors, full sun. No more than 20% shade.
Temperature: Germination, 65°F (18°C). Outside, will survive light frost. Best over 50°F (10°C).
Water: Allow container almost to dry out between waterings.
Humidity: Do not spray flowers.
Soil: Loam-based No. 1 or soil-less potting compost.
Feeding: Feed every 14 days in soil, starting 6 weeks after planting. In soil-less, feed weekly, starting 3 weeks after planting out. Liquid feed best, at half maker's recommended strength.
Propagation: In mid-spring, sow fine seed thinly in prepared tray. Do not cover with compost. Place in propagator or plastic bag at 65°F (18°C) in light shade, not full sun. Germination takes 8 days. Prick out seedlings as soon as large enough to handle, into small pots or 2in (5cm) apart in trays. Reduce to 50°F (10°C) and give maximum light. Will grow at 45°F (7°C) but slowly.
Tidying: Remove wet flowers after rain.
Varieties: Many hundreds. Multifloras have smaller flowers but are very prolific. Resisto Rose Pink most rainproof. Grandifloras have large flowers but are less weather-proof.

Growing from seed

1. Sow thinly in prepared, drained compost in seed. Place fine seed on palm of hand and tap edge with index finger of other hand so seed falls evenly. Do not cover seed with compost.

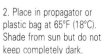

2. Place in propagator or plastic bag at 65°F (18°C). Shade from sun but do not keep completely dark.

3. When seeds germinate (8 days) remove propagator cover. Prick out singly when seedlings large enough to handle.

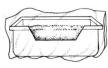

what goes wrong

Young plants grow slowly. Too cold. Plants will survive light frosts but grow better if above 50°F (10°C)

Leaves grow lush but few flowers appear. Overfeeding. Do not feed until plant has been in soil for 6 weeks, then feed regularly with half-strength liquid feed.

Plant wilts and droops. Too hot and dry. Water well but allow soil to dry out between waterings. Plant survives well in dry weather.

Young plant looks thin and weedy. Too dark. Move to lighter position with full sunlight.

Small winged green flies on leaves and inside flower. Leaves sticky. Aphid. Spray with systemic insecticide and repeat after 14 days if pest has returned.

White ghost spots on flowers. Alternaria disease. Spray with benomyl once.

Flowers turn colourless and soggy, all flowers affected. Heavy rain damage. Remove old blooms and new buds will soon open. Protect plants from heavy rain if possible.

Yellow blotches on leaves, dark patches on flower stems. Tobacco mosaic virus. No cure, but plant will not be badly affected. Sterilize container before planting more petunias or tobacco plants in it or disease will spread.

Plant turns yellow from base upwards, leaves look limp. Root rot from overwatering. Check drainage in container is clear and allow soil to dry out between waterings. Petunias prefer to be too dry rather than too wet.

Light brown streaks on leaf stems and plant stem, later turning black. Advanced stage of alternaria disease. Spray with benomyl or, if flowering finished, remove plants.

Upright philodendron

Philodendrons are some of the easiest plants to grow in the house and so can be recommended for a beginner. The upright or bush type is a very useful plant and will normally survive in quite a dark position. Though not as popular as the climbing varieties, it is well worth growing. It has thick, slightly fleshy leaves which grow to about 15in (38cm) across on 2ft (60cm) stems. Older plants may produce even larger leaves, so are best grown on their own. Stems which lean too far out over the edge of the pot can be tied to a cane. When inserting canes, take care not to damage the roots. Cuttings can sometimes be grown from the small shoots at the base of the leaf stems, but they are difficult to root.

Light: Prefers good light position away from direct sunlight. Will tolerate positions away from the window.

Temperature: Winter minimum 55°F (12°C). Up to 75°F (24°C) in summer, provided good humidity is maintained.

Water: Twice a week in summer while growing, once a week in winter. Do not allow plant to stand in water.

Humidity: Mist with tepid water twice a week all the year round.

Feeding: Every 14 days in the growing season (spring and summer) with houseplant food diluted according to the maker's instructions.

Soil: Loam-based No. 2 or peat-based compost with fertilizer of No. 2 strength included.

Repotting: Annually in spring until plant is in 7in (18cm) pot. Then just replace topsoil in pot each spring.

Cleaning: Use damp cloth, supporting leaf from underneath. Use leafshine not more than once every two months.

This type of upright Philodendron has leaves about 15in (35cm) across. Healthy leaves are bright, glossy green, with deep indentations around the edges so that they are split almost to the centre vein. Young leaves are scarcely indented at all but develop their characteristic shape as they grow older.

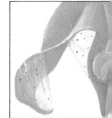

Webs under leaves, leaves start to discolour. Red spider mite. Spray with diluted malathion or systemic insecticide every 14 days until clear.

what goes wrong

Leaves look dull and do not grow in spring. Too cold. Move to warmer place, at least 55°F (12°C).

Stems grow long and floppy.
Too dark. Move to lighter
position but not full sun.
Need not be by window but
does need some light to
flourish.

Cleaning
Clean the leaves with a
damp sponge or cloth,
supporting them from
underneath. Use leafshine
but not more than once a month.

corch marks on leaves.
irect sunlight. Do not spray
sunlight and keep plant in
hadier position.

Leaves droop. Too hot and
dry. Soak plant in bucket of
water for 10–15 minutes,
then drain. Water more often
and keep in cooler place.

Leaves turn yellow then
drop. Too wet, overwatered.
Check drainage holes in pot
are clear and allow to dry
out before watering again. In
winter allow top layer of soil
to dry out between
waterings.

New leaves stay small or
none appear. Needs feeding
or repotting. Check roots
and repot in spring if
crowded together. Feed
regularly when growing.

431

Climbing philodendron

Philodendrons are a very large family of plants, many of which make excellent houseplants. They are generally divided into upright and climbing types. Many new varieties of climbing Philodendron have been specially bred as houseplants; all need the support of canes or moss poles and most grow quickly into large, handsome plants. The large leaved types have pointed leaves that are mainly green but may be so dark as to be nearly black, red or almost golden. Growing up to 2–3ft (60–90cm) a year, they make ideal plants for office or showroom displays.

Large-leaved climbing Philodendrons, like this *Philodendron erubescens* 'Emerald Queen' are quick growers, making up to 2-3ft (60-90cm) a year in good conditions.Strong support from a cane or moss pole is essential.

Light: Best in indirect light (not direct midday sun) but will survive in semi-shade.
Temperature: In winter 55–65°F (13–18°C); in summer up to 75°F (24°C).
Water: Keep moist in summer, watering regularly twice a week while growing. Allow soil surface to dry out in winter, watering once a week.
Humidity: Spray twice weekly all the year round; in winter use tepid water.
Feeding: Feed every 14 days in growing season (spring and summer) using liquid houseplant food at maker's recommended strength.
Soil: Loam or peat-based No. 2.
Repotting: Young plants need repotting at least once a year in spring. When they have grown too large to handle easily, replace top 2–3in (5–7cm) compost each year with fresh and feed regularly.
Cleaning: Wipe leaves with a damp cloth. Use leafshine not more than once a month.

Making a moss pole

1. Choose cane long enough to reach to top of plant from pot base and tie a piece of string about 9in (22cm) from end.

2. Take enough sphagnum moss to cover rest of cane and loosen it with stick or pencil. Bind moss along cane with string, tying off at top with a firm knot.

3. Position cane when repotting and tie plant loosely to pole in several places.

what goes wrong

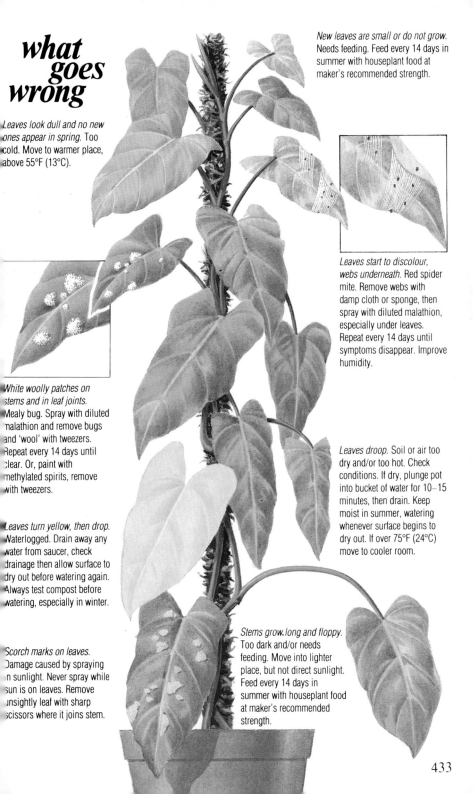

Leaves look dull and no new ones appear in spring. Too cold. Move to warmer place, above 55°F (13°C).

New leaves are small or do not grow. Needs feeding. Feed every 14 days in summer with houseplant food at maker's recommended strength.

Leaves start to discolour, webs underneath. Red spider mite. Remove webs with damp cloth or sponge, then spray with diluted malathion, especially under leaves. Repeat every 14 days until symptoms disappear. Improve humidity.

White woolly patches on stems and in leaf joints. Mealy bug. Spray with diluted malathion and remove bugs and 'wool' with tweezers. Repeat every 14 days until clear. Or, paint with methylated spirits, remove with tweezers.

Leaves droop. Soil or air too dry and/or too hot. Check conditions. If dry, plunge pot into bucket of water for 10–15 minutes, then drain. Keep moist in summer, watering whenever surface begins to dry out. If over 75°F (24°C) move to cooler room.

Leaves turn yellow, then drop. Waterlogged. Drain away any water from saucer, check drainage then allow surface to dry out before watering again. Always test compost before watering, especially in winter.

Scorch marks on leaves. Damage caused by spraying in sunlight. Never spray while sun is on leaves. Remove unsightly leaf with sharp scissors where it joins stem.

Stems grow.long and floppy. Too dark and/or needs feeding. Move into lighter place, but not direct sunlight. Feed every 14 days in summer with houseplant food at maker's recommended strength.

433

Sweetheart plant

This plant comes from the West Indies and is the most popular of all the Philodendrons. It grows rapidly, requires minimum care and does reasonably well in darker areas. When growing well it will soon cover a trellis with its dark green, heart-shaped leaves. Being a vigorous climber it needs supporting at all times, and has small aerial roots which will attach themselves to whatever is used. Recently it has been grown as a trailing plant for hanging baskets but if grown like this, keep it bushy by pinching out the leading shoots 2 or 3 times in summer. It also does well in hydroculture.

The Sweetheart plant has heart-shaped leaves some 4–5in (10–12cm) long which should be a strong, bright green. Avoid plants that look leggy or have yellowing leaves. This small-leaved species can be either trained as a climber or allowed to trail from a hanging pot.

Light: Keep away from direct sunshine but otherwise will stand most positions. Grows best in a window that does not receive direct sun.

Temperature: Winter minimum 65°F (18°C) though will survive down to 55°F (13°C). Summer maximum 75°F (24°C).

Water: Twice a week in summer while growing. In winter keep drier, watering once a week or less. Always test compost before watering to check that surface has dried out.

Humidity: Spray overhead twice a week all year round. In winter use tepid water.

Feeding: In summer feed with liquid houseplant food every 14 days, diluting to maker's recommended strength.

Soil: Loam or peat-based No. 2. Make sure compost is porous.

Repotting: Repot once a year in spring until too large to handle easily. Then simply replace top 2–3in (5–7cm) soil, being careful not to disturb roots. Make sure pot has good drainage.

Cleaning: Wipe leaves with damp cloth. Use leafshine not more than once a month.

Changing the topsoil

1. When plant is too large to remove from pot, carefully scrape away 2–3in (5–7cm) compost from top of pot.

2. Add fresh compost leaving ½–¾in (1–2cm) between compost and rim to allow space for watering.

3. Firm compost around roots with palms and water well. Add liquid food to water to replace nutrients and continue to feed every 14 days during the growing season.

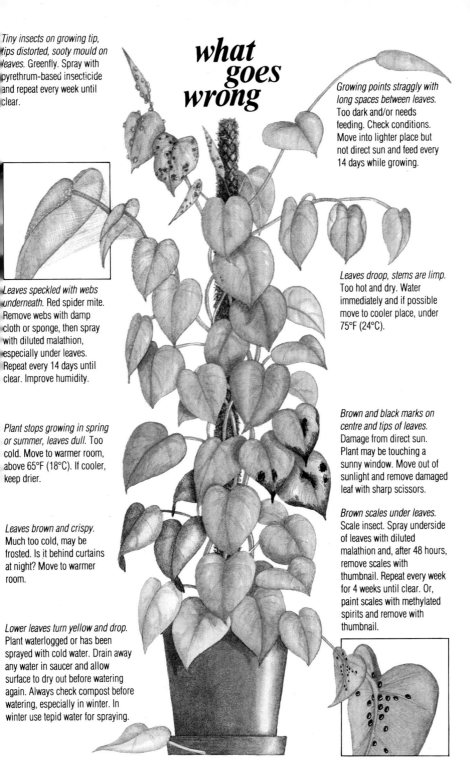

Tiny insects on growing tip, tips distorted, sooty mould on leaves. Greenfly. Spray with pyrethrum-based insecticide and repeat every week until clear.

what goes wrong

Growing points straggly with long spaces between leaves. Too dark and/or needs feeding. Check conditions. Move into lighter place but not direct sun and feed every 14 days while growing.

Leaves speckled with webs underneath. Red spider mite. Remove webs with damp cloth or sponge, then spray with diluted malathion, especially under leaves. Repeat every 14 days until clear. Improve humidity.

Plant stops growing in spring or summer, leaves dull. Too cold. Move to warmer room, above 65°F (18°C). If cooler, keep drier.

Leaves brown and crispy. Much too cold, may be frosted. Is it behind curtains at night? Move to warmer room.

Lower leaves turn yellow and drop. Plant waterlogged or has been sprayed with cold water. Drain away any water in saucer and allow surface to dry out before watering again. Always check compost before watering, especially in winter. In winter use tepid water for spraying.

Leaves droop, stems are limp. Too hot and dry. Water immediately and if possible move to cooler place, under 75°F (24°C).

Brown and black marks on centre and tips of leaves. Damage from direct sun. Plant may be touching a sunny window. Move out of sunlight and remove damaged leaf with sharp scissors.

Brown scales under leaves. Scale insect. Spray underside of leaves with diluted malathion and, after 48 hours, remove scales with thumbnail. Repeat every week for 4 weeks until clear. Or, paint scales with methylated spirits and remove with thumbnail.

Hare's foot fern

The hare's foot fern grows from a furry rhizome which lies half buried in the compost and in time spreads over the surface of the pot. New stems emerge tightly coiled and unfurl to grow into long, brownish, slender stalks up to 2ft (56cm) long, bearing elegant green fronds which add another 16–20in (40–50cm) to the total length. On the undersides of the fronds small orange-brown spores appear on either side of the central vein. Fronds die away one by one and are replaced by new growth from the rhizome.

The Hare's foot fern has graceful, bright green fronds on long stems which are green when young, but turn brown as they grow. The stems emerge from a furry rhizome which lies half buried in the compost and will spread to cover the pot surface. Healthy leaves should look bright and fresh and in spring and summer may have lines of orange spores on the undersides.

Light: High level of diffused light essential. Keep out of direct sunlight.

Temperature: 55–65°F (13–18°C) from early spring to late autumn. Hotter than 70°F (21°C), the leaves will shrivel. Winter minimum 50°F (10°C)

Water: 3 times a week in summer to keep soil moist and once or twice a week in winter, allowing top ½in (1cm) to dry out between waterings. Do not stand in water or expose plant to continual dripping of water.

Humidity: Spray daily with tepid soft water from late winter to early autumn. Stand pot in saucer of pebbles almost covered with water.

Feeding: Every 14 days in summer only, with liquid houseplant food diluted with water. Use half the amount recommended by the maker.

Soil: Equal parts of loam-based No. 2, peat, leafmould and coarse potting sand.

Repotting: In spring into pot two sizes larger, since rhizomes can spread to cover whole surface of compost. Every 2 or 3 years divide rhizomes and repot into well-drained 5in (13cm) pots. Each section of rhizome should have roots and 2–3 stems.

Cleaning: Spray daily with soft water. No leafshine.

Humidity
1. Provide constant humidity around pot by standing pot on saucer of pebbles, half covered in water. Do not allow base of pot to touch water.

2. Or, place pot in outer container packed with damp peat.

No new growth in spring though all conditions correct. Soil too heavy. Repot using correct mixture.

what goes wrong

Stems too crowded in pot, rhizome fills pot. Needs repotting or dividing. Do this every 2–3 years in spring.

New leaves pale. Too dark. Needs good diffused daylight but not direct sun.

Tips of fronds turn black. Food too strong. Feed only every 2 weeks in growing season and use food diluted at half recommended strength.

Foliage dries up and turns brown. Air too dry. Spray daily with water and provide extra humidity by standing on wet pebbles. Or keep in steamy bathroom or kitchen.

Fronds begin to rot away. Too wet or standing in water. If using wet pebbles to provide humidity, make sure pot base is clear of water.

Fronds turn black and shrivel. Leafshine damage. Do not use. Clean only by spraying with soft tepid water.

Plant wilts. Too dry and too hot. Keep soil moist and water daily in summer. Move to cooler place (70°F, 21°C maximum).

Flies hopping around soil surface. Whitefly. Add pyrethrum-based insecticide to water every 14 days until clear. Do not use malathion and do not spray leaves.

Leaflets dry up one by one. Too much direct sunlight. Move to shadier place. Do not spray in sunlight.

437

Phoenix canariensis

Canary Island date palm

This plant requires a large home since it grows to 15ft (4½m) as a house-plant. It is a very chunky plant when mature with a large and heavy root ball: an 8-ft (2½m) specimen could weigh as much as 3cwt (152kg) and would need to be planted in a pot the size of a small dustbin! As it develops, a trunk forms as the lower leaves die. These should be removed with a saw or very sharp knife. The palm will stand quite low temperatures, and can be put outside in the summer even in northern countries. They grow slowly; about 6–10in (15–25cm) a year.

Light: Indirect daylight when young; takes full sunlight when over 4 years old.

Temperature: Cool in winter – about 50°F (10°C). Summer maximum 80°F (27°C), allowing plenty of fresh air round plant if very hot.

Water: At least twice a week in summer to keep evenly moist. In winter water only when surface soil appears dry, about once in 14 days.

Humidity: Spray twice a week with tepid water if temperature over 80°F (27°C). Do not spray in winter.

Feeding: Every 14 days in summer with liquid houseplant food diluted with water according to maker's instructions.

Soil: Heavy, peatless loam like loam-based No. 3. Use reddish clay/loam for larger plants from southern Europe.

Repotting: Annually for small specimens. With larger specimens in planters, change topsoil.

Cleaning: Spray with tepid soft water, or use household duster on a stick to keep your distance from sharp leaves. No leaf-shine.

The Canary Island date palm has pale green new leaves which turn darker green as they mature and develop and may have brown, fibrous hair at the edges. Healthy leaves have a natural gloss but should never be treated with leafshine or they will turn black and dry out.

Changing the topsoil

1. In spring soil will need renewing. Remove top 2in (5cm) with trowel, being careful not to damage roots.

2. Replace with new compost. Firm gently around roots. Do not water for 2 days, to encourage roots to grow into new soil. Feed regularly.

Bottom fronds dry up. Natural as long as rest stay healthy. Remove old dead frond with sharp knife or saw, cutting as close to trunk as possible.

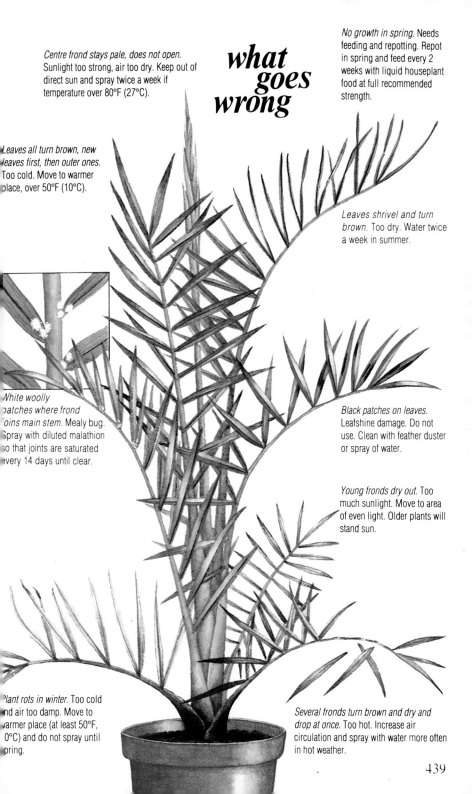

Centre frond stays pale, does not open. Sunlight too strong, air too dry. Keep out of direct sun and spray twice a week if temperature over 80°F (27°C).

what goes wrong

No growth in spring. Needs feeding and repotting. Repot in spring and feed every 2 weeks with liquid houseplant food at full recommended strength.

Leaves all turn brown, new leaves first, then outer ones. Too cold. Move to warmer place, over 50°F (10°C).

Leaves shrivel and turn brown. Too dry. Water twice a week in summer.

White woolly patches where frond joins main stem. Mealy bug. Spray with diluted malathion so that joints are saturated every 14 days until clear.

Black patches on leaves. Leafshine damage. Do not use. Clean with feather duster or spray of water.

Young fronds dry out. Too much sunlight. Move to area of even light. Older plants will stand sun.

Plant rots in winter. Too cold and air too damp. Move to warmer place (at least 50°F, 0°C) and do not spray until spring.

Several fronds turn brown and dry and drop at once. Too hot. Increase air circulation and spray with water more often in hot weather.

439

Phoenix roebelinii

Pygmy date palm

This is a thin-leaved plant growing from a bulbous stem. New sucker shoots tend to sprout from the base and should be removed or the plant will weaken. Do not confuse these suckers with other plants growing in the same pot, as these palms are often sold two or three to a pot, to give a denser display of foliage. Unlike other *Phoenix* varieties, *P. roebelinii* (sometimes incorrectly called *P. humitis*) does not have sharp leaves on its fronds. New fronds appear from the centre of the plant, growing slightly taller than existing ones. The plant grows only to about 2ft (60cm) high and is relatively easy to care for. Its main requirement is humidity but it dislikes extremes of temperature.

The Pygmy date palm has soft, graceful fronds which appear more delicate and fragile than they actually are. They grow from a bulbous stem and the plants do not normally become large enough to develop a trunk.

Light: Diffused daylight when young. Will grow slowly in shaded position.

Temperature: Winter minimum 55°F (13°C), summer maximum about 70°F (21°C), provided in humid position.

Water: Twice a week in summer, about once every 10–14 days in winter. Plant should almost dry out between waterings in winter.

Humidity: Spray daily with tepid soft water to help humidity. Stand in saucer of pebbles almost covered with water, or put pot into a larger container with damp peat between the two.

Feeding: Every 14 days in summer with liquid houseplant food diluted with water according to maker's instructions.

Soil: 3 parts loam-based No. 2 with 1 part peat.

Repotting: Annually in early spring into clay pot one size larger.

Cleaning: The daily spray for humidity will keep leaves clean. If dusty, wipe carefully with damp cloth. No leafshine.

Fronds dry out and turn crisp. Needs water. Plunge into bucket of water for half an hour, then drain.

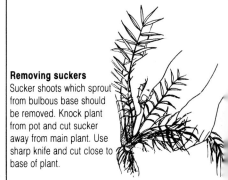

Removing suckers
Sucker shoots which sprout from bulbous base should be removed. Knock plant from pot and cut sucker away from main plant. Use sharp knife and cut close to base of plant.

440

No new fronds in spring and summer. If early spring, repot. If summer, feed regularly until following spring, then repot.

Young leaves turn brown and dry out before developed. Sunlight too strong. Move to area of diffused daylight until leaves fully develop.

what goes wrong

Small yellowish dots on leaves, webs underneath. Red spider mite. Spray with diluted malathion every 14 days, especially under leaves.

Lower leaves turn brown and dry out. Air too dry. Spray regularly, especially in summer and place pot on wet pebbles.

White woolly patches on leaf joints. Mealy bug. Spray with malathion every 14 days until clear, and add malathion to water for pot every 14 days until clear.

Plant droops, looks lifeless, starts to turn yellow. Too wet, roots stagnating. Allow to dry out before watering again. Water less often in winter than summer.

Fronds turn black and dry out. Leafshine damage. Do not use. Clean with spray of soft tepid water.

Pilea cadierii

Aluminium plant

This attractive, compact plant is easy to grow and does well in mixed bowls with other types of plants. As it is inclined to become a little straggly, the young shoots should be picked out in mid-summer to make the lower stems grow more bushily. The leaves are oval in shape, measuring about 1½in long by ¾in wide (37mm x 18mm) and are dark green with silvery markings. They grow in pairs up the stems, with several stems sprouting together in one pot. There are several varieties of the plant including a miniature version, *P. cadierii nana* and *P. mollis* or 'Moon Valley' an exciting new one with crinkled leaves.

Light: Does well on windowsill out of direct mid-day sun. Tends to grow leggy if away from light. Leaves must not touch window glass in winter.

Temperature: Winter minimum 60°F (15°C), though survives at lower temperatures if water withheld. Summer maximum 70°F (21°C).

Water: 2–3 times a week in summer. Once a week in winter, though compost should never dry out.

Humidity: Spray daily in summer and about once a week in winter unless in very hot room (70°F, 21°C), when a daily spray will help. Shake off surplus water if plant in direct sunlight.

Feeding: Every 14 days when growing in spring and summer with liquid houseplant food diluted according to the maker's instructions.

Soil: 3 parts loam-based No. 2 mixed with 1 part peat.

Repotting: In spring. Prune back stems by half before repotting so that plant grows bushily again.

Cleaning: Humidity spraying sufficient. If very dirty or dusty, use small dry paintbrush. No leafshine.

Healthy Aluminium plants have clean, clearly marked leaves. In spring and summer they should have vigorous growing tips and should look neat and compact. New leaves are paler at first, developing their colour as they grow.

New leaves small. Needs feeding or repotting. If rootball is tangled with no soil clinging to roots, repot in spring with new compost.

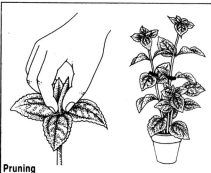

Pruning

If plant is growing straggly with more stem than leaf, pinch out growing tips. New shoots will grow from lower down the stem.

In spring, cut straggly plant back to half their height before repotting. Cut with scissors just above a pair o' leaves.

Plants grows straggly with long spaces between leaves. Too dark. Move to lighter place. Prune very straggly stems and pinch out growing tips to encourage bushy growth.

Plant collapses, all leaves and stems droop. Frosted, plant is dead.

what goes wrong

White woolly patches on leaves and stems. Mealy bug. Wipe off with cotton wool dipped in methylated spirits or spray with diluted malathion every 14 days until clear.

Leaves distorted and sticky with green insects. Greenfly. Spray with pyrethrum or systemic insecticide every 14 days until clear.

Single leaf turns black in winter. Plant in window with leaf touching cold glass. Move away from window.

Patches of grey mould on leaves. Botrytis, caused by overwatering. Allow to dry out before watering again and dust affected leaves with sulphur dust.

Scorch marks on leaves. Leafshine. Do not use. Clean only by spraying or with a dry paintbrush. Pick off damaged leaves.

Leaves droop. Needs water. Soak well in bucket of water for 10–15 minutes, then drain. Water more often and spray regularly.

Leaves turn black and drop off. Too cold. Move to warmer room, at least 60°F (15°C).

443

Australian laurel

This green-leaved plant is often associated with cut flowers in winter for it is the standard foliage used by most florists. However, it makes a good, shrubby or tree-like indoor plant, especially in its variegated form. It needs plenty of light but does well in cool winter temperatures, so is well suited to a porch, sun-room or conservatory. Its small, pale green leaves grow close together on woody stems and in summer it grows rapidly. In the wild Pittosporums grow up to 30ft (10m) high and even indoors may need pruning in spring to keep them to a manageable size. Cut stems just above a leaf.

Light: Must be in a very light position and will take full sun. Will drop its leaves if too dark.

Temperature: Minimum winter temperature 40°F (4°C) and even slight frost if protected by polythene. Up to 75°F (24°C) in summer but requires plenty of air and high humidity if indoors.

Water: Keep moist at all times, watering 2–3 times a week in summer – once a week in winter. If down to minimum temperature do not water at all.

Humidity: If in central heating in winter or if over 70°F (21°C) in summer spray daily. In other circumstances spray twice a week.

Feeding: Every 14 days in growing season using liquid houseplant food at maker's recommended strength.

Soil: Loam-based No. 2. They need heavy loam to hold them upright.

Repotting: When young repot every spring. When too large to handle easily, replace top 2–3in (5–7cm) as new leaves start to grow.

Cleaning: The spraying should keep it clean, but leafshine can be used once a month.

Australian laurels grow over 3ft (1m) indoors and need very good light, full sun if possible. The leaves are familiar to many people who have never seen them growing as a houseplant since they are widely used as foliage in florists' displays.

Leaves are limp and hang down. Soil too dry. Plunge pot into bucket of water for 10–15 minutes, then drain. Keep constantly moist in summer, watering every day if it dries out in hot weather. Do not allow to stand in water. Spray daily with soft, tepid water.

White woolly patches under leaves. Mealy bug. Spray with diluted malathion and remove bugs and 'wool' with tweezers. Repeat every 14 days until symptoms disappear. Or, paint bugs with methylated spirits and remove with tweezers.

Leaves pale and drop off. Not enough light. Move to a position in diffused daylight but not direct sun.

Leaves droop and turn yellow.
Too wet, overwatered. Allow
surface to dry out before
watering again. If temperature
below 40°F (5°C), keep dry.
Otherwise water 2–3 times a
week in summer, once a week
in winter.

what goes wrong

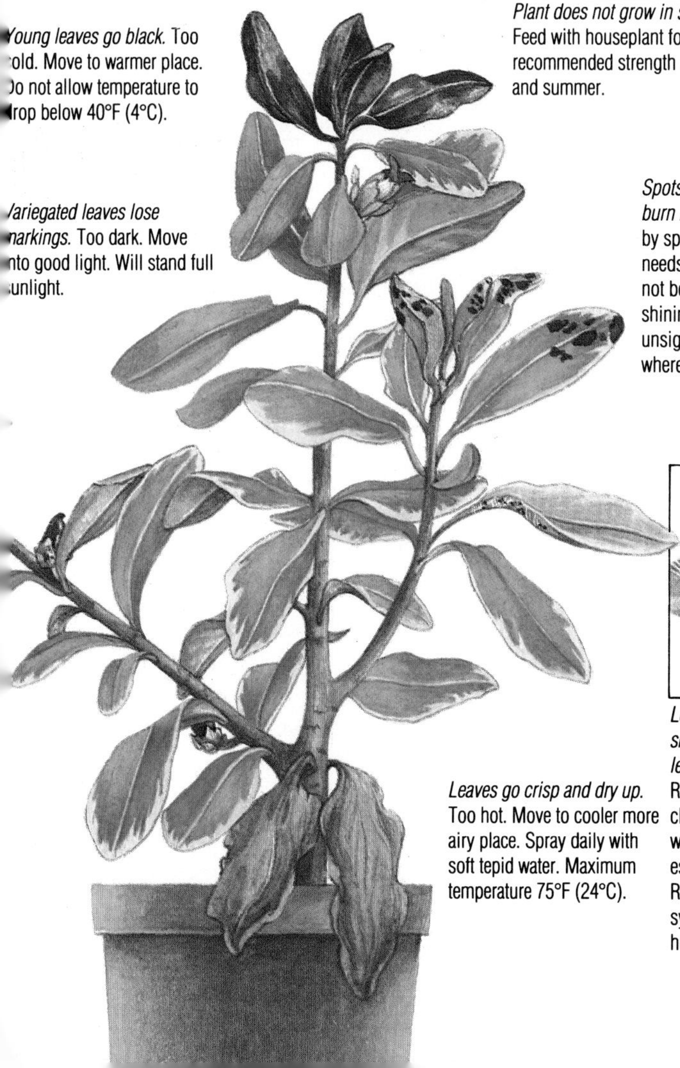

Young leaves go black. Too
cold. Move to warmer place.
Do not allow temperature to
drop below 40°F (4°C).

*Variegated leaves lose
markings.* Too dark. Move
into good light. Will stand full
sunlight.

Humidity
Pittosporums need constant
humidity. Spray them daily
in hot weather and stand
pot on saucer of pebbles or
gravel half covered in water.
Do not allow pot base to
rest in water or compost
will waterlog and roots rot.

Plant does not grow in summer. Needs feeding.
Feed with houseplant food at maker's
recommended strength every 14 days in spring
and summer.

*Spots on leaves that look like
burn marks.* Damage caused
by spraying in sunlight. Plant
needs high humidity but must
not be sprayed when sun is
shining on leaves. Remove
unsightly leaf with scissors
where it joins stem.

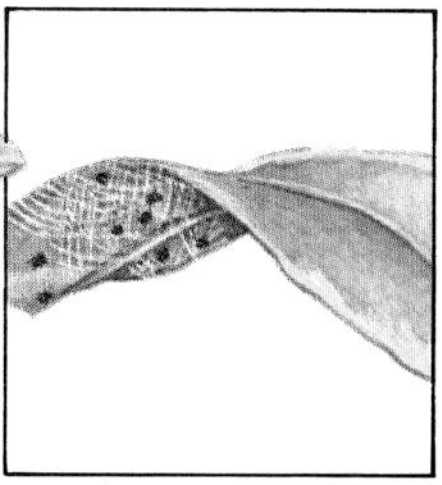

Leaves go crisp and dry up.
Too hot. Move to cooler more
airy place. Spray daily with
soft tepid water. Maximum
temperature 75°F (24°C).

*Leaves fade, with webs and
small insects underneath
leaves.* Red spider mite.
Remove webs with damp
cloth or sponge, then spray
with diluted malathion,
especially under leaves.
Repeat every 14 days until
symptoms disappear. Improve
humidity.

445

Platycerium bifurcatum

Stag's horn fern

This native of Australia is striking in appearance and grows best in a hanging container. It can also be grown on a piece of cork bark. It is natural for the leaves at the base of the main 'horns' to appear brown and crispy: they are sterile leaves developed to support the main leaves. The down-like hair on the main leaves must not be removed or the plant will die. Unlike most ferns, it does not mind a dry atmosphere. It is sometimes difficult to water, as the sterile leaves grow right over the compost with no gaps for the watering can spout to penetrate. The best way of watering is to plunge the pot into a bucket of water once a week or to water from below.

Light: Full light, even sunshine. Hung close to the glass roof, they will shade a greenhouse or conservatory.

Temperature: Winter minimum 60°F (15°C). In summer keep between 65–75°F (18–24°C).

Water: Plunge pot once a week into water, unless pot has a drip tray allowing watering from below. Dry out between waterings.

Humidity: No special treatment as plant stands dry air. If central heating 75°F (24°C) or above, spray once a week with soft water.

Feeding: Once a month in spring and summer with houseplant food diluted with water according to maker's instructions.

Soil: 1 part chopped sphagnum moss to 2 parts peat-based compost ideal.

Repotting: Once every two years for young plants. Adult plant has little root and prefers to be left alone.

Cleaning: Spray once a month with soft water, or gently use feather duster. Never wipe leaves. No leafshine.

The Stag's horn fern has down-covered green fronds which grow from the centre of the brownish back leaves. The fronds divide rather like the antlers of a stag and make an unusual display, especially if attached to a piece of cork bark or driftwood. The larger Elk's horn fern needs a slightly higher winter temperature.

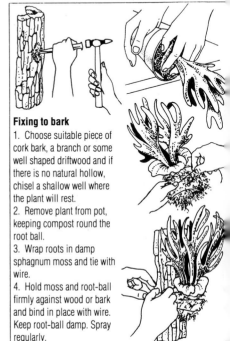

Fixing to bark
1. Choose suitable piece of cork bark, a branch or some well shaped driftwood and if there is no natural hollow, chisel a shallow well where the plant will rest.
2. Remove plant from pot, keeping compost round the root ball.
3. Wrap roots in damp sphagnum moss and tie with wire.
4. Hold moss and root-ball firmly against wood or bark and bind in place with wire. Keep root-ball damp. Spray regularly.

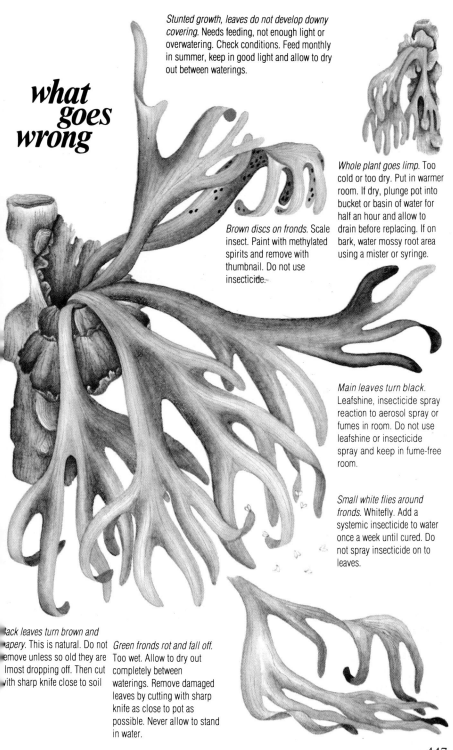

Stunted growth, leaves do not develop downy covering. Needs feeding, not enough light or overwatering. Check conditions. Feed monthly in summer, keep in good light and allow to dry out between waterings.

what goes wrong

Brown discs on fronds. Scale insect. Paint with methylated spirits and remove with thumbnail. Do not use insecticide.

Whole plant goes limp. Too cold or too dry. Put in warmer room. If dry, plunge pot into bucket or basin of water for half an hour and allow to drain before replacing. If on bark, water mossy root area using a mister or syringe.

Main leaves turn black. Leafshine, insecticide spray reaction to aerosol spray or fumes in room. Do not use leafshine or insecticide spray and keep in fume-free room.

Small white flies around fronds. Whitefly. Add a systemic insecticide to water once a week until cured. Do not spray insecticide on to leaves.

Back leaves turn brown and papery. This is natural. Do not remove unless so old they are almost dropping off. Then cut with sharp knife close to soil

Green fronds rot and fall off. Too wet. Allow to dry out completely between waterings. Remove damaged leaves by cutting with sharp knife as close to pot as possible. Never allow to stand in water.

447

Swedish ivy

This plant has been used as a house-plant almost from the beginning of indoor gardening but has never become very common. Though its leaves look ordinary, it makes a lovely hanging basket plant and produces delicate mauve flowers from the end of trailing stems in late autumn/early winter. Its pale green leaves are faintly aromatic and must be handled with care as they snap or break easily. It is a native of Australia. Other varieties include one with variegated leaves and one with darker green leaves.

Swedish ivy has pale green serrated, slightly aromatic leaves which must be handled with care as they snap and break easily. Grown mainly for its trailing foliage, it produces delicate mauve flowers in late autumn/early winter.

Light: Best in a window that does not receive midday summer sun; tolerates some shade.

Temperature: Up to 70–80°F (21–27°C) in summer. Winter minimum 55°F (13°C).

Water: Water thoroughly twice a week in summer, once a week in winter so that soil surface dries out well between waterings. Remember to check hanging baskets regularly as they dry out quickly.

Humidity: Will survive in normal room humidity but a twice weekly spray helps to keep them clean and bright.

Feeding: Give liquid houseplant food every 21 days in summer at half maker's recommended strength.

Soil: Loam-based No. 2 with 10 per cent added peat and soft sand.

Repotting: Once a year in spring but if plants are becoming leggy, repropagate from young tip cuttings. Pinch out the growing tips two or three times in summer to make a bushier plant. Large plants can also be divided in spring.

Cleaning: Spraying sufficient but if very dusty, flick with feather duster. No leafshine.

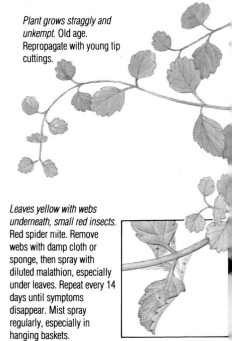

Plant grows straggly and unkempt. Old age. Repropagate with young tip cuttings.

Leaves yellow with webs underneath, small red insects. Red spider mite. Remove webs with damp cloth or sponge, then spray with diluted malathion, especially under leaves. Repeat every 14 days until symptoms disappear. Mist spray regularly, especially in hanging baskets.

Plant is limp and collapses. Too dry. Water immediately. Allow compost surface to just dry out before watering again. In winter water only once a week.

Leaves pale, plant grows slowly. Too dark. Move to window that does not get direct sun.

Propagation
Young stem tips root easily in spring. Cut off tip 3–4in (7–10cm) long just below a leaf, trim to leaf, remove lowest pair of leaves and insert in mixture of peat and sand. Keep warm and moist until new shoots grow.

what goes wrong

Leaves dry and crisp. Damage by sunlight. Move into an area of diffused daylight, out of harmful rays of sun. Remove damaged leaf where it joins stem.

Leaves limp and drooping. Too hot. Move to cooler place, below 80°F (27°C). Spray twice weekly, especially in hot weather. If in window, shade from midday summer sun and spray in early morning or evening.

Leaves spotted with brown marks. Leafshine damage. Do not use. Clean only by spraying with soft tepid water. Remove damaged leaf where it joins main stem.

Mildew on stems, rot sets in. Botrytis. Plant too cold and damp. Spray with fungicide, then keep in warmer place (above 55°F, 13°C) and spray with water less frequently. Allow soil surface to dry out between waterings.

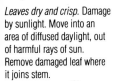

Leaves drop off while still green. Needs feeding. Feed with houseplant food at half maker's recommended strength every 21 days in the growing season, spring and summer.

Leaves turn yellow and drop off. Plant waterlogged, standing in water. Drain away any water in saucer and allow surface of soil to dry out before watering again. Then keep moist but never allow pot base to stand in water. Always throw away excess that drains through after watering.

449

Pleiospilos

This is another South African plant that mimics stones. It is similar to Lithops but the plant bodies look like pieces of broken, weathered grey rock instead of smooth pebbles and are about 2in (5cm) high and 2½in (6cm) across. *Pleiospilos hilmari* is more attractively coloured than most species, with purple tinges overlaying a minutely spotted surface. It produces its bright yellow flowers freely in late summer. The main causes of problems for growing this plant are: not enough light, and water at the wrong time, which causes the body to split, or even to rot completely. Other species are *Pleiospilos bolusii*, grey and angular, *P. nelii*, rounded, grey-brown, *P. willowmorensis*, with longer leaves than most, *P. prismaticus* and *P. simulans*, and others.

Pleiospilos hilmari. These small stone-like plants, known as Living rocks, are often hard to distinguish from the pebbles around them. They sometimes grow in clumps but single, 2 or 3-headed plants are most common. The bright yellow flowers appear from between the thick leaves in late summer.

Light: A sunny windowsill is needed for best results, although there is a danger of scorching in spring, especially if a period of cloudy weather is followed by some days of strong sunshine.

Temperature: Minimum 40°F (4°C) for safety. Give fresh air in summer.

Water: Do not water until early summer, then only once every two or three weeks, making sure the soil has dried out between waterings. Tail off in late autumn; do not water in winter and spring.

Feeding: Only if not repotted for 3 years; use high potash fertilizer, only twice during summer.

Soil: Use good loam-based No. 2 potting compost, or soil-less compost, with 50% coarse, gritty sand added.

Repotting: Every year when young; after 3 years, repot every other year. Leave dry for 2 weeks after repotting in late spring.

Propagation: Old clumps may be increased from cuttings, but best from seed.

Two pairs of leaves actively growing at the same time on each head. Caused by watering before old leaves have shrivelled. When old leaves die, stop watering until they have dried up completely.

what goes wrong

Plant shows little sign of growth, and on repotting white woolly patches are found on roots. Root mealy bug. Wash all soil off roots, swirl roots in contact insecticide, and allow to dry before repotting in fresh compost and washed pot. Leave dry for two weeks before watering again.

Growing from seed
1. Sow seed thinly in spring on surface of prepared tray or half pot. Tap sides of tray to settle seed.

2. Water from base with fungicide diluted as for 'damping off' of seedlings, until surface is damp. Place tray or pot in polythene bag with ends folded underneath to seal in moisture. Leave in light (not direct sun) a 70°F (21°C).

Leaves become elongated and lose colour. Too dark. Move into full sunlight gradually over 2 weeks. May also occur if too hot and wet in winter.

No flowers. Not enough light or watered at wrong time. Check conditions. If in shade, move over 2 weeks into full sunlight. Keep dry from early winter to early summer.

White woolly patches in crevices and between new and old leaves. Mealy bug. Remove with small paintbrush dipped in methylated spirits, and spray with contact or systemic insecticide. Repeat every 2–3 weeks until clear.

Leaves split and crack open. Water at wrong time of year or overwatering. Allow to dry out then give less water each time and keep dry in winter. Not fatal but will not heal up.

Plant marked. Either mealy covering damaged by handling or sunscorch. Shade from midday sun in early summer. Give fresh air in hot weather.

Plant turns black and soft. Too wet in summer or winter or too cold and humid; roots rotting. Keep above 40°F (4°C) in winter in dry atmosphere. Treat roots (see Introduction).

Leaves wither, turn brown and die. Natural. Each pair of leaves lasts only 1 year, then dies down. Do not remove old leaves until they pull away easily.

451

Plumbago capensis

Cape leadwort

Said to be a remedy against lead poisoning, this plant's name is derived from the Latin *plumbum*, 'lead'. It is a climbing or trailing shrub which is usually bought growing on a wire hoop. The pale blue flowers are carried in spikes at the ends of the trailing stems. In the greenhouse it can be trained along the rafters or a wall. It should be cut back to within 6in (15cm) of pot after flowering and kept cool and drier for a rest period in the winter. Frequent watering and increased heat from the following spring will produce prolific new growth. Flowers appear on the current season's growth.

Light: Full light, avoiding midday sun in summer. Keep in shady situation in winter, when dormant.

Temperature: Keep at 45°F (7°C) in winter, increasing to 55–70°F (13–21°C) in early spring until autumn.

Water: Twice a week in spring and summer, keeping compost moist at all times, but pot must not stand in water. Water in winter only when compost surface has dried out, about once every 10 days.

Humidity: Spray with soft tepid water daily in spring and summer. Avoid flowers.

Feeding: Every 14 days after the first flower buds appear, with liquid fertilizer diluted to maker's instructions. Stop feeding in autumn and winter.

Soil: Equal parts leafmould, peat, sand and loam-based No.3.

Repotting: In early spring into pot one size larger, up to maximum pot size 10in (25cm). Then repot into same size pot annually, with fresh soil. Plant grows successfully only when root ball is compact. Put plenty of broken crocks into bottom of pot.

Cleaning: Humidity spraying, out of direct sunlight, adequate. No leafshine.

The Cape leadwort is a climbing or trailing shrub with pale blue or lavender-coloured flowers which are carried as spikes on the end of the stems. The vigorous growth should be pruned hard after flowering as the flowers only appear on the current season's growth.

White cotton-wool patches where leaf joins stem. Mealy bug. Spray with diluted malathion and remove bugs and 'wool' with tweezers. Repeat every 14 days until symptoms disappear. Or, paint bugs with methylated spirits and remove with tweezers. When spraying, avoid flowers and buds.

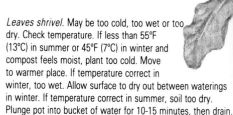

Leaves black when temperature and humidity correct. Leafshine damage. Do not use. Clean only by spraying with soft, tepid water. Remove damaged leaf.

Leaves shrivel. May be too cold, too wet or too dry. Check temperature. If less than 55°F (13°C) in summer or 45°F (7°C) in winter and compost feels moist, plant too cold. Move to warmer place. If temperature correct in winter, too wet. Allow surface to dry out between waterings in winter. If temperature correct in summer, soil too dry. Plunge pot into bucket of water for 10-15 minutes, then drain.

Few flowers in spring and summer. Should have been pruned previous year. Prune current season's flower stems when flowering finished to encourage new growth on which next year's flowers form. Do not prune in spring before flowering.

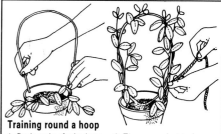

Training round a hoop
1. Push ends of wire hoop or thin cane so that they are ⅔ down pot on opposite sides. Bend plant stem to one side of hoop and gently twist around.

2. To secure plant to hoop, tie twine to one end of hoop and thread it along, looping it loosely around stem. Do not tie knots or stem may be damaged.

what goes wrong

Flower buds do not open. Too cold and too dark. Move to warmer place, at least 65°F (18°C) in summer, 70°F (21°C) if possible. Make sure plant is in good light.

New leaves small. Needs feeding. Feed with houseplant food diluted to maker's recommended strength every 14 days after first flower buds appear.

Flower buds covered with sticky green insects. Greenfly. Spray with pyrethrum-based insecticide or diluted malathion. Repeat one week later, then every week until clear.

Leaves turn brown and crisp, flower buds drop. Too hot and air too dry. Move to cooler place (less than 70°F, 21°C) if possible, with good ventilation. Spray with soft, tepid water and improve humidity by standing pot on saucer of wet pebbles.

Lower leaves rot. Waterlogged, plant standing in water. Happens especially in winter. Drain away any water in saucer and allow surface of compost to dry out before watering again. Then keep moist in summer but allow surface to dry out between waterings in winter. Always throw away excess water that drains through pot into saucer after watering.

453

Portulacaria afra

The only species of this South African genus comes in either a green-leaved form, or the more attractive, variegated, yellow and green leaved form shown here. It is slow-growing, making a low 'bonsai' type of plant some 10in (25cm) across and 5–6in (12–15cm) tall in 5 to 10 years. The flowers, which are rare in cultivation, are similar to groundsel, yellow and daisy-like. This beautiful succulent plant is grown for its foliage and is an ideal subject for a half-pot or bowl, or even a hanging basket.

Portulacaria afra variegata looks like a miniature Jade tree. It is a slow grower, taking some 5 years to grow into a 5in (13cm) pan or half-pot but looks attractive both in a normal pot and in a hanging basket. Flowers are rare when grown indoors.

Light: A sunny position is needed for best results, but provided it gets an hour or two of sunshine each day it will grow well.

Temperature: A minimum of 40°F (4°C) is needed. Give fresh air in summer.

Water: Start watering in spring. Water fortnightly in spring and summer, weekly in hottest weather. Tail off in autumn, and in winter water once a month to prevent soil drying out.

Feeding: Use high potash fertilizer 2 or 3 times in summer.

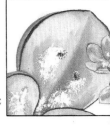

White woolly patches among leaves. Mealy bug. Remove with small paintbrush dipped in methylated spirits, and spray with contact or systemic insecticide. Repeat every 2 weeks until clear.

Soil: Use good loam-based No. 2 potting compost, or soil-less compost, with 30% coarse, gritty sand.

Repotting: Every spring when young, leave 2 or 3 years when stems reach about 9in (22cm). Do not water for 2 weeks after repotting. Be careful not to knock off leaves when repotting as they are fragile.

Propagation: Lengths of stem about 2in (5cm) can be cut off in spring and summer, dusted with hormone rooting powder, left to dry for a few days, then rooted in dry compost. Water after about 3 weeks when roots start to appear. Also possible from seed, if obtainable, but it is rarely available. The tiny seedlings should not be allowed to dry out for the first 6 months.

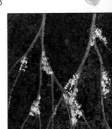

Bottom leaves fall, little new growth. Needs repotting or feeding. Repot every spring in fresh compost and feed 2 or 3 times a year with high potash plant food. If conditions correct, inspect roots for root mealy bug (white woolly patches on roots). Wash all soil off roots, swirl in contact insecticide, and allow to dry before repotting in fresh compost and washed pot. Leave dry for two weeks.

Propagation

1. When taking cuttings in spring or summer, cut stem with sharp knife just below a leaf. Dust both cut ends with hormone rooting powder to prevent infection.

2. If growing from seed, water half pot or tray regularly by standing in outer container of water until surface is damp.

what goes wrong

Leaves turn black and fall, stem ends turn black and go soft, roots rot. Too cold and probably too wet. Keep above 40°F (4°C). Pare off blackened part of stem and dust with hormone rooting powder containing fungicide. If roots rotted, see Introduction.

Stems grow long with few, pale leaves. Too dark or, in winter, too hot and wet. Keep in full light all year round but if in shade, move into sunlight gradually over 2 weeks to prevent scorching. In winter keep dry, below 50°F (10°C) if possible.

Leaves become crisp and brown, then fall. Too dry for too long. If summer or spring soak in bowl of water for half an hour, then drain and allow almost to dry out before watering again. Water more regularly. In winter water once a month to prevent soil drying out completely.

Brown patches on leaves. Sun scorch. Move to more airy place and shade from hot sun for 2 weeks. Then move gradually back, over period of 2 weeks.

Round pieces missing from leaf edges, stem swollen; little new growth. Vine weevil. Sprinkle insecticide powder around base of pot and water soil with systemic insecticide to kill larvae in stem. Or slice stem from base until larvae found and reroot.

Fairy primrose

Primulas are a large group of flowering plants which grow wild in many parts of the world. Most are hardy plants but a few are suitable as houseplants. Two of the best for indoors are *Primula obconica* (see p.458) and *Primula malacoides*, the Fairy primrose. Although usually bought as a plant in flower, Fairy primrose can be grown from seed and will produce many sprays of bloom in late winter/early spring, lasting 6–10 weeks. After germination in early summer, the young plants should be kept in a cool, airy place such as an unheated porch or conservatory and brought into a light room when the flower buds are formed.

The pink, white or mauve flowers of the Fairy primrose grow in clusters on 10in (25cm) stems which appear 6–10 at a time from among the soft, pale green leaves. The flowers open from the bottom of the stems and last several weeks. Both stem and buds are covered naturally with a white powder which should not be confused with mildew.

Light: Good light at all times, but protect seedlings from direct sunlight in summer.
Temperature: Will not thrive in warm conditions. Maximum 45–50°F (7–10°C) for best growth.
Water: Young plants should dry out between waterings, once a week sufficient. Increase as buds form, but no more than 2–3 times a week, as overwatered plants are susceptible to root rot. Never stand pot in water.
Humidity: Keep in a well ventilated room. Do not spray, as moisture on leaves increases vulnerability to fungus diseases.
Feeding: From the time first buds appear until flowering is finished, feed weekly with dilute liquid houseplant food at maker's recommended strength.
Soil: Loam-based No.2 or soil-less potting compost.
After flowering: Remove dead flowers to encourage new buds. Fairy primrose is an annual, and will not flower again. Discard plant when flowering is finished and no more buds are seen.

Leaves distorted with dark streaks. Virus disease. No cure so destroy plant to prevent it from spreading to other plants.

Plant turns black. Frost damage. Fairy Primrose needs cool conditions, but will not survive frost. Do not shut behind curtains on a cold night and do not leave outside.

Brown spots on leaves. Leaf spot fungus disease. Humid conditions make plant susceptible, so increase ventilation. Do not spray leaves with water. Spray plant with iprodione.

Foliage greyish and limp. Too dry. Increase watering to 2–3 times a week. Soil should be just moist at all times.

what goes wrong

Seedlings stop growing.
Pythium disease, possibly
contracted from unsterile soil
or water. Always grow in
sterile compost and use
clean, fresh water. Discard
seedlings and sow again.

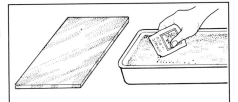

Propagation
Sow seed very thinly in early
summer. Do not cover with
compost but place sheet of
glass over tray to retain
moisture. Prick out 2in (5cm)
apart when large enough to
handle, then, when tray
crowded, pot singly into
4½in (11cm) pots, where
plant can stay for flowering.

*Flower buds hang limp,
especially just before
flowering. Foliage may be
soggy.* Botrytis. Spray
benomyl. Do not overwater or
spray water on leaves. Move
to more airy place.

Plant wilts, flowers collapse.
Root rot, usually caused by
overwatering. Badly affected
plants may not recover. Allow
soil to dry, then begin
watering again gradually. Soil
should be barely moist.

*Leaves small and dull, flowers
very small.* Needs feeding.
Feed weekly with dilute liquid
houseplant food while in
flower.

*Buds do not develop, or are
few and pale.* Too dark. Keep
in good light, but not in direct
sunlight.

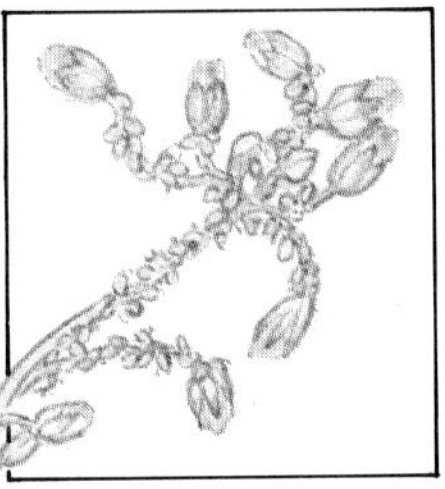

*Small wingless insects on
leaves or buds.* Greenfly.
Spray with pyrethrum-based
insecticide. Spray again in 10
days if greenfly are still
visible.

Leaf stalks long and weak, flowers deteriorate. Too
hot. Keep at maximum 45–50°F (7–10°C).

*Small white insects present,
white scales on undersides of
leaves.* Whitefly. Spray with
pyrethrum-based insecticide
at weekly intervals until plant
is clean.

457

Primula obconica

Rash primrose

This long-lasting, robust plant is less popular than it deserves to be because its leaves may cause a skin rash if touched. However, this affects only about 10% of the population, and if you are not susceptible it is well worth growing. Unlike other indoor Primulas, it can be grown through the winter to flower the following year. Roots can be divided after spring flowering or seed can be sown in midsummer for the following spring. Sow in trays and do not cover seed with compost. Germination may take 3–4 weeks (at 50–55°F, 10–13°C) and seedlings are ready for pricking out when 2 true leaves are fully developed. Pot in 4½in (11cm) pots when trays are crowded but do not put in a larger pot until roots fill the compost.

Light: Full light at all times, but shade from strong sun in summer.
Temperature: Best growth at 50–55°F (10–13°C). Will tolerate slightly colder temperatures while resting; no frost.
Water: Compost should be moist but not waterlogged. Water 2–3 times weekly in warm weather, less in winter.
Humidity: Good ventilation essential. Do not spray.
Feeding: Feed weekly with liquid houseplant food at maker's recommended strength. Start 3 weeks after plant in final pot, continue while growing and flowering. Do not feed while overwintering.
Soil: Loam-based No.2.
After flowering: Remove dead flowers to encourage new buds to form. After all flowering is finished, cut back flowering stems, decrease watering, and move plant to a cool, light situation to rest. Increase watering and begin feeding when growth begins again in spring.

A native of China, *Primula obconica* grows about 12in (30cm) tall when in flower. The flowers grow on tall stems and are white, pink, mauve or blue. Flowering lasts for several months, usually beginning in spring. The fine hairs on the undersides of the leaves may cause irritations.

Foliage greyish and limp, flowers hang limply. Too hot or too dry. Mover to a cooler position out of direct sun. Increase watering so that soil is always moist.

Brown spots on leaves. Leaf spot fungus disease. Humid conditions make plant susceptible so increase ventilation. Spray with iprodione.

Pale green or yellow spots on leaves, fuzz underneath. Downy mildew. Dust over plant with copper lime dust. Never spray with water, which makes Primula vulnerable to fungus infection.

Small white insects present, white scales under leaves. Whitefly. Spray with pyrethrum-based insecticide at weekly intervals until plant is clean.

458

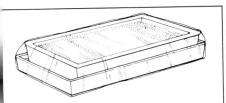

Watering seed trays
Place trays in plastic bags until seedlings germinated but keep compost moist on surface. To water, stand tray in container with an inch (2½cm) water and leave until compost surface looks damp.

Growth weak but conditions are good. Plant may not be firm in soil. Check soil surface for C-shaped grubs of vine weevil and dust with gamma HCH if found. If leaves also dark, too cold. Move to warmer spot.

Bushy leaf growth but few flowers. Over-feeding. Feed at weekly intervals with liquid houseplant food diluted to recommended strength.

Flowers turn brown at edges. Either sun damage or chemical damage. Protect from direct sun. If spraying chemicals, never spray when plant is in strong light. Spray in evening.

Foliage pale, flowers small. Plant needs feeding. Feed weekly with liquid houseplant food diluted to maker's recommended strengths.

what goes wrong

Small wingless insects on any part of plant. Greenfly. Spray with pyrethrum-based insecticide at 10-day intervals until plant is clean.

Leaves distorted with streaks or spots. Virus disease. Plant may still flower, but destroy afterwards. Insects can spread disease to other plants so take precautions.

Round yellow spots on leaves. Leaf hopper insect, which is uncommon. Spray with diluted malathion.

Leaves droop and turn yellow. Overwatering. Water enough to keep compost just moist. Ensure that drainage is good.

Plants wilt badly during the day, sometimes recovering at night. Root rot fungus, often caused by overwatering. Allow to become nearly dry, then begin watering gradually so soil is kept barely moist.

Polyanthus

Polyanthus and primroses are well known signs of spring and though the flowering season is short, they are well worth an early place in boxes and tubs. It is preferable not to buy plants in flower in spring as they are difficult to establish. The true primrose *(Primula acaulis)* is of the same family as the Polyanthus and needs the same treatment.

Light: Maximum possible in spring. 40% shade in high summer when plants are resting or establishing themselves in a new place.

Temperature: Not above 55°F (13°C). Shade in summer. Will stand frost.

Water: Cool, moist soil. Flower buds drop off if soil too dry before flowering.

Humidity: Spray leaves in hot weather to help keep it cool.

Soil: Loam-based No. 3 or, better still, soilless potting compost.

Feeding: After flowering, put layer of fertilizer made of fish, blood and bonemeal on top of container. Do not feed from early autumn to later winter, then feed with fertilizer diluted to maker's recommended strength every 5 days until in full flower.

Propagation: Sow in late spring/early summer. Prepare seed tray and sow very thinly. Cover with 1/8in (2mm) moist compost, seal in plastic bag and keep in cool (45°F, 7°C), sunless place until germination (10–20 days). Compost should stay moist without watering. Prick out when large enough to handle into small pots or 2in (5cm) apart in trays. Or, divide existing plants after flowering.

Tidying: Cut off dead flowers. Remove dead leaves at the end of winter.

Varieties: Hardy, Giant Bouquet, Kelscott, Giant Yellow. Almost hardy, Pacific hybrids.

Polyanthus are 5–9in (13–23cm) at flowering stage with bright green leaves and flowers in a wide range of colours. The flowers are usually clustered on each stem, though single blooms on a stem, like the true primrose, are possible.

Flower buds damaged, may be eaten away completely. Birds, especially sparrows. May occur whenever buds visible but only one colour may be attacked. Tie black cotton thread on sticks 2in (5cm) above plant to prevent attack. Chemicals effective only for short periods.

Leaves droop, soil dark and sour. Waterlogged. Check drainage and water less often. Keep moist but not soaked.

Whole plant turns suddenly yellow and wilts. Root rot disease. Remove carefully from container and destroy. Water soil with fungicide, diluted as maker recommends.

what goes wrong

Divided crowns do not produce healthy green leaves by early autumn. Planted in hot sun or slug damage. Plant divided plants in shade and apply slug pellets monthly. Bottom leaves will shrivel naturally in late winter and should be removed.

Division

1. After flowering, remove plant carefully from container and shake soil from around roots.

2. Gently pull roots and stems apart. Plant in shady part of garden or in pot and keep moist and cool through summer. Plant in position in mid-autumn. Remove dead bottom leaves in spring.

Leaves and buds covered in tiny green insects. Aphid. Spray with diluted malathion or general insecticide. If attacked in autumn, buds and flowers may be distorted following spring. Spray monthly in summer to prevent attacks.

Edges of young leaves have dry, shrivelled patches in spring. Handled in frost. Do not touch frosted leaves.

Leaves almost hide flowers. Too dark or too hot in confined space. No cure but improve conditions next year.

Holes in leaves. Slugs or snails. Put down slug pellets as maker recommends but keep away from pets and fish ponds.

Leaves pale green with veins nearly white. Needs feeding. Feed every 5 days in spring while growing.

Fluffy grey mould in crown. Botrytis due to lack of air movement round plant. Remove decaying tissue and spray with benomyl and iprodione. Repeat after 10 days.

Flower buds drop. Too dry. Keep soil moist, especially when buds appear.

461

Pteris cretica

Ribbon fern

Over 250 species of *Pteris* exist. *P. cretica* is a robust-looking variety, and is quite easy to keep in the home provided it is kept moist at all times. *P. cretica albolineata* is a variegated variety and *P.c. crispata* has irregularly shaped leaves that end in an extra leaflet. *Pteris* has fairly thick leaves and will take a good deal of neglect. When buying it, look for healthy, undamaged foliage.

Light: Diffused light best, though will survive in a very shaded position. Keep out of sunlight. *P. cretica albolineata* needs less light than other variegated plants and dislikes direct sun.

Temperature: Winter minimum 50–55°F (10–13°C), summer maximum 70°F (21°C).

Water: Daily in summer, 2 or 3 times a week in winter, to keep soil always moist. Do not stand in water.

Humidity: Spray daily with tepid soft water to keep as humid as possible. Stand on a saucer with pebbles almost covered in water or put pot into outer container with damp peat between the two. The more humid the atmosphere, the more healthy the plant.

Feeding: Every 14 days in summer only, with houseplant food diluted with water. Use half the amount recommended by the maker.

Soil: Compost of 1 part loam-based No. 1, 2 parts sterilized peat, 1 part sharp sand. Peat-based compost will also suit.

Repotting: Every spring into one size larger plastic pot. Do not firm new compost down too much or roots will be stifled.

Cleaning: Spray with soft water. Be very careful if wiping leaves as the frond stems are very brittle and break easily. No leafshine. Plant is very susceptible.

This is the variegated version of the normal green Ribbon fern, having a narrow white centre stripe down its leaves. Although the leaves look delicate, they are actually quite thick and tough and will tolerate a wide variety of light and temperature conditions. Healthy plants will have several stems growing together with bright leaves showing no signs of discoloured tips.

what goes wrong

Small brown discs on back of leaves. Scale insects. Paint with methylated spirits and remove with thumbnail. For other insects add pyrethrum-based insecticide to water every 14 days until clear. No malathion.

Leaves turn black. Leafshine damage or polluted atmosphere. Clean only by spraying and do not use aerosols in same room as plant.

462

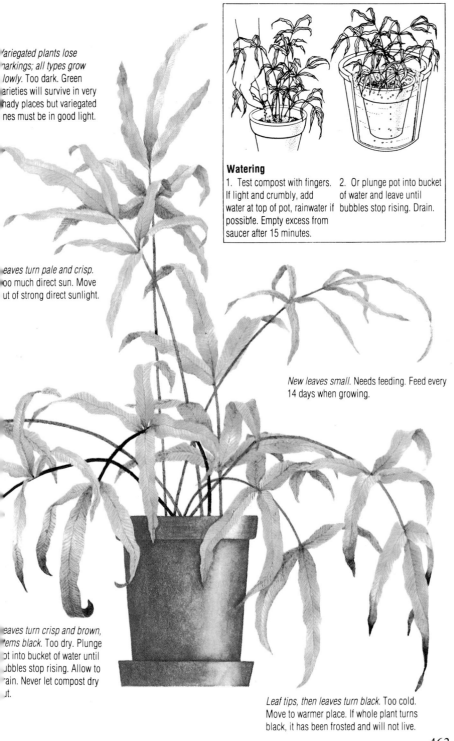

Variegated plants lose markings; all types grow slowly. Too dark. Green varieties will survive in very shady places but variegated ones must be in good light.

Leaves turn pale and crisp. Too much direct sun. Move out of strong direct sunlight.

Watering
1. Test compost with fingers. If light and crumbly, add water at top of pot, rainwater if possible. Empty excess from saucer after 15 minutes.

2. Or plunge pot into bucket of water and leave until bubbles stop rising. Drain.

New leaves small. Needs feeding. Feed every 14 days when growing.

Leaves turn crisp and brown, stems black. Too dry. Plunge pot into bucket of water until bubbles stop rising. Allow to drain. Never let compost dry out.

Leaf tips, then leaves turn black. Too cold. Move to warmer place. If whole plant turns black, it has been frosted and will not live.

Pteris tremula

Australian bracken

The fronds of this plant are similar to common bracken though less leathery and much smaller. The maximum length of the fronds is about 18in (46cm), whereas bracken grows to 48in (over 1m) and cannot be grown in pots. *P. tremula* makes a most attractive potted fern, with its delicate leaflets bushing out to make a symmetrical plant. The fronds are liable to snap off if accidentally brushed against. If it grows too bushy for its pot, it can be divided in spring by gently pulling the roots and stems apart.

Australian bracken ferns look like miniature versions of wild bracken. Healthy fronds are bright green but shrivel and turn black or brown if conditions are too hot and dry. The spores grow easily and may self-sow beside the parent plant or in the pots of other plants nearby.

Light: Diffused light out of direct sunlight.
Temperature: Winter minimum 50°F (10°C), summer maximum 70°F (21°C), or slightly higher if humidity is high, as in a greenhouse or conservatory.
Water: Daily in summer and 2 or 3 times a week in winter to keep moist at all times. Do not stand in water.
Humidity: Spray daily with tepid soft water, and stand pot in saucer of pebbles almost covered with water. Better still, plant pot into larger pot with damp peat in between or into self-watering planter. High humidity is essential for successful growth. Instructions for using a self-watering planter are on p.19.
Feeding: Every 14 days in summer and once a month in winter with houseplant food diluted with water. Use half the amount recommended by the maker.
Soil: Mixture of 1 part loam-based No. 1, 2 parts sterilized peat, 1 part sharp sand. Can also use peat-based compost.
Repotting: Annually in spring into plastic pot one size larger.
Cleaning: Humidity spraying should be adequate. Soft summer rain, above 55°F (13°C), washes leaves well. No leafshine.

Leaflets turn brown and shrivel. Too dry. Keep soil moist always. If many fronds die, cut them off close to soil and plunge pot into basin of water every day for 15 minutes until new growth appears. Allow to drain.

Humidity
Humidity is especially important for this plant. Spray daily in hot weather and provide constant humidity by putting in outer pot packed with damp peat.

Tips of leaflets shrivel then turn black, young leaflets especially affected. Too hot and dry. Spray regularly and move to cooler place.

New leaflets small and do not develop same shape as adult ones. Needs feeding.

Foliage looks burned, with blackened fronds. Leafshine or malathion have damaged leaves. Do not use.

Leaflets pale, growth slow and distorted. Too dark. Move to lighter place but not direct sunlight.

Leaflets turn black from tips. Too cold. Move to warmer place. If whole plant turns black at same time, frosted. Will not recover.

Small white insects fly around plant. Whitefly. Spray every 14 days with pyrethrum-based insecticide until clear.

Fronds pale with shrivelled leaflets. Too much direct sun. Move to shadier place with some diffused light.

Small brown discs on leaflets. Scale insect. Paint with methylated spirits and remove with thumbnail. Do not use malathion.

what goes wrong

Rebutia

Rebutias are among the best cacti for beginners: they grow well on a sunny windowsill and flower freely from the time they are 1in (2½cm) tall. They grow in clusters but rarely need more than a 5 or 6in (13cm) pot. Their spines are weak and flexible and flower colours range from red, orange, pink to yellow and white. *Rebutia perplexa* (p.467) is a recent introduction now widely available.

Light: A sunny windowsill or greenhouse will give best flower production.

Temperature: If kept dry they will take temperatures of below freezing, but for safety keep above 40°F (4°C) in winter. Keep below 100°F (38°C) in summer and give fresh air whenever possible.

Water: Water weekly in summer (fortnightly if in pans of 5in (13cm) or more), monthly in spring and autumn, with none at all in winter.

Feeding: Use a high potash fertilizer (as used for tomatoes) 3 or 4 times in the spring and summer.

Soil: Use 3 parts soil-less or good loam-based No. 2 potting compost with 1 part coarse, gritty sand (not builders' or seashore).

Repotting: Repot every year in next size pan or half-pot until 5in (13cm) pan is reached, when every other year will do unless plant has grown right up to or over the sides of its container. If it has not filled container, replace it in the same sized pan with new compost after shaking the old soil off the roots.

Cleaning and pest control: Spray once a month to keep dust-free and incorporate an insecticide 2 or 3 times a year to combat pests. Most Rebutias are particularly susceptible to red spider and also to mealy bug.

Other species: Without exception the 50 or more species available from cactus nurseries

Rebutia albiflora was almost unknown 20 years ago but has quickly become a favourite. Its tiny stems have glassy white, bristle-like spines and it flowers freely at only ½in (1cm) tall when it is a year or two old. It is easily propagated from the lightly attached offsets but is susceptible to red spider.

Rebutia flavistyla is a fairly recent introduction now freely available. It will produce its rich reddish-orange flowers at 2 or 3 years old, when it will be an inch or so (3cm) wide.

cluster freely and will flower easily. A good selection of the many to choose from would be: *R. perplexa*, *R. albiflora*, with tiny, acorn-sized heads, white spines and flowers; *R. marsoneri* and *R. aureiflora*, with rich deep yellow flowers; *R. krainziana*, with short, neat white spines, dark bodies and blood red flowers; *R. kupperana*, with long, bristly spines, brown and yellow, and fiery red flowers; *R. haagei*, small cone-shaped heads and salmon-pink flowers; *R. violaciflora*, with lilac-pink flowers; *R. muscula*, with dense, short white spines and orange flowers; *R. kariusiana*, with pale pink flowers and *R. flavistyla* with reddish-orange flowers.

Rebutia haagei is one of a group of Rebutias sometimes labelled Mediolobivia which make dense clusters of brownish-grey stems and produce many red or pink flowers. In this species they fade from deep to pale salmon-pink, each bloom lasting a week or more. They flower at 2 or 3 years old when they are barely 1in (2½cm) tall.

Rebutia perplexa grows as clusters of small, green heads with yellow spines. Its lovely rose-pink flowers grow from around the base after about a year's cultivation, the late spring flowering season lasting from a week to a month. A healthy plant will also produce new, brightly coloured spines at the centre of each head. Like all Rebutias it is susceptible to red spider mite and if the skin begins to turn brown all over, this is usually a sign that the pest is present.

Lady palm

This genus of five species of palm originated in southern China and Japan. Neat and attractive, they form large clusters of delicate slender stems in clumps and grow to a height of about 3ft (90cm). The leaves, growing from the multiple thick cane-like trunks, are divided into between 5 and 7 segments. The bases of old leaves remain to form a covering for the trunk in the form of woven fibres. The trunk is about as thick as a thumb and rod-like. The palm, which is sometimes called the ground rattan cane, should be kept out of strong sun, as this will turn the leaves yellow. A variegated variety with yellow and green markings is also sometimes available.

Light: Keep out of sunlight in summer. Full light in winter.

Temperature: Winter minimum 45°F (7°C). Spring and summer temperature of 50–60°F (10–16°C).

Water: Daily in summer, keeping soil constantly moist. Three times a week in winter. Do not stand in water or the roots will become waterlogged.

Humidity: Spray twice daily in summer with tepid soft water to maintain high humidity. Three times a week sufficient in winter. Stand pot on saucer of pebbles almost covered in water, or plant into self-watering container.

Feeding: Weekly in summer with houseplant food diluted with water according to maker's instructions.

Soil: Mixture of good loam such as loam-based No. 2 with equal parts of peat and sand. Perfect drainage important.

Repotting: Annually, with plenty of broken crocks in bottom of pot for good drainage.

Cleaning: Humidity spraying adequate. No leafshine.

468

The Lady palm has smaller leaves than many palms, growing in clusters on delicate, slender stems. They are very sensitive to atmospheric pollution and react badly to any kind of aerosol spray. Healthy plants have glossy green leaves, with no brown or blackened tips.

what goes wrong

Leaves have brown patches. Leafshine or atmospheric pollution. Do not use aerosols of any kind. Keep in fume-free room.

Removing dead fronds

When old leaves dry up and die, cut them off with sharp scissors or secateurs close to main stem.

If leaf tips turn brown and unsightly, clip off ends with scissors. Do not cut into healthy green area.

Webs under leaves, leaves then turn yellow. Red spider mite. Spray every week under leaves with pyrethrum-based insecticide until clear. Water soil once with malathion diluted to half recommended strength.

White woolly patches in leaf joints. Mealy bug. Paint with methylated spirits and remove wool with tweezers. Or water soil with malathion diluted to half recommended strength every 14 days until clear.

Leaf tips fail to open. Needs water and humidity. In summer spray twice a day and water daily.

New leaf tips turn brown. Needs water and humidity. In summer spray twice a day with soft tepid water and water daily.

Brown discs under leaves, marks on surface. Scale insect. Paint under leaves and on stem with methylated spirits and remove with thumbnail.

Leaves turn black. Too cold. Minimum winter temperature 45°F (7°C), or in summer 50°F (10°C).

Irregular chalky white circles on leaves. Lime màrks from spraying with hard water. Use only soft water.

Leaves turn yellow. Too much light. Needs good light but not direct sun.

Older leaves dry out. Natural for old leaves to die one at a time, as new ones produced. If several dry out at same time, too hot or air too dry. Spray twice daily and move to cooler place.

No new leaves appear in growing season. Needs feeding. Feed every week in summer.

Rhododendron simsii

Azalea

This spectacular winter-flowering house-plant is a member of the Rhododendron family but unlike other rhododendrons and azaleas, it is not hardy and will not survive frost if planted in the garden. Its most important requirement is copious amounts of soft water, both watered on and sprayed. It grows very slowly and would naturally flower in spring, but is usually 'forced' to produce flowers from early winter.

Light: Plenty of diffused light but keep out of direct sun.

Temperature: Maintain 55°F (13°C) all winter, though up to 60–65°F (16–18°C) can be tolerated for short periods if humidity is high. Once in bud, keep under 55°F (13°C).

Water: Copiously. Best method is to plunge pot into bucket of soft, lime-free water so that compost surface is covered. Leave until bubbles stop rising (about 10 minutes) then drain for half an hour before replacing in usual position. Do not leave for long periods standing in water. Do not allow compost to dry out: water every day all year round if necessary to keep it moist.

Humidity: Spray daily all year round with soft water, avoiding flowers. Stand pot on saucer of wet pebbles.

Feeding: Start feeding when flower buds form in early autumn, then feed weekly until spring. Reduce to fortnightly and stop feeding at midsummer. Use liquid houseplant food diluted to maker's instructions.

Soil: Equal parts of leafmould, peat and pine needles, with ¼ part sharp sand added.

Repotting: In summer, sink pot in ground outside in shady place. Keep watered and sprayed. In early autumn repot in 1 size larger pot. Clay pots are best.

Cleaning: Humidity spraying adequate. No leafshine.

Azaleas are winter-flowering indoor plants which do best in a cool atmosphere and give great pleasure at a time when few plants are in flower. Plants are available to 18in (45cm) in height and diameter, although more expensive standards and pyramids can also be obtained.

Flowers have black marks. Leafshine or insecticide damage. Do not use leafshine at all and do not spray flowers with insecticides of any kind.

Leaves have black marks. Leafshine damage. Do not use.

Leaves and flowers dry up and fall. Insufficient watering, too hot and air too dry or too wet. Check conditions. If dry, plunge pot into bucket of water and leave until bubbles stop rising. Allow to drain before replacing in position. Repeat daily in hot weather and spray daily all year round with tepid soft water. Keep in cooler place, around 55°F (13°C) ideal. If compost completely waterlogged, plant may show same symptoms: drain water from saucer and allow compost surface to dry out before watering again.

Leaves become hairy. Natural, do not remove them

Plant grows straggly and out of shape. Needs pruning. Prune after flowering, removing lanky stems that grow from flower clusters.

New leaves stay small, flowers do not form. Needs feeding. Feed once a week from time first buds appear and while flowering with liquid houseplant food diluted in water or with a foliar feed when spraying. After flowering feed fortnightly. Stop feeding in midsummer.

Watering

Water by plunging pot into large bowl or bucket so that water covers pot rim. Spray leaves. Leave for 15 minutes, then take pot out and allow it to drain. Always use soft water.

what goes wrong

Flowers fail to open. Waterlogged, standing in water or too hot. Check conditions. Always drain away excess water 10–15 minutes after watering. Spray daily with tepid soft water and keep at around 55°F (13°C). If waterlogged, allow compost surface to dry out.

Leaves turn pale green. Too dark or lime damage, eventually killing plant. If in dark place, move to lighter position; will take full sun. Check compost is lime-free and water and spray only with soft water.

White rings on leaves. Azalea leaf miner. Spray leaves with diluted malathion. Repeat once after 1 week. Do not spray flowers.

Brown husks around flowers. Natural. They will fall as flower develops.

Leaves turn black. Too cold. Move to warmer place, over 50°F (10°C).

Leaves have yellow speckles and webs underneath. Red spider

Flies hopping around plant. Whitefly. Spray with pyrethrum-based insecticide, avoiding flowers if possible. Repeat every 14 days until clear.

mite. Spray with diluted malathion, avoiding flowers which will burn. Repeat weekly for 4 weeks. Continue daily spraying with tepid soft water.

471

Rhoeo spathacea

Moses in the bullrushes

A pretty plant from Mexico that is closely related to the familiar Wandering Jew (Tradescantia). Unfortunately it is not so easy, and is really only suitable for someone with considerable experience of growing indoor plants. Its common name comes from the little white flowers which appear at the base of the leaves, half hidden in a boat-shaped bract. Great care must be taken with watering, especially in winter when overwatering can cause rotting. It grows first as a rosette of leaves but gradually produces a short stem, with the leaves and flowers growing on top. Offsets from around its base can be used to start new plants.

Moses in the bullrush plants are best treated as small specimen plants, that is, left to stand alone rather than planted together with others in a mixed bowl. They need careful watering, especially in winter, and soon rot if given too much at too low a temperature.

Light: Full light to partial shade. Keep out of midday summer sun.

Temperature: Winter minimum 60°F (16°C). In summer, ordinary room temperature, 70°F (21°C).

Water: Keep moist at all times watering 2–3 times a week in summer. In winter take great care particularly if temperature is near minimum. Water only once a week at most, with tepid (preferably soft) water. Always test compost.

Humidity: Spray at least twice weekly, summer and winter, more often if near maximum. In winter use tepid water.

Feeding: Every 14 days in spring and summer using liquid houseplant food at half maker's recommended strength.

Soil: Loam or peat-based No. 2.

Repotting: Once a year in spring when plant has outgrown its pot. If growth is slow leave for a year.

Cleaning: The spraying should keep it clean. Do not use leafshine.

Speckling or small burn marks all over plant. Leafshine damage. Do not use. Clean only by spraying with soft tepid water. Remove damaged leaf at base with sharp knife.

Leaves pale and plant looks tired. Not enough light. Move to a position in diffused daylight but not direct sun.

Small insects and webs under leaves. Red spider mite. Remove webs with damp cloth or sponge, then spray with diluted malathion, especially under leaves. Repeat every 14 days until symptoms disappear. Improve humidity by standing pot on saucer of wet pebbles and spray regularly.

Plant grows leggy and loses lower leaves. Old age. Propagate new plant from offshoots at base.

Plant becomes top heavy and won't stand up. Needs repotting. Move to larger pot and firm compost around base.

Propagation

1. When plant has flowered, offsets often grow around its base. When these are about 4in (10cm) tall, pull gently away, taking care not to damage their tiny roots.

2. Plant them in small pots containing drainage and compost of equal parts peat and sand. Leave in shade without water for 2 days, then treat as adult plants.

Leaf tips brown, leaves droop and curl. Soil and/or air too dry. Check compost and if dry, water well, then check compost regularly and keep moist in future. If over 70°F (21°C) spray daily.

what goes wrong

Brown marking on centre and edges of leaves. Damage caused by spraying in sunlight. Plant needs high humidity but must not be sprayed when sun is shining on it. Remove unsightly leaf at base with sharp knife.

Leaves curl inwards, darken and die. Too cold. Move to warmer place. Do not allow temperature to drop below 60°F (16°C).

Plant rots at stem. Compost too moist. Allow surface of soil to dry out before watering again. May need water 2–3 times a week in summer but not more than once a week in winter.

473

Miniature rose

Miniature roses are the only type that grow successfully as houseplants. Growing to 9–12in (23–30cm) high, they produce single, double or clusters of flowers, according to the variety. Their main requirements are good light and high humidity during the growing period in spring and summer. Once the flowers are over, the pots should be taken outside and sunk to their rims in soil; a layer of moist peat should be added to the top of the compost and they should be fed with fertilizer diluted to half normal recommended strength. If this is not possible, keep them in as cool a place as possible after flowering, to give them a 2 month dormant period. In early spring, prune away half the new growth from the previous year, cutting with scissors or secateurs just above a new bud.

Light: Full daylight, including sun.
Temperature: Winter indoors at 45°F (7°C), or outdoors (see above). In early spring gradually increase temperature as growth begins. Summer maximum 70°F (21°C).
Water: 2–3 times weekly in summer, once a week in winter, just enough to stop compost from drying right out.
Humidity: Spray daily in spring and summer, avoiding flowers, especially in strong sun, as droplets may burn plant. Stand pot on saucer of damp pebbles.
Feeding: Every 14 days in spring and summer when growing with liquid houseplant food at maker's recommended strength.
Soil: Equal parts of loam-based No. 2 and peat-based composts.
Repotting: Annually in early spring into next size pot. They flower best if potbound, so do not use too large a pot.
Cleaning: Humidity spraying sufficient. No leafshine.

Miniature rose bushes, up to 12in (30cm) high, make unusu indoor plants and, provided they can be kept in light, hum conditions, produce flowers every two months throughout the year. In drier conditions they should be put outside aft flowering in summer and brought back indoors when a ne crop of buds appears.

White powdery mould on leaves and buds. Mildew. Caused by dry roots, poor feeding and hot days followed by cold nights. Spray immediately with fungicide and repeat weekly until clear.

Black powdery mould on younger stems. Sooty mould. This forms on sticky substance left by greenfly. Spray twice weekly with diluted malathion and fungicide until clear.

Centre of leaves pale. Magnesium shortage. Use special rose fertiliser containing magnesium. Some tomato fertilisers are suitable – check contents on label.
Young leaves pale green with red spots. Nitrogen shortage. Feed every 14 days with liquid houseplant food in spring and summer and use correct compost.

what goes wrong

Plant grows straggly with no flowers. Too dark. Move into light window where it will get full sun.

Plant wilts, though leaves do not fall. Needs water. Water 2–3 times a week in summer, once a week in winter but do not allow to stand in water.

Green insects covering buds and flower stems. Greenfly. Spray every week with systemic insecticide until clear. Water same mixture into soil once a week until clear.

Leaf veins turn pale yellow or cream. A harmless virus disease. Needs feeding.

Leaves have large yellow patches. Too much lime in soil. Use a standard rose fertiliser every two weeks in spring and summer. If problem persists, apply one dose of sequestered iron.

Leaves turn brown and crisp. Too hot and air too dry. Summer indoor maximum temperature 70°F (21°C). Spray daily in spring and summer – though not in bright sunshine. Stand pot

on damp pebbles to provide extra humidity.

Flower petals eaten. Thrips. Very common in hot summer on indoor plants. Spray every week with diluted malathion until clear.

Black burn patches on leaves. Leafshine damage. Do not use. Clean only by spraying with soft water.

Veins turn yellow, leaves develop large yellow areas. Waterlogged. Never stand plant in water. And allow surface soil to become dry between waterings.

Leaves crinkled with brown marks. Frost damage while overwintering. If outside in long, frosty periods, cover plants with straw and wrap in sacking.

Leaves have large black spots surrounded with yellow. Leaves fall. Black spot. If not treated, all leaves will fall and plant will die. Spray twice a week with fungicide and improve air circulation around plant. Remove and burn affected leaves and stems.

475

Ruellia mackoyana

Trailing velvet plant

Named after Jean de la Ruelle who was botanist and physician to Francis I of France in the early 16th century, these free-flowering plants were fairly common in Victorian times but had all but disappeared from flower shops until quite recently. Attractive both for the beauty of their flowers and their silvery veined leaves, they are now coming back into favour. Watch especially for greenfly which attack the tender growing tips of the stems.

Light: Full diffused, not direct sun. In winter give 8 hours light, using artificial lighting to prolong flowering.
Temperature: At least 55°F (13°F) and in summer between 55 and 65°F (13–18°C). Maximum 70°F (21°C) for short periods if humidity high.
Water: From early spring for 6 weeks water as compost is about to dry out (every 10 days). Otherwise 2 days after surface feels dry (every 5 days).
Humidity: High if temperature over 65°F (18°C). Spray twice weekly with soft water when 55–65°F (13–18°C), daily if higher. Stand pot on saucer of wet pebbles all year round. Do not spray in rest period. Do not spray flowers.
Feeding: Fortnightly except during rest period. Dilute houseplant food to maker's recommended strength.
Repotting: In early autumn. After 2 years take cuttings in summer and root in peat/sand mixture. Pot up after 12 weeks in normal compost and feed.
Soil: Loam-based No. 2 mixed in equal parts with moss.
Cleaning: Humidity spray adequate. Use only soft water. Do not use leafshine.

The trailing velvet plant flowers in winter but its silver-veined leaves make it attractive all year round. To prolong its flowering period, use artificial lighting to give more 'daylight' hours in winter.

White powdery mould on leaves and stems. Botrytis, plant too cold and damp. Spray with fungicide, then place in warmer position and spray with water less often. Allow compost surface to dry out between waterings. Minimum temperature 55°F (13°C). Remove damaged leaves.

Spotty burn marks on flowers and leaves. Caused by spraying in bright sunlight. Move into area of diffused light and remove damaged leaf or flower.

Humidity
Stand pot on saucer of pebbles half covered in water all year round. Do not allow pot base to stand in water. If temperature over 65°F (18°C) provide higher humidity by daily spraying. Do not spray in spring rest period. Protect flowers from spray.

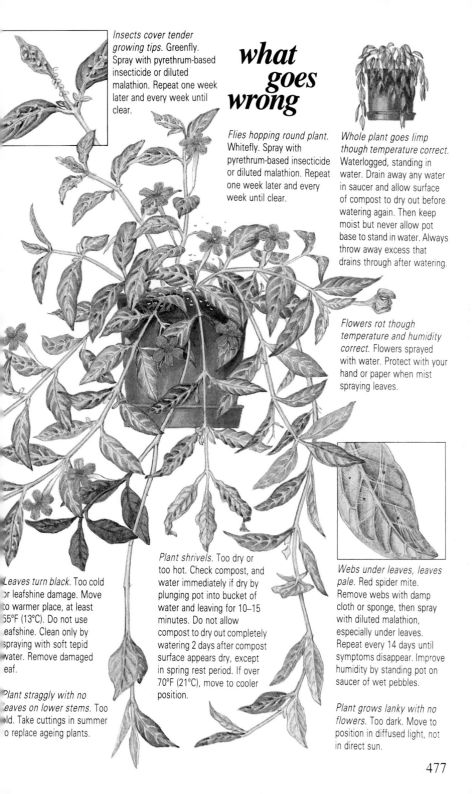

Insects cover tender growing tips. Greenfly. Spray with pyrethrum-based insecticide or diluted malathion. Repeat one week later and every week until clear.

what goes wrong

Flies hopping round plant. Whitefly. Spray with pyrethrum-based insecticide or diluted malathion. Repeat one week later and every week until clear.

Whole plant goes limp though temperature correct. Waterlogged, standing in water. Drain away any water in saucer and allow surface of compost to dry out before watering again. Then keep moist but never allow pot base to stand in water. Always throw away excess that drains through after watering.

Flowers rot though temperature and humidity correct. Flowers sprayed with water. Protect with your hand or paper when mist spraying leaves.

Leaves turn black. Too cold or leafshine damage. Move to warmer place, at least 55°F (13°C). Do not use leafshine. Clean only by spraying with soft tepid water. Remove damaged leaf.

Plant straggly with no leaves on lower stems. Too cold. Take cuttings in summer to replace ageing plants.

Plant shrivels. Too dry or too hot. Check compost, and water immediately if dry by plunging pot into bucket of water and leaving for 10–15 minutes. Do not allow compost to dry out completely watering 2 days after compost surface appears dry, except in spring rest period. If over 70°F (21°C), move to cooler position.

Webs under leaves, leaves pale. Red spider mite. Remove webs with damp cloth or sponge, then spray with diluted malathion, especially under leaves. Repeat every 14 days until symptoms disappear. Improve humidity by standing pot on saucer of wet pebbles.

Plant grows lanky with no flowers. Too dark. Move to position in diffused light, not in direct sun.

477

African violet

The original species of this plant, found in the mountains of East Africa, was blue; it has been hybridised to produce plants which do not drop their flowers so quickly and come in a range of colours, including pink, red, white and bi-colour varieties, and with single and double flowers. A relatively small pot, warmth and high humidity are all necessary for good flower production; a pinch of Epsom salts added once to the water in early summer will encourage the plant to flower.

The African violet is one of the world's most popular houseplants, yet it is often reluctant to flower. Warmth is the principal secret (60°F, 16°C all year round) coupled with a special watering technique and high humidity.

Light: Full light in summer, avoiding spring and summer sun. Will tolerate winter sunshine.

Temperature: Maintain 60°F (16°C) all year. Tolerates a minimum 55°F (13°C) and a maximum of 80°F (27°C) if humidity is high.

Water: Stand pot in a saucer and fill saucer to brim twice a week all year. After half an hour, tip out excess, as pot must not stand in water. Do not water top of pot.

Humidity: Do not spray. Achieve essential high humidity by standing pot on saucer of pebbles almost covered with water. Remove to another saucer for watering. Alternatively, put pot into another pot with damp peat between.

Feeding: Add liquid houseplant food every 2 weeks in spring and summer to water used for watering. Throw away excess. Use maker's recommended strength.

Soil: Peat-based potting compost.

Repotting: About every 2 years, only when plant looks really overcrowded in pot. Use shallow pots. Maintain overall rosette of leaves by removing leaves pointing towards centre of plant whenever necessary.

Cleaning: Dust with camel hair brush. No spraying, no leafshine. Remove dead flowers.

Leaves turn pale. Too much light or needs feeding. If in sun, move to position in diffused light. If new leaves also small, feed. Use liquid houseplant food at recommended strength every 2 weeks in the growing season and when in flower.

Leaves turn black. Leafshine damage. Never spray with leafshine or water. If dusty, remove by carefully brushing leaves with soft camel-hair brush.

New leaves small and very crowded. Needs repotting. Repot in spring into next size pot, but keep pot bound.

Watering

Water twice weekly all year round. Stand pot in saucer and fill saucer to brim with water. Leave for half an hour, then drain away excess. Do not leave standing in water.

Humidity

Plant needs high humidity but must not be sprayed. Put pebbles in saucer and stand pot on top. Add water to saucer until it is half way up pebbles. Do not let bottom of pot touch water.

Healthy plant does not flower. Pot too large. Plant flowers better when slightly pot bound. Do not repot for 2 years.

No flowers but plant in correct sized pot and in correct conditions. Add pinch of Epsom salts to water once only to trigger flowering season.

Flowers small and sparse. Usually occurs if second flush of flowers in same season. Remove faded flowers and feed every 2 weeks throughout summer with houseplant food at recommended strength.

Flowers have translucent marks. Water damage. Do not allow water to get on flowers. Plant needs humid atmosphere but do not spray.

what goes wrong

Leaves and flowers rot. Too frequent watering and watering from top. Water twice a week all year round by standing pot in saucer of water for half an hour. Do not water from above. Discard water after half an hour.

Brown marks on leaves. Water damage, especially if in sunny position. Never spray with water. Keep humidity high by standing pot on a saucer of damp pebbles. Water from below.

Healthy plant suddenly turns yellow. Gas fumes or cold draughts. Move to protected position in fume-free room.

Leaves curl or look limp and dry. Needs watering or too hot and air too dry. Water twice a week all year round, always from below. If temperatures near 80°F (27°C) improve humidity by standing on saucer of damp pebbles. Do not spray.

Leaves look limp and weedy. Too cold. Move to warmer place. Do not allow temperature to drop below 55°F (13°C).

Salvia

Salvias come originally from Brazil and though naturally perennials, are quickly killed by frost; in countries with cold winters they are therefore best grown as annuals. Modern varieties seldom exceed 12in (30cm) high, so are ideal for windowboxes.

Light: Maximum possible at all times.

Temperature: Germination, 70°F (21°C). Young plants, 60°F (16°C). Outside, protect from cold winds. No frost.

Water: Keep moist, not waterlogged.

Humidity: Seedlings, young plants: light syringing. Stop when flowering.

Soil: Loam-based No.3 or soil-less potting. Even better, equal parts of both.

Feeding: Start feeding young plants while still in tray, using liquid fertilizer at half maker's recommended strength. Ten days after final planting, start feeding at full recommended strength every 10 days in soil, every 5 in soil-less.

Propagation: Cuttings are difficult to overwinter so seeds sown in mid-spring are better. Use soil-less potting compost and cover seed with ¼in (½cm) fine compost, pressed down lightly. Place in plastic bag and cover with thick paper. Keep at 70°F (21°C). After germination (7–10 days) put in full light. Prick out singly into 3½ (9cm) pots or in trays 3in (8cm) apart as soon as they can be handled (about 15 days after sowing). Keep at 70°F (21°C) for 1 more week, then 60°F (16°C) until put outside.

Tidying: Snap off dead flower spikes to encourage branching.

Varieties: Volcano, midgreen foliage, bright scarlet, dwarf, compact and early. Blaze of Fire, slightly taller than Volcano, vigorous, compact. Midget, very dwarf and early. Carabinierre, dark foliage, very strong, grows with large spike. Dress Parade, mixture of cream, salmon, pink, scarlet, purple.

Salvias are bushy plants 9–15 (23-38cm) tall and produce clusters of flowers in a pyramid-shaped spike. Flower buds show early and when buying, choose plants whose bud colour is visible but not advanced; the leaves should be a fresh green, going right down to the base of the stem.

Pinpoint yellow or white spots on leaves. Underside is mealy. Red spider mite. Spray with diluted malathion at 10 day intervals until completely clear.

Upper leaves and growing points show yellow and pale green markings. Sometimes occurs after a check in growth due to cold. Condition usually disappears when warm weather returns.

Grey mould appears on flowers or foliage. Botrytis. Carefully remove any affected parts to avoid dropping spores on other plants and then spray with benomyl.

Plant wilts in hot sunshine. Needs more water. Keep soil always moist. Leaves will turn yellow if left without water for too long.

Seedlings develop dark and shrivelled area around base. Pythium or other root and stem rots. Seedlings will not recover. Remove affected plants and those near them. Spray compost with soil fungicide. If time, sow again in sterile compost and use only tap water for watering and spraying.

Leaves turn black and plant collapses. Frost. Protect from frost in spring.

Pricking out
1. When seedlings are large enough to handle, remove carefully from seed tray, holding them by the seed leaves.

2. Prepare 3½ (9cm) pots or tray, with holes for planting seedlings. Plant each one singly in pot or 3in (8cm) apart in tray. Moisten compost and leave in shade for 2 days.

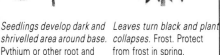

what goes wrong

Small insects clustered round growing points, possibly inside flowers. Aphids. Spray with pirimicarb or diluted malathion. Pirimicarb will not harm bees.

Flower stem distorted possibly with sunken area underneath flowers. Capsid bug. Spray with systemic insecticide.

Leaves have ragged holes, stem possibly rasped away. Slugs or snails. Place slug pellets as maker recommends.

Dark streaks and misshapen leaves. Virus. No action can be taken but flowering may not be affected. Destroy plants at end of season.

Bottom leaves turn yellow, upper leaves are grey/ green. Needs feeding. Increase number but not strength of feed.

Whole stem black, leaves yellow, flowers droop. Waterlogged. Check drainage. Plant will not recover. If others not yet affected allow soil to almost dry out before watering again. Yellow leaves also sign of dryness.

481

Sansevieria trifasciata

Mother-in-law's tongue

This is an easy plant which should be in everyone's collection as its leaf shape is strikingly different from most houseplants. It is very tolerant of most conditions except overwatering. If it is watered too much, especially in winter, the leaves may rot. Surprisingly, however, it does well in hydroculture (see p.18). It has an interesting star-like yellow flower which grows on a stem rising straight up from the soil beside the leaves. This stem should be removed with a sharp knife when the flowers have died. Because of their special watering needs, they are difficult to use in mixed plantings unless the pot is isolated from the surrounding compost in an outer container of dry sand. The other plants around it can then be watered normally.

Mother-in-law's tongue has tall, spiky leaves with black markings in the centre and a band of cream at the edge. Occasionally all-green plants are seen but these are usuall the result of propagation from cuttings. To maintain the cream markings, propagation must be by division. A shorterleaved variety, *S.hahnii*, needs similar care.

Light: Flourishes in full sunlight but will survive in shade.
Temperature: Winter minimum 60°F (16°C) but will survive down to 50°F (10°C). In summer, normal room temperatures up to 75°F (24°C).
Water: Never overwater – if in doubt, don't water. About once a week in summer, only every 21 days in winter sufficient. Make sure drainage is good.
Humidity: Likes a dry atmosphere. Do not spray.
Feeding: Feed every 21 days in summer with liquid houseplant food at maker's recommended strength.
Soil: Loam-based No. 2.
Repotting: Prefers to be in a small pot and is best left until pot bursts. About every 2–3 years will do. Make sure compost is firmed down well around plant as it tends to become top-heavy and can fall over.

Leaf cuttings
1. Cut across base of healthy leaf with sharp knife and cut leaf into 1in (2½cm) sections. Make small slit in cut edges that were towards base.

2. Insert sections half into tray of sand, slit edge downwards.

3. Water well and cover. Keep at 70°F (21°C) until growing well. When they have 2 or 3 new leaves they can be lifted and repotted separately in small pots.

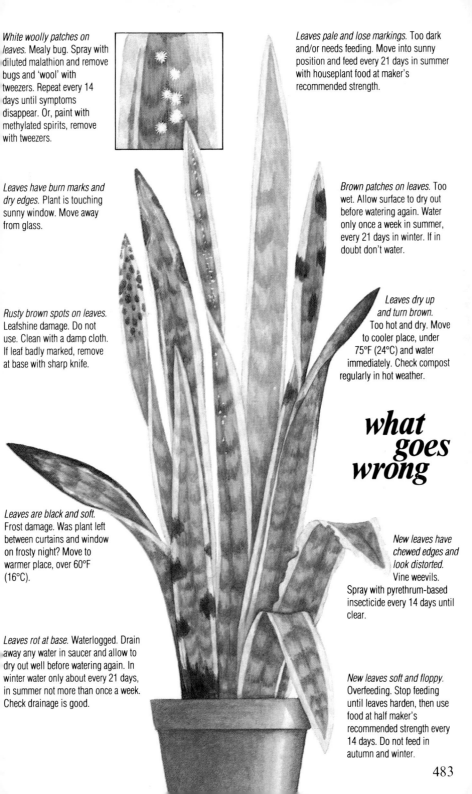

White woolly patches on leaves. Mealy bug. Spray with diluted malathion and remove bugs and 'wool' with tweezers. Repeat every 14 days until symptoms disappear. Or, paint with methylated spirits, remove with tweezers.

Leaves have burn marks and dry edges. Plant is touching sunny window. Move away from glass.

Rusty brown spots on leaves. Leafshine damage. Do not use. Clean with a damp cloth. If leaf badly marked, remove at base with sharp knife.

Leaves are black and soft. Frost damage. Was plant left between curtains and window on frosty night? Move to warmer place, over 60°F (16°C).

Leaves rot at base. Waterlogged. Drain away any water in saucer and allow to dry out well before watering again. In winter water only about every 21 days, in summer not more than once a week. Check drainage is good.

Leaves pale and lose markings. Too dark and/or needs feeding. Move into sunny position and feed every 21 days in summer with houseplant food at maker's recommended strength.

Brown patches on leaves. Too wet. Allow surface to dry out before watering again. Water only once a week in summer, every 21 days in winter. If in doubt don't water.

Leaves dry up and turn brown. Too hot and dry. Move to cooler place, under 75°F (24°C) and water immediately. Check compost regularly in hot weather.

what goes wrong

New leaves have chewed edges and look distorted. Vine weevils. Spray with pyrethrum-based insecticide every 14 days until clear.

New leaves soft and floppy. Overfeeding. Stop feeding until leaves harden, then use food at half maker's recommended strength every 14 days. Do not feed in autumn and winter.

Saxifraga stolonifera

Mother of thousands

Saxifragas are usually thought of as alpine plants, hugging a rocky scree covered in snow and ice in winter. They are therefore an unusual family of plants for the house, though this variety makes a good indoor plant. In summer it produces dainty white flowers and a mass of young plantlets grow on runners, slender stems which hang over the sides of the pot. If grown in a hanging basket, the runners and plantlets hang down attractively, while in a large bowl or trough, the plant will spread to cover a wide area. The leaves are green with lighter green or white vein markings and are slightly hairy. There is a variegated version with smaller leaves which needs a slightly higher minimum temperature.

Light: Windowsill shielded from hot summer sun ideal.

Temperature: Winter minimum 45°F (8°C), summer ideal 55–60°C (12–15°C), as plant prefers cool temperatures. Does not like hot central heating and may dry up in 70°F (20°C).

Water: 3 times a week in summer. In winter allow to dry out between waterings. Every 10–14 days probably enough unless rooms are very warm (70°F, 20°C). Test compost regularly. Good drainage is essential to prevent rot. Make sure that plants in hanging baskets are watered regularly as they dry out quickly in summer.

Humidity: Not important, provided temperature moderate. A fortnightly spray keeps foliage fresh in hot weather.

Feeding: Once a month in summer with houseplant food diluted with water. Use half as much food as the maker recommends.

Soil: Loam-based No. 2 compost.

Repotting: Annually in spring.

Cleaning: Spray with water if dusty or dirty. No leafshine.

The Mother-of-thousands, sometimes called the Strawberry plant because its runners are like those of the garden strawberry, has dark green leaves with lighter green markings along the veins. A fortnightly mist spray with water will keep them clean and dust-free.

what goes wrong

Leaves pale and dull. Too dark. Move to lighter place but shield from hot summer sun. Pale, brownish leaves also caused by hot direct sunlight.

Leaves distorted and sticky with green insects. Greenfly. Spray with pyrethrum or systemic insecticide every 14 days until clear. Plant is very susceptible.

White woolly patches on leaves and stems. Mealy bug. Remove with cotton wool dipped in methylated spirits or spray with diluted malathion every 14 days until clear.

Plant collapses, leaves limp, stems rot. Too wet, overwatered. Allow soil to dry out before watering again. Check drainage and water less often.

Plant flops. Too dry. Soak in bowl of water for half an hour, then drain well. Water more regularly.

Propagation

1. Prepare small pot with drainage material and compost of ½ sand, ½ loam-based No. 2. Place next to parent plant and position plantlet in centre. Firm compost round it and water well.

2. When plantlet grows new leaves, sever runner close to new plant.

Burn marks on leaves. Leafshine damage, or direct sun. Do not use leafshine and move out of sunlight.

Stems grow straggly and leaves do not group together closely. Too hot (over 70°F, 21°C). Move to cooler place.

Webs under leaves, leaves begin to discolour. Red spider mite. Spray with diluted malathion every 14 days until clear. If temperature high (68–70°F, 18–21°C) spray every week to improve humidity.

Grey mould on leaves around base; leaves turn brown and shrivel. Botrytis, plant too wet and humid. Move to warmer place (55–60°F, 12–15°C) and allow to dry out before watering. Spray with systemic fungicide.

No runners or new leaves in spring and summer. Needs feeding. Feed every month in summer.

Leaves look ragged and many die. Old age. Propagate new plants from runners and throw old one away.

Schefflera arboricola

Umbrella tree

Umbrella trees have increased in popularity over recent years as new varieties have been introduced, some more compact, some with attractive variegated leaves. Their larger relative, *Schefflera actinophylla*, grows to 8ft (2½m) tall with leaves up to 8in (20cm) long; but *S. arboricola* is a more manageable height, around 4ft (120cm) in a pot or tub. Often marketed under the alternative names *Heptapleurum* or *Brassaia* they are good plants to grow in hydroculture and are tolerant of less than perfect conditions in the home and office.

The Umbrella tree grows up to 4ft (120cm) tall and may make a foot (30cm) or more in a season. Its green or variegated leaves have about 7 leaflets which fall in a graceful umbrella shape over the stem. Smaller varieties are often available.

Light: Like most plants it prefers good indirect light with some morning sun but will tolerate a more shady position.
Temperature: Between 55–65°F (13–18°C) in winter; in summer normal room temperature, but increase ventilation if over 80°F (27°C).
Water: Keep moist, watering 2–3 times a week in summer, once a week in winter.
Humidity: Spray with soft water twice a week all year round. In dry, centrally-heated rooms, stand pot on saucer of wet pebbles for constant humidity.
Feeding: In summer, when growing, feed every 14 days with houseplant food diluted to half recommended strength.
Soil: Either loam or peat-based No. 2.
Repotting: Young plants need repotting twice a year as they grow up to a foot (30cm) a year. Older plants need repotting only once a year or every other year. When too large to handle easily, replace top 2–3in (5–7cm) soil in spring and feed regularly throughout the summer. Taller plants may need a cane. Insert when repotting, taking care not to damage roots.
Cleaning: Spraying will keep it clean. Use leafshine not more than once a month.

Variegated leaves lose colour. Too dark. Move into good indirect light; best with some sunlight every day but not direct midday sun.

Leaves have too few leaflets on young plant. These are the juvenile leaves, quite normal on young plant. Adult leaves have about 7 leaflets.

Cleaning
Spray leaves regularly for humidity and to keep them dust free. For extra shine, add liquid leafshine — but not more than once a month.

Plant becomes lanky with long spaces between leaves. Too hot. Move to a cooler, more airy place. Spray twice weekly with soft tepid water. If over 80°F (27°C) give fresh air.

White woolly patches on leaves and where leaves join stem. Mealy bug. Spray with diluted malathion and remove bugs and 'wool' with tweezers. Repeat every 14 days until symptoms disappear. Or, paint bugs with methylated spirits and remove with tweezers.

what goes wrong

Plant limp, leaves hang down. Too dry. Plunge pot into bucket of water for 10–15 minutes, then drain. Keep soil constantly moist in summer, watering every day if it dries out in hot weather. Do not allow to stand in water. Spray daily with soft tepid water.

Leaves pale or even yellow. Needs feeding. Feed with houseplant food diluted to half maker's recommended strength every 14 days in the growing season, spring and summer.

Brown scales on stems, leaf stalks and under leaves. Scale insect. Spray underside of leaves with diluted malathion and, after 48 hours, remove discs with thumbnail. Repeat every week for 4 weeks until clear.

Leaves distorted, and sticky with green insects. Greenfly. Spray with pyrethrum-based insecticide or diluted malathion. Repeat one week later and every week until clear.

Leaves yellow with webs underneath. Red spider mite. Remove webs with damp cloth or sponge, then spray with diluted malathion, especially under leaves. Repeat every 14 days until symptoms disappear. Improve humidity by standing pot on saucer of wet pebbles and spray regularly.

Leaves turn yellow, droop and fall. Too wet. Allow surface to dry out before watering again and check drainage in pot. Do not stand in water. If plant is cold, leaves may drop one by one while still green.

487

Schizanthus hybridus

Butterfly flower

The Butterfly flower or Poor man's orchid is a native of Chile and can be grown outdoors or indoors as a pot plant. Plants bought in flower in early summer will, if kept cool and light and not overwatered, continue to flower through to late autumn. It can also be grown from seed in early autumn and grown in a cool porch or conservatory to flower in early spring indoors on a light windowsill. Sow seed in trays of seed compost and place tray in a plastic bag or propagator. Keep at 50–60°F (10–16°C) and prick out into 2in (5cm) containers when seedlings are large enough to handle. As they grow, move to 4½in (9cm) pots where dwarf varieties can remain for flowering. For taller types move to 6in (15cm) pots when roots fill pot.

Butterfly flower or Poor man's orchid, grows to 24in (60cm) high, though modern dwarf varieties, at 12in (30cm) are more suitable for indoors. It is very sensitive to polluted atmospheres but if grown correctly, will be so covered in its spikes of pink or lilac flowers that the small, slightly sticky leaves are almost hidden.

Light: Maximum light at all times. Protect young plants from strong sunlight.
Temperature: Germination at 50–60°F (10–15°C). Grow on through winter at 45°F (7°C). Plants will not flower at high temperatures.
Water: Keep soil just moist until plants are in final pots, then water every 2–3 days. Ensure good drainage.
Humidity: Cool, dry conditions essential. Spraying makes them vulnerable to fungus infections.
Feeding: To ensure good flowering, feed with liquid houseplant food at maker's recommended strength every week while in small pots, then every 4 days until last flowers have died.
Soil: Loam-based No.2 or soil-less.
After flowering: Remove dead flowerheads to encourage new buds to form. Butterfly flower is a perennial usually treated as an annual and will rarely flower again indoors. Discard after flowering.

what goes wrong

Leaves turn yellow, growth stops. Too wet. Water 2–3 times a week, and do not let pot stand in water.

Plant grows straggly, no flower buds appear. Much too dark. Butterfly Flower needs full light at all times to bloom.

Flowers turn brown and papery at edges. Spraying of insecticide in full sun. Always spray in evening. Ensure good ventilation, and never spray with water.

Small, wingless insects on leaves, buds or flowers. Greenfly, which are very common on Butterfly Flower. Spray weekly with pyrethrum-based insecticide if seen.

Top leaves wilt and turn bronze. Spotted wilt virus disease, which usually affects only plants grown outdoors. No cure, so destroy plant before virus spreads.

Plant looks sickly. Leaves and flowers brown at edges. Check conditions. May be too hot, especially if plant was purchased in flower. Move to a cooler place. Butterfly Flower will not thrive in gas or traffic fumes, so move to a fume-free position.

Leaves turn greyish-green with brown edges, flowers drop. Needs feeding. Feed every 4 days with liquid houseplant food diluted to recommended strength.

Entire plant looks limp and dull. Either much too hot or too cold. Established plants do best at about 50°F (10°C). Good ventilation essential. Butterfly Flower dislikes central heating. Move plant to better conditions.

White froth in leaf axils in spring. Froghopper, which usually attacks only outdoor-grown plants. Wash off froth with water, avoid chemical spraying.

White powder on leaves and especially stems. Powdery mildew. Spray with dinocap or other fungicide. Plants which are allowed to dry out are particularly susceptible, so keep soil moist.

Plant droops, flowers are floppy. Too dry. Water every 2–3 days once plant is in final pot, more often in hot weather.

Base of stem looks sunken and reddish brown. Root rot fungus disease. If stem still supports plant, treat with copper compound fungicide. Disease may come from contaminated soil or water. Always use sterile compost and clean water.

Schlumbergera

The name Schlumbergera is now accepted as the correct one for the well-known Christmas cactus (Zygocactus) which, as its common name implies, comes into flower in Europe's mid-winter. In fact, though some flower for Christmas, for others the natural flowering season is later.

They grow wild in the jungles of Brazil so need rather different treatment from desert cacti. They need peat-based, soil-less composts, watering all the year round and slightly less light than other cacti and are generally treated more like an ordinary indoor plant. There are many different forms to choose from as breeders have produced numerous hybrids, usually with toothed stems and flower colours ranging from white through pinks and reds to purple. All have the familiar segmented stems, with flowers appearing at the ends of segments grown earlier in the year.

There are many coloured hybrid Schlumbergeras to choose from but some of the most sought after are the paler forms, like this S. 'Wintermarchen'. They will flower a year or two after rooting, when they have made a few new stems.

Light: They do well on a sunny windowsill indoors but if grown in a greenhouse should be kept out of long periods of continuous sunlight: 2–3 hours a day are about right. Shade the greenhouse lightly in the hottest months.

Temperature: Keep above 40°F (4°C) in winter but a temperature of about 50°F (10°C) is better, especially for producing flowers at around Christmas time. Keep below 100°F (38°C) in summer, giving fresh air whenever possible.

Water: Water once a month in winter to prevent soil from drying out completely, fortnightly in spring and autumn. In summer water every week, allowing soil just to dry out between waterings.

Feeding: Use high potash fertilizer once a month in the spring, summer and autumn. Do not feed while flowering.

490

Soil: Soil-less, peat-based compost is best with no additional material. Some growers prefer leafmould, which is more like their natural surroundings.

Repotting: Schlumbergeras grow quickly and may reach 12in (30cm) across in 3–4 years. Repot each year into next size pot, handling the root ball carefully as they dislike having their roots disturbed. The base of the plant becomes woody with age and it is a good idea to propagate new plants.

Cleaning and pest control: Spray at least once a week to keep them fresh and dust-free. Incorporate an insecticide 2 or 3 times a year to combat pests and a systemic fungicide to prevent the orange and brown spotting which sometimes affects them.

Other species: The many hybrids of the popular Christmas cactus all flower in mid-winter but a later-flowering species, known as the Easter cactus, blooms in spring and has bright red flowers.

Stem segments
A month after flowering, take cutting of 2 segments, cutting at joint with a sharp knife.

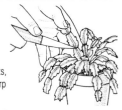

2. Dust both cut ends with hormone rooting powder containing fungicide and leave to dry for 2 days. Place end of cutting gently into almost dry soil-less compost, planting about ½in (1cm) deep. Water after 2 weeks.

These plants appreciate a weekly spray with distilled or rainwater – tap water tends to leave marks. Spray more often in warm weather, in the evenings.

Two similar plants worth looking out for are *S. (Rhipsalidopsis) rosea,* with lilac pink flowers and stem segments each only an inch (3cm) long and *S. (Epiphyllanthus) obovatus* which looks like a small-stemmed Opuntia and has scarlet flowers.

A healthy Schlumbergera will make new segments on all its stems and will flower in winter. The flowers appear at the ends of the newest segments and last for 1 or 2 weeks.

Scirpus cernuus

Mini bulrush

Bulrushes are a family of water-loving plants that thrive in bogs or on marshy land. This miniature variety can be used in aquariums as it will actually grow in water but is a good indoor pot plant as well and will last a long time if kept damp and in a humid atmosphere. Its grass-like leaves grow upright at first, then bend gracefully over, reaching 6–10in (13–25cm) long. It grows best in clay pots and is most attractive when quite small and young as it becomes untidy and straggly with age. Although the stems trail, the plant needs too much water to grow successfully in a hanging basket.

Light: Will stand full sun but better in indirect light. Will survive 4–6 weeks in a shady corner.

Temperature: Very tolerant, down to 45°F (8°C) in winter, though better around 55°F (13°C). If over 75°F (24°C), increase humidity.

Water: Moist at all times, summer and winter as it grows continuously unless temperature at minimum. Water 2–3 times a week all year round.

Humidity: Spray daily, twice a day in hot weather.

Feeding: Give liquid houseplant food every 3 weeks at maker's recommended strength while plant is growing. This may be all year round in normal room temperatures.

Soil: Loam-based No.2. Roots need firm compost.

Repotting: Every 6 months but best to divide plant into two rather than use a larger pot. Use clay pot if possible and make sure drainage is good.

Cleaning: Spraying should keep it clean. Leafshine spray can be used once a month but too frequent use will mark leaves.

The grass-like stems of the miniature Bulrush plant produce tiny cream-coloured flowers at their tips. Though the stems trail gracefully, they are not really suitable for hanging baskets, since they need to grow in compost that is constantly very moist.

Plant looks straggly, untidy and tired. Needs repotting and splitting in half. Small plants look more attractive than larger ones.

what goes wrong

Whole sections look burned, but still green on either side. Damage by sunlight. Move into an area of diffused daylight, out of harmful rays of sun. Remove damaged leaf.

Division

1. When plant gets large and straggly, divide roots and stems in spring. Remove from pot and gently tease away old soil from around roots. Prepare 2 pots with compost and drainage.

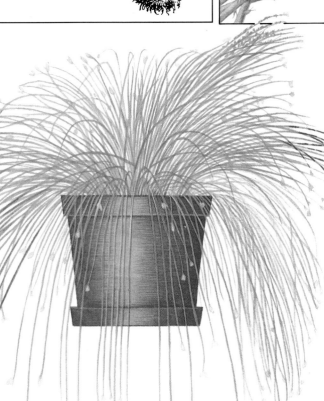

2. Gently pull roots and stems in half with your hands, dividing plant into 2 equal portions. Repot each half separately and leave in shade without water for 2 days to encourage roots to explore compost.

Plant does not grow. Needs feeding. Feed with houseplant food at maker's recommended strength every 3 weeks while growing.

All outside leaves go brown in summer. Too hot. Move to a cooler place with more ventilation. Spray daily with soft, tepid water. Maximum temperature 75°F (24°C).

Little green insects among the leaves. Greenfly. Spray with pyrethrum-based insecticide or diluted malathion. Repeat one week later and every week until clear.

Brown rust marks on leaves. Too much leafshine; only use once a month.

Leaves lose their colour. Not enough light. Move to a position in very good light. Plant will stand direct sunshine.

Plant looks limp and dried up. Soil too dry. Plunge pot into bucket of water for 10–15 minutes, then drain. Keep constantly moist in summer, watering every day if it dries out in hot weather. Spray daily with soft tepid water.

493

Sedum morganianum

This is one of a vast genus of succulent plants, widespread in both tropical and temperate climates. *Sedum morganianum* from Mexico is one of the most attractive of the tender species which all have fleshy stems or leaves. It needs to be kept indoors or in a greenhouse, and is an ideal subject for a hanging basket. It does better out of the full glare of the sun in summer, but must have a good light position all year. The stems will grow up to about 3ft (1m) and cover a base area of about 8in (20cm). Other good species, not for hanging baskets, are *Sedum rubrotinctum*, especially 'Aurora', *S. hintonii*, and *S. furfuraceum*.

Sedum morganianum or Donkey's tail, makes a splendid hanging pot plant. Be careful not to allow it to dry out completely in winter or the leaves will become crisp and fall leaving unsightly areas of bare stem. Pink flowers appear from the ends of the stems but only on very large mature plants: its leaves are its main indoor attraction.

Light: To bring out the best colouring full sunshine is needed at all times.

Temperature: Many species will take temperatures near freezing, but are better kept at a minimum 40°F (4°C) in winter. Give fresh air in summer.

Water: Spray heavily monthly in winter, or give just enough water to keep the soil from drying out completely once a month or every six weeks. Water fortnightly in spring and summer, weekly in hottest weather. Tail off in autumn. See also Introduction.

Feeding: Not needed if repotted each year. Use high potash fertilizer if not repotted, not more than twice in summer.

Soil: Use good loam-based No. 1 potting compost, or soil-less compost, with 30% coarse, gritty sand.

Repotting: Every spring until they are in 5in (13cm) half pot or pan, then every other year. Always use shallow pots as the roots are short. Do not water for 2 weeks after repotting.

Propagation: By whole stem cuttings or leaf-cuttings.

Taking cuttings

1. Cut stem 2in (5cm) from end, between leaves in late spring or early summer. Dust cut ends with hormone rooting powder to prevent infection, leave to dry for 2 days, then place cutting on dry compost. Do not water until roots appear.

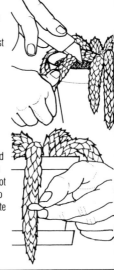

2. Or, ease off leaf from healthy stem with fingers and lay flat on dry compost, with base touching surface. Do not water until roots form and do not remove old leaf until quite dried out.

what goes wrong

No growth, leaves fall leaving tuft at stem end. If lower stem soft or blackened, overwatered. Allow to dry out well before watering again and pare away blackened stem (see Introduction). In winter water only once a month. If conditions correct and stem firm, check roots for root mealy bug.

No flowers. Too dark. Move to full sun over 2 weeks. Needs sunshine all year round.

Stems short, have not grown in spring and summer. Compost unsuitable or has not been repotted or fed. Repot following spring in fresh compost or feed twice during summer. Do not feed in winter.

New leaves small, little new growth in spring. Needs repotting in half-pot or pan with fresh compost. Take care not to damage the leaves when repotting and choose pot only one size larger each time.

Leaves next to glass light brown and shrivelled. Sunscorched, probably after cloudy period. Shade for 2 weeks, then move back gradually to full sun. In hot summer weather, shade from midday sun.

White woolly patches among leaves. Mealy bug. Remove with small paintbrush dipped in methylated spirits and spray with insecticide. Repeat 2–3 times in spring and summer.

Long gaps of bare stem between leaves. Too dark. Move to sunny place over 2 weeks.

Hanging baskets
Plants in hanging baskets dry out more quickly than those in standing containers. Check compost regularly and water when pot dries out in summer. In winter, spray monthly, especially if over 50°F (10°C) to prevent leaves from falling.

Leaves shrivel and fall. Too dry. Soak in bowl of water for ½ hour, then drain and give more water each time soil dries out. In winter moisten soil monthly, to keep leaves plump.

Leaves wrinkle, turn black and fall; stem ends black and soft. Too cold and wet or too humid. Move to warmer place, around 50°F (10°C) in winter and allow to dry out if soil wet. Pare away blackened area and dust with fungicide.

495

Selaginella uncinata

Rainbow moss

Looking like growing moss, *Selaginella* (also known as Peacock fern) can be grown in soil or on cork bark. Without a very humid atmosphere, however, they will turn brown and die. Thus, an ideal situation for them is a bottle garden or fern case where the humidity is constantly high and the plant is protected from draughts. A number of varieties are available, most of them in varying shades of green, though some have a decidedly blue tinge. If the plant grows very quickly it can be cut back by half without damage. Any fronds and leaflets that dry up can also be trimmed off.

Rainbow moss grows as a mass of spreading bright green fronds and when healthy, will have no sign of brown or shrivelled leaflets. The shimmering colour which is caused by light bouncing off its minute scale-like leaves gives it its alternative name of the Peacock fern.

Light: Medium light for successful growth. Do not keep in a dark corner, in a very light position or in full sunlight.
Temperature: Winter minimum 55°F (13°C), summer maximum 65°F (18°C).
Water: Daily in spring and summer unless in fern case or bottle garden. Once a week in winter. Must be kept moist at all times.
Humidity: Very high level essential for successful growth. Steamy kitchen would be suitable, though fern case, cool greenhouse ideal. Keep out of very dry room where even daily spraying would be insufficient.
Feeding: Every 14 days in summer only with houseplant food diluted with water. Use half the amount recommended by the maker.
Soil: Peat-based compost mixed with one-third by volume of chopped sphagnum moss to ensure open mixture.
Repotting: Every two years in spring, into well-drained pot. If in fern case or bottle garden, replace some of top soil with fresh compost mixture.
Cleaning: Spray with tepid soft water. Do not use a feather duster as this could break brittle stems. No leafshine.

Tips of fronds shrivel. Too dry. Needs watering every day in growing period.

Some leaflets on frond turn black and die. Leafshine damage. Do not use.

Leaflets and stems black. Too cold. In winter 55°F (13°C) minimum. Place in warmer room and keep humidity high. Remove unsightly stems with scissors.

ronds turn brown all at once and whole
lant dries out. Too hot. Move to cooler
lace (not more than 65°F, 18°C) if possible.

eaflets remain pale. Too dark. Move to
ghter place but not in direct sun.

**Replacing top soil in
bottle garden.**

1. Carefully remove top inch
(2½cm) soil using wooden
spoon on end of cane.

2. Add new compost and firm
around plant with cotton reel
tied to cane.

what
goes
wrong

Fronds dry up, starting at tip
and gradually going black.
Direct sun. Move to shadier
place.

Small flies around soil
surface. Whitefly. Add
systemic insecticide to water
every 14 days until clear. Do
not spray leaves or they will
'burn'.

lant looks 'tired' and dull.
oil too compact, preventing
ealthy root development.
epot in correct mixture.

Leaflets brown and shrivelled. Insufficient
humidity. Needs very damp atmosphere.
Spray daily and place pot on wet pebbles.

Leaflets do not grow. Needs
feeding. Feed every 14 days
in summer with houseplant
food at half recommended
strength.

497

Selenicereus

This is the famous, clambering cactus known as Queen of the Night, because of its enormous, white, scented flowers which bloom for one night only. It is a vigorous grower and in the right conditions will make yards of growth each year. For best results it needs either a large pot or to be planted in a corner of a greenhouse. The stem must be looped in and out around a large trellis or cane or twined along the sides and ridge bar of a greenhouse. Old, woody growth should be cut out every year and the plant treated rather like a cultivated blackberry or climbing rose. If it is not pruned it will quickly become a tangled mess. The different species come from Cuba, Haiti, Mexico and Texas where they grow rooted in the soil and clamber among the upper branches of trees.

This plant, believed to be *Selenicereus grandiflorus*, clambers along the ridge bar of a 12ft (3½m) greenhouse where it is trained back and forth. The huge flowers, 8–12in (20–30cm) across, are produced in summer and open on warm evenings to fill the greenhouse with their perfume.

Light: Full sunlight at all times is needed, on a sunny windowsill or porch. In a greenhouse the root can be planted in a shady corner so long as the stem is trained into the lightest position possible. Without full light it will not produce its flowers.

Temperature: It will stand 40°F (4°C) in winter but is best at 45–50°F (7–10°C). Keep below 100°F (38°C) in summer and give fresh air whenever possible.

Water: In spring and summer water once a fortnight, or once a month if in a big pot 9in (23cm) or more. Allow soil to dry out between waterings. In early autumn stop watering to allow pot to dry out before temperatures fall too much, then keep dry in winter.

Feeding: Feed monthly in spring and summer with high potash fertilizer (as used for tomatoes).

Soil: Use soil-less or good loam-based No. 2 potting compost with no added grit or sand.

Repotting: Repot every year in spring until roots fill a 9in (23cm) pot. Then change so every 3 years, replacing plant in same size pot unless roots have outgrown it. Cut ol wood when repotting. In years plant is no repotted, cut out old wood in spring, stems are tangled and unsightly.

Cleaning and pest control: Spray week with water in spring and summer incorporating an insecticide 2 or 3 times year to combat pests.

Other species: There are half-a-dozen or s names but it is difficult to be sure of th accuracy of any in cultivation. All loo similar and all produce the large flowers fo which they are famous. Named specie sometimes found are *S. grandiflorus*, *S macdonaldiae* and *S. pseudospinulosus*.

Training

1. Start training when plant is 3ft (1m) long. First repot into large pot with room for root ball and space around for growth.

2. Insert 2 pliable canes (as used for basket-making) at opposite sides of pot, pushing them well down. Tie them firmly at top where they cross.

3. As stem lengthens, weave it around the canes. It is important to train while still young and flexible as older stems become woody.

Selenicereus pteranthus should flower after 3–5 years, when its stems are 2–3ft (60–90cm) long. The flowers, about 10in (25cm) across, appear 2 or 3 at a time in the summer, the flowering season lasting about a month. The flowers open in the evening, bloom for the night and by morning are finished.

Cineraria

This very popular flowering pot plant requires cool, airy conditions to grow successfully and will soon die in high temperatures. Plants are usually bought in flower or bud in late winter or early spring but they can also be grown from seed. Sow in trays in mid-spring to early summer, dusting seeds lightly with seed compost. Keep at 55°F (13°C) and prick out when large enough to handle, into small containers. Repot in 3 stages as roots fill pots, until in final 6in (15cm) pots where they will flower the following spring. Because they are very susceptible to various fungus diseases and to attacks by pests, particularly greenfly, spray with fungicides and insecticides every 3–4 weeks while growing.

Cinerarias grow 6–8in (15–20cm) tall but may be more in diameter, with flower heads 8–10in (20–25cm) across. They produce a succession of small, daisy-like flowers over a period of 6–10 weeks in spring, with colours ranging from pink, red, mauve and blue to white.

Light: Good light at all times, but protect flowers from direct sunlight.
Temperature: Cineraria will not thrive in high temperatures. Maximum 55°F (13°C), best around 45°F (7°C) in winter.
Water: Keep compost just barely moist until in final pot, then water every 2–3 days while in flower. Good drainage essential.
Humidity: Prefers cool, dry situation. Do not spray as this increases vulnerability to fungus diseases.
Feeding: Not necessary with purchased plants, as overfeeding makes leaves grow coarse and ugly. If growing from seed, feed every other week with houseplant food at half maker's recommended strength from the time first buds appear.
Soil: Loam-based No.2 or soil-less potting compost.
After flowering: Remove dead flowers to encourage new buds to form. When all flowering is finished, discard, as plant will not flower again.

Small white flies around plant. White scales may be seen under leaves. Whitefly. Spray with pyrethrum-based insecticide at 3-day intervals until no more flies or scales seen. Do not spray in sunshine.

Silvery streaks on leaves. Onion thrips, especially likely in high temperatures. Spray with diluted malathion and repeat in 10 days.

what goes wrong

Yellow spots on leaves, veins dark. Tomato spotted wilt virus. No cure so destroy plant. Not common.

Leaves wilt, flowers droop or die. Too hot, dry or too wet. Check. Keep below 55°F (13°C) with compost just moist.

Leaves dark, plant not thriving. Too cold. Move to a warmer place, but not over 55°F (13°C). If leaves are black, suspect frost damage and discard plant.

Stem turns black at base. Plant wilts in sunshine. Phytophthora, likely if soil too wet or drainage is poor. Try to prevent as there is no cure.

Leaves small and grey-green, flower head small. Not fed while growing. Next year feed with half-strength liquid feed when buds form. Feeding will not improve mature plant.

Flowers turn pale and may droop. Too much direct sun. Keep in a shady position when in flower.

Watering
Always test compost before watering, especially if plant is drooping. An overwatered plant, a dry plant and a plant in moist compost but full sun will all droop their leaves in the same way. Make sure you discover the correct cause.

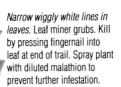

Small wingless insects on buds and leaves. Greenfly, to which Cineraria is very susceptible. As a precaution, spray plants weekly with pyrethrum-based insecticide.

Narrow wiggly white lines in leaves. Leaf miner grubs. Kill by pressing fingernail into leaf at end of trail. Spray plant with diluted malathion to prevent further infestation.

Small orange blisters on surface of leaves, powdery yellow spots under leaves. Cineraria rust fungus disease. Spraying with water makes plants vulnerable. Spray with fungicide. Do not let powder fall on other leaves.

Stems and leaf stalks grow long and thin, few flowers. Too dark. Move to a light position but protect from sun.

Leaves have holes especially around edges. Caterpillar, likely if plant has been outdoors. Find and destroy.

Senecio maritima

Silverleaf

The Silverleaf, a native of Southern Europe, is a perennial but as it becomes woody and rather straggly after its first year, it is usually grown as an annual. It can be grown from seed or cuttings, will stand moderate frosts and thrives in almost any type of soil.

Light: Full light. Shade cuttings until rooted.

Temperature: Germination, 55°F (13°C). Cuttings taken in midsummer need no extra heat. Protect from severe cold. Will stand moderate frost.

Water: Keep moist to dry.

Humidity: Dry, no spraying.

Soil: Any loam-based or soil-less compost. If plant kept for several years, add fresh compost for 3rd season.

Feeding: Feed every 14 days with liquid fertilizer diluted to maker's recommended strength.

Propagation: Sow seed in early spring, soon after days lengthen. Cover with enough compost to hide seed and keep at 55°F (13°C). Prick out when large enough to handle and keep in cool, airy room until putting outside in mid-spring. Plant in container by late spring. For cuttings, cut off non-flowering shoots about 3–4in (8–10cm) long in midsummer. Strip off lower pair of leaves, and dip end in rooting powder. Plant singly into small peat pots of seedling compost or place several round outside of 4in (11cm) pot, water well and leave in shady spot. Keep moist and rooting will occur in 3 weeks. Pot singly in 3½in (9cm) pots if rooted in groups and grow outdoors until late autumn, when they need protection.

Varieties: Silver Dust, very dwarf and finely cut leaves (6in, 15cm). Candicans (10in, 25cm). Diamond, broadly cut leaves (12in, 30cm). Heights are first year's growth. Mature height double.

The attractive silvery white foliage of the Silverleaf remains on the plant all year round, providing a foil for summer flowers and a patch of brightness in winter. Its own deep lemon yellow flowers appear in its second year.

Small green lice on young seedlings. Aphid. Spray once with diluted malathion or pirimicarb. A repeat attack is unlikely as plant gets older.

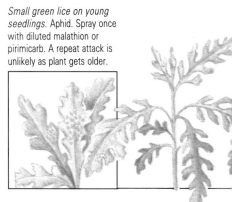

Leaves are dark grey/green instead of silvery white. In seedlings this is natural and colour will appear well before planting time. In older plants, over rich compost especially if feeding was regularly high in nitrogen. Feed with potash sulphate, watering well. Choose balanced feed in future.

what goes wrong

Changing the topsoil

If keeping from year to year, renew top 3in (7½cm) soil in container after 2nd winter. Carefully remove soil, teasing it from around roots. Add fresh compost, firming round roots. Water well.

Fine yellowish streaks in leaves. Thrips. Usually occurs during hot weather. Spray with diluted malathion during the evening and repeat after 14 days.

Small dark spots on leaves, especially on young seedlings. Leaf spot fungus, probably alternaria. This disease can be seed or air borne. Always buy treated seed. Spray with iprodione or bordeaux mixture.

Leaves have brown edges. Too concentrated feed or insecticide, or spraying insecticide in full sun in the heat of the day. If in winter, possibly frost scorch, in which case do not prune off affected stems until early spring. Spray only in early morning or evening; always follow instructions when feeding or spraying insecticides.

Leaves lose colour and plant wilts. Container too dry. Soak well and leave to drain to just moist before watering again.

Holes in foliage, flower buds eaten. Caterpillar. Pick off pest and dust carefully with gamma-BHC if badly infested. Keep away from vegetables.

Base of plant becomes brown and soggy, soil is scummy. Waterlogged. Senecios prefer moist/dry rather than moist/wet soil. Make sure drainage holes are clear and allow container to dry out before watering again.

Mature plant lies along the tub, especially when flower stems growing. Plant straggles naturally with age. Could be staked, or if unsightly, cut off flower stems.

Gloxinia

One of the most beautiful of summer plants, the Gloxinia can, with a little care and attention, be kept going for more than a season. The size and quality of its blooms deteriorate after two or three years, when it may be better to start again. It is also difficult to transport as its wide, flat leaves crack and break easily. The plant's trumpet-shaped flowers are carried singly on stems about 8in (20cm) above the leaves. They are available in many colours, including red, white, mauve, pink and multi-colours.

Gloxinias have velvety, trumpet-shaped flowers and wide leaves with distinct vein markings. As the first flower opens, there should be many new buds growing at its base. The dark green rather fleshy leaves should be firm and undamaged, with no curled or discoloured edges.

Light: Good light position, avoiding direct mid-day sun.

Temperature: 60–70°F (15–21°C) summer indoors. Plants should die down in autumn, and the tubers be stored in a dry place, minimum temperature 40°F (6°C). Move to temperature of 70°F (21°C) in early spring to start new growth.

Water: 3 times a week in summer, reducing in autumn until completely dried off. Water must not go on crown (centre) of plant.

Humidity: Mist spray every day with tepid water when growing, avoiding flowers. Shake surplus off leaves. Provide local humidity by standing pot on saucer of pebbles almost covered with water or in outer container with damp peat.

Feeding: Weekly when growing in spring and summer with liquid houseplant food diluted according to the maker's instructions.

Repotting: 2–3 times in first year for young plants grown from seed or cuttings. Repot old tubers each year in fresh compost when winter rest period is over. Use same sized pot as before, allowing tuber to fit comfortably across width of pot. Half bury tubers in compost, leaving top exposed.

Cleaning: Humidity spraying sufficient. No leafshine.

what goes wrong

Leaves cracked or split. Plant has been knocked or damaged while moving. Be careful of plants fragile leaves.

Leaves distorted and sticky with green insects. Greenfly. Spray with pyrethrum or systemic insecticide every 14 days until clear.

Repotting

1. Repot tubers in early spring, just before new growth starts. Prepare pot same size as before, wide enough for tuber to fit easily with at least 1½in (3cm) space around it for stems and shoots to grow. Put good drainage layer in bottom and layer of peat-based compost ⅔ way up pot.

2. Place tuber on compost and add more until it is half buried. Do not cover it completely, but firm compost around it so that roots are well covered.

3. Leave without water for 2–3 days then water and bring into warmer room (70°F, 21°C) to encourage shoots to appear. Water once or twice a week.

4. When shoots are growing well, increase watering to 2 or 3 times a week, so that compost is always moist but not waterlogged.

Leaves and buds rot. Too cold and/or water on crown of plant. Move to warmer place (at least 60°F, 15°C) and allow soil around crown to dry out before watering again. Water from below, not top of soil. In winter, allow soil to dry out completely.

Brown rings on leaves. Tomato spotted wilt virus. No cure, destroy plant immediately. Or leafshine damage. Do not use.

Flowers marked and stained. Caused by spraying flowers with water. Do not spray or if water gets on to them, shake it off immediately.

New leaves small and pale. Needs feeding. Feed every week in spring and summer with liquid houseplant food.

Small flowers on short stems. Too dark. Move to lighter position, in window but out of direct midday sun.

Leaves curl and go limp. Too sunny and too dry. Water (from below) and move out of direct sun.

505

Solanum capsicastrum

Winter cherry

The Winter cherry is one of 900 plant species in a family which includes the potato. It produces flowers in summer, followed in autumn by attractive berries which remain on the plant through the winter and even into early spring. Although not poisonous, they should not be eaten as they can cause a violent stomach upset. Winter cherries must not be kept in too warm a position; outside they will grow in window-boxes in winter, provided they are kept frost free. After the berries have fallen, the plants should be cut back to half their original size. Cut each stem just above a leaf. In autumn, pinch out tips of non-flowering stems.

Light: Full light, including direct sunlight. Cool but sunny window ideal.
Temperature: Winter minimum 40°F (5°C), though 55°F (13°C) ideal. Summer maximum 65°F (18°C), especially inside.
Water: 2–3 times a week in spring and summer so that plant never dries out. Once every 14 days in winter to keep just moist.
Humidity: Spray daily in summer with soft water in early morning. Stand pot in saucer of pebbles almost covered with water but do not allow pot base to touch water. Or put pot in outer container or trough of damp peat.
Feeding: Weekly in spring and summer with liquid houseplant food diluted according to maker's instructions.
Soil: 3 parts loam-based No. 2 with 1 part peat.
Repotting: Annually in spring, with gravel in pot for drainage. 5in (13cm) pot adequate for adult plant.
Cleaning: Humidity spraying sufficient. No leafshine.

The Winter cherry's tiny white flowers appear in midsummer and are followed by a crop of berry-like fruits which change colour slowly from green to bright orange-red. These stay on the plant all through the winter as long as it is kept in a cool but humid position.

No berries form after flowering. Flowers not pollinated. Spray flowers with tepid soft water or brush each in turn with soft paint brush to transfer pollen.

what goes wrong

Plant stunted with yellow rings on leaves. Tomato spotted wilt virus. No cure. Burn plant.

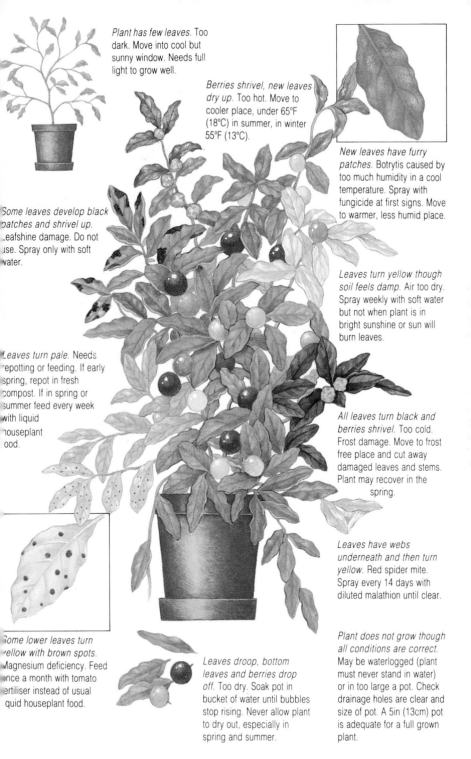

Plant has few leaves. Too dark. Move into cool but sunny window. Needs full light to grow well.

Berries shrivel, new leaves dry up. Too hot. Move to cooler place, under 65°F (18°C) in summer, in winter 55°F (13°C).

New leaves have furry patches. Botrytis caused by too much humidity in a cool temperature. Spray with fungicide at first signs. Move to warmer, less humid place.

Some leaves develop black patches and shrivel up. Leafshine damage. Do not use. Spray only with soft water.

Leaves turn yellow though soil feels damp. Air too dry. Spray weekly with soft water but not when plant is in bright sunshine or sun will burn leaves.

Leaves turn pale. Needs repotting or feeding. If early spring, repot in fresh compost. If in spring or summer feed every week with liquid houseplant food.

All leaves turn black and berries shrivel. Too cold. Frost damage. Move to frost free place and cut away damaged leaves and stems. Plant may recover in the spring.

Leaves have webs underneath and then turn yellow. Red spider mite. Spray every 14 days with diluted malathion until clear.

Some lower leaves turn yellow with brown spots. Magnesium deficiency. Feed once a month with tomato fertiliser instead of usual liquid houseplant food.

Leaves droop, bottom leaves and berries drop off. Too dry. Soak pot in bucket of water until bubbles stop rising. Never allow plant to dry out, especially in spring and summer.

Plant does not grow though all conditions are correct. May be waterlogged (plant must never stand in water) or in too large a pot. Check drainage holes are clear and size of pot. A 5in (13cm) pot is adequate for a full grown plant.

507

Soleirolia soleirolii

Mind-your-own-business

This bright green plant grows almost like a weed in a greenhouse but is a useful plant in a bowl or trough. It is a mass of tiny round leaves which grow on very thin stems and quickly hide any ugly exposed soil or edging. It is a relative of the nettle, comes from Corsica and is very easily propagated by division in spring. It likes a cool, moist position and will not do well where there are gas fumes. It is sometimes called *Helxine soleirolii*. A similar and related plant is *Nertera depressa*. This grows more slowly but in late summer and autumn is covered with tiny orange berries. It, too, needs very moist conditions

Mind-your-own-business is an excellent plant for covering bare patches of compost in a trough or large pot; take care to plant it only with other moisture loving species, though, as it needs to be kept very damp all the year round.

Light: Grows in most positions although is most vigorous in good indirect light. Keep away from direct sunlight after watering. Will tolerate shade.

Temperature: Minimum in winter 45°F (7°C), summer maximum 70°F (21°C). May burn in summer if in direct sun.

Water: Keep moist at all times, watering 3–4 times a week in summer, once a week in winter. Never let it dry out.

Humidity: Spray daily if temperature over 70°F (21°C), otherwise once a week is sufficient.

Feeding: Not really necessary but if fed every 14 days with liquid houseplant food diluted to maker's recommended strength, it will grow faster.

Soil: Loam-based No. 2.

Repotting: Repot in spring. It is best to divide plant before repotting. Separated pieces quickly form compact new plants.

Cleaning: The leaves are too small to wipe but spraying should keep them dust-free. No leafshine.

Plant shrivels, leaves hang down. Soil too dry. Plunge pot into bucket of water for 10–15 minutes, then drain. Keep always moist in summer, watering every day if it dries out in hot weather. Do not allow to stand in water. Spray regularly.

Leaves turn black in winter Too cold. Move to warmer place, above 40°F (4°C).

Plant wilts. Too hot and dry. Move to cooler place, below 70°F (21°C). Water and spray immediately.

Root division

1. These plants grow rapidly to cover the pot with foliage and it is best to divide them each year to keep them to a manageable size. Do this in spring, before repotting. First prepare 2 pots with drainage and layer of loam-based No. 2 compost. Water plant.

2. Remove plant from pot and tease away excess soil from around roots with a rounded stick or pencil.

3. Gently pull stems and roots apart, leaving a good section of both roots and stems on each half.

4. Repot each one separately and leave in shade without water for 2 days to encourage roots to explore new compost.

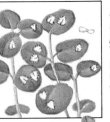

Leaves covered with small insects which fly out when plant is moved or touched. Whitefly. Spray with pyrethrum-based insecticide or diluted malathion. Repeat weekly until clear.

Rusty marks spotting leaves. Leafshine damage. Do not use. Clean only by spraying with soft, tepid water. Remove damaged leaf at base of stalk.

what goes wrong

Leaves turn yellow and die. Plant waterlogged, standing in water. Likes to have moist soil but must not stand in water or roots will rot. Make sure drainage is good. Always check soil before watering, especially in winter when it will not dry out so quickly.

Burns on part of foliage. Damage by strong sunlight. Move into area of good indirect light, out of harmful rays of sun. Remove damaged leaves at base of leaf stalks.

Sonerila margaritacea

Pearl plant

A delightful but unfortunately delicate plant which is well worth trying to grow. It has small oval dark green leaves, covered with silvery dots which suggest pearl seeds, and reddish stems. The leaves are not more than 3in (7cm) long but are usually plentiful. It flowers briefly in the autumn with clusters of pretty little pink flowers but is attractive all the year round. It comes from Java and therefore likes warm moist conditions away from direct sunlight. It can be propagated from stem tip cuttings taken in spring and summer and rooted in a mixture of peat and sand. Since older plants tend to lose their lower leaves, it is wise to do this after 2 or 3 years if you want to keep an attractive, bushy plant.

The Pearl plant's seed-pearl markings make it a good plant to put in a mixed bowl, as a contrast to those with plainer green leaves. It also benefits from the extra humidity the other plants provide. If grown alone, it needs a moist, humid atmosphere.

Light: Does not like direct light and mid-day sun can kill. Best in partial shade.
Temperature: Winter minimum of 60°F (16°C). Below this leaves will drop. Summer maximum 75°F (24°C).
Water: Keep moist at all times, watering 2–3 times a week in summer, once a week in winter. Good drainage is essential.
Humidity: Likes a moist atmosphere. Spray every other day. Also if possible stand plant on saucer of wet pebbles.
Feeding: Every 14 days when growing in summer with liquid food at maker's recommended strength.
Soil: Loam-based No. 2.
Repotting: Once a year in spring, although as the plant tends to get rather leggy, it is often better to propagate new plants from cuttings than to pot up old plants.
Cleaning: The spraying should be enough. Do not use leafshine.

what goes wrong

Leaves curl, look dull and limp. Too hot. Move to cooler room, below 70°F (21°C) if possible and spray every other day.

Leaves drop off in winter. Too cold. Move to warmer place. Do not allow temperature to drop below 60°F (16°C).

Plant grows thin and straggly with small, pale leaves. Needs feeding. Feed with houseplant food diluted to maker's recommended strength every 14 days when growing in summer.

Leaves all over plant are limp. Compost and air too dry. Water immediately and spray regularly with water. Allow compost surface to just dry out before watering again. In winter water only once a week, but spray regularly.

Plant collapses. Waterlogged, standing in water. Drain away any water in saucer and allow surface of soil to dry out before watering again. Then keep moist but never allow pot base to stand in water. Always throw away excess that drains through after watering.

Plant grows tall and leggy with no bottom leaves. Old age. Repropagate from stem tip cuttings.

Little red insects under leaves. Red spider mite. Remove webs with damp cloth or sponge, then spray with diluted malathion, especially under leaves. Repeat every 14 days until symptoms disappear. Improve humidity.

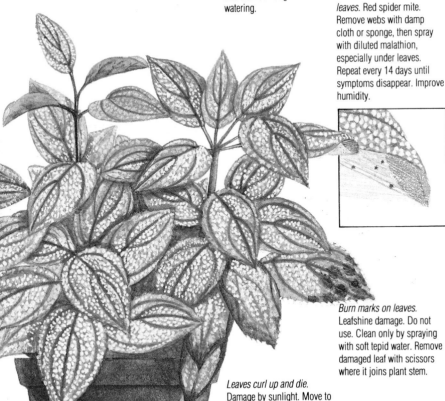

Burn marks on leaves. Leafshine damage. Do not use. Clean only by spraying with soft tepid water. Remove damaged leaf with scissors where it joins plant stem.

Leaves curl up and die. Damage by sunlight. Move to an area of diffused daylight, out of harmful rays of sun. Remove damaged leaf.

511

Sparmannia africana

Indoor lime tree

The indoor lime is a very beautiful plant which makes a splendid feature in a room. Unfortunately it is not as widely available as it deserves to be – but is well worth asking for. It needs plenty of light but tolerates quite low temperatures. A native of South Africa, it may produce clusters of white flowers with purple stamens, when over 3 years old, especially if it is kept slightly pot-bound. If it is growing too big for the available space, it can be pruned in spring. Use secateurs and cut at an angle just above a leaf or side branch. Dust cut with sulphur dust to protect from any infection. It grows quickly and will need a strong cane to support it and a heavy pot.

The leaves of the elegant Indoor lime are like those of the outdoor lime tree in shape, and are delicate green covered with fine hairs. It does not need high temperatures but good light is essential for healthy growth. In ideal conditions it will grow to 6ft (2m) in a pot or tub.

Light: Good natural light, but midday sun in summer may burn the leaves.
Temperature: In winter down to 45°F (7°C) if soil allowed to dry out completely between waterings. Summer maximum 75°F (24°C).
Water: In summer, never allow to dry out, watering 3 times a week. In winter water once a week unless below 50°F (10°C), when every 10 days is sufficient.
Humidity: Spray 2–3 times a week in summer, but not when sun is on leaves.
Feeding: Add liquid houseplant food to the water every 14 days in spring and summer, diluting to maker's recommended strength.
Soil: Loam-based No. 3, a rich soil.
Repotting: It grows quickly, so repot at least twice during first year. After this, repot once a year in spring. If not repotted for 3 years, then fed weekly, plant should flower.
Cleaning: Dust lightly with feather duster – leaves and young stems break easily. No leafshine.

Rusty marks on leaves. Leafshine damage. Do not use. Clean by carefully dusting with feather duster. Remove damaged leaf where it joins stem.

Repotting a large plant
1. A large plant can be replaced in its original pot with fresh compost. Wait until soil is dry, then remove plant and lay on flat surface covered with paper. Remove old compost with stick.

2. Prune longest roots with secateurs. Wash out pot, fill with fresh compost and replace plant. Leave in shade without water for 2 days to recover.

White woolly patches where leaf joins stem. Mealy bug. Spray with diluted malathion and remove bugs and 'wool' with tweezers. Repeat every 14 days until symptoms disappear. Or, paint bugs with methylated spirits and remove with tweezers. Keep away from other plants.

Leaves turn yellow, plant grows lanky. Too dark. Move into lighter place, but shade from midday summer sun.

New leaves are small or do not appear. Needs feeding. Feed every 14 days in spring and summer.

what goes wrong

Leaves look translucent, plant droops. Too cold. Move to warmer place, above 45°F (7°C). Do not leave between curtains and window on frosty nights.

Leaves dry up and curl. Too hot. Move to cooler place, below 75°F (24°C) and spray 2–3 times a week in hot weather.

Leaves have brown, scorched patches. Damage caused by spraying in sunlight, too much direct sun or air too dry. Plant needs humidity but never spray when sun is on leaves. Shade from midday summer sun and spray 2–3 times a week in hot weather.

Leaves mildewed. Overwatered, waterlogged. Allow soil surface to dry out before watering again and in winter allow to become almost dry between waterings.

Leaves drop. Too dry. Plunge pot into bucket of water for 10–15 minutes, then drain. Keep soil constantly moist in summer, watering 3 times a week. Spray 2–3 times a week.

513

Spathiphyllum wallisii

Sail plant

This is a good dual-purpose plant for its leaves arc attractive and it has graceful white flowers which are long-lasting and almost continuous from the time the plant is about 6 months old. The flowers are carried on a long stem, the outer part (the spathe) is white and the central spadix cream; with age they both turn a delicate green. When each flower withers, cut its stem off with scissors or secateurs, close to the compost. Dead leaves should also be removed in the same way. A large plant that is outgrowing its pot can be divided in spring. Roots and stems should be gently pulled into 2 sections, then repotted separately and kept at about 70°F (21°C), in shade, until they show signs of new growth. The Sail plant is a good plant to grow in hydroculture.

A healthy Sail plant has bright, glossy green leaves and, i summer, should show signs of new flowering stems amon the leaves. Each flower lasts for 5 to 6 weeks, changing colour from white to green with age. As each one dies, it should be cut off at the base of its stem with sharp scisso This encourages new flower stems to grow in its place.

Light: Semi-shade in summer, full light in winter. No direct summer sun.

Temperature: Winter minimum 55°F (13°C), though best at 60–65°F (16–18°C). Summer 65–70°F (18–21°C). If higher, humidity must also be high.

Water: 2–3 times a week in summer, once a week in winter, to keep moist at all times.

Humidity: Spray daily when temperature over 70°F (21°C); otherwise 3 times a week in summer, twice a week in winter. Stand pot on saucer of pebbles almost covered with water.

Feeding: Every 14 days in summer with liquid houseplant food diluted according to the maker's instructions.

Soil: 4 parts loam-based No. 3 and 1 part peat.

Repotting: Annually in spring as the plant starts into growth into next size of pot. Ensure good drainage in bottom of pot.

Cleaning: Wipe leaves with damp cloth. No leafshine.

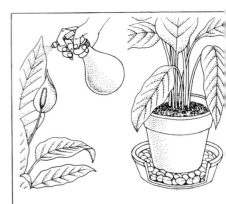

Humidity

Sail plants need humidity all the year round. Spray daily if over 70°F (21°C); if cooler, spray 3 times a week in summer, twice a week in winter.

To provide permanent loca humidity, stand pot on sauc of pebbles. Add water to saucer, almost covering pebbles but don't let base pot touch water.

what goes wrong

Plant grows new leaves but produces no flowers. Either old, needs feeding or too dark. If 3–4 years old, divide plant. Needs full light in winter, semi-shade in summer. Feed every 14 days in summer.

Brown marks on flowers. Leafshine damage. Do not use.

Leaves and flowers droop and flop. Topsoil dry. Needs water. Water and spray more often to keep soil always moist in summer. If soil feels dry, plant too hot. Move to cooler place (under 70°F, 21°C if possible) and spray regularly.

Leaves distorted and sticky with green insects. Greenfly. Spray with derris or pyrethrum every 14 days until clear.

Leaves yellow with webs underneath. Red spider mite. Spray every 14 days with diluted malathion or systemic insecticide until clear.

Leaves go pale and slightly yellow. Too much direct summer sunlight. Move to shadier position.

Leaves droop and flop. Top soil very wet with mould and rotting on surface. Much too wet, waterlogged. Check drainage hole in bottom of pot is clear. Allow plant to dry out completely before watering.

Leaves dull, soft and rotten. Much too cold. Move to warmer place, 60–65°F (16–18°C) best in winter. Use tepid water for watering in winter and do not allow plant to dry out.

515

Stapelia pulvinata

Another of the 'carrion-flowered' succulents, so-called because the flowers look and smell like rotting meat. *Stapelia pulvinata* produces large, hairy, starfish shaped red to reddish-brown flowers on its fine, velvety stems. Their unpleasant smell attracts flies and you may find that fly eggs have been laid on the plant. The hatching maggots have nothing to feed on and soon die. If the flowers have been pollinated, long seed-pods like cattle-horns form in pairs, splitting eventually to let out the thistle-like seeds. Many species are available.

Light: For good flowers these plants need a sunny position. A little shading is needed in the hottest weather (over 90°F, 32°C) if in a greenhouse.

Temperature: A minimum of 40°F (4°C). Give fresh air if over 80°F (27°C).

Water: Fortnightly in spring and summer, weekly in hottest weather, but always make sure soil has dried out. Tail off in autumn, keep dry in winter unless stems droop. Then give just enough to revive them – once a month should be sufficient. Incorporate systemic fungicide 2 or 3 times in spring and summer. See also Introduction.

Feeding: Use high potash fertilizer 3 or 4 times in spring and summer.

Soil: Use good loam-based No. 2 potting compost, or soil-less compost, with 40% coarse, gritty sand.

Repotting: Every spring in size larger half-pot or pan until in 6 or 8in (15cm) size. Then best to repropagate from shoots. Do not water for 2 weeks after repotting.

Propagation: Cut young shoots 2–3in long and leave to dry for 2 days. Dust base with hormone rooting powder containing fungicide, then place on dry compost until roots begin to form (2–3 weeks). Start watering.

Stapelia pulvinata. This carrion-flower's hairy, red or reddish-brown flowers grow on velvety stems at the base of the plant. The plant itself will grow quite large with stems up to 6in (15cm) tall and it is important to repot each year into a larger container to allow for fresh growth, as flowers develop on the newer stems.

Stems become elongated, pale green, especially at tips; no flowers produced. Too little light. Move gradually to lighter position over 2 weeks.

All stems shrivel in summer though conditions and care correct. Remove from pot and look for white woolly patches among roots (root mealy bug). If found, wash soil off roots, swirl in insecticide diluted in water and leave to dry before repotting in clean pot and fresh compost.

Stems do not grow in spring and summer. Needs repotting or feeding. Repot every spring into size larger pot with fresh compost and feed 3–4 times in spring and summer.

what goes wrong

Taking cuttings
Use young shoots 2–3in (5–8cm) long for cuttings in spring or summer. Cut as close to base as possible, dust both cut ends with hormone rooting powder to prevent infection, then leave dry for 2 days. Then place cutting in dry compost and do not water until new roots appear.

Stems turn brown and shrivelled in summer. Too dry. Plunge pot into bowl of water for half an hour, then drain. Water when pot dries out in spring and summer, so test compost regularly in hot weather. Stems may turn bronze if suddenly exposed to direct hot sun and may scorch if in stuffy place. Give fresh air when temperature over 80°F (27°C).

In winter months stem goes first yellow, then black. Too cold; plant may have been shut behind curtains. Move to warmer position, over 40°F (4°C) or bring inside before drawing curtains at night.

White woolly patches on stems, especially around base. Mealy bug. Remove with small paintbrush dipped in methylated spirits. Remove plant from pot and discard soil, which may contain eggs of pest. Dip stems in insecticide, leave for 3 days to dry before repotting in fresh soil and clean pot.

Stems turn black and soft. Overwatering and too cold. Check roots and if rotted separate healthy stems. Pare away roots until healthy tissue reached. Dust with hormone rooting powder and use as cuttings. Keep dry, above 40°F (4°C) in winter.

Tips of stems die back in winter. Too hot. Try to keep in cool room, below 50°F (10°C) in dry resting period. But keep in good light.

Tiny black flies around plant and on surface of soil: plant may be collapsing. Sciara or mushroom fly. Roots have probably rotted, so lift stems and pare from the base until no trace of larvae or brown rot is seen. Dust with hormone rooting powder and leave to dry for 3 days, before treating as cuttings.

517

Stenocactus

Plants of this genus are unique among cacti in having numerous wavy ribs down their sides: some have as many as 50 closely packed ridges. In the Mexican desert where they grow wild, the cacti are able to expand like a concertina to hold water when this is available and to contract in the more frequent periods of drought. Spines vary from species to species. Plants such as *Stenocactus xiphacanthus* (p.519) have thick spines sparsely scattered over its body. Others have a dense covering of thin spines. They are quite small plants, rarely outgrowing a 5in (13cm) pot and taking 7–8 years to reach this size. They are sometimes labelled by an alternative name: Echinofossulocactus.

Light: A sunny windowsill or greenhouse is essential for best results.

Temperature: Keep above 40°F (4°C) in winter and below 100°F (38°C) in summer, giving fresh air whenever possible.

Water: Water weekly in hot summer months, fortnightly in spring and autumn. Keep dry in winter.

Feeding: Use high potash fertilizer (as used for tomatoes) once a month in spring and summer.

Soil: Use 3 parts soil-less or good loam-based No. 2 potting compost with 1 part coarse, gritty sand (not builders' or seashore).

Repotting: Repot every year in spring until plant is in a 4in (10cm) pot. Then repot every other year. If roots do not fill pot, shake old soil carefully off and replace in same pot with fresh compost.

Cleaning and pest control: Spray monthly to keep dust-free, incorporating an insecticide 2 or 3 times a year to combat pests. Brush out dead mealy bugs from between ribs if they have been a problem. If left they can cause moulds to form.

Other species: The main attraction of these

Stenocactus vaupelianus has pale yellow flowers and dense spines in glassy white and brown, obscuring the wavy ribs beneath. It flowers at an inch or two (3–8cm) tall, when 3 or 4 years old. Occasional spraying keeps the spines bright and fresh.

Stenocactus lamellosus is a good example of a plant with the thin, wavy ribs which characterize this genus. Flowers are freely produced after plants get to about 2in (5cm) tall, and are 3 or 4 years old. The plant here is about 3in (8cm) wide.

Stenocactus xiphacanthus is one of the larger species in this genus, growing eventually to 8 or 9in (20–23cm) tall in a pot. It flowers after 3 or 4 years, when it is only about 2in (5cm) across. Flowering season is spring and may last for up to a month. Three or four flowers usually appear at the same time from the centre of the plant though on large plants up to 10 may bloom simultaneously.

The wavy ridges of these plants trap any debris that comes their way and, if they have been attacked by mealy bug, the pests are difficult to remove when killed. Brush out when plant is well watered, so that the ribs are open. If left, they may cause mould.

cacti is their rib formation and spines. The flowers are similar to each other, usually white, striped prominently with purple or purple-pink; some species have plain yellow or cream flowers. A good selection in addition to *S. xiphacanthus* (above) is: *S. vaupelianus* or *S. albatus*, with dense, fine spines and yellow flowers; *S. multicostatus*, with a great many fine, wavy ribs and purple flowers; *S. caespitosus*, an offsetting species which produce clumps of wavy-ribbed heads and white flowers; *S. crispatus* with strong spines and purple flowers; *S. lamellosus* with pinkish flowers; *S. violaciflorus* with white flowers striped with purple and *S. zacatecasensis* with fewer ribs than most and pale violet-pink flowers.

Growing from seed

1. Sow seed thinly on surface of prepared tray and tap sides to settle it in grit. Water from base with fungicide diluted to strength recommended for 'damping off' of seedlings, until surface shows dampness.

2. Cover tray with polythene to seal in moisture. Keep in light (not sunlight) at 70°F (21°C) and do not water unless condensation on cover dries up or is patchy. Prick out after 6 months.

Stephanotis floribunda

Madagascar jasmine

Well-known for its waxy, bell-shaped scented white flowers, the essential constituent of most summer bridal bouquets, Madagascar jasmine is not an easy plant to grow in the home. It requires plenty of light and careful watering, especially in winter when too much can be fatal. It is best when allowed to climb up the walls of a greenhouse or conservatory where its clusters of blooms will hang down all summer. In the house, it can be trained up a cane or round a hoop and, in a good, light window, should grow successfully. In good conditions its shoots can grow 2ft (60cm) a year, eventually reaching 20ft or more (over 6m).

Madagascar jasmine has clusters of pretty white, waxy flowers among bright green leaves. When buying, look for a plant with healthy young buds, not those in full flower. In the home it needs a very good, light position out of direct midday sun and careful watering to keep it in good condition.

Light: Plenty. Place on sun-facing window-sill, shaded from mid-day sun in height of summer.

Temperature: Winter minimum 55°F (13°C); summer minimum 60°F (15°C), maximum 75°F (24°C).

Water: 2–3 times a week in summer, once a week in winter with tepid, soft water. Water less if temperature falls below minimum so that compost almost dries out.

Humidity: Spray daily in summer, once a week in winter with tepid soft water, avoiding clusters of flowers. Stand pot on saucer of pebbles almost covered with water. Do not allow base of pot to touch water.

Feeding: Every 14 days in spring and summer when growing and flowering with houseplant food diluted with water. Use half as much food as maker recommends.

Soil: Loam-based No. 1 compost.

Repotting: When young and very vigorous, repot twice a year in spring and summer. Annually in spring sufficient after 2 years.

Cleaning: Humidity spraying sufficient. If very dirty, wipe with damp cloth. No leafshine.

Brown spots on flowers. Leafshine damage. Do not use.

Brown scales on stems and under leaves. Scale insect. Paint with cotton wool dipped in methylated spirits or spray every 14 days with diluted malathion until clear.

520

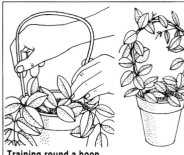

Training round a hoop

1. Push ends of wire hoop or thin cane so that they are ⅔ down pot on opposite sides. Bend plant stem to one side of hoop and gently twist around.

2. To secure plant to hoop, tie twine to one end of hoop and thread it along, looping it loosely around stem. Do not tie tight knots or stem may be damaged.

Leaves dull and limp, flowers dry up. Air too dry. Spray daily in summer, once a week in winter and stand pot on saucer of wet pebbles to provide extra humidity.

New leaves turn yellow. The effect of tap water. Water once with a weak solution of sequestered iron (use half the amount recommended on the bottle) then use only lime-free water.

Leaves turn yellow with webs underneath. Red spider mite. Spray every 14 days with diluted malathion until clear.

Flower buds shrivel. Too hot and dry. Move to cooler place (below 75°F, 24°C) if possible and water 2 to 3 times a week in summer to keep soil always moist.

Flower buds drop off without opening. Plant moved around too much or too cold. Keep in warmer place (60°F, 15°C at least in summer) and do not move plant around from place to place when it comes into flower.

what goes wrong

Leaves turn yellow and drop. Too dark or too wet, overwatered. Check conditions and move to lighter place. If compost very wet, allow to dry out before watering again.

White woolly patches on leaves and stems. Mealy bug. Remove with cotton wool dipped in methylated spirits or spray every 14 days with diluted malathion until clear.

521

Cape primrose

This plant's exotic-looking flowers stand high above large, rather incongruous, bright green, somewhat distorted leaves. The leaves are very brittle, so great care needs to be taken of the plant in the home. The commonest flower colour is blue, but white and red varieties are available occasionally. Propagation is unusual: a leaf is cut along the length of the centre vein with a sharp knife and the leaf put in sharp sand with the exposed vein just buried along its length. With bottom heat, plantlets will grow along the leaf. In low light levels, a sheet of tinfoil put between the top of the pot and the leaves will reflect light on the underside of the leaves, greatly helping culture.

The Cape primrose's lush green leaves are rather few in number but in summer set off well the delicate blue flower White and red varieties are also available. When buying, look carefully for damaged leaves as they are brittle and break easily.

Light: Full light, avoiding midday sun.
Temperature: 65–70°F (18–21°C) all summer, with maximum 75°F (24°C). Winter minimum 60°F (16°C).
Water: 2 or 3 times a week with soft tepid water to keep moist in summer, but plant must not stand in water. In winter, water when compost surface is dried out: about once a week.
Humidity: Must be high. Spray twice a week in spring and summer when not in flower. When in flower, stand pot on saucer of pebbles almost covered with water, or put pot into an outer pot with moist peat between.
Feeding: Monthly in spring and summer with liquid food diluted to half maker's instructions.
Soil: 4 parts peat-based potting compost to 1 part sharp sand.
Repotting: Annually in spring up to maximum pot size 4in (10cm); in effect, after second year, use same pot with fresh soil.
Cleaning: Carefully brush leaves with camel-hair paint brush. No leafshine.

what goes wrong

Leaves turn black. Too cold. Move to warmer place, at least 60°F (16°C). Or leafshine damage. Do not use. Clean by dusting carefully with feather duster or camel hair brush.

Leaves sticky. Greenfly. Spray with pyrethrum-based insecticide or diluted malathion. Repeat one week later, then every week until clear.

Leaves shrivel, flowers fall off. Compost too dry. Water immediately and keep always moist but not waterlogged in summer. In winter, water only once a week, allowing surface to begin to dry out.

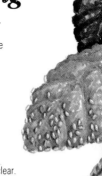

Leaf propagation

1. Cut down centre of main vein and dip cut surface in hormone rooting powder.

2. Place in tray of sharp sand with cut vein just covered. Keep warm (60°F, 16°C) and moist. New plantlets grow along vein.

Plant looks limp. Cold draughts or smoke affected. Move to protected position in fume-free room.

Leaves pale, no flowers. Not enough light. Move to position in good light. Plant will stand sunlight except at midday.

Leaves very large, no flowers. Too much food and pot too large. Do not repot for 2 years. Reduce feeding to half maker's recommended strength, once a month only.

Leaves turn brown, flowers fall. Too hot. Move to cooler place with more ventilation. Spray daily with soft, tepid water. Maximum temperature 75°F (24°C).

Flies hopping round compost surface. Whitefly. Spray with pyrethrum-based insecticide or diluted malathion. Repeat one week later.

One or two leaves rot at base. Waterlogged, standing in water. Drain away any water in saucer and allow compost to dry out on surface before watering again. Water only once a week in winter. Never stand pot in water.

Leaves and flower stems rot away. Botrytis. Too cold and damp. Spray with fungicide, then place in warmer room and spray less often. Allow surface to just dry out between watering in winter and keep at least 60°F (16°C). Remove damaged leaves at compost level.

523

Sulcorebutia

Ten years ago only a handful of Sulcorebutias were known and they were rare in cultivation. Now there are some 40 or 50 to choose from and they are becoming increasingly popular with collectors since they are extremely free flowering. They come originally from the mountains of Bolivia where they grow at about 9000ft (about 2800m) and were at first grouped with Rebutia species (p.466) but are now considered to be a separate genus.

Sulcorebutias grow only slowly, taking 8 to 10 years to fill a 6–8in (15–20cm) pan but they flower when they are less than an inch across, often when they are only 2 years old. Flower and spine colours vary: *Sulcorebutia rauschii* (p.525) with its bright, electric pink flowers, is perhaps the best looking of them all.

Sulcorebutia glomeriseta has an absolutely impenetrable covering of fine, bristly spines. The many, rich yellow flowers are produced sporadically throughout the summer when it is 2 or 3 years old and an inch (2½cm) wide.

Light: As mountain cacti they are used to very bright light so they need the sunniest possible windowsill to ensure compact growth and good flowers. Do not shade in the greenhouse.

Temperature: They will survive below freezing temperatures in an unheated greenhouse but must be kept quite dry. In summer keep below 100°F (38°C) and give fresh air whenever possible.

Water: Keep dry in winter and water once a month in spring and autumn. In summer, water weekly (fortnightly if in 5in (13cm) pots or more), making sure soil dries out between waterings.

Feeding: Feed 3 or 4 times in spring and summer with high potash fertilizer (as used for tomatoes).

Soil: Use 2 parts soil-less or good loam-based No. 2 potting compost to 1 part coarse gritty sand (not builders' or seashore).

Repotting: Repot every year until in a 5in (13cm) pot, then every other year will be

Sulcorebutia canigueralii is a popular, easily grown species with short spines and purple-brown or green stems. The bicoloured flowers are freely produced at 2 or 3 years old, when the plant is only about an inch (2½cm) tall.

enough. If roots do not fill pot, repot in same sized container with fresh soil.

Cleaning and pest control: Spray monthly with water to keep dust-free and incorporate an insecticide 2 or 3 times a year to combat pests.

Other species: A good selection of the many now available is: *S. alba*, with white spines and pink or red flowers; *S. canigueralii*, with brown spines and two-coloured flowers, red with a yellow throat; *S. arenacea*, with wonderfully neat, short, white spines and yellow flowers; *S. candiae*, with yellow spines and flowers; *S. flavissima*, with bright yellow spines, pink flowers; *S. lepida* with dark brown spines and deep purple-red flowers; *S. glomeriseta*, with flexible, bristly spines and yellow flowers; *S. pulchra*, with deep red flowers; *S. mizquensis*, with short white spines and lilac flowers; and *S. rauschii* (below).

Repotting

1. Loosen pot from around root ball by squeezing it gently on one side, then the other, then ease root ball out sideways into gloved hand. Try to grasp root ball not plant.

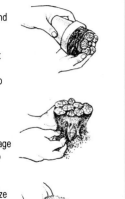

2. If loose soil is around root, crumble it gently, being careful not to damage roots. If no loose soil, do not try to loosen it.

3. Prepare clean pot 1 size larger and add 1–2in (2½–5cm) fresh soil. Place plant on soil and trickle new soil around roots. Firm gently around plant. Do not water for 2 weeks.

Sulcorebutia rauschii flowers when it is only about ½in (1cm) tall, after 2 years growth. The flowers appear in spring or summer, the season lasting for a month or more. Heads grow to about 1½in (4cm) wide and form clumps of offsets which will eventually fill a 6in (15cm) pot. *S. rauschii* comes in several different forms, with purple or green bodies and black or golden spines. All have the striking electric pink flowers.

525

Syngonium vellozianum

Goose foot plant

This handsome climber is a little more demanding than other climbing plants and needs a humid atmosphere to grow well. It produces 6 or 7 new leaves a year, making around 12in (30cm) of new growth and supports itself by producing aerial roots which cling on to whatever the plant is climbing. It needs to be supported as it climbs and a moss-covered pole or a thin cane are both suitable. It can also trail from hanging baskets. The easiest variety has all green leaves; variegated plants grow more slowly and need good light to keep the patterning of their leaves. All-green plants do well in shadier places, out of direct sun. It is a good plant to grow in hydroculture.

Goose foot plants may have either plain green leaves or leaves patterned in green and creamy white. The variegated ones are slightly more delicate than the all-green ones and grow more slowly. Healthy plants should have plenty of bright, unmarked leaves and be firmly tied to a cane or moss pole.

Light: Keep out of direct sunlight. Tolerates shaded positions, especially the plain green varieties.

Temperature: Winter minimum 60°F (15°C). Optimum summer temperature 65–70° (18–21°).

Water: 3 times a week in summer with tepid water. Once a week in winter, also with tepid water. Allow the top layer of compost to dry out between waterings in winter.

Humidity: Spray daily. Stand pot in saucer of pebbles almost covered with water, but do not allow base of pot to touch water.

Feeding: Every 21 days in spring and summer when growing, with liquid houseplant food diluted with water. Use half as much food as the maker recommends.

Soil: 4 parts loam-based No. 2 compost to 1 part extra peat.

Repotting: Annually in spring. If growing fast so that roots show through pot base by midsummer, repot a second time.

Cleaning: Humidity spraying sufficient. If leaves get dusty or dirty, wipe with damp cloth. No leafshine.

Humidity

Goose foot plants need constant humidity. Spray every day all the year round.

For extra local humidity, stand pot on saucer of pebbles almost covered with water. Don't let the pot base touch the water or roots will be waterlogged.

For larger plants, stand pot in outer container packed with damp peat.

Leaves turn pale with webs underneath. Red spider mite. Spray every 14 days with diluted malathion until clear. Plant is very susceptible. Spray with water daily and increase humidity by standing pot in saucer of damp pebbles.

Stems grow straggly with long spaces between the leaves. Too dark. Move to lighter place but not full sunlight.

what goes wrong

Plant droops and leaves look dull, curl and turn brown at edges. Stems rot at top. Too cold and wet, or in a draught. Move to warmer, draught-free place and allow to dry out before watering again. Water only once a week in winter.

Leaves turn brown and brittle. Too hot and dry, air too dry. Water more often and increase humidity by spraying and standing pot on saucer of damp pebbles. Move to cooler place if possible (under 70°F, 21°C). Cut off dead leaves.

Leaves look bleached. Too much direct sunlight. Move out of sun, into shadier position.

Leaves so pale they are almost transparent. Needs feeding. Feed regularly when growing, but use only half strength food.

Tagetes patula

French marigold

The marigold family are natives of Mexico and so luxuriate in hot conditions and do not need much moisture. Single flowered varieties are virtually unaffected by rain (and resistant to rain-induced diseases) but the double and larger flowered ones are soon damaged. All will succumb to the slightest frost. Two other Tagetes are commonly grown: *T. signata* is small flowered and dwarf; *T. erecta*, the African marigold, is taller with large double flowers. Except for its very dwarf varieties, it is not suitable for window-boxes.

French marigolds are bushy plants about 10in (25cm) high. The flowers, from 1½–2in (4–5cm) across, are almost always yellow or orange but may have red or maroon markings. They are single or double according to variety.

Light: Maximum. Can stand 20% shade if light brilliant for rest of day.

Temperature: Indoors light and air more important than warmth. Outside, choose sheltered area. No frost.

Water: Seedlings, just moist. For mature plants, soak container thoroughly and re-water only when soil nearly dry.

Humidity: Dry. Do not spray double flowers or they may rot.

Soil: Loam-based No. 1.

Feeding: Monthly with liquid fertilizer at half maker's recommended strength; or plant sticks.

Propagation: Seed is large and easy to grow. Sow in prepared seed tray in early spring. Cover with compost and keep at 60°F (16°C). Germination takes 3 days. Prick off singly into small pots or trays not more than 10 days after sowing. Give maximum light and air. Plant out after frost has finished.

Tidying: Snap off dead heads to encourage more flowers.

Varieties: Single, Cinnabar, orange, gold. Pascal, Susie Wong, Ruffled Red. Double: Golden Ball, Orange Beauty, Queen Sophia, Gold and Boy series.

Holes in buds and leaves. Caterpillar damage. Pick off pest and spray plant with liquid derris or dust with derris dust. Inspect regularly.

Buds puckered, leaves distorted. Aphid. Spray with insecticide. Repeat 10 days later if pest persists.

Plant wilts slightly but stays green. Slug attacking main stem. Place slug pellets around as maker's instructions. Keep away from pets and fishponds. Stake plant until recovered.

Plant wilts and droops. Too hot and dry. Water well, soaking container to bottom but allow soil to dry out before watering again.

Protection

French marigolds will die if frosted so protect young plants at night when frost expected. If in cold frame, close lid and wrap with hessian or newspaper and sheet of plastic. If no frame, cover with cardboard box, with newspapers and plastic as extra protection.

Plant turns black and collapses. Frost damage. Plant will not survive frost so protect young plants in spring. Remove dead plant from container.

Leaves lush and healthy but few flowers. Soil too rich or fed too often. Feed once a month with half-strength fertilizer or use plant sticks.

Pinpoint white markings on leaf surface, underside mealy and pinkish-grey. Webs. Red spider mite. Spray with dimethoate or use liquid derris as maker recommends.

what goes wrong

Plant does not grow bushy or produce flowers. Soil too rich or fed too often. Feed monthly with fertilizer at half maker's recommended strength or use plant sticks.

Double flowers turn brown and rot. Water damage. Do not spray or water overhead large-flowered types. Protect from heavy rain.

Leaves turn yellow and droop. Too wet, overwatered. Allow soil to dry out between waterings and keep plant in sunny position.

One branch hangs limp, rest healthy. Botrytis where branch joins main stem. Cut off affected branch cleanly and treat rest of plant with benomyl.

Plant turns yellow from base. Phytophthora root rot. Remove affected plant and treat all plants in container with cheshunt compound.

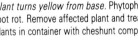

529

Testudinaria elephantipes

This intriguing succulent has a large, swollen corky stem shaped rather like an elephant's foot. It generally lies dormant between spring and late summer or autumn, then sends up a vine with heart-shaped leaves and tiny flowers. In mature plants the vine may grow up to 10ft (3m) long before dying down again in late winter. Regular watering and feeding while the vine is growing increases the size of the plant's corky stem – its main attraction. One or two other species are occasionally seen.

Testudinaria elephantipes, Elephant foot plant. In late summer or autumn, stems shoot up from the corky tuber and may grow up to 8 or 10ft (3m) in a season. The stems need some sort of support, either on a cord suspended from above or trained around a curved bamboo cane.

Light: Full sun best, but will also grow well on a windowsill out of direct sun – but not shaded from the light.

Temperature: A minimum of 40°F (4°C) for safety, although if root is dry it will take temperatures to nearly freezing.

Water: Start when there are signs of growth, usually but not always in late autumn. Water every 2 weeks while vine is growing and producing leaves, but always allow to dry out between waterings. Test soil regularly as in cloudy weather it stays damp for longer. When leaves turn brown and fall in spring, water once more to make sure it is not just too dry, then stop until growth begins again. See also Introduction.

Feeding: use high potash fertilizer 2 or 3 times when vine is growing.

Soil: Use good loam-based No. 2 potting compost, or soil-less compost, with 30% coarse, gritty sand.

Repotting: Every year in early years until 6in (15cm) pot is reached, then every 2 or 3 years will do. Do not water for 2 weeks after repotting.

Propagation: Only possible from seed, which is often available from specialist nurseries.

Leaves brown and fall. In autumn and winter too dry or too wet. Check conditions. If dry, increase amount of water each time, but allow to dry out thoroughly between waterings. If soil soggy, inspect roots and cut away rot. In spring leaves fall naturally but check compost and continue watering in case caused by dryness. If leaves continue to fall, stop watering until new shoots appear in autumn.

Stem soft and squashy, no leaves grow in autumn/winter. Overwatered or watered at the wrong time; or too cold. The plant will have died. Check watering instructions carefully before growing a new plant. Always allow to dry out between waterings.

Leaves scorched, stems die back. Too sudden exposure to strong sun and too stuffy an atmosphere. Move out of strong sunlight and gradually move back over 2 weeks. Keep in more airy place. Remove unsightly leaves and stem with sharp scissors or secateurs.

Leaves have brown or white marks. Caused by insecticide spray or hard water. Not fatal.

Vine stem has long spaces between pale leaves and does not grow well. Too dark. Move gradually over 2 weeks into full sunlight.

what goes wrong

Green insects on leaves and vine stems. Greenfly. Spray with pyrethrum-based insecticide, and repeat every 10 days until clear.

Removing the stem
When stem begins to turn yellow and die in late winter, stop watering and allow compost to dry out. Cut stems near corky base with secateurs or sharp scissors.

Vine stem grows quickly and needs support. Insert cane or plant trellis in pot or provide hanging cord. Tie stem loosely to support, making sure knot is against cane, not plant stem.

Corky stem does not enlarge. Needs feeding. Feed 2–3 times in autumn and winter, when new leaves growing.

531

Black-eyed Susan

The Black-eyed Susan is a native of Africa and will not survive frost. However, once the danger of frost has passed, it can be planted out into containers and will climb a balcony rail or trellis or trail attractively from a tub. Cuttings taken in summer can be overwintered indoors: a cool, double-glazed window ledge is ideal. Do not leave taking cuttings too late in the season as the parent plant will be destroyed by frost at the beginning of autumn. Though tender, the plant is not especially affected by pests and diseases.

Light: Bright, especially indoors.
Temperature: Germination, 65–70°F (18–21°C). Outside, 50–90°F (10–32°C). Protect from strong winds.
Water: Do not overwater. A plant drooping from dryness will quickly recover when watered.
Humidity: Light spray after hot day (over 75°F, 24°C). Use clean water or flowers will mark.
Feeding: Every 10 days in loam, every 5 in soil-less. Dilute as maker recommends.
Soil: Loam-based No. 2 or soil-less potting compost.
Propagation: Sow seed in early spring, in prepared seed tray. Cover with ⅛in (2mm) dry compost and place in propagator or plastic bag at 65–70°F (18–21°C). Prick off singly into small pots when large enough to handle and grow in light. In late spring start to harden off, putting outside in sheltered spot by day, indoors at night. After 1 week, leave outside overnight in cold frame or under cardboard box covered with thick, dry material whenever frost threatens. Or, take cuttings in summer.
Tidying: Remove yellow leaves.
Varieties: Alata, creamy yellow. Gibsonii, deep orange.

The Black-eyed Susan is a trailing, twining plant with thin, wiry stems which can reach 4ft (over 1m) in ideal conditions. The deep creamy yellow flowers have a round 'eye' of such deep purple it looks black and are followed by seed pods like miniature Chinese lanterns.

Growing point distorted with clusters of small insects. Dark sooty, sticky deposit on leaves. Aphid. Spray with diluted general insecticide according to maker's instructions.

Taking cuttings

1. In midsummer take cutting 4in (10cm) long from tip of shoot, just below pair of leaves. Remove lowest leaves and dip bottom ½in (12mm) in hardwood rooting compound.

2. Insert 1in (2½cm) into pot of seedling compost. Water and keep at 70°F (21°C) until rooted. Keep cool (45–50°F, 7–10°C) indoors in winter, treating as seedling next spring.

what goes wrong

Leaves pale, new leaves small. Needs feeding. Feed every 10 days in loam, every 5 in soil-less compost. Do not increase strength of feed.

Leaves turn yellow. Too dry or needs feeding. Check conditions. Water if soil dry. If soil correct, feed regularly. Do not increase strength of feed.

Few flowers, hidden by leaves. Too dark. Move to lighter place.

Leaves purple at edges. Cold winds. Will recover if weather improves. If cold continues, move to sheltered place if possible.

Flowers brown on edge of petal. Insecticide sprayed in sun. Spray only in dull, still weather or in evening. Or, too strong mixture. Follow maker's instructions. Severe scorching may kill plant.

Leaves turn black and soggy. Frost damage. Protect young plants in late spring and early autumn. Remove dead plants.

Flowers lose brightness and leaves look dull. Too hot. Spray in evening.

Flowers marked with brown spots. Sprayed with dirty water. Make sure water for spraying is clean.

Leaves grey and brittle with pinpoint white spots above, pinkish-grey underneath. Red spider mite. Spray with liquid derris or systemic insecticide every 10 days until new growth is green again.

Plant droops. Too dry or waterlogged. Check soil. If dry, water at once and plant will recover. If wet, check drainage holes and allow soil to dry out before watering again.

533

Tillandsia cyanea

Blue flowered torch

A member of the Bromeliad family, the Blue flowered torch originates in Peru, where it grows on tree branches. The foliage is rather uninteresting and somewhat messy, but the spathe, formed of a series of spear-shaped carmine-coloured bracts, will suddenly produce, one after the other, deep blue, exotic-looking flowers with a white spotted throat. These gorgeous flowers are a splendid reward for having to live with an otherwise untidy specimen. Propagation is by potting up offsets in spring after the parent plant has died. The life cycle is three years from offset to flowering.

The Blue flowered torch has a rather messy looking mass of foliage but its broad bract produces purple flowers which are quite outstanding in their colour density. Like other bromeliads it flowers only once in its life cycle but new plants can be grown from its offsets.

Light: Full light, including sunlight. Will survive happily in indirect daylight if it is reasonably bright.

Temperature: Best between 70 and 75°F (21–24°C) though will grow in summer temperatures as low as 65°F (18°C). Minimum winter temperature 55°F (13°C).

Water: Twice weekly in summer to keep moist, pouring water into centre of plant and allowing it to trickle into compost. In winter, water only when surface has dried out, about once every week to 10 days.

Humidity: Spray daily with soft water in spring and summer, not in autumn or winter.

Feeding: Every 14 days in summer only with liquid houseplant food diluted to half maker's instructions.

Soil: 4 parts peat-based potting compost to 1 part chopped sphagnum moss.

Repotting: Pot up offset in spring and repot after 1 year. Do not repot in second year. Plant has very small roots, just enough to hold it upright.

Cleaning: Humidity spraying adequate. No leafshine. Remove unsightly brown tips with sharp scissors.

Offsets

1. When parent plant dies and offset is about half its size, remove offset and its roots from parent with sharp knife.

2. Pot in new pot, firming compost around base. Water well and keep pot covered with polythene for 2–3 days to provide extra humidity.

Plant rots. Botrytis, plant too cold and damp. Spray with fungicide, then place in warmer atmosphere, best around 70–75°F (21–24°C) but never below 55°F (13°C). Do not spray until plant begins to recover and allow surface of compost to dry out between waterings.

534

Side shoot appears from base and parent plant dies. Natural life cycle. Wait until parent plant is shrivelled in spring, then remove shoot with sharp knife.

Webs on plant. Red spider mite. Remove webs with damp cloth or sponge, then spray with diluted malathion, especially under leaves. Repeat every 14 days until symptoms disappear.

Plant turns black in winter. Too cold. Move to warmer place; do not let temperature fall below 55°F (13°C). If temperature correct, leafshine damage. Do not use.

Plant does not flower in first year. It will flower once in 3 years, at end of its life cycle. After flowering it will produce suckers from base.

Flower bract does not produce flowers. Too cold and dark and air too dry. Move to warmer place, in full light. Keep at temperature of between 70–75°F (21–24°C). Plant will stand full sunlight. Spray daily with soft, tepid water and provide extra humidity by standing pot on saucer of wet pebbles. Do not spray in bright sunlight.

*what
goes
wrong*

Whole plant shrivels. Air too dry and too cold or needs water. Move to warmer place, best between 70–75°F (21–24°C) in summer, not less than 55°F (13°C) in winter. Spray daily with soft, tepid water. Check compost. In hot weather (75°F, 24°C) keep moist but otherwise allow surface to dry out between waterings.

Plant shrivels in midsummer though all conditions correct. Fumes and too

Improve humidity by daily spraying with soft, tepid water.

Ants running up and down flower bract. Dust base of plant with ant powder.

much direct light. Needs plenty of fresh air in hot weather, in fume-free room if possible. Shade from direct sunlight in midsummer. Some brown leaf tips are natural. Remove with sharp scissors.

535

Tolmeia menziesii

Piggy-back plant

Piggy-back plants get their common name from the way new plantlets grow on top of older leaves in spring and summer. The plantlets sprout from the point where the leaf joins its stem and if not removed, give the leaf a 'layered' look. The heavier leaves hang down over the edge of the pot and make this an ideal plant for a hanging basket. When well grown, they can produce almost a curtain of green. New plants may be easily propagated from the young plantlets, either by cutting off the parent leaf and standing its stalk in water, or in a mixture of moist sand and peat moss.

Light: Very tolerant of most conditions, although it can be burned by strong sunlight through glass. Plants kept in shady places will have paler leaves.

Temperature: Winter minimum as low as 33°F (1°C) provided water is withheld but ideally not less than 50°F (10°C). Plant prefers not to be too hot and stuffy in summer, so should be out of direct sun if temperature over 75°F (24°C).

Water: About twice a week in summer, once a week in winter, to allow top layer of compost to dry slightly between waterings. Use tepid water in winter.

Humidity: Stand pot in saucer of pebbles almost covered in water, especially if over 75°F (24°C). Never let pot base touch water or roots will be waterlogged.

Feeding: Every 14 days in spring and summer when growing with liquid houseplant food. Use half as much food as the maker recommends.

Soil: Loam-based No. 2 compost.

Repotting: Annually in spring, taking care not to damage runners carrying plantlets.

Cleaning: Occasional spray with water, about once every 14 days sufficient. No leafshine.

The leaves and stalks of the Piggy-back plant are covered with soft hairs. In spring and summer, small plantlets grow on top of the older leaves and can be used to propagate new plants. Healthy plants have well coloured green leaves growing close together at the centre, with new plantlets forming on some of the outer ones.

Leaves turn brown and curl. Too hot. Move to cooler place, less than 75°F (24°C) if possible. In summer, stand outside.

Dark brown burn marks on leaves. Leafshine damage. Do not use.

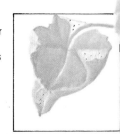

Leaves curl with webs underneath. Red spider mite. Spray with diluted malathion every 14 days until clear.

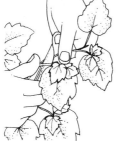

Propagation

1. In spring or summer, prepare small pot with drainage layer and compost made of half peat moss, half sharp sand.

2. Choose leaf with healthy plantlet attached and cut whole leaf off, with 1in (2½cm) stalk.

3. Make small hole in compost with stick or pencil and insert leaf stalk. Leaf with plantlet should lie closely on soil surface. Firm soil around stalk.

4. Water well. Keep soil moist but not saturated, with pot in good light. In 2–3 weeks, plantlet will grow new leaves. About 6 weeks later, repot in loam-based No. 2 compost. Do not remove parent leaf until it is quite dried up.

what goes wrong

New leaves stay small and plant does not grow well or produce plantlets. Needs feeding or repotting. Check roots are not crowded in pot. Feed every 14 days in spring and summer.

Scorch marks on leaves. Direct sun through glass. Move out of hot summer sun.

Leaves and stems rot in winter. Too cold and wet; or water used too cold. Move to warmer place, at least 50°F (10°C) and do not water again until soil feels dry. Use tepid water in winter.

Crawling insects on compost and edge of pot. Earwigs. They damage roots. Dust with derris or pyrethrum every 14 days until clear.

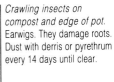

537

Tradescantia albiflora

Wandering Jew

This is one of the oldest, best-known and easiest to grow of houseplants. There are many varieties with a wide range of colours and growth habits. In most varieties, the oval, pointed leaves are multi-coloured, and if green leaves appear, they should be removed. Some varieties have small fluffy pinkish/purple flowers. They make ideal subjects for a hanging basket and are also a good ground cover plant for a mixed bowl or trough. As they tend to become a bit leggy when over a year old, it is best to repropagate each year. Cuttings 1½in–2in (3–4cm) long put 5 to a pot will soon root and grow to form a compact new plant. They can also be rooted in water. Cover a jar of water with kitchen foil and insert cuttings through small holes. Repot when roots form.

Light: Tolerates fairly dark position; becomes leggy and variegations tend to revert to all-green if too dark.
Temperature: Winter minimum 50°F (10°C). Normal room temperature in summer, or put out-of-doors.
Water: Twice a week in summer, once a week in winter. Tolerates a little neglect.
Humidity: Spray every 14 days. Stand on saucer of pebbles almost covered with water but do not let pot base touch water or roots will be waterlogged.
Feeding: Every 14 days in the growing season (spring and summer) with liquid houseplant food diluted according to the maker's instructions.
Soil: Loam-based No. 2 or peat-based with fertilizer at No. 2 strength added.
Repotting: Best to repropagate in spring into 3in (8cm) pots. Then repot in early summer into 4in (11cm) pots.
Cleaning: Mist spray every 14–21 days with tepid water. No leafshine.

The leaves of this *Tradescantia albiflora* 'Quicksilver' are attractively striped in green and white. Other varieties may be green with yellow, grey or even a pretty pink tinge. Trandescantias are such easy plants to keep that they are sometimes neglected. Healthy plants should be compact, with leaves growing to the bottom of their stems and no dried or discoloured patches.

Leaves turn brown, shrivel and wilt; edges yellow or brown. Air too dry. Spray with water more often to increase humidity and stand pot on saucer of damp pebbles.

Leaves very pale with scorch marks. Too much direct sunlight. Move to position out of direct sun.

Propagation
To start new plants from old, straggly stems, cut stem tip including at least two pairs of leaves and growing tip, just below a leaf. Remove lowest pair of leaves to give enough bare stem to plant and insert in small pot of new compost. Keep moist and new leaves will soon start to grow.

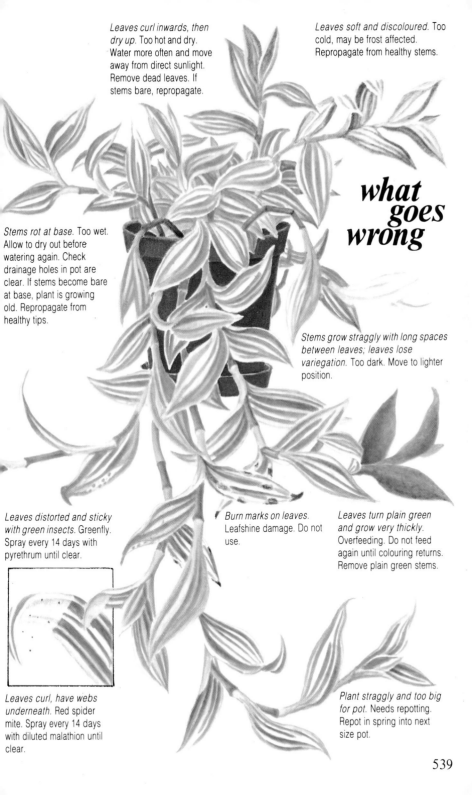

Leaves curl inwards, then dry up. Too hot and dry. Water more often and move away from direct sunlight. Remove dead leaves. If stems bare, repropagate.

Leaves soft and discoloured. Too cold, may be frost affected. Repropagate from healthy stems.

what goes wrong

Stems rot at base. Too wet. Allow to dry out before watering again. Check drainage holes in pot are clear. If stems become bare at base, plant is growing old. Repropagate from healthy tips.

Stems grow straggly with long spaces between leaves; leaves lose variegation. Too dark. Move to lighter position.

Leaves distorted and sticky with green insects. Greenfly. Spray every 14 days with pyrethrum until clear.

Burn marks on leaves. Leafshine damage. Do not use.

Leaves turn plain green and grow very thickly. Overfeeding. Do not feed again until colouring returns. Remove plain green stems.

Leaves curl, have webs underneath. Red spider mite. Spray every 14 days with diluted malathion until clear.

Plant straggly and too big for pot. Needs repotting. Repot in spring into next size pot.

539

Tropaeoleum

Nasturtium

The Nasturtium is a fast-growing climbing or trailing plant, a native of South America. With its gaudy coloured flowers it gives a brilliant display at little cost. If you do not require a climber, the similar *Nasturtium nana* is a dwarf, more bushy species, while for covering a trellis the even faster-growing *Tropaeoleum canariense* (Canary creeper) with its bright yellow flowers is superb. All three plants need the same basic treatment.

Light: Maximum. Sunshine essential for lots of flowers.
Temperature: Germination, 45°F (7°C). No frost. Will stand hot conditions well.
Water: A sappy plant which needs moisture in soil; keep container moist.
Humidity: Dry air, no spraying.
Feeding: Once a month at maker's recommended strength. More frequent feeding leads to lush leaves but few flowers.
Soil: Loam-based No. 1.
Propagation: Sow pea-sized seeds direct into container loam 1in (24mm) deep in late spring. Water compost 24 hours beforehand and allow to drain. Allow 6 seeds to a 12in (30cm) diameter tub or 16 to a 4ft (120cm) trough and thin to 3 and 8 seedlings respectively. Number of seeds for other sized containers can be worked out from this. Or sow indoors individually in small pots in mid-spring, moving to cold frame when 3in (7cm) high. Plant out in early summer.
Tidying: Cut off dead flowers once a week. This prolongs flowering.
Varieties: Gleam hybrids, trailing. Tom Thumb, compact. The smallest varieties grow to only 6in (15cm) so are suitable for windowboxes as well as larger containers. Choose a variety which suits your situation. *Tropaeoleum canariense* is always a climber or trailer.

540

Nasturtiums have almost white stems and brilliant green leaves with contrasting paler veins. Some, like these, have variegated leaves. The flowers, about 3in (7cm) across, range from pale yellow through gold, orange and scarlet to a rusty brown-red. Sun lovers, they produce lush leaves but few flowers if kept in shade.

Holes in leaves and flowers. Caterpillar damage. Caterpillars eat away buds, flowers and stem. Pick off all you can find and spray with derris or dust with derris powder. Ragged flowers may have been eaten by earwigs hidden inside flowers or between box and sill. Spray with diluted malathion and remove debris where pest may hide.

Grey powdery deposit on stems and leaf stalks. Powdery mildew. This may retard growth and should be sprayed as soon as noticed with copper-based fungicide, diluted to maker's instructions.

Watering

Nasturtiums need moist soil but make sure container is well drained. Check surface of soil daily in hot weather and if it feels dry and crumbly, add water. If it becomes heavy and does not dry in cold weather, check drainage holes and allow container to dry out before watering again.

Plant collapses, leaves turn black. Frost damage. Plant will not survive frost. Protect your plants until danger of frost is over. Remove plants at end of summer season.

Very large lush leaves and few flowers. Soil too rich. Do not feed for at least a month, then feed only once a month.

Flowers under leaves and hardly visible. Plant in too much shade. Mover to sunnier position. Needs full sunshine whenever possible.

what goes wrong

Leaves turning yellow over all plant. Soil too wet and cold. Allow to dry out before watering again and check drainage layer in container is not blocked or container standing in water.

Stems crinkled and rubbery at soil level. Stem rot. Soil probably waterlogged from poor drainage. Spray stems with benomyl and improve drainage in container.

Black, sappy looking flies in clusters on plant; plant turning black. Black aphid. Spray with diluted malathion or rub aphids between fingers to kill them. If no insecticide, spray with diluted detergent.

White wriggly lines on leaves. Leaf miner grubs inside leaf tissue. Press grub at end of trail between finger and thumb or spray with diluted systemic insecticide.

Flower buds and growing tips of stems distorted. Aphid. Spray with general insecticide and repeat after 10 days.

Tulipa

Tulip

The many thousands of different tulips grown world-wide today are all descended from tulips which grow wild in central Asia. All are hardy late winter to spring flowering bulbs but many can be grown indoors, though taller ones tend to fall over if grown in too warm a room. For growing indoors, choose bulbs marked 'Single Early' or 'Double Early', and look for the shorter varieties. It is also possible to buy specially treated or prepared bulbs for indoor flowering. Pot up in early autumn, placing 6 bulbs in a 5in (12cm) pot or bowl. Keep in a cold, dark place for at least 8 weeks. Uncover but keep in a cool, shady room for about 2 weeks, until the bud is through the neck of the bulb.

Tulips produce cup-like flowers on upright stems. The best varieties to choose for pot cultivation are those which grow to a height of 6–12in (15–30cm), as taller stems tend to fall over. Even when limited to these dwarf types, the range of colours available is extensive.

Light: Total darkness for 8 weeks, diffused light for 2 weeks, then full light to flower.
Temperature: Cold, 40–45°F (5–7°C) after potting. Maximum 65°F (18°C) for flowering. Flowers last longer in cool temperatures.
Water: Soak compost after planting, then no water until brought into light. Water 2–3 times a week to keep compost moist.
Humidity: Cool, dry, well ventilated spot essential. Do not spray.
Feeding: If bulbs are to be saved, feed weekly with liquid houseplant food at maker's recommended strength from the time bud appears until foliage dies back.
Soil: Loam-based No.2 or soil-less compost. Grow prepared bulbs in special bulb fibre but do not save.
After flowering: Cut dead flowerheads. Allow foliage to die back, then cut off. Lift bulb, separate offsets, and store in a cool, dry place for repotting in autumn. Offsets are difficult to flower in pots and treated bulbs will not flower again indoors.

what goes wrong

Yellow blisters on leaves which may burst. Rust fungus disease. Spray with zineb. Do not use copper fungicides, which can damage tulips.

Holes in leaves. If plants have been outdoors, look for slime trails of slugs or snails and put down slug pellets if present.

Flower bud weak and does not rise from foliage, or no bud at all. Bulb may not have been fed in previous season, or may have contracted pythium disease from unsterile soil. Always plant healthy bulbs in sterile compost. Another cause may be pots brought into heat too soon. Bud should be clear of neck of bulb before placing in final position.

Leaf tips and flowers shrivel on plant bought in flower. Plant forced incorrectly. Do not buy plants in flower, look for those still at young bud stage.

Plant yellows, may have dark streaks near base of stem. Much too wet. Water only 2–3 times a week to avoid waterlogging. Destroy badly affected plants.

Flowers become spotted with a different colour. Virus disease, of which many can attack tulips. No cure, discard bulb after flowering and take precautions to prevent spread by greenfly.

Petals become papery. Too hot. Maximum temperature 65°F (18°C) for flowering, although flowers will last longer if cooler.

Buds turn brown and fail to open, flowers collapse. Much too dry. Water 2–3 times a week to keep soil moist.

Tips of leaves turn brown, brown spots on flower, petals may begin to shrivel. Tulip fire fungus disease. No cure so destroy bulbs. High humidity makes plants susceptible.

Small wingless insects on any part of plant. Greenfly. Spray with pyrethrum-based insecticide at 10-day intervals.

Leaves soft and droopy. Stem elongated and soft. Too dark. Move to a position in full light. Support stems by tying to a cane.

543

Uebelmannia

This is a recently discovered genus and, though it is difficult to grow on its own roots indoors, it has become quickly popular. When grown naturally it is susceptible to overwatering and possibly to low temperatures and grows very slowly — only about ½in (1cm) a year. It is usually found grafted onto a different kind of cactus and when grown like this presents few problems. It grows to the size of a grapefruit in about 5 years and occasionally even produces offsets. Uebelmannias are grown essentially for the beauty of their form, colouring and spines since flowers rarely appear on cultivated plants and when they do are small and yellow, growing in the top centre of the plant. *Uebelmannia pectinifera* (p.545) is by far the most popular species available.

Uebelmannia pseudopectinifera may in fact be a variety of the similar *U. pectinifera* (right). It differs in being olive green and less spiny than the other plant but, like it, rarely flowers in cultivation.

Light: A sunny windowsill or greenhouse is essential for good colour and compact growth.

Temperature: It is thought that winter minimum should be 50°F (10°C) but they will usually stand 45°F (7°C) without harm. Keep below 100°F (38°C) in summer and give fresh air whenever possible.

Water: If plant is growing on its own roots, water only once a fortnight in summer, monthly in spring and autumn. Keep dry in winter. If on a graft, water every week in summer and fortnightly in spring and autumn. But keep dry in winter.

Feeding: Use high potash fertilizer (as used for tomatoes) once a month in spring and summer.

Soil: Use soil-less or good loam-based No. 2 potting compost mixed with coarse gritty sand (not builders' or seashore). If on a graft use 2 parts compost to 1 part sand; if on its own roots use half and half.

Repotting: Repot every year, being careful

Uebelmannia buiningii is a much smaller growing plant with the rich purple body colouring of *U. pectinifera* but with fewer, wispy yellow spines and fewer ribs. The plant here is on a graft and is about 1½in (4cm) wide.

ot to disturb roots if plant is not grafted. If has not outgrown its pot, shake old soil off oots and replace,in same container. When a n (13cm) pot is reached, repot every other ear.

leaning and pest control: Spray monthly to eep dust-free, incorporating an insecticide

2 or 3 times a year to combat pests.

Other species: *U. pectinifera* is by far the most common but others sometimes offered are *U. gummifera, U. meninensis, U. flavispina, U. buiningii* and *U. pseudo-pectinifera.* All are very similar in appearance and growth habit.

Uebelmannia pectinifera is a handsome, dark purple to black skinned cactus with neat rows of spines down its ribs. It grows slowly to about 3–4in (7–10cm) tall and across but if it is not grafted will rarely increase more than ½in (1cm) in a year. The yellow flowers are rare indoors but come in summer from the centre of the plant when it is fully grown.

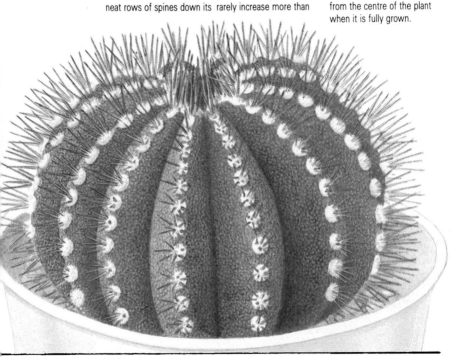

Grafting
1. Remove top inch (2½cm) of a tall type of cactus and cut a slice from the bottom of the Uebelmannia with a sharp, clean knife.

2. Immediately place the Uebelmannia's cut surface firmly on the other stump, making sure the rings near the centre of the stems overlap.

3. Hold firmly in place with elastic bands until new growth appears. Do not damage outer tissue with too tight or too narrow a band.

4. To improve appearance of plant on graft, use deep pot and bury rootstock in gravel below pot rim so that only the Uebelmannia is visible.

Scarborough lily

This beautiful native of South Africa is easy to grow and is ideal for a light, warm position such as a sunny windowsill. It needs a cooler resting period but the leaves do not die down completely. Plant new bulbs in mid-summer in just moist fibrous compost, then do not water until new leaves start to grow. A large bulb needs a 5in (13cm) pot and should be planted with the tip showing above the surface. It will produce a mass of striking bright red blooms in late summer and can be left in its pot for 3–4 years. Change the top inch (2½cm) compost in spring.

Light: Full light, including direct sun but shade from midday sun in summer.
Temperature: 55°F (13°C) for 2 months in rest period. Up to 75°F (24°C) while growing and flowering. Move out of direct sun if higher.
Water: 2–3 times a week in spring and summer to keep moist. In winter only every 10–14 days; do not allow to dry out completely. Start watering again more often as new leaves appear.
Humidity: Give plenty of air. Spray leaves with clean water if over 80°F (27°C). Do not spray flowers.
Feeding: Every week from early spring to late autumn, with houseplant food at maker's recommended strength.
Soil: Loam-based No. 2 mixed with 50% peat. Or soil-less potting compost.
After flowering: When flowers die and stem yellows, cut stem as close to bulb as possible. Reduce watering so that soil almost dries out each time and reduce feeding to every month. When leaves start to turn yellow naturally, stop feeding and move to cooler place for resting.

The Scarborough lily produces new leaves each spring and late summer, a flower stem carrying up to 10 red, white or pink flowers. It grows to about 12in (30cm) high and keeps some leaves all the year round. When buying growing plant choose them with the flower buds still unopened. Bulbs for next year's flowers should be about 1½in (3cm) in diameter with brown, dry outer skins.

Black patches on leaves. Leafshine damage do not use. Clean by spraying with soft tepid water when not in flower. When flowering, wipe leaves with damp cloth.

Offsets
If offsets around parent bulb are crowding pot, remove them in spring. Pot them singly in 3½in (9cm) pots, where they will flower in 2–3 years.

After flowering
Allow flower stem to dry out. After about 5 weeks when stem is yellow, cut it off just above top of bulb with sharp knife or razor blade. Do not use scissors.

Plant wilts and ceases to grow. Leaves eventually turn brown. Too hot. Maximum summer temperature 80°F (27°C) if kept always moist; better at 75°F (24°C).

Flower stem does not form. Bulb too small or plant not fed in previous spring and summer. Feed every week now to give flower spike next year.

Leaves turn yellow before flowers appear. Too dry and needs feeding. Feed every week from spring until flower spike appears and water as soon as soil surface appears at all dry.

Leaves droop. In summer, too dry. Water whenever soil surface begins to dry out. In autumn leaves droop naturally as plant loses some leaves. Reduce watering gradually so that soil is nearly dry in winter.

what goes wrong

Flower rots. Atmosphere too humid, or flowers sprayed with water. Keep in good airy place and do not spray plant while in flower.

Bulb rotted in early spring. Overwatered in winter. When next bulb purchased remember to keep almost dry in winter, watering once every 2–3 weeks only.

Leaves turn black. Too cold. Is pot in a draught? Has it been shut behind curtains on a cold night? Vallota will suffer in these conditions. Move pot to warmer place.

Keep summer average temperature at 75°F (24°C) if possible. In winter, keep at least 55°F (13°C).

Flower buds stay pale and do not open. Too dark. Keep in good light position. Will enjoy sunlight but shade from fierce midday sun.

Webs under leaves. Red spider mite. Remove webs by wiping both sides of leaves with cotton wool dipped in diluted malathion and spray every 14 days with systemic insecticide until clear.

Grey fungus around tip of bulb. Botrytis, plant too cold and wet in spring and summer or overwatered in dormant period. Spray affected areas every week with systemic fungicide until clear. Move to more airy place. Keep almost dry in winter.

547

Verbena

Verbenas grow on average 12–14in (30-45cm) in height and through recent breeding work are becoming more bushy, less straggling plants. They are not easy to grow from seed and seedlings emerge erratically. To avoid root disturbance at planting out time, prick them out into individual pots so that the roots can be planted intact. If buying plants, try to find those grown in this way, not crowded all together in a tray.

Light: A sunny spot. Needs maximum light.
Temperature: Germination, 70°F (21°C). As soon as seedlings appear, 65°F (18°C). One week after pricking out, 55°F (13°C). Keep out of draughts. No frost.
Water: Soak container thoroughly, then allow to dry out before watering but do not leave dry for too long. Good drainage essential.
Humidity: Dislikes high humidity. Keep in airy place while indoors.
Soil: Gritty, loam-based No. 2 or soil-less potting compost.
Feeding: Start 2 weeks after planting in final container, then every 10 days in soil, every 5 in soil-less. Use liquid fertilizer at maker's recommended strength.
Propagation: Sow seeds as soon as days start to lengthen on well moistened seedling compost. Cover with ⅛in (2mm) compost and keep moist so hard seed coat softens. Place in propagator at 70°F (21°C) and cover. Bring tray into light when first seedlings appear (about 1 week). Prick out when large enough to handle into individual pots.
Tidying: Remove seed heads after flowers have died.
Varieties: Royal Bouquet, upright, good colours with white 'eye'. Derby Salmon, Derby Scarlet, both bushy, no 'eye'. Tropic, slightly taller.

Verbena's small flowers are grouped at the top of a flower stem and open gradually to form an elongated head of brilliant colours, from white, pale pink to red and from pale blue to deep purple. Flowering season lasts without a break from early summer to late autumn.

New leaves small and pale, slow growth. Needs feeding. Use liquid fertilizer every 10 days at recommended strength.

Young plants stop growing. Examine soil surface for tiny almost transparent grubs, larvae of mushroom fly, feeding on roots. Water soil with malathion diluted to maker's instructions. (Small black flies may also be seen on surface.)

Newly potted seedlings fall over and stem near compost thin and soft. Pythium or damping off disease. Remove affected seedlings and those near them and water soil with fungicide. Never water young seedlings from a rain butt; tap water is safe.

548

White powder clinging to stems and leaves of mature plants. Mildew. Verbenas are very susceptible. Spray with inocap and continue every 10 days for rest of season.

Plant grows straggly, not bushy. Too dark. Move into sunny position.

what goes wrong

Older leaves of plant late in season show yellowing of veins in leaf, leaves look generally bronzed. Possibly magnesium deficiency. Water soil with solution of Epsom salts made by mixing 1 level tablespoon (40ml) with 1 gal (5l) water.

Tiny white spots on leaves, underside mealy and grey. Red spider mite. Spray with derris every 10 days as soon as first seen.

White froth on growing points where leaf joins the stem. Froghoppers, hidden in froth. Trap between thumb and forefinger. Spray with liquid derris if severe infestation. Insect is able to jump quite a distance when disturbed.

Plants stop growing, leaves lifted upwards, soil looks black. Too much water. Check drainage in container. Withhold water until nearly dry.

Plant droops after repotting or transfer. Repotted when dry or plant too cold to repot. Always soak plant well before moving to new containers.

Leaves droop and have a grey appearance. Too dry. Water more often to keep soil moist but not waterlogged. Mildew will develop if dry for long periods.

Leaves blacken and plant collapses. Frost. Protect from spring frosts.

Pansy

Pansies are totally hardy in a temperate climate and produce flowers from late winter to the end of summer. Being small (4–6in, 10–15cm) they are ideal for windowboxes or small containers. They are easily raised from seed and grow best in dappled shade, not in hot, dry positions. Buy plants that are short and bushy with deep green leaves. If they already have open flowers they will be difficult to establish.

Light: In summer, dappled shade or half shade, half sun. In autumn, winter and early spring, full light.

Temperature: Germination, 50°F (10°C). Cool and airy while growing. Will stand frost.

Water: Keep soil moist.

Soil: Rich, fibrous soil. Loam-based No. 3 with ⅓ coarse peat added or soil-less compost based on coarse sphagnum peat.

Feeding: Feed every week in soil, every 4 days in soil-less, using liquid fertilizer diluted to maker's recommended strength.

Propagation: Sow thinly in early spring or midsummer in prepared seed tray. Cover seed lightly with dry compost and cover tray with thick paper. Keep at 50°F (10°C). Prick out singly into 3½in (9cm) pots or 2in (5cm) apart in seed trays. Water well and keep shaded for 2 days. If indoors, place in light window but not full sunlight. Outside, keep out of summer sun. Or, take cuttings.

Tidying: Pick off seed pods to encourage more flowers to grow.

Varieties: Celestial Queen, lavender and Orion, yellow, will flower in late winter from midsummer sowing. Swiss Giants, Majestic Giants, Imperial Orange, Prince, and Sunny Boy all have 'marked' flowers. Paramount Azure Blue, Golden Crown and all the Dream Strain colours are clear of the dark marking.

The garden Pansy's flat flowers are made up of 5 overlapping petals which form a near circle. The most popular are those with a dark marking resembling a face but a range of self-coloured hybrids is also available.

Spots on leaves. Either ramularia or phillosticta, both leaf-spotting fungi, encouraged by too high humidity. Spray with a general fungicide and try to improve air circulation around plants.

Holes in leaves and eaten areas on stems. Slugs or snails. Scatter slug pellets round following maker's instructions. Keep away from pets and fishponds. Slugs will feed off the roots of the pansy throughout the winter if not checked. When weather is mild and damp, place a few pellets around and look out for slime trails.

Plant becomes yellow and falls over. Phytophthora root disease. No cure at this stage. Remove carefully and drench soil with cheshunt compound. Treat roots and stems of any other pansies in container.

Cuttings

1. In spring or summer cut off non-flowering shoot just below a leaf joint, not more than 3in (8cm) long.

2. Remove lowest leaf and dip cut end of stem in rooting powder.

3. Insert cuttings round edge of 3½in (9cm) pot so that lowest leaf is level with compost.

4. Keep moist and cool. Pot separately in 3½in (9cm) pots after 2–3 weeks, when rooted.

what goes wrong

Opening flowers chewed and buds also damaged. Earwigs, in leaves or under debris during day, come out to feed at night. Clear up debris and spray with gamma-BHC or diluted malathion to maker's instructions. Gamma-BHC will taint food crops.

Foliage turns pale green and new flowers are smaller. Needs feeding. If feeding regular, was compost good quality? Top dress container with fresh compost.

Plant becomes yellow and looks distorted. Root aphid. Spray with diluted malathion.

Powdery deposit on stems and/or leaves. Powdery mildew. This can be made worse by keeping plant too dry. Spray with benomyl or iprodione. Keep soil moist.

Buds drop before opening. Too dry at root. Keep soil moist always.

Blotches of yellow on top of foliage with brown pustules on the underside. Pansy rust. This will gradually reduce flowering and plant will be unsightly. Spray with dinocap fungicide.

Plant wilts and droops. Needs watering. Do not allow to dry out completely in hot sunshine.

Small insects on leaves, growing points small. Aphids. Spray with diluted malathion or derris following maker's instructions. Repeat in one week. Pansy is very susceptible.

Plant grows weak and straggly. Too hot while developing. Keep seedlings cool until they are well established with leaves and buds beginning to develop.

Flaming sword

In the wild, this plant (a bromeliad) grows on the jungle trees of tropical South America. It is a striking plant, with a brilliant orange flower spike or spathe rising some 18in (45cm) out of the central rosette formed of horizontally striped dark brown and green leaves. The flower itself is small, yellow and looks rather like a lobster's claw coming out of the side of the spathe. One of the easiest Bromeliads to grow, a Flaming sword plant provides a good contrast of shape and form in mixed plantings. Like other bromeliads, it dies down after flowering (2–2½ years) but produces new offsets at its base. When choosing a new plant, inspect its central well carefully. The spike should be just appearing, not fully grown with flowers, and certainly not already fading.

Light: Good light position with some sunshine, though not full mid-day sun.
Temperature: Best to maintain constant 60°F (15°C). Winter minimum 55°F (13°C), summer maximum 70°F (21°C).
Water: Keep centre of rosette filled at all times, except when flower stem is appearing, changing water weekly. Water compost once a week in summer, keep drier in winter, watering every 10–14 days. Use clean lime-free water only.
Humidity: Spray overhead weekly.
Feeding: Every 14 days in summer add liquid houseplant food to water for central well. Use half as much food as maker recommends.
Soil: Peat-based compost.
Repotting: Twice as plant grows to flowering size, i.e. at about 6-month intervals.
Cleaning: Wipe leaves with damp cloth. Do not use leafshine.

The Flaming sword produces its flower spike (below) when it is about 2 years old but even without a flower, is an attractive houseplant. Its striped green and brown leaves enclose a central well which must be kept full of clean, lime-free water.

Brown scales under leave Scale insect. Remove with cotton-wool dipped in methylated spirits or spray every 14 days with systemic insecticide until clear.

what goes wrong

Leaves shrivel and tips turn brown. Too dry. Keep water in central rosette, changing every week. Water compost once a week in summer, once every 10 to 14 days in winter.

Removing the flower stem
When flower spike has died, cut its stem at base with secateurs.

Offsets
Offsets can be cut from the parent when they are about half the parent's size and have roots of their own. Separate with a sharp knife, making sure offset has its roots attached. Pot in new pot. Water and keep warm (75°F, 24°C).

Flower stem discoloured, flowers die as they come out. Leafshine damage. Do not use.

Leaves fade and become pale. Too dark. Move to position with good light. Will take some direct sun, though not hot mid-day sunlight.

Leaves shrivel up. Too hot. Keep under 70°F (21°C) in summer. Constant 60°F (15°C) ideal. If plant not moved to cooler place, may die.

Central rosette starts to die and young side shoots appear at base. This is natural after about 2 years. Do not remove young shoots until centre rosette of parent plant has died completely.

Leaves fade and have webs underneath. Red spider mite. Spray every 14 days with diluted malathion or derris.

Base of rosette rots. Too cold and too wet – usually fatal. Empty water from central well and allow soil to dry out. If it recovers and young side shoots appear, place in warmer position, 60°F (15°C)

Spineless yucca

These are interesting and easy plants to keep in the home, and less dangerous indoors than the other indoor yucca, the spiky *Yucca aloifolia*. Canes between 1 and 5ft (30–90cm) are imported from the West Indies, forced into growth in a greenhouse and, when they have a good head of green, potted singly or two or three together. When canes of different heights are potted together they make an attractive display. Always make sure that the plant you buy is well rooted in its pot. Yucca canes will not grow taller but more leaves will grow from each rosette.

Light: Need good light including sunlight except at midday in summer. Will survive for 4–5 weeks in a shady place. Can be put outside in summer.

Temperature: Keep between 50–60°F (10–16°C) in winter; normal room temperature in summer or outdoors on a balcony or patio.

Water: Keep moist in summer, watering every 2–3 days if soil seems to be drying out. In winter every 10 days should be enough.

Humidity: In summer spray once or twice a week; once a month in winter unless over 65°F (18°C), when weekly spraying will keep them fresh.

Feeding: Feed weekly in summer using liquid houseplant food at half maker's recommended strength.

Soil: Loam-based No. 2.

Repotting: Once a year when young. After 3–4 years, remove top 2–3in (5–7cm) compost and replace with new. Always firm compost well down around base of cane, especially with tall plants.

Cleaning: Wipe leaves carefully with damp cloth. No leafshine.

Yuccas make a handsome display, especially if canes of different heights are planted together. The leaves of this species are not dangerous, bending easily at the touch of a finger, but the spiky *Yucca aloifolia* has leaves that are dangerously sharp.

White woolly patches in centre of leaves. Mealy bug. Spray with diluted malathion and remove bugs and 'wool' with tweezers. Repeat every 14 days until symptoms disappear. Or, paint bugs with methylated spirits and remove with tweezers. Keep away from other plants.

what goes wrong

Rosettes (especially young ones) turn black and rot. Too wet. Allow surface to dry out before watering again. Water 2–3 times a week in summer, only once every 10 days in winter.

A yucca garden
1. Choose 3 plants of different heights and a pot large enough to hold them with at least 3in (8cm) between for root growth. Pot must be heavy or it may be unstable.

2. Remove plants from pots and position first one in compost. Firm well in. Add second and third plants around it, firming compost well round them. Fill pot with compost and leave in shade without water for 2 days.

Brown scales under leaves and on stems. Scale insect. Spray underside of leaves with diluted malathion and, after 48 hours, remove scales with thumbnail. Repeat every week for 4 weeks until clear. Or, paint scales with methylated spirits and remove with thumbnail.

Grey mould on leaves. Botrytis. Too cold and damp. Spray with fungicide, then move plant to warmer room (over 50°F, 10°C) and spray less often. Allow soil to dry out in winter between waterings.

Rusty marks on leaves. Leafshine damage. Do not use. Clean with damp cloth if dusty.

Leaves pale. Too much direct sun. Need good light but while indoors keep out of midday summer sun. Outdoors will stand full sun.

Leaves dry up in winter. Too hot. Keep at 50–60°F (10-16°C) in winter. If temperature over 65°F (18°C) spray weekly.

Lower leaves yellow. Too dark. Move to lighter place, plant will stand full sun. Remove yellow leaves with sharp knife where they join cane.

Plant falls over. Not sufficiently rooted in pot. Replace carefully in pot and firm soil well down around base of cane. Place in full light to encourage root growth.

New leaves do not grow. Needs feeding or, if feeding regular, too cold. Check conditions. Feed weekly in summer with houseplant food at half maker's recommended strength and keep above 50°F (10°C) in winter.

Zebrina pendula

Wandering sailor

These attractive plants look very like the familiar 'Wandering Jew' (Trades-cantias) and are closely related to them, but with larger and stronger leaves. They flourish in good light, which brings out the bright purple and cream of their leaves. If in too shady a position, or in winter when the days are short, the leaves may turn almost green. But when better conditions return, the bright colours reappear. They are at their most attractive massed in a hanging basket in a good, light position. If stem tips are regularly replanted, the pot will be kept full and bushy, with no bare, brown stems visible. Remember to check the compost regularly in hanging pots and baskets, as they dry out quickly. A layer of damp pebbles or gravel in the drip tray will help provide humidity.

The colouring of the Wandering sailor plant's leaves improves in good light. They are best in a hanging basket where 3 or 4 pots together provide a mass of purple trailing stems.

Light: Must have plenty of light, including full sunlight except at midday in summer.
Temperature: Winter minimum 55°F (13°C). In summer normal room temperature, but best below 70°F (21°C).
Water: Keep moist all year round. Water twice a week in summer, once a week in winter.
Humidity: Like humid atmosphere. Stand pot on wet pebbles all year round.
Feeding: Add liquid houseplant food to water every 14 days in spring and summer, diluting to maker's recommended strength.
Soil: Loam-based No. 2.
Repotting: Best to repropagate every 2nd or 3rd year instead of repotting, as they become straggly with age. Root 4 or 5 cuttings in a 3in (7cm) pot, repot after 6 months into 5in (13cm) pot, then leave.
Cleaning: Spray if dusty with tepid water. No leafshine.

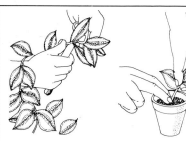

Propagation
1. When plant looks bare at base, cut off 3–4in (5–7cm) length from stem tip, including at least 2 pairs of leaves and the growing tip. Cut just below a leaf or joint.

2. Trim to just below leaves, then remove lowest pair and insert stem end in small pot of fresh compost. Keep moist and new growth will show in 2–3 weeks.

Stems grow straggly with long spaces between leaves. Too dark. Move into lighter place, but not direct sun.

Burn marks on leaves. Leafshine damage or too much direct midday sun. Do not use leafshine: clean only by spraying with soft tepid water if dusty. Remove damaged leaf where it joins stem. Keep plant in good indirect light.

Stems rot at base. Waterlogged, standing in water. Drain away any water in saucer and allow surface to dry out before watering again. Always throw away excess water from saucer after watering.

Leaves lose markings and grow thickly. Overfeeding. Dilute food to half recommended strength. Feed only every 14 days.

what goes wrong

Leaves distorted with sticky green insects. Greenfly. Spray with pyrethrum-based insecticide or diluted malathion. Repeat weekly until clear.

Leaves soft and discoloured. Much too cold, possibly frosted. Repropagate from healthy stem tips.

Brown tips and patches on leaves. Too dry. Keep moist all year round.

Leaves curl inwards, then dry up. Too hot, air too dry, or too cold. Check conditions. If over 75°F (24°C) move to cooler more airy place. Improve humidity and keep over 55°F (13°C).

Leaves curl, webs underneath. Red spider mite. Remove webs with damp cloth or sponge, then spray with diluted malathion, especially under leaves. Repeat every 14 days until symptoms disappear. Improve humidity.

Plant is straggly, stems bare at base, falling out of pot. Needs repotting or cut stems back to 3in (7cm) from pot so that they will grow new leaves. Or propagate from stem tips.

557

Zinnia elegans

Zinnia

Zinnias come from Mexico and so are not suitable for a cold, windy position or one shaded by trees or buildings for much of the day. They grow rapidly and seeds should not be sown before mid-spring or the plants may be ready to put outside before it is warm enough for them. Do not try to check their natural growth or they may become diseased.

Light: Maximum at all times.
Temperature: Germination, 65–70°F (18–21°C). Seedlings, 55°F (13°C). No frost.
Water: Keep soil always just moist. Never overwater.
Humidity: Keep dry, do not spray or water overhead when in flower.
Soil: Rich, well-drained. Loam-based No. 3 or soil-less potting compost.
Feeding: In loam-based No. 3, start 3–4 weeks after planting out, using liquid fertilizer at maker's recommended strength, then feed every 10 days. Feed soilless 10 days after planting out, then every 5 days.
Propagation: Sow seed thinly in mid-spring in drained soil-less seedling compost. Cover with ¼in (6mm) compost and lightly press with flat board. Do not place in plastic bag but cover tray with thick paper and place in propagator at 65–70°F (18–21°C). Germination takes 2 days. Remove paper immediately and place tray in light, airy room with no draughts. Prick out 2in (5cm) apart within 2–3 days and start to harden off when plants about 5in (12cm) tall. Do not put outside until all danger of frost passed.
Tidying: Remove dead flowers.
Varieties: Goblin, Lilliput, Pumila and Peter Pan are all good dwarf windowbox varieties. Giant Dahlia Flowered, Giants of California, Tetra State Fair, very large flowers for patio and balcony. Mixed colours.

Zinnia flowers measure up to 5in (13cm) across, in colours ranging from white to yellow, rose, scarlet and violet. They are long lasting when cut but need bright light and a sunny position to flourish.

Plant does not grow well in spring, flowers small and pale. Too dark and too cold. Protect from cold winds and place in good sunny position. Plants will not do well in shade.

Seedlings fall over and die. Pythium disease. Caused by unsterile conditions or contaminated water. Never use stored water for seedlings. Remove affected seedlings and those around them. Water soil with fungicide.

Plant collapses, leaves black. Frost. Protect from frost in spring.

Buds and flowers malformed, often tilted to one side. Leaves tattered. Capsid bug. Spray with insecticide every 10 days until early autumn. Do not use malathion which may cause leaf scorching.

Flower petals have ragged edges and small holes. Earwigs, hidden between windowbox and sill or under decaying leaves. Dust plant carefully with gamma-BHC or set trap by putting a little dried grass or straw in a jar, supporting it upside down on a small cane. Next morning many of these pests will have installed themselves in the new home. They can then be destroyed by emptying into boiling water.

Grey spots on flowers and brown edges. Flower scorch fungus, occurs in a humid season. Spray with bordeaux mixture or iprodione. If flowers are spotted without brown edges disease is likely to be botrytis but treatment is the same.

Foliage pales, new flowers smaller. Needs feeding. Feed more often with fertilizer diluted to manufacturer's recommendation. Do not increase strength.

White or grey fluffy mould on stems. Stem turns brown. Botrytis well developed. Zinnia is highly susceptible. Carefully cut off all affected parts of the plant, avoiding sharp movements if possible as spores disperse easily. Spray with a fungicide and continue every week or 10 days for the rest of season.

Clusters of small insects round bud. Aphid. Spray with insecticide. Do not use malathion.

Mottled leaves with yellow rings, distorted growth. Spotted wilt virus. No cure. Destroy plant.

Bottom of stem blackened. Plant is sickly. Phytophthora stem and root rot. Caused by unsterilized soil or contaminated water. No cure. Remove and treat soil with a fungicide.

Plant looks yellow and sickly, possibly with mould at base of stem. Soil is dark and sour. Overwatered. Check drainage in container and allow to dry out before watering again.

Young plants, especially soon after moving out of doors, develop small spots, enlarging to circles. Alternaria disease. It can be seed or airborne. Spray plant with bordeaux mixture. White spots may also be caused by chemical spray or hail.

Stems of plants eaten off at ground level. Slugs or snails if slimy trail present on soil, container or ground. Otherwise suspect cutworm. Put down slug bait as maker recommends. Keep away from pets and fishponds. For cutworm spray plant with systemic insecticide.

Buying houseplants

All kinds of shops now sell houseplants. Large or unusual plants are best purchased from florists or garden centres but supermarkets, shops and even petrol stations offer excellent value. Cacti and other succulents are best bought from specialist centres or by mail order.

Before buying a plant consider where it will stand. Think about the room conditions—the light, heat or draughts it may be subjected to. Make sure it will not grow too large or too tall for the space available. If you are a beginner, choose a plant that is simple to look after. Don't buy one that needs special conditions until you have some experience. If you are given one as a present, look up its entry immediately. Even a few days in the wrong atmosphere may damage some species.

Look carefully at the plant you intend to buy. It should be firm in its pot, which should be clean. The compost on top should be fresh, not sprouting weeds or moss, none of the leaves should be marked, torn, yellow or faded. Beware of small plants in large pots: they may have just been repotted and the roots will not have grown properly into the fresh compost. Cacti and other succulents should be standing in good light and should not look 'stretched' at the tips. Blackened leaves may mean they have been outside in the cold and fatally damaged.

Always insist that your plant is properly wrapped up, with a double layer of paper if necessary. Large plants should be supported with a cane—and take care that the plant does not catch cold in the winter as you take it from shop to home. As soon as you get it home, check it for pests; cacti should have the roots inspected too. Keep them away from other plants until you are sure they are pest free.

Finally, make sure you know the plant's correct name so that you can look it up and give it the care it needs in your home. In this book each plant is indentified under both its scientific and its common name.

Chemicals

All chemicals used to control pests and diseases may be harmful to other plants, insects, animals or humans. Always read the labels carefully and follow the instructions. Keep chemicals in their original containers (*never* in unlabelled or wrongly labelled bottles) and keep them out of reach of children.

Fungicides:

Benomyl. Moderately safe. Can irritate throat.

Bordeaux mixture. Harmful if swallowed.

Cheshunt compound. Harmful if swallowed. Do not smell.

Dinocap. May irritate skin, eyes, nose and mouth. Wear mask and goggles.

Iprodione. May irritate nose and throat. Harmful to fish.

Insecticides and pesticides:

Derris. Controls aphids, helps with red spider mite, caterpillars, thrips. Relatively safe for humans, toxic to fish.

Dimethoate. Controls red spider and aphid. Dangerous to humans and animals.

Gamma-BHC (or HCH). Kills earwigs, cutworm, caterpillars, leather-jackets. Toxic if inhaled. Taints food crops and persists in soil for many years.

Malathion. Controls wide range of pests. Toxic to some plants, harmful to humans, bees, fish.

Metaldehyde. Controls slugs and snails. Harmful if swallowed to humans, animals, fish, birds. Used in slug pellets.

Pirimicarb. Kills aphids only. Relatively safe.

Acknowledgements

Colour artwork by Bob Bampton, Jane Fern, Steve Kirk, Stewart Lafford, Josephine Martin, Jane Pickering, Andrew Riley and Paul Wrigley. **Line artwork** by Marion Neville, Patricia Newton, and Norman Bancroft-Hunt. **Photographs** by David Cockcroft with additional photography by Gordon Rowley, The Harry Smith Horticultural Collection, Bill Weightman and A-Z Botanical Photographic Collection.